palgrave macmillan law masters

employment law

Hc

Series editor: **Marise Cremona**

Business Law   Stephen Judge
Company Law   Janet Dine and Marios Koutsias
Constitutional and Administrative Law   John Alder
Contract Law   Ewan McKendrick
Criminal Law   Jonathan Herring
Employment Law   Deborah J Lockton
Evidence   Raymond Emson
Family Law   Kate Standley and Paula Davies
Intellectual Property Law   Tina Hart, Simon Clark and Linda Fazzani
Land Law   Mark Davys
Landlord and Tenant Law   Margaret Wilkie, Peter Luxton and Desmond Kilcoyne
Legal Method   Ian McLeod
Legal Theory   Ian McLeod
Medical Law   Jo Samanta and Ash Samanta
Sports Law   Mark James
Torts   Alastair Mullis and Ken Oliphant
Trusts Law   Charlie Webb and Tim Akkouh

If you would like to comment on this book, or on the series generally, please write to lawfeedback@palgrave.com.

palgrave macmillan law masters

employment law

deborah j lockton

Formerly Professor of Employment Law,
Leicester De Montfort Law School

Ninth edition

This edition first published 2014 by PALGRAVE MACMILLAN

Palgrave Macmillan in the UK is an imprint of Macmillan Publishers Limited, registered in England, company number 785998, of Houndmills, Basingstoke, Hampshire RG21 6XS.

Palgrave Macmillan in the US is a division of St Martin's Press LLC, 175 Fifth Avenue, New York, NY 10010.

Palgrave Macmillan is the global academic imprint of the above companies and has companies and representatives throughout the world.

Palgrave® and Macmillan® are registered trademarks in the United States, the United Kingdom, Europe and other countries.

ISBN: 978–1–137–35412–9 paperback

This book is printed on paper suitable for recycling and made from fully managed and sustained forest sources. Logging, pulping and manufacturing processes are expected to conform to the environmental regulations of the country of origin.

A catalogue record for this book is available from the British Library.

Typeset by Cambrian Typesetters, Camberley, Surrey.

Printed and Bound in Great Britain by TJ International Ltd, Padstow.

Contents

Part V   Trade unions and the law of industrial action   333

In the last edition of this book I stated that there had been considerable change since the previous edition. Likewise with this edition there have been major changes. Perhaps the most controversial of these is the introduction of tribunal fees, so that those wishing to pursue a claim in a tribunal will have to pay an issuing fee and a further hearing fee should their claim go to a full hearing. The introduction of the fees was unsuccessfully challenged. In addition, the continuity requirement for unfair dismissal has been increased to two years and the compensatory award capped. Due to the decision of the European Court of Human Rights in *Redfearn*, there is now no continuity requirement where there is a dismissal on the grounds of political belief. Changes to the TUPE Regulations were enacted in January 2014. As I have stated before, employment law is never dull!

As usual, there are many people to thank for their patience and understanding. My students, who are my most effective critics, and my colleagues, who have continued to support me. Keith and James have put up with my mutterings about major pieces of legislation causing major rewrites, and have provided necessary sustenance. Despite all of this support, any mistakes are my own.

The law is as I understand it to be on 1 January 2014.

Deborah J Lockton

Table of cases

Table of legislation

Part I

Introduction

Chapter 1

Sources and institutions of employment law

The law governing the relationship between an employer and employee has become increasingly complex over the last 50 years or so as more and more provisions have been introduced. In addition, employment law comes not only from common law and statute but also from a variety of additional sources such as codes of practice. Over the years, specific institutions have also been introduced into the area, some with an adjudicative function, such as the employment tribunals and Employment Appeal Tribunal (EAT), and some, such as the various Commissions, which have a variety of functions, including overseeing legislation and helping applicants. All of these factors can appear to make the subject somewhat daunting, but together they make it dynamic and one which is constantly changing. This changing nature of the subject is, in reality, very important, as the relationship between an employer and employee does not stand still but evolves over the years. Most employers nowadays do not regard their employees as their property, and the law has changed with changing attitudes, introducing basic employment rights and providing specialised forums in which those rights can be enforced quickly and cheaply. As such, it is necessary to spend some time looking at the different sources and institutions of employment law today.

1.1 Common law

Although the area of employment law contains a great many statutory provisions, a large number of statutes are recent, in that they came on to the statute books in the past 40 years. Before then, there were very few pieces of legislation governing the employment relationship, and it was up to judges to interpret contractual provisions and to imply terms into a contract where the document was silent. While many older cases would not be followed today – given the changing nature of the employment relationship – judges are still required to interpret terms that the parties may, or may not, have included in the contract.

But this implies that judges have no function in the many areas of the employment relationship that are governed by statute. This is misleading. The employment relationship is a fluid, ever-changing one, and statutes, to some extent, reflect this. The most common phrase in the Health and Safety at Work etc Act 1974 is 'as far as reasonably practicable'; when considering whether an employee has been unfairly dismissed, a tribunal is required by section 98(4) of the Employment Rights Act (ERA) 1996 to consider whether the 'employer acted reasonably or unreasonably in treating the reason relied on as a sufficient reason for dismissing the employee; and that question shall be determined in accordance with equity and the substantial merits of the case'. Such words as 'reasonably' or phrases such as 'as far as reasonably practicable' lead to a wealth of law on interpretation, and as such the common law is an important source of employment law.

1.2   Legislation

Given the large amount of legislation enacted in the last 40 years, governing every facet of the employment relationship, statutes are a primary source of employment rules. In addition to statutes, there is a wealth of delegated legislation. Statutory instruments may amend existing statutory provision, where existing authority is in place, because of a change in government policy, or UK legislation may be amended to comply with European directives – the Equal Pay (Amendment) Regulations 1983 and the Transfer of Undertakings (Protection of Employment) Regulations 2006 being two examples.

1.3   Codes of practice

A code of practice is not legally binding. It is intended to provide guidance for employers and to promote good industrial relations. Although not legally binding, however, a code may be used in evidence. The ACAS Code on Disciplinary and Grievance Procedures 2009, for example, is referred to by tribunals in an unfair dismissal claim. An employer who has not complied with the Code may find the compensation awarded against him increased by up to 25 per cent. Various bodies have the authority to issue codes of practice – the Secretary of State for Employment, the Advisory, Conciliation and Arbitration Service (ACAS), the Equality and Human Rights Commission (incorporating since October 2007 the Commission for Racial Equality, the Equal Opportunities Commission and the Disability Rights Commission), and the Health and Safety Commission. There are codes covering a variety of areas, including discipline, trade union ballots, picketing and discrimination.

1.4   European Union law

The United Kingdom joined the European Community by the European Communities Act 1972. This provides that any EU treaty shall have legal effect in the United Kingdom without further enactment. Thus treaty articles are directly applicable and will override national law. This means that individuals in Member States have rights under certain treaties in addition to rights created by national statute. This is seen, for example, in the area of equal pay. In addition to the three routes to equal pay provided by the Equality Act 2010 (previously the Equal Pay Act 1970), all individuals have an additional route under Article 157 of the Treaty on the Functioning of the European Union (TFEU) (formerly Article 141 TEC), which provides that men and women shall receive equal pay for equal work.

In addition to treaty articles, the Council of Ministers (or in rare circumstances the European Commission) may issue directives. These are binding as to the result that Member States must achieve but not prescriptive as to the method by which such States achieve that result; for example, the Equal Pay Directive (75/117) reiterated the principle of equal pay for equal work. The original UK Equal Pay Act did not achieve that result, and after action against the UK by the Commission (*Commission of the European Communities v United Kingdom* [1982] IRLR 333) the Act was amended by the Equal Pay (Amendment) Regulations 1983 (now the Equality Act 2010). As it is the responsibility of the Member State to bring the purpose of the directive into its law, an individual within a Member State has no right to sue a private employer for breach of a directive. The employer is, after all, only complying with national law. It has been decided, however, that a state should not profit from its own wrongdoing, and therefore an individual may sue the state (or an organ of the state) if that body employs the individual. This means that employees of emanations of the state have the additional right to sue the state or the organ of the state qua employer for a breach of the relevant directive (*Marshall v Southampton & South West Hampshire Area Health Authority* [1986] QB 401; *Foster v British Gas plc* [1991] ICR 84).

The Court of Justice of the European Union (CJEU), comprising the European Court of Justice (ECJ) and the General Court, has the jurisdiction to give rulings on the interpretation of treaty articles, directives and regulations. The Commission or any Member State may take another Member State to the Court for a breach of treaty obligations or a breach of the obligations under a directive. In addition, a court in a Member State may refer a case to the ECJ for guidance on interpretation and the ECJ will give a ruling, after which the national court will give its decision.

1.5 The European Convention on Human Rights 1950 and the Human Rights Act 1998

The European Convention on Human Rights (ECHR) was signed by the then Member States of the Council of Europe in 1950 and came into force in 1953. Until the passing of the Human Rights Act 1998, the only challenge under the Convention was against the state, and any claim for a breach of Convention rights had to be pursued in the European Court of Human Rights (ECtHR) – a costly and lengthy process. Such challenges were successfully made and had an impact on UK practices, and in some cases legislation was introduced as a result of such challenges. For example, in *Smith and Grady v UK* [1999] IRLR 734 there was a successful challenge against the questioning of members of the armed forces about their sexuality, such being an infringement of Article 8 of the Convention which guarantees the right to respect for an individual's private life. The challenge led to the removal of the ban against employing homosexuals in the armed forces. Similarly in *Halford v UK* [1997] IRLR 471, Halford successfully challenged the practice of monitoring employees' telephone calls as an infringement of Article 8. Such monitoring, and the use of information gained that way, is now covered by the Data Protection Act 1998, the Regulation of Investigatory Powers Act 2000 and the Telecommunications (Lawful Business Practice) (Interception of Communications) Regulations 2000, which give employers power to monitor employee communications as long as employees are aware of such monitoring. A further major change in UK law was as a result of *Young, James and Webster v United Kingdom* [1983] IRLR 35, which successfully challenged the closed shop (a device whereby a union could insist an employer employed only members of that union) as an infringement of Article 11 ECHR which provides, *inter alia*, a right to be or not to be a member of a union.

The Human Rights Act (HRA) 1998 effectively incorporates the Convention into UK law. It came into force in 2000. By section 3 of the Act, all courts and tribunals, in determining questions which arise in connection with a Convention right, must take into account judgments from the ECtHR. In addition, by sections 6 to 8, all public authorities must act in a way which is in compliance with the Convention. Both courts and tribunals are deemed to be public authorities.

While the full impact of the HRA 1998 on tribunal proceedings has to date appeared negligible, there have been a number of cases at the time of writing. In *De Keyser Ltd v Miss Wilson* [2001] IRLR 324, the complainant had presented a complaint to the tribunal, alleging constructive dismissal arising from stress. The respondent had asked for a doctor to examine the complainant, and the doctor's subsequent report gave a great deal of detail about the complainant's personal life which both the doctor and the respondent felt was the cause of the stress. The complainant asked the tribunal for a fresh expert to be appointed because she felt that the original doctor was prejudiced against her. The tribunal, however, took the unprecedented step of striking out the ET3 (employer's response) as a breach of Article 8 (right to respect for private life). The EAT overturned the decision for a number of reasons. First, the letter of instruction from the respondent to the doctor was sent a week before the HRA 1998 came into force. Second, the report did not contain any information given in confidence. Third, the employer was not a public authority. Fourth, the tribunal could have directed that another expert be appointed. Fifth, the tribunal had not considered whether a fair trial of the issues was still possible and, lastly, the right to respect for private life is qualified by the right of both parties to a just trial of the issues between them. Thus, even if the Act had been in force at the time of the respondent's instructions, it would appear from the decision that it would have made no difference to the outcome. The decision would suggest, moreover, that Article 6 (right to a fair trial) qualifies Article 8. This will be particularly important in cases of dismissal on health grounds (discussed in Chapter 9).

The application of Article 6 of the Convention was also discussed in *Tehrani v UK Central Council for Nursing, Midwifery and Health Visiting* [2001] IRLR 208. The case confirmed that disciplinary proceedings before the Council's Professional Conduct Committee fell within Article 6, as they could result in Ms Tehrani's removal from the register of nurses and were thus a determination of her civil rights. However, although she was entitled to a hearing before an impartial and independent tribunal, the internal tribunal did not have to meet all of the necessary requirements as there was a statutory right to appeal to a court of law, which itself complies with Article 6.

Article 6 has also been applied in cases of legal representation in two more recent cases – *Kulkarni v Milton Keynes Hospital NHS Trust* [2009] EWCA Civ 789 and *R (on the application of G) v The Governors of X School* [2009] EWHC 504. In the case of *Kulkarni*, there was an *obiter dictum* from the Court of Appeal that if internal disciplinary hearings (in the case, a doctor being disciplined for incapability) are so serious that it could lead to an employee losing his livelihood (ie in the case, being struck off), then that person has a free-standing right to legal representation under Article 6. Likewise, in *R (on the application of G)*, where a music assistant at a school was dismissed, having been found guilty of kissing a 15-year-old boy, the High Court held that the employee should not have been denied legal representation by the school, because the school was under a duty to report the decision to the Secretary of State for Children, Schools and Families, which could lead to the employee being placed on the register of persons unsuitable to work with children. As such, the school's procedures were part and parcel of those of the Secretary of State, and thus could lead to the employee losing his livelihood.

In *X v Y* [2004] IRLR 625, the Court of Appeal considered the application of section 98(4) of the ERA 1996 where there had been alleged breaches of the employee's rights under the HRA 1998. In this case the employee, who worked with 16–25-year-old young offenders, had failed to reveal to his employers that he had a conviction for gross indecency with another man in a public toilet. When his employers discovered the conviction he was dismissed. The employee argued that his employers were in breach of Articles 8 and 14 (rights against discrimination). While the Court of Appeal recognised that section 98 must be interpreted to give effect to the ECHR, in this case the act which gave rise to the dismissal did not take place in the employee's private life and he had received a caution which was highly relevant to his employment. The fact that the employee wished to keep the act private did not prevent it from being public. In *Pay v Lancashire Probation Service* [2004] IRLR 129, Pay was a probation officer whose job involved working with sex offenders. In his spare time he was involved in a company which sold products relating to sado-masochism over the Internet and appeared at fetish clubs, pictures of which were published on the Internet. When his employer discovered this Mr Pay was dismissed. He argued in the EAT that the dismissal was a breach of his rights under Articles 8 and 10 – the right to respect for private life and the right to freedom of expression. Both arguments were rejected by the EAT. In *McGowan v Scottish Water* [2005] IRLR 167, McGowan was suspected of falsifying his time sheets over call-outs, so his employer, a public authority, undertook covert surveillance of his home. The surveillance confirmed the employer's suspicions and McGowan was dismissed. He alleged a breach of Article 8. The EAT held that there was a breach of Article 8 but that the employer's actions were justified, as it was protecting its assets. Another Court of Appeal decision was *Copsey v WWB Devon Clays Ltd* [2005] EWCA Civ 932. In this case the employee, a practising Christian, refused to change his shift patterns to include Sunday working. He was offered a number of other jobs by the company but refused them, because none could guarantee he would not have to work on a Sunday. He was eventually dismissed and claimed he had been unfairly dismissed for exercising his right under Article 9 (freedom of religion). His appeal was dismissed. Mummery LJ felt that the article was not engaged. Rix LJ felt that the article did apply but that the claim for unfair dismissal failed.

The ECJ considered the impact of Article 11 – freedom of assembly and association – in *ASLEF v UK* [2007] IRLR 361. In the case Lee, who was a train driver and a member of ASLEF, was discovered to be an activist in the British National Party (BNP) and had stood as a candidate in elections. His activities in relation to anti-Nazi protestors had been reported to the police. ASLEF took the view that such activities were likely to bring the union into disrepute and were a breach of the union rules. Consequently, Lee was expelled from the union. An employment tribunal on two occasions held that Lee had been unlawfully excluded from the union contrary to section 174 of the Trade Union and Labour Relations (Consolidation) Act (TULR(C)A) 1992. The original section 174 stated that it was unlawful to expel a member because of his membership of a political party. ASLEF applied to the ECtHR, saying that it was prevented from expelling a member because of membership of a political party that had views which were contrary to its rules, and that this was an infringement of Article 11.

The ECtHR stated that the expulsion did not breach Lee's freedom of expression under Article 10 and that he had suffered no real detriment apart from loss of membership, as ASLEF bargained for all train drivers whether union members or not. It did, however, uphold the union's right to choose its members, and held that the balance between competing Convention rights had not been struck and there was a breach of Article 11. As a result, section 174 of the TULR(C)A 1992 was amended by the Employment Act 2008. The amended section 174 does allow a union to exclude or expel an individual due to membership or past membership of a political party, if such membership is contrary to a rule or an objective of the union. The provisions are discussed in more detail in Chapter 13.

Conversely, however, in the case of *Redfearn v UK* [2012] ECHR 1878 the ECtHR decided that UK law does not provide adequate protection against dismissal on the grounds of membership of a political party. Redfearn was employed by Serco as a bus driver in Bradford. When he was elected as a councillor for the BNP Serco dismissed him, arguing that he was at risk of attack because of his political views, which were now in the public domain. He had insufficient service to claim unfair dismissal and so he brought a race discrimination claim, which failed. The ECtHR held that the lack of protection from unfair dismissal interfered with Redfearn's right to freedom of assembly under Article 11 and that there is an obligation to provide at least a means for an independent assessment of the proportionality of such a dismissal. In other words, the judgment is saying that Redfearn should have had the right to challenge the dismissal, not that such a dismissal would be automatically unfair.

It is arguable that political beliefs are incorporated into the definition of 'philosophical belief' (see Section 5.2.7 below) under the Equality Act 2010; however, under the Enterprise and Regulatory Reform Act 2013, section 13, the two-year continuity period for unfair dismissal does not apply where the reason for the dismissal is, or relates to, an employee's political opinions or political affiliations, where the effective date of termination is after 25 June 2013.

1.6   Employment tribunals

Industrial tribunals were renamed 'employment tribunals' on 1 August 1998 by the Employment Rights (Dispute Resolution) Act 1998, and any reference to 'industrial tribunals' in existing legislation changed to 'employment tribunals' on that date. Employment tribunals became part of the legal system of the UK by the Industrial Training Act 1964, and at that time they had very little jurisdiction. Their functions have grown, and they now have the jurisdiction to hear claims arising out of breaches of most aspects of the employment relationship. Most commonly, they will hear claims for unfair dismissal, redundancy payments, equal pay and discrimination claims, breach of employment protection rights and claims in relation to unlawful deductions from wages. Until 1994 they were excluded from hearing claims for breaches of contract, which had to be heard in the ordinary civil courts. This lack of jurisdiction caused problems for an applicant who had both a breach of statute claim and one of breach of contract. In *Treganowan v Robert Knee & Co Ltd* [1975] IRLR 247, an applicant was found to be fairly dismissed but the tribunal felt that she should have been given notice and not dismissed instantly. She was entitled to six weeks' notice by her contract, and as such was entitled to six weeks' wages as damages for the employer's breach of contract. The tribunal, however, had no jurisdiction to hear the breach of contract claim or award damages for that breach. Ms Treganowan had to go to the civil courts. The anomaly created by this lack of jurisdiction was often commented upon by the courts.

Breach of contract jurisdiction was given to the tribunals by the Employment Tribunals (Extension of Jurisdiction) (England and Wales) Order 1994. This Order is now to be read in conjunction with the Employment Tribunals Act 1996. The changes create concurrent jurisdiction in the tribunals and the courts. Tribunal jurisdiction is, however, limited. First, it arises only when the contract is terminated (see *Capek v Lincolnshire County Council*

[2000] IRLR 590 and *Miller Bros and PF Butler v Johnson* [2002] IRLR 386). Second, the type of claim that a tribunal can hear is also restricted. A tribunal can hear claims for a breach of the employment contract or any other contract connected with employment; claims for a sum due under such a contract, or claims for recovery of such a sum in pursuance of any enactment relating to the terms of performance of such a contract (Employment Tribunals Act 1996, s 3(2)). Breach of contract includes a breach of a term implied in a contract or under any enactment or otherwise; a term modified by or made under any enactment or otherwise; and a term which, although not contained in the contract, is incorporated into the contract by another term of the contract (s 3(6)).

Certain claims are specifically excluded from the tribunal jurisdiction:

- damages or sums due in respect of personal injuries;
- breach of a term requiring the employer to provide living accommodation for the employee, or imposing an obligation on the employer or employee in connection with the provision of living accommodation;
- breach of a term relating to intellectual property (including copyright, rights inperformances, moral rights, design rights, registered designs, patents and trade marks);
- breach of a term imposing an obligation of confidence; and
- breach of a term which is a covenant in restraint of trade.

In all of the above cases only the courts have jurisdiction.

A claim is brought by issuing an originating application, normally within three months of the effective date of termination of the contract. If there is no effective date of termination because, for example, the contract has been frustrated, then within three months from the last day that the employee worked an employer cannot originate a claim for a breach of contract in the tribunal but can issue a counter-claim. Such a claim must be lodged within six weeks of the employer's receiving a copy of the originating application. The tribunal has the discretion to extend both time periods if it feels that it was not reasonably practicable to present the claim or the counter-claim in time.

Breach of contract claims are heard by the chair of the tribunal alone, unless the chair considers that a full tribunal should hear the case (s 4(3)(d) and s 4(5)). In making the decision as to whether the case should be heard by a full tribunal, the chair must consider the likelihood of a dispute arising on the facts or over an issue of law, any views of the parties as to whether the case should be heard by one person and whether there are proceedings which might be heard at the same time which cannot be heard by the chair alone. The maximum damages a tribunal can award in a breach of contract claim is, at present, £25,000.

ACAS conciliation is available (s 18) and parties may also reach their own agreement to settle by a settlement agreement (renamed from 'compromise agreement' in July 2013) (see Section 9.3 below). Appeals lie to the EAT on a point of law.

The tribunal consists of a legally qualified chairperson and two lay members, one of whom is a nominee of an employer's organisation and the other a nominee of a trade union. The Tribunals, Courts and Enforcement Act 2007 received Royal Assent in July 2007. This inserted section 3A into the Employment Tribunals Act 1996, which renamed tribunal chairpersons 'employment judges' and was implemented on 1 December 2007. By section 4(3) of the Employment Tribunals Act 1996, in addition to breach of contract claims, certain other claims may be heard by the employment judge alone. Originally these included claims in relation to deductions from wages, claims on the insolvency of an employer, and claims in relation to interim relief pending determination of an unfair dismissal complaint or revocation or variation of an order arising from such a complaint. However, by section 3 of the Employment Rights (Dispute Resolution) Act (ER(DR)A) 1998 and the Employment Tribunals (Constitution and Rules of Procedure) (Amendment) Regulations 2008, the types of claim which can be heard by the judge alone have been augmented as follows and are now found in section 4 of the Employment Tribunals Act 1996:

- the right not to suffer unauthorised or excessive deductions in respect of trade union subscriptions;
- the employer's failure to pay remuneration under a protective award;
- the right to receive written particulars, a statement of changes to the particulars or an itemised pay statement;
- the right to guarantee payments;
- the right of remuneration for suspension on medical grounds;
- the right to a redundancy payment;
- an application for an employer's payment against the Secretary of State for Employment;
- the appointment of an authorised person to conduct certain proceedings under the ERA 1996 where an employee has died and has no personal representative;
- a failure to pay compensation for failing to inform or consult over a transfer of an undertaking;
- stage 1 equal value claims; and
- holiday pay claims.

In addition, the employment judge may hear any claim alone if the parties agree in writing, and may sit with one other member only if the parties present or represented at the hearing agree (Employment Tribunals Act 1996, s 4(6)). Section 7 of the 1996 Act also provides that the tribunal may dispense with an oral hearing where the parties have given their written consent (even if they subsequently withdraw it), and may determine a case hearing evidence only from the applicant where:

1. the party against whom proceedings are brought has not contested the case; or
2. the applicant is not seeking relief that the tribunal has the power to grant or the applicant is not entitled to any such relief.

Section 7 also allows for tribunal rules to provide that the tribunal can determine a case hearing only the parties where the tribunal is, on undisputed facts, bound by a court decision to dismiss the case or the proceedings relate only to a preliminary issue.

The role of the tribunal has been described as that of an industrial jury, and as such it is more informal than a court, with no requirement of legal representation, although such representation is allowed. Legal aid is not available for an employment tribunal claim. When a claim is presented, a conciliation officer from ACAS will attempt to conciliate between the parties, and because of the success of this procedure the majority of cases are settled without reaching the tribunal. Should the parties reach an agreement with the help of ACAS, that agreement is binding between the parties. Until recently, this was the only way a claim could be settled without going to a hearing. Section 203 of the ERA 1996 generally renders void any agreement which purports to oust the jurisdiction of the tribunal. It is now possible, however, for the parties to reach an agreement without the help of ACAS. The section now provides that an agreement to settle will be binding, provided that it is in writing, the employee has received advice from a relevant independent adviser who has explained the effect of the agreement, and the adviser is insured and has been identified by the agreement (s 203(3)). Section 9 of the 1998 Act has extended the category of persons who may be advisers for the purposes of settlement agreements by amending section 203 of the ERA 1996. Prior to the Act only lawyers could be advisers, but the category now includes trade union officials, employees and advice workers.

The Enterprise and Regulatory Reform Act 2013 has introduced a number of changes to tribunal procedure which will be brought in over a period of time. Perhaps most controversial is the introduction of fees, which is, at the time of writing, subject to challenge in both England and Scotland (see further below). The 2013 Act amends the Employment Tribunals Act 1996 by the insertion of section 18A. This requires all claimants, *before* instituting tribunal proceedings, to send information to ACAS which will then be passed on to a conciliation officer with the aim of trying to resolve the claim. At present conciliation occurs only once a claim has been lodged in the tribunal. In certain situations there is no requirement to go to early conciliation (s 18A(7)); however, where such a requirement exists, a claimant cannot institute proceedings unless ACAS has issued a certificate stating that the matter cannot be resolved or the prescribed time limit for conciliation has expired. Even after the time limit has expired, the conciliation officer may continue to try to get the parties to reach an agreement. The time limit by which claims have to be submitted to a tribunal is consequently increased. At the time of writing, it is expected that this early conciliation scheme will be introduced in April 2014.

Since the end of July 2013 a claimant has had to pay a fee to lodge a claim, and a further fee if the claim goes to a hearing. In certain cases these fees may be remitted. Under the Employment Tribunals (Constitution and Rules of Procedure) Regulations 2013, all claims presented to a tribunal are vetted. Regulation 10 provides that a claim will be rejected if it is not on the prescribed form, or if information is missing from the form. In addition, Regulation 11 provides that a claim will be rejected if the fee or remission application has not been received. At the time of writing the fees were:

- Issue fee
  Type A claims (for example, unlawful deductions and redundancy pay) £160
  Type B claims (for example, unfair dismissal, whistle-blowing and discrimination) £250
- Hearing fee
  Type A claims £230
  Type B claims £950

A recent challenge in the Scottish Court for an interim interdict in the judicial review application brought by Fox and Partners against the introduction of tribunal fees was refused (*Fox Solicitors Ltd Re Judicial Review* [2013] CSOH 133). In addition the judge delayed a full hearing of the case for six months because of a similar challenge by

UNISON in England which was listed for hearing in October 2013. That case was unsuccessful.

In addition, Regulation 12 provides that tribunal staff may refer a claim form to an employment judge, who may reject a claim if it is one which the tribunal has no jurisdiction to consider, or it is in a form which cannot be sensibly responded to or is otherwise an abuse of process. The judge is required to give written reasons for rejecting the claim (Reg 27). The claimant has 14 days in which to apply for a reconsideration of the decision to reject (Reg 13). The same rules apply to a response to a claim (Regs 17–19), with a requirement to give reasons for a dismissal of a response (Reg 28).

By Regulation 37, at any stage of the proceedings, either on its own initiative or at the request of a party, a tribunal may strike out all or part of a claim on the grounds that:

1. it is scandalous, vexatious or has no prospect of success;
2. the manner in which the proceedings have been conducted by or on behalf of the parties has been scandalous, vexatious or unreasonable;
3. there has been non-compliance with the rules or with an order of the tribunal;
4. the claim has not been actively pursued; or
5. the tribunal feels that it is no longer possible to have a fair hearing (see *Elliott v The Joseph Whitworth Centre Ltd* [2013] All ER(D) 117).

Furthermore, the rules have introduced what are called 'unless orders'. By Regulation 38 the tribunal may specify that if a tribunal order is not complied with by the date specified, the claim or response shall be dismissed. The party has the right to apply to the tribunal, in writing, within 14 days to have the dismissal set aside on the basis that it is in the interests of justice to do so.

The tribunal or either party may apply for a preliminary hearing (Reg 54). At such a hearing, the tribunal will assess the strength of the claim and advise the parties accordingly. Preliminary hearings are conducted by the employment judge, and a party to such a review may be required to pay a deposit of up to £1,000 if he wishes to continue with what the tribunal decides is a weak case. The aim is to weed out weak cases, as parties may think twice about continuing their action if to do so could mean the loss of £1,000.

Regulation 2 of the Employment Tribunals (Constitution and Rules of Procedure) Regulations 2013 creates an overriding objective that tribunals deal with cases 'justly'. This means that tribunals must ensure that parties are on an equal footing, keep down expense, deal with cases in ways that are proportionate to the complexity of the issues, and deal with cases expeditiously and fairly. This will allow tribunals to move parties on where the issue argued is not difficult, and allow the parties to argue more fully where the issues are more complex.

Tribunal regulations introduced in 2001 gave employment tribunals more teeth and created a statutory duty for the tribunal to consider awarding costs in some circumstances. Prior to this, tribunals had only a discretion to award costs. These powers are now reproduced in the Employment Tribunals (Constitution and Rules of Procedure) Regulations 2013. Prior to 2001, tribunals had a discretion to award costs of up to £500 where the claim was considered to be frivolous or vexatious. Under the 2013 Regulations, tribunals may award costs where either a party or a party's representative has acted improperly. The tribunal must also consider awarding costs where parties or their representatives have acted 'vexatiously, abusively, disruptively or otherwise unreasonably, in either the bringing of the proceedings or the way that the proceedings have been conducted; or any claim or response had no reasonable prospect of success' (Reg 76). The costs a tribunal can award are up to £20,000. In addition, the tribunal may award a preparation time order at £33 per hour and a wasted costs order against a party's representative (Regs 78–80). A 'representative' means one who is paid for his services (Reg 80(2)).

Section 16 of the of the Enterprise and Regulatory Reform Act 2013 empowers tribunals to impose financial penalties on employers where they breach a worker's rights and there are 'aggravating features'. The penalty is 50 per cent of any awards, with a maximum of £5,000, which is halved if paid within 21 days. Originally the Department for Business, Innovation and Skills (BIS) announced that it had no plans to implement this provision, but in October 2013 the Minister for Employment Relations tweeted that this provision will come into force in April 2014.

In April 2007 the Compensation Act 2006 came into force. This requires that any representative of an employee in an employment claim must be authorised by a Regulator, who is formally the Secretary of State for Constitutional Affairs. Such authorised persons must comply with rules regulating their conduct.

Since April 2009 the requirement that the claimant had to register a tribunal award in the county court or High Court to enforce it has been removed (Employment Tribunals Act 1996, s 15(1)). Claimants can now proceed immediately to enforcement. In addition, the Ministry of Justice announced that High Court Enforcement Officers would from April 2009 take on recovery of claims by tribunals or in out-of-court claims.

1.7 The Employment Appeal Tribunal (EAT)

The EAT hears appeals on a question of law or a question of law and fact from the employment tribunal. It consists of the president, who is a High Court judge or a Lord Justice of Appeal, and two or four lay members. The lay members are again drawn from employers' representatives and trade unions. Section 12 of the Enterprise and Regulatory Reform Act 2013 amends section 28 of the Employment Tribunals Act 1996 and provides that all cases in the EAT shall be heard by a judge sitting alone, unless the judge directs that a case should be heard by the judge and two or four members (s 28(3)). With the consent of the parties, a judge may sit with only one or three lay members (s 28(4)). In addition, the Lord Chancellor can direct by order that proceedings specified in the order be heard by the judge and two or four members.

By section 33 of the Employment Tribunals Act 1996, if, on the application of the Attorney-General, the EAT is satisfied that a person has persistently and without reasonable cause instituted vexatious proceedings or made vexatious applications in either the employment tribunal or the EAT, a restriction of proceedings order may be made. This order prevents any proceedings being initiated or continued by the person in question without the consent of the EAT, and may be for a specified period or may remain in force indefinitely. There is no appeal against the making of such an order. In *Attorney-General v Wheen* [2001] IRLR 91, the Court of Appeal decided that the power under section 33 does not breach the right to a fair trial under Schedule 1, Article 6 to the HRA 1998.

The decisions of the EAT are binding; appeal lies to the Court of Appeal and from there to the Supreme Court. (Note that from October 2009 the House of Lords became the Supreme Court of the United Kingdom.)

The changes to tribunal powers, already discussed in relation to employment tribunals, are also applicable to the EAT, and the Employment Act 2002 gave the Secretary of State power to introduce regulations giving the EAT similar powers to award costs against an applicant's representative and to give more flexibility in case management. These were introduced by the Employment Appeal Tribunal (Amendment) Rules 2004.

As in employment tribunals, in July 2013 fees were introduced for issuing and pursuing appeals in the EAT. These comprise a fee of £400, to be paid on a date specified in a notice following receipt by the EAT of the notice of appeal, and a fee of £1,200, to be paid on a date specified following the EAT's direction that the matter proceed to a hearing.

In *Barke v Seetec Business Technology Centre Ltd* [2005] IRLR 633, the Court of Appeal said that the EAT has a discretionary power, in the exercise of case management, to adjourn an appeal and ask an employment tribunal to amplify its reasons for a decision.

1.8   The civil courts

In addition to the appellate function of the ordinary courts, both the civil and the criminal courts have jurisdiction in the area of employment law. Even though the tribunals have jurisdiction to hear breach of contract claims, they do not have jurisdiction to hear claims for damages for personal injury and these claims are heard by the civil courts. The High Court additionally has the jurisdiction to issue injunctions to restrain unlawful industrial action.

Breaches of the Health and Safety at Work etc Act 1974 may involve civil and criminal claims. Criminal prosecutions are brought in the magistrates' court or, on indictment, in the Crown Court.

1.9   Advisory, Conciliation and Arbitration Service (ACAS)

ACAS came into existence in 1974 and was placed on a statutory footing by section 1 of the Employment Protection Act 1975. ACAS is now charged with the duty of improving industrial relations; the words 'in particular by exercising its functions in relation to the settlement of trade disputes' (TULR(C)A 1992, s 209) were removed by section 26 of the Employment Relations Act 1999.

ACAS consists of a Council which comprises a chairperson and up to nine members appointed by the Secretary of State. Three members are appointed after consultation with employers' organisations, three after consultation with workers' organisations and three are neutral members. As its name suggests, ACAS has a variety of functions, considered in the following sections.

1.9.1   Advice

By section 213 of TULR(C)A 1992, ACAS may give advice, on request or by its own volition, to employers or workers or their associations, on any matter concerned with, or likely to affect, industrial relations. It may also publish general advice. In addition, section 251A of the 1992 Act allows ACAS, on the direction of the Secretary of State, to charge a fee for the exercise of any of its functions.

1.9.2   Conciliation

By section 210 of TULR(C)A 1992, ACAS can conciliate where a trade dispute exists or is apprehended. Again, ACAS may become involved by its own volition or at the request of any party. A charge may be made for this service. ACAS also appoints conciliation officers who conciliate when a claim is presented to an employment tribunal (s 211). From May 2014 ACAS conciliation will be compulsory prior to a claim being issued in the employment tribunal.

1.9.3   Arbitration

At the request of one or more parties to a trade dispute, but with the consent of them all, ACAS may refer any matter to an arbitrator or to the Central Arbitration Committee. Such referral may take place only after the parties have exhausted all agreed procedures, unless there is a special reason why those procedures should not be followed (TULR(C)A 1992, s 212). Sections 7 and 8 of the Employment Rights (Dispute Resolution) Act 1998 set out a framework within which ACAS may establish a scheme whereby parties can submit their case to binding voluntary arbitration rather than take their claim to an employment tribunal. The Act states that such arbitration may cover unfair dismissal complaints, although the Secretary of State may extend the category of claims.

The ACAS arbitration scheme came into existence in May 2001. At present it covers only unfair dismissal. Arbitration is an alternative to a tribunal claim and thus, should the parties agree to arbitration, they must sign an agreement (a COT3 or a settlement agreement) taking the claim out of the tribunal system. That arbitration is in place of a tribunal claim, not in addition to it. An arbitrator's finding is enforceable in the same way as a tribunal decision, and the powers to award reinstatement, re-engagement or compensation are almost identical to those applicable in a tribunal.

The scheme, however, has its limitations which have led to criticism. Although arbitration is quicker and less formal, this can lead to some parties feeling a sense of injustice. There are no procedural rules and parties cannot cross-examine witnesses. Arbitrators are not bound by existing law or precedent and can only decide if a dismissal is fair or unfair, although they must have regard to the ACAS Code of Practice on Disciplinary Powers and Grievance Procedures and the *Discipline at Work* handbook. This means that provisions in the ERA 1996, which render dismissals automatically unfair in certain circumstances (see Chapter 9), will not bind an arbitrator, neither will the 'band of reasonable responses test' which allows a tribunal to find a dismissal fair if dismissal would be one of the sanctions a reasonable employer would have used in the circumstances. Further, an arbitrator cannot decide any jurisdictional points, such as whether the claimant is an employee or has sufficient service. An arbitrator can decide only whether the dismissal was fair or not.

The limits of the jurisdiction of the arbitrator appear to have resulted in few parties choosing to go to arbitration, preferring instead to take their claims to a tribunal. The limits mean that any case involving dismissal and another claim can be decided only partially by arbitration. Where a claim involves, for example, unfair dismissal and an unlawful deduction from wages, the issue in respect of whether there has been an unlawful deduction can be heard only by a tribunal. Further, if there is an issue regarding whether a dismissal has actually occurred, for example in a constructive dismissal situation, this must first be decided by a tribunal before the claim can be arbitrated. It is inconceivable that in such cases parties will use both the tribunal and arbitration in respect of the claim, and they are likely to use only the tribunal system.

A further criticism surrounds appeals. There is no right of appeal from the decision of an arbitrator except in cases where there has been a serious irregularity, such as in the conduct or the process of the hearing. The logic behind this is that arbitrators are not bound by existing law but must have regard only to the Code and the handbook. However, while tribunals must have regard to the Code, there are circumstances where an employer may successfully argue he has treated an employee fairly in breach of the Code. It is unlikely that such an argument would be successful in arbitration, particularly as arbitrators do not have to be legally qualified and would appear to raise the status of the Code and the handbook to the equivalent of near-binding legal status.

At the time of writing the scheme has been operating for some years and has heard fewer than 100 cases. All arbitration hearings and awards are confidential, and so until detailed research has been carried out, the success or otherwise of the scheme cannot be measured.

1.9.4   Inquiries

By section 214 of TULR(C)A 1992, ACAS may inquire into industrial relations generally, or into any particular industry or undertaking. The findings may then be published after taking into account the views of the parties involved.

1.9.5   Codes of practice

ACAS is one of the bodies empowered to issue Codes of Practice by section 199 of TULR(C)A 1992. There are four ACAS Codes covering disciplinary powers and grievance procedures, disclosure of information for collective bargaining purposes, time off for trade union duties and activities, and settlement agreements

1.10   Central Arbitration Committee (CAC)

The CAC was established by the Employment Protection Act 1975 (it is now regulated under s 259 of TULR(C)A 1992). It consists of a chairperson and members from both sides of industry. It has the jurisdiction to hear complaints from trade unions of failure on the part of an employer to disclose information for collective bargaining purposes. Should the employer fail to comply with a declaration of the CAC, the union may present a claim to the Committee that certain terms should become part of individual contracts of employment, and if the CAC finds the claim well founded, the award it makes automatically becomes a term of each individual contract (TULR(C)A 1992, s 185). In addition, the CAC has seen two major developments to its jurisdiction. By the Employment Relations Act 1999, it has jurisdiction to adjudicate on disputes arising from the statutory recognition procedure; and by the Transnational Information and Consultation of Employees Regulations 1999 and the Information and Consultation of Employees Regulations 2004 it now has jurisdiction in respect of certain issues such as confidentiality of information.

1.11   Certification Officer

Until recently, the Certification Officer had one main function – the issuing of certificates of independence to trade unions. Throughout the rest of this book, readers will note that many rights which accrue to trade unions and their members are given to independent trade unions. By section 5 of TULR(C)A 1992, an independent trade union is one which:

(a) is not under the domination or control of an employer or group of employers or of one or more employers' associations, and

(b) is not liable to interference by an employer or any such group or association (arising out of the provision of financial or material support or by any other means whatsoever) tending towards such control.

A trade union applies to the Certification Officer for a certificate of independence. He must decide whether the trade union is independent and issue a certificate if it falls within the statutory definition. If he feels that the union is not independent, he must give reasons for his refusal to issue a certificate. In coming to a decision, he can make any inquiries he sees fit, and can take into account any information given by other trade unions which may wish to challenge the assertion of independence.

In addition to the power to grant certificates of independence, the Certification Officer was granted additional powers by the abolition of two posts under the Employment Relations Act 1999. Prior to 1999 there were two additional Commissioners: the Commissioner for the Rights of Trade Union Members, and the Commissioner for Protection Against Unlawful Industrial Action. The 1999 Act abolished both of these posts, but the jurisdiction of the Commissioner for the Rights of Trade Union Members passed to the Certification Officer. The Certification Officer now has the jurisdiction to hear complaints brought by individuals on infringement of the laws relating to balloting for the political fund, union amalgamations and the appointment of union officers. He may also hear complaints from individual trade union members of breaches of a trade union's own rules such as disciplinary rules. His powers have been strengthened, in that he can now issue enforcement orders to ensure compliance with his decisions. An appeal from his decision lies to the EAT on a point of law.

1.12   The commissions

There are two commissions established to oversee and advise on specific areas of legislation:

▶ the Health and Safety Commission (HSC – see Section 1.12.1); and
▶ the Equality and Human Rights Commission (EHRC – see Section 1.12.2).

1.12.1   The Heath and Safety Commission (HSC)

The HSC was established by the Health and Safety at Work etc Act 1974. Its duties are the supervision of the promotion of health and safety at work. It consists of a chairperson and nine members, three from either side of industry and three appointed after consultation with local authorities. Like the other commission it has a duty to oversee the legislation and submit proposals for reform, to give advice and assistance, to disseminate information and to carry out research. The enforcement of the statutory provisions is carried out by the Health and Safety Executive. This consists of a director and two assistant directors.

1.12.2 Equality and Human Rights Commission (EHRC)

The EHRC was established by the Equality Act 2006. From October 2007 it took over the responsibilities of the Commission for Racial Equality, the Equal Opportunities Commission and the Disability Rights Commission. Its powers are wider than those of its predecessors in that in addition to responsibilities in respect of sex, race and disability discrimination, it also has responsibilities in respect of religion or belief, sexual orientation and age.

The EHRC has similar powers to its predecessors in that it can conduct inquiries, investigations and assist litigation. It can also issue an unlawful act notice which is similar to the old power to issue a non-discrimination notice, although, unlike the old power, it also has the jurisdiction to require a person to develop an action plan and the power to enter an agreement not to take legal action if the person agrees to stop committing the discriminatory act and take such steps as are specified by the Commission.

Summary

1.1 There is a variety of sources of employment law, ranging from statutes to non-legally binding codes of practice.

1.2 European Union law has had a major impact on UK employment law, particularly in the areas of transfer of undertakings, health and safety, discrimination and equal pay.

1.3 In addition to the ordinary courts, employment law has specialised adjudicative forums in the form of employment tribunals and the EAT.

1.4 The Health and Safety Commission is responsible for monitoring the operation of the Health and Safety at Work etc Act. Since October 2007, the EHRC has replaced the Equal Opportunities Commission, the Commission for Racial Equality and the Disability Rights Commission, and has a duty to monitor anti-discriminatory legislation in the areas of sex, disability, sexual orientation, religion or belief and age, thus creating a single commission with responsibility for promoting equal opportunities.

Further reading and references

Baker, 'Access vs Process in Employment Discrimination: Why ADR Suits the US but not the UK' (2002) 31 ILJ 113

Burton, 'The Employment Appeal Tribunal: October 2002–July 2005' (2005) 34 ILJ 273

Ewing, 'The Human Rights Act and labour law' (1998) 27 ILJ 275

Lightman and Bowers, 'Incorporation of the ECHR and its Impact on Employment Law' (1998) EHRLR 560

MacMillan, 'Employment Tribunals: Philosophies and Practicalities' (1999) 28 ILJ 33

Further reading and references cont'd

O'Cinneide, 'The Commission for Equality and Human Rights' (2007) 36 ILJ 141

Palmer, 'Human Rights: Implications for Labour Law' (2000) 59 CLJ 168

Skidmore, 'Labour Law in the Courts: National Judges and the European Court of Justice' (2003) 32 ILJ 334

Vickers, 'Unfair Dismissal and Human Rights' (2004) 33 ILJ 52

Part II

The employment relationship

Chapter 2

The nature of the relationship

2.1 Distinction between employees and independent contractors

It may seem a fairly obvious statement, but the two parties who make up an employment relationship are an employee and an employer. Such a distinction may not be so obvious, however, if the word 'worker' is used instead of 'employee'. Often lay people use the words interchangeably, but for a student of employment law the definition of 'employee' is vitally important and must be distinguished from that of a self-employed person or an independent contractor. This is because a variety of legal and economic consequences flow from the distinction. An employee works under a contract *of* service, whereas an independent contractor works under a contract *for* services. The major differences between the two types of contract are set out in the following sections.

2.1.1 Insurance and welfare benefits

Employees are entitled to jobseeker's allowance, statutory sick pay and a state retirement pension as long as they have paid Class 1 National Insurance Contributions (NICs). Such contributions are assessed on the employee's earnings and should be deducted at source by the employer. In addition the employer makes a contribution. By contrast, independent contractors are responsible for their own contributions and pay the lower-rate Class 2 NICs. These payments give only limited rights to certain welfare benefits and do not entitle the contributor to jobseeker's allowance or statutory sick pay.

2.1.2 PAYE

Employers must deduct tax at source from the wages of those of their employees who are so liable. It is very often because of tax liability that problems occur in this area. To take an example, a taxi driver may be given the option of having tax deducted at source or being responsible for his own payments and receiving his wages gross. He decides to take the latter option. At first sight this choice may seem perfectly reasonable, but it will be seen in Section 2.2 below that it is the law that decides on the status of a person and not the parties themselves, and should the law decide that our taxi driver is an employee, despite being paid gross, that leads to a variety of legal complications, not least that the employer may be committing a criminal offence for failing to deduct tax at source.

In *Jennings v Westwood Engineering* [1975] IRLR 245, a person was given the option of receiving his pay net or gross. He chose the latter option. Some time later he was dismissed. He sued for unfair dismissal, arguing that despite the situation he was in fact an employee. (Independent contractors have no protection against unfair dismissal, as will be seen in Section 2.1.6 below.) The court held, looking at the realities of the relationship, that Mr Jennings was indeed an employee. However, as Mr Jennings had not had tax deducted at source and had not paid any tax, the purpose of his contract had been illegal because there was an intention to defraud the Inland Revenue (now HM Revenue and Customs (HMRC)). As all students of contract will be aware, a contract set up for an illegal purpose is void and no rights can arise from it. As such, Mr Jennings could not rely on his rights not to be unfairly dismissed. *Jennings* should be distinguished from *Hewcastle Catering Ltd v Ahmed* [1992] ICR 626, where the Court of Appeal distinguished between contracts which were formed for an illegal purpose and contracts which were legal at their inception but which were performed illegally. The Court held that in the latter case, the innocence of the employee would be a defence and the contract would be saved. Thus in that case, waiters who were dismissed, and where it was later discovered that the employer was committing VAT fraud, could still sue for unfair dismissal. The cases of *Enfield Technical Services v Payne/Grace v BF Components Ltd* [2007] All ER 394 may, however, throw some doubt on *Jennings*. In the joined cases the Employment Appeal Tribunal (EAT) held that to defeat an unfair dismissal claim on the grounds of an illegal contract, there must be some misrepresentation or hiding of the true relationship. A mislabelling of the relationship or an arrangement which deprives HMRC of monies is not enough to render the contract illegal. (This decision was confirmed by the Court of Appeal, [2008] EWCA Civ 393.)

2.1.3   Vicarious liability

Employers can be made vicariously liable for the torts of their employees committed during the course of their employment. As a general principle, there is no such liability for independent contractors.

2.1.4   Safety

The standard of care employers must exercise in relation to their employees' safety, both at common law and under statute, is generally higher than that owed to independent contractors.

2.1.5   Terms in the contract

In addition to the terms the parties themselves have negotiated, the law implies a host of terms into the employment relationship. The law will rarely interfere in a contract between an employer and an independent contractor.

2.1.6   Employment protection rights

An employee enjoys a large number of employment protection rights. These include the right not to be unfairly dismissed, the right to redundancy payment, statutory maternity pay, statutory sick pay, security of employment after maternity leave, protection of the right to belong or not to belong to a trade union, and rights to time off. Independent contractors have no such protection, with one notable exception. Everyone is protected under anti-discriminatory legislation where they are providing personal services (*Quinnen v Hovells* [1984] IRLR 227; and see also *BP Chemicals v Gillick* [1995] IRLR 128).

2.1.7   Employee shareholders

The Growth and Infrastructure Act 2013 introduced a new type of employment status from 1 September 2013. It inserts new section 205A into the Employment Rights Act (ERA) 1996. This provides that an employer can award a person at least £2,000 in shares in exchange for that person giving up a number of employment protection rights. This offer may be made to existing employees or to new employees, and there is protection for existing employees who refuse to change their status but no protection for an applicant for a job who is rejected because he or she does not want employee shareholder status. An agreement cannot be accepted by the employee until seven days has elapsed, and any acceptance prior to the seven-day deadline is not binding. Furthermore, an agreement is not binding unless the employee has received advice from an relevant independent adviser. The employer is required to pay the reasonable costs of this advice, even if the employee does not take up the offer of employee shareholder status.

The employer has to give the employee a written statement with full details of the shares and the rights they carry, such as whether they are voting shares, whether they will attract a dividend and whether there are restrictions on selling them, and also a written statement setting out the employment protection rights the employee will be relinquishing. These rights are the right not to be unfairly dismissed under section 94 of the ERA 1996 (unless the reason for the dismissal is a refusal to accept employee shareholder status, in which case the normal two-year continuity rule does not apply), the right to statutory redundancy pay under section 135, the right to time off to undertake study or training under section 63D and the right to request flexible working under section 80F. Furthermore, the normal eight-week notice period to be given to an employer when an employee is returning from maternity leave or adoption leave is increased to 16 weeks for employee shareholders. In addition to protection from unfair dismissal for refusing to change status, a new section 47G protects employees from suffering a detriment because of such refusal.

HM Revenue and Customs will, if asked, undertake a valuation check prior to employee shareholder shares being awarded. The first £2,000 worth of shares do not attract income tax, and employee shareholder shares worth up to £50,000 on acquisition are free from capital gains tax when sold.

At the time of writing this new type of employment status had just been introduced and has attracted a lot of criticism. The present government got its way, but only after it had made a number of concessions to appease the House of Lords. It will be interesting to see how workable this new type of status will be and how many employers will take up the opportunity. In reality it will be attractive only to a small employer.

2.2   Tests for determining status

It can be seen from the discussion in Section 2.1 above that it is important for both parties to know at the outset whether the relationship is that of employer–employee. Even employee shareholders are, for most purposes, employees. It has also been noted that it is the courts who determine that status; the name the parties give to the relationship is, normally, irrelevant. The courts over the years have devised a series of tests to apply to a relationship to determine the status of the parties within it.

2.2.1   Control test

The early cases, where the courts began looking at the nature of the relationship, arose in the context of vicarious liability, and in some ways it was obvious to look at the control the employer exercised over the worker. In *Performing Rights Society v Mitchell and Booker* [1924] 1 KB 762, McCardie J said that 'the final test, if there is to be a final test, and certainly the test to be generally applied, lies in the nature and degree of detailed control over the person alleged to be a servant'. The basis of the test was whether the employer not only controlled when a job was done, but also how it was done. If a large amount of control existed in relation to the method and content of the work, the person was in an employment relationship.

The control test, as a single test, worked well where there were unskilled workers but fell down when workers became more skilled than the persons employing them. The control test taken to its logical conclusion was shown not to work in *Hillyer v Governors of St Bartholomew's Hospital* [1909] 2 KB 820, where it was held that nurses were not employees of a hospital when carrying out operating theatre duties. Although the courts took the realistic approach in *Cassidy v Minister of Health* [1951] 2 KB 343, increased technology meant that in a large number of cases control did not determine the true nature of the relationship and a more realistic test was needed.

2.2.2   Organisation test

As it became obvious that the control test, on its own, was inadequate for a modern industrial society, the judiciary tried to develop a new test which took into account industrial reality. To this end Denning LJ developed what became known as the organisation or integration test in 1952, in a case called *Stevenson, Jordan & Harrison Ltd v Macdonald and Evans* (1952) 1 TLR 101. There, he said that 'under a contract of service a man is employed as part of the business and his work is done as an integral part of the business but under a contract for services his work, although done for the business, is not integrated into it but only accessory to it'. Although as a test it overcame the problems with the control test, Denning LJ did not explain what he meant by 'integration' or 'organisation' and so the test was never widely used.

2.2.3   Multiple test

Over the years, the courts have realised that no one factor can be identified to denote an employment relationship. Such a relationship is complex and consists of a variety of factors depending on the nature of the job and the relative skills of the employer and the employee. It is this multiplicity of factors that the judges now look to, and consequently the predominant test used is known as the multiple test, indicating that one factor alone cannot identify the type of relationship. The test began in the case of *Ready Mixed Concrete (South East) Ltd v MPNI* [1968] 2 QB 497. The appellants were arguing that the lorry drivers they employed were independent contractors and so the appellants were not liable for paying their NICs. McKenna J looked at a variety of factors to determine the status of the lorry drivers. On the facts there were some factors indicating an employment relationship and others indicating that the drivers were self-employed, as shown below:

Employee factors
- Lorry painted in company colours
- Lorry for exclusive company use
- Had to obey orders
- Minimum payment of £1,500 per year

Self-employed factors
- Bought lorry by company loan
- Maintained own lorry use
- Could delegate driving duties
- After the minimum payment, paid on amount of concrete carried

McKenna J then identified three conditions which must be present for the relationship to be one of employment:

1. the employee agrees to provide his skill in consideration of a wage;
2. there is an element of control exercised by the employer; and
3. provisions in the contract are consistent with its being a contract of service.

On the basis of the final condition, McKenna J decided that the lorry drivers were self-employed because they could delegate driving duties, and the basis of an employment relationship is that the duties within it cannot be delegated. The decision has since been criticised, but not the essence of the test. Later cases have seen judges looking at a host of factors within a relationship and balancing them to identify whether there are more factors indicating a person is self-employed rather than an employee or vice versa. Cooke J summarised the approach of the courts in the case of *Market Investigations Ltd v MSS* [1969] 2 QB 173, when he said that the question to be determined by the court was whether a person was in business on his own account. If so, then there was a contract for services and not a contract of service.

These pronouncements by judges, however, are in many ways not helpful as they leave the question: What factors indicate that a person is an employee rather than self-employed? Certainly, it is the law that decides on the status of a person and not the parties themselves, although the starting point is the terms of the agreement, unless it is shown that the agreement is a sham. Recently, in *Troutbeck SA v White and Todd* [2013] EWCA Civ 1171, the Court of Appeal stated that the control element of McKenna's test does not mean that the employer has to exercise actual control but that there is a contractual right of control. In the case the claimants were caretakers of a small estate on behalf of owners who visited once or twice a year. The agreement set out the claimants' responsibilities and duties, and there were several references in the agreement to 'employment'. The Court held that the claimants were employees, as neither party disputed that the agreement did not reflect the true nature of their relationship, unlike in *Autoclenz v Belcher* (below).

The fact that the parties think that a person is an independent contractor will be one of the factors the court will take into account. In *Ferguson v John Dawson Ltd* [1976] IRLR 346, a builder's labourer agreed to work as a self-employed worker. He was injured when he fell off a roof. No guardrail had been provided, which was in breach of a duty owed to employees under the Construction (Working Places) Regulations 1966. The employer argued that the plaintiff was self-employed and that consequently no duty was owed to him. The Court of Appeal disagreed. In reality the plaintiff was an employee, and a statement as to the status of a person was a factor but not a conclusive factor. It appears, however, that if there is ambiguity as to whether the relationship is one of employment, the courts will resolve such ambiguity by looking at what the parties consider the relationship to be. This comes from a statement by Lord Denning MR in the case of *Massey v Crown Life Insurance Co* [1978] ICR 590, although this has been doubted in later cases, particularly by Stephenson LJ in *Young & Wood Ltd v West* [1980] IRLR 201 when he said: 'It must be the court's duty to see whether the label correctly represents the true legal relationship between the parties.' In *Protectacoat Firthglow Ltd v Szilagyi* [2009] EWCA Civ 98, Szilagyi worked for Protectacoat and claimed unfair dismissal. The company argued that it did not employ him, as he had signed a partnership agreement which showed he was a partner and not an employee. Szilagyi argued that because Protectacoat supplied his van and tools and had control over him, and he was not free to work elsewhere, this made him an employee. The Court of Appeal had to decide whether the agreement was a sham. It stated that normally the nature of the relationship can be found in the contract between the parties, but if it is claimed that the agreement does not reflect the true relationship, the court or tribunal has to decide what the true relationship is. It is up to the court to decide the true intentions of the parties, not only when the document was drawn up but, if appropriate, during the course of the relationship. This has led to cases where it has been held that ministers of religion can be employees if this was the intention of the parties (*Percy v Board of National Mission of the Church of Scotland* [2006] ICR 134). Conversely, the Supreme Court has more recently decided that the detailed internal arrangements of the Methodist Church led it to conclude that there was no intention to create legal relations between the Church and one of its ministers, in *Methodist Conference v Preston* [2013] UKSC 29. Each case turns on its own facts.

An agreement which is shown to be a sham should be wholly disregarded when deciding what the true nature of the relationship is, although Sedley LJ in *Protectacoat* (above) said that the more helpful position is to look at the true nature of the relationship and not consider whether the agreement is a sham. Nevertheless, on the facts in *Protectacoat* the Court decided that the agreement was meant to conceal the actual relationship and that Szilagyi was an employee. Likewise in *Autoclenz v Belcher* [2009] EWCA Civ 1046, car valeters had a contract which stated that they were not required to turn up for work and could send a substitute, but which also required them to notify the company if they were going to send someone else. The Court of Appeal held that the two terms were inconsistent, and the former did not reflect the true relationship between the parties as in reality no substitution had ever taken place. As such, the tribunal was entitled to look at the reality and conclude that the substitution clause did not reflect the true relationship between the parties. There was no need to establish that the clause was deliberately trying to mislead. The decision was upheld by the Supreme Court ([2011] UKSC 41).

The courts, therefore, decide the status of the relationship by looking to see if a person is really in business on his own account. This involves looking at a variety of factors such as investment, ownership of tools, who bears the risk of loss and who stands to make a profit. Whereas in a large number of cases these questions are easily answered, in some situations it is difficult to come to any firm conclusions. Homeworkers, for example, are a group of persons who, on the face of it, appear to be self-employed. In *Airfix Footwear Ltd v Cope* [1978] IRLR 396, it was held that homeworkers were employees because work was provided on a regular basis and in reality the employer decided on the way in which the job was to be done, and the time and place of performance. In *Nethermere (St Neots) Ltd v Taverna and Another* [1984] IRLR 240, the Court of Appeal again decided that homeworkers were employees because although there was no legal obligation on the employer to provide work, a mutuality of obligations existed in reality based on the long-standing relationship between the employer and the workers concerned. This mutuality of obligations – that the employer will provide the work and the employee will provide his services – is the essence of an employment relationship, and if it is lacking then the court will decide there is a contract for services. Thus in *Little v BMI Chiltern Hospital* (2009) UKEAT/0021/09/DA, the fact that the employer could and did send workers home halfway through their shift, without pay, when their services were not required, negatived the existence of mutuality of obligations. In *O'Kelly and Others v Trusthouse Forte plc* [1983] IRLR 369, the plaintiff was a regular casual worker who was given preference when work was available. In a claim for unfair dismissal, the tribunal held that the casual workers were self-employed, even though they worked solely for one employer because of the long hours they had to work. The most important factor for the tribunal, in reaching this conclusion, was that there was no obligation on the employer to provide work and no obligation on the casual workers to offer their services. This lack of mutuality was the clear reason for the decision, despite the facts that the employer had total control over the workers while they were at work and it would be difficult to describe a casual worker as in business on his own account. Again, in *Carmichael and Leese v National Power plc* [2000] IRLR 43, the House of Lords decided that guides employed on a 'casual as required' basis were self-employed because of the lack of mutuality.

Lack of mutuality has led to decisions that agency temporaries are self-employed (*Wickens v Champion Employment* [1984] ICR 365), although the case of *McMeechan v Secretary of State for Employment* [1997] IRLR 353 said that this is not a general proposition. There, the fact that there was a weekly wage, obligations of fidelity and confidence, a power of dismissal and a grievance procedure led the court to conclude that the agency worker was an employee of the agency. In *Serco Ltd v Blair* (1998) IDS Brief 624, the EAT held that agency workers who had a written agreement with the client company in which they were placed by the agency did not have an employment relationship with the client. The EAT held that the test in *Ready Mixed Concrete* (above) was not satisfied, in that the client did not exercise a sufficient degree of control over the agency workers, the workers were free not to accept the placement and the agency could terminate the agreement. However, in *Motorola Ltd v Davidson* [2001] IRLR 4, an agency worker who had a written agreement with the client, Motorola, to comply with all reasonable instructions, was held to be employed by Motorola because there was a sufficient degree of day-to-day control. *Dacas v Brook Street Bureau (UK) Ltd* [2008] EWCA Civ 35 seemed potentially to give protection to agency workers when the Court of Appeal suggested that, because of mutuality of obligations and the control exercised by the client over the worker, Ms Dacas was an employee of the client and not of the agency. While this would appear clear-cut, in the case of *Bunce v Postworth Ltd and Skyblue* [2005] EWCA Civ 490 (CA), the Court found that as there was no mutuality nor any real control exercised by the agency over Mr Bunce, he was not an employee of the agency. The same conclusion was reached in the race discrimination case of *Mingeley v Pennock and Ivory t/a Amber Cars* [2004] IRLR 373, where the Court of Appeal held that where someone is free to work when it suits him and does not have an obligation to work, he cannot be an employee.

After *Dacas* there was a spate of cases involving agency workers. In *James v Greenwich Borough Council* [2008] EWCA Civ 35, Mrs James was an agency worker who had worked for Greenwich Council for five years. The EAT upheld the tribunal decision that there was no implied contract of employment between Mrs James and the Council. The EAT said it was inappropriate to imply a contract when the end-user could not insist on the agency supplying a particular worker, and went on to say that implying mutuality of obligations between the worker and the end-user is inconsistent with a normal agency arrangement and that a tribunal can infer a contract between the worker and end user only if, after the relationship has commenced, there are words or conduct which would entitle the tribunal to conclude that the agency arrangements no longer reflect how the work is performed. Elias P also said that such circumstances would be rare and that the passage of time does not justify the implication of a contract. This decision was upheld by the Court of Appeal and was followed in *Craigie v London Borough of Haringey* [2007] All ER 82, *Heatherwood & Wexham Park Hospitals NHS Trust v Kulubowlia* (2007) UKEAT 0633/06 and *Astbury v Gist* (2007) UKEAT 0619/06, all EAT decisions. The EAT has also held that volunteer workers do not have contracts of employment in *South East Sheffield Citizens' Advice Bureau v Grayson* [2004] IRLR 353, confirmed by the Supreme Court in *X v Mid Sussex CAB* [2012] UKSC 59.

The most recent agency case is the Court of Appeal decision in *Tilson v Alstom Transport* [2010] EWCA Civ 1308. In the case the claimant, who was provided to the end-user by an agency, had worked for the end-user for just over two years before he was dismissed by the end-user. He had begun work as a technical engineer but had been promoted to fleet health manager. In that role he had permanent employees reporting to him whom he could discipline and dismiss, and he could order materials and negotiate contracts on behalf of the company. He was responsible to his line manager and had to, for example, obtain his permission before taking annual leave. He had been offered a permanent contract by the end-user, but had refused it because in essence it would have meant a reduction in pay. It was clear that there was no express contract between the claimant and the end-user, but the claimant argued that as he was so integrated into the business, a contract of service could be implied, and thus he could claim unfair dismissal. The Court of Appeal stated that although the worker was integrated into the business, on the facts, given that he had rejected a contract of employment, a contract would not be implied.

The position of agency workers is therefore not clear-cut, as tribunals are bound by the Court of Appeal. Consequently, if *Dacas*, *McMeechan* or *Davidson* applies, such workers are employees of either the agency or the client; and if none of those cases is applicable, such workers are self-employed under *Bunce*, *Wickens*, *Blair* and the EAT decisions noted above, and thus have limited employment protection. Some protection will exist. The Working Time Regulations 1998 (see Chapter 4) specifically provide that workers who are supplied by an agency to do work for a principal and who would not otherwise be covered by the Regulations because of the absence of a contract with the agent or principal, are taken to be employed, for the purposes of the Regulations, by whoever is paying them (Reg 36). Similar provisions are also included in the National Minimum Wage Act 1998. Certain rights introduced by the Employment Relations Act 1999 and anti-discrimination legislation apply to workers or those who agree to provide services personally. Without the existence of an employment relationship, however, protection in respect of unfair dismissal and redundancy is not available.

The government originally intended to introduce measures amending the Employment Agencies Act 1973, to make the contractual position of agency workers clearer. The

Conduct of Employment Agencies and Employment Businesses Regulations 2002, however, did not achieve this completely. The Regulations give increasing differentiation between employment agencies and employment businesses. An *employment agency* provides a work-finding service for work-seekers and provides workers for employers, thus creating a contractual relationship between the work-seeker and the employer. This may or may not be an employment relationship depending on the factors in *Davidson* or *Blair* above. In a case prior to the Regulations, a contractor who hired himself out, through an agency, was not regarded as an employee of a third party because there was no contractual relationship between him and the hirer (*Hewlett Packard Ltd v O'Murphy* [2002] IRLR 4). An *employment business*, on the other hand, engages its own workforce which it supplies to hirers. Regulation 15 provides that the agreement between the employment business and the worker must state whether the relationship is one of a contract of service, a contract for services or an apprenticeship. If it is a contract for services, certain basic terms must apply relating to pay and holidays, but it leaves the worker taken on by an employment business on a contract for services little protection in a dismissal situation. The Agency Worker Regulations 2010, introduced in 2011, give agency workers who have been employed by the end-user for a continuous 12 weeks on an assignment the protection of the same rights as permanent employees employed by the end-user. Regulation 5 gives such workers the right to the same working and employment conditions as permanent workers, to include pay, working time and holiday entitlement, in addition to employment protection rights such as flexible working, redundancy rights, rights to time off, etc.

Lack of protection still exists, however, in certain types of employment. In *Hellyer Brothers Ltd v McLeod* [1987] 1 WLR 728, trawler men who entered into separate crew agreements for each voyage were found to be self-employed and therefore not entitled to a redundancy payment, despite the fact that they invariably returned to the same employer year after year. Lack of mutuality was the key factor.

The Privy Council highlighted the factors the courts take into account in the case of *Lee v Chung & Shun Chung Construction and Engineering Co Ltd* [1990] IRLR 236. In this case the worker was a mason who suffered an injury while working on a building site. The Privy Council looked back to the judgment in *Market Investigations* (above) and asked itself the question whether the plaintiff was in business on his own account. The Privy Council continued:

> Other matters which may be of importance are whether the worker provides his own equipment, whether he hires his own helpers, what degree of financial risk he takes, what degree of responsibility he has for investment and management and whether and how far he has the opportunity to profit from sound management in the performance of his task.

By looking at all these factors the Privy Council decided that the plaintiff was an employee. In *Hall (Inspector of Taxes) v Lorimer* [1994] IRLR 171, however, the court stressed that the factors should not be gone through mechanically. Here the employee worked as a vision mixer. He used the equipment of the television company that employed him and was paid a lump sum plus travelling expenses for each job he did. He was registered for VAT, had his own pension and sickness policies, took bookings from home and had no long-term contracts with any single company. None of his own money was used in the production of any of the programmes he mixed, neither did he stand to make a profit or loss from any of the programmes. The Special Commissioners had found that Lorimer was self-employed. The Inland Revenue appealed against this decision, arguing that it was the production company who controlled when and where he worked, provided the equipment and had the financial stake in the programme. The court held it could not run through a checklist of items to determine if a person was self-employed: 'The whole picture has to be painted and then viewed from a distance to reach an informed and qualitative decision in the circumstances of the particular case.' The Special Commissioners, on the evidence before them, had reached a conclusion and there was no evidence that their decision was unsustainable on the facts. As such, the court would not interfere with that decision.

More recently the Court of Appeal has overturned the EAT by holding that a lap dancer is not an employee. In *Stringfellow Restaurants Ltd v Quashie* [2012] EWCA Civ 1735, Ms Quashie was a lap dancer at 'Stringfellows' nightclub. She was claiming unfair dismissal, and the preliminary issue was whether she was an employee. The EAT held that she was an employee because on the nights she worked there was a contract of employment as she had to perform the work personally, 'Stringfellows' was obliged to provide her with work and there was an element of control as she was subject to disciplinary sanctions. However, the Court of Appeal disagreed. Whereas Elias LJ found that when Ms Quashie was working there was a contract and some mutuality, 'Stringfellows' was under no obligation to pay her as she negotiated her own fees with her clients and therefore bore the risk of being out of pocket. Elias LJ said '[i]t would, I think, be an unusual case where a contract of service is found to exist when the worker takes the economic risk and is paid exclusively by third parties'.

Other cases have talked about the irreducible minimum needed to constitute a contract of employment. In *Carmichael and Leese* (above), mutuality was seen as the irreducible minimum; while in *Express Echo Publications Ltd v Tanton* [1999] IRLR 367, the Court of Appeal regarded personal service by the employee as the irreducible minimum, so that a power to delegate job duties was fatal to an employment claim. This was also the case in *Staffordshire Sentinel Newspapers Ltd v Potter* [2004] IRLR 752, where a contract which allowed substitutes with company approval (and where such substitutes had been used) was held not to be a contract of employment because it did not require personal service. This would seem to go against *Macfarlane v Glasgow City Council* [2001] IRLR 7, however, where an earlier EAT stated that a limited or occasional power of delegation is not inconsistent with a contract of employment. This was supported by *Byrne Brothers (Formwork) Ltd v Baird* [2002] IRLR 96. The issue in this case was slightly different in that it considered the definition of 'worker' for the purpose of the statutory rights introduced by the Employment Relations Act 1999. Section 230 of the ERA 1996 defines a worker as working under a contract of employment or 'any other contract … to do or perform personally any work or services for another party to the contract …'. In *Baird* the issue was whether a building contractor, who was permitted in his contract, with the express permission of the employer, to engage another person to do the job when he was unable to do it himself, fell within the definition in section 230. The court held that he was a worker, and distinguished *Tanton* on the basis that in *Tanton* the person could delegate not only when he was unable to do the job but also when he was unwilling to do the job. Thus, in *Baird* a limited power to delegate was not inconsistent with an obligation of personal service. So too in *Redrow Homes (Yorkshire) Ltd v Wright* [2004] IRLR 721, the Court of Appeal decided that bricklayers were workers, not self-employed, even though their contracts permitted substitution and even though substitutes had never been used. By contrast, in *Community Dental Centres Ltd v Sultan-Darmon* [2010] All ER (D) 99, the EAT held that an unfettered right of substitution in a contract meant that the claimant could not be a worker within the meaning of section 230(3) of the ERA 1996 as he was not obliged to 'perform personally any work or services'.

A useful decision in this area is the case of *Ministry of Defence Dental Services v Kettle* [2007] All ER 301. Dr Kettle responded to an advertisement for a part-time dentist issued by the Ministry of Defence. According to the employment judge, the advertisement was worded in such a way as to indicate that the successful applicant would be employed under a contract of employment. Dr Kettle was successful in her application. The documentation she signed, however, described her as a contractor and explicitly allowed her to delegate her services to a suitably qualified substitute, although she pointed out that she would never be able to find a substitute and when she was on holiday the Ministry provided cover. She paid her own tax and insurance. Although the contract was to run from March to September it was abruptly terminated in June. The tribunal held that she was an employee, despite the substitution clause in the contract, on the basis of the wording of the advertisement and the conduct of the parties. The Ministry appealed to the EAT. Richardson J looked at the decision in *Carmichael and Leese* and said that where there is a document which is said to be contractual, it is a question of fact for the tribunal whether the parties intended the document to be an exclusive record of their agreement. If it is then generally a tribunal can only look at the document and interpret it, but if the tribunal decides that the parties do not intend the document to be exclusive then the tribunal can look at other materials, oral exchanges and conduct. The EAT concluded that it was clear from the advertisement and the conduct of the parties that the documentation did not reflect the intention of the parties. It did not, for example, state how many hours Dr Kettle was to work, although this was stated in the advertisement and agreed between the parties. It also referred to Dr Kettle as an organisation, which clearly she was not, and Dr Kettle, when she questioned the appropriateness of the documentation, pointed out it would be impossible for her to provide a substitute. As such there was both mutuality of obligations between the parties and control exercised by the Ministry, and consequently Dr Kettle was an employee.

It would appear, therefore, that a clause allowing substitution may not prevent a person's being an employee if, in reality, such substitution is impossible. However, in *Archer-Hoblin v MacGettigan* (2009) UKEAT 0037/09/0307, Slade J, in the EAT, stated that the construction of substitution clauses must be carried out using the normal rules of construction, and unless such a clause is a sham, an unfettered right of substitution is inconsistent with an obligation to perform the work personally. However, while what happened in practice could not be used to construe the meaning of the clause, it could be looked at to determine whether the clause was a sham. He then remitted the case to a fresh tribunal to determine whether the substitution clause was a sham (although note *Autoclenz* above).

It may appear that this is a grey area of the law and that no situation is clear-cut. What we can glean from the cases, however, is that the courts, when using the multiple test, look at a wide range of factors, of which control, mutuality of obligations and personal service seem to be the most important.

Summary

2.1 An employee has far greater rights than an independent contractor, and so it is important to determine the status of the parties in the relationship.

2.2 The consequences of a wrong analysis can be criminal liability, and the contract may be rendered void on the basis of illegality.

2.3 The courts decide the nature of the relationship, not the parties.

2.4 The courts have used various tests over the years to help them to decide the true nature of the relationship before them.

2.5 The present test used by the courts is the multiple test. This involves the court looking at a variety of factors, of which the most important are control, personal service and mutuality of obligations.

Exercises

2.1 What are the differences between an employee and an independent contractor?

2.2 What are the three tests used by the courts over the years to determine the nature of the relationship?

2.3 Florence works from home. Her employers, Roundabout Products, sell Christmas crackers. Florence has worked for the company, making up crackers, for six years. She receives no holiday or sick pay and is paid per 100 crackers she assembles. She uses no machinery in her work. Although she can work when she wishes, over the past four years she has worked constantly from October to January, averaging 500 crackers per week; and then when demand has dropped, she has worked intermittently throughout the rest of the year when work has been available, averaging 200 crackers per week. Roundabout Products has informed Florence that they are closing their operation and they will no longer require her services. Florence wishes to claim a redundancy payment. Advise Florence whether she will be entitled to make a claim for a redundancy payment.

Further reading and references

Albin, 'The Case of Quashie: Between the Legalisation of Sex Work and the Precariousness of Personal Service Work' (2013) 42 ILJ 180

Bogg, 'Sham Self Employment in the Supreme Court' (2012) 41 ILJ 328

Davidov, 'Who is a Worker?' (2005) 34 ILJ 57

Davies, 'Casual Workers and Continuity of Employment' (2006) 35 ILJ 196

Deakin, 'Does the Personal Employment Contract Provide a Basis for the Reunification of Employment Law?' (2007) 36 ILJ 68

Fredman, 'Labour Law in Flux: The Changing Composition of the Workforce' (1997) 26 ILJ 337

Freedland, 'From the Contract of Employment to the Personal Work Nexus' (2006) 35 ILJ 1

Hakim, 'Employment Rights: A Comparison of Part-Time and Full-Time Employees' (1989) 18 ILJ 69

Jones, 'Temporary Agency Labour: Back to Square One?' (2002) 31 ILJ 183

Further reading and references cont'd

Leighton and Wynn, 'Classifying Employment Relationships – More Sliding Doors or a Better Regulatory Framework?' (2011) 40 ILJ 45

Reynolds, 'The Status of Agency Workers: A Question of Legal Principle' (2006) 35 ILJ 320

Wedderburn, 'Labour Law 2008: 40 Years on' (2007) 36 ILJ 397

Wynn and Leighton, 'Will the Real Employer Please Stand Up?' (2006) 35 ILJ 301

Chapter 3

Terms of the contract

3.1 Express terms

The employment relationship is a contractual one and as such must have all the basic elements of an enforceable contract to make it legally binding. In strict contractual terms, the offer is made by the employer and is formally or informally accepted by the employee. This acceptance may be oral or in writing, or conversely the employee may signify his acceptance merely by turning up for work on the appointed day. The consideration within the contract is the promise to pay wages on the part of the employer, and the promise to provide his services on the part of the employee. Once the acceptance has taken place there is a legally binding agreement, and a claim will lie against the party who breaches that agreement, even though it may only just have come into existence. In *Taylor v Furness, Withy & Co Ltd* (1969) 6 KIR 488, a dock worker was sent by the Dock Labour Board to a new employer. The employer sent him a letter welcoming him and an identity card to sign. When the employee arrived to begin his employment, the employer discovered that he had let his union membership lapse and, under the terms of the Dock Labour Scheme, the employer could not employ him. The employee was therefore sent home. He sued the employer for a week's wages, the notice he was entitled to under the contract. The employer argued that as the plaintiff had never worked, the contract had not come into existence. It was held that, by signing the identity card, the plaintiff had accepted the employer's offer, and at that time a legally binding contract came into existence. The plaintiff was thus legally entitled to one week's notice which he did not receive and the court awarded a week's pay as damages. Similarly, in *Sarker v South Tees Acute Hospitals NHS Trust* [1997] IRLR 328, Sarker was offered a job by the Trust which she accepted, but the job offer was withdrawn before the start date. It was held that the Trust was in breach of contract.

A complex case *is Dresdner Kleinword Ltd and Commerzbank AG v Attrill and ors* [2013] EWCA Civ 394, where the issue was whether statements made by the employer were intended to create legal relations and had become contractually binding. To simplify a complex set of facts, there were discussions in August 2008 that Commerzbank was going to acquire Dresdner Kleinword. This caused some disquiet amongst employees. The sale was agreed on 31 August 2008 and the shares transferred in January 2009. The contracts of all employees entitled them to discretionary annual bonuses, but they also contained a clause allowing the employer to vary the contract unilaterally; and if such a variation affected a group of employees, such variation would be communicated by notice boards and intranet. Due to the disquiet amongst employees and to ensure that there would not be a mass exodus of staff, the Dresdner Board agreed a bonus pool of €400 million, and this was communicated to the employees by intranet, stating that that fund would be distributed 'no matter what'. On 20 October 2008 an e-mail was sent to all staff stating that the bonuses would be announced in December 2008 and included in January's pay. However, the banking crisis then hit, and in December 2008 employees were sent a letter saying that the size of the bonus pool was subject to the bank's earnings not reducing. Eventually, in January 2009 the Board agreed to reduce the pool by 90 per cent. The Court of Appeal held that the announcements and statements to all workers were sufficiently precise to constitute contractual terms and that there was an intention to create legal relations. The workers had given consideration by staying with the bank and not seeking employment elsewhere. The fact that the bank's circumstances had changed did not mean that it could no longer honour its contractual promise of a guaranteed minimum bonus pool.

The essence of any contract is the terms within it, for they show what the parties intended. However, an employment contract is unlike most other contracts. Although the parties will have negotiated the main terms, we shall see that a large number of terms will be implied into the agreement from all sorts of different sources and will not have been individually negotiated by the parties at all.

Express terms are the terms agreed by the parties. The employee is unlikely to have accepted the job without knowing his salary and hours of work, and therefore these will have been agreed by the parties before the commencement of the relationship. From an employer's point of view it is better to have agreed as many terms as possible. It ensures certainty, so that both parties know where they stand at the outset. Express terms, however, may cause problems. If the term itself is ambiguous, the courts will interpret the term should a dispute arise. Many an employer has discovered that his idea of 'reasonable overtime' differs greatly from both his employee's interpretation and that of the court (see, for example, *Johnstone v Bloomsbury Area Health Authority* [1991] ICR 269). Likewise, because the express terms do show the parties' intentions, if the term is inaccurate, that can lead to problems. In *Stubbes v Trower, Still & Keeling* [1987] IRLR 321, a firm of solicitors, in offering articles, omitted to provide expressly that the applicant had to pass the Law Society Final Examination before he could begin. The Court of Appeal held that this was not a requirement of the articles.

In addition to pay and hours, often the parties will have stated the details of the job. This means that should an employee refuse to perform duties to which he has agreed, the employer will have a claim for breach of contract. In *Wiluszynski v London Borough of Tower Hamlets* [1989] IRLR 259 there was a NALGO dispute and, as part of industrial action, some employees were refusing to answer councillors' questions. These duties took up about half an hour of a 37-hour week. Before the action started, the council informed the employees that if they did not perform the full range of their duties they would be held to be in breach of contract and would not be paid. The plaintiff took part in industrial action for five weeks and the council refused to pay him for any of the other duties he had performed. The Court of Appeal upheld the council's action. Answering councillors' questions was a material part of the employee's duties, and he had refused to perform that material part. As such, the employee had committed a repudiatory breach of contract. In such circumstances the employer has the choice of accepting the breach as terminating the contract, or waiving the breach. In the case the council had made it clear that it considered the breach would terminate the relationship. Furthermore, by allowing the employee to continue working, the employer had not waived the breach and affirmed the contract. It was unrealistic to expect the employer of large numbers of employees to identify and physically eject those taking industrial action. Therefore, when the employee was working during the industrial action, he was doing so voluntarily and was not entitled to payment.

Wiluszynski should be distinguished from the earlier cases of *Sim v Rotherham Metropolitan Borough Council* [1986] IRLR 391 and *Miles v Wakefield Metropolitan District Council* [1987] IRLR 193, in both of which employees were refusing to perform part of their duties as part of industrial action. In *Miles*, superintendent registrars were refusing to perform weddings on Saturdays; in *Sim*, teachers were refusing to cover for absent colleagues. In both cases the employer deducted a proportion of pay, representative of the non-fulfilment of contractual duties, and the action was upheld by the court.

The three cases demonstrate two important points. First, if the employee refuses to perform some of his duties, that is a breach of contract and the employer is entitled to assess his damages and withhold the pay which represents the duties not performed. This is the decision in *Miles* and *Sim*. Second, if the employer feels that the employee is refusing to perform a material part of his duties, and he informs the employee that this is the case and that he regards the employee's breach as repudiatory, then the employer is entitled to withhold all of the employee's wages until he is prepared to fulfil all the terms of his contract. The employer must ensure, however, that he does nothing to waive the breach, and if possible should prevent the employee from doing any work. This is the decision in *Wiluszynski*. Whereas the court seems to be prepared to accept the employer's contention that certain duties are a material part of the employee's contract, there may be a challenge where the employer is deducting a proportion of wages for non-performance, if the employee feels that the deduction is not truly representative of the amount of lost work.

Apart from the above, express terms usually cause no problems and can help both parties because they cannot be ousted by implied terms. In *Deeley v British Rail Engineering Ltd* [1980] IRLR 147, an advertisement was displayed for a sales engineer (export). The plaintiff applied for and was given the job, but his contract described him as a sales engineer. He argued that his job was limited to export because of the advertisement and applied to the court to clarify the position. The court held that the contract prevailed. The express term was clear and it could not be overridden by an implied term. It should be noted, however, that the interpretation of an express term may be subject to the implied duties discussed in Chapter 4 (see *Johnstone v Bloomsbury Area Health Authority* and *St Budeaux Royal British Legion Club Ltd v Cropper* (1995) IDS Brief 552).

The law, to a large extent, allows parties to negotiate any terms they wish, subject to the restrictions noted below, and a clear agreement showing both sides' intentions can save a lot of trouble. There are three main statutory restrictions on the express terms in an employment contract. These are:

1. The employer cannot restrict his liability for the death or personal injury of his employees caused by his negligence. Further, he may restrict or limit his liability for damage to his employees' property only if such a term is reasonable in the circumstances (Unfair Contract Terms Act 1977, s 2).
2. Certain express terms must not infringe the Equality Act 2010.
3. No term of the contract can take away an employee's right to take action in the courts or the employment tribunal (Employment Rights Act (ERA) 1996, s 203).

3.1.1   Variation of terms

The employment relationship is an ever-changing one, particularly with the introduction of new technology which will often affect the way the employee performs his job. One of the problems with express terms in the contract is that, if they are very specific, they may not allow for the flexibility inherent in the relationship. On contractual principles, any changes in the terms of the contract must be mutually agreed, and the employer who attempts a unilateral variation may find a constructive dismissal claim being brought against him. In some situations, the courts may be prepared to agree that the employee's conduct shows that he has accepted the variation if, for example, he has continued to work, without protest, after the change has been made. In all cases, however, it is a question of fact as to whether the employee's conduct does indicate acceptance of the change. In *Jones v Associated Tunnelling Co Ltd* [1981] IRLR 477, the Employment Appeal Tribunal (EAT) stressed that continuing to work is not necessarily an implied assent to a unilateral variation by the employer, particularly where the variation does not have immediate effect. This was applied in *Harlow v Artemis International Corporation Ltd* [2008] IRLR 629, where the High Court held that an employer's variation of an enhanced redundancy scheme could not be said to be accepted by the employee merely because the employee had not objected to the variation. In *Marriott v Oxford & District Co-operative Society Ltd* [1970] 1 QB 186, the Court of Appeal held that the fact that an employee worked for three weeks under protest, after the unilateral change by his employer, in no way constituted implied consent to the variation in the contractual terms.

Minor changes may be possible within the contract itself. In *Cresswell v Board of Inland Revenue* [1984] IRLR 190, the court held that a change from manual calculation of tax codes to computerised calculation was not a breach on the part of the employer, provided the employer gave the necessary training to the staff. The basis of this decision is an implied term in all contracts of employment that employees will adapt to new methods of doing their job. As will be shown in Section 4.3.2 below, an employee is also expected to do tasks which are incidental to his job duties, and asking that such tasks be performed is within the employer's contractual rights. These situations, however, are not variations but the courts recognising the necessary flexibility within the express terms themselves. Where the employer wishes to have the right to make more radical changes from time to time, he should have an express term in the contract allowing such changes to be made. The two most common ways these terms appear are in the form of flexibility clauses and mobility clauses. The former give flexibility in the area of the employee's job duties and the latter in the place of work. In the case of flexibility clauses, the courts have been less willing to grant that they allow the employer a great deal more scope than the implied term that an employee can be asked to perform tasks which are reasonably incidental to his main job duties (see *Haden Ltd v Cowan* [1982] IRLR 314).

In relation to mobility clauses, the courts are more generous as long as the employer exercises his rights reasonably in the circumstances by, for example, giving sufficient notice before requiring a person to move halfway round the country (*United Bank v Ahktar* [1989] IRLR 80). What is reasonable conduct on the part of the employer will depend on the circumstances, and a short move will not require notice. In *White v Reflecting Roadstuds Ltd* [1991] ICR 733, the EAT said that it would not imply a term that the employer would exercise his rights under the express terms of the contract reasonably if this was not needed to make the contract work properly. The EAT distinguished *Ahktar* on the basis that without the implication of reasonableness on the part of the employer, the contract would have been impossible to perform. In other words, expecting Mr Ahktar to start a job in a branch at the other end of the country without giving him sufficient time to sell his house and move his family made it impossible for the employee to perform his side of the bargain. In Mr White's case, the move to another department did not involve extra travelling or relocation. The contract allowed the employer to make such a move, and it was not necessary to imply a term that such a right would be exercised after giving notice. It should be noted, however, that the enforcement of mobility clauses, even through express terms in the contract, could be potentially discriminatory on the grounds of sex following the Court of Appeal decision in *Meade-Hill v British Council* [1997] IRLR 522. The case decided that to require a woman to comply with a mobility clause was potential sex discrimination as she was unlikely to be the breadwinner. Note, however, the date of the case. Such an assumption nowadays might in itself be sex discrimination!

If the employer wishes to have the ability to make changes in areas other than job duties or place of work, he will need an express provision to do so unilaterally, although the exercise of such a right is subject to the implied duty of trust and confidence (see Section 4.2.10), and an employer cannot exercise the right in such a way as to render performance of the employee's contractual duties impossible (*St Budeaux Royal British Legion Club Ltd v Cropper*, Section 3.1 above). Such a term may be expressed in the contract itself or may come from another document, such as a collective agreement. In *Bateman v ASDA Stores Ltd* [2010] IRLR 370, the employer wanted to harmonise the pay and work structures of all its employees. It introduced amendments to the employment which ensured that no employee suffered a reduction in pay. Out of all the employees, 9,300 agreed to the changes but 8,700 did not, and so the company imposed the changes unilaterally. The employer had issued a company handbook, sections of which were stated to be the main terms and conditions of employment. The handbook also gave the employer the right to 'revise, amend or replace' the content of the handbook as a result of a number of events, including the needs of the business. The company, invoking this term unilaterally, altered the terms of those employees who had not expressly agreed to the changes. Silber J stated that such a term, even though contained in a company handbook, allowed the employer to make unilateral changes, provided they were properly implemented and the employer acted in a way which did not destroy the implied duty of trust and confidence.

3.2　Collective agreements

Collective agreements are the result of joint negotiation between two sides of industry, that is, the union and employer or employer's association. They are defined by section 178(1) of the Trade Union and Labour Relations (Consolidation) Act (TULR(C)A) 1992 as 'any agreement made by or on behalf of one or more trade unions and one or more employer or employer's association and relating to one or more of the matters specified below'. The section goes on to give a list of the specified matters, which include terms and conditions of employment, engagement or termination of engagement of workers, allocation of duties and so on.

Such agreements have two major functions. On one level they deal with issues pertinent to the union as an entity and the employer. They will deal with matters such as negotiation rights, when the agreement will be renegotiated and so on. Such issues are not important to the relationship of the individual employee and his employer, and as such do not bind the individual parties. On the other hand, many terms of the agreement will be relevant to the individual employee, that is, terms such as pay rises and hours of work. It is therefore important to see how such terms become part of an agreement that binds the individual parties.

3.2.1 Enforceability between the collective parties

A collective agreement operates on two levels. It is first an agreement between the union and the employer or employer's association. For certain purposes the union is treated as if it were a body corporate (TULR(C)A 1992, s 10), and as such it is the union independent from its human members and officers which makes the agreement at this level. Apart from a short period during the currency of the Industrial Relations Act 1971, collective agreements are not legally enforceable between the collective parties (TULR(C)A 1992, s 179(1)). While the Industrial Relations Act was in force, agreements were presumed to be legally binding unless there was a clause to the contrary. Many agreements of the time contained such a clause, which became known as a TINA LEA clause ('this is not a legally enforceable agreement'). This means that between employer and union, agreements have no legal force and are little more than 'a gentleman's agreement'. In *British Leyland (UK) Ltd v McQuilken* [1978] IRLR 245, the company agreed to close down a department. Skilled employees were to be given the option of redundancy or retraining. Some employees who had originally chosen redundancy wanted to change their minds, but they were not allowed to by the company. They sued for a breach of the collective agreement which, they argued, had become part of their contracts of employment. The court held that the agreement was a policy plan rather than an agreement giving individual rights, and therefore could not be enforced individually. In addition, because a collective agreement is not a legally binding contract, it could not be enforced by the union.

3.2.2 Enforceability between the individual parties

In addition to being an agreement between the collective parties, the negotiations with the union are likely to affect individual employees. Pay rises, for example, will affect all of the employer's workers. The problem that arises, however, is how the individual worker can enforce the pay rise against his employer. It is the union who is the other party to the agreement, and not the employees. Even if the agreement is legally binding at the collective level, on the basis of privity the individual employee cannot enforce an agreement to which he is not a party, even if the agreement is for his benefit. Section 1 of the Contracts (Rights of Third Parties) Act 1999 does not apply to collective agreements as they are not legally enforceable between the collective parties, as noted in Section 3.2.1 above. This means that the only way the individual can enforce the relevant provisions against his employer is if those provisions have become part of the employment contract between them. This, however, is not as straightforward as it seems. Before looking to see whether a term has become incorporated, a court must first decide whether the term is appropriate for incorporation. Thus it is a two-stage process: Is the term appropriate for incorporation into an individual contract of employment? If so, has the term been incorporated?

The issue of the appropriateness of the term for incorporation has caused what appear to be conflicting decisions. Deakin and Morris (2012) say that it is necessary to distinguish between those terms which are procedural in nature (such as redundancy selection policies) and those which are substantive, laying down rights for employees such as pay and hours. While this appears to be clear-cut, in reality this is not so. *McQuilken* (Section 3.2.1 above) decided that a policy allowing employees to choose redundancy or retraining was exactly that, and thus inappropriate for incorporation. In *Alexander v Standard*

Telephones and Cables Ltd [1990] ICR 291, while Aldous J rejected an application for an injunction, he was prepared to say that a redundancy selection policy of 'last in first out' could be capable of incorporation into an individual's contract. (This was later rejected in *Alexander v Standard Telephones and Cables Ltd (No 2)* [1991] IRLR 286.) However, in *Anderson v Pringle of Scotland* [1998] IRLR 64, the Court of Session not only held that 'last in first out' had been incorporated into the individual contract but also restrained the employee's dismissal in breach of the term. Despite this – and it is argued that a term which takes seniority into account is substantive and not procedural as it does confer rights on individuals – *Rover Group plc v Kaur* [2005] IRLR 40 yet again decided that a redundancy policy was inappropriate for incorporation, although in *Harlow* (Section 3.1.1 above) the High Court held that an enhanced redundancy payment scheme was apt for incorporation. This is supported by *Allen v TRW Systems* [2013] IRLR 699. In the case TRW had, in 1999, agreed a policy with its works council for enhanced redundancy payments. This agreement was added to the employee handbook and repeated in letters to employees on a number of occasions. The EAT held that provisions on redundancy payments were apt for incorporation, and it was irrelevant that such provision was in the employee handbook and not in the statement of terms and conditions. The express promise in the handbook, reiterated in subsequent letters, led to employees having a reasonable expectation that such payments would be made. In other words, a redundancy selection scheme is a policy issue and not appropriate, but it seems that any payments under such a scheme are deemed to be appropriate for incorporation into an individual's contract.

The Court of Appeal in *Malone and Ors v British Airways plc* [2010] EWCA Civ 1225 appears to add a further dimension. In the case, minimum crew numbers were set by the regulator in the jurisdiction of the manufacture of the planes. These were set for Boeing planes, but a collective agreement between British Airways (BA) and the unions set higher minimum numbers, though allowing for numbers below the minimum set out in the agreement when there was a 'significant event outside the control of BA' after BA had informed the union that it was going to reduce the numbers below the minimum set out in the agreement. To save money, BA reduced the crew complement on its planes. Although the number was below that stated in the agreement, it was not below the minimum number specified by the regulator. The cabin crew argued that the collective agreement had become part of their contract and therefore BA were in breach of contract.

The Court of Appeal held that although the provision impacted on the working conditions of the crew and was therefore appropriate for incorporation, the disastrous consequences for the business if the provision were enforceable individually led it to the conclusion that the parties could not have intended it to be individually enforced, and thus it could only have been intended as an undertaking to cabin crew collectively and so binding in honour alone.

Thus the Court of Appeal seems to say that a tribunal should not only look to see if a term is appropriate for incorporation, but also at the intention of the parties, once the tribunal looks at the consequences of such incorporation. For example, in *Malone* the Court of Appeal looked at the hypothetical possibility of an individual or small group of cabin crew being able to bring a flight to a halt by refusing to work under-complement, which the Court felt was 'so serious as to be unthinkable'. It is suggested that the consequences consideration will be important, as without doubt the union in *Malone* intended the clause to be part of the contract.

A further issue is what happens when there are two terms within a collective agreement which are inconsistent? Which term is enforceable? This was the situation in *Anderson v London Fire and Emergency Planning Authority* [2013] EWCA Civ 321. In the case the Authority had entered into a three-year pay agreement with two unions. In the final year the pay increase was to be 2.5 per cent or a figure worked out by a formula (which turned out to be 1.575 per cent). The Authority offered 1.85 per cent due to financial restraints, and the employees sought 2.5 per cent.

The Court of Appeal held that the deal was a fixed one for three years and was certain in that it gave two clear choices; as such, it was appropriate for incorporation. Kay LJ considered what a reasonable man would have made of the agreement and came to the conclusion that a reasonable man would not have considered that the agreement gave the employer an unfettered right to choose between the two options. The increase had to be the higher percentage because this was the only meaning which made industrial sense.

Once it has been decided that the term is appropriate for incorporation, and that is what the parties intended, there are various ways in which terms at the collective level may become incorporated into the individual's contract.

3.2.3   Implied incorporation

This is the most complex way of incorporating the terms of a collective agreement. The basis of such incorporation is that there is evidence that both parties have accepted the agreement as binding. On the part of the employer this is not difficult, as he is usually one of the parties who negotiated the agreement at the collective level and obviously agrees to be bound by it. The problem lies with the individual employee. What evidence is needed to show that he intends certain parts of the agreement to bind him? At one time it was thought that if the employee continued working once the collective agreement had been negotiated, this indicated acceptance on his part of the relevant provisions. More recently, however, the courts have argued that that may be a dangerous route to follow, as taken to its logical conclusion it could mean that an employee is bound by provisions in an agreement he did not know existed.

In *Joel v Cammell Laird* [1969] ITR 206 it was decided that before an employee can be bound by a collective agreement, there must be:

1. specific knowledge of the agreement;
2. conduct on the part of the employee which shows that he accepts the agreement; and
3. some indication of incorporation into the contract.

Further, in *Duke v Reliance Systems Ltd* [1982] IRLR 347 it was held that the employee should have knowledge of the existence of the term if not its content. This may still work unfairly, though. For example, an employee may know of the existence of a term relating to pay. He may mistakenly assume the term covers a pay rise, whereas in fact it covers a reduction in pay. From the decision in *Duke* he will be bound. He knows of the existence of the term; it is irrelevant that he does not know its content.

While the courts have tried to restrict implied incorporation, one point should be made. The above principles apply only to union members. The courts have long held that provisions of a collective agreement cannot be impliedly incorporated into a non-unionist's contract, and that the only way a non-unionist can be bound is by express incorporation. In *Singh v British Steel Corporation* [1974] IRLR 131, the plaintiff had left the union. Some time later the union negotiated a change in the shift system. Singh refused to accept the change and was eventually dismissed. It was held that the union agreement did not alter the terms of his contract. As a non-union member, the only way his contract could be altered was by express agreement on his part, which he obviously had not given. He was still bound by his original terms and conditions, that is, the old shift system. It should also be added, however, that given that all the rest of the workforce had accepted the new system, it was held to be a fair dismissal under 'some other substantial reason' (see Section 9.5.5).

The decision in *Singh* has been taken a step further and has been held to apply to an employee who is a member of a union other than the one which negotiated the collective agreement. In *Miller v Hamworthy Engineering Ltd* [1986] IRLR 461, the plaintiff's union, along with the other union on the site, had negotiated a reduction in the working week. Some time later, the second union negotiated a further reduction on its own. The plaintiff refused to accept the new hours that had not been negotiated by his union. The Court of Appeal held he was not bound by the new hours. For the purposes of a collective agreement negotiated by a union other than his own, he was to be treated as a non-union member, and as such he had to incorporate the second agreement expressly into his contract. The more recent case of *Henry v London General Transport Services Ltd* [2002] IRLR 472 may, however, limit *Singh* and *Miller*. In that case, changes to contractual terms made by way of collective agreement were incorporated into individual contracts by virtue of custom (see Section 3.5 below). Thus if a custom can be established whereby collectively agreed variations (in this case a pay reduction) are implied into both union and non-union members' contracts, this will be upheld by the courts.

3.2.4 Express incorporation

The major problem with implied incorporation is evidence that the employee has accepted the change in his terms and conditions of employment. Express incorporation of the agreement provides such evidence. Such incorporation is a simple process and merely requires a statement in the contract or the statutory statement to the effect that the relevant negotiations by union X shall be part of the individual's contract. In 1993 the contents of the statutory statement were amended. These amendments are now contained in sections 1–6 of ERA 1996, which state the items which must be included in the statutory statement of terms and conditions (see Section 3.4 below) and specifically provide that the employee must be given particulars about collective agreements which directly affect terms and conditions. However, in *Worrall v Wilmott Dixon Partnership* [2010] All ER (D) 107 Silber J said that to incorporate the term of a collective agreement, the term must be brought to the employee's attention or agreed. It was insufficient for the term to be in a company handbook. As such, an enhanced redundancy payment was not incorporated into the employees' contracts as there was no evidence that it had been brought to their attention or agreed by them. He further stated that on a transfer under the Transfer of Undertakings (Protection of Employment) Regulations 2006 (a 'TUPE transfer' – see Section 9.2.5) a collective agreement becomes frozen so that any future changes do not apply to the transferred employees and thus the new employer. This has now been confirmed by the ECJ. In *Alemo-Herron v Parkwood Leisure Ltd* (2013) Case C-426/11, there was a transfer of Lewisham Council's leisure services to the private sector. There were clauses in the employment contracts obliging the employer to be bound by the agreements of the national negotiating body. The ECJ held that such clauses are static, as any other interpretation would conflict with Article 16 of the Charter of Fundamental Rights of the European Union under which an employer must have the right to conduct a business and assert its interests effectively in a contractual process to which it is a party. As such, a transferee cannot be bound by an agreement to which it was not a negotiating party.

If the test above is satisfied, sometimes the whole of the agreement will be expressly incorporated, at other times it may be only part of the agreement. In *NCB v Galley* [1958] WLR 16, the employee, by his contract, agreed to be bound by 'such national agreements for the time being in force'. This was held to incorporate the relevant collective agreement.

The test in *Worrall* should prevent problems arising out of the fact that the agreement provides employees with certain rights but the employee is unaware of the existence of those rights. In *Scally and Others v Southern Health & Social Services Board and Another* [1991] 3 WLR 778, doctors employed in Northern Ireland had made contributions to the statutory superannuation scheme. By collective agreement they had the right to improve their pension entitlement by buying added years, but this right had to be exercised within a certain time limit. None of the doctors was aware of this right. They claimed damages against the health boards for breach of an implied term, that is, the employer had a duty to tell them such a right existed. The House of Lords said that in a modern world it is common for people to have contracts negotiated collectively. They could not be expected to know all the details unless these were pointed out to them. In this situation, if the agreement gave a valuable right to the employee of which the employee had to take advantage, and the employee could not, in all the circumstances, reasonably be aware of the right unless it was drawn to his attention, the employer was under a duty to make that right known to the employee. By providing the employee with the particulars about any collective agreement which affects his terms and conditions of employment, the onus will be on the employee to take up any rights the agreement confers upon him.

Once the provision has become part of the individual's contract, contractual principles apply. This has three consequences for the employer. First, the fact that the collective agreement is stated to be binding in honour only has no effect on the legal enforceability at the individual level. Once the provision becomes a contractual term it is legally binding and has no reliance on the legal enforceability of the collective agreement. This is obviously the case, and is supported by the judgments in *Marley v Forward Trust Group Ltd* [1986] IRLR 369.

Second, if either party at the collective level withdraws from the agreement, this has no effect on the terms incorporated into the individual's contract. In *Burrough's Machines Ltd v Timmoney* [1977] IRLR 404, the employer was a member of an employer's association which had negotiated a lay-off procedure. Some time later the employer left the association, but it was held that he was still bound by the procedure in relation to his employees because his leaving the association did not affect the employment contracts. In *Whent v T Cartledge* [1997] IRLR 153, employees were transferred to a new employer. The then Transfer of Undertakings (Protection of Employment) Regulations 1981 (SI 1981/1794 – see Section 9.2.5) applied, and therefore the employees were transferred on their existing terms and conditions. One of the terms of the contract incorporated a collective agreement between the old employer and the GMB union that the National Joint Council (NJC) pay rates applied. After the transfer, the new employer derecognised the GMB and told the employees that the NJC rates would no longer be paid, freezing the employees' pay despite an NJC rise. It was held that the provision to pay NJC rates was a term of the contract and the new employer's refusal to pay the rate, despite derecognising the union, was a breach of that contract. Any other conclusion in either of the above cases would, of course, give either party the right to alter the terms of the contract unilaterally (see *Gibbons v Associated British Ports* [1985] IRLR 376).

Third, the incorporation may affect the interpretation of the provision. Collective agreements tend to be loosely drafted, but once certain parts become contractual terms, they are interpreted as such. In *Hooper v British Railways Board* [1988] IRLR 517, a term regarding sick pay was incorporated into the employee's contract from an agreement made with the Railway Staff Joint Council. It was badly drafted, however, and did not reflect what happened in practice. The Court of Appeal held that the term had to be interpreted in the normal contractual way, objectively as it stood and without reference to the subsequent behaviour of the parties. The application of contractual rules was also seen in *Ali v Christian Salvesen Food Services Ltd* [1997] IRLR 17. In this case, a collective agreement which had been incorporated into the employees' contracts provided for annual hours based on a notional 40-hour week. The annual hours were 1,824, and once these hours were worked overtime rates applied to the excess hours. Some employees were made redundant before the year was out. They had worked more than 40 hours a week but had not reached the total annual hours by the time of their redundancy. They sued for an unlawful deduction from their wages when they were not paid overtime for the weeks they had worked in excess of 40 hours. At first instance the employment tribunal held that overtime was not payable until the employees had worked 1,824 hours and that a term could not be implied that overtime would be paid for hours in excess of 40 per week where there was an early termination of the contract. The employees appealed, arguing that such an implied term was needed on grounds of business efficacy. This argument was upheld by the EAT but rejected by the Court of Appeal, which stated that as the contract did not mention early termination the omission must have been deliberate and a term did not need to be implied for the contract to work.

Interpretation of terms in a collective agreement arose again in *O'Brien v London Borough of Haringey* (2013) UKEAT 0167/12/0702. In the case the school for which Mrs O'Brien worked was anxious to create links with schools across the world as part of a British Council initiative. If such links were accredited by the British Council, it would guarantee funding for three years. While Mrs O'Brien was on holiday in Gambia, another teacher had established links with a school out there. Mrs O'Brien learned about the British Council initiative when she returned to her school, and with the approval of her head teacher she contacted the head of the school in Gambia, agreeing to share lesson plans and materials. She intended to return to Gambia in the February half-term, and agreed with the Gambian head that she would take materials with her and visit the school. She discussed this with her own head teacher, who said that the school could not pay for her trip, but Mrs O'Brien said she did not mind paying for it herself. She flew out on the last working day before half-term, with the permission of her head teacher in order to have the day off with full pay.

While in Gambia Mrs O'Brien spent five hours in the school over two sessions. She contracted a contagious virus, and it was uncontested that she had caught it from the Gambian school children. Clause 10 of a collective agreement which applied to Mrs O'Brien stated that if she contracted a contagious disease during the course of her employment, she would receive full sick pay. The school argued that she was not acting in the course of her employment when she contracted the virus. However, clause 9 of the collective agreement, which covered injury during the course of employment, defined in depth what the phrase meant and stated that it included extra-curricular or voluntary activity connected with the school. The EAT held that if the employer did not want that construction to apply to clause 10, it should have made it clear in the agreement. Mrs O'Brien was entitled to full pay during her illness.

3.2.5 Agency

As seen from the above, there are problems in incorporating the relevant provisions of a collective agreement into an individual contract. Whereas express incorporation is the simplest way, in practice implied incorporation is the most common, leading to a wealth of case law on what type of conduct implies acceptance and what knowledge the employee must have before it can be said that his conduct represents acceptance of this agreement or this term. The courts at one time did try to make their task easier by arguing that when the union negotiated, it was doing so as an agent of its members. The attractiveness of this argument is undeniable. It avoids the problems seen above and means that any agreement negotiated collectively automatically binds the member as the union's principal, whether he knows of the negotiation or not. The proposition has major flaws, though. First, it would only apply to members at the place of work when the agreement was negotiated; employees taken on after the negotiation would have to accept the agreement separately when starting their employment. Second, the proposition does not address the issue of non-union members. How would the union act as their agent? Would non-union members have to appoint the union as agent, and would the appointment be general, for a particular item such as pay, or for a particular agreement? Last, what is the basis of the agency in the case of a union member? Is it the contract of membership which would give unfettered authority in any negotiation or would the member have to give authority each time negotiations started, or, conversely, is authority presumed unless the member withdraws it before negotiations begin? The problems, as can be seen, are numerous. While some judges feel agency is a neat way of dealing with the issues, most have recognised the inherent problems. While agency as a concept will work where there is a small unionised workforce, it becomes impractical where there are large numbers of employees, some unionised and some not, with perhaps two or more unions operating on one site. The present state of the law on this issue was voiced by Arnold J in *Burton Group Ltd v Smith* [1977] IRLR 191, when he said:

> There is no reason at all why, in a particular case, union representatives should not be the agent of an employee … But that agency does not stem from the mere fact that they are union representatives and that he is a member of the union; it must be supported in the particular case by the creation of some specific agency.

3.2.6 Conflicting collective agreements

A further problem exists when there are two collective agreements, perhaps a locally negotiated agreement and a nationally negotiated one, and the agreements conflict. Which one prevails? In *Clift v West Riding County Council* (1964) *The Times*, 10 April, the court held that a local agreement prevailed over an earlier national agreement because the local one was later in time. This decision was not followed by the Court of Appeal, however, in the later case of *Gascol Conversions Ltd v Mercer* [1974] IRLR 155. In that case the Court held that a national agreement prevailed over a later local one. Given this authority, it is probable that this is the position of the law at the moment.

3.2.7   No-strike clauses

The law is very specific on how a 'no-strike' or 'peace' clause in a collective agreement becomes part of an individual's contract. The law is found in section 180 of TULR(C)A 1992. This provides that such a clause will become part of the individual contract if the following five conditions are met:

1. The collective agreement is in writing.
2. The agreement expressly states that the terms are to be incorporated into the individual's contract.
3. A copy of the collective agreement is reasonably accessible to the employees concerned.
4. The agreement is made by an independent trade union.
5. The individual contract expressly or impliedly incorporates the terms of the collective agreement.

If all the above apply, the provision becomes part of the employment contract. It must be remembered, however, that a strike is a repudiatory breach by the employee. While the 'peace' clause may make an employer feel safer, it gives him no more rights than he already has, consequently the effect of the statutory provision is minimal.

3.3   Incorporation of other documents

In addition to collective agreements, the employer will often have other documents around the workplace to which he wishes his employees to adhere. He will be able to enforce such documents, however, only if they have become part of the individual contract. The two most common documents around a workplace will be the works rules and the employer's disciplinary and grievance procedures.

3.3.1   Works rules/staff handbooks

The status of the works rules is a somewhat grey area at the moment. Certainly, they do not appear to be contractual per se, and therefore must be incorporated into the individual's contract. If they are not incorporated, they are orders from an employer to his employees. In the leading case in this area – *Secretary of State for Employment v ASLEF (No 2)* [1972] 2 QB 455 – Lord Denning MR expressed the view that the rules were in 'no way terms of his contract. They are only instructions to a man on how he is to do his work'. Other cases have adopted this approach. In *Peake v Automotive Products* [1978] QB 233 it was held that the rule book was non-contractual and merely set out administrative arrangements for running the factory. Such an interpretation means that the employer has the right to alter the rules unilaterally, without consulting his employees. Further, the employer does not lose a remedy against those employees who refuse to comply with the works rules if they are defined as non-contractual. It is an implied duty on the part of the employee that he obeys all lawful, reasonable orders issued by his employer. Failure to do so is a breach of contract.

Whatever the status of the works rules, the employer will have the ultimate remedy of dismissal. While that may seem to paint a black picture for employees, even if the courts and tribunals do decide that the rules in a particular case are merely instructions from the employer, they will use the test of reasonableness to curb excesses of management power and they will not allow an employer to act autocratically. In *Talbot v Hugh M. Fulton Ltd* [1975] IRLR 52, an employee was dismissed for wearing his hair long, which was in breach of the works rules. It was held that his dismissal was unfair. The rule did not state the exact length of hair considered to be acceptable, and in addition such a rule would be reasonable only if there was a safety or hygiene risk.

The above comments do not mean that works rules are never contractual. Just as collective agreements can become incorporated into the contract, so too can the works rules. Where the rule book was given to the employee or referred to when the contract of employment was formed, and the employee acknowledged the rule book as part of his conditions of employment, it is likely that the courts would hold that the rules had contractual effect. This will certainly be the case where the employee signs a document agreeing to be bound by the rules. In these cases, however, not all the rules will necessarily become contractual terms. Rule books, like collective agreements, will often be vague, and certain parts of the rules may be inappropriate for inclusion in the contract. In *Cadoux v Central Regional Council* [1986] IRLR 131, the employee's contract was subject to the Conditions of Service laid down by the National Joint Council for Local Authorities Administrative, Technical and Clerical Services, as supplemented by the Authorities Rules, as amended from time to time. The issue that arose out of this rather complicated clause was whether the employer could unilaterally withdraw a non-contributory life assurance scheme for staff. It was held that, given that the Joint Council could unilaterally alter the rules from time to time, the parties could not have intended them to have contractual effect. However, in *Keeley v Fosroc International Ltd* [2006] EWCA Civ 1277, the Court of Appeal held that where a staff handbook contained details of an enhanced redundancy payment, there was a presumption that it had contractual status. (See also *Allen v TRW Systems* in Section 3.2.2 above.)

The importance of the status of the works rules is demonstrated by *Cadoux*. While the remedy for breach of the rules may be the same whatever the definition given to them, the power of the employer is restricted once they are classified as contractual. Then the employer may alter his rules only by mutual agreement. An example of how crucial the definition may be is given by *Selwyn* (2012). What if the employer introduces a search policy into the rules? If the employee refuses to be searched, is he in breach of an express term in the contract, or is he refusing to obey an order? If he is refusing to obey an order, is the order reasonable? If the rules are non-contractual, the employer will have to show his order is both lawful and reasonable before he can compel an employee to obey it. Clearly there is a variety of issues arising out of this area which still need addressing by the courts.

3.3.2 Disciplinary and grievance procedures

By section 3 of the ERA 1996, the employer must give details of the disciplinary and grievance procedures to all of his employees at the start of their employment. In respect of disciplinary procedures, some incorporation into the contract may be advantageous for an employer, particularly in relation to disciplinary sanctions. Should the employer wish to impose a sanction which will involve a reduction or loss of pay, for example demotion or suspension without pay, he needs contractual authority or the employee's written consent. Failure to have this authority or consent will be a breach of section 13 of ERA 1996 in relation to deductions from wages and will entitle the employee to sue for recovery.

Once disciplinary procedures are in the contract they must be adhered to, and this may be seen as a disadvantage for the employer, as all employees will potentially be able to claim a breach of contract, even those with insufficient continuity to present a claim for unfair dismissal. In *Jones v Lee and Guilding* [1980] IRLR 67, the plaintiff was a headmaster who was dismissed when he divorced and remarried. His contract gave him a right to a hearing before the local education authority before the decision to dismiss was taken, but the plaintiff was not afforded this opportunity. The Court of Appeal granted an injunction restraining the school managers from dismissing the employee before a hearing had taken place. In *Gunton v London Borough of Richmond* [1981] 1 WLR 28, damages were assessed for wrongful dismissal to include a period of time the employee would have been employed if his contractual disciplinary procedure had been implemented. The House of Lords decided in the case of *West Midlands Co-operative Society Ltd v Tipton* [1986] IRLR 112 that failure to allow an employee to exercise his contractual right of appeal renders a dismissal unfair. All of the above show the different remedies available to an employee should the employer fail to comply with contractual disciplinary procedures.

Apart from compliance with section 13, however, it can be to an employer's advantage that the disciplinary procedures are contractual. The procedures will not only lay down details about hearings and so on, but will also give a list of examples of misconduct and those standards of behaviour and workmanship which the employer finds unacceptable. This will put the employer in a much stronger position in an unfair dismissal claim, for he will be able to show that the employee is in breach of contract.

Contractual grievance procedures may also be advantageous to an employer. In *Witham v Hills Shopfitters* (unreported) the employee resigned after being at the receiving end of foul language. Without pursuing the company grievance procedure, the employee claimed unfair dismissal, arguing that the language constituted a constructive dismissal. It was held that the language was not unusual for the shopfloor and, furthermore, that the employee should have pursued the company's internal procedures before resigning and presenting a claim to an employment tribunal. Furthermore, the EAT in *WA Goold (Pearmak) Ltd v McConnell* [1995] IRLR 516, held that the failure on the part of the employer to provide a grievance procedure was a breach of the duty of mutual respect which entitled the employee to resign and claim constructive dismissal.

3.4 Statutory statement of terms and conditions

By section 1 of the ERA 1996, every employee should receive a statement of the basic terms and conditions of employment within eight weeks of the commencement of relationship. The detailed requirements of section 1 were brought in to implement EC Directive 91/533, which requires employers to inform employees of the essential elements of the contract of employment. Certain employees are excluded from section 1, including employees who work for less than four weeks. The matters the statement must contain are as follows:

- identification of the parties;
- the date on which the period of continuous employment began, stating whether any continuous employment with a previous employer counts and, if so, when the continuous period began;
- the scale and rate of remuneration or the method of calculating the remuneration;
- the intervals at which remuneration is paid;
- any terms and conditions relating to hours of work;
- any terms and conditions relating to entitlement to holidays, including public holidays and holiday pay;
- the title of the job the employee is employed to do, or a brief description of the work he is employed to do; and
- either the place of work or, if there is more than one place, an indication of such and the address of the employer.

The terms above must be set out in one document, known as the 'principal statement'. In addition, the following additional information must be given to employees, but may be given in instalments, so long as this is done by the end of the eighth week:

- terms relating to incapacity for work due to sickness or injury, including any provision for sick pay;
- pensions and pension schemes;
- period of notice the employee must give and is entitled to receive;
- if the employment is temporary the period it is expected to last, or the termination date of a fixed-term contract;
- any collective agreements which directly affect the terms and conditions of employment and, if the employer is not a party, the persons by whom they were made;
- where the employee is required to work outside the United Kingdom for a period of more than one month, the length of the period, the currency in which he is to be paid, any benefits or extra remuneration paid because he is working outside the United Kingdom, and any terms and conditions relating to his return; and
- details of the disciplinary and grievance procedures.

The employer may, by the statement, refer the employee to the provisions of another document, for items not in the principal statement, which the employee has reasonable opportunities to read during the course of his employment or which is made reasonably accessible to him. This means that the employer can put items in, for example, a staff handbook, which he either gives to the employee or makes accessible. If there are any changes in any of the items, the employer must inform the employee of the change, in writing, within one month of the change happening.

The statement is not contractual. In *System Floors Ltd (UK) v Daniel* [1981] IRLR 475, Browne-Wilkinson J said about the statement that:

> It provides very strong prima facie evidence of what were the terms of the contract between the parties ... Nor are the statements of the terms finally conclusive: at most they place a heavy burden on the employer to show that the actual terms of the contract are different from those which he had set out in the statutory statement.

The importance of the words spoken by Browne-Wilkinson J above is demonstrated by the case of *Robertson and Jackson v British Gas Corporation* [1983] IRLR 302. The statutory statement was silent regarding a bonus which had been incorporated into the plaintiffs' contracts from a collective agreement. It was held that where there is a conflict between the statement and the contract, the contract prevails. This approach was confirmed by the ECJ in *Kampelmann v Landschaftsverband Westfalen-Lippe* [1998] IRLR 333 and demonstrated by the ECJ decision in *Lange v Georg Schünemann GmbH* [2001] IRLR 244, where it was held that the fact that the obligation to work overtime was not reduced to writing did not nullify a contractual term agreed orally by the employee.

If the employee does not receive his statement, he may apply to an employment tribunal. The tribunal will then determine what particulars should be included. If the tribunal does not have sufficient evidence to determine what the parties would have agreed, it must determine what should have been agreed, according to Stephenson LJ in *Mears v Safecar Security Ltd* [1982] IRLR 183. This has since been doubted in another Court of Appeal decision, *Eagland v British Telecom* [1993] ICR 644, where Parker LJ pointed out that the remarks of Stephenson LJ were *obiter* and he doubted that a tribunal had the power to invent terms if the intentions of the parties were not discoverable. The Court of Appeal further decided in *Mears* that, given that a tribunal will hear a complaint because of the employer's breach of statutory duty, any doubt as to content should be resolved in favour of the employee. However, in *Southern Cross Healthcare v Perkins and ors* [2010] EWCA Civ 1442, the Court of Appeal held that tribunals do not have the power of contractual interpretation when the terms are clear. In the case the claimants were entitled to five days' extra holiday entitlement due to long service. When the Working Time Regulations 1998 were amended to increase holiday entitlement to 28 days, the employer increased the holiday entitlement of all of its employees, including the claimants. The claimants argued that they were entitled to extra holiday due to long service. The Court of Appeal held that the tribunal had no jurisdiction to construe the contractual term in that way.

Tribunals have the power to award compensation where the lack of, incompleteness of or inaccuracy of the statutory statement becomes evident in certain tribunal claims, such as unfair dismissal or discrimination. It is important to note that this allows a tribunal to look at the statement in a number of statutory claims and not only in claims relating specifically to the statement or lack of one. Where there is an incomplete or inaccurate statement compensation may be increased by two to four weeks' pay. Where a statement has not been issued, compensation may also be increased by two to four weeks' pay. In addition, where the remedy for the original complaint is not financial compensation, the tribunal may award two to four weeks' pay.

3.5   Custom

It is sometimes argued that the terms of a contract of employment may be found in the custom and practices of a particular industry. In the old case of *Sagar v Ridehalgh* [1931] 1 Ch 310, a custom allowing the employer to deduct from workers' wages for bad workmanship was held to be a term of the contract. In *Marshall v English Electric Ltd* [1945] 1 All ER 653, an established practice of using suspension as a disciplinary sanction was held to be a term in the employee's contract. It is fair to say, however, that custom as a source of contractual terms per se is used less and less, although working practices within an industry may be used to interpret an ambiguous express term. For a custom to become a contractual term, it must be certain, well-known and reasonable; a deduction for bad workmanship today would probably not be upheld as a term of the contract because of the uncertainty in the phrase itself. What constitutes 'bad'?

Even if the courts do accept a custom as a contractual term, there seems to be judicial uncertainty as to exactly when the custom becomes part of the contract. Is it once it has become certain, well-known and reasonable, or does the individual employee have to know of the custom and accept it as part of his contract? The cases can perhaps be summarised as deciding that normally the employee should know of the custom and have accepted it, and evidence of this must be brought before the courts before the employee will be contractually bound. It is important to note that merely working, knowing of the custom, may not be sufficient to show the employee's acceptance of it into his contract. In *Samways v Swan Hunter Shipbuilders Ltd* [1975] IRLR 190, the employee had been a labourer and was given the job of charge-hand, with a consequent rise in pay of £4 per week. Because of a reduction in work, the employers withdrew his additional money and offered him his old job as a labourer. The employee sued for a redundancy payment, but the employers argued that the extra money was temporary by virtue of custom and practice within the industry, and gave evidence of other workers who had been made up to charge-hands and then reverted to labouring work with the reduction in pay. The tribunal held that the fact that men had reverted to being labourers in the past was not sufficient to establish a custom. Furthermore, their conduct was not an indication that they were contractually bound to accept the change in status but could be explained by the fact that they wished to remain in employment. However, in the more recent case of *Henry v London General Transport Services Ltd* (Section 3.2.3 above), the Court of Appeal upheld a custom which was 'reasonable, certain and notorious' incorporating a pay reduction agreed collectively into all contracts of employment. The Court of Appeal stated that incorporation could not be undermined by showing some individuals did not know of the practice, or did not intend or wish it.

3.6 Implied terms

Although many individual contracts will have covered all eventualities by express terms, some circumstances may arise which have not been envisaged by the parties and therefore there is no term to cover them. In these cases the court 'fills in the gaps' and tries to establish what term the parties would have provided if they had thought about it. This function of the court to imply terms on an individual basis should be distinguished from the function to imply common law duties discussed in the next chapter. The duties discussed later are implied into every contract of employment by the common law. The implied terms discussed below are terms specific to an individual contract and to individual parties.

The courts rely on two old contractual tests to determine the content of the missing term:

1. The term is necessary to give the contract business efficacy (the test from the old case of *The Moorcock* (1889) 14 PD 64).
2. The term is so obvious that it goes without saying, so that if you asked an officious bystander if the term should be in, he would answer 'Oh, of course'. This test comes from the case of *Shirlaw v Southern Foundries Ltd* [1939] 2 KB 206.

It is true to say that the business efficacy test lost favour after the case of *Lister v Romford Ice and Cold Storage Co Ltd* [1957] AC 555 and that the preferred test is the obvious consensus one. While the courts will profess that they are merely putting into the contract what the parties would have intended, this is obviously a legal fiction, as presumably if the parties knew the term they wanted, there would be no need to use the court in the first place! The tests are merely an aid for the courts to fill in the blanks. The problem with both tests, however, is that although they tell the court that a particular term should be included in the contract, they do not tell the court what the content of that term should be. In *Shell UK Ltd v Lostock Garage Ltd* [1977] 1 All ER 481, Lord Denning MR said that where an employment contract was silent, the courts should ask what would be reasonable in the circumstances. Although this view has been followed since, there is a vast difference between what is obvious and what is reasonable.

To establish the content of the term, the courts will start with how the parties have worked the contract in the past. In *Mears v Safecar Security Ltd* (Section 3.4 above), the Court of Appeal refused to imply a term that the employee was entitled to sick pay, because sick pay had never been paid in the past. If there is no evidence of past conduct, the courts will imply a term they feel is necessary and one the parties would have agreed if they were being reasonable (*Courtaulds Northern Spinning Ltd v Sibson* [1988] IRLR 305). Finally, the courts may imply particular terms into the contract of a professional employee by reference to the nature of the profession. In *Sim v Rotherham Metropolitan Borough Council* (Section 3.1 above), the High Court implied a term that teachers should cover for absent colleagues, as this would be seen by people outside the profession as part of the duties of a teacher. Note, however, that the court will not imply a term to distort the meaning of a clear express term (*Ali v Christian Salvesen Food Services*, Section 3.2.4 above).

Summary

3.1 Normal contractual rules apply to the employment relationship and the contract becomes binding as soon as the offer by the employer is accepted, expressly or impliedly, by the employee.

3.2 The terms of the contract come from a variety of sources.

3.3 Express terms in the contract should be clear and unambiguous.

3.4 Partial performance by the employee of the express terms relating to job duties may allow the employer to deduct a proportional amount of pay, or, if the duties are deemed to be a material part of the contract, the employer may treat the contract as repudiated.

3.5 Express terms cannot be ousted by implied terms.

3.6 Certain statutory provisions restrict the content of express terms.

3.7 The law recognises the inherent flexibility needed within the relationship, and a variation in working methods is within the employer's contractual rights. Any other variation must be mutually agreed; and even if such variation is allowed by the contract, the courts may imply that the employer should exercise his rights reasonably.

3.8 Collective agreements are a major source of employment terms. Their provisions need to become part of the individual's contract to be enforceable against the employer. This is normally done by express or implied incorporation. In the case of non-unionists, it must be done by express incorporation, unless a custom exists which varies all contracts.

3.9 A no-strike clause must comply with the statutory requirements to be enforceable.

Summary cont'd

3.10 Works rules and disciplinary and grievance procedures may become part of the contract. The court will assess whether they are appropriate for incorporation, and whether the documents were given to the employee at the time the contract was made or reference was made to the documents within the contract.

3.11 The statutory statement is non-contractual but gives evidence of the contractual terms.

3.12 Certain customs may become part of the contract if they are certain, well-known and reasonable.

3.13 The courts may use the old contractual tests to imply terms into the contract to cover situations the parties have not envisaged. The content of such terms is decided on past conduct and reasonableness.

Exercises

3.1 To what extent is the contract of employment an individually negotiated agreement between two parties?

3.2 How far is it true to say that the rights of an employee come from status rather than contract?

3.3 Engineers working for Heavy Engineering Ltd have received a Christmas bonus every year for the past 10 years. This year the company has told the employees that no bonus will be paid.

The company has recently issued a new rule which has been posted on the notice board. The rule states that the management reserves the right to require any employee to submit to a body search on leaving company premises in order to check that company property is not concealed on an employee's person.

Advise the company on the contractual implications of these changes.

Further reading and references

Barmes, 'The Continuing Conceptual Crisis in the Common Law of the Contract of Employment' (2004) 67 MLR 435

Deakin and Morris, *Labour Law* (Hart Publishing 2012)

Dolding and Fawlk, 'Judicial Understanding of the Contract of Employment' (1992) 55 MLR 562

Emir, *Selwyn's Law of Employment* (Oxford University Press 2012)

Honeyball, 'Employment Law and the Primacy of Contract' (1989) 18 ILJ 97

McLean, 'An Employer's Right to Be Unreasonable' (1992) 49 CLJ 23

Napier, 'Incorporation of Collective Agreements' (1986) 15 ILJ 52

Reynold and Hendy, 'Reserving the Right to Change Terms and Conditions: How Far Can an Employer Go?' (2012) 41 ILJ 79

Russell, 'Malone and ors v British Airways plc: Protection of Managerial Prerogative?' (2011) 40 ILJ 207

Wilson, 'Contract and Prerogative: A Reconsideration of the Legal Enforcement of Collective Agreements' (1984) 13 ILJ 1

Wynn-Evans, 'Implication and Omission in Collectively Negotiated Contracts' (1997) 26 ILJ 166

Chapter 4

Implied duties in the contract of employment

4.1 Personal nature of the contract

It has already been seen that the courts have power to impose terms on the parties where the contract is silent (Section 3.6). The power previously discussed applies on a contract-specific basis, so the courts are implying terms into an individual contract only, not into every contract of employment. By contrast, over the years, the courts have decided that some terms are so important that they should be in every contract, and if the parties have omitted them the courts will insert the relevant provision. These terms have been called 'implied duties' to distinguish them from the terms discussed in Chapter 3.

The nature and the content of the duties have changed over the years as the law has moved away from the attitude that the relationship is one of master and servant and towards the idea that it is a relationship between two equals. It will not go too far down the equality line, however. Whilst it has recognised an inequality of bargaining power between the parties, the law has only gone some way towards balancing that inequality. It will be seen that statute has moved in to give employees minimum rights which cannot normally be contracted out of. For example, women generally have a right to equal pay with men, and certain employees have a right not to be unfairly dismissed and a right to redundancy pay. In addition to statute, the common law has developed the implied duties to protect employees during the performance of the contract. It would be unwise, however, to imagine that the courts have created a charter of employment rights. While duties are imposed upon the employer, the law similarly imposes duties upon the individual employee. Breach of these duties on either side will create a potential claim for breach of contract.

The duties discussed below are duties imposed during the performance of the contract and which limit how either side exercises its rights. To some extent, this is an unusual function of the law and demonstrates the unique nature of a contract of employment. On its most basic interpretation, a contract of employment is a personal contract. Both parties agree to provide personal services for each other. This aspect has already been seen in *Ready Mixed Concrete (South East) Ltd v MPNI* [1968] 2 QB 497 (see Section 2.2.3), where McKenna J refused to hold that lorry drivers were employees, because they could delegate their driving duties under the contract. Given the fact that an employment contract is one where each party is chosen for individual attributes, such a term in the lorry drivers' contracts demonstrated that the relationship could not be one of employment. It has also been seen in *Express Echo Publications Ltd v Tanton* [1999] IRLR 367 (Section 2.2.3), where the Court of Appeal regarded personal service as the irreducible minimum in a contract of employment.

Given that the contract is unique to the two parties within it, it follows that, from basic contractual principles, the courts cannot force the parties to continue the contract should they no longer wish to do so. This has been recognised by statute and is at present to be found in section 236 of the TULR(C)A 1992, which provides that no court by an order of specific performance shall compel the parties to continue the contract, or, likewise, no court shall order an injunction to prevent a breach or threatened breach of a contract by an individual employee, if either order would have the effect of compelling an employee to work or attend a place for the purpose of doing work. In *Whitwood Chemical Co v Hardman* [1891] 2 Ch 416, a manager's contract contained a clause that he agreed to devote the whole of his time to company business. He intended to work for a rival in his spare time, so his employer sought specific performance of the clause. It was held that the action did not lie. Likewise, if an injunction would have the effect of specific performance, in that it would compel the parties to continue the contract, it will not be granted. In *City & Hackney Health Authority v National Union of Public Employees* [1985] IRLR 252, a shop steward obtained an injunction to restrain his employers from preventing his entering the premises when he was suspended. The employers appealed to the Court of Appeal which lifted the injunction. To allow it to stand would have forced the employer to allow the employee to attend the place of work, and would therefore have had the effect of an order of specific performance.

There is, however, one situation where the court will compel the parties to continue the contract. This is where the employer is blatantly ignoring the employee's contractual rights and preventing him from pursuing a remedy provided by the contract itself. The court will exercise its power only in exceptional circumstances, and in the majority of situations will decide that a better remedy is damages for a breach of contract. In *Hill v CA Parsons & Co Ltd* [1972] Ch 305, an employee refused to join the union when there was a closed shop in existence. The employers gave him one month's notice of dismissal. The court felt that, given the employee's position as a senior engineer, he was entitled to six months' notice, and granted an injunction restraining the employers from treating the contract as terminated until after that date. The court conceded, however, that there were exceptional circumstances in that there was no loss of confidence between the parties and the employers had dismissed him because of union pressure. In *Jones v Lee and Guilding* [1980] IRLR 67 (Section 3.3.2), an injunction was granted to prevent a dismissal taking place until the contractual disciplinary procedures had been observed. In *Irani v Southampton & South West Humpshire Health Authority* [1985] IRLR 203 a similar decision was reached. Here the employer had not lost confidence in the employee, the procedures were contractual and damages would have been an inadequate remedy. Given this decision, it can be seen that the normal remedy will be damages, and only if that is inadequate will an order to continue the contract be granted. It should be noted, moreover, that in most cases where an injunction has been granted, this has been to continue the contract for only a relatively short space of time. One exception to this is the case of *Powell v Brent London Borough Council* [1988] ICR 176. There, an employee was promoted. The council then feared that the appointment was in breach of their equal opportunities policy, rescinded the promotion and re-advertised the post. Meanwhile the plaintiff continued to do the job and sought an injunction to restrain the council from treating her as demoted. There was nothing to show that she was unable to do the new job, or that the council did not have confidence in her. The injunction was granted. The later case of *Hughes v London Borough of Southwark* [1988] IRLR 55 supported this decision. In that case the court granted an injunction to prevent the employers from requiring the employees temporarily to staff community areas and so stop their normal hospital work. All of these cases show that the court will compel the employer to continue the contract if there has been no loss of confidence in the employee (see also *Wadcock v London Borough of Brent* [1990] IRLR 223 and *Alexander v Standard Telephones and Cables Ltd* [1990] ICR 291). Courts, however, cannot grant an order in favour of the employer because of section 236 of the 1992 Act (above).

4.2   Duties of the employer

4.2.1   Duty to provide work

Very often you hear lay people and the media talk about the right to work. If, however, there is a right to work, jurisprudentially there must be a corresponding duty on the employer to allow the employee to exercise that right, as for every right there must be a corresponding duty. If my neighbour has a right of way over my property, I must be under a corresponding duty to allow him to exercise his right. In the area of employment, it has been emphatically stated by the majority of judges that there is no right to work and therefore no duty of the employer to provide work. The clearest exposition of the law was by Asquith J in *Collier v Sunday Referee Publishing Co Ltd* [1940] 2 KB 647, when he said: 'Provided I pay my cook her wages regularly, she cannot complain if I choose to take all or some of my meals out.'

Following Justice Asquith's judgment, Lord Denning in particular seemed anxious to establish that there was a right to work. In *Nagle v Fielden* [1966] 2 QB 633, a woman argued that a rule of the Jockey Club that prevented women from holding licences to train horses, prevented her from earning her living. Lord Denning MR held that such a rule was in restraint of trade and void. In the later case of *Langston v Chrysler United Kingdom* [1974] 1 All ER 980, which was referred to the Court of Appeal by the National Industrial Relations Court, Lord Denning MR said: 'We have repeatedly said in this court that a man has a right to work which the courts will protect – I would not wish to state the decided view, but merely state the argument.' The case was referred back to the National Industrial Relations Court, where Sir John Donaldson P decided that suspension of an employee on full basic pay was a breach of the contractual term to earn extra payment for night-shift and overtime working.

It seems, therefore, that despite attempts by Lord Denning, the courts have been reluctant to establish a general right to work. The courts have always recognised, however, that there is a duty to provide work in certain types of cases. Two exceptions to the general rule were given in the case of *Turner v Sawdon* [1901] 2 KB 728, and since then the courts have expanded the group of situations where the employer is under a duty to provide work for his employee, as the opportunity to work is seen to be as important as the salary received. The exceptions are as follows:

1. The work is needed to maintain the employee's publicity and reputation. In *Herbert Clayton & Jack Waller Ltd v Oliver* [1930] AC 209, the employee, who was playing the lead in a play, was given a lesser part at the same salary. It was held that the employer was in breach of contract, as the nature of the job was as important as the salary in terms of the publicity the employee needed.
2. The work is needed to enable the employee to earn the wage. This covers the situation of piece-workers or workers on a commission-only basis, where the failure to provide work will mean that the employee receives no pay (*Devonald v Rosser & Sons* [1906] 2 KB 728). This will apply, however, only if the commission is the sole means of earning the salary. In *Turner v Sawdon* a salesman was on a fixed salary plus commission. He

was given no work to do but still received the fixed salary. It was held that the employer was not in breach of contract.

3. There are *dicta* in *Langston* to suggest that if the nature of the job is such that the employee needs the work to develop or maintain his skills, the employer will be in breach of contract if he fails to provide it. This would cover the situation of apprentices or trainees, although the extension of the principle to the maintenance of skills does extend the potential situations.

4. Later cases seem willing to accept that *Turner v Sawdon* did not lay down a definitive list. In *Pedersen v London Borough of Camden* [1981] ICR 674, it was suggested that it may be a breach of contract to deprive an employee of a substantial proportion of his job, based on the view that a man does not work for wages alone. This view was relying on the earlier case of *Breach v Epsylon Industries Ltd* [1976] IRLR 180, where an employer moved a large part of his operation to Canada, leaving the employee with little to do. On appeal to the EAT, Phillips J said that *Turner v Sawdon* envisaged exceptions to the general principle, but the case was old and in more modern times there may be facts where it is easier to find that there is an implied obligation to provide work. In other words, the courts seem prepared to extend the exceptions first laid down in the case if they feel the circumstances are appropriate. This can be seen in the Court of Appeal decision in *William Hill Organization Ltd v Tucker* [1998] IRLR 313. In the case, Tucker had to give six months' notice to his employer. When he resigned to take up a job with a competitor, William Hill told him that they required six months' notice from him but that he would not be expected to work during that period. In other words, Tucker had been put on 'garden leave'. William Hill then sought an injunction to prevent Tucker working for a competitor during his notice period. The High Court found that there was no express clause in Tucker's contract which allowed the employers to require him to take garden leave and therefore they were obliged to provide him with work during the notice period. Failure to do so amounted to a breach of contract, and thus Tucker was entitled to terminate his contract immediately. The employers appealed. The Court of Appeal noted that social conditions had changed since the older cases in the area and that the courts had been increasingly ready to recognise the importance to an employee of work as well as pay. Looking at Tucker's contract, the Court felt that it created an obligation on William Hill to provide Tucker with work during his notice period. This was because the skills the job required had to be exercised frequently, which was supported by a clause in the contract which stated that the employer would ensure that the employee had every opportunity to develop his skills; the employee had to work such hours as were necessary to carry out his job duties, which appeared inconsistent with the employer's contention that the employee could draw his wages but not be required to work; and the employer had a contractual right to suspend in disciplinary cases. The Court felt such a specific power would be unnecessary if the employers could put employees on garden leave. Consequently, the Court dismissed the employer's appeal. It would appear, however, that if the employer had had a specific contractual provision allowing garden leave then the employer's appeal would have been upheld, although the Court pointed out that the issue of an injunction to prevent the employee working during the notice period (in other words the injunction would restrain competition) should be justified on grounds similar to those necessary in relation to a covenant in restraint of trade.

4.2.2 Duty to pay wages

Although there is no general duty on the employer to provide work, his duty to pay wages is fundamental to the bargain, and if persistently broken will entitle the employee to sue for a repudiatory breach of contract. Normally the contract itself will state the amount of pay the employee is entitled to receive. This will come either from individual negotiation between the employer and the employee, or from a collective agreement. If the contract is silent as to the amount of pay, the law will imply that reasonable remuneration should be paid. The court will assess the value of the employee's services on an action for quantum meruit – literally suing for what the service was worth.

Since April 1999 the amount of pay an employee is entitled to receive has been governed by the National Minimum Wage Act (NMW Act) 1998 and the National Minimum Wage Regulations 1999. The Act by section 1 covers workers, which term is wider than the traditional definition of 'employee' in employment law (see Section 2.1). In *Redrow Homes (Yorkshire) Ltd v Wright* [2004] IRLR 721 (see also Section 2.2.3), the Court of Appeal confirmed an earlier EAT decision that bricklayers were covered by the term 'worker' under Regulation 2(1)(b), in that they worked under a contract, they undertook to perform the work personally, and the other party to the contract was not a client or customer of a business undertaking carried on by the individual. The definition does not cover pupil barristers, however (*Edmunds v Lawson, QC* [2000] IRLR 391). The power to issue regulations is found in section 2 of the NMW Act 1998, and the power to extend the coverage of the legislation by regulations is provided in section 41.

Essentially the NMW Act 1998 applies to a worker's gross standard pay, which includes incentive payments based on output or performance, but certain benefits are excluded from the calculation, such as tips paid directly by the customer to the worker (but not tips distributed through the payroll); premium payments for shift and overtime working (but not standard pay for such working); and other benefits in kind such as company cars and private health insurance, although there are permitted offsets for certain benefits in kind. In *Leisure Employment Services v HM Revenue and Customs* [2007] EWCA Civ 92, the employer provided accommodation for the employee. While the employee received a wage, £3 per week was deducted for the cost of gas and electricity, which took the wage received below the national minimum wage. The Court of Appeal held that the employer could not count the £3 a week towards the national minimum wage and the employer was in breach of the legislation. Likewise, tips paid to a tronc master (that is a person who controls the pool of tips) cannot be part of the minimum wage, because ownership of the money has passed to the tronc master and therefore the money is no longer paid by the employer (*Annabels (Berkeley Square) Ltd & Others v HMRC* [2009] EWCA Civ 361). Conversely, tips paid as part of a bill and paid over to the employer who later distributes them can be part of the national minimum wage according to the ECJ in *Nerva & Others v UK* [2002] IRLR 815. It follows, therefore, that tips paid directly to the worker by the customer cannot be part of the national minimum wage. Since 2009 it has been illegal to use tips to make up the national minimum wage.

The definition of 'working time' for the purposes of calculating the worker's hourly rate is based on the definition used in the EU Working Time Directive (93/104/EC), that is, any period when a worker is working at the employer's disposal and carrying out his duties. The national minimum wage is also payable when a worker is required to be at his place of work, even if no work is available. By Regulation 15 of the National Minimum

Wage Regulations 1999, if workers sleep on the premises, the NMW Act 1998 applies when they are awake and required to be available for work. In *Wright v Scottbridge Construction Ltd* [2001] IRLR 589, a nightwatchman was allowed to sleep during his hours of employment. His contract required him to be on site to respond to any alarm calls. It was argued that, on interpretation, his working time was only the time he was awake. The EAT, however, said that Regulation 15 applies specifically to the situation where an employer allows an employee an allocated period of time for sleep. In the situation where the employee is required to be on site and is permitted to sleep at any time if he wishes, he is entitled to receive the national minimum wage for the whole of the period he is required to be at the site (*Anderson v Jarvis Hotels* (2006) UKEAT 0062/05). However, in *South Manchester Abbeyfield Society v Hopkins and Ors* (2010) UKEAT 0079/10/3011, housekeepers at sheltered accommodation who were required to be on call, during which time they were provided accommodation, could not take into account all of the hours they spent on call for the purposes of the NMW Act. The EAT held that the respondents could claim only for such hours that they were awake for the purposes of working. It remitted the case back to the tribunal to decide whether any payment was due.

The hourly rate is determined by calculating the average pay over the normal pay period, as agreed between the worker and employer, up to a maximum of one calendar month. Homeworkers and others paid by output must be paid no less than the national minimum wage on average for the pay reference period. By the National Minimum Wage Regulations 1999 (Amendment) Regulations 2004, workers below the age of 18 who have ceased to be of compulsory school age qualified from October 2005.

The 2004 Regulations also ensure that homeworkers and piece-workers must be paid a rate linked to the national minimum wage. From October 2004 an employer can no longer set the rate of pay at four-fifths of the time it takes an average worker to complete a set piece of work; instead, it must pay homeworkers the minimum wage for all hours worked, or 120 per cent of the national minimum wage for the number of hours it takes an average worker to complete an agreed block of work.

Enforcement of the national minimum wage is through a variety of procedures. Workers have contractual rights (NMW Act 1998, s 17), plus enforcement via Part II of the Employment Rights Act (ERA) 1996 (unlawful deductions from wages). In addition there is a national minimum wage statement as part of the itemised pay statement (NMW Act 1998, s 12) and a right not to suffer a detriment or unfair dismissal as a result of enforcing the 1998 Act (ss 23, 24 and 25). Employers are required to keep records (s 9) to which the worker has a right of access (ss 10 and 11). Officers have the power to issue enforcement and penalty notices and to take proceedings on behalf of workers (ss 19–22). There are also criminal sanctions for non-compliance (ss 31–33).

4.2.3   Itemised pay statement

If the pay is stated in the contract then few disputes arise. By section 8 of the ERA 1996, every employee who works eight hours a week or more has the right to an itemised pay statement at or before every payment of salary. It must state the gross and the net amount of pay, the amount of any variable or fixed deductions and the purposes for which those deductions are made. If different parts of the net payment are paid in different ways, the statement must give details of the amount and method of each part-payment. Where there are fixed deductions, for example union contributions, the employer need not give a statement each time a deduction is made, but may give a general statement covering those deductions for a period of 12 months. Such a general statement should include the amount of the deduction, the intervals at which it is paid and its purpose (ERA 1996, s 9(5)). The statement should also include the national minimum wage rate (see above). If the employer fails to give an itemised pay statement, or there is a dispute as to its contents, the employee may apply to an employment tribunal (ERA 1996, s 11). The tribunal can declare the particulars which should have been in the statement (*Coales v John Wood & Co* [1986] IRLR 129) and order the employer to make up any unnotified deductions from the employee's pay in the 13 weeks preceding the tribunal hearing.

4.2.4 Normal working hours/weekly pay

In addition to issues relating to the national minimum wage, another problem which may arise is in relation to statutory compensation should the relationship come to an end. Statutory compensation is based on the concept of the employee's weekly pay, and this may not be clear from the statement itself, particularly where the employee is paid hourly and the wage usually includes some provision for overtime. In *Tarmac Roadstone Holdings Ltd v Peacock* [1973] 2 All ER 485, Lord Denning MR stated that for overtime to be part of the normal working hours of the employee it had to be obligatory on both sides. There are therefore three possible situations:

1. Overtime is voluntary on both sides.
2. Overtime is voluntary on the part of the employer but a contractual obligation on the part of the employee.
3. Overtime is obligatory on both sides, that is, the employer is under a contractual obligation to provide it and the employee is under a contractual obligation to work it.

In the third situation only is the overtime part of the employee's weekly pay. The judgment in *Tarmac Roadstone Holdings Ltd* is further endorsed by section 234 of the ERA 1996. Section 234(1) and (2) provide that the normal working hours are the number of hours to be worked before overtime becomes payable. In *Fox v C Wright (Farmers) Ltd* [1978] ICR 98, an agricultural worker was employed under a contract which did not specify a minimum number of hours a week but which stated that overtime would be paid for hours worked in excess of 40. He regularly worked 50–60 hours a week, but the EAT held that his normal working hours were 40. There is an exception, however, in section 234(3) where the contract lays down a minimum number of obligatory hours which includes a number of hours payable as overtime. In this situation, the normal working hours are the obligatory hours even though they include overtime. For example, if the contract states that the working week is 40 hours but that overtime will be paid after 35 hours, the normal working hours are 40.

Apart from the provisions relating to overtime in section 234, sections 221–224 of the 1996 Act give three different methods of calculation of the normal working hours/weekly pay:

1. If there are normal working hours and the remuneration does not vary, the weekly pay is the normal payment under the contract when the normal hours are worked. Any

further payments made on a regular basis, for example a bonus, will be added to the weekly pay (*Donelan v Kerby Constructions Ltd* [1983] IRLR 191) (s 221).

2. If there are normal working hours but the remuneration varies with the amount of work, for example in the case of piece-workers, the weekly pay is the pay for the normal working hours payable at the average hourly rate. The average hourly rate is calculated by working out the total number of hours worked in the preceding 12 weeks, the total pay received and thus the average pay per hour (*May Gurney Ltd v Adshead* [2006] All ER 388) (s 222).

3. If there are no normal working hours, the weekly pay is calculated by establishing the average weekly pay received by the employee over the preceding 12 weeks (s 224).

Ignoring the problems which can arise in relation to overtime and which have already been discussed, two further points should be noted. First, as the tribunal is calculating the weekly pay based on the average hourly rate, although the provisions specifically exclude non-contractually binding overtime this does not exclude commission or contractually binding bonus payments (*Amalgamated Asphalt Companies Ltd v Dockrill* (1972) ITR 198 and *Weevsmay Ltd v Kings* [1977] ICR 244). In *Horkulak v Cantor Fitzgerald International* [2004] IRLR 942, the Court of Appeal stated that a discretionary bonus can be contractual if it is mentioned in the contract. In that case the employee's contract provided that 'the company may, in its discretion, pay you an annual discretionary bonus'. The Court of Appeal held that if the bonus was something the employer could pay on a whim it would not be in the contract. The bonus was clearly intended to be part of the salary structure and the discretion to be exercised in a rational and bona fide way. Section 229(2) of the ERA 1996 further provides that if the bonus or commission is payable outside the 12-week calculation period, it should be apportioned for calculation purposes. In simple terms, therefore, if the employee is entitled to an annual bonus of £1,040 this is translated as £20 a week and is part of the calculation. Indirect benefits should also be taken into account, but non-cash benefits are not part of the calculation, nor are benefits (for example tips) from persons other than the employee's employer. A service charge which the employer is contractually bound to distribute among his employees is, however, part of the weekly pay.

Second, the provisions require the tribunal to look at the preceding 12 weeks to calculate the normal working hours and hence the weekly pay. This means that the tribunal must look to weeks where the employee actually worked, and thus base its calculation on the preceding 12 working weeks (*Secretary of State for Employment v Crane* [1988] IRLR 238). If in the preceding 12 weeks the amount of work has decreased then those weeks will still be used for the calculation, even though they do not reflect the employee's normal wage.

4.2.5 Deductions from pay

The original Wages Act 1986 was brought in to remedy deficiencies in the Truck Acts 1831–1940. The provisions in relation to deduction from wages are now contained in the ERA 1996. The provisions have far-reaching consequences for many contractual terms, in that there must be a statutory or contractual right to deduct from wages before any such deductions may be made. This has implications should an employer wish to impose a disciplinary sanction such as suspension without pay, demotion or a deduction for bad workmanship. Since the case of *Robertson v Blackstone Franks Investment Management Ltd* [1998] IRLR 376, it appears that the provisions protect not only employees but those who personally provide services, given that this is the definition of 'worker' in section 230(3) of the ERA 1996.

By section 13(1) of the 1996 Act, an employer must not make a deduction from the wages of an employee unless the deduction is:

1. required or authorised by statute (for example PAYE); or
2. required or authorised by a provision in the contract of employment which has been given to the employee or notified to the employee previously in writing; or
3. agreed to by the employee in writing before the making of the deduction.

There is a corresponding duty on the employer in section 15 not to receive payment from the employee apart from in the circumstances above.

The wording of the contractual provision or agreement must be precise. In *Potter v Hunt Contracts Ltd* [1992] IRLR 108, when the employee joined Hunt he had to repay the cost of an HGV driving course to his previous employer. Hunt agreed to give him a loan for this purpose, the terms of which provided that if Potter left within 24 months, 'you shall be required to return the fee, less any repayments made'. When Potter left the company within 24 months he received no wages, because the sum owed exceeded his pay. The EAT held that the employer had no right to deduct monies, only to receive repayment. Furthermore, any agreement to deduct from wages must have been entered into before the happening of the event which caused the deduction, according to the significant decision of the EAT in *Tobacco and Confectionery Ltd v Williamson* [1993] ICR 371. In this case the employee was the manager of a store where large stock deficiencies were found in December 1988 and February 1989. In March 1989 he signed a document giving his employers the right to deduct £3,500 from his wages at £20 per week. In May 1989 there was a further deficiency and the employee was dismissed, the employer withholding all of his wages in reliance on the March document. Section 13(6) of the ERA 1996 states that any agreement by the worker to deduct shall not operate to authorise a deduction before the agreement was signed. The employers argued that this meant that the agreement had to pre-date the deduction. The EAT disagreed. The agreement had to pre-date the event that had led to the deduction, that is, deductions made in respect of deficiencies prior to March 1989 were unlawful and the employer had no right to withhold the employee's wages in respect of those deficiencies.

Section 14 of the 1996 Act then contains a list of exceptions. The provisions of section 13(1) do not apply to deductions in respect of:

- overpayment of wages or expenses;
- disciplinary proceedings held by virtue of any statutory provision;
- a statutory requirement to deduct from wages to pay over to a public authority;
- payments agreed to by the employee which are to be made over by the employer to a third party;
- a strike or other industrial action in which the employee took part; or
- the satisfaction of a court or tribunal order requiring the employee to pay something to the employer.

Again, there is a corresponding provision in relation to the acceptance of such payments by the employer (s 16).

The list in section 14 does not give the employer the right to deduct such payments, it merely means that such deductions do not infringe section 13(1). Such deductions cannot be heard by the tribunal and an action lies in the county court, because the deduction may still be illegal. For example, an overpayment of wages is within section 14 but in some cases the employer will have lost the right to claim back the overpayment. In *Avon County Council v Howlett* [1983] IRLR 171, the employee was a teacher who had been regularly overpaid while off sick following an accident. The overpayment amounted to £1,007. The council sought to reclaim the money. The Court of Appeal held that where the money was accompanied by an express or an implied representation that the recipient was entitled to treat the money as his own, the employer was prevented from recovery. In the case, the employee, without any idea that the overpayment had been made, or that the council would seek recovery, had changed his position so that repayment would be inequitable. The overpayment was a result of a mistake of fact on the part of the council, in that it had failed to realise that Mr Howlett had been off sick for more than six months. The employee had spent the money, believing it to be his, though the court intimated that the decision might have been different if the defendant still had the money in his possession.

The question of a deduction being made owing to a strike or other industrial action arose in the case of *Sunderland Polytechnic v Evans* [1993] IRLR 196. The employer had deducted a full day's pay from the employee after the employee had taken part in a half-day strike. The employee argued that there had been an illegal deduction of half a day's pay since she had not agreed to the deduction in advance. In other words, the employee was arguing that deduction of half a day's pay was within section 14, but not the deduction of the other half-day's pay. The EAT held that whether the deduction was lawful or not was a question to be determined. If the reason for the deduction was industrial action then it fell within section 14 whether the deduction was lawful or not, and therefore the tribunal had no jurisdiction. A similar decision in relation to overpayment was reached in *SIP (Industrial Products) v Swinn* [1994] ICR 473. It is for the tribunal to decide whether it has jurisdiction. In *Gill v Ford Motor Company Ltd* and *Wong v BAE Systems* [2004] IRLR 840, the EAT rejected the employers' contention that a tribunal had no jurisdiction to hear the claims. In *Gill*, production stopped because of unofficial industrial action which meant that no one could work, but Gill contended he was not taking part in the action. In *Wong*, BAE deducted from the employee's his wages because of an overpayment of a bonus. In both cases the EAT said the facts were unclear and remitted them back to the tribunal to decide the facts.

In addition to section 13 deductions, the ERA 1996, sections 17–22 give further protection to workers in retail employment. Where a deduction is made in respect of cash shortages or stock deficiencies, the maximum which may be deducted is 10 per cent of the gross amount of wages for that particular day. However, the deductions can continue over successive pay days until the full amount is recovered, and the 10 per cent limit does not apply to the final payday if the employee's contract is terminated (s 22).

The provisions have been widely criticised. They deal with the mechanics of how an employer collects money from his employees rather than his entitlement to do so. Prior to changes in the law relating to employment tribunal jurisdiction, the provisions led to a variety of cases in its relatively short life on questions of interpretation. The major problem was whether the provisions applied to given situations. If there was an illegal deduction within section 13, the employee could complain to an employment tribunal, normally within three months of the deduction's being made. Any other deduction made had to be recovered in the normal courts. Before the tribunals had jurisdiction in breach of contract cases, many problems arose concerning the definition of 'wages' and 'deduction'.

The starting point for a tribunal when it heard a claim was given by the EAT in the cases of *Barlow v AJ Whittle* [1990] IRLR 79 and *Alsop v Star Vehicle Contracts Ltd* [1990] IRLR 83. A tribunal had to ask itself three questions:

1. What is the wage due?
2. Is there an entitlement to a deduction or repayment?
3. Was that deduction properly made?

The above questions, however, meant that the tribunal had first to decide whether there had been a deduction, and whether that had been from the employee's wages.

Section 27 of the ERA 1996 lists payments which may be regarded as wages. In particular section 27(1)(a) refers to 'any fee, bonus, commission, holiday pay, or any other emolument referable to [the worker's] employment, whether payable under his contract or otherwise'. A number of cases since the Act was passed have discussed whether wages in lieu of notice are wages for the purpose of the legislation. In the House of Lords' decision in *Delaney v Staples (t/a De Montfort Recruitment)* [1992] 1 AC 687, their Lordships decided (confirming the Court of Appeal decision) that payment in lieu was a substitution for damages for breach of contract. Such payment did not arise out of employment but as a result of the termination of employment, and as such could not fall within section 27 even if the employer had a contractual right to give wages in lieu. While the decision is undoubtedly correct, it left the employee who had had deductions made from a final payment in lieu in the situation where he had to take action in the normal courts. If, however, there was also a deduction of, for example, holiday pay, the employee could sue for this deduction in the tribunal. This meant that many employees were taking two separate actions against their employer in two different forums, and this was hardly a satisfactory state of affairs. In *Delaney*, the House of Lords ended with a plea that the jurisdiction of the tribunals be extended to hear breach of contract claims, a plea which has been answered to some extent; but given that the tribunals have breach of contract jurisdiction only when the contract has been terminated, the above discussion is still pertinent for those deductions made while the contract is still subsisting. In *Coors Brewers v Adcock* [2007] EWCA Civ 19, 600 employees claimed that they had not been given the correct bonuses under an implied contractual promise to carry on with a bonus scheme operated by a previous employer. As they were still employed, the tribunal could not hear a breach of contract claim and thus heard the action under the unlawful deductions jurisdiction. The Court of Appeal held that such claims were claims for unliquidated damages, as unlawful deductions jurisdiction applied only to claims for a specific sum of money or an identifiable sum (*per* Wall LJ). As there needed to be an investigation into the amount of the underpayment, the proper route was a breach of contract claim. which had to be taken to the county court and not the tribunal as the employees were still employed.

The position as regards deductions from sums due and payable after the termination of the contract has been decided by the Court of Appeal in the *Robertson* case, above.

Further problems have arisen in relation to whether a payment which is stated to be ex gratia can be wages for the purpose of the provisions. An immediate reaction would probably be a resounding 'no', but this may not always be the case, as demonstrated in *Kent Management Services Ltd v Butterfield* [1992] ICR 272. In this case the ex-employee complained that on his dismissal the employers had refused to pay him outstanding commission. The employers argued that commission and bonus schemes were discretionary and ex gratia because a document attached to his letter of appointment stated that such payments would not be made in exceptional circumstances, such as bankruptcy. The employer therefore argued that as such payments were discretionary, they could not be contractual. The EAT looked at the definition of wages in section 27(1)(a) of the ERA 1996. Wood P said that such schemes must be fairly common, and that while they were in being, the anticipation of both parties must be that in normal circumstances the commission, etc would be paid. This was the situation here. No exceptional circumstances existed to prevent payment, therefore the expectation of both the parties must have been that the commission would be paid. As such it was wages and there had been an unlawful deduction. This decision has been confirmed by *Bannerman Co Ltd v Mackenzie* (1995) IDS Brief 552.

Later cases have brought more payments into the arena of unlawful deductions. In *Taylor Gordon & Co v Timmons* [2004] IRLR 180, the EAT stated that the provisions applied to deductions from statutory sick pay (SSP). In *HMRC v Stringer & Others* [2009] UKHL 31, the employee was employed by the Revenue from 1976 until he was dismissed four days into his leave year on 4 November 2002. He had been absent on sick leave for more than a year at the time of his dismissal. While the Revenue accepted that holiday pay was payable, the question was under what statutory provisions liability lay. The Revenue contended that holiday pay was not wages and therefore a claim could not be made under ERA 1996 but had to be made under Regulation 30 of the Working Time Regulations 1998. The House of Lords unanimously held that holiday pay was wages for the purposes of unlawful deductions and a claim could be pursued under the ERA 1996 or the 1998 Regulations. The practical effect of this decision is that whereas a claim under Regulation 30 must be made within three months of the date on which the leave should have been taken, a claim under ERA 1996 may be brought within three months after the deduction is made, or three months after the last deduction is made if there is a series. The decision therefore allows a claimant to take advantage of the more generous time limits under the ERA 1996.

Lastly, the EAT has recently decided that pension contributions are not wages and so cannot be reclaimed as an unlawful deduction under the legislation (*Somerset County Council v Chambers* [2013] All ER (D) 260).

In relation to total deductions the law is somewhat unclear. The EAT has held that in cases where there is a non-payment (for example, where the employer has paid none of the money due because he feels that the employee owes him that money) this is not a deduction. The Court of Appeal, however, held in the *Delaney* case (above) that non-payment was a 100 per cent deduction, and as such the tribunal had the jurisdiction to hear the complaint. The House of Lords did not hear this point on appeal and it therefore appears that this is still the law.

4.2.6   Payment during sickness

There is no presumption that an employee will be paid by his employer while he is sick. While an employee may be entitled to SSP, this will give only the statutory level of payment and will often be considerably less than the employee's wage. It is therefore important to see if there is a term in the contract providing for payment during sickness. Such a term may be express or implied, but before a court will imply a term that the employee will be paid during sickness, there must be evidence that the parties intended this to be the case. In the leading case of *Mears v Safecar Security Ltd* [1982] IRLR 183 the employee was ill for six months. During that time he did not ask for payment, he did not send in medical certificates, and when he asked his colleagues about sick pay, they told him it was not available and had never been paid in the past. The Court of Appeal held that as there was no express term on sick pay, it was necessary to see if there was an implied term. To see if there was such a term the court had to look at the conduct of the parties. Given that the employer had never paid sick pay in the past and given that the conduct of the employee indicated that he did not expect to receive sick pay, no term was implied.

The SSP scheme was introduced by the Social Security and Housing Benefits Act 1982. The aim of the scheme is to pass the administration of the old sickness benefit on to the employer. Since April 2014 all employers bear the cost and there is no recoupment from the government. In outline, the scheme provides that a qualifying employee is entitled to SSP for the first 28 weeks of sickness and after that period he will receive state sickness benefit. Certain employees are excluded from the scheme. These include pensioners, persons who do not pay NICs and employees who are not employed because of a trade dispute at their place of work, unless they have no direct interest in its outcome.

To claim, the employee must be suffering from some disease or physical or mental disability rendering him incapable of performing any work he could reasonably be expected to do under his contract of employment. In addition, the employee must satisfy the following three conditions:

1. There must be a period of incapacity for work which is a period of four or more consecutive days of incapacity, which may include Sundays and holidays. Two periods of incapacity are treated as one if they are not separated by more than two weeks.
2. The period of incapacity must fall within a period of entitlement, which commences with the start of the period of incapacity for work and ends with the occurrence of the first of the following:
    (a) the day the employee returns to work;
    (b) after 28 weeks during a three-year period;
    (c) the termination of the contract;
    (d) when a pregnant employee reaches the beginning of the eleventh week before the expected week of confinement; or
    (e) the day the employee is detained in custody or leaves the EU.
3. SSP is payable only in respect of qualifying days. These are normally agreed with the employer and include all working days. The first three qualifying days are waiting days, SSP being payable on the fourth day.

The amount payable is a daily rate but depends on weekly earnings. The general rule is to take the last pay day before the period of sickness and average the weekly earnings over a period of the preceding eight weeks. To claim entitlement the employee must inform the employer that he is unfit for work. The employer can fix a time limit during which he must be notified, but in the absence of a time limit the employee must inform the employer within seven days. The employer can specify the mode of notification. Disputes as to SSP are decided at first instance by an adjudication officer, with an appeal to the Social Security Appeal Tribunal and a final appeal to a Social Security Commissioner.

4.2.7   Pay during lay-offs or short-time working

The general rule at common law is that the employer must pay the wages of staff who are available for work even if no work is provided by the employer. There is no common law right of lay-off. If there is an interruption in the provision of work, the employee is still entitled to payment (*Devonald v Rosser & Sons*, Section 4.2.1 above). It appears, however, that if the failure to provide work is totally outside the control of the employer, the courts will imply a term that the employees are not entitled to be paid. In *Browning v Crumlin Valley Collieries* [1926] 1 KB 522, a colliery had to close down when a serious land fault made the mine dangerous. It was held that the failure to provide work was totally outside the employer's control and, as such, the implied term that the employees were entitled to payment would not apply. Thus the situation at common law is that there is an implied duty that the employer will pay wages unless the failure to provide work is outside his control. It should be noted that if the employer finds it inconvenient to provide the work, not impossible, the common law term will apply.

Given that the above term is implied into the contract by the common law, it follows that such a term may be ousted by an express term to the contrary. In *Hulme v Ferranti Ltd* [1918] 2 KB 426, an employee was employed on terms that if there was no work he would not be paid. He was laid off as the result of a strike at his place of work, and it was held that he was not entitled to payment during the period of the lay-off. The law, however, will restrict the employer's exercise of such a contractual right, and it appears from the more modern case of *Dakri (A) & Co Ltd v Tiffen* [1981] IRLR 57 that the right can be exercised only for a reasonable length of time. After such a time has elapsed, the employee is entitled to treat the non-payment by his employer as a repudiatory breach and may, if he has the continuity (see Section 9.2), sue for a constructive dismissal.

Although the common law position is still important in this area, it has to some extent been superseded by the right to a guaranteed payment given by sections 28–35 of the ERA 1996 (discussed in Chapter 7).

4.2.8   Duty to indemnify

There is some legal argument as to whether the common law implies a duty that the employer should indemnify his employee against expenses incurred during the performance of his contract. While the majority of contracts will expressly cover the situation of travelling and accommodation expenses, the problem arises when the expense has not been envisaged by the contract, for example if a lorry driver is fined for overloading or for a defective tyre. *Selwyn* argues that there is an implied duty to indemnify, but that the duty does not apply where the employee has the choice of performing the job in a lawful or unlawful way and by choosing the unlawful way he incurs an expense such as a fine. *Selwyn* (2012) gives two cases as authority for his proposition that such a duty exists. The first, *Gregory v Ford* [1951] 1 All ER 121, was a case where an employee injured a third party owing to his negligent driving. His employer did not have third party insurance as required by legislation. As a result, the employee was sued personally, and it was held that there was an implied term in the contract of employment that the employer would not require the employee to do an illegal act, which in this case had been broken. The damages resulting from the employer's breach were the damages the employee had to pay to the plaintiff. The second case cited by *Selwyn* is *Re Famatina Development Corporation* [1914] 2 Ch 271. There, a consulting engineer was asked to prepare a report on the conduct of the managing director, and as a result the managing director brought an action for libel against the engineer. It was held that the engineer was entitled to be indemnified against the cost of defending the action. Of the two cases, *Re Famatina* is more directly related to the question of indemnity; however, Hepple argues that in that case the position of the engineer was more akin to that of an agent, and there has always been a principle in the law of agency that an agent should be indemnified for expenses incurred during the performance of his agency. It is difficult to come to any firm conclusion. Taking the *Ford* case, it would appear that if the employee incurs expense by doing an unlawful act at the instruction of his employer, he is entitled to be reimbursed, but on the basis of an implied term that the employer will not ask the employee to commit an unlawful act. Apart from this situation, it appears that if the employee is in the position of an agent, he is entitled to be indemnified, but because of the agency relationship and not because of an employment relationship. The position does not appear to be as clear-cut as it might at first seem.

4.2.9   Duty in relation to references

While employers are under no duty to provide references (unless there is a contractual obligation to do so) in practice most employers do. The case of *Spring v Guardian Assurance Co* [1994] 3 All ER 129 has imposed duties upon employers who provide references for their employees. In the case, Spring had worked for Guardian Assurance and left to sell policies for another insurance company. As required by LAUTRO, Guardian Assurance provided a reference for Spring, which doubted, among other things, his honesty and his selling tactics. The reference was described by the House of Lords as 'the kiss of death' to his future career. Although the writer of the reference honestly believed what he had written, he had been negligent in ascertaining the facts.

The majority of the House of Lords held that the writer of a reference owed a duty to the subject of that reference to exercise reasonable care. They applied the test in *Caparo Industries v Dickman* [1990] 1 All ER 568 for establishing a duty of care: that the damage is foreseeable, there was a sufficient closeness of proximity between the parties, and that it was fair and reasonable to impose such a duty. The argument that the imposition of such a duty would deter employers from writing references was not considered to be a serious enough risk to prevent the duty being imposed. While it was not established whether Spring worked under a contract of employment or a contract for services, the court felt that this was irrelevant and the duty would apply in both situations. Furthermore, although the duty was imposed in tort, it was held that the duty could also be implied into some contracts.

Since *Spring* there have been a number of cases refining the duty. In *Bartholomew v London Borough of Hackney* [1999] IRLR 246, the Court of Appeal held that a reference must be true, accurate and fair, not giving a misleading impression, although there is no duty that the reference must be full and comprehensive. This was expanded in *Kidd v Axa Equity and Law Life Assurance Society* [2000] IRLR 301, when the High Court stated that the duty owed by a referee is 'not to give misleading information … whether as a result of the unfairly selective provision of information, or by the inclusion of facts or opinions in such a manner as to give rise to a false or mistaken inference in the mind of a reasonable recipient'. The import of this is seen in *TSB Bank v Harris* [2000] IRLR 157. In this case the bank provided a reference containing mere factual information. This included the fact that a number of complaints had been made against the employee, some of which were upheld and some of which were outstanding. The reference made no assessment of the employee's ability. In accordance with the practice of the bank, the employee was unaware of the complaints against her. The employee did not get the other job, and when she discovered the content of the reference she resigned and claimed constructive dismissal. The EAT held that the bank was in breach of the duty of mutual respect (Section 4.2.10 below) by revealing complaints of which the employee was unaware in a reference to a prospective employer. Although the contents of the reference were accurate, the reference could not be said to be reasonable and fair (*Bartholomew*). There was a further breach of the duty since the employee had not been given the opportunity to answer the complaints. It has also been held in *Coote v Granada Hospitality* (No 2) [1999] IRLR 452 that refusal to provide a reference after the termination of the relationship, because the ex-employee had brought a discrimination case against her employers, was victimisation under the Sex Discrimination Act 1975 (see Chapter 5) (now the Equality Act 2010).

4.2.10 Duty of mutual respect/trust and confidence

At the beginning of the Industrial Revolution, the employment relationship was seen as a relationship of servitude, and this was reflected in the names the law chose for the parties in the relationship. For many years the law thought of an employment relationship as being between a master and his servant rather than between an employer and an employee. In fact the law itself reflected the servile nature of the relationship in the judgments made over a hundred years ago. In *Turner v Mason* (1845) M & W 112, for example, it was held that an employer was entitled to sack a domestic servant who, in breach of her contractual provision requiring her to be on duty 24 hours a day, took a day off to visit her dying mother. Fortunately, the law has moved forward somewhat since that decision, to the extent that the law now imposes a duty on the employer to treat the employee with respect. It is often referred to as the 'duty of mutual respect', but the word 'mutual' merely demonstrates that the duty now applies to both parties and not merely to the employee, as was almost certainly the case until the 1970s. While reflecting the change in attitude of the courts, the duty has really arisen in the context of unfair dismissal, where the employee will argue that the employer's treatment of him has destroyed the trust and confidence the parties need to maintain the relationship, and as a result the employee argues that there has been a constructive dismissal.

The idea that the relationship is one that can be maintained only if there is trust and confidence is not new. As long ago as 1888, in the case of *Boston Deep Sea Fishing and Ice Co v Ansell* (1888) 39 Ch 339, the court talked of a breach of the confidential relationship between an employer and employee, and went on to find that should an employee commit an act which destroyed that relationship, such a breach was repudiatory, entitling the employer to dismiss. It was not until the 1970s, however, that the law decided that such a breach could be made on the part of the employer. The first time this was addressed by a court was in the case of *Donovan v Invicta Airways* [1970] 1 Lloyds Rep 486, when the Court of Appeal considered whether consistent complaints about the employee by the employer constituted a repudiatory breach, entitling the employee to resign and claim constructive dismissal. On the facts it was held that there was no breach by the employer, not because the duty did not exist, but rather because on the particular facts it had not been broken. Cases since *Donovan* have found a breach on the part of the employer, and the duty was accepted as an implied term in the contract by the Court of Appeal in the case of *Woods v WM Car Services* [1982] IRLR 413. Conduct such as telling an experienced employee before his subordinates that he is incapable of doing the job has been found to be a breach (*Courtaulds Northern Textiles Ltd v Andrew* [1979] IRLR 84), as has describing a senior officer as wholly unsuitable for promotion without any evidence to support that finding (*Post Office v Roberts* [1980] IRLR 515). Perhaps the leading case in this area is *Bliss v South East Thames Regional Health Authority* [1987] ICR 700, where the Court of Appeal held that refusing to allow a doctor to return to work after he had been suspended, because he refused to submit to a psychiatric examination, was a repudiatory breach by the employer. There was no evidence of mental instability on the part of the doctor, and thus no evidence that such an examination was necessary.

The fact that this is an ever-expanding duty has been demonstrated by a number of cases. In *WA Goold (Pearmak) Ltd v McConnell* [1995] IRLR 516, it was held that failure to provide a grievance procedure, given that there is a statutory duty to do so by section 3 of the ERA 1996, was a breach of the duty of mutual respect entitling the employees to resign and claim constructive dismissal. Likewise, in *Blackburn v Aldi Stores Ltd* (2013) UKEAT 0185/12/JOJ the EAT concluded that a failure to provide an adequate appeal process in a grievance procedure amounted to a breach of trust and confidence entitling the employee to resign and claim constructive dismissal. In *Malik v BCCI* [1997] IRLR 462, an employer's fraudulent conduct was held to be a breach of the duty, and so the ex-employee was entitled to claim damages for his difficulty in finding alternative work because of the loss of reputation he suffered when it was known that he had been employed by that employer. *TSB Bank v Harris* (Section 4.2.9 above) decided that a failure to allow an employee to answer complaints made against him or her, and listing those complaints in a reference without any judgement as to the ability of the employee, is also a breach. Furthermore, in *Morrow v Safeway Stores* [2002] IRLR 9, the EAT held that any breach of the duty is repudiatory and thus a constructive dismissal. In *University of Nottingham v (1) Eyett and (2) Pensions Ombudsman* [1999] IRLR 87, on the other hand, it was held that the duty of mutual respect does not extend to a positive obligation on the part of the employer to warn an employee that he is not exercising his rights, in connection with the contract of employment (in the case, the date at which to take early retirement), in the most advantageous way. However, in the later case of *BC plc v O'Brien* [2001] IRLR 496 the EAT upheld the decision of an employment tribunal that the singling out of an employee by not offering him a revised contract of employment, providing for enhanced redundancy payments, was a breach of the duty. Mr Recorder Langstaff, QC said:

it is difficult, if not impossible, to draw any satisfactory distinction between an obligation positively expressed: a requirement not to take a certain course of action may be, in effect, a requirement to permit another.

Nevertheless, the tribunal emphasised that there is no implied duty that an employer will act reasonably towards his employees. In *London Borough of Waltham Forest v Omilaju* [2004] EWCA Civ 1493, the Court of Appeal talked about the 'last straw' where a final act by an employer, after a series of other acts, causes the employee to resign and claim constructive dismissal on a breach of the duty of mutual trust and confidence. The Court stated that the act which constituted the last straw did not have to be unreasonable or blameworthy, but a blameless act by an employer could not constitute a last straw. Thus the refusal of an employer to pay for an employee's attendance at a tribunal could not be the last straw as the employer was not contractually bound to pay him.

4.2.11 Duty to ensure employees' safety

4.2.11(a) Extent of the duty

While the provisions in the 1996 Act protect an employee health and safety representative from unfair dismissal while pursuing his duties (see Chapter 9), the ordinary employee's safety is protected in two ways. First, by the common law of negligence. This derives from the case of *Donoghue v Stevenson* [1932] AC 562, and requires that an employer take reasonable care to protect his employees who are reasonably foreseeable victims should the duty of care be broken. This duty is translated into an implied term in the contract of employment, and if broken can be seen as a repudiatory breach of contract. In *British Aircraft Corporation v Austin* [1978] IRLR 332 the employer did not investigate a complaint about the suitability of protective glasses. It was held that the conduct was a repudiatory breach of contract which entitled the employee to resign and claim constructive dismissal.

In addition to the common law implied term, statute protects employees in the form of the Health and Safety at Work etc Act 1974. Both statute and common law run side by side, but their aims are different: the common law exists to provide the employee with compensation once he is injured; the Act exists to prevent the injury happening in the first place and creates criminal, not civil, liability. As such, the two systems complement each other and interrelate, so that often an employee will allege both a breach of contract and a breach of statute. In *Smith v Vange Scaffolding & Engineering Co Ltd and Another* [1970] 1 WLR 733, the employee was injured when he fell over a cable when walking back to work. It was held that the employers were in breach of their common law duty in failing to provide safe premises; in addition, they were in breach of their statutory duty imposed by the Construction (Working Places) Regulations 1966 by failing to provide safe access and egress to and from the employee's place of work.

In some situations the employer may have complied with his statutory duties but still failed to come up to the standard of a reasonable employer. In *Bux v Slough Metals* [1973] 1 WLR 1358, the employer complied with his statutory obligation to provide goggles; however, the employee did not wear the goggles because they misted up. The Court of Appeal held that while the employer had not broken his statutory duties, he was negligent at common law for failing to insist that the goggles were worn. As a result of this negligence, the employee lost the sight of his eye when he was splashed with molten metal, and thus the employer was liable.

Although only the common law duty is implied into the contract of employment, given the interrelationship of the common law and statute, it is proposed to discuss both aspects below.

4.2.11(b) The common law

The common law standard is a negligence standard; in other words, the employer must do all he can to prevent foreseeable injury. The important word is 'foreseeable' – an employer will not necessarily be liable for every injury that his employees incur. For example, it may be that the state of knowledge in an area is such that it is not known that a certain process can cause injury until that injury occurs. Such an injury will not be foreseeable and the employer will not be liable. In addition the law requires the employer to act reasonably in all the circumstances. In *Latimer v AEC* [1953] AC 643, a factory was flooded by a heavy rainstorm. The employer asked his employees to return to work, warning them that the factory floor was dangerous in places. The employer had put sawdust on the floor, but could not get enough to cover the whole factory so that some areas of floor were untreated. The employee was injured when he slipped on an untreated area of floor. It was held that the employer had done all that was reasonable. The only other alternative would have been to close down the factory until the floor had dried out, and it was unreasonable to expect the employer to do this.

The employer is also entitled to assume the employee has a modicum of common sense. In *O'Reilly v National Rail* [1966] 1 All ER 499, a group of workers found an unexploded bomb in a scrapyard where they worked. They challenged Mr O'Reilly to hit it with a hammer. He did so, with the inevitable result. It was held that the employer was not liable for failing to tell his employees not to go around hitting unexploded bombs – he was entitled to assume that the employees would know the inherent dangers in such a practice! Likewise in *Vinnyey v Star Paper Mills* [1965] 1 All ER 175, an employee was injured when he slipped while mopping a floor. It was held that the employer was entitled to assume that the employee knew how to mop a floor properly.

However, the employer owes his duty to each individual employee and not to his employees as a whole. If he therefore knows that an employee is particularly susceptible to risk, he must take added precautions. In *Paris v Stepney Borough Council* [1951] AC 367, the employee in question had one eye. He lost the sight of his only eye while chipping off rust from underneath a bus. Despite the fact that it was not normal to provide the employees with goggles, the Court held that a reasonable employer would have provided this employee with goggles, given that any injury would leave him totally blind. The employer was therefore liable.

Given that the employer should act to prevent only foreseeable injury, it follows that if knowledge in the area has not advanced sufficiently to identify the injuries which may be caused, the employer cannot be liable. In *Down v Dudley Coles Long* (1969) (unreported) the employee suffered partial deafness from using a hammer-assisted drill. The employer did not provide ear-defenders because, at the time, medical knowledge was such that it was not known that such drills could cause deafness. It was held that the employer was not liable. On the other hand, once the knowledge becomes available, the employer will not be acting reasonably if he does not act quickly. In *Wright and Cassidy v Dunlop Rubber Co and ICI* (1972) 13 KIR 255, the employers had been informed by the manufacturers that certain chemicals they were using could cause cancer. The manufacturers advised that all employees involved with the chemical should be screened. The employers did not institute screening for some time. It was held that the employers had not acted reasonably. Once the injury was foreseeable, the employers should have taken immediate steps to protect their employees. Likewise in *Baxter v Harland & Wolff plc* [1990] IRLR 516, the employee had been subjected to high levels of noise since 1937 which had resulted in appreciable hearing loss. In 1963 the Ministry of Labour published guidelines regarding levels of noise at work. The defendants took no precautions. The Court of Appeal held that the defendants were liable because there was sufficient medical and scientific information, post-1963, which the defendants had failed to address to see what precautions they should have taken. This was taken a step further in *Bowman v Harland & Wolff plc* [1992] IRLR 349, where employees alleged that the employers were negligent in failing to recognise that they risked contracting vibration white finger from working with pneumatic drills and failing to take precautions. The Northern Ireland High Court held that by January 1973 a reasonable employer in the defendant's position would have appreciated the problem and instituted preventative action. Hence the employer was liable for damage sustained from that date.

The cases above raise two important issues. How far can the employer balance the cost of protecting his employees against the likelihood of injury occurring and its potential seriousness; and how far should the employer keep up to date with knowledge in the area? These questions were considered by Swanwick J in the case of *Stokes v Guest, Keen & Nettlefold (Bolts & Nuts) Ltd* [1968] 1 WLR 1776. He listed five factors which should be taken into account when looking at this area:

1. The employer should take steps to ensure his employee's safety in the light of the knowledge he has or ought to have.
2. The employer can follow recognised practice unless this is clearly unsound.
3. Where there is developing knowledge, the employer must keep up to date and apply it.
4. If the employer has greater than average knowledge of the risk, he must take greater than average precautions.
5. The employer must weigh up the risk (in terms of the likelihood of the injury occurring and its potential seriousness) against the cost of taking precautions and the effectiveness of those precautions.

Perhaps the most ambiguous point is the last one. This allows the employer to balance the cost of precautions against the likelihood and seriousness of injury. It can be demonstrated by comparing *Latimer* (above) with the case of *Bath v British Transport Commission* [1954] 2 All ER 542. In *Bath*, an employee was killed when he fell from the top of a high, narrow dock. The employer provided no protection whatsoever for his employees. It was argued that the cost of taking precautions was prohibitive. The court, however, decided that given that injury was likely to occur and could be foreseen as being very serious when it did happen, the employer was under a duty to protect his employees whatever the cost. In *Latimer*, by contrast, injury was not likely to happen, but if it should occur it was unlikely to be serious. Thus the employer was entitled not to incur the considerable cost of closing down the factory. The key points, therefore, are how likely it is that injury will occur and how serious it will be if it happens.

While the implied term is a general term to ensure the employee's safety, the House of Lords in *Wilsons and Clyde Coal Co v English* [1938] AC 57 identified three specific aspects of the duty – competent staff, adequate plant and equipment, and safe system of work. To this list we can add a fourth aspect – the provision of a safe place of work.

4.2.11(b)(i) Safe place of work

It has been seen from *Latimer* (above) that the courts will take a variety of factors into account when assessing whether the employer has acted reasonably in the circumstances. When looking specifically at the maintenance of safe premises, the court will investigate whether the employer has an adequate reporting system, how he reacts when complaints are reported and whether he has effectively maintained his premises. Part of the employer's grievance procedure, therefore, should provide for complaints about the place of work, and the employer should investigate those complaints if and when they arise. In *Franklin v Edmonton Corporation* (1966) 109 SJ 876, the employer stated that complaints had to be in writing, but later accepted oral complaints. An employee complained orally that the brakes on his lorry were defective, but the employer did nothing. Eventually the employee had an accident due to the defective brakes. It was held that the employer was liable for failing to act on the complaint when received. (The damages were reduced by two-thirds because of the employee's contributory negligence, in that he did not put the complaint in writing and he continued to drive the lorry knowing the brakes were defective.)

In addition to an effective reporting system, the court will look at the employer's maintenance system. In *Braham v Lyons & Co Ltd* [1962] 3 All ER 281, an employee dropped a food substance on the floor. The floor supervisor immediately sent a maintenance man to clean it up, but before he reached the place another employee had slipped on the spilled substance and was injured. It was held that the employer was not liable; he had done all he reasonably could to protect his employees. More recently, in *Lowles v Home Office* [2004] EWCA Civ 985, a prison worker, while deep in conversation, tripped on a step while entering work and was injured. There was a sign saying 'Please Mind the Step' and the worker had used the entrance before. The Court of Appeal held the employers 50 per cent liable for the injury because they had failed to ensure the doorway was 'suitable for the purpose for which it was used'.

One aspect of ensuring a safe place of work which came to the fore in more recent times was that of smoking, and the effects of passive smoking on employees. While *Dryden v Greater Glasgow Health Board* [1992] IRLR 469 decided that there was no implied term in an employment contract that a worker had a right to smoke at work, and *Waltons and Morse v Dorrington* [1997] IRLR 488 established that employees had a right not to work in a smoky environment, no court or tribunal stated that employees were entitled to a smoke-free working environment. The law did not appear to grasp the nettle in respect of whether smoking at work was a health and safety issue. It was not raised in *Dorrington*, since there was no evidence that the employee had suffered an injury to her health. The amount of evidence in respect of passive smoking does suggest, however, that it is a health and safety issue, and that an employer who failed to protect his employees would have been in breach of his common law safety duties and in breach of section 2(2)(e) of the Health and Safety at Work etc Act 1974 (discussed at Section 4.2.13 below). This issue has since been resolved by the introduction of the ban on smoking in public places in July 2007.

Given that the employer must provide a safe place of work for his employees, the question which now must be asked is how far that duty extends to ensuring that other premises where his employees may work are safe. Many employees work in other places, for example in people's homes (for example, plumbers, electricians and so on) or in other employers' premises to service machinery and so on. It appears that while the employer's duty does extend to other premises where his employee may work, for obvious reasons the duty is reduced. What is important, however, is that the employer cannot leave it up to the employee to protect himself just because he is working on premises over which the employer has no control. In *General Cleaning Contractors v Christmas* [1953] AC 180, the employer operated a window cleaning company. He provided safety belts for his employees, but on one particular building there were no safety hooks on which to attach the belts. The employee was injured when a defective window sash fell on his fingers whilst he was working on that building, causing him to lose his grip. It was held that the employer was liable. He could not abdicate his responsibility to the employee on the spot to devise a safe way of doing the job. It was the responsibility of the employer, once he knew of the problem, to devise a way of making the job safe. This case was confirmed in the Court of Appeal in *King v Smith and Another* (1994) *The Times*, 3 November.

Obviously, in these situations the employer will often know of the problem only once it has been brought to his attention, and therefore the court will again look closely at the employer's system of reporting safety hazards and how he reacts to such complaints. In *Smith v Austin Lifts Ltd* [1959] 1 All ER 81, the employee maintained lifts supplied by his employer to other premises. One day he reported to his employer that the doors on the machine house at particular premises were dangerous, and his employer reported this to the occupier. On the employee's next visit the doors had not been repaired, so he tied them together to prevent the doors from being used and again reported to his employer, who again told the occupier. On his third visit, the rope had been taken off the doors and they had jammed. The employee was injured when he fell off a ladder while trying to unjam the doors. Four out of five judges in the House of Lords held that his employer was liable for failing to check the premises to see whether the hazard had been removed before sending his employee back there.

4.2.11(b)(ii) Safe plant and equipment

All machinery, tools and equipment used by the employee should be reasonably safe for use. In *Bradford v Robinson Rentals Ltd* [1967] 1 All ER 267, a driver was required to drive on a long journey, in very cold weather, in a van which the employer knew had a broken heater. As a result the driver suffered frostbite. It was held that the employer was liable for his injury. In *Sherlock v Chester City Council* [2004] EWCA Civ 201, a joiner severed his thumb and finger using a bench saw. The wood had been bending, but rather than ask for help or move to another bench, the employee continued sawing, with the injury being the result. It was held that the employer was liable for 40 per cent of the damages because the joiner had not been trained in the use of the bench saw, nor in carrying out a risk assessment. The employee's lack of experience or otherwise was irrelevant. The employer could not rely on experienced and skilled workers to discharge the employer's duty.

In the past, if plant or equipment had a hidden defect which was totally unknown to the employer, and he had purchased from a reputable supplier, the employer had acted reasonably and was not liable for any subsequent injury to the employee (*Davie v New Merton Board Mills* [1959] AC 604). Once the defect had become apparent, however, the employer was liable if he failed to take immediate action. In *Taylor v Rover Car Co* [1966] 2 All ER 181, the employer had purchased a batch of chisels. He was unaware that they were badly hardened until one shattered, without causing injury. The employer did not withdraw the chisels from use and a second one shattered, injuring an employee. It was held that the employer was liable. If injury had occurred when the first chisel shattered, there would have been no liability because, until then, the employer was unaware of any defect. Once a problem had occurred, a reasonable employer would have realised that potentially all the chisels were affected and withdrawn them from use.

The problem with the proposition that the employer was liable only if he knew of the defect is that it left the injured employee with no contractual remedy. He could, of course, sue the manufacturer of the tools or equipment in negligence, but this is frequently difficult to establish, and therefore many injured employees are left with no compensation. As a consequence the Employer's Liability (Defective Equipment) Act 1969 was passed. In essence, this provides that if an employee is injured during the course of his employment as a result of a defect in equipment provided by his employer, and the defect is attributable to the negligence of a third party, the injury will be deemed to be due to the negligence of the employer. At the same time the Employer's Liability (Compulsory Insurance) Act 1969 was passed, requiring all employers to take out insurance to cover personal injury claims from their employees. Although this may seem hard on the employer who is not to blame for the employee's injury, he (or his insurance company) can, of course, sue the manufacturer of the defective equipment and so recover the compensation he has paid to his employee.

4.2.11(b)(iii) Safe system of work

This essentially means that the employer should provide safe working methods. The court will look at a variety of factors, including layout of the workplace, training and supervision, warnings and the provision of safety equipment. The court is basically looking at how the employer conducts his business and whether he does all he can to protect his employees. In *Goodchild v Organon Laboratories Ltd* [2004] EWHC 2341 (QB), a sales representative, who had been told by her doctor not to lift heavy weights following an operation, had been lifting heavy boxes with a colleague. The colleague left for a short time and the representative lifted a heavy box on her own, causing back injury. The employer was held 90 per cent liable on the basis that the Manual Handling Operations Regulations 1992 state that an employer must avoid the need for employees to undertake manual handling which could cause injury.

Given that the benchmark is reasonableness on the part of the employer, two fairly obvious points should be noted. First, a reasonable employer tells his employees where the safety equipment is kept. This may seem like a blindingly obvious proposition, but there have been cases where this has not happened. In *Finch v Telegraph Construction & Maintenance Co Ltd* [1949] 1 All ER 452, the employee was a grinder and was injured when a piece of flying metal struck him in the eye. The employer provided goggles, but had not told the employees where they were kept. It was held that the employer was liable for the employee's injury. Second, to some extent the employer can assume that the employee has some common sense and therefore does not have to warn him against clearly obvious dangers. It has already been seen in *O'Reilly* that an employer was not liable when his employee hit an unexploded bomb with a hammer! In *Lazarus v Firestone Tyre and Rubber Co Ltd* (1963) *The Times*, 2 May, an employee was injured when he was knocked down in the rush to get to the canteen. The employer was not liable for failing to tell him of the potential risk in trying to get lunch!

While the common law places a duty on the employer, the employee too has some responsibility for his own safety. In *Smith v Scott Bowyers Ltd* [1986] IRLR 315, the employee was injured when he slipped on a greasy floor. The employer knew of the risk and provided the employees with wellingtons which had ridged soles. Smith had been provided with such a pair of wellingtons, but they had worn smooth on the soles and had become dangerous. The employer would have renewed the wellingtons on request, but Smith had not asked for a replacement pair. It was held that the employer was not liable. He was not under a duty to inspect the wellingtons every day to see if they needed replacing and was entitled to assume that his employees would take some responsibility for their own safety.

The situations listed above are, however, extreme cases. Most situations fall between the two extremes of total non-protection and assuming that the employee has a modicum of common sense. The majority of cases, therefore, raise the issue of how far the employer must go to protect his employees. Ignoring the issue of balancing cost and likelihood of injury, does the employer fulfil his common law duty merely by providing the equipment and telling his employees where it is, or does he need to go further and insist that it is used?

The answer to this depends on the obviousness of the risk to the employee and the likely seriousness of the injury. If the risk of the injury is obvious to the employee and not likely to be serious if it occurs, the employer will have fulfilled his duty by providing the equipment and telling the employee where it can be found, leaving the employee to use it if he wishes. In *Qualcast (Wolverhampton) Ltd v Haynes* [1959] AC 743, the employee was injured when he was splashed on the legs with molten metal. The employer provided protective spats but the employee chose not to wear them. It was held that the employer was not liable. The risk of injury was obvious to the employee (who was an experienced workman) and the injury was not serious. On the other hand, if the risk is not obvious, or the injury would be serious, the employer should insist that safety precautions are taken and supervise the employees to ensure that they are following orders. In *Berry v Stone Maganese Marine Ltd* (1971) 12 KIR 13, the employee was working in high noise levels. The employer provided ear-defenders but did nothing to ensure their use. The employee suffered a loss of hearing due to working without the defenders. The employer was held liable. The seriousness of the potential injury and the risk of its occurring would not be obvious to the employee. The employer should have alerted the employee to the dangers of what he was doing and insisted that ear-defenders be worn.

The law is realistic, however. There will be a stage where the employer has done all that can be done bar physically putting the safety equipment on employees and watching them every moment of the working day. If an employee will not wear the equipment, despite the entreaties of the employer, and is subsequently injured, the employer will have done all a reasonable employer would have done and will not be liable. The ultimate sanction the employer can impose will be dismissal. Although he does not have to use this sanction to protect the employee, dangerous practices by one employee can lead to others being injured and the employer may find himself in breach of the duty to provide competent employees (see Section 4.2.11(b)(iv)). Many employers now make failure to comply with safety rules a disciplinary offence so that they can employ the sanction of dismissal should everything else prove ineffective.

The importance and scope of this aspect of the employer's duty may be seen in two cases. In *Johnstone v Bloomsbury Area Health Authority* [1991] ICR 269, the number of hours that the employee was required to work was held to be a breach of the employer's duty. Browne Wilkinson LJ argued that the employer should interpret the express terms of the contract reasonably. Stuart-Smith LJ went further and stated that the express term relating to hours was subject to the implied duty of the employer to take reasonable care to ensure the health and safety of employees. In *Walker v Northumberland County Council* [1995] IRLR 35, an employee who had suffered a nervous breakdown due to the pressure of work returned and was given the same level and amount of work, with little support being put in place by the employer. In the end the employee suffered another nervous breakdown and had to retire on the grounds of ill-health. It was held that the employer was in breach of the safety duty he owed to his employee. Given the first nervous breakdown, it was reasonably foreseeable that without extra staff the plaintiff's health would suffer, and there was no reason why the employer should not be liable for psychiatric damage to the employee as well as physical damage. This was followed in *Ratcliffe* (1998) *The Times*, 25 August, where a primary school deputy head won a £100,000 out-of-court settlement after suffering two nervous breakdowns, allegedly caused by bullying in the workplace. In *Waters v Commissioner of Police of the Metropolis* [2000] IRLR 720, the House of Lords held that an employer could be liable for psychological harm caused by failing to take a complaint of sexual assault by a fellow officer seriously, and by allowing the employee to be subjected to victimisation and harassment by other officers after she had made the complaint (see also *Cross v Highlands and Islands Enterprise* [2001] IRLR 336 and Chapter 5). However, *Sutherland v Hatton* [2002] EWCA Civ 76 restricted the imposition of liability. In that case the Court of Appeal held that, for liability to arise, there must exist plain indications of impending harm arising from stress. Even then, the employer will be liable for breach of the duty only if he fails to take reasonable steps to overcome the risk of ill-health. In determining what is reasonable, regard must be had to the gravity of the harm, the size of the risk and the cost to the employer of rectifying the situation.

Since *Sutherland* a number of other cases have reached the courts. In *Barber v Somerset County Council* [2004] UKHL 13, the House of Lords said that employers had to take the initiative rather than wait and see as suggested by the Court of Appeal, and in *Simmons v British Steel* [2004] ICR 585 their Lordships confirmed this, saying that while physical injury had to be reasonably foreseeable for employers to be liable, this was not essential in cases of psychiatric injury. Employers became liable to take action once they were aware of the employee's condition. In *Intel Corporation (UK) Ltd v Daw* [2007] EWCA Civ 70, Daw had a nervous breakdown caused by an excessive workload. The employer was aware of Daw's history of depression and the High Court found Intel to be negligent. Intel appealed, arguing that it had a confidential counselling service which Daw had chosen not to use. The appeal was rejected on the grounds that offering such a service was insufficient to discharge the employer's duty of care. In *Hartman v South Essex Mental Health and Community Care NHS Trust* [2005] EWCA Civ 6, the Court of Appeal stated that courts are still finding it difficult to apply the appropriate principles to stress claims. The Court reiterated that the duty on employers is to prevent foreseeable injury, and employers are liable if a failure to take action leads to an employee suffering foreseeable loss. An employer may be aware of this through the way work is organised, or because the employee has a health problem, although it is the responsibility of the employee to make the employer aware of the health problem, and complaining about overwork or possible risk to health is not sufficient. In *Hartman* the employee had a breakdown. She had told the Occupational Health Department about problems and a previous breakdown, but because she was passed as fit to work, this was not passed on to the Trust. When aware of potential problems, the Trust offered counselling and leave, both of which she refused. She suffered no difficulties at work and could not identify an event at work which had caused her breakdown. As such the Trust was not liable. The employer was also not liable in *Deadmen v Bristol City Council* [2007] EWCA Civ 822. In the case the employee suffered from depression after an allegation of sexual harassment was made against him. He claimed damages for breach of contract, arguing that the way the employer handled the complaint against him, in breach of contract, had led to his suffering stress. The Court of Appeal held that a policy to handle complaints of harassment 'sensitively' was aspirational and did not form part of the contract. Although having a panel of two rather than three members was a breach of contract, it was not reasonably foreseeable that the claimant would suffer stress as a result. Further, the employer was not in breach by leaving a letter stating its decision on the employee's desk. It was the content of the letter and not the way that content was disclosed which was important. However, in *Melville v Home Office* [2005] EWCA Civ 6, the Court of Appeal stated that if the employer could foresee the risk of harm, because of the nature of the job, the employer did not have to foresee harm to a particular employee. Thus an employer was liable for the breakdown of a healthcare worker in a prison, who had the job of removing the bodies of suicide victims. His illness was caused by the last suicide and the employer was held to be liable.

The Court of Appeal in *Dickens v O₂ plc* [2009] IRLR 58, however, seems to suggest that the *Hatton* requirements of reasonable foreseeability, breach and causation may not be as strict as first thought. In finding O₂ liable for stress-induced injury, the Court stated that in relation to reasonable foreseeability it was sufficient that the employee had previously complained about the stress of the job, had regularly been late coming to work and had told her manager she did not know how long she could keep going before she became ill. The breach of duty occurred when O₂ did not send her home pending investigation by occupational health, even though she had not been signed off by her GP. The Court also decided that there was a sufficient causal connection with the failure of O₂ to act, which had materially contributed to the employee's subsequent illness. Further, in *Corr v IBC Vehicles Ltd* [2008] UKHL 13, the House of Lords held that an employer was liable for the suicide of an employee who became depressed after a serious accident at work. Mr Corr suffered a severed ear when an automated arm unexpectedly struck his head. As a result he suffered disfigurement and severe headaches, and had problems sleeping. After he had been hospitalised for depression, he took his own life in 2002, some six years after the original accident. The House of Lords said that the employer had breached the duty of care owed to Mr Corr to prevent both physical and psychological injury. Mr Corr would not have committed suicide had it not been for the accident at work. An employer is liable when it can reasonably foreseeable damage caused by the commission of a tort, but liability does not rest on the necessity to foresee the precise form of that damage. Suicide is something which is reasonably foreseeable for someone with severe depression, and the depression was as a result of an accident caused by the employer's negligence. Consequently, the employer was liable. All of these cases demonstrate that the law is this area is still in a state of flux.

4.2.11(b)(iv) *Reasonably competent fellow employees*

Apart from any vicarious liability which may arise should an employee injure one of his colleagues during the course of employment, the employer may also be primarily liable if it can be shown that he knew one of his employees was potentially dangerous and did nothing to protect the rest of the workforce. Competence obviously begins with the employee's ability to do the job safely; if the employer has not provided sufficient training, and while performing work duties the employee injures someone, the employer will be liable. In *Hawkins v Ross Castings Ltd* [1970] 1 All ER 180, an employee was injured following the spillage of molten metal. The injury was partly due to the fact that the plaintiff was working with a 17-year-old Indian who spoke little English, and who had not been trained in the task of carrying and pouring molten metal. It was held that the employer was liable, as the failure to ensure that the employees were competent had been a cause of the accident.

Competence, however, is defined more widely than the employees having the ability and training to do the job safely. Practical jokes which go wrong can be just as dangerous and cause just as serious an injury. In *Hudson v Ridge Manufacturing Co Ltd* [1957] 2 QB 348, an employee, who was known to be a practical joker, injured an employee when one of his jokes went wrong. The employer was liable for the consequent injury. The important point to note from both *Hawkins* and *Hudson*, however, is the employer's knowledge. In both cases the employer knew the failings of the employee involved and should have taken steps to protect the other employees. By contrast, in *Coddington v International Harvester Co of Great Britain Ltd* (1969) 6 KIR 146, the employee, as a joke, kicked a tin of burning thinners close to X. X kicked the tin away and it injured a third employee. The employer was not liable for the injury. The employee had never before played a practical joke and the employer had no knowledge that he was a source of potential danger to other employees.

4.2.11(b)(v) Defences to a common law claim

If the employee is injured and sues his employer for breach of his common law duties, there are three defences the employer can raise. First, he can deny negligence. In other words, the employer is arguing that he has done all a reasonable employer would do to protect his employee and yet the injury still occurred. He may show, for example, that the costs of providing total protection outweighed the risk of injury and its likely seriousness, as seen in *Latimer* (Section 4.2.11(b) above). Or he may argue that he is following expert advice or recognised current practice. In *Brown v Rolls-Royce Ltd* [1960] 1 All ER 577, an employee contracted dermatitis from the use of oil. There was a barrier cream which could have been used, but the employer did not provide it on the advice of his medical officer who did not think that it worked. It was held that the employer was not liable.

The second defence the employer can raise is an admission of technical negligence but an argument that the injury was, in reality, solely caused by the employee's own negligence. This argument is often raised when the employer commits a breach of the Factories Act 1961. Under that legislation liability is strict, and the mere fact that a provision has been broken establishes liability without the need to prove negligence. For example, section 14(1) of the Factories Act 1961 states:

> Every part of dangerous machinery shall be securely fenced unless it is in such a position or of such a construction as to be safe to every person employed or working on the premises as it would be if securely fenced.

In *Horne v Lec Refrigeration Ltd* [1965] 2 All ER 898, an employee was killed when he failed to operate a safety procedure as he had been trained to do. His employers were in breach of section 14(1) of the Factories Act 1961 as the machine was not fenced at the time of his death. The lack of the fence was due to action of the employee, who had removed it. It was held that although the employers were in breach of their statutory duty, it was not this breach that was the cause of the employee's death but the removal of the fence by the employee. As such, the employee's own negligence had been the cause of the accident and the employer was not liable.

The two defences above extinguish liability. The third defence reduces rather than totally eliminates the employer's liability. This is the partial defence of contributory negligence under the Law Reform (Contributory Negligence) Act 1945. This provides that fault for the injury may be apportioned between the employer and the employee, where the negligence of the employee has been partially to blame for the injury (see *Sherlock, Lowles* and *Goodchild*, Section 4.2.11(b)(i)–(iii) above). In the *Bux* case (Section 4.2.11(a) above), it will be remembered that the employer was liable for failing to insist that goggles were worn. The employee, however, was found to be 40 per cent responsible for his own injury, and his damages were reduced accordingly, the employer paying only 60 per cent. The raising of the defence of contributory negligence is quite common in this area, particularly where the employee has ignored the use of safety equipment but the employer has not checked to see if the equipment is being used. The percentage by which the employee's damages may be reduced depends on the extent of his blameworthiness, a matter which is decided by the court.

On normal contractual principles, an express term will override an implied term; this is one area, however, where an employer cannot exclude his common law liability by an appropriately worded term in the contract. The Unfair Contract Terms Act 1977 provides, by section 2, that a person cannot, by reference to a contractual term or notice, exclude or restrict liability for death or personal injury resulting from negligence.

4.2.11(b)(vi) *Vicarious liability*

While the law imposes the duty to employ reasonably competent workers upon the employer, this duty does not help the employee who may be injured by the negligence of one of his colleagues if the employer had no knowledge of the lack of competence (*Coddington*, Section 4.2.11(b)(iv) above). Likewise, it does not help a third party who may be injured by the negligence of one of the employer's employees. While the injured party may sue the original tortfeasor, it is unlikely in the majority of cases that the employee who caused the injury will have the funds to support a claim for compensation, or that he will be insured against such risks. Employers, on the other hand, will have insurance which can support a compensation claim. It is really as a result of these financial considerations that the law has developed the principle of vicarious (substituted) liability. Although it arises in other situations, its most common application is in the area of employment, where the employer can be made vicariously liable for the tortious wrongs of his employees committed within the course of their employment. The basis of the liability is control. In theory, while the employee is performing his job, he is under the control of his employer, and therefore, should he perform his duties negligently, the employer, who has the ultimate control, should be liable. As we have seen, in a modern-day industrial society, the issue of control by an employer over how employees perform their job is probably more of a legal fiction than industrial reality, but the basis of vicarious liability remains, almost certainly because of the financial considerations discussed above.

It would be easy simply to impose liability on the employer every time an employee commits a tortious act while at work. The law does not go that far, however. There is a limit on the employer's liability, in that he is vicariously liable only for the torts of his employees committed within the course of employment. The phrase 'course of employment' has produced many interpretations by the court and does not mean 'committed while at work'. At its simplest, the phrase refers to when the employee is doing an act authorised by his employer, in a manner authorised by his employer. The employer, however, will also be liable if the employee commits a tort while performing an authorised act in an unauthorised way, unless the employer has expressly forbidden the employee to do that act. For example, in the old case of *Limpus v London General Omnibus Co* (1862) 7 LT 641, a bus driver injured a queue of passengers when he negligently drove into them. It was held that the employer was liable. The driver was authorised to drive. Once that authorisation was given, the employer could not argue that he wished the employee to drive in a certain way, that is, not negligently. The authorisation was to drive, and because when he was driving the employee injured third parties, he was within the course of his employment. By contrast, in *Beard v London General Omnibus Co* [1900] 2 QB 530, the employee, a bus conductor, was expressly forbidden to drive. He injured a third party when he was reversing a bus in the depot. It was held that as he was performing an unauthorised act at the time of the commission of the tort, he was not acting within the course of his employment and the employer was not vicariously liable.

The issue of the commission of authorised acts in an unauthorised mode was discussed by the Privy Council in relation to industrial action in the case of *General Engineering Services Ltd v Kingston & Saint Andrew's Corporation* [1989] IRLR 35. Can industrial action such as a go-slow be deemed to constitute performing an authorised act in an unauthorised way? In the case, action was brought against an employer when, as a result of a go-slow operated by the fire brigade, it took 17 minutes to reach a fire instead of three minutes, and consequently the plaintiff's business burned to the ground. The reason it had taken so long for the fire brigade to reach the fire was that they were stopping and starting for the whole of the journey. The Privy Council held that the firefighters were not performing an authorised act in an unauthorised way. The go-slow was an unauthorised and illegal act, and had no connection with the authorised activity of reaching a fire as soon as possible. This decision is not surprising.

The courts have, in the past, argued that although the employee's action appears to be authorised, in essence it is alien to his job duties and therefore outside the course of employment. Often this is because the employee has performed his duties excessively and the excess will take him outside the course of his employment. In *Keppel Bus Co v Sa'ad Bin Ahmed* [1974] 1 WLR 1082, a bus conductor got into a fight with a passenger who objected to the way the conductor had treated another passenger on the bus. To end the fight, the conductor hit the passenger over the head with his ticket machine. It was held that the employer was not vicariously liable. While the conductor could use reasonable force to prevent trouble on the bus, here he had started the trouble and used excessive force to make his point. Likewise, in *Daniels v Whetstone Entertainments* (1962) 106 SJ 284, an employer was not liable when a bouncer at a nightclub chased a customer after he had left the club peacefully and attacked him in the street. When the bouncer had originally hit the customer in the club, during a fight he was trying to break up, he was within the course of his employment; however, by chasing the customer along the street after the fight had died down, the employee had taken himself outside the course of his employment. In the particularly nasty case of *Tower Boot Co Ltd v Jones* [1995] IRLR 529, some employees had committed acts of extreme racial harassment, including whipping the plaintiff and branding him with a hot screwdriver. The EAT held in no way could the attacks be described as part of the employees' duties and thus there was no vicarious liability. While this decision appears to be legally correct, it leaves the victim of such harassment with little or no chance of gaining financial compensation for his injuries. The Court of Appeal reversed the decision ([1997] IRLR 168), stating that the concept of employer's liability under then Race Relations Act 1976 was wider than the concept of vicarious liability at common law. As such, the Court plugged a serious loophole in the protection of employees.

While the Court of Appeal in *Jones* decided that the common law definition of the 'course of employment' was too restrictive and did not apply in a statutory context, more recently the House of Lords redefined the common law definition. In *Lister v Helsey Hall Ltd* [2001] IRLR 472 their Lordships held that the correct approach to determine whether an employee's wrongful act is committed during the course of his employment is to concentrate on the relative proximity between the nature of the employment and the act committed. As such, a boarding school was liable for the sexual abuse of boys by a school warden, because the nature of the employment meant that the employee had close contact with the boys, and this created a sufficiently close connection between the acts of abuse and the work he had been employed to do to make it fair to hold the employers liable (see also *Dubai Aluminium Ltd v Salaam* [2003] 2 AC 407). The decision overrules the earlier Court of Appeal decision in *ST v North Yorkshire County Council* [1999] IRLR 98, in which the Court held that indecent assault was not an unauthorised way of doing an authorised act. *Lister* brings the statutory and common law definitions more into line with each other. However, it also has the effect of creating vicarious liability for the criminal acts of employees.

A further development arising from *Lister* comes from *Majrowski v Guy's and St Thomas's NHS Trust* [2005] EWCA Civ 251. In this case the employee claimed to have been bullied by his manager. He argued that his manager had subjected him to harassment as defined under the Protection from Harassment Act 1997, for which his employer was vicariously liable. The Court of Appeal held that the House of Lords in *Lister* established that the test was the closeness of the connection between the employee's duties and his wrongdoing, not based on some fiction based on implied authority, and where the connection was established it was immaterial whether the employee's act was authorised or expressly forbidden by the employer, or civilly or criminally illegal. As such, an employer could be vicariously liable for a breach of a statutory duty imposed only on his employee if there was sufficient connection with the employment that it was fair and reasonable to impose such liability.

Given that until recently the underlying basis of vicarious liability was the authorisation of the act by the employer, it followed that if the employer expressly forbade the act, there was no authorisation and thus no liability. In *Conway v George Wimpey* [1951] 1 All ER 56, a driver was expressly forbidden to carry people in his van. The plaintiff was injured by the driver's negligent driving when travelling as a passenger in the van. It was held that there was no vicarious liability. The employee was doing a prohibited act and thus there was no authorisation from his employer. This principle needs qualification, however. It appeared that if the prohibited act benefited the employer, vicarious liability would still lie. In *Rose v Plenty* [1976] 1 WLR 141, a milkman, contrary to an express prohibition, took a 13-year-old boy with him to help deliver the milk. The boy was injured owing to the milkman's negligent driving. It was held that despite the prohibition, the employer was vicariously liable for the milkman's negligence. So too in *Stone v Taffe* [1974] 1 WLR 1575, the manager of a public house was held to be in the course of his employment when a customer was injured by falling down unlighted steps some two and a half hours after licensed closing time. It remains to be seen, however, after *Lister* and *Majrowski*, whether such a prohibition will end what the House of Lords described as the relative closeness of the connection between the nature of the employment and the employee's wrongdoing, or whether the prohibition will have no effect on the employer's liability.

The employee will not, however, be acting within the course of his employment if during working hours he goes off on a 'frolic of his own' – in other words, if he does something unconnected with his job duties which is of no benefit to his employer. In *Hilton v Thomas Burton (Rhodes) Ltd* [1961] 1 WLR 705, the plaintiff's husband was killed by the negligent driving of one of his colleagues. The employer was not vicariously liable, as the accident occurred while the employees were driving back from a café following an unauthorised break. The case raises the issue, however, of whether the employee will be in the course of his employment when on meal breaks or travelling. In *Smith v Stages and Another* [1989] IRLR 177, the House of Lords considered the question of whether an employee was within the course of his employment when he was injured by a fellow employee while travelling from home to a workplace other than his normal one. In this case the driver was on duty while driving to the workplace at the request of his employer, thus the employer incurred vicarious liability for his actions. Normally, however, an employee travelling from home to work would not be in the course of his employment unless he was paid for that time or using the employer's transport. Once on the employer's premises, however, the employee is benefiting his employer, even if he has not yet started work, and is therefore within the course of his employment. In *Compton v McClure* [1975] ICR 378, the plaintiff was injured when struck by a car on the employer's premises. The car was driven by a fellow employee who was late for work. It was held that the employer was vicariously liable for the negligent driving of his employee.

What is the situation when the employer lends his employees to another employer? In *Mersey Docks & Harbour Board v Coggins & Griffith Ltd* [1947] AC 1, the primary employer had lent a crane and its driver to the secondary employer. The employee was negligent and an accident occurred. The House of Lords held that the primary employer was vicariously liable for the employee's negligent operation of the crane. The employee remained the employee of the primary employer and hence under his control. The primary employer was also liable, on a different basis, in *Morris v Breaveglen* [1993] IRLR 350, where firm A lent an employee to firm B to use certain machinery, knowing the employee was not competent. The employee was subsequently injured when working for the secondary employer. It was held that the primary employer was liable in negligence, even though the employee was under the control of the secondary employer, because it was the negligence of the primary employer, in lending out an employee to do a job the primary employer knew him to be incapable of performing, which had caused the employee's injuries.

The *Morris* case above, however, is unusual, and normally the question of control is used to determine liability. In *Sime v Sutcliffe Catering Scotland Ltd* [1990] IRLR 228, the employee was injured when she slipped on some food dropped by a fellow employee. The management of the catering had been put out to Sutcliffe, but there was an agreement that Sutcliffe would retain the existing catering staff, including the employee. The catering company then bought in additional staff. It could not be established whether the employee who had dropped the food and so started the chain of events was an employee of the catering company or of the primary employer. The question for the court was whether the catering company could be vicariously liable for the actions of an employee it did not employ. The Court of Session held that the issue turned not on who was the actual employer at the time, but on who had sufficient control to be the effective employer at the relevant time. The day-to-day running of the canteen was the responsibility of the catering company, which had complete control over how all the catering workers worked. As such the company was vicariously liable, whether it was the legal employer of the negligent employee or not. However, a more recent case questioned this. In *Viasystems (Tyneside) Ltd v Thermal Transfer (Northern) Ltd* [2006] EWCA Civ 1151, a fitter working for a third defendant caused damage through his negligence. At the time he was supervised by the second defendant, and the Court of Appeal held that both the second and third defendants were vicariously liable for his negligence. The point was clarified in *Hawley v Luminar Leisure Ltd* [2006] EWCA Civ 18, where the issue was where vicarious liability lay in respect of a serious assault carried out by a doorman in a nightclub. The doorman's services were provided by a security firm, but he wore the uniform of the nightclub and was subject to the orders of the nightclub manager. The defendant argued that either the security firm should be solely vicariously liable, or under *Viasystems* liability should be split. The Court of Appeal said that although it was a heavy burden upon an employer to show that control had passed to the second employer, this was the case here and Luminar were solely vicariously liable.

4.2.12 The Working Time Regulations 1998

The Working Time Regulations 1998 ('the Regulations') were brought in to implement the EU Working Time Directive (93/104/EC) and the Young Workers' Directive (94/33/EC). They came into force on 1 October 1998. The Regulations cover workers as a wider group of individuals than employees. The definition of 'worker' is found in Regulation 2; it includes employees and anyone who works under an express or implied contract whereby the individual undertakes to do or personally perform any work or services. Special provision is made for agency workers. Domestic workers in a private household are excluded from the Regulations, although they are entitled to rest breaks, rest periods and paid annual leave.

The 1998 Regulations limit working time. This is defined in Regulation 2 as:

- any period when a worker is working or at the employer's disposal and carrying out his activities or duties;
- any period during which the worker is receiving relevant training;
- any other periods treated as working time by a relevant agreement.

Agreements are the method by which the 1998 Regulations can be supplemented or derogated from. There are three types of recognised agreement in the Regulations: a collective agreement, a workforce agreement and a relevant agreement. A collective agreement has already been defined in Chapter 3. A workforce agreement, by Schedule

1, must be in writing, have effect for a specified period which does not exceed five years, must apply to all the workforce or all the relevant members of the workforce who belong to a particular group, and must be signed by the workforce representatives or, if the employer employs fewer than 20 employees, either the appropriate representatives or a majority of the workforce, the workforce having been provided with a copy beforehand. A relevant agreement is either a workforce agreement which applies to the worker, a provision of a collective agreement which is part of the employment contract, or any other agreement between the employee and employer which is in writing and legally enforceable (presumably an express term in the contract itself or a separately negotiated contract).

The limit imposed on the working week by the Working Time Regulations 1998 is 48 hours. This must be expanded upon, however. First, the 48-hour limit is a limit on average working time. The average is calculated over a reference period of 17 weeks, although this may be derogated from and certain workers are excluded because they have unmeasured working time, for example family workers, managing executives and workers officiating at religious ceremonies. In addition, an individual may opt out of the 48-hour week. This is covered by Regulation 5. For a valid individual opt-out there must be an agreement in writing; the agreement must specify its length, or it may be of indefinite length subject to the right of the employee to bring it to an end by giving notice which must not exceed three months; the employer must keep records of the workers who have opted out and the terms of their agreement; and the records must be available for inspection by the relevant inspector appointed by the Health and Safety Executive or any other relevant authority.

In addition to regulating the working week, the 1998 Regulations cover rest breaks and periods, night work and annual leave. By Regulation 10, adult workers are entitled to a daily rest period of at least 11 consecutive hours in each 24-hour period (12 hours for workers aged under 18). Shift workers are exempt when they change shift or the shifts involve periods of work split up over the day, provided they are given equivalent periods of rest. Workers are also entitled to an uninterrupted weekly rest period of no fewer than 24 hours (48 hours if aged under 18) in each seven-day period averaged over 14 days (Regulation 11), and are entitled to rest breaks during the day where the working time is more than six hours. The break should be negotiated by collective or workforce agreement, but if none is in force, should be for an uninterrupted period of not less than 20 minutes (Regulation 12).

In respect of nightworkers (that is, workers working between 11 pm and 6 am), Regulation 6 specifies that the normal working hours should not exceed an average of eight in any 24-hour period. The 17-week reference period is used to calculate the average. If the work involves special hazards or heavy strain, working hours must not exceed eight in any 24-hour period. In addition, the employer must give the worker the opportunity of a free health assessment before starting night work and regular assessments thereafter, and if a night worker is suffering from health problems which are connected with night work, he or she is entitled to be transferred whenever possible to suitable day work.

Originally, all workers were entitled to three weeks' (15 days) paid annual holiday. This was first extended to four weeks (20 days), then from October 2007 the entitlement increased to 24 days and from October 2008 the entitlement became 28 days. This is an additional 1.6 weeks over and above the EU minimum of four weeks introduced into UK law. Originally the right arose only after a qualifying continuity period of 13 weeks. This qualifying period was challenged before the ECJ in *R v Secretary of State for Trade and Industry, ex parte BECTU* [2001] IRLR 559. The ECJ ruled that the Working Time Directive did not permit restrictions to be imposed on the granting of annual leave. As a result, after consultation, the government amended the Regulations and the qualifying period was removed. The Working Time Regulations 1998 state that to claim the right to annual leave, the worker must give the employer twice as much notice as the leave they want to take, for example four weeks' notice that the employee wishes to take a two-week holiday, unless otherwise provided for by agreement. While the Directive lays down that there cannot be payment in lieu of annual leave unless the contract is terminated, it allows national legislation to lay down conditions for entitlement to leave (Article 7). Further, in *Gibson v East Riding of Yorkshire Council* [2000] IRLR 598, the Court of Appeal held that the right to annual leave contained in the Directive was not sufficiently precise to have direct effect, since a worker's entitlement to leave could be ascertained only once his or her working time was known. Once the working time is known, however, the right to paid holiday cannot be contracted out of. In *Witley & District Men's Club v Mackay* [2001] IRLR 595, the applicant was dismissed for dishonesty and his holiday pay withheld as provided by his contract. The EAT upheld his complaint that the withholding of holiday pay was a breach of Regulation 35(1)(a), and any contractual term to the contrary was void in so far as it sought to avoid the employer's obligations under the Regulations. Furthermore, in *Leisure Leagues UK v Maconnachie* (2002) *The Times*, 3 May, the EAT held that pay for a day's contractual leave should be based on the number of working days in the year and not the calendar days (overruling *Thames Water Utilities v Reynolds* (1996) IDS 561).

Holiday pay is payable even if due to sickness the worker has not worked during the holiday year (*HMRC v Stringer & Others*, Section 4.2.5 above); this was extended by the ECJ, however, in *Pereda v Madrid Movilidad SA* [2010] 1 CMLR 3. In *Stringer*, the House of Lords held that the easiest way to comply with the decision of the ECJ was for employers to allow employees to take holiday while on sick leave, as it is inconsistent with the Working Time Regulations to carry over annual leave (Reg 13(9)(b)). In *Pereda* the employee was due to take annual leave from 16 July–14 August, but had an accident and was off sick from 3 July–13 August, so his holiday coincided with most of his annual leave. His employer refused his request for an alternative holiday period and the employee challenged the decision in the Spanish labour court, which asked the ECJ for a preliminary ruling as to whether the employer's decision was a breach of the EU Working Time Directive. The ECJ held that annual leave and sick leave have totally different purposes. The former is to allow an employee to rest, the second allowed him to recover from illness. Employees who have been unable to take holiday because of illness should be allowed to take holiday at a later date, even if this means carrying holiday over to the next holiday year if the employee cannot take holiday during the current year. In *Stringer* the ECJ did not decide this point, and thus the *Pereda* decision takes *Stringer* a step forward. Note, however, the EAT decision in *Sood Enterprises v Healey* [2013] UKEAT 0015/12/B1. In the case the claimant had been off sick for 18 months when he resigned. The EAT held that although ordinary annual leave (ie the EU minimum of four weeks – Reg 13) which cannot be taken due to sickness automatically carries forward into the next holiday year, the additional 1.6 weeks granted by UK law (Reg 13A) carries forward only if there is an agreement between the parties, which in this case there was not.

There have been a number of cases on 'rolled-up' holiday pay, that is, pay which is not separate but paid as part of an hourly rate. In *Marshalls Clay Products Ltd v Caulfield* [2004]

ICR 436, the EAT gave the following advice so that employers could ensure that when they paid rolled-up holiday pay, all the provisions of the Working Time Regulations 1998 were met:

▶ the rolled-up holiday pay must be clearly incorporated into the individual contract and expressly agreed;
▶ the percentage or amount of holiday pay must be identified in the contract and preferably the pay slip;
▶ it must be a true addition to the hourly rate;
▶ records of holiday taken must be kept; and
▶ reasonably practicable steps must be taken to require workers to take their holiday before the end of the relevant holiday year.

In *Smith v AJ Morrisroes & Sons Ltd; JJ Cafferkey & Co Ltd v Bryne; Wiggins v North Yorkshire CC* [2005] IRLR 72, Smith was paid a daily rate which included holiday pay. His employer told him that his holiday pay would be retained until he actually took his holiday. The EAT held that since there was no difference in the actual rate of pay before and after his employer told him his holiday pay would be withheld, there was no genuine provision for holiday pay in the contract and Mr Smith was entitled to sue for a deduction from wages. In Mr Byrne's case his rate of pay included holiday pay at 8 per cent; however, as the employer offered no evidence that it had complied with the guidelines in *Marshalls Clay Products Ltd*, the EAT found in his favour. Mr Wiggins' contract had no express provision for holiday pay but did contain a number of other documents which together complied with *Marshall Clay Products Ltd*; these gave details of the calculations of amounts and the arrangements for payments. As such, the employer was compliant with the 1998 Regulations. However, in *Clarke v Frank Staddon Ltd* [2006] All ER 749 (ECJ), [2006] EWCA Civ 1470 (CA), both the ECJ and the Court of Appeal held that rolled-up holiday pay is contrary to the Directive and unlawful, and that holiday pay must be paid in respect of the period when leave is actually taken, although an employer who has paid rolled-up holiday pay in a manner that clearly identifies the pay for holidays can offset amounts already paid against future payments. Thus rolled-up holiday pay is a breach of the Working Time Regulations 1998.

Although the Regulations will cover a large number of workers, they allow for exclusions and derogations. Certain workers are excluded by Regulation 18. These include those working in service activities, such as the police or armed forces, and certain sector activities such as air, rail, road and sea. Regulation 21 also excludes certain workers or activities from the Regulations or parts of them. These include service providers such as gas, electricity and water suppliers; areas where there are foreseeable surges in activity, such as tourism and agriculture, and security workers; or unforeseeable circumstances beyond the employer's control. However, the Working Time (Amendment) Regulations 2003 extended the working time measures to all non-mobile workers in road, sea, inland waterways and lake transport, and to all workers in the railway and offshore sectors. If Regulation 21 applies then the workers are not covered by the provisions on the length of night work, daily and weekly rest periods, and rest breaks. Regulation 23 also allows the employer and employees to exclude or modify certain provisions by collective agreement. The 48-hour week cannot be modified in this way, but the reference period for averaging hours may be increased to 52 weeks by a collective or workforce agreement.

Employees can enforce entitlement by complaint to an employment tribunal. However, in *Barber v RJB Mining (UK) Ltd* [1999] IRLR 308, the High Court held that the right not to be required to work more than 48 hours a week was a term of the individual's contract of employment, and therefore the limits set down in the Regulations are enforceable as contractual rights by workers. The Working Time Regulations 1998 make it unlawful to subject an employee to a detriment because of refusal to work beyond the limits set in the Regulations, refusing to work during rest breaks, refusing to sign an agreement, being a candidate in an election of workplace representatives, alleging contravention of a right under the Regulations or taking proceedings. The same protection exists against dismissal, and dismissal for any of the above grounds is automatically unfair, with no continuity required. Enforcement is carried out by the Health and Safety Executive, and Regulation 9 imposes an obligation on employers to keep records showing the limits on weekly working and night work, including the assessments of nightworkers.

The Working Time Regulations 1998 are complex. They were brought in to implement the Working Time Directive which was adopted under the health and safety provisions contained in Article 118a of the Treaty of Rome (now Article 153 TFEU). As such, they are a valuable extension of an employee's health and safety rights, and an addition to the employer's common law duties.

4.2.13 The Health and Safety at Work etc Act 1974

As with the Working Time Regulations 1998, the provisions of the Health and Safety at Work etc Act (HASAWA) 1974 cannot be seen as implied duties in the contract of employment; it would therefore be incomplete to talk about the employer's liability in relation to the safety of his employees without a brief overview of the statutory provisions. Breach of the common law implied term can also lead to criminal prosecution for breach of the legislation, and therefore the two areas are necessarily interlinked.

The 1974 Act was introduced as a result of the Robens Committee 1970, which reported in 1972. The Committee found that the law on health and safety was piecemeal and badly structured, with 11 pieces of major legislation supplemented by over 500 statutory instruments.

The majority of the law based liability on occupation of premises. The Committee proposed a unification of the law, basing liability on employment instead. It felt the aim of the law should be accident prevention, which should be underpinned by enforcement powers and criminal liability. It did not feel that the purpose of any changes should be to provide compensation for an employee who was injured as a result of a breach of the proposed legislation. This is why the common law duty on the part of the employer is so important today.

The Committee's recommendations were embodied in HASAWA 1974. The aims of the Act are twofold: to lay down general duties applicable across the whole of the area of employment, and to provide a unified system of enforcement under the control of the Health and Safety Executive and local authorities. General duties are imposed upon various types of people, for example employers, suppliers and manufacturers, with the aim of ensuring, in so far as is reasonably practicable, a safe working environment.

Section 2(1) lays down the general duty on employers:

> It shall be the duty of every employer to ensure, so far as is reasonably practicable, the health, safety and welfare of all of his employees.

Section 2(2) then specifies particular duties, as follows:

▶ The provision and maintenance of plant and systems of work so that they are safe and without risk to health.

▶ The making of arrangements for the use, handling, storage and transport of articles and substances.

▶ The provision of information, instructions, training and supervision.

▶ The maintenance of places of work under the employer's control in a safe condition, with safe and risk-free means of access and egress.

▶ The provision and maintenance of a safe, risk-free working environment with adequate welfare facilities and arrangements.

The phrase to which all of these duties are subject is 'so far as is reasonably practicable'. This necessarily involves an examination of the common law to discover what action is deemed to be reasonably practicable in what circumstances, and the judgments, whether under the common law or the statute, come to similar conclusions. In *Associated Dairies v Hartley* [1979] IRLR 171, the employer supplied safety shoes for which he charged £1 a week. An employee was injured when a truck went over his foot when he was not wearing the shoes. The employee argued he could not afford to pay for the shoes, and an improvement notice was served on the employer, requiring him to provide the shoes free of charge. The employer appealed against the improvement notice. The Court of Appeal upheld the employer's appeal. The cost of providing the shoes was estimated at £20,000 in the first year and £10,000 per year thereafter. Comparing the cost of providing the shoes with the likelihood of injury occurring and its seriousness should it occur, it was not reasonably practicable for the employer to provide shoes free of charge. This is a similar decision to that in *Latimer v AEC* (Section 4.2.11(b) above) – a decision under the common law.

The basis of the duties under section 2(2) is that of employment – it covers duties owed by an employer to his employees; the duties extend beyond the employment relationship however. Section 3(1) provides that employers should conduct their business in such a way, 'in so far as is reasonably practicable to protect persons other than their own employees from risks to their health and safety'. The provision relates back to the specific duties in section 2(2). The interaction of the two sections may be seen in the case of *R v Swan Hunter Shipbuilders Ltd and Telemeter Installation Ltd* [1982] 1 All ER 264. Eight men were killed by a fire caused by the failure of the subcontractor (Telemeter) to turn off the oxygen supply overnight. Both Swan Hunter and Telemeter were convicted under the Act and appealed against their convictions. The Court of Appeal held that the provision of a safe system of work in section 2(2) involved the provision of information and instructions. This provision of information and instructions should be to the employer's employees by virtue of section 2(1). In addition, the same information and instructions should be available to other employees involved in the employer's undertaking by section 3(1). By failing to supply such information, the employers would be liable unless they could show that supplying it was not reasonably practicable.

Section 2(2) also covers the provision and maintenance of plant so that it is reasonably safe. This means that the employer will be in breach of his duty under section 3(1) if he lends out equipment which injures a third party. In *R v Mara* [1987] 1 All ER 478, a company had a contract to clean International Stores on weekdays. The loading bay was in constant use during the week, so there was an agreement that the employees of International Stores would clean the bay using equipment provided by the cleaning company. On Saturday, an employee of International Stores was electrocuted when using the cleaning equipment. The cleaning company was convicted for a section 3 offence. An argument that was raised in the case was that the cleaning company did not work on a Saturday and was therefore not conducting its undertaking within the wording of section 3 when the accident occurred. The Court of Appeal rejected this argument. The Court said that the company conducted its undertaking by cleaning on weekdays and by leaving its equipment for use by its client's employees at weekends. The company had therefore broken the duty it owed to its client's employees.

Previous legislation based liability on occupation of premises, as has already been stated. Robens disagreed with liability based solely on occupation, but felt that such liability should go hand in hand with the general liability of employers. As such, section 4(1) places a general duty on those who occupy premises. They should ensure 'so far as is reasonably practicable the safety of premises, any means of access and exit from the place of work, and of any plant or substance provided for use on the premises'. This duty is owed to all persons and not just those employed by the occupier. In *Austin Rover Group Ltd v HM Inspector of Factories* [1990] 1 AC 619, Austin Rover was prosecuted for a breach of section 4 when the employee of a contractor working on Austin Rover premises was killed by a flash fire. The House of Lords, hearing the appeal against conviction, said that when looking at the reasonableness of the precautions taken by the occupier to render his premises safe, account must be taken of the knowledge of, and control over, the use of his premises that the occupier has. An occupier cannot be made liable if the injury which occurs arises from totally unforeseen and unexpected events which could not be prevented. A flash fire was an unforeseen and unpreventable event, and therefore the appeal was allowed.

Liability is imposed not only on those who physically occupy premises, but also on those who are responsible for the maintenance of such premises, or for the access to and exit from the premises (s 4(2)). In addition, liability is imposed on those responsible for safety and absence of risk concerning plant or substances used on the premises (s 4(3)).

Protection of those other than employees is continued in section 5. This imposes a general duty on those who control work premises to use the best means practicable to prevent the emission of offensive or noxious substances, and to render harmless any such substances which are so emitted. This general duty overlaps with the more specific duties laid down by the Control of Pollution Act 1974.

The Act attempts to increase protection by imposing duties on designers, manufacturers, importers and suppliers. By section 6(1), designers should ensure, as far as is reasonably practicable, that an article's design is safe and without risk to health. By section 6(2), information must be available indicating the uses for which an article has been made and tested, and stating the conditions for safe use. Duties are imposed upon designers and manufacturers to undertake research to identify and minimise the risks to health and safety, and similar duties are imposed on an importer or a supplier.

The 1974 Act therefore imposes a chain of responsibility from the design and manufacture of an article to its installation, use and maintenance. It can be seen, however, that the duties under the Act overlap, and this demonstrates the stated aim of the legislation of accident prevention. For example, if an employee of a subcontractor is injured when using a machine owned by an occupier, there may be a breach of duty by the designer of the machine, by the manufacturer, by the occupier of the premises and by the employee's own employer. The principle of the Act is that the more people are entrusted with the duty to ensure safety, the less likely it is that an accident will happen. The fact that other people owe duties towards the employee will be no defence in an action for breach of statutory duty. In the *Swan Hunter* case (above), the employers argued that they had no duty to inform the employees of the subcontractor about the dangers of the build-up of oxygen since the subcontractor was under a duty to inform them because he employed them. It was held that this did not discharge Swan Hunter of its duties under the Act.

The duty owed to employees goes further in that, by section 2 of the Act, if the employer employs five or more persons he should have a general policy on health and safety and bring this policy to the notice of his employees (s 2(3)). The policy should identify who is responsible for health and safety, and should point out particular health and safety problems and the arrangements for dealing with them. The policy should also cover such matters as training, supervision, inspection procedures, safety precautions and consultative arrangements. In addition, it should tell employees how they may complain about any health and safety risk to which they feel they are being exposed.

While the common law imposes no duty on employees to look after their own safety, failure to do so may mean that any damages could be wiped out by the employer raising the defence of contributory negligence. Given that the aim of the statutory provisions is not to provide compensation, the Act places a duty on the individual employee to have regard to his own safety and that of others around him. Any breach of this statutory duty will form the basis of the employer's common law defence of contributory negligence (Section 4.2.11(b)(v) above). By section 7, every employee, while at work, is under a duty:

1. to take reasonable care for the health and safety of himself and other persons who may be affected by his acts or omissions at work; and
2. as regards any duty or requirement imposed on his employer or any other person by or under any of the relevant statutory provisions, to cooperate with him so far as is necessary to enable that duty or requirement to be performed or complied with.

This places a clear duty on the employee to have regard for his own safety as well as that of his colleagues or third parties, and in addition imposes a duty of cooperation upon all employees to help all persons comply with their statutory duties. This reinforces the Robens philosophy that health and safety should be a joint venture between employers and employees, and gives the employer more leverage when trying to impose safety procedures on his workforce. Often employers will make breaches of safety procedures a disciplinary offence, and in some cases it may be fair to dismiss the employee if the breach of procedure could have serious consequences. In *Roger v Wicks and Wilson* COIT 228 90/97, wilful breach of a no-smoking policy imposed for safety reasons was held to be a justifiable reason for dismissal.

4.2.14 Corporate Manslaughter and Corporate Homicide Act 2007

The Corporate Manslaughter and Corporate Homicide Act 2007 ('the 2007 Act') came into force in April 2008 as a result of concerns regarding the difficulties in obtaining prosecutions of individuals when serious management failings led to death. Prior to the Act, prosecutions were only possible against individuals who were the 'directing mind and will' of the company, and as such were notoriously difficult to achieve. The 2007 Act creates organisational liability. An organisation will commit the offence of corporate manslaughter or homicide if the way in which its activities are managed or organised causes the death either of an employee or of member of the public. In other words, the organisation must be guilty of gross negligence and its conduct fall far below what could reasonably be expected.

This does not replace the liability of individuals under HASAWA 1974 (Section 4.2.13) and does not create new duties. Importantly, it allows the Crown Prosecution Service to take an organisation to court; and if found guilty, the organisation is subject to an unlimited fine. The court can also require the organisation to publicise details of its conviction and take steps to remedy the failings which led to the death.

4.3   Duties of the employee

4.3.1   Duty of cooperation

The law has always required that an employee should serve his employer faithfully and act in a loyal manner. More specific duties discussed below have been developed out of this proposition. The idea that an employee should always cooperate with his employer was first expounded in detail, however, by the Court of Appeal in the case of *Secretary of State for Employment v ASLEF (No 2)* [1972] 2 QB 455. The issue arose because under the Industrial Relations Act 1971, which was in force at the time, the Secretary of State could order a cooling-off period where the employees were acting in breach of contract. The trade union ASLEF was conducting a work-to-rule, and argued that there was no breach of contract as the employees were merely following the rule book to the letter and nothing more. All the judges in the Court of Appeal held that the employees were in breach of contract. Lord Denning MR said that if the employee took steps wilfully to disrupt his employer's undertaking, he would be in breach of contract. Buckley LJ said that there was an implied term in all contracts that the employee should serve his employer faithfully and promote the employer's commercial interests.

While rarely mentioned specifically, the duty of cooperation again reared its head in the case of *Ticehurst v British Telecommunications plc* [1992] IRLR 219. The employee was a BT manager and also a union official. The union instigated a number of one-day strikes and also a withdrawal of goodwill. British Telecommunications wrote to the employees saying that if they did not fully comply with the terms of their contracts, the company would consider them to be taking industrial action and that they would be sent home without pay until they were prepared to work normally. Ticehurst went on strike, and when she returned to work she refused to sign an undertaking that she would work normally and take no further industrial action. As a result she was sent home. At the end of the dispute, she sued for the money BT had deducted for the time she had not been at work. At first instance it was held that as she was ready, willing and able to work, BT had no right to deduct her pay. British Telecommunications appealed against that ruling to the Court of Appeal. The Court held that Ticehurst had demonstrated that if she returned to work she would withdraw her goodwill. This amounted to a breach of the implied term that she would serve her employer faithfully. It was necessary to imply such a term in managers' contracts because they are in charge of other employees and therefore must exercise judgement and discretion when they give orders. Managers were bound to exercise their discretion to further the employer's interests, and as Ticehurst had indicated that she would withdraw her goodwill, she would not be promoting her employer's interests and the employers were entitled to refuse to accept this part-performance.

While the principle of non-payment for part-performance has already been noted (in Section 3.1), this case goes further. Yet again the Court of Appeal has implied a term of cooperation into employees' contracts, and this, taken to its logical conclusion, will mean that any industrial action on the part of the employee, even if it is within the bounds of the contract, such as a work-to-rule or a go-slow, will be a breach of contract. It is important to note, however, that the Court appears to have restricted the *ASLEF* decision. In 1972 the Court of Appeal talked of such a term being in every contract of employment, whereas in *Ticehurst* it went to great lengths to point out that Ticehurst was a manager and therefore the term should be implied.

4.3.2 Duty to obey reasonable lawful orders

The duty to obey the employer's orders is the most fundamental duty of the employee. Providing his services in the manner required by the employer is the employee's consideration within the contract, just as providing wages is his employer's consideration. Given that the duty is fundamental, it follows that should the employee refuse to obey a legitimate order, the common law entitles the employer to dismiss without notice. By refusing to obey orders the employee is essentially saying that he does not wish to be bound by the contractual terms any longer and is thus committing a repudiatory breach. The classic example of this is a strike. The employer, subject to unfair dismissal provisions discussed in Chapter 9, is entitled to accept the strike as a breach which terminates the contract. The modern statement of the law is by Lord Evershed MR in *Laws v London Chronicle* [1959] 1 WLR 698:

> [W]ilful disobedience of a lawful and reasonable order shows a disregard ... of a condition essential to the contract of service, namely the condition that the servant must obey the proper orders of the master, and that unless he does so the relationship is, so to speak, struck at fundamentally.

The duty is not, however, to obey all orders of the employer, but only those that are reasonable and lawful. Furthermore, the duty is to obey orders and not requests. To establish whether the duty has been broken, it is necessary to ask first if the order is reasonable, and this generally means asking whether the order is within the contractual obligations of the employee.

Very often the order will be in relation to the employee's job. The starting point is therefore what the contract states the job duties to be, and a refusal to perform such duties will be, in the main, a breach of contract. The courts, however, recognise that the employee needs to be flexible, and may decide that the duties are wider than those expressly listed in the contract. Certainly an employee will be expected to perform duties which are reasonably incidental to his main job duties, and it has already been seen in the case of *Sim v Rotherham Metropolitan Borough Council* [1986] IRLR 391 (see Section 3.1) that the courts may imply duties into particular types of contracts and will expect the employee to adapt to new methods of performing his job (*Cresswell v Board of Inland Revenue* [1984] IRLR 190; see Section 3.1.1). Some employers try to foresee any future problems by the use of a flexibility clause in the contract. In essence, this is normally a wide clause requiring the employee to perform any task ordered by the employer. Taken to their logical conclusion, however, these clauses could mean that the employee could be asked to do anything, and such an interpretation has fundamental consequences in the case of redundancy. Consequently, the Court of Appeal limited the application of flexibility clauses in the case of *Haden Ltd v Cowan* [1982] IRLR 314 when it decided that such clauses had to be referred back to the employee's main job duties. This means that, even with the widest of flexibility clauses, a lecturer could not be told to clean his or her office, as cleaning duties are totally unrelated to lecturing duties.

In addition to orders in relation to the job, there may be other areas where the employee refuses to obey, for example, mobility or overtime requirements. The starting point again is the contract, remembering that the courts may imply a term if they feel that that would have been the parties' intention. In *Courtaulds Northern Spinning Ltd v Sibson* [1988] IRLR 305, the employee was asked to transfer to another site which was within easy travelling distance of his home. The contract was silent as to mobility between sites, but the employee had worked on the site in the past. The Court of Appeal held that because of his past conduct, there was an implied term in the contract requiring him to move sites, and refusal to do so was a breach of contract. Certainly, refusal to move where there is an express mobility clause will normally be, on the face of it, a breach of contract, as would be refusal to work contractually binding overtime. The courts may, however, decide that an employee has been fairly dismissed even though he is refusing to do something which is outside the ambit of his contract. In *Horrigan v Lewisham London Borough Council* [1978] ICR 15, the employee was a driver who was contracted to work until 4.30 pm but in practice rarely finished at that time. He was paid overtime rates after 4.30 pm, but there was no contractual requirement for him to work overtime. After 10 years of working overtime, the employee began working only his contractual hours and was eventually dismissed. It was held that his dismissal was fair given the difficulties that would be faced by the employer in not knowing from day to day whether the employee would be available to complete his round.

While the contract, therefore, is the starting point, the courts interpret the word 'reasonable' in a flexible way, and this can mean that the employee will be required to carry out duties which are not within his contract. But this works both ways, and there have been situations where the courts have decided that even though the order is within the contractual authority of the employer, it is still unreasonable and the employee is not in breach of contract in refusing to obey it. In the old case of *Ottoman Bank Ltd v Chakarian* [1930] AC 277, the employer ordered the employee, an Armenian, to stay in Constantinople where he had been previously sentenced to death. It was held that the order, although within the employer's contractual rights, was not reasonable in the circumstances and the employee was entitled to refuse to obey it.

In addition to the requirement that the order is reasonable, it must also be lawful, and the employee can legitimately refuse to obey an order which requires him to act illegally, even if the order is within his contractual obligations. In *Morrish v Henlys (Folkestone) Ltd* [1973] IRLR 61, an employee was dismissed when he refused to obey an order to falsify the account books at the garage where he worked. It was held that his dismissal was unfair as he was not in breach of contract by refusing to comply with the order.

4.3.3 Duty to exercise reasonable care and skill

In addition to the duty to obey reasonable, lawful orders the law imposes a duty on the employee that he will perform his work with reasonable care and skill. This duty can arise in three situations. First, and at its simplest, the law requires the employee to take reasonable care of his employer's property (for example tools and equipment). In *Superlux v Plaisted* (1958) *The Times*, 12 December, a salesman negligently left his van unlocked, and as a result a stock of vacuum cleaners was stolen. It was held that the employee was in breach of contract. In some cases the act of negligence may be so serious that it warrants dismissal, but minor acts of neglect will not justify the employer sacking the employee unless there is a series of such minor acts (*Lowndes v Specialist Heavy Engineering Ltd* [1977] ICR 1).

The second situation involves the skill part of the duty. An employee impliedly promises that he is able to do the job where he is not being trained, and failing to reach an acceptable standard of performance is a breach of that implied promise. Under the common law, such a breach would entitle an employer to dismiss instantly (*Harmer v Cornelius* (1858) 5 CBNS 236), but nowadays the procedural protection which arises from the statutory unfair dismissal provisions (see Chapter 9) will aid an incompetent employee to some extent.

The third situation when a breach of this implied duty may arise is when the employee performs his work negligently and in doing so injures a third party, who may be a fellow employee or nothing to do with the employer. In these cases, the employer may find himself liable to his injured employee for failing to provide a competent colleague (see Section 4.2.11(b)(iv)), or in either situation may find himself vicariously liable (see Section 4.2.11(b)(vi)). While in theory the employer could, in either of these situations, sue the employee who caused the injury for his breach of contract, it has been seen that in practice, since the case of *Lister v Romford Ice and Cold Storage Co Ltd* [1957] AC 555 (see Section 3.6), this rarely, if ever, happens where physical injury occurs and the injured party is another employee. In other cases, however, the courts have upheld an action for damages against the employee. In *Janata Bank v Ahmed* [1981] IRLR 457, a bank manager performed his duties negligently and was dismissed. The bank sued him for its loss of £34,640, and the Court of Appeal upheld the claim. The employer's loss had been caused by the employee's failure to exercise proper care and skill, as implied by his contract.

4.3.4 Duty not to accept bribes or secret commission

The employee should accept rewards only from his employer and is under an implied duty not to accept payment from another source, even if the payment does not influence him. The basis of the duty is that the employee must serve his employer faithfully, and it is inconsistent with this duty that he should receive payment from another source for performing his job. In *Boston Deep Sea Fishing and Ice Co v Ansell* (1888) 39 Ch 339, the employee was accepting payment for placing orders with a supplier and was receiving dividends from shares he owned in another supplier of his employer. It was held that his dismissal was justified. Breach of this duty is considered to be so serious by the courts that it will normally justify instant dismissal. The payment must be secret, however, and if the employer knows that the payment has occurred and accepts it, the duty is not broken; for example, it is accepted in a number of jobs that employees will receive tips.

While the duty is a simple one to state, in practice it may be difficult to enforce. Many employees will receive gifts from customers or suppliers, and will often receive free meals and drinks. While technically a breach of contract will have occurred, few employers would pursue a remedy against the employee. In practice many employers will tell those employees likely to be put in this position what is and is not acceptable. Should an employee then step out of line, he will be in breach of contract.

4.3.5 Duty not to disclose confidential information

The law recognises that if the employee divulges confidential information he has acquired during the course of his employment, this may harm the employer's interests, and therefore the duty not to disclose such information applies not only during the currency of the relationship, but also once the relationship has ended. The extent of the duty was discussed in detail in *Faccenda Chicken Ltd v Fowler* [1987] Ch 117. Mr Fowler was a salesman who left Faccenda Chicken to set up a business in competition. He recruited a number of his ex-employer's staff, and most of his customers had previously been customers of his ex-employer. Faccenda Chicken sued for damages for the misuse of sales information relating to prices and customers. The Court of Appeal dismissed the claim. The Court laid down that as a matter of principle, the duty of the employee once he had left the relationship was more restricted than during his employment. The Court distinguished between two types of confidential information. The first is information of a highly confidential nature which should be treated as if it were a trade secret, and the employee can be restrained from divulging this information even though the relationship has ended. The second type of information is that which is confidential, so that it would be a breach of this duty to disclose it while in employment, but not a breach to use it after the relationship has ended. If the employer wants to protect himself after the relationship has terminated, he should insert a restraint covenant in the contract to bind the employee once he has left. Such covenants are discussed in Section 11.3. If there is no such covenant then, to see if a breach of duty has occurred, the court must look at:

1. the nature of the employment;
2. the nature of the information;
3. whether the information can be isolated from other information which the employee is free to use; and
4. whether the employer impressed upon the employee the need for confidentiality.

In a large number of cases, it may be difficult to distinguish between the two types of information, but the judgment means that in relation to ex-employees, the duty will not normally protect the employer in the majority of cases. In the few successful cases, a clear breach has occurred during the currency of the relationship, and this has led the court to be more willing to find that the employee is liable. In *Robb v Green* [1895] 2 QB 315, a manager copied his employer's customer list before leaving his employment. He then set up in competition and solicited the customers on the list. His ex-employer successfully obtained an injunction against him. Similarly in *Sanders v Parry* [1967] 2 All ER 803, an assistant solicitor set up on his own, taking with him one of the practice's main clients whose affairs he had looked after. It was held that he was in breach of duty.

Although the duty may be restricted in relation to ex-employees, the only restriction in respect of existing employees is that the information must be confidential. This leaves the question, however, as to what information is deemed to be confidential. Certainly it includes information which the law allows an employer to protect by a restraint covenant. This means any information which the law regards as the employer's property, and consequently includes trade secrets, secret processes and customer lists. There may be other information, however, which the employer regards as confidential and which, if divulged, could injure the employer's business. In *Marshall (Thomas) (Exports) Ltd v Guinle* [1979] Ch 227, the court identified certain factors which should be considered in deciding if the information is confidential and in need of protection:

1. The owner of the information must reasonably believe that the release of the information would benefit a competitor or cause harm to himself.
2. The owner must reasonably believe that the information is confidential and not already public knowledge.
3. The information must be judged bearing in mind the practice of the particular trade or industry.

Given the factors listed above, it is irrelevant whether the item disclosed is simple or could be discovered by the person to whom the information is divulged with some research. In *Cranleigh Precision Engineering Ltd v Bryant* [1965] 1 WLR 1293, the employee divulged the right type of clamp to use to keep the inner and outer skins of swimming pools together. The materials and type of clamp were common in the industry, but had not been used for that purpose before. It was held that the employee was in breach of contract. The courts feel that information which the employer regards as confidential and which, if divulged, would put the recipient in a stronger position than others should be protected. The attitude of the courts was summed up by Roxburgh J in *Terrapin Ltd v Builders Supply (Hayes) Ltd* [1960] RPC 128 when he said that 'a person who has obtained information in confidence is not allowed to use it as a springboard for activities detrimental to the person who made the confidential communication'.

One problem which exists in determining whether the employee is in breach of duty is separating out confidential information from the skills the employee has learned during his employment and which he is entitled to use for the benefit of his new employer. For example, if the employee has learned a process during his employment, is this a skill he has acquired or is it confidential information? In *Printers & Finishers Ltd v Holloway* [1964] 3 All ER 731, the ex-employee, a manager, had knowledge of the employer's flock-printing process, skill in using a flock-printing plant, plus information from documents acquired from his ex-employer. His former employer successfully obtained an injunction only in respect of the information contained in the documents. The other information was skill the employee had acquired during his employment which he could use for the benefit of his new employer. In this case the dividing line was quite clear-cut, but in many cases it will not be.

Prior to 1998, there was one exception when the duty not to disclose confidential information did not apply. This was where the information must be disclosed by law, or it was in the public interest that the information should become known. In *Initial Services Ltd v Putterill* [1968] 1 QB 396, an ex-employee gave details to a newspaper of restrictive trade practices operated by his ex-employer. Such practices were in breach of the Restrictive Trade Practices Act 1968. It was held that the disclosure was not a breach of the employee's duty as the information should be divulged in the public interest. Likewise, employees are required to divulge information by certain statutes such as HASAWA 1974. To do so will not be a breach of duty on the part of the employee.

The Public Interest Disclosure Act 1998 has increased protection for employees who disclose information that their employer is likely to regard as confidential (so called whistle-blowing). The Act inserted new sections into the ERA 1996. Employees are protected if they make a qualifying disclosure. In *Bolton School v Evans* [2007] ICR 641, the Court of Appeal discussed what is meant by 'disclosure'. Evans was an IT teacher. He resigned and claimed constructive dismissal after he had been given a final warning when he disabled some of the service accounts on the school's computer network from a pupil's computer. He had done this to show flaws in the network's security. He argued he had suffered a detriment as a result of disclosing the school's breach of its data protection obligations. The school claimed he had been disciplined for his misconduct in hacking into the system. Buxton LJ said that the word 'disclosure' should be given its common meaning, and this meant words spoken to the employer about the breach and did not extend to the surrounding circumstances. As such Evans had not made a disclosure.

A 'protected disclosure' is defined by section 43B of the ERA 1996 as any disclosure of information which, in the reasonable belief of the worker making the disclosure, tends to show one or more of the following:

- A criminal offence has been committed, is being committed or is likely to be committed.
- A person has failed, is failing or is likely to fail to comply with a legal obligation.
- A miscarriage of justice has occurred or is likely to occur.
- The health or safety of an individual has been or is likely to be endangered.
- The environment has been or is likely to be damaged.
- Information showing any of the above has been or is likely to be deliberately concealed.

It is important to note that the standard used is subjective, and the question for a tribunal will be whether the employee has a reasonable belief (*Babula v Waltham Forest* [2007] IRLR 346). There are also two exceptions when the disclosure is not protected. This is where the person making the disclosure commits a criminal offence by making it, and where it is a disclosure in respect of which legal professional privilege would apply.

In order to qualify for protection there are specified procedures the employee must have followed. The aim of the legislation is to encourage the employee to go through appropriate channels first, and thus an employee will gain protection more easily if he discloses to a person within employment rather than going outside to, for example, the press. The provisions are considered further in the following sections.

4.3.5(a) *Disclosure to employer or other responsible person (s 43C)*

The aim of this provision is for the employee to make the disclosure to the person responsible for preventative action. This will normally be the employer, but may be another person to whom the employer has delegated responsibility.

4.3.5(b) Disclosure to a legal adviser (s 43D)

4.3.5(c) Disclosure to a Minister of the Crown (s 43E)

This will apply when the employer is an individual appointed by a Minister of the Crown.

4.3.5(d) Disclosure to a prescribed person (s 43F)

The persons who fall within this category are defined by an order made by the Secretary of State for Employment.

4.3.5(e) Disclosure in other cases (s 43G)

If the worker believes the allegation to be true, the conditions in the section are met, the worker does not make the disclosure for personal gain and it is reasonable in all the circumstances to make the disclosure, it will be protected. The Enterprise and Regulatory Reform Act 2013 removes the requirement that the disclosure must be in good faith; instead, it gives a discretion to a tribunal to reduce any compensation by up to 25 per cent where the disclosure is not made in good faith.

The conditions are that at the time he makes the disclosure:

- the worker reasonably believes that he will be subjected to a detriment if the disclosure is made to the employer or a prescribed person;
- if there is no prescribed person, the worker reasonably believes that evidence will be concealed or destroyed if the disclosure is made to the employer; or
- the worker has previously disclosed substantially the same information to the employer or a prescribed person.

In deciding whether it was reasonable for the worker to make the disclosure the tribunal should take account of:

- the identity of the person to whom the disclosure was made;
- the seriousness of the relevant failure;
- whether the failure is continuing or likely to reoccur;
- whether the disclosure is a breach of the employee's duty of confidentiality;
- any action the employer could have taken or could reasonably be expected to take as a result of the previous disclosure; and
- whether when making the disclosure to the employer the worker complied with any procedure laid down by the employer.

4.3.5(f) Disclosure of exceptionally serious breaches (s 43H)

If the disclosure is serious enough to bypass the procedures, it will be protected if the worker reasonably believes the allegations are true, the worker does not make the disclosure for personal gain, the matter disclosed is of an exceptionally serious nature and in all the circumstances it was reasonable to make the disclosure. The identity of the person to whom the disclosure is made is a relevant factor when considering whether it was reasonable to make the disclosure. Again, the tribunal has the discretion to reduce compensation by up to 25 per cent if the disclosure is not made in good faith.

Section 47B of the ERA 1996 provides protection for the employee who has suffered a detriment because of a qualifying disclosure. Section 103A states that the dismissal of an employee in those circumstances shall be unfair, and the employee has protection from selection for redundancy. The normal continuity period does not apply. In *Kuzel v Roche Products Ltd* [2007] IRLR 309, the EAT stated that where a claimant has shown that the reason put forward by the respondent was not one of the five fair reasons for dismissal but a reason falling within section 103A, the employer must either prove the real reason for the dismissal or disprove the section 103A reason. If he is unsuccessful, the dismissal is for the section 103A reason.

Section 43J of the ERA 1996 provides that any term in an employment contract preventing disclosure is void. In *Lucas v Chichester Diocesan Housing Association Ltd* (2004) EAT 0713/04, Lucas reported concerns about financial irregularities in a project to a senior manager, who then informed the project manager. The manager cut Lucas's hours, and after Lucas raised further issues she was dismissed. She claimed a breach of section 103A. The employment tribunal found that her disclosures were motivated by her worsening relationship with her manager, but the EAT found that there were no relationship problems at the time of the first complaint and the employer had not raised bad faith (which would now give the tribunal a discretion to reduce compensation by up to 25 per cent). Furthermore, in *Miklaszewicz v Stolt Offshore Ltd* [2001] IRLR 656, the Court of Appeal held that the Act can apply to protect a disclosure made before the Act was in force where an employee was dismissed as a result of that disclosure after the Act came into force.

4.3.6   Duty not to work for a competitor

Generally the employer cannot restrict what the employee does in his spare time, and the employee can take on a second job without interference from his employer. There are, however, two exceptions to the rule. The first is that the employee cannot work for a competitor of his employer in his spare time. In *Hivac Ltd v Park Royal Scientific Instruments Ltd* [1946] Ch 169, employees were working for a competitor in their spare time. Although the first employer sued the second employer and successfully obtained an injunction to restrain future employment of his employees, the court was in agreement that the employees were in breach of contract.

Given that an employee may not work for a competitor, it also follows that he may not set up in competition in his spare time. In *Adamson v B&L Cleaning Services* [1995] IRLR 193, a foreman at a contract cleaning firm was dismissed for seeking to obtain an existing contract when it came up for tender. The EAT held that the dismissal was fair, in that intending to leave and set up in competition would not be a dismissible offence, but here the employee had overstepped the mark by breaching the duty of fidelity. The emphasis, however, is that spare-time employment must harm the employer, and without evidence of such harm the duty will not be broken. This is seen in *Helmet Integrated Systems Ltd v Tunnard* [2007] IRLR 126. The defendant had been employed as a salesman for a company which produced safety helmets. There was an express term in his contract that he would not undertake work which would affect or be in competition with his employer. He was also under a duty to inform his employer of competitor behaviour. While employed he had an idea for a new helmet, and got drawings made and applied for funding. He then resigned and set up his own company. The Court of Appeal held that he was not in breach of his contractual duty of fidelity. His actions while employed were merely preparing for competition and not actually in competition. Further, although he was required to inform his employer about competitor behaviour, this duty did not extend to disclosing his own behaviour. This is supported by *Lonmar Global Risks Ltd v West and Ors* [2010] EWHC 2878, a restraint of trade case. Here the High Court stated that unless an employee is a fiduciary (such as a director or a senior manager), there is no duty to report his own misconduct or that of fellow employees, as a fiduciary duty did not arise from the relationship of employer and employee per se. Presumably, if the employer inserts a term in the contract to the effect that such misconduct should be disclosed, this then becomes an issue of breach of an express term rather than breach of an implied duty.

The second situation which may arise is that the employee gets another job in his spare time which has nothing to do with his employer's business. In this situation there is very little the employer can do, unless he has an express provision in the contract forbidding such employment. The only way this type of work could be a breach of an implied term is if the second job made the employee so tired he became incapable of performing his main job. He would then be in breach of the implied duty to perform his work with reasonable care and skill (see Section 4.3.3).

The cases above all involved situations when the employee was under a contract of employment and still under a duty to work. If, however, the employer has relieved the employee of the duty to work, there would be no breach on the part of the employee if, despite the fact that a relationship still existed with the employer, the employee worked for a competitor, unless the employer made it clear that this was forbidden. In *Hutchings v Coinseed Ltd* [1998] IRLR 190, the employee resigned, giving a month's notice. Her contract provided that during the notice period the employers were not obliged to provide her with work, and could require her to stay at home and not work for a competitor (so-called 'garden leave'). The employers, on receipt of her letter of resignation, replied, stating that the employee was not required to work her notice and that she would be paid in lieu. On the same day the employee started work with a competitor and the employers withheld her payment in lieu.

The Court of Appeal held that the employer's letter made it clear that the employee was not required to work for them, and it did not say that she should not take up other employment. As such, she was free to work for a competitor, as the letter from the employer varied the terms of her contract. It would appear, however, that if the employer's letter had reiterated the garden leave clause, or stated that the employee could not work elsewhere until the end of the notice period, the employee would have been in repudiatory breach.

4.3.7 Inventions

At common law the duty of fidelity meant that any ownership of inventions made by an employee during the course of employment was vested in the employer (*British Syphon Co Ltd v Homewood* [1956] 1 WLR 1190). Often collective agreements modified the common law and protected the employee to some extent, to enable a share in any profits made from the invention, but without such an agreement, the invention was seen as part of the employee's general duty to promote his employer's interests. The position has now been changed by the Patents Act 1977 and the Copyright, Designs and Patents Act 1988.

Section 39 of the 1977 Act provides that in two circumstances the invention belongs to the employer. These circumstances are where the invention:

1. was made in the course of the normal duties of the employee, or outside those normal duties but within the course of duties specifically assigned to him, and in both cases the invention reasonably resulted from the carrying out of those duties; or
2. was made during the course of the duties of the employee and at the time of making the invention the employee had a special obligation to further the interests of his employer's undertaking.

In all other circumstances the invention is owned by the employee. In *Reiss Engineering Co Ltd v Harris* [1985] IRLR 232, the court decided that the employee's normal duties are those he is actually employed to carry out. In the case the employee invented a valve while he was under notice of redundancy. It was held that the invention belonged to the employee because it did not arise out of his normal duties and he was under no obligation to further his employer's interests.

Even if the invention is owned by the employer, section 40 of the Patents Act 1977 provides that the employee can apply to the Patents Court or the Patents Office for compensation where the invention belongs to the employer under section 39 but is proved to be of outstanding benefit to the employer, or where the invention is owned by the employee but he has assigned it to the employer for inadequate compensation in relation to the benefit obtained by the employer from the invention. The amount of compensation is determined by taking into account the criteria listed in section 41.

Copyright is covered by the 1988 Act. Section 11 provides that the copyright in any work is owned by the author, unless it is written by the employee in the course of his employment and the employee was employed for the purpose of writing such work, in which case the copyright is owned by the employer, subject to any agreement to the contrary.

While the Acts simplify the position, they still provide problem areas in terms of what the employee's normal duties are, when the employee is under a special obligation to further his employer's interests and when something is produced in the course of the employee's employment. Many employers avoid these problems by providing specifically in the contract what type of work is deemed to be owned by the employer, or conversely that the employee is under a special obligation to further the employer's interests.

Summary

4.1 A contract of employment is a contract for personal services and the law normally will not compel the parties to continue the contract by the use of specific performance or injunction.

4.2 The law implies duties into all contracts of employment, and they will be imposed on the parties unless ousted by an express term.

4.3 The law imposes duties on both the employer and the employee.

4.4 The consideration by the employer is the payment of wages, and therefore generally there is no duty on the employer to provide work, only pay.

4.5 The ERA 1996 prevents unauthorised deductions from an employee's pay by the employer.

4.6 The law now recognises that both parties owe a duty of respect towards each other.

Summary cont'd

4.7 The common law imposes detailed duties on the employer to look after the employee's safety. These duties complement the duties imposed by HASAWA 1974.

4.8 The employer will be vicariously liable for the acts of employees committed during the course of their employment if there is a sufficient connection between the act committed and their employment.

4.9 The duties imposed upon the employee come under the general heading of fidelity. This means that the employee owes duties of obedience, loyalty, and care and skill to his employer.

Exercises

4.1 Paul is a weekly-paid production worker in an engineering factory. During the last six months he has been laid off on three separate occasions, but has received no wages during the course of any of the three periods of lay-off. On the first occasion, he was laid off when the factory was closed after a week-long rail strike made it impossible for half the workforce to get to work. On the second occasion, he was laid off for three consecutive weeks as a result of a fall in demand for the company's products, caused by the last-minute cancellation of a large order by an overseas customer. On the last occasion, he was laid off intermittently over a period of six weeks as a result of sporadic industrial action by other workers at the plant, who forced the closure of certain parts of the plant at regular intervals. Paul is a highly skilled worker who had only been laid off once previously, last year, when again he received no wages, although he made no complaint. Now, however, he wishes to sue his employers for breach of contract. Advise Paul.

4.2 Bill and Ben work for Flowerpot Ltd as roofers. In winter the roofs are dangerous. Six months ago, Flowerpot provided safety belts for the roofers to wear. They showed the employees how to use the belts and where they were kept, and put up a notice saying belts should be worn at all times. Bill is illiterate and was away on a training course when the belts were first issued. Ben thinks it spoils his image to wear the belts because he likes impressing Weed, who works in the canteen, by dancing on the roof. Last week both Bill and Ben were working on a roof. Neither of them was wearing belts. Ben was dancing about, trying to attract Weed's attention, when he distracted Bill. Both fell from the roof and were seriously injured. Consider the liability of Flowerpot Ltd.

Further reading and references

Barmes, 'Common Law Implied Terms and Behavioural Standards at Work' (2006) 36 ILJ 1

Barnard, 'The Working Time Regulations 1998' (1999) 28 ILJ 61

Barnard, 'The Working Time Regulations 1999' (2000) 29 ILJ 167

Barrett, 'Clarification of Employer's Liability for Work-Related Stress' (2002) 31 ILJ 285

Barrett, 'Employer's Liability After *Hatton* v. *Sutherland*' (2005) 34 ILJ 182

Brodie, 'The Personal Employment Contract' (2004) 33 ILJ 87

Brodie, 'Health and Safety, Trust and Confidence and *Barber* v. *Somerset County Council*: Some Further Questions' (2004) 33 ILJ 261.

Further reading and references cont'd

Brodie, 'The Enterprise and the Borrowed Worker' (2006) 35 ILJ 87

Brodie, 'Mutual Trust and Confidence: Catalysts, Constraints and Commonality' (2008) 37 ILJ 329

Cabrelli, 'The Implied Duty of Mutual Trust and Confidence: An Emerging Overarching Principle?' (2005) 34 ILJ 284

Clarke, 'Breach of Confidence and the Employment Relationship' (2002) 31 ILJ 353

Emir, *Selwyn's Law of Employment* (Oxford University Press 2012)

Holland and Chandler, 'Implied Mobility Clauses' (1988) 17 ILJ 253

Lewis, 'The Public Interest Disclosure Act 1998' (1998) 27 ILJ 325

Lewis, 'Freedom of Speech and Employment' (2003) 32 ILJ 72

Lewis, 'Providing Rights for Whistleblowers: Would An Anti-Discrimination Model be more Effective?' (2005) 34 ILJ 239

Lewis, 'Whistleblowers, Reasonable Belief and Data Protection' (2006) 35 ILJ 324

Lewis, '10 years of the Public Interest Disclosure Act 1998 Claims: What Can We Learn from Statistics and Recent Research?' (2010) 39 ILJ 325

Middlemiss, 'The Truth and Nothing but the Truth? The Legal Liability of Employers for Employee References' (2004) 33 ILJ 59

Rodgers, 'The Notion of Working Time' (2009) 38 ILJ 80

Simpson, 'The National Minimum Wage Five Years On: Reflections on Some General Issues' (2004) 33 ILJ 22

Part III

Constraints on the employment relationship

Chapter 5

Discrimination

5.1 The concept of discrimination

The common law principle of freedom of contract applies equally to employment contracts, consequently, at common law, the employer can employ, or refuse to employ, anyone for whatever reason he wishes, including reasons based on the sex or race of that person. Such a proposition nowadays, however, would offend most people's sense of fairness, and over the past few decades the law has sought to intervene to restrict an employer from exercising his common law rights.

The original impetus to bring in legislation in this area came from international law. The Universal Declaration of Human Rights 1948 states that everyone is entitled to all rights and freedoms, 'without distinction of any kind, such as race, colour, sex, language, religion, political or other opinion, national or social origin, property, birth or status'. Such statements are reiterated by the International Labour Organization's Conventions of 1958 and 1980. Without doubt, however, the most important influence on national law has been the UK membership of the European Union.

An EC Directive of 1976 (EEC 76/207) required the implementation of the principle of equal treatment for men and women in all aspects of employment. Article 288 TFEU states that directives are binding on Member States as to the result, but the method of implementation is left up to the particular Member. Failure to implement a directive fully will lead to action against the Member State by the European Commission. In relation to the United Kingdom this has happened twice in the area of equal opportunities, once in the area of equal pay, discussed in Chapter 6, and once in the area of sex discrimination, when the European Court of Justice (ECJ) decided that the UK had failed to comply with Article 4(b) of the Equal Treatment Directive, in that legislation did not outlaw discriminatory treatment in collective agreements, internal rules of undertakings or rules governing independent occupations and professions. Furthermore, the ECJ has held that the Directive can be directly enforced where the employer is an organ of the state and the Directive is clear. This issue is discussed later (Section 6.8.2). Note, however, that the Supreme Court has recently held that only those who are paid are protected. In *X v Mid Sussex Citizens Advice Bureau* [2012] UKSC 59, the Court held that volunteers were not protected as they do not fall within the word 'occupation' in the Framework Directive.

To comply with its international and European obligations, Britain introduced a series of legislation, all of which was replaced by the Equality Act 2010 which came into force on 1 October 2010. While there have been a few cases under the Act at the time of writing, cases under the old law will be used to show how the 2010 Act may be interpreted.

In addition to those areas covered by the Equality Act 2010, the Part-time Workers (Prevention of Less Favourable Treatment) Regulations 2000 prohibit discrimination on the basis that a person works part-time, and the Fixed-term Employees (Prevention of Less Favourable Treatment) Regulations 2002 mean that it is also illegal to discriminate on the basis that a person is on a fixed-term contract.

The legislation used is monitored and kept under review by the Equality and Human Rights Commission.

5.2 Protected characteristics

The Equality Act 2010 protects against discrimination on the basis of nine protected characteristics (s 4). The protected characteristics are:

- Age
- Disability
- Gender reassignment
- Marriage and civil partnership
- Pregnancy and maternity
- Race
- Religion or belief
- Sex
- Sexual orientation

Each characteristic is then defined and will be discussed below. Unless stated otherwise, references in this chapter to sections of an Act are to provisions of the Equality Act 2010.

5.2.1 Age

Section 5 defines 'age' as being a reference to a particular age group or to a person within a range of ages, ie over 65 or 18–21. However, it will also include people who share a characteristic associated with an age group, such as pensioners, according to the Employment Code of Practice. In *Live Nations (Venues) UK Ltd v Hussain* (2008) UKEAT 02034/08, the EAT gave some guidance as to conduct which might or might not justify a finding of age discrimination:

1. An employer that genuinely believes employee A is guilty of age discrimination against employee B, and dismisses employee A for that reason, cannot be said to be discriminating against employee A because of his or her age.
2. An unjustified or unreasoned belief that an employee has ageist tendencies may render dismissal unfair, but it does not justify an inference that the reason for the dismissal is the employee's age.
3. If an employee's dismissal for suspected ageism justified an inference of age discrimination by the employer, it might restrict an employer in dealing with a suspected discriminator for fear it would be found to be discriminating.
4. Any reference to an employee being 'too old to change' could, in an appropriate case, provide some basis for inferring age discrimination.

5.2.2 Disability

The definition of 'disability' largely reflects previous legislation. It should be noted that an action lies only if a person is discriminated against because he or she is disabled (although see *Coleman v Attridge Law* in Section 5.4 below). Therefore it allows the employer to discriminate positively in favour of a disabled person.

To be protected against discrimination, an individual must be a person who has a disability (s 6(1)) or a person who has had a disability (s 6(2)). A disability is defined as either a physical or mental impairment, which has a substantial and long-term adverse effect on the person's ability to carry out normal day-to-day activities (s 6(1)). In other words, the physical or mental impairment must be the cause of the substantial and long-term adverse effects. The 2010 Act does not define either physical or mental impairment. The concept of mental impairment caused problems in the past. For example, in *Goodwin v Patent Office* [1999] IRLR 4, the EAT held that an employee dismissed because of paranoid schizophrenia had been dismissed on the grounds of disability. It is still important, however, to note the case of *Dunham v Ashford Windows* [2005] IRLR 608. There, the EAT emphasised that a tribunal hearing a mental impairment case based on learning difficulties should always seek expert evidence of an identified condition.

In *J v DLA Piper UK LLP* [2010] IRLR 936, the EAT laid down the following propositions:

▷ A GP is fully qualified to express an opinion on whether a patient is suffering from depression.
▷ It remains good practice for a tribunal to state conclusions separately on questions of impairment and adverse effects, and on questions of substantiality and the long-term nature of adverse effects.

Nevertheless, a tribunal should not keep to rigid stages, and if there is a dispute about the existence of an impairment, it makes sense to start with an investigation as to whether the claimant's ability to carry out normal day-to-day activities is adversely affected.

The impairment must have a substantial and long-term adverse effect on the employee's ability to carry out normal day-to-day activities. The Equality Act 2010, unlike the old law, does not contain a list of what constitute normal day-to-day activities. What constitutes 'substantial' is not defined in the Act either. Schedule 1, paragraph 2 defines what is meant by 'long term', however. The effect must have lasted at least 12 months, or be likely to last either 12 months or for the rest of the person's life. In *SCA Packaging v Boyle* [2009] UKHL 37, the House of Lords stated that the word 'likely' should be interpreted as meaning 'could well happen' rather than 'more likely than not', so establishing a much lower threshold and giving more people protection. In *Richmond Adult Community College v McDougall* [2008] IRLR 227, the Court of Appeal stated that the point in time for determining whether the effect of an impairment is likely to last 12 months is the time of the decision complained of, and a tribunal should make its decision based on evidence as to the circumstances at that time. However, the fact that someone has a life-long condition, controlled by medication, which makes a person more prone to infections which have once had a substantial adverse effect on that person's ability to carry out normal day-to-day activities, does not make that person disabled, according to the EAT in *Sussex Partnership NHS Foundation Trust v Norris* [2012] EmpLR 179. There needed to be sufficient evidence that if the infections were to recur they would be serious enough to have a substantial adverse effect.

The EAT, in *Aderemi v London and South East Railway* [2013] All ER (D) 201, has stated that when a tribunal is assessing whether a claimant is disabled, it should concentrate on what an employee cannot do, not on what he can do. In the case, Mr Aderemi worked on the station gate checking passenger tickets, which involved him in standing for the duration of his nine-hour shifts. He developed a back problem which meant that he could not stand for long periods, and eventually he was dismissed on the ground of capability. The tribunal dismissed his claim for unfair dismissal and disability discrimination. In respect of the latter ground, the tribunal concluded that his impairment did not have a substantial adverse effect on his ability to carry out normal day-to-day activities, and gave a long list of the activities he could do. The EAT held that the tribunal had looked at the issue of disability in the wrong way. Rather than concentrating on what the claimant could do, it should have concentrated on what he could not do. He could not, for example, stand for more than 30 minutes, nor could he bend or lift. This would have substantially affected him not only at work, but also in his ability to carry out normal day-to-day activities. Futhermore, the EAT held, in *Walker v Sita Information Networking Computing Ltd* [2013] All ER (D) 317, that when establishing whether a claimant is disabled, a tribunal should focus on the *effect* of a person's symptoms and not on their cause. As such, it upheld an appeal that a claimant who was obese, and who suffered from a range of symptoms because of his obesity, could be disabled. Langstaff P stated that the first question a tribunal should ask is whether the individual has an impairment, and the second is whether that impairment is physical or mental. The cause of that impairment is relevant only in so far as a tribunal may find that a person does not suffer from a disability because there is no recognisable cause. However, Langstaff P refused to accept that obesity is a disability per se, though he did state that it may make it more likely that someone is disabled.

In some cases the disability will be well recognised, such as blindness, and the employee will be registered as disabled. Problems arise, however, when the situation is not so obvious. In *O'Neill v Symm & Co Ltd* [1998] IRLR 233, an employment tribunal considered that chronic fatigue syndrome and ME (myalgic encephalomyelitis) could be a disability for the purposes of the Act. This finding was upheld by the EAT, but the appeal tribunal went on to say that nothing in its judgment, nor that of the employment tribunal, should be taken as establishing that chronic fatigue syndrome is generically a disability which falls within the ambit of the legislation. A tribunal must consider each case in relation to the particular complainant and the impairments relative to that complainant. In *Tarling v Wisdom Toothbrushes Ltd t/a Wisdom* (1997) IDS Brief 597, the employee had a club foot which resulted in progressive deterioration of her bone structure. As a result she had sciatica, which made it difficult for her to stand for the long periods of time required to do her job. The employment tribunal found that she was disabled for the purposes of the Act. In *Clark v Novacold Ltd* [1998] IRLR 420, too, the employment tribunal and the EAT accepted that an applicant who did manual work and who, after injuring his back at work, could not walk short distances or lift heavy loads, a condition which would last more than 12 months, had a disability for the purposes of the Act. Conversely, in *Foord v JA Johnston & Sons* (1998) IDS Brief 611, an employment tribunal considered that an applicant with fallen arches, which meant that she was unable to stand or be on her feet for prolonged periods of time, was not disabled. She was able to cope with her normal working hours of 8 am to 2 pm, and she had experienced difficulties on only one occasion she worked an extra two hours. In *Goodwin v Patent Office* (above), the employment tribunal held that the applicant who suffered from paranoid schizophrenia was not disabled within the meaning of the Act. Although recognising that the applicant had a mental illness, his work was of a satisfactory standard and he could carry out domestic activities without assistance. The reason for his dismissal was not his inability to work to the required standard but complaints from female staff that he stared at them and made unwelcome social advances. On appeal the EAT reversed the decision and emphasised that the fact that a disabled person can carry out certain day-to-day activities does not mean that his or her ability to do so has not been impaired. Disabled persons often adjust their lives and circumstances to enable them to cope. This does not mean that their condition is not a disability. In *Hewett v Motorola Ltd* [2004] IRLR 545, the EAT said that 'understand', as a normal day-to-day activity, is not limited to an ability to understand information, knowledge or instructions. Someone who has difficulty in understanding normal social interaction, such as someone with Asperger's Syndrome, should be regarded as having their understanding affected. Further, in *Kapadia v London Borough of Lambeth* [2000] IRLR 14, the EAT allowed an appeal against a tribunal decision that the applicant was not disabled. The tribunal had ignored medical evidence and come to an opinion based on how the applicant had given evidence.

Schedule 1, paragraph 6 to the 2010 Act provides that a person who has cancer, HIV infection or multiple sclerosis is to be deemed to have a disability. This protects persons who have progressive conditions, in that there is no longer a need to show an effect on the ability to perform normal day-to-day activities and thus they will be protected from the time of diagnosis. Schedule 1, paragraph 3 also states that a severe disfigurement is to be treated as having a substantial adverse effect on the ability of the person to carry out normal day-to-day activities. This of course gives rise to the question of what is a substantial disfigurement.

In *Swift v Chief Constable of Wiltshire Constabulary* [2004] IRLR 540, the EAT considered the position in relation to recurring conditions. This is an important decision where the condition does not fit the definition of 'progressive conditions' above. The EAT said that a tribunal had to ask itself four questions. First, was there at some stage an impairment which had a substantial adverse effect on the complainant's ability to carry out normal day-to-day activities? Second, did the impairment cease to have such an effect and, if so, when? Third, what was the substantial adverse effect? Fourth, is that substantial adverse effect likely to recur? A substantial adverse effect is likely to recur if it is more probable than not that the effect will recur, although the tribunal does not need to be satisfied that the recurrence will last 12 months. The tribunal must look to see if the effect will recur and not the illness, which may run its course but leave behind an impairment.

5.2.3   Gender reassignment

Section 7 states that a person has the protected characteristic of gender reassignment if that person is proposing to undergo, is undergoing or has undergone gender reassignment.

5.2.4   Marriage and civil partnership

This protects only those who are married or who have undergone a civil partnership ceremony (s 8). It does not protect those who are engaged or living together. The original Sex Discrimination Act 1975 prohibited discrimination on the grounds of sex or marital status. The Act did not, however, prevent discrimination on the grounds that a person is single – marital status means being married. In *Bick v School for the Deaf* [1976] IRLR 326, the employee was dismissed just before her wedding day because of a policy operated by the school of not employing married staff. It was held that the applicant had no action for discrimination on the grounds of marital status, as she was still single at the date of her dismissal. However, a subsequent tribunal decision held that such action was discrimination on the grounds of marital status. In *Turner v Stephen Turner* (2005) 138 EOR 31, the complainant was dismissed when it was announced that she was to marry her employer's son. The tribunal dismissed the complaint of sex discrimination as there was no evidence that the employer would not have treated a male employee, in similar circumstances, in the same way. The tribunal did find, however, that there was discrimination on the grounds of marital status. The tribunal found that there was no binding authority on the point but that Article 12 of the ECHR provides:

> Men and women of marriageable age have the right to marry and to found a family according to the national laws governing the exercise of this right.

As such, the tribunal found that to give effect to the Human Rights Act 1998, the law had to be interpreted as protecting those who were about to marry. To find differently would be contrary to the mischief at which the 1998 Act was aimed. This interpretation does not seem to be replicated in the Equality Act 2010, however, and it will be interesting to see if there is a challenge on the basis of non-compliance with the Human Rights Act 1998.

5.2.5　Pregnancy and maternity

These are defined in the relevant sections on prohibited conduct below (Section 5.4.5).

5.2.6　Race

Section 9 defines 'race' as including colour, nationality and ethnic or national origins, so removing the anomaly that existed under the previous law. In *Mandla v Dowell Lee* [1983] 2 AC 548, the House of Lords held that Sikhs were a racial group; and in *Commission for Racial Equality v Dutton* [1989] IRLR 122, the Court of Appeal held that gypsies were within the definition of 'racial group' given that the definition under the Act referred to ethnic origins, and gypsies have a long history, their own customs and a unique dialect. The Court of Appeal in *Dawkins v Department of Environment* [1993] IRLR 284 decided that Rastafarians, on the other hand, were not a racial group for the purposes of the legislation. Their history goes back only 60 years, and there is nothing to distinguish Rastafarians from others of Jamaican or Afro-Caribbean descent. However, Rastafarians are classed as a religious group.

5.2.7　Religion or belief

Section 10 replicates the old law. 'Religion' includes a lack of religion. 'Belief' means any religious or philosophical belief, or a lack of belief. Originally the philosophical belief had to be similar to a religious belief, but the word 'similar' was removed by the Equality Act 2006. This has led to speculation that political beliefs may be protected. In *Redfearn v UK* [2012] ECHR 1878, Redfearn was employed by Serco, providing transport services in Bradford. When he was elected as a councillor for the British National Party (BNP) he was dismissed, Serco citing health and safety concerns as the reason for his dismissal.

Redfearn did not have the continuity of employment to claim unfair dismissal (see Section 9.2) and his race discrimination claim failed. The ECtHR held that lack of unfair dismissal protection interfered with the right to freedom of assembly and association in Article 11 of the ECHR. As such, there is an obligation to protect against dismissal motivated by a person's membership of a political party. (This has now been introduced by the Enterprise and Regulatory Reform Act 2013.)

The protection afforded appears to be against discrimination on the basis of the complainant's religion, etc and not that of the discriminator; however, in *Saini v All Saints Haque Centre* [2009] IRLR 74, the EAT held that as the legislation prevents discrimination 'on the grounds of religion or belief', this does not require the unwanted conduct to be on the grounds of the employee's own religious beliefs. Thus an employee was discriminated against when he resigned after being pressured to provide evidence in order for his employer to dismiss a manager because he was a Hindu. Using an employee to help to implement a discriminatory policy was discrimination on the grounds of religion. There is no definition in either the Directive or the Act as to the meaning of religion, religious belief or philosophical belief, but they will encompass a wide range of beliefs, and tribunals will be required to have regard to Strasbourg jurisprudence in applying Article 9 of the ECHR (freedom of religion). In *Grainger v Nicolson* [2010] IRLR 5, the EAT held that a genuine belief in man-made climate change could be a philosophical belief. Under ECtHR case law, Article 9 protects druidism (*Campbell v UK* (1987) 53 DR 241); pacifism (*Arrowsmith v UK* (1978) 19 DR 5); veganism (*X v UK (Commission)* Appl 18187/91); the Divine Light Zentrum (*Omkarananda and the Divine Light Zentrum v Switzerland* (1981) 25 DR 105); and the Church of Scientology (*X and the Church of Scientology v Sweden* (1979) 16 DR 68). The ECtHR has also said that Article 9 is a 'precious asset for atheists, agnostics, sceptics and the unconcerned' (*Kokkinakis v Greece* (1994) 17 EHRR 397). Thus the Act protects not only those who hold religious beliefs, but equally those who do not. While the ECtHR case law gives tribunals guidance, the lack of definitions in the Act could lead to a lot of litigation.

An unfair dismissal case shows the interface between the Act, Article 9 of the ECHR and other UK law. In *Copsey v WWB Devon Clays Ltd* [2005] EWCA Civ 932, a claim of unfair dismissal was brought by a Christian employee who refused to accept shift changes requiring Sunday working, and who was dismissed as a result. The Court of Appeal held that the dismissal was fair, but for different reasons. Mummery LJ held that the employer was bound by jurisprudence of the ECtHR, ending with *Stedman v UK* [1997] 23 EHRR CD, holding that Article 9 does not apply because an employee is always free to resign. Rix LJ felt that this was not what the ECtHR cases said, but held on the facts that the employer had tried to accommodate the employee when changing his hours, and although Article 9 did apply, it was not breached. Neuberger LJ dealt with UK law and held that a dismissal is fair if an employer strikes a reasonable balance between the needs of the business and the employee's religious beliefs. Thus it is unclear at present how the different pieces of law interlink.

In the case of *Eweida and others v UK* [2013] ECHR 37, the ECtHR held that UK law does not give sufficient protection for employees who wish to manifest their religion. In the case, two employees, Eweida and Chaplin, wished to wear visible crosses in breach of their employers' uniform policies. Eweida worked for British Airways and Chaplin was a geriatric nurse. A third employee, Ladele, was a registrar whose employer required her to perform civil partnership ceremonies; and McFarlane worked for Relate and was unwilling to provide sex counselling for same-sex couples. Article 9 of the Convention provides a right to freedom of thought, conscience and religion, but a qualified right to manifest one's religion or beliefs. This is subject to 'only such limitations as are prescribed by law and are necessary in a democratic society in the interests of public safety, for the protection of public order, health or morals, or for the protection of the rights and freedoms of others'. The ECtHR in previous decisions had held that where the interference with an individual's right occurred in the workplace, the possibility of changing jobs removed that interference; however in this case the court held that the possibility of moving jobs must be balanced with whether the restriction imposed by the employer was proportionate. In Eweida's case the domestic court had placed too much weight on British Airways' desire to project a certain image, and there was no evidence that the wearing of other items, such as turbans and hijabs, had damaged that image. Thus in the case the state had breached its obligations under Article 9 to protect Eweida's rights. In Chaplin's case, the reason for asking her to remove the cross was in the interests of health and safety, and therefore the interference was necessary and her rights were not breached. In the cases of McFarlane and Ladele, differences in treatment on the basis of sexual orientation require very serious reasons by way of justification. States have a wide margin of appreciation when it comes to competing Convention rights, and in both cases the margin of appreciation had not been exceeded. This has also been seen in the Court of Appeal decision of *Black and anor v Wilkinson* [2013] EWCA Civ 820, where the Court held that a Christian hotelier's decision to offer double bedrooms only to married couples and not homosexual couples was unlawful. Likewise in *Mba v The Mayor and Burgesses of the London Borough of Merton* [2013] All ER (D) 68, the EAT held that it was not discrimination to require a Christian worker to work on Sundays, although this decision was handed down before *Eweida* was heard in the Strasbourg Court.

5.2.8 Sex

By section 11, this includes both men and women.

5.2.9 Sexual orientation

Section 12 replicates the old law. 'Sexual orientation' refers to a person who is gay, lesbian, heterosexual or bisexual.

5.3 Prohibited conduct

The Equality Act 2010 covers employees and applicants (s 39) but the scope of the Act is wider. In the employment sphere, both contract workers (s 41) and those who work for employment service providers (s 55) are protected too. In addition, section 83(1)–(2) covers those who are under a contract to perform work personally. In *Quinnen v Hovells* [1984] IRLR 227, it was held that the legislation would protect the self-employed, provided they are providing personal services (see also *Harrods Ltd v Remick and Others* [1997] IRLR 583). Furthermore, as protection comes from statute and not from the contract, an illegality within the contract (for example, failing to pay tax and NICs) will not prevent an action being brought under the Act (*Leighton v Michael* [1996] IRLR 67).

Furthermore, should an employer commit an act of discrimination and then transfer his business, liability for the act passes onto the transferee (*DJM International Ltd v Nicholas* [1995] IRLR 76).

5.3.1 Burden of proof

By section 136(2):

> If there are facts from which the court could decide, in the absence of any other explanation, that a person (A) contravened the provision concerned, the court must hold that the contravention occurred.

Once a person has established a prima facie case of discrimination, the court must uphold the complaint unless the respondent shows that he did not commit the act. In other words, the burden of proof shifts to the employer once the claimant has established a prima facie case of discrimination.

Under the previous legislation there were a number of cases on the burden of proof. In *University of Huddersfield v Wolff* [2004] IRLR 534, the EAT held that the burden shifts once the tribunal has concluded that a prima facie case of less favourable treatment (on the grounds of one of the protected characteristics) has been made out and has set out the relevant facts on which it has made its findings, so that the employer knows what it has to justify. Only at that stage must the tribunal consider the employer's explanations (see also *Sinclair Roche & Temperley v Heard* [2004] IRLR 763). In *Rihal v London Borough of Ealing* [2004] IRLR 642, the Court of Appeal stated that a tribunal is obliged to consider all the evidence about the conduct of the alleged discriminator before or after the event complained about, and should not look at incidents in isolation where there are allegations of discrimination over a period of time, as to do so would give a fragmented picture. However, the same Court, in *Bahl v Law Society* [2004] IRLR 799, also stated that unreasonable treatment of the complainant alleging discrimination, if there is nothing else to explain it, cannot of itself lead to an inference of discrimination, even in the absence of evidence from the employer in the case at issue that it would treat a member of the opposite sex in the same way. In addition, the tribunal must find that subjectively consideration on the grounds of one of the protected characteristics was in the mind of the discriminator.

It appears, however, that, despite the above, the evidence needed to shift the burden of proof is not that onerous. In *Webster v Brunel University* EAT 0730/04, the complainant was employed as a help-desk officer, providing IT support to administrative staff. She complained that while giving advice over the telephone to accommodation staff, she heard laughter in the background and heard someone say 'Paki'. The tribunal dismissed her complaint on the basis that the accommodation office was a public place and someone other than a member of staff could have uttered the offending word. The EAT, however, said that once the tribunal had established the facts, it had to ask itself if the employer could have been responsible. Once the complainant had shown the speaker could have been an employee, the burden shifted to the employer to prove it was not. This seems a very low threshold. Further, in *Dattani v Chief Constable of West Mercia Police* [2005] IRLR 327, the EAT pointed out that a tribunal may also find inferences of discrimination from evasive or equivocal replies from the employer to any questions from the complainant.

The Court of Appeal in *Igen Ltd v Wong* [2005] IRLR 258 refined previous EAT guidance to tribunals (in *Barton v Investec Henderson Crosthwaite Securities Ltd* [2003] IRLR 332) on how to approach the burden of proof in discrimination claims, as follows:

1. It is for the claimant who complains of discrimination to prove on the balance of probabilities facts from which the tribunal could conclude, in the absence of an adequate explanation, that the respondent has committed an act of discrimination against the claimant which is unlawful by virtue of the Act. These are referred to below as 'such facts'.
2. If the claimant does not prove such facts, he or she will fail.
3. It is important to bear in mind in deciding whether the claimant has proved such facts that it is unusual to find direct evidence of discrimination. Few employers would be prepared to admit such discrimination, even to themselves. In some cases the discrimination will not be an intention but merely based on the assumption that 'he or she would not have fitted in'.
4. In deciding whether the claimant has proved such facts, it is important to remember that the outcome at this stage of the analysis by the tribunal will therefore usually depend on what inferences it is proper to draw from the primary facts found by the tribunal.
5. It is important to note the word 'could' in section 136(2) (above). At this stage the tribunal does not have to reach a definitive determination that such facts would lead it to the conclusion that there was an act of unlawful discrimination. At this stage a tribunal is looking at the primary facts before it to see what inferences of secondary fact could be drawn from them.
6. In considering what inferences or conclusions may be drawn from the primary facts, the tribunal must assume that there is no adequate explanation for those facts.
7. These inferences can include, in appropriate cases, any inferences that it is just and equitable to draw from an evasive or equivocal reply to a questionnaire or the questions in section 138.
8. Likewise, the tribunal must decide whether any provision of any relevant code of practice is relevant. This means that inferences may also be drawn from any failure to comply with any relevant code of practice.
9. Where the claimant has proved facts from which conclusions could be drawn that the respondent has treated the claimant less favourably on the ground of a prohibited characteristic, the burden of proof moves to the respondent.
10. It is then for the respondent to prove that he did not commit, or as the case may be, is not to be treated as having committed, that act.
11. To discharge that burden it is necessary for the respondent to prove, on the balance of probabilities, that the treatment was in no sense whatsoever on the grounds of a protected characteristic since 'no discrimination whatsoever' is compatible with the Directive on the Burden of Proof in Cases of Discrimination Based on Sex (97/80/EC). (This burden of proof now applies across all the protected characteristics.)
12. That requires a tribunal to assess not merely whether the respondent has proved an explanation for the facts from which such inferences can be drawn, but further that it is adequate to discharge the burden of proof on the balance of probabilities that a protected characteristic was not a ground for the treatment in question.

13. Since the facts necessary to prove an explanation would normally be in the possession of the respondent, a tribunal would normally expect cogent evidence to discharge that burden of proof. In particular, the tribunal will need to examine carefully explanations for failure to deal with the questionnaire procedure and/or code.

This clearly establishes a two-part process whereby the claimant first has to prove on the balance of probabilities that there has been discrimination which has been committed by the employer or for which the employer is responsible. In *ACCEPT v Consiliul National pentru Combaterea Discriminarii* [2013] Case C-81/12, ACCEPT was a gay rights organisation. Becali, a prominent figure in FC Steaua and one who had a management role, said publicly that he would close the club before accepting a gay man on the team. Becali had no authority over recruitment, but the ECJ held that his comments did not prevent his remarks from raising a presumption of discrimination, given his close and publicly known association with the club. Once discrimination is presumed, the burden then passes to the employer to show that there was none.

5.3.2 Presentation of complaint

A complaint of discrimination must be presented within three months of the act of discrimination or the last act of discrimination. Any act done over a continuing period is treated as being done at the end of that period (s 123). This can cause problems, however. In *Calder v James Finlay Corporation* [1989] IRLR 55, the employers operated a subsidised mortgage scheme which by an unwritten rule excluded women. The employee lodged a complaint five months after being refused the mortgage but within three months after leaving the employment. It was held that the refusal of the mortgage was a continuing act which continued during the whole of the time she was employed, and ceased only when she left her employment.

The question of a continuing act arose again in *Littlewoods Organisation v Traynor* [1993] IRLR 154. Here an employee had brought a grievance under the company procedure, complaining of discrimination by a supervisor. Remedial action was promised but never taken. In January 1990 the employee took voluntary redundancy and then entered a complaint of discrimination in the employment tribunal. The act had taken place more than three months before proceedings were commenced. The EAT, however, held that where remedial action was promised and never carried out, the possibility of further discrimination existed, and that per se could constitute continuing discrimination. The complaint was therefore not out of time.

In *Cast v Croydon College* [1998] IRLR 318, it was held to be a continuing act of discrimination when an employer refused on three separate occasions to allow an employee to job-share after returning from maternity leave, so that the three-month time limit started to run from the date of her resignation, prompted by the refusal. Furthermore, in *Aziz v FDA* [2010] EWCA Civ 304, Aziz had made allegations about three union officials who had failed to provide her with support on three different occasions. She argued that it was a continuing act of discrimination extending over a period of time. While the Court of Appeal found that the tribunal was entitled to find that the three acts were separate incidents, it did note that when considering whether separate incidents are a continuing act, a relevant, though not conclusive, factor is whether the same individuals were involved in the incidents.

Conversely, in *Sougrin v Haringey Health Authority* [1992] IRLR 416, the Court of Appeal held that the appointment of a nurse at a particular grade and the refusal of her appeal against that grade was a one-off act and not a continuing one. The fact that she continued to be paid at a lower salary than a white staff nurse was a consequence of a one-off act and not the act itself. Moreover, in *Tyagi v BBC World Service* [2001] IRLR 465, the Court of Appeal distinguished *Calder* and *Cast* in respect of a complainant who claimed that a discriminatory recruitment policy, which resulted in a post not being offered to him, was a continuing act allowing him to claim out of time. The Court held that there was a difference between a practice which prevented an existing employee from gaining promotion under section 139(2)(b), and a policy which prevented a non-employee from gaining a job. The former would be a continuing act, whereas the latter was not, and thus any claim had to be presented within three months of the refusal of the job.

Thus in *Okoro and anor v Taylor Woodrow Construction and ors* [2012] EWCA Civ 1590, the appellants were employed through an agency to work for Taylor Woodrow. A dispute arose, and on 7 April 2008 the appellants were told they were banned from the site. Another agency sent them to the site on 18 April and they were again told that they were banned. They presented race discrimination claims on 6 August 2008. The Court of Appeal held that there was not a continuing act. The ban was a one-off act, and therefore the race discrimination claim was out of time.

5.4 Direct discrimination

Direct discrimination occurs when a person is treated less favourably because of a protected characteristic. The relevant provision is section 13(1) of the Act. In *Sidhu v Aerospace Composite Technology Ltd* [2000] IRLR 602, the Court of Appeal stated that to find direct discrimination the complainant must show that he has been treated less favourably than a person who does not possess his protected characteristic, and that the reason for the less favourable treatment is the complainant's protected characteristic. To discover if the treatment of the complainant is less favourable, a comparison must be made with the treatment of other persons who do not share the protected characteristic and where there is 'no material difference between the circumstances relating to each case' (s 23(1)). In *Lockwood v DWP* [2013] EWCA Civ 1195, the employment tribunal in an age discrimination claim took into account age-related differences between the claimant and her comparator such as the fact that she was less likely to have family ties and would have less difficulty gaining a new job after redundancy when compared to her comparator because she was younger. The Court of Appeal held that as section 23(1) states that there should be no material differences between the claimant and her comparator, the tribunal had wrongly relied on the differences between her and her comparator. Once the correct comparator exercise had been conducted, it was found that Lockwood had suffered less favourable treatment, although such treatment was objectively justified.

In most cases, the comparison exists between people in the same circumstances, or a hypothetical comparator in similar circumstances. Where the protected characteristic is disability, the comparison also includes a comparison of abilities (s 23(2)). In any case, it is irrelevant if the alleged discriminator has the same protected characteristic as the claimant (s 24(1)). Therefore, if the protected characteristic was race and an employee had been assaulted for non-racial reasons, and had retaliated and subsequently had been dismissed, if this was because of a policy adopted by the employer which disregarded provocation and other mitigating circumstances, this was a non race-specific policy and could not found a race discrimination claim without evidence that persons of a different race in the same circumstances had been treated more favourably.

One act is sufficient and the motive behind the action is irrelevant; there is no defence once the claim has been proved, unless there is an occupational requirement or an exception applies (see Sections 5.12 and 5.13 below). In *Greig v Community Industries* [1979] IRLR 158, the applicant was on a work experience scheme for painting and decorating. She was withdrawn from the scheme when the only other girl left 'for her own good'. It was held that she had suffered direct discrimination and the motive behind the action was irrelevant. This is supported by *Amnesty International v Ahmed* [2009] IRLR 884, where it was held that the refusal to appoint a Sudanese woman to the post of Sudanese researcher, because of the risk that the organisation would appear to lack impartiality, was direct discrimination on the grounds of race. The motive of the employer was irrelevant. Trivial differences in treatment are not discriminatory, however, according to Lord Denning MR in the famous (or infamous) case of *Peake v Automotive Products* [1978] QB 233. In this case, Mr Peake claimed direct discrimination on the basis that the women in his factory were allowed to leave five minutes earlier than the men. The employer argued that the reason was that the women would be trampled in the rush if they did not leave at a different time from the men. The Court of Appeal held that there was no discrimination on three grounds: first, rules for safety and good administration could not be discriminatory; second, 'it would be very wrong if this statute were to obliterate the chivalry and courtesy which we expect mankind to give to womankind'; third, the *de minimis* principle. The first reason was considered dangerous by later critics of the judgment, because it suggested that motive was a valid consideration in deciding whether discrimination had occurred. This is clearly against the legislation. The second reason given quite frankly wipes out the whole purpose of anti-discriminatory provisions. While Lord Denning admitted he may have gone too far in *Peake* in the later case of *MOD v Jeremiah* [1980] ICR 13, he still supported the decision on the grounds of *de minimis*. While five minutes a day may not seem a lot, it adds up to 25 minutes a week which, taken over a 47-week year, is a lot of paid time to which the men were not entitled.

It has been decided that assumptions based on sex may also constitute direct discrimination. In *Horsey v Dyfed County Council* [1982] IRLR 395, Mrs Horsey was denied a place on a training course by her employers because, under county council rules, she was required to remain in her job for two years after completing the course. Her employers discovered that her husband had recently obtained employment in London, and assumed that he was the breadwinner and that his wife would resign and join him after completing the course. Mrs Horsey was never asked her intentions. It was held that she had been discriminated against. Likewise, assuming that a woman with young children will be an unreliable employee is sex discrimination (*Hurley v Mustoe* [1981] IRLR 208). On the other hand, it is not discriminatory to take into account natural differences between the sexes. In *Schmidt v Austicks Bookshops Ltd* [1977] IRLR 360, it was held not to be discriminatory to tell women they could not wear trousers to work when men were also subjected to rules on dress. In *Dansie v Metropolitan Police* [2009] All ER (D) 117, the EAT held that a male employee had not been discriminated against when told to cut his hair, in compliance with a dress code, even though a female employee would not have been so required, provided that the dress code was balanced equally between the sexes. The EAT held that the correct legal test is whether, applying contemporary standards and conventions, as well as the specific needs of the profession in question, the employer's dress code as a whole was asking its employees to display an equivalent level of smartness, as per *Smith v Safeway plc* [1996] ICR 868.

The concept of a person's sex was widened by the case of *P v S and Cornwall County Council* [1996] IRLR 347. Here, the applicant was dismissed when he informed his employer that he was about to undergo gender-reassignment surgery and live his life as a woman. The employment tribunal considered that a claim did not lie under the existing legislation but referred the question to the ECJ as to whether discrimination on the grounds of gender reassignment could be in breach of the Equal Treatment Directive. The ECJ held that P had been discriminated on the grounds of sex for two reasons. First, given that a fundamental principle of EU law is equality and the right not to be discriminated on the grounds of sex, it followed that a person was protected not only because of the sex to which they were born, but also because of the sex they chose to become. Second, the fact that P showed that she received less favourable treatment in comparison with persons of her former sex showed that the treatment she suffered was based on her sex. The Equality Act 2010 now specifically prohibits less favourable treatment on the grounds of gender reassignment. In *A v Chief Constable of West Yorkshire Police* [2004] IRLR 573, the House of Lords stated that EU law requires that a transsexual person must be recognised in his or her reassigned gender for the purposes of sex discrimination law. Thus in a case of a transsexual person, the complainant's treatment must be compared to the treatment afforded to the sex to which he or she used to belong.

After *P v S* it was thought that logically the principle of equality would also protect against discrimination on the grounds of sexual orientation. On this basis two cases were referred to the ECJ. In *Grant v South-West Trains Ltd* [1998] IRLR 206, Grant argued that a policy of paying benefits only to heterosexual partners of employees was in breach of the Equal Pay Directive (75/117/EEC). While the Advocate General gave the opinion that there was such a breach, the ECJ declined to follow that opinion and ruled that Community law, as it then stood, did not cover discrimination based on sexual orientation. In a similar case, *R v Secretary of State for Defence, ex parte Perkins* [1998] IRLR 508, the High Court originally referred the same issue to the ECJ in respect of the forces' ban on homosexuals. Again the Advocate General gave the opinion that such a ban was contrary to the Equal Treatment Directive, but that whether the ban could be justified on the basis of ensuring combat effectiveness was outside the scope of both the EC Treaty and the Directive. Following the ruling in *Grant*, however, the ECJ asked Lightman J in the High Court whether he wished to withdraw the reference. Lightman J, in considering the issue, said it must be reasonably inferred that the word 'sex' in both the Equal Pay and the Equal Treatment Directives was intended to have the same meaning, and thus, albeit reluctantly, he was bound to withdraw the reference.

Nevertheless, there appeared to be some protection from the case of *Smith v Gardner Merchant* [1998] IRLR 510. Smith, who was gay, was employed as a barman. Following a complaint about his conduct from a female member of staff, Smith was subjected to disciplinary proceedings, during which he alleged that the member of staff had made offensive remarks about his homosexuality and had punched him on one occasion. The company upheld the female member of staff's complaint, choosing not to believe the applicant's complaints, and dismissed Smith for gross misconduct. Smith complained of sex discrimination to an employment tribunal which decided it did not have the jurisdiction to hear the complaint, a position upheld by the EAT. Smith appealed to the

Court of Appeal. The Court of Appeal held that the tribunal had understandably but wrongly come to the decision that it did not have jurisdiction. The tribunal had concluded that Smith was being treated differently from a man who was not gay, and that but for his homosexuality the less favourable treatment would not have happened. As such, there would be no protection. However, the Court of Appeal held that the proper question to ask was whether Smith was treated differently from a woman in similar circumstances; if so, was this different treatment on the grounds of his sex. The correct comparator in Mr Smith's case, therefore, was a lesbian. If it could be shown that the member of staff who subjected the applicant to harassment would have treated a lesbian in the same way, there was no discrimination. If, however, she would not have harassed a lesbian, Mr Smith had been treated less favourably on the grounds of his sex. Likewise, if Mr Smith could show that the decision in not believing his allegations taken by his employers was predominantly because he was a man, and not because he was gay, again he had suffered less favourable treatment because of his sex. On the basis of the decision, the Court of Appeal remitted the case back to the tribunal. It should be noted that this case did not conflict with *Grant* or *Perkins*. There was still no protection against discrimination on the grounds of sexual orientation, but if it could be argued that the less favourable treatment was directed at gay men and the treatment of a gay woman would be different (or vice versa), the complainant would be protected.

In *Governing Body of Mayfield School v Pearce* [2001] IRLR 669 (CA), a teacher complained of homophobic abuse by pupils. The Court of Appeal held that no action lay under then legislation because there was no evidence that a gay man would not have suffered the same sort of abuse (*Smith*, above). However, the Court went on to say that at the time of the complaint the Human Rights Act 1998 was not in force, and thus there was no duty on the tribunal to interpret UK law in such a way as to ensure compatibility; but if the complaint had arisen after the Act had come into force, the abuse would have been a breach of Schedule 1, Part I (Articles 8 and 14 ECHR) and the complainant would have been able to seek redress. In addition to potential protection under the Human Rights Act 1998, protection was given in 2003 in the Employment Equality (Sexual Orientation) Regulations of that year and is now found in the Equality Act 2010.

In the important case of *James v Eastleigh Borough Council* [1990] 2 AC 751, the House of Lords discussed the interpretation of the words on the grounds of a protected characteristic in the previous legislation. In the case, Mrs James was entitled to free admission to the local swimming pool because at 61 she had reached the state pension age for women, which was then 60. Her husband, on the other hand, who was the same age as his wife, could not get free admission until he reached the state retirement age for men, which was then 65. There was no intention to discriminate on the part of the Council, it was merely giving concessions to pensioners and Mr James did not become a pensioner by the state rules until he reached 65. The House of Lords established what became known as the 'but for' test. The House affirmed that the test for discrimination is objective and motive or intention is irrelevant. If the reason for the less favourable treatment is the complainant's protected characteristic then there is discrimination. In other words, but for Mr James's sex, would he have received the concession? The answer is 'yes'. It was because he was a man that the concession did not apply. Second, their Lordships held that to use a criterion to decide an advantage, which is itself discriminatory, means that the action resulting from the use of that criterion must also be discriminatory. In other words, the state retirement age was discriminatory because it gave men less favourable treatment.

To give someone a concession based on the state retirement age therefore perpetuated the discrimination. In the employment field, many employers give concessions based on length of service. This is not discriminatory, provided that when calculating length of service, time women have out for maternity leave is counted in the calculation. If it is not then women will have to be employed longer to acquire the concession. This is less favourable treatment and is based on a selection criterion which is discriminatory because it puts women at a disadvantage. From the *James* case, if the criterion is discriminatory, so too is any action flowing from the use of that criterion.

The application of the 'but for' test may be seen in *Coyne v Home Office* [2000] ICR 1443. In that case, Coyne complained of sexual harassment by a member of staff. Her supervisor told her manager that Coyne was to blame and that she should be relocated. Her complaint was not dealt with for over two years and she was subsequently dismissed. Coyne argued that the failure to deal with her complaint of sexual harassment constituted sex discrimination. The Court of Appeal held that in order for a claim to lie, Coyne had to show that but for her sex the complaint of harassment would have been investigated. Here, however, there was no evidence that the Home Office would have treated a complaint by a man in a more favourable way. The detriment she suffered was the failure of the Home Office to investigate her complaint, but the evidence did not show that this failure was due to her sex. How far the 'but for' test will be relevant to interpretations under the Equality Act 2010 has yet to be seen.

Under the old law, the Sex Discrimination Act (SDA) 1975 and the Race Relations Act (RRA) 1976 used similar wording but there was an important difference. The SDA 1975 referred to less favourable treatment of a woman on the grounds of her sex, whereas the RRA 1976 referred to less favourable treatment on racial grounds. The importance of the distinction was seen in the case of *Showboat Entertainment Centre v Owens* [1984] 1 WLR 384, where an employee was dismissed for failing to obey an order not to admit young black men into an amusement arcade. The Court of Appeal held that, on the wording of the RRA 1976, discrimination had occurred if the reason for the less favourable treatment was race – the Act did not specify that it had to be the complainant's race. The employee had been dismissed because he refused to obey an order which was racially discriminatory, therefore he had been dismissed on racial grounds (see also *Weathersfield Ltd t/a Van Truck Rentals v Sargent* [1999] IRLR 94). While the judgments were to be welcomed, the basis of them led to the question of whether the same decision would have been reached if Mr Owens or Mrs Sargent had been dismissed or had suffered for refusing to obey an order not to discriminate against women, as the reason for the dismissal would not have been on the basis of the claimant's sex. Section 13 of the Equality Act 2010 removes this inconsistency, as the test for direct discrimination is less favourable treatment because of a protected characteristic. This not only protects against situations such as *Showboat Entertainments* (above), but also where there is discrimination based on a person's association with another who has a protected characteristic. In *Coleman v Attridge Law* [2008] IRLR 722, Coleman successfully claimed disability discrimination, after reference to the ECJ, on the basis of less favourable treatment because of the time off she had to take in order to look after her disabled son. The ECJ held that the then Disability Discrimination Act 1995 did not give effect to the Framework Directive which is intended to protect those who are associated with disabled persons. The Equality Act 2010 thus gives protection to all who associate with persons who have a protected characteristic and are discriminated against on the grounds of that association.

5.4.1   Exceptions

While normally direct discrimination cannot be defended unless there is an occupational requirement (OR), section 13 does provide exceptions where direct discrimination may be justified in relation to age, pregnancy or childbirth, and disability.

In respect of age, direct discrimination can be justified if the employer can show it was a proportionate means of achieving a legitimate aim (s 13(2)). See, for example, *Rolls Royce plc v UNITE* [2009] IRLR 576.

In respect of disability, a non-disabled person has no claim if the reason for the claim is that the discriminator has treated a disabled person more favourably than the claimant (s 13(3)). See, for example, *Archibald v Fife Council* [2004] IRLR 651.

Lastly, a man cannot claim discrimination because of special treatment afforded to a woman in connection with pregnancy or childbirth (s 136)).

5.4.2   Discrimination arising from disability

Section 15 of the Equality Act 2010 is a new provision which did not exist under the previous law. It states that a person discriminates against a disabled person if he treats the disabled person unfavourably because of something arising in consequence of the person's disability and the employer cannot show that the treatment is a proportionate means of achieving a legitimate aim. However, a claim will not lie if the employer can show that he did not know, or could not be reasonably expected to know, that the person was disabled.

This replaces the old law on disability-related discrimination which no longer exists. However, some of the old case law may still be relevant to an interpretation of section 15. In *Reedman v Fresh Connection Ltd* (1997) (unreported), the employment tribunal stated that there was no need for any ill intention or improper motive on the part of the employer, but there had to be a causal connection between the less favourable treatment and the disability. According to the EAT in *O'Neill v Symm & Co Ltd* [1998] IRLR, to establish this causal connection it is necessary for the employer to know about the complainant's disability at the time of the less favourable treatment, a requirement re-iterated in section 15. Furthermore, the reason for the less favourable treatment must relate to the person's disability and not to some other factor. For example, in *Hanlon v University of Huddersfield* (1998) (unreported), a disabled employee was suspended because of his refusal to perform a contractual duty. By contrast in *Clark v Novacold* [1999] IRLR 318, the employee was dismissed because of his absence from work, which was caused by his disability; and in *Cox v Post Office* (1998) IDS Brief 609, an employment tribunal found that a postman had been dismissed because of his disability since his absences were caused mainly by his asthma, and if these absences had been ignored when invoking the irregular attenders procedure he would have received only an informal warning. However, in *O'Hanlon v HM Revenue and Customs* [2007] IRLR 404, the claimant, who was off work with clinical depression, argued that the employer had discriminated against her on the grounds of disability when it adhered to the normal sick pay policy of six months on full pay and six months on half pay. Her argument was that as her absence was disability-related, the employer should have paid her 12 months' full pay. The EAT (confirmed by the Court of Appeal) held that the reduction in pay because of sick absence when the employee was disabled was discrimination on the grounds of disability but that it was justified, as to pay full pay would go against the policy of the legislation, which is to assist the integration of disabled persons into the workplace, and would also be a disincentive for disabled people to return to work.

In *Reedman*, the employment tribunal said that once it is shown that the applicant is disabled and a prima facie case of less favourable treatment has been established, the tribunal should look to the employer for an explanation. If that explanation is inadequate, it is reasonable to infer that the reason for the less favourable treatment is the applicant's disability. This is the application of the burden of proof in section 136, that is, if the complainant establishes a prima facie case, the burden shifts to the employer to prove the reason for the treatment was not related to the person's disability.

Prior to amendments to the old legislation in 2003 there was no statutory definition of a 'comparator'. In *O'Neill*, the EAT discussed the relevant comparator. The EAT said:

> An employer can be held to have treated a disabled employee, for a reason related to that disabled employee's disability, less favourably than in comparable circumstances he would treat an otherwise comparable employee, without knowing of the fact of the disability.

Therefore in *Clark*, the employment tribunal compared the employee's treatment with that of a non-disabled, long-term sick employee who had had the same amount of absence and like the applicant was unlikely to return in the foreseeable future. Clark appealed to the EAT, arguing that the employment tribunal had used the wrong comparator. He argued that as his inability to attend work was because of his disability, it was inappropriate to compare him with someone who was also absent for a non-disability reason; the comparator should be someone at work and able to carry out the normal functions of the job. The EAT, however, rejected Clark's argument and upheld the employment tribunal decision that the correct comparator was a non-disabled employee who was off sick for the same length of time as Clark, and who was unlikely to return in the foreseeable future. The EAT itself, however, said that it was 'without great confidence' that it rejected Clark's arguments.

Clark appealed to the Court of Appeal ([1999] IRLR 318). The Court reversed the decision of the EAT. It said that the test for less favourable treatment is based on the reason for the treatment of the disabled person and not on the fact of his disability: 'It does not turn on a like for like comparison of the treatment of the disabled person and of others in similar circumstances.' Thus the correct comparator was a person who has not been absent from work or who has the same absence record when any disability-related absences are ignored. This was also the decision of the EAT in *British Sugar plc v Kirker* [1998] IRLR 624, which did not consider its earlier decision in *Clark*. The House of Lords' decision in *London Borough of Lewisham v Malcolm* [2008] UKHL 43 overruled *Clark*. Their Lordships stated that the correct comparator was someone who was not disabled and had been off for the same length of time as the disabled person. They also reiterated that the employer must know of the disability before he or she can be guilty of discrimination. While a housing case, the EAT in *Child Support Agency v Truman* [2009] IRLR 277 held that *Malcolm* applied in employment cases. Clark HHJ said that 'in our judgement the narrower comparator favoured by the majority in *Malcolm* applies equally in the employment context. The wider comparator used in *Novacold* should no longer apply (unless and until the legislation is further amended by Parliament)'. However, *Malcolm* severely limited protection for a large number of disabled people, although it was argued that the duty to make reasonable adjustments (see Section 5.6

below) could alleviate its effect. The government was not happy with consequences of the *Malcolm* decision. As such, section 15 does not require a comparator in order for the claimant to allege discrimination.

Section 15(1)(b) provides the employer with a defence if he can show that the less-favourable treatment is a proportionate means of achieving a legitimate aim. While the cases discussed below are under the old law, it is felt that some can be applied to the new provision in section 15.

The employment tribunal in *Terry v Sheldon School* (1998) (unreported) stated that the test of the defence under the old law was much stricter than the concept of reasonableness under section 98(4) of the ERA 1996. However, in *Jones v Post Office* [2001] IRLR 384, the Court of Appeal held that when looking at the defence, the task facing tribunals is 'not very different to the task which they have to perform in cases of unfair dismissal', in which they have to adopt a 'range of reasonable responses approach'. The Court said that in both cases the tribunal may come to a different conclusion from the employer, but it must 'respect the opinion of the employer in the one case if it is within the range of reasonable responses and in the other if the reason given is material and substantial'. According to the employment tribunal in *Holmes v Whittingham & Porter Ltd* (1998) IDS Brief 609, this strict test is because the aim of the legislation is not to promote equality for disabled employees but to require the employer to take steps to protect disabled employees. Thus, in the case, although the tribunal found that Holmes had been fairly dismissed for the purposes of the ERA 1996, in that the employer had acted reasonably within the provisions of section 98(4) of that Act, the employer had not justified his less favourable treatment.

Health and safety reasons have been held to justify dismissal in a number of employment tribunal cases (for example, *Smith v Carpets International UK plc* (1998) IDS Brief 611 and *Reilly v EXI Ltd* (1997) (unreported)). Furthermore, in *Fozard v Greater Manchester Police Authority* (June 1997) *Personnel Management*, Jane, a disabled applicant who was not shortlisted for a job which involved word processing because of her inability to produce accurate written work, was not discriminated against, as although some of the errors were due to her disability, others were due to carelessness, and the employer's need for accuracy was material to the particular case and substantial. Conversely, in *Holmes* (above), while reliance on a company medical report, prepared by a general practitioner, was sufficient to defeat an unfair dismissal claim, it was not sufficient to satisfy the defence in a disability claim. The employers should have obtained a specialist's report before acting, and therefore the dismissal of the disabled applicant was unjustified treatment (see also *Vickary v British Telecommunications plc* [1999] IRLR 680).

5.4.3 Gender reassignment: absence from work

Section 16 offers protection where an employer treats a transsexual person less favourably due to absences that are because of gender reassignment (for example, hormone treatment) than the employer would treat that person if the absences were due to sickness or injury, and it is not reasonable for that person to be treated less favourably.

Note that there is a need for the comparison with the treatment the claimant would have received if the absence was due to sickness or injury, and the employer has the defence of reasonableness.

5.4.4 Pregnancy and maternity

By section 18, an employer discriminates against a woman if, in the protected period in relation to a pregnancy of hers, he treats her unfavourably because of the pregnancy or because of an illness suffered by her as a result of her pregnancy (s 18(2)). If the treatment of the woman is as the result of a decision taken during the protected period, it is to be regarded as occurring during the protected period even if the actual implementation of the decision occurs after the protected period (s 18(5)). The protected period starts when the pregnancy begins, and finishes at the end of additional maternity leave or when the woman returns to work if that is earlier (s 18(6)). If she does not have the right to ordinary and additional maternity leave, it ends two weeks after the end of the pregnancy. During this period a woman cannot claim sex discrimination as a result of pregnancy or illness arising from it (s 13(8); s 18(7)).

An employer also discriminates against a woman if he treats her unfavourably because she is seeking to exercise, has exercised or sought to exercise her right to compulsory, ordinary or additional maternity leave (s 18(3)(4)). Note that there is no need for the woman to rely on a comparator.

Until 2005, when pregnancy and maternity became specific forms of protection under previous legislation, discrimination on the grounds of pregnancy or maternity was based on the concept of sex discrimination, a claim now barred by the Equality Act 2010 (see above). However, it is felt that some of the old cases will still be relevant when interpreting the new provisions. The original decision in *Brown v Rentokil* [1995] IRLR 211 was that the dismissal of a pregnant woman, who had exhausted her period of sick leave, was dismissal for sickness and not pregnancy. Mrs Brown appealed to the House of Lords, which referred a number of questions to the ECJ, in particular whether it was contrary to the Equal Treatment Directive to dismiss a woman during her pregnancy as a result of absence through illness arising from that pregnancy, and whether it was relevant that the dismissal occurred in accordance with a contractual provision entitling the employer to dismiss, irrespective of gender, after a stipulated number of weeks of absence.

The ECJ ([1998] IRLR 445) referred to the EC Pregnant Workers Directive (92/85/EC) and noted that Article 10 prohibited dismissal during the period from the beginning of the pregnancy to the end of maternity leave (save in exceptional circumstances not connected with the woman's condition). Hence the dismissal of a woman during pregnancy for absences due to such incapacity 'must therefore be regarded as essentially based on the fact of pregnancy'. In respect of pathological conditions caused by pregnancy or childbirth which arise after the end of maternity leave, the action would then lie as a claim for discrimination on the grounds of the protected characteristic of sex. The question then is whether the female worker's absences are treated in the same way as those of a male worker; if they are, then there is no sex discrimination. Absences during the pregnancy and during maternity leave cannot be taken into account for the computation of the sickness period for dismissal under a contractual procedure. In deciding *Brown*, the ECJ went against its earlier decision of *Handels- og Kontorfunktionaerernes Forbund i Danmark (acting on behalf of Larsson) v Dansk Handel & Service (acting on behalf of Fotex Supermarket A/S)* [1997] IRLR 643. The decision is now embedded in the Equality Act 2010. It is interesting to note, however, that prior to the ECJ ruling in *Brown*, the EAT decided that the dismissal of a woman suffering from post-natal depression and who thus failed to return to work after her maternity leave period, was a pregnancy-related dismissal and therefore sex discrimination (*Caledonia Bureau Investment & Property v Caffrey* [1998] IRLR 110). Note also *Patefield v Belfast City Council* [2000] IRLR 664, where it was held that the replacement of a contract worker with a permanent employee while she was on maternity leave, and when the employer knew she wished to return, was sex discrimination. This would now be a dismissal on pregnancy or maternity grounds as it occurred during maternity leave.

In respect of actions other than dismissal, again the ECJ, in the case of *Caisse Nationale d'Assurance Vieillesse des Travailleurs Salariés v Thibault* [1998] IRLR 399, has held that a woman who was deprived of the right to an annual performance assessment, and consequently the possibility of qualifying for promotion, because she was on maternity leave, was discriminated against. If she had not been on maternity leave, she would have been assessed and could have qualified for promotion the following year. Furthermore, in *GUS Home Shopping Ltd v Green* [2001] IRLR 75, it was held that an employer had discriminated when a discretionary bonus was not paid to Green when she was on maternity leave. The bonus was paid on the successful transfer of the marketing department in which she worked to another office. The transfer had occurred while she was on maternity leave, and the only reason she was not paid it was because she had been absent at the relevant time. The EAT held that the bonus scheme could not be divorced from the contract of employment as all it required was the proper performance of the employee's responsibilities under the contract.

5.5 Indirect discrimination

The second type of discrimination recognised by the legislation is discrimination against a particular group which shares a protected characteristic, and which prejudices the complainant, hence the title 'indirect discrimination'. The definition of this type of discrimination is to be found in section 19 of the Act.

For indirect discrimination to be actionable, the following four conditions must be satisfied:

1. the employer applies a provision, criterion or practice (PCP) which he applies or would apply equally to persons with whom the claimant does not share the protected characteristic;
2. which puts, or would put, persons with whom the claimant shares the characteristic at a particular disadvantage when compared to other persons who do not share it;
3. which puts the claimant at that disadvantage; and
4. which the employer cannot show to be a proportionate means of achieving a legitimate aim.

The protected characteristics are those in section 19(3), which are all the protected characteristics in section 4 excluding pregnancy and maternity.

Thus in *Price v CSC* [1978] IRLR 3, the imposition of an age requirement of 17–28 for promotion to executive officer was held to be indirect discrimination, as more women than men would be out of the labour market having children between those ages. Such age limits could also be indirect race discrimination, if potential applicants were immigrants who were unlikely to have the necessary qualifications for the job by the age of 28, because they had entered the educational system at a later age than the indigenous population.

While examples are easy to state, it is necessary to examine the four conditions in more detail.

5.5.1 Provision, criterion or practice

Given that to claim successfully, the claimant must show a discriminatory provision, etc is being applied, it is necessary for the courts to identify the offending provision properly. This has been demonstrated in equal pay claims, where an argument may be raised that pay structures can create indirect discrimination. For example in the equal pay case of *Jenkins v Kingsgate Clothing Productions Ltd* [1981] IRLR 228 (ECJ), it was held that a pay structure which paid less to part-timers could be justified if there was a sound economic reason for the difference, and it was irrelevant that this created indirect discrimination. A similar case was decided in the ECJ in the form of *Enderby v Frenchay Health Authority and Secretary of State for Health* [1994] 1 All ER 495. In this case, one of the arguments of the complainant speech therapists was that by placing them on a lower salary scale, indirect discrimination occurred because speech therapists are predominantly female. In *Jenkins*, the requirement was one of full-time working, and although there was no such identifiable requirement in *Enderby*, the therapists won their claim. This is an important case because the real argument, of course, is that women tend to be concentrated in traditionally low-paid work and that the provisions of the legislation are insufficient to deal with this problem. This will be discussed in the next chapter.

In *British Airways plc v Starmer* [2005] IRLR 863, a female pilot asked to reduce her hours by 50 per cent after having a baby. The employer refused on the basis that it would be difficult to reorganise schedules and it would be expensive to train replacements. After she sued for indirect sex discrimination, the company introduced a policy saying that pilots could reduce their hours by only 25 per cent for safety reasons. The EAT held that the decision not to allow her to go part-time was a PCP, even though the company argued that at the time of its refusal, there was no policy in place and the decision had been a one-off based on the employee's request. This shows a liberal interpretation of 'provision, criterion or practice'. In *Chief Constable of West Yorkshire Police v Homer* [2009] IRLR 262, the EAT held that the requirement to have a law degree to move on to a higher salary band did not put a 61-year-old employee at a particular disadvantage because of his age, even though he could not obtain the degree before he retired. Elias P said that the requirement of a law degree was not something required only of those over a certain age, nor was it more difficult for an older person to obtain the qualification. The EAT did state, however, that had the claimant established the disadvantage, it would have concluded that such discrimination was not justified as the requirement was not a proportionate means of achieving the recruitment and retention of appropriately qualified staff. However, on appeal (*Homer v Chief Constable of West Yorkshire Police* [2012] UKSC 15), the Supreme Court held that there was age discrimination, but remitted the case for a tribunal to consider whether such discrimination was justified.

5.5.2 The comparative group

The issue of the comparative group is confusing. Is the comparison the workforce nationally, the workforce locally, or the workforce within the particular workplace? The problem rests on the fact that tribunals choose the relevant comparative group, which can lead to some confusing decisions, although the tribunals should look to the group that the employer is targeting, which may be national or local depending on the employer's business.

The definition which was in force between 2001 and 2005 required the claimant to show that a larger proportion of persons sharing the protected characteristic, compared with others who did not share that characteristic, was disadvantaged by the provision, etc. In *Rutherford v Secretary of State for Trade and Industry (No 2)* [2004] IRLR 892, the Court of Appeal held that the sections of the ERA 1996 which then excluded those who had reached the age of 65 from unfair dismissal or redundancy compensation (now repealed) did not have a disparate impact on men. The relevant pool of comparison was the entire workforce to which the requirement applied – that is, not just those disadvantaged by the age limit. On that comparison the differences were very small and did not show a disparate impact on men. The amended definition does not require the complainant to show proportions, so it is debatable whether *Rutherford* would be decided the same way today. However, a pool still needs to be established to show that a particular group has been put at a disadvantage.

Nevertheless, while a claimant no longer has to produce statistical evidence, there is still the risk that the pool identified by the claimant is not the one the tribunal will chose, albeit that it was established in *Starmer* that the pool may be a hypothetical one. In *Grundy v British Airways* [2008] IRLR 74, Sedley LJ said 'one of the striking things about both race and sex discrimination is that … three decades of litigation have failed to produce any universal formula for locating the correct pool'.

In *Hardys & Hansons v Lax* [2005] EWCA Civ 846, the Court of Appeal held that the range of reasonable responses test, applicable when assessing the fairness of a dismissal (see Chapter 9 and Section 9.6), does not apply to the defence in indirect discrimination. Thomas LJ held that the principle of proportionality requires the tribunal to take into account the business needs of the business, but it has to make its own decision as to whether the proposal (in this case for a full-time appointment) is reasonably necessary. A tribunal cannot consider only whether the employer's views are within a range of reasonable responses. He added that where the employer is relying on the economic needs of the business, it would be expected to adduce sufficient evidence to enable the tribunal to 'set out at least a basic economic analysis of the business and its needs'.

The idea of a requirement of full-time working being discriminatory to women was accepted in *Holmes v Home Office* [1984] IRLR 260. In *Meade-Hill v British Council* [1997] IRLR 522, the Court of Appeal confirmed the decision of the EAT and decided that the imposition of a mobility clause was indirectly discriminatory because it was common knowledge that more women than not were secondary earners who would therefore find it difficult to comply with such a requirement to be mobile. Furthermore, in *Whiffen v Oxfordshire CC* (2001) *The Times*, 3 April, it was held that a redundancy selection policy selecting fixed-term workers first was indirectly discriminatory to women. This decision was supported by the implementation of the Fixed Term Work Directive (99/70/EC) in October 2002.

The tribunal may reject the comparative group as being inappropriate, as seen in *Rutherford* (above). In *Pearse v Bradford Metropolitan District Council* [1988] IRLR 379, one requirement of eligibility to apply for a post of senior lecturer was that the applicants had to work full-time at the college run by the local authority. Pearse claimed that the requirement was discriminatory, and produced statistics that out of the academic staff,

21.8 per cent of women could apply compared with 46.7 per cent of men. The EAT held that the comparative group was too wide. The group should have been those staff with the necessary qualifications to apply and not all academic staff. The complainant had therefore failed to show that the requirement was indirectly discriminatory. *Jones v University of Manchester* [1993] IRLR 218 was the first case where the Court of Appeal was required to decide the relevant comparative group. In this case the university had advertised a post requiring a graduate between the ages of 27 and 35. Mrs Jones had been a mature student who graduated at 41. She argued that the job was asking for mature graduates, that is, those who had graduated after the age of 25, and as such the age limit of 35 was indirect discrimination against women because fewer mature women students than mature male students would complete their degree by that age. The Court of Appeal held that the applicant was choosing too narrow a comparative group. The advertisement was asking for graduates and not those who had graduated after the age of 25. To place any other interpretation would involve redrafting the advertisement. As such, there was no discriminatory effect on women.

5.5.3 Proportionate means of achieving a legitimate aim

The third stage in the establishment of an indirect discrimination claim is that the provision, etc is not a proportionate means of achieving a legitimate aim. In the early case of *Steel v Union of Post Office Workers* [1978] ICR 181, the employers operated a rule which gave the choice of postal rounds to the most senior post staff. Seniority was based on length of service as a permanent employee. Mrs Steel had been employed since 1961 but, because of Post Office rules, women could not hold permanent status until 1975. Mrs Steel lost her choice of round to a man who had been employed since 1973, who, on the rules, had two years' seniority over Mrs Steel. The EAT said that, in looking at the defence, a tribunal had to distinguish between a provision which was necessary and one which was merely convenient for the employer. In the case, it was not necessary to base seniority on permanent length of service; it was merely convenient because it had always been calculated in that way. Mrs Steel had therefore been the victim of indirect discrimination.

In *Bilka-Kaufhaus v Weber von Hartz* [1987] ICR 110 (ECJ), the ECJ, in interpreting Article 141 TEC (now Article 157 TFEU – the principle of equal pay for male and female workers), stated that the employer would have to show 'objectively justified' grounds to make out the defence, in that the employer must show that any factors which have a disparate effect on one group 'correspond to a real need on the part of the undertaking, and are appropriate with a view to achieving the objectives pursued and are necessary to that end'. This interpretation was supported in *Hampson v DES* [1989] IRLR 69, where Balcombe LJ held that this 'requires an objective balance to be struck between the discriminatory effect of the (provision) and the reasonable needs of the party who applies that condition'. This balancing is to be done by the tribunal, as indicated by the EAT in *Cobb v Secretary of State for Employment and Manpower Services Commission* [1989] IRLR 464 when it said:

> It is for the tribunal to carry out the balancing exercise involved, taking into account all the surrounding circumstances and giving due emphasis to the degree of discrimination caused against the object or aim to be achieved – the principle of proportionality.

In *Allonby v Accrington and Rossendale College* [2001] IRLR 364, the Court of Appeal gave guidance on the principle of proportionality. The Court held that once the tribunal had identified the provision that had a disparate impact, the tribunal had to demonstrate that it had objectively weighed the justification for the provision against its discriminatory effect. At the minimum this meant conducting a critical evaluation of whether the employer's reasons demonstrated a real need. If there was a real need, the tribunal should consider the seriousness of the disparate impact and make an evaluation of whether those reasons were sufficient to outweigh it. If the tribunal gets the balance wrong, the EAT will intervene. Thus in *Saint Matthias Church of England School v Crizzle* [1993] ICR 401, there was a condition that any applicant for the post of head teacher had to be a communicant (that is a Christian receiving Holy Communion). Crizzle was an Asian and a Christian but was not a communicant, and therefore he brought a claim of indirect racial discrimination. His complaint was upheld by the tribunal, which decided that the requirement that the head teacher be a communicant was not necessary for efficient education and was therefore not justifiable. The EAT disagreed. The EAT held that the school was concerned with spiritual worship as well as efficient education. This was a legitimate objective, and the means of achieving it – that is, requiring the head teacher to be a communicant – was reasonable when weighed against the discriminatory effect.

In *Azmi v Kirklees MBC* [2007] All ER 484, the EAT held that a Muslim teaching assistant had not been directly discriminated against on the ground of religion or belief by a requirement that she remove her veil when teaching. While it concluded that the requirement was indirectly discriminatory, it was justified as a proportionate means of achieving the legitimate aim of raising the educational achievements of the pupils. In *Chondol v Liverpool City Council* [2009] All ER (D) 155, it was held that a social worker who was specifically prohibited from overt promotion of religious beliefs in his work, was not dismissed contrary to the regulations when he was sacked for inappropriately promoting the Christian religion. Similarly in *London Borough of Islington v Ladele* [2009] IRLR 154, the EAT held that a registrar who was disciplined for refusing to conduct marriages between same-sex couples, which was contrary to her Christian beliefs, had not been the subject of discrimination. She had refused to comply with the Council's Dignity for All policy, and her complaint was not that she had been treated differently from others but rather that she had not been treated differently. Likewise in *Eweida v British Airways plc* [2009] IRLR 78, a claimant lost her claim of religious discrimination after being barred from wearing a cross at work. The EAT said that her claim should have been one of indirect discrimination, and she had failed to prove that a group was put at a particular disadvantage.

In *Seldon v Clarkson, Wright and James* [2012] UKSC 16, the Supreme Court considered that a requirement for partners to retire at 65 could constitute age discrimination unless there was a legitimate aim to achieve and the age limit was a proportionate means of achieving that aim. However, the assumption that performance declined with age was not justification as there was no evidence to support that claim. The case was remitted back to the tribunal to consider if the other aims raised by the respondents justified the rule. However, a lot of cases on age discrimination have upheld the employer's defence. In *Rolls-Royce plc v UNITE* [2009] EWCA Civ 387, the Court of Appeal has upheld UNITE's argument that although a LIFO (last in first out) redundancy selection procedure was indirect age discrimination, it was a proportionate means of achieving the legitimate aim of carrying out compulsory redundancies peaceably. In *Kucukdeveci v Sweden GmbH & Co* (Case C-555/07) [2010] IRLR 346, the ECJ held that although it was a legitimate aim to afford employers greater flexibility in personnel management by alleviating the burden on them in respect of dismissal of young workers who were more likely to be more mobile in relation to job changes, legislation which allowed employers to disregard all years of service before the age of 25 when calculating notice requirements was not a proportionate means of achieving that aim. However, in *Wolf v Stadt Frankfurt am Main* [2010] IRLR 44 the ECJ held that the upper age limit of 30 for those joining the fire service in jobs which required fire-fighting on the ground and rescuing people, was justified. This was because the legitimate aim was the operational capacity and proper functioning of the fire service. Given that anyone recruited had to undergo two years' training, evidence showed that if recruited under the age of 30, they would be able to fulfil the physical demands of the role for 15 or 20 years and thus could replace older firefighters over the age of 45 who, evidence showed, had reduced lung capacity and were therefore unable to continue in that role. Thus the age limit was a proportionate means of achieving the legitimate aim. Likewise in *Kraft Foods v Hastie* (2010) UKEAT 002/10/0607, a rule which capped the amount of redundancy pay so that it did not exceed wages payable up to retirement was a proportionate means of achieving protection of employees' income after redundancy, and it was not improper to have a rule which saved the company the expense of giving a windfall to a redundant employee. Similarly in *Woodcock v Cumbria Primary Care Trust* [2012] IRLR 491, the claimant was dismissed for redundancy with no consultation because, if consultation had been undertaken, his notice of termination would have expired after his 50th birthday, which would have meant that his redundancy pay would have increased from £220,000 by at least another £500,000. There was a genuine redundancy situation, and the decision to dismiss him had already been taken before the Trust realised the significance of the timing. Consequently, it deliberately dispensed with the consultation to save costs. The aim of saving money, in combination with the genuine need for redundancy, was found to be a legitimate aim. The lack of consultation was appropriate because it would not have made a difference.

The government abolished the default retirement age in October 2011. The decision in *Rosenbladt v Oellerking Gebaudereinigungsges mBh* Case 45/09 [2010] All ER (D) 101 may help employers in this respect. The ECJ held that while a compulsory retirement age was prima facie age discrimination, it might be justified if:

1. the retirement age had been negotiated with the union;
2. the employee will receive a pension (on the facts a state pension); and
3. compulsory retirement has been widespread in the relevant country for a long time without having had any effect on the levels of employment.

In *EC v Hungary* [2012] All ER (D) 345, the ECJ held that lowering the compulsory retirement age for judges from 70 to 62 was age discrimination. The aims behind doing so were legitimate: it was wished, first, to standardise the age limit for professions in the public sector and, second, to establish a more balanced age structure facilitating access for younger lawyers into the profession. However, while lowering the age was proportionate in respect of the first aim, it was not in relation to the second. There was no staggering of the change, and so in the short term there would be a lot of vacancies which would be filled with younger lawyers, and this would not create a more balanced age structure.

In *Seldon v Clarkson, Wright and James* [2013] UKSC 16, Seldon, under the terms of the partnership agreement, was forced to retire at age 65. He claimed age discrimination. In the Supreme Court, Lady Hale considered the Strasbourg jurisprudence and concluded that two legitimate aims which appeared to come from the European Court were inter-generational fairness and dignity. In *Seldon*, the partners argued that having a defined retirement age was pursuing the legitimate aims of (i) creating vacancies which would be filled by younger lawyers, and (ii) allowing a partner to leave with dignity, so alleviating any need for performance management. As such her Ladyship concluded that the partnership had established legitimate aims, and remitted the case back to the tribunal to establish whether the imposition of a retirement age of 65 was a proportionate means of achieving such aims. (The tribunal did so uphold.)

5.5.4 Disadvantage to the claimant

The final hurdle in an indirect discrimination claim is that the claimant must suffer a disadvantage because of the application of the provision, etc. By this last hurdle the 2010 Act limits the pool of complainants to those who actually apply for a job, etc and are turned down because of the application of the provision, etc.

The Act refers to a claimant suffering a disadvantage because of the provision, etc being applied. The House of Lords, however, made it clear in *Mandla v Dowell Lee* [1983] 2 AC 548 that the fact that someone can theoretically comply with the provision, etc, does not mean that that person has not suffered a disadvantage. In the case it was theoretically possible for a Sikh boy to comply with the condition of having short hair, but not reasonable to expect him to do so, given the requirement of the Sikh religion that hair remains uncut.

The problem in this area is what exactly constitutes a disadvantage. In *De Souza v AA* [1986] IRLR 103, it was held that suffering distress was not a detriment under the old law. Whether it would now be held to constitute a disadvantage, which seems to connote a lesser test, has yet to be seen. In *Clymo v Wandsworth London Borough Council* [1989] IRLR 241, the EAT held that a refusal to allow a woman in a managerial post the opportunity of job sharing was not subjecting the claimant to a detriment. The tribunal accepted the argument that job sharing was not available for managers, and if the facility was not available to others on her grade, she had not suffered a detriment by being denied it. This discussion on the meaning of 'detriment' leads to a circular argument and creates loopholes in the legislation. The argument that there can be no detriment if the facility is not in existence must be fallacious.

5.6 Duty to make reasonable adjustments

The duty to make reasonable adjustments is a form of positive discrimination in favour of disabled persons. The duty is found in section 20 of the Equality Act 2010, and replicates and enhances the previous law. The duty comprises three requirements.

1. The first requirement arises where a PCP puts a disabled person at a substantial disadvantage compared to a non-disabled person; the employer is required to take such steps as are reasonable to remove the disadvantage (s 20(3)).
2. The second requirement arises where a physical feature puts a disabled person at a substantial disadvantage compared to a non-disabled person; the employer is required to take such steps as are reasonable to remove the disadvantage (s 20(4)), for example, installing a wheelchair ramp.

3. The third requirement arises where the disabled person would, but for the provision of an auxiliary aid, be put at a substantial disadvantage; the employer is required to take such steps as it is reasonable to have to take to provide the auxiliary aid (s 20(5)). Auxiliary aid includes an auxiliary service.

By section 20(7), an employer cannot require a disabled person to pay for the costs of making reasonable adjustments.

Thus the claimant must show substantial disadvantage for the duty to come into play. This means a substantial disadvantage when compared to a non-disabled person. In *Newcastle upon Tyne Hospitals NHS Foundation Trust v Bagley* [2012] EqLR 634, the claimant was a radiographer who had been injured in an accident at work which resulted in a long period of absence. During her absence she was paid a Temporary Injury Allowance, which topped up her sick pay to 85 per cent of her pay but which was available only to those who were absent from work and not to those who were on reduced hours due to sickness. The absence was initially for four months, after which the claimant made a phased return to work; she was then told that in order to receive full pay, she would need to take annual leave when she was not working. After she had used up all her annual leave she was off work for a further 21 months. During this time she did not work part-time because of the financial consequences – that is she would only have received a reduced salary and not 85 per cent of her full pay which she received because she was absent. The employment tribunal held that the employer had failed to make reasonable adjustments by not adjusting the claimant's pay to at least 85 per cent of her full pay when she was on reduced hours due to sickness, so that she could return to work part time. The EAT disagreed. It held that the claimant had not been put at a substantial disadvantage when compared with non-disabled people as the policy applied to everyone.

By Schedule 8, paragraph 20 to the 2010 Act, a person is not subject to the duty to make reasonable adjustments if the person does not know, and could not reasonably be expected to know, that a person is disabled or is likely to be placed at a substantial disadvantage.

In *Environment Agency v Rowan* [2008] IRLR 218, the EAT stated the matters that must be identified by a tribunal to determine whether the duty arises:

1. the PCP applied by or on behalf of the employer;
2. the physical feature of premises occupied by the employer;
3. the identity of non-disabled comparators (where appropriate); and
4. the nature and extent of the substantial disadvantage suffered by the claimant.

In *Eastern & Coastal PCT v Grey* [2009] IRLR 429, the EAT stated that the defence in Schedule 8, paragraph 20 requires each of the four following limbs to be satisfied, that is, that the employer:

- does not know that the person is disabled;
- does not know that the disabled person is likely to be at a substantial disadvantage compared with non-disabled persons;
- could not be reasonably expected to know that the disabled person had a disability; and
- could not be reasonably expected to know that the disabled person is likely to be placed at a substantial disadvantage in comparison with non-disabled persons.

While the above indicates when the duty applies, Schedule 8 provides that employers do not have to make reasonable adjustments in certain circumstances. The EAT, in *DWP v Alam* (2009) UKEAT 0241/09/0911, stated that there are two questions which must be asked when deciding whether the schedule applies.

▶ Did the employer know both that the employee was disabled and that his disability was liable to affect him in the manner set out in section 20(1)?
▶ If not, ought the employer to have known both that the employee was disabled and that his disability was liable to affect him in the manner set out in section 20(1)?

The EAT also stated that the requirements are not cumulative (as was assumed after the *Grey* decision). If an employer could not reasonably have been expected to know that the employee's disability would have the effect set out in section 20(1), no duty to make reasonable adjustments arises.

In *Kenny v Hampshire Constabulary* [1999] IRLR 76, the EAT held that the duty applies only to job-related arrangements and does not require the employer to provide a carer to deal with an employee's personal needs. It is suggested that this interpretation is outside the spirit of the Act, in that if a disabled person cannot use a toilet without help, that person cannot work.

The duty arises when the employer knows, or could be reasonably expected to know, that the person has a disability and as a result that person is placed at a substantial disadvantage. In *Archibald v Fife Council* [2004] IRLR 651, Mrs Archibald had been a roadsweeper when a complication after surgery left her virtually unable to walk. Subsequently, she undertook administrative work and was assessed as 'more than capable of carrying out work in an office environment'. The Council's office jobs were on a higher grade than manual ones, and it was the Council's policy that all employees seeking redeployment on a higher salary had to go through competitive interviews. Mrs Archibald went through a number of interviews and was unsuccessful; she was eventually dismissed. Mrs Archibald argued disability discrimination on the basis that she should not have to go through interviews for a job she was qualified to do. The House of Lords held that the duty to make an adjustment is triggered where an employee becomes so disabled that she can no longer meet the requirements of her job description. The arrangements used by her employer in selecting employees for the jobs fell into the definition of 'provision, criterion or practice'. Mrs Archibald was placed at a substantial disadvantage when she could no longer meet a requirement of her job description that she was physically fit, as she was liable to be dismissed.

The duty to make reasonable adjustments arises even if there is nothing an employer can do to prevent the disabled person being placed at a disadvantage, and the duty may require an employer to treat a disabled person more favourably to remove the disadvantage. This necessarily involves a measure of positive discrimination. The comparator in this case is not confined to non-disabled persons doing the same job, and thus a measure the employer can take is transferring the employee to another job. As such, a reasonable adjustment would be a transfer without competitive interview, and such a transfer could be sideways, upwards or downwards. However, in *NTL Group v Difolco* [2006] EWCA Civ 1508, the employee, who was partially paralysed and could work only part time, was made redundant. She was given the opportunity to apply for another job which was advertised as full time, but she was told that if she got the job the employer would consider making it part time. She refused to apply for the job unless it became part time before she applied, and claimed that her employer had failed to make reasonable adjustments. The Court of Appeal stated that the employer had not failed in its duty. Until the claimant applied for the job, the duty did not arise. In *Spence v Intype Libra Ltd* [2007] All ER 261, an employee who had become disabled argued that his employer had failed to make reasonable adjustments by not obtaining and consulting on a medical report before dismissing him. The EAT held that the employer was not in breach of the duty, but gave leave to appeal to the Court of Appeal. The appeal was not pursued.

Other cases under the original legislation show how the duty was interpreted. In *Tarling v Wisdom* (1997) IDS Brief 597, the employee could have worked with the provision of a special chair. The employer had sought advice from the Department for Education and Employment (DfEE), a medical opinion, and advice from the Shaw Trust which provides financial support for employers with disabled employees. The DfEE advised that two special chairs were available, one at a cost of £1,000, but which was available on a four-week free trial, and another at a cost of £500. The employer thought that both chairs would be difficult to move between workstations and gave the applicant a number of ordinary chairs. Eventually the applicant was dismissed on the grounds of poor performance. The tribunal found that the employer had failed in its duty to make reasonable adjustments, particularly as the most expensive chair would have cost the employer about £200 with assistance from the Shaw Trust. In *Williams v J Walter Thompson Group Ltd* [2005] IRLR 376, the complainant needed special equipment and training in Lotus notes because she was blind. The employer claimed its failure to provide this was justifiable because of the costs involved. The Court of Appeal rejected this, stating that the company knew the claimant was blind when it employed her, but did no investigation and made no plans to deal with this before or after her employment started. The decision in *Archibald* has already been noted above. In *Nottinghamshire County Council v Meikle* [2004] IRLR 703, Mrs Meikle had a visual impairment and mobility problems. She argued that her employer had failed to make reasonable adjustments since 1993 in respect of, *inter alia*, providing large-print documents, adjusting the timetable so she did not have to walk too far to classrooms and she had classrooms with proper equipment, and giving her additional non-teaching time to complete paperwork in daylight. She started proceedings, then was off work with eye strain. As such, she was put on half pay. Mrs Meikle eventually resigned and claimed constructive dismissal, in addition to failure to make reasonable adjustments. The Court of Appeal, upholding the EAT, said that there had been a breach by the employer of the duty to make reasonable adjustments. It also held that putting Mrs Meikle on half pay was a failure to make a reasonable adjustment which placed Mrs Meikle at a substantial disadvantage. It further held that a persistent failure to carry out reasonable adjustments amounted to a fundamental breach of the obligation of trust and confidence, and was therefore a constructive dismissal.

There is no duty on employers to be proactive, merely to react once the substantial disadvantage is known or could reasonably be known. In *Ridout v TC Group* [1998] IRLR 628, the applicant stated on her application form that she had photosensitive epilepsy which was controlled by medication and that she was disabled. She was interviewed in a room lit by fluorescent lighting, and when she entered the room she commented that she might be affected by the lighting. She was not offered the job and claimed under the Act that the employer had failed to make reasonable adjustments. The EAT held that she had not been discriminated against. The Act did not require a disabled person to go into detailed explanations about the adjustments required, neither did it require the employer to ask questions as to what adjustments should be made. The employment tribunal was entitled to conclude that a reasonable employer would be unaware of the effect of fluorescent lighting on the applicant's rare form of epilepsy. Furthermore, the duty arises only when the person with a disability is placed at a substantial disadvantage.

One of the issues which may arise is that the person's disability may lead to the contract being frustrated. However, this would seem to undermine the protection the law gives to disabled employees. The EAT has recently held that the doctrine of frustration can apply, but only if the duty to make reasonable adjustments has not been breached. In *Warner v Armfield Retail and Leisure Ltd* (2013) UKEAT 0376/12/0810, the employee was working as a manager for a small company specialising in shop and pub refurbishments. His job included some carpentry work and a great deal of mobility. He had a stroke in February 2010 and was unable to continue in his role. An employment tribunal dismissed his claim for unfair dismissal and disability discrimination on the grounds that the contract had been frustrated. The employee appealed, arguing that the contract could not be frustrated once the duty to make reasonable adjustments had arisen. The EAT disagreed, stating that the doctrine could apply, although in the case of a disabled employee there was an additional requirement to consider whether the employer was in breach of its duty to make reasonable adjustments.

5.7 Harassment

There are three forms of harassment in the Equality Act 2010:

▶ **Unwanted conduct harassment** is defined in section 26(1) as follows:

(1) A person (A) harasses another (B) if—
   (a) A engages in unwanted conduct related to a relevant protected characteristic, and
   (b) the conduct has the purpose or effect of—
      (i) violating B's dignity, or
      (ii) creating an intimidating, hostile, degrading, humiliating or offensive environment for B.

▶ **Sexual harassment** is defined in section 26(2) as follows:

(2) A also harasses B if—
   (a) A engages in unwanted conduct of a sexual nature, and
   (b) the conduct has the purpose or effect referred to in subsection (1)(b).

In relation to both unwanted conduct harassment and sexual harassment, in deciding whether the conduct has the effect referred to in section 26(1)(b), the court should take into account the perception of the victim (B), the other circumstances of the case, and whether it is reasonable for the conduct to have that effect (s 26(4)).

▶ **Non-submission harassment** is defined in section 26(3) as follows:

(3) A also harasses B if—
   (a) A or another person engages in unwanted conduct of a sexual nature or that is related to gender reassignment or sex,
   (b) the conduct has the purpose or effect referred to in subsection (1)(b), and
   (c) because of B's rejection of or submission to the conduct, A treats B less favourably than A would treat B if B had not rejected or submitted to the conduct.

Note that harassment cannot occur where the protected characteristic is maternity or pregnancy, or marriage or civil partnership.

Section 40(1) protects applicants for jobs from harassment by the employer.

There are a number of points to note about the definition of 'harassment'. First, it is clear that the harassment need not be intentional. Second, it is not confined to action based on the complainant's race or sex, etc, therefore harassment can occur when, for example, jokes about the race of a friend of the complainant create an offensive environment. Third, the statute particularly directs the tribunal to take into account the perception of the complainant, introducing a subjective element. However, it is important to note that this is qualified by an objective element, in that despite the perception of the complainant the conduct will constitute harassment only if such perception is reasonable.

Underhill P, in *Richmond Pharmacology v Dhaliwal* [2009] IRLR 336, analysed the statutory definition of 'unwanted conduct harassment'. Dhaliwal was a project manager at a contract research organisation. In August 2007 she gave a month's notice, which was in breach of an oral agreement that she would give two months' notice of an intention to resign. This put a strain on the relationship between her and the medical director, which was exacerbated by problems with untaken holiday and whether Dhaliwal should come into work during a tube strike. There was also a perception that her work had started to deteriorate. There was a short meeting between Dhaliwal and the medical director during which she was asked to make sure she worked out her notice. The medical director, feeling that after she left their paths would still cross, said, 'We will probably bump into each other in the future, unless you are married off in India.' This caused the claimant a great deal of distress and the meeting was ended. She pursued a grievance which was not settled to her satisfaction, and she later lodged a complaint in the tribunal.

The tribunal found that the claimant in the past had told the medical director that her parents wished to see her married and that she would be visiting India in the near future. However, the tribunal also found that her distress had been caused by the implication that she would be sent to India for a forced, as opposed to an arranged, marriage and upheld her complaint. It awarded compensation of £1,000 and the company appealed.

Underhill P stated that the complaint could be broken down into three specific elements:

1. The unwanted conduct.
2. The purpose or effect of that conduct, ie did it violate the claimant's dignity or create an adverse environment for her (the proscribed consequences)?
3. The grounds for the conduct, ie was it on the grounds of the claimant's race, or ethnic or national origins?

He then went on to make four other points. First he said that case law prior to the statutory definition was unlikely to be helpful, as was any case law under the Protection from Harassment Act 1997. Second, it was important to note the breakdown in point 2. above as to both purpose or effect. A respondent may be liable even if he did not intend his conduct to cause distress but also liable if he did so intend but the proscribed consequences did not occur, as it would be surprising for a tribunal to find, in the case of an intention, that the proscribed consequences had not occurred. Third, a respondent should not be liable merely because the proscribed consequences occurred, but it should be reasonable that those consequences occurred. The criterion is objective, because the tribunal has to consider whether, if the claimant experienced those feelings or perceptions, it was reasonable for her to do so. Thus if a claimant is unreasonably prone to take offence, even if she did have those feelings, there will be no harassment. Further, if the perpetrator did not intend to cause offence, it may be unreasonable for the claimant to take offence. Fourth, the reason for the conduct involves an inquiry by the tribunal. If a perpetrator intended to cause offence but not on the grounds of the claimant's race (or any other prohibited ground), there is no liability. In some cases this will mean an inquiry into the mental processes of the perpetrator, but in other cases the grounds will be established without such inquiry. An example is *James v Eastleigh Borough Council* (Section 5.4 above), where the age distinction discriminated between men and women, and there was no need to look into the mental processes of the council.

The EAT in *Dhaliwal* found that the words did have the connotation of a forced marriage and upheld the tribunal's decision. It is yet to be seen how Underhill's analysis will be greeted by the higher courts.

In *English v Thomas Sanderson Blinds* [2009] IRLR 206, the Court of Appeal upheld a claim for harassment made by English. He had been subjected to homophobic banter because he had attended a boarding school and lived in Brighton. Mr English was not gay and his colleagues knew this. The Court of Appeal upheld his complaint of harassment on the basis of the protected characteristic of sexual orientation. Note also that the conduct, although unwanted, does not have to intend to violate a person's dignity, etc if the effect is such. Note also *Dhaliwal* above.

There are other avenues open to a victim of harassment. In *Waters v Commissioner of Police of the Metropolis* [2000] IRLR 720 (Section 5.11.4 below), the House of Lords stated that an employer could be liable in negligence if it could foresee harassment taking place and did nothing to stop it. More recently, in *Majrowski v Guy's and St Thomas's NHS Trust* [2006] IRLR 695, the House of Lords held that an employer could be vicariously liable for the harassment caused by an employee to another under the Protection from Harassment Act 1997.

5.8   Victimisation

Section 27 of the Equality Act 2010 defines 'victimisation'. Victimisation is subjecting a person to a detriment because that person has done a 'protected act' or the employer thinks that he or she has done a protected act. In other words, victimisation is not based on a protected characteristic as are the other forms of discrimination. A protected act is:

- bringing proceedings under the Act;
- giving evidence or information in connection with proceedings under the Act;
- doing any other thing for the purposes of or in connection with the Act;
- making an allegation (whether express or not) that the employer or another person has contravened the Act.

This means that the complainant must show that a person who has not done the act would be treated differently. In *St Helens MBC v Derbyshire* [2007] UKHL 16, female catering staff argued that they were entitled to a bonus scheme operated for roadsweepers because their work was of equal value. While many claims were settled, some were not, and those workers continued their claims. Before the hearing, they received letters from a senior council official stating that if their claims were successful it could lead to redundancies and deprive children of school dinners. The House of Lords held that this amounted to victimisation.

In *Chief Constable of West Yorkshire v Khan* [2001] IRLR 830, the House of Lords confirmed that the correct test was to see if a person who had not done the act would be treated differently. However, their Lordships rejected the 'but for' test applied by the Court of Appeal as they considered it too low a threshold. In the case the employee was not provided with a job reference because he was pursuing a race discrimination claim and the employer wished to preserve its position. If the 'but for' test was applied, 'but for' the race discrimination claim (the protected act) the reference would have been provided. However, the reason references were withheld was so that the employer might preserve its position. Their Lordships therefore concluded that the correct interpretation was that the less favourable treatment was 'by reason that' the applicant had carried out the protected act.

In the leading case of *Aziz v Trinity Taxis* [1988] ICR 534, a person was dismissed for making secret recordings to be used in discrimination proceedings. The employers showed that they would have dismissed anyone who had taped conversations, whatever the final purpose of the tapes. The Court of Appeal held that there was no victimisation. Aziz had been dismissed because he had recorded conversations, and not because those recordings were to be used in any proceedings under the Act. By contrast, in *London Borough of Lambeth v D'Souza* [1999] IRLR 240, the applicant had brought several successful race discrimination complaints against his employer. He alleged further discrimination and was suspended by his employer as a troublemaker. He brought a victimisation complaint and was dismissed. His complaint of victimisation was upheld by the employment tribunal and the House of Lords, although the House of Lords rejected his claim that the failure to comply with a reinstatement order was a separate act of victimisation. The Court of Appeal, however, has stated that the concept of victimisation requires the discriminator to have a motive which is consciously connected with the legislation. In other words, it must be shown that the fact that a protected act was done or believed to have been done by the complainant at the very least influenced the alleged discriminator in his unfavourable treatment of the complainant (*Nagarajan v London Regional Transport* [1998] IRLR 73). This interpretation, however, was rejected by the House of Lords ([1999] IRLR 572). Their Lordships said that it was not necessary for the applicant to show a conscious motivation on the part of the discriminator, because motivation is irrelevant in respect of other areas of the legislation. It is sufficient to establish that the protected act was done and that this was an important cause of, or significant influence on, the less favourable treatment. This, however, is now subject to *Khan* (above), as in *Khan* their Lordships appeared to be suggesting that motivation is important in that the less favourable treatment is in reaction to the protected act.

This appears to create a difference between victimisation and other forms of discrimination where motive is irrelevant. It also appears that to constitute victimisation, the act complained of must be legally actionable (*Waters v Commissioner of Police of the Metropolis* [2000] IRLR 720). While this seems to place a restriction on such claims, the Court of Appeal decision in *Rank Nemo (DMS) Ltd v Coutinho* [2009] EWCA Civ 454 appeared to increase protection in certain circumstances. Coutinho won his claim for unfair dismissal and race discrimination, and was awarded just over £72,000 in compensation. The award was not paid, and so he pursued a victimisation claim based on the non-payment. The respondents relied on *D'Souza* (above), but this was rejected by the Court of Appeal. Mummery LJ distinguished *D'Souza* on the basis that statute provided a remedy for the failure to comply with a reinstatement order, whereas in Coutinho's case there was no statutory remedy, hence he could pursue his claim as victimisation.

There is no protection if the information is false or the allegation is made in bad faith (s 27(3)). Note that there is no need for a comparator.

5.9　Relationships which have ended

Section 108 of the Equality Act 2010 replicates the old law and protects ex-employees from discrimination by their former employer.

By section 108(1), an employer must not discriminate against another if:

(a) the discrimination arises out of and is closely connected to a relationship which used to exist between them, and
(b) conduct of a description constituting the discrimination would, if it occurred during the relationship, contravene [the] Act.

By section 108(2), an employer must not harass an ex-employee. It is irrelevant in both cases whether the conduct started before or after the relationship had ended (s 108(3)).

While this seems to provide wide protection for ex-employees, the case of *Rowstock Ltd v Jessemey and EHRC* [2013] IRLR 439 seems to indicate its limitations. There, the EAT held that section 108 does not provide protection in respect of post-termination victimisation. Jessemey was dismissed at age 65 at a time when this was the default retirement age. At that time such a dismissal was fair if the statutory procedures were followed, but Rowstock did not follow the procedures, and Jessemey claimed unfair dismissal and age discrimination. As a result, Rowstock provided a very unfavourable reference. Jessemey then claimed victimisation, but the employer, with whom the EAT agreed, said that section 108(7) specifically disapplied the anti-victimisation provisions where the relationship had ended. Section 108(7) reads:

(7) But conduct is not a contravention of this section in so far as it also amounts to victimisation of B by A.

This is clearly not compatible with the Equal Treatment Directive. Having said that, two months later a differently constituted EAT in the case of *Onu v Akwiku* (2013) UKEAT 0283/12/RN held that post-relationship victimisation *is* covered. In the case the claimant was a domestic servant who brought a claim of post-termination victimisation. The employment tribunal held that victimisation was not made out and the claimant appealed. On appeal the respondent argued the claim did not lie due to section 108(7). The EAT said that there were two stages to the interpretation of the Act. First, it had to be interpreted as a purely domestic statute. Second, if this conflicted with the Equal Treatment Directive then the tribunal should consider whether the Act could be interpreted in accordance with the UK's obligations under the Directive. The EAT then held that on domestic construction the Equality Act 2010 did allow claimants to bring a claim for post-termination victimisation and *Jessemey* had been wrongly decided. Leave has been granted to appeal.

By sections 212 and 108(4) of the 2010 Act, the employer is under a duty to make reasonable adjustments for an ex-employee if the ex-employee continues to be placed at a substantial disadvantage. For example, the ex-employee may need access to the premises to talk to witnesses.

5.10 Acts of discrimination

The Equality Act 2010 lists a series of discriminatory acts which can be committed by an employer; these are found in section 39 and examined in further detail below.

5.10.1 In relation to applicants

5.10.1(a) In the arrangements the employer makes for deciding to whom to offer employment (s 39(1)(a))

Jobs must be generally available to everyone unless there is a genuine occupational qualification for the job (see Section 5.12 below). 'Arrangements' include interviews, advertisements (where the EHRC can take action – see Section 5.14.2) and application forms. In *Saunders v Richmond-upon-Thames Borough Council* [1978] ICR 75, a woman applied for a job as a golf professional. She was asked certain questions not asked of the male applicants, such as how did she feel men would react to a woman as a golf professional? It was held that these questions were pertinent to the job and not discriminatory. In *Gates v Wirral Borough Council* (1982) (unreported), however, it was held that it was discriminatory to ask questions of a woman such as 'What will you do when the children are sick?', when those questions were not also asked of a man. To some extent, however, this judgment is not particularly helpful. While it establishes that these questions may be discriminatory when asked only of women, it suggests that asking men the same questions eliminates the discrimination. This, of course, is a nonsense because it is the answers to the questions that will affect an employer's decision. Even in today's more enlightened society, the majority of men are unlikely to take full responsibility for childcare and the bulk of the work will still fall on the woman within a partnership. The EHRC in its Employment Statutory Code of Practice (para 16.62) recommends that questions at interview should only relate the job description and asking questions for example about childcare could lead to a discrimination claim. Whether this would be the case if the same questions were asked of both sexes is not discussed.

5.10.1(b) As to the terms on which an employer offers a person employment (s 39(1)(b))

Any terms offered to a person that are different from those offered to others, and which are based on a protected characteristic, are prima facie discriminatory. For example, offering women flexible start and finish times but not offering the same to men. The exception in relation to sex discrimination is pay, unless the woman's contract contains a sex equality clause by virtue of the Act. In respect of disability, it is possible to offer a disabled person more favourable terms than that of an able bodied person because there is no right to claim discrimination on the grounds of non-disability.

5.10.1(c) By not offering employment (s 39(1)(c))

An employer commits an act of discrimination if he refuses to employ a person solely because of a protected characteristic. In *Batisha v Say* [1977] IRLR 6, a woman was turned down for a job as a cave guide because 'it was a man's job'. It was held that discrimination had occurred. Similarly in *Owen & Briggs v James* [1982] IRLR 502, a woman was discriminated against on the grounds of race when she was rejected for a job (despite having a better shorthand speed than the successful applicant) when it was shown that the person who had interviewed her had said to the successful applicant, 'Why take on a coloured girl when English girls are available?' The employer's argument, that there could be discrimination only where race was the sole factor involved, was rejected by the Court of Appeal. It is sufficient that a protected characteristic is an important factor in the employer's decision.

A problem arises under these particular provisions where a person is rejected on the grounds of protected characteristic but no one is appointed to the job. The problem arose in earlier cases because of the requirement that the complainant had to show that he or she had been treated less favourably than a person in the same or not materially different circumstances. In other words, if a woman applied for a job and was rejected because she was a woman, how could she argue she had been treated less favourably than a man when a man also did not get the job? Two early tribunal cases in this area are often cited as conflicting, although they may be reconciled. In *Roadburg v Lothian Regional Council* [1976] IRLR 283, a man and a woman applied for a job. The woman was told she was unsuitable because she was a woman. The man was offered the job, but the post was then frozen and in fact the post was not filled. The tribunal held that there had been discrimination. In *Thorn v Meggit Engineering Ltd* [1976] IRLR 241, again a woman was rejected for a job because she was a woman, but no one was appointed to the post. The tribunal held that there had been no discrimination. The woman had not been treated less favourably than a man because a man had not been appointed either. While these cases may appear to be in conflict, they may be distinguished; in *Roadburg* the man was offered the job while the woman was not. This still left the law in the ridiculous position that if no one was offered the job, there could be no discrimination. The position has now been clarified by the EAT decision in *Brennan v Dewhurst Ltd* [1984] ICR 52. In this case a girl applied for a job as a butcher's assistant. She was not offered the job because she was female, but after her interview the post was frozen. It was held that the interview was the incident of discrimination. While this case will be of help where there is evidence from the interview stage of a job application, if that evidence does not exist, the fact that the post is not filled will make it very difficult to prove discrimination. However, in *BP Chemicals v Gillick* [1995] IRLR 128, it was held that an agency worker who, through the agency, had worked for the respondents, and who had then gone on maternity leave, had been discriminated against by the respondents when they told the agency they did not want her to return. This is an important case because obviously the plaintiff was already employed by the agency.

5.10.2 In relation to employees

5.10.2(a) As to the terms of his employment (s 39(2)(a))

This means the same as discussed above in Section 5.10.1(b).

*5.10.2(b) In the way the employer affords the employee access, or by not affording the
           employee access to opportunities for promotion, transfer or training, or any other
           benefits, facilities or services (s 39(2)(b))*

5.10.2(b)(i) Promotion, transfer or training

It is a breach of the legislation to choose or not choose employees for promotion, transfer
or training because of a protected characteristic, and, as already seen, this will include
rejecting a person because of an assumption made by the employer which has
discriminatory connotations (*Horsey v Dyfed County Council*, Section 5.4 above). In *R v
CRE, ex parte Westminster City Council* [1985] IRLR 426, a black roadsweeper applied for
the post of cleansing operative within the Council. He was offered the job, but a
representative of the National Union of Public Employees (NUPE) objected to his
appointment, ostensibly on the grounds of his poor attendance record. The Assistant
Director of Cleansing felt that the union was objecting to the appointment on racial
grounds, but because he feared industrial action if the appointment went ahead, he
withdrew the offer of the job. It was held that a discriminatory act had been committed,
and the fact that the intention had been to preserve industrial peace was irrelevant.

There are two exceptions to the requirement not to discriminate in relation to
promotion, transfer or training in sections 158 and 159 (discussed in Section 5.10.2(d)
below).

5.10.2(b)(ii) Benefits, facilities or services

While the first part of section 39(2)(b) is very specific, this second part is deliberately wide.
'Benefit' was given a broad interpretation by the EAT in the case of *Peake* (Section 5.4
above), when Phillips J said that benefit 'meant no more than advantage'; and although
the decision was overturned on appeal, it is suggested that the definition is still pertinent.

To have separate facilities for different races is unlawful, even if those facilities are equal
in quality, although the decision in *Pel Ltd v Modgill* [1980] IRLR 142 shows that the
employer is under no duty to remove de facto segregation. Obviously different facilities
can be provided for different sexes, although they should be of equal quality.

5.10.2(c) Dismissing an employee (s 39(2)(c))

Unlike the unfair dismissal provisions (see Chapter 9), there is no continuity requirement
for pursuing a claim for a discriminatory dismissal, and a complainant may pursue a
claim despite not having the required continuity. The reason for the dismissal must be a
protected characteristic, however. In *Gubala v Crompton Parkinson Ltd* [1977] IRLR 10, an
employer chose to select a woman for redundancy, despite the fact that she had longer
service than her male counterpart, because the man was the breadwinner in his family. It
was held that she had been discriminated against. By contrast, in *Goult v Reay Electrical*
[1977] IRLIB 80, a woman was dismissed when it was discovered that she had married an
employee of a competitor of her employer. It was held that the reason for her dismissal
was not her sex or marital status but rather whom she had married. This should be
contrasted, however, with the later case of *Skyrail Oceanic Ltd v Coleman* [1981] IRLR 398,
where a woman was dismissed when she became engaged to an employee of a rival firm.
The two employers decided that, given that her husband would be the breadwinner, she
should be the one to lose her job. The Court of Appeal decided that the reason for her

dismissal was primarily an assumption based on her sex, and she had therefore suffered discrimination. Dismissal includes constructive dismissal (s 39(7)). Constructive dismissal is discussed further at Section 9.4.3.

5.10.2(d) Subjecting a person to any other detriment (s 39(2)(d))

The meaning of the phrase 'subjecting to a detriment' was given a broad interpretation in the case of *Burton v De Vere Hotels* [1996] IRLR 596. Two waitresses were working at a function at which Bernard Manning appeared as a guest act. The waitresses complained that Manning made racist jokes and comments about them, as did members of the audience. Both waitresses argued that the employer had subjected them to a detriment – that is, racial harassment by a third party. The EAT held that the words 'subjecting to' connoted control, therefore an employer subjected his employee to a detriment if he caused or allowed harassment to happen in circumstances where he could control whether it happened or not. It was not necessary to imply foresight on the part of the employer, although foresight might be relevant in determining the amount of control he could exercise. The question to ask was whether the event was sufficiently under the control of the employer that he could, by the application of 'good employment practice', have prevented or reduced the extent of the harassment. In the particular case the employer could have told the assistant manager to withdraw the waitresses from the function. He had not done so, therefore he subjected them to the detriment of harassment. This case had far-reaching implications, in that the harassment was not by a person under the employer's control but by a third party on the employer's premises. However, in *Pearce v Governing Body of Mayfield School* [2003] IRLR 515, the House of Lords disapproved of *Burton*. While the House of Lords upheld the decision of the Court of Appeal in holding that Ms Pearce had not been the victim of sex discrimination, it went further and stated that even if the conduct of the pupils had amounted to sex discrimination, the school would not have been liable for their actions. Their Lordships stated that the school would be liable only if it could be shown that it had omitted to act on the grounds of Ms Pearce's sex.

The definition of 'detriment' within the provisions has had a chequered history. In a direct discrimination claim the complainant has to show that one of the acts of discrimination in section 6 or section 4 has occurred. Therefore the concept of what constitutes a detriment is important. The Court of Appeal developed a test of whether a reasonable worker would feel placed at a disadvantage (*MOD v Jeremiah*, above Section 5.4; *De Souza v AA*, above Section 5.5.4), but this itself raises the question of what constitutes a reasonable worker. In *Shamoon v Chief Constable of the Royal Ulster Constabulary* [2003] IRLR 285, while the House of Lords stated that there did not need to be any physical or economic consequence to constitute a detriment, their Lordships did reiterate the 'reasonable worker' test, although stating that the victim's view is important.

In addition to the above, section 39(3) and (4) protect applicants and employees against victimisation in any of the above acts.

5.10.2(e) Positive action

While section 39 protects applicants and employees, sections 158 and 159 allow an employer to take positive action in general, and specifically in relation to recruitment and promotion. By section 158(1) and (2), if a person reasonably thinks that:

- persons who share a protected characteristic suffer disadvantage connected to the characteristic;
- persons who share a protected characteristic have needs that are different from the needs of persons who do not share it; or
- participation in an activity by persons who share a protected characteristic is disproportionately low,

the Act allows a person to take action which is a proportionate means of achieving the aim of:

- enabling or encouraging persons who share the protected characteristic to overcome or minimise that disadvantage;
- meeting those needs; or
- enabling or encouraging persons who share the protected characteristic to participate in that activity.

This is a new section and case law will be needed to see what sort of action will be allowed.

In addition, section 159 allows for positive action in relation to recruitment and promotion. It states that if a person reasonably thinks that:

- persons who share a protected characteristic suffer a disadvantage connected to the characteristic; or
- participation in an activity by persons who share a protected characteristic is disproportionately low,

the Act allows a person to treat the person with the protected characteristic more favourably in connection with recruitment or promotion than a person without the protected characteristic (s 159(3)). However, this only applies where:

1. both parties are as qualified as each other;
2. the employer does not have a policy of treating persons with the protected characteristic more favourably than those without it; and
3. the action in question is a proportionate means of achieving a legitimate aim.

This section allows an employer, where there are two equally qualified people, to give priority to one who has a protected characteristic where persons with that characteristic have been disadvantaged in the past, However, giving priority must be a proportionate means of achieving a legitimate aim. This is a controversial provision and is likely to be the basis of a lot of case law. It also goes against the basic premise that has always underpinned equality law in the past, that of equality of treatment.

5.11   Other unlawful acts

In addition to the specific acts of discrimination which may be committed by an employer during recruitment to, or in the course of, employment, the 2010 Act lists other unlawful acts that may be committed.

5.11.1   Instructing, causing or inducing discrimination

Section 111 makes it unlawful for a person to instruct, cause or induce someone to discriminate against, or harass or victimise another, or attempt to do so. In addition to any action taken under this provision, an employee who refuses to obey an order to discriminate on racial grounds, and thus suffers a detriment, will also have a claim, as seen from the cases of *Showboat Entertainment Centre v Owens* [1984] 1 WLR 384 and *Weathersfield Ltd t/a Van Truck Rentals v Sargent* [1991] IRLR 94.

It is likely that this section will also cover discriminatory advertisements which were a specific unlawful act under the old legislation. An advertisement is discriminatory if it indicates, or may reasonably be understood to indicate, that there is an intention to discriminate, unless a particular characteristic is an occupational requirement for the job (see Section 5.12 below). In *Equal Opportunities Commission v Robertson* [1980] IRLR 44, the respondent placed an advertisement stating that he wanted 'a good bloke (or blokess to satisfy fool legislators)'. It was held that this might reasonably be understood to mean that women need not apply. The advertiser will not incur liability if there is an indication in the advertisement that there is no intention to discriminate, for example a statement that the employer is an equal opportunities employer. Furthermore, the publisher will not be liable if he can show that he relied on a statement by the person who placed the advertisement that it was not unlawful, and it was reasonable for the publisher to rely on that statement.

Action may be taken by the recipient of the instruction, etc, by the victim or by the EHRC.

5.11.2   Aiding contraventions

Under section 112 of the Equality Act, a person must not knowingly help another to do anything which contravenes the Act. However, if a person relies on a statement that the action does not contravene the Act and it is reasonable to rely on that statement, section 112 is not breached.

The person making the statement commits a criminal offence if he knowingly or recklessly makes a statement which is false or misleading in a material way (s 112(4)). In *Anyanwu v South Bank Student Union* [2001] ICR 391, the House of Lords considered the liability under the predecessor to section 112. The appellants were students of the university who were employed by the union after being elected to their posts. The university raised allegations of misuse of funds and bullying against them, and after instigating disciplinary proceedings the university expelled the appellants and banned them from university premises. As a result, the union sacked them. They claimed against the union as their employer, but also claimed against the university for a breach of what is now section 112, arguing that the university had knowingly aided the union in committing an unlawful act. The House of Lords said that 'knowingly aids' in the provision meant that the person had given 'some kind of assistance to the other person which helps him to do it … All that is needed is an act of some kind, done knowingly, which helps the other person to do the unlawful act' (*per* Lord Hope). In other words, there is no requirement that the person aiding should have any knowledge of the unlawful act or desire that it takes place; as the expulsion by the university had helped the union in dismissing the appellants, the university was liable under what is now section 112.

However, in a case heard a week before (*Hallam v Cheltenham Borough Council* [2001] ICR 408), the House of Lords upheld a trial judge's decision that there must be an element of joint enterprise when considering that provision. This was supported by the Court of Appeal in *Bird v Sylvester* [2008] IRLR 232, where it was held that the execution, by a solicitor, of a client's racist instructions did not make the solicitor an aider of an unlawful act.

5.11.3 Enquiries about disability and health

Section 60 of the 2010 Act prohibits an employer from making enquiries about the health of the applicant before offering work. An employer does not commit disability discrimination by asking about the health or disability of an applicant, but his conduct in response to the answers may constitute discrimination. However, there is no breach if the questions are asked to establish whether the applicant will be able to comply with a requirement to undergo an assessment, or to establish what reasonable adjustments will have to be made, whether the applicant will be able to carry out an intrinsic function of the job or to monitor diversity (s 60(6)). A breach of section 60 may be pursued only by the EHRC and not an individual.

5.11.4 Liability of an employer

An employer or principal will be liable for any unlawful act committed by his employees/agents in the course of their employment, unless the employer can show he took all reasonable steps to prevent those unlawful acts being done (s 109). An important interpretation of the predecessor to these provisions was given in *Tower Boot Co Ltd v Jones* [1997] ICR 254. Jones was subjected to severe racial harassment by his colleagues. He was branded with a hot screwdriver, whipped with flex and had metal bolts thrown at him. Despite his being moved to another part of the factory the harassment continued, and Jones resigned having been employed for only one month. The EAT held that the liability of the employer under what is now section 109 was that of vicarious liability. As such, Jones had to establish that the harassment occurred during the course of the employees' employment. This meant that the acts committed had to be authorised by the employer and performed in an authorised way, or acts authorised by the employer but performed in an unauthorised way. The EAT then held that the nature of the acts was such that they could not be described as authorised acts done in an unauthorised manner, and thus the employer could not be held liable. This was despite the fact that the employer knew about the harassment and had done little to prevent it. The judgment was severely criticised and left a very large gap in protection for employees against harassment from colleagues. On appeal to the Court of Appeal, the decision was reversed. The Court of Appeal held that there was insufficient similarity between vicarious liability and liability under the Act to impose tortious principles on the statutory provisions. A purposive approach was needed, and 'in the course of employment' should be given its everyday meaning, that is, during employment. As such, the employer was liable, as any other interpretation would seriously undermine the legislation.

In *Canniffe v East Riding of Yorkshire Council* [2000] IRLR 555, the EAT held that, to see whether an employer has taken reasonable steps to prevent the unlawful acts, the proper approach is first to identify whether the employer took any steps at all and, if steps were taken, then to consider whether there were any further steps which it would have been reasonably practicable to take. Whether the steps would have been effective is irrelevant, and an employer cannot argue that he has failed to take steps because, even if he had, the unlawful acts would still have taken place.

Liability has since been extended. In *Chief Constable of Lincolnshire Police v Stubbs* [1999] IRLR 81, the EAT held that an employer could be liable for harassment which took place in a social situation, if this could be regarded as an extension of work (in this case a leaving party). However, in *Sidhu v Aerospace Composite Technology Ltd* [2001] ICR 167, the Court of Appeal held that the employer was not liable for racial harassment during a works outing, even though the employer had disciplined those concerned. Such conduct was not during the course of the perpetrators' employment.

Thus the more generous interpretation in *Jones* may still leave an employee unprotected. This is shown by *Waters v Commissioner of Police of the Metropolis* (Section 5.7 above), where the employer was not liable for a serious sexual assault committed outside working hours on the complainant by a fellow employee. The House of Lords held that as the assault took place outside working hours, it could not be held to have been committed during the employee's employment. Furthermore, as the employer could not be liable, the complainant could not have been victimised under the Act, despite the fact that she had complained repeatedly about the assault and was taken off special duties following her complaints. Their Lordships did find the employer liable at common law, however (see Section 4.2.11(b)(iii) in Chapter 4). This shows why the more generous interpretation in *Jones* is important, as if the employer is not liable, then neither is the perpetrator, since the legislation only prevents discrimination by employers and not employees. Should the employer be liable, however, the perpetrator can be ordered to pay compensation.

5.12 Occupational requirements (ORs)

The legislation recognises that in some cases a job must be done by a person who has a particular characteristic. If the employer can show that this is the case, he will have a defence to a direct or indirect discrimination claim. Unlike the old law, where the legislation laid down circumstances in which the employer might plead the defence, the Equality Act 2010 is much more general.

Schedule 9, Part 1 states that a person does not contravene a provision making it unlawful to discriminate in relation to recruitment, opportunities for promotion, transfer or training and dismissal, by applying to work a requirement to have a particular protected characteristic, if he shows that having regard to the nature or context of the work:

1. it is an occupational requirement;
2. the application of the requirement is a proportionate means of achieving a legitimate aim; and
3. the person to whom the requirement is applied does not meet it, or the employer has reasonable grounds for not being satisfied that the person meets it.

For example, in *Wylie v Dee & Co (Menswear) Ltd* [1978] IRLR 103 a woman was turned down for a job in a menswear shop. The employer argued that the job would require her to measure men's inside legs and therefore an occupational requirement (OR) existed. The tribunal found that the shop had changing cubicles and seven male assistants who could be called upon to do the appropriate measurements if required. An OR did not exist and there had been an act of discrimination. By contrast, in *Times v Hodgson* [1981] IRLR 530 a male supervisor, with longer service than his female counterpart, was chosen for redundancy. The reason was that all other female supervisors had left and the employers had to retain one woman to deal with the problems of the female workers, to take them to the first-aid room and to take urine samples from them when they had been working with toxic substances. The tribunal held that the employer had discriminated against the man but that an OR existed. Likewise from the field of race discrimination, in *London Borough of Lambeth v CRE* [1990] IRLR 231, the council advertised the post of group manager and assistant head of housing benefits for Asian or Afro-Caribbean applicants only. The council argued that over half the tenants were of Asian or Afro-Caribbean descent and that staff had to be sensitive to their problems. The Court of Appeal held that as the holders of the posts would have very few dealings with the public, the council was guilty of unlawful discrimination. By contrast, in *Tottenham Green Under Fives' Centre v Marshall* [1991] IRLR 162, the EAT held as 84 per cent of the children were of Afro-Caribbean or African descent, an OR existed and the council could restrict the job to persons of the same racial group.

An employer cannot use this exception to discriminate in relation to the terms of employment or to subject a person to a detriment (Sch 9, para 1(2)).

5.12.1 Religion or belief

The 2010 Act replicates the old law in creating special ORs where employment is for the purposes of an organised religion.

Schedule 9, paragraph 2 allows an employer to apply a requirement to be of a particular sex, or not to be a transsexual, or a requirement related to the employee's marriage, civil partnership or sexual orientation if the requirement is to comply with the doctrines of the religion or to avoid a conflict with the strongly held religious convictions of a significant number of the religion's followers. Note that there is no requirement that the OR is a proportionate means of achieving a legitimate aim. This is very similar to the old law and applies in very limited circumstances.

There is also an OR in respect of employment where there is an ethos based on religion or belief. Schedule 9, paragraph 3 allows an employer with an ethos based on religion or belief to apply a requirement to be of a particular religion or belief, but only if the requirement is a proportionate means of achieving a legitimate aim.

This OR existed under the old legislation. Parliamentary debate indicated that this was intended to apply only to priests, but the wording is much wider and a challenge was mounted arguing that this did not comply with the Framework Directive. In *R (on the application of Amicus – MSF section) v Secretary of State for Trade and Industry* [2004] IRLR 430, the High Court held that the OR is compatible with the Directive. It is narrow, and when interpreted to ensure compatibility with the Directive it can be seen to afford an exception in very limited circumstances. This is because of the words 'for the purposes of an organised religion'. As such, the employment of, for example, a teacher in a faith school would not be employment for the purposes of an organised religion. The fact that the employer must apply the requirement to comply with the doctrines of the religion is an objective test, so that the employer must show that the employment of a person not meeting the requirement would be incompatible with the doctrines of the religion. This is very narrow in scope. Further, to apply a requirement to avoid conflicting with the strongly held religious convictions of a significant number of the religion's followers requires precise examination of the precise nature of the employment, and is an objective test which will be difficult to satisfy. As such, the OR is not incompatible with the Directive.

5.12.2 Armed forces

Schedule 9, paragraph 4 makes it lawful for the armed forces to apply a requirement excluding women and transsexuals from service in the armed forces, provided it is a proportionate means of ensuring the combat effectiveness of the armed forces.

5.13 Exceptions to the legislation

There are areas in the 2010 Act when the laws preventing discrimination do not apply. These are found in Schedule 9, Parts 2 and 3.

1. National security is exempt (s 192).
2. Age. It is not unlawful to discriminate on the basis of age in certain situations. It is not age discrimination to base benefits on length of service (for example *Cadman v Health and Safety Executive* [2006] IRLR 969), have a different national minimum wage for young people, enhanced redundancy pay based on age, and to provide life assurance for employees who take early retirement due to ill-health. The provision of childcare facilities which are limited by the child's age is also not age discrimination (Sch 9, Pt 2).
3. Maternity and marriage/civil partnerships. Other exceptions in Schedule 9, Part 3 relate to non-contractual payments to women on maternity leave and payments dependent on marriage/civil partnership.

5.14 Enforcement and remedies

5.14.1 Enforcement by an individual

When an individual presents a complaint of discrimination to an employment tribunal, a conciliation officer will attempt to conciliate. If this fails, the tribunal has three main remedies that it may award the complainant:

- an order declaring the complainant's rights;
- financial compensation;
- a recommendation of action to be taken by the respondent to reduce the adverse effect of the discrimination.

If the respondent fails to comply with a recommendation, compensation may be increased by section 124(7). In *D'Souza* (Section 5.8 above), the council refused to comply with an order to reinstate the complainant. He was originally awarded £358,289 in compensation. This included loss of pension and future loss of earnings that he would sustain in the four years and 10 months he had left until he retired. This sum was later reduced, however, by the Court of Appeal. If the complaint is one of indirect discrimination and the respondent shows that there was no intention to discriminate, the tribunal must first consider if a declaration or recommendation is sufficient before considering whether to order compensation (s 124(4) and (5)).

General principles on the award of compensation can be found in the judgment of May LJ in the case of *Alexander v Home Office* [1989] IRLR 190. The purpose of an award is restitution, but given the difficulties of quantification in this area, awards should be restrained. Awards may be made for injury to feelings. In *Vento v Chief Constable of West Yorkshire Police (No 2)* [2003] IRLR 102, the Court of Appeal reiterated the guidance given in *Alexander*, saying that damages for discrimination have some similarity to those awarded in personal injury cases. The maximum award should be in the region of £25,000 for serious cases and the lowest should be £500 for isolated incidents. Awards below £500 should not be made.

Damages are not confined to pecuniary loss, and sometimes aggravated damages may be appropriate if the defendant has behaved in a high-handed, malicious, insulting or oppressive manner when compared to the conduct, character and circumstances of the complainant. For example, in *McLaughlin v London Borough of Southwark* (1997) *The Times*, 11 December, the total award of £234,000 included a sum for aggravated damages because the council refused to disclose certain documents. An award of aggravated damages was also considered appropriate in the case of *City of Bradford Metropolitan County v Arora* [1989] IRLR 442, but it was held by the Court of Appeal that such an award in discrimination cases was appropriate only in the event of outrageous conduct on the part of the employer. This statement on the award of aggravated damages was subject to doubt, however, from the later Court of Appeal decision in *AB v South Western Water Services Ltd* [1993] 1 All ER 609. The Court held that the effect of the decision in *Rookes v Barnard* [1964] 1 All ER 367 was that aggravated damages could only be awarded for torts recognised at that time (1964). Legislation on sex and race discrimination came into force after 1964. Consequently, in *Deane v Ealing London Borough Council* [1993] ICR 329, Wood P decided that aggravated damages could not be awarded for a breach of anti-discriminatory legislation. However, this is now subject to *Kuddus v Chief Constable of Leicestershire Constabulary* (2001) IDS Brief 690. While the case is not an employment decision, it is of importance to issues of compensation in discrimination cases. Briefly, Kuddus was asking for aggravated damages when he discovered that a police constable had forged his signature on a document withdrawing a complaint about the police. The Chief Constable, while accepting that there had been a forgery, successfully argued in both the High Court and the Court of Appeal that aggravated damages could not be awarded because the tort of misfeasance in public office was not a tort for which aggravated damages could be awarded prior to 1964, the date of the *Rookes* decision. Kuddus appealed to the House of Lords. Lord Slynn, giving the leading judgment, stated that he did not think that anything in Lord Devlin's analysis in *Rookes* required that in addition to the categories of conduct for which aggravated damages can be awarded, there was an additional requirement that the claim should amount to a tort for which aggravated damages were available before 1964. He concluded on this basis that the Court of Appeal in *AB v South Western Water Services Ltd* had not been justified in restricting an award in such a way. Such a limitation would affect the future development of the law. Thus, Kuddus's claim for aggravated damages was not precluded on the basis that the claim was not a tort for which aggravated damages were available prior to 1964. The issue of whether aggravated damages are now available for statutory torts such as those created by anti-discrimination legislation was not resolved by their Lordships. Lord Mackay was of the view that such damages would be available only if expressly authorised by statute. Lord Scott, on the other hand, felt that such a claim would lie if the conduct fell within one of the categories laid down by Lord Devlin in *Rookes*. In *Scott v Commissioners of Inland Revenue* [2004] IRLR 713, however, the Court of Appeal accepted that aggravated damages could be awarded, and stressed that they were intended to deal with cases where the injury was inflicted by conduct that was 'high-handed, malicious, insulting or oppressive' and should be awarded separately from damages for injury to feelings.

Commonly, tribunals make substantial awards against an employer and only a small award against the discriminator. However, in *Way & IntroCate Chemicals v Crouch* [2005] IRLR 603 the EAT held that it was proper to make both the employer and discriminator liable for the full amount on a joint and several basis, as this will allow the complainant to sue the discriminator in the case of employer bankruptcy. In the case, the EAT made an award against the employer and its managing director after the claimant was dismissed for refusing to have a relationship with the director. The EAT held that a tribunal should apportion the share of the award between the respondents. This apportionment should be on the basis of culpability and not on the basis of financial strength. Whether in reality this decision helps complainants is debatable, as it is highly unlikely that an employee will have the finances to pay the compensation and a complainant could end up with little or nothing. It is hoped that in these situations a claimant will be advised to pursue the employer for the full amount, and thus place the burden on the employer to pursue a claim against the discriminator.

The actual amount awarded will depend on the detriment which is caused and the injury to the complainant's feelings. In *Wileman v Minilec Engineering Ltd* [1998] IRLR 144 the compensation awarded was £50, whereas in *Noone v North West Thames Regional Health Authority* [1988] IRLR 195, £3,000 was awarded. The large award made in *McLaughlin* (above) is unusual and the average award is much lower.

A major problem lies with the available remedies. First, the normal detriment suffered in these cases will be the loss of a job or a promotion. The Court of Appeal in *Noone* held that the Health Authority could not be ordered to offer the next available vacancy to the complainant, and this was followed by the EAT in the later case of *British Gas plc v Sharma* [1991] IRLR 101. There was a second problem in that a tribunal had no power to add interest to awards made by it. By section 139 of the 2010 Act there is now power to make regulations to deal with this deficiency in the legislation.

5.14.2 Enforcement by the Equality and Human Rights Commission

The functions of the EHRC were discussed in Chapter 1. In addition, only the Commission can take action under section 60 (enquiries about disability and health). It has wide powers to carry out formal investigations and issue non-discrimination notices.

Formal investigations are a vital part of the EHRC's functions. They are the means by which discrimination in large areas of employment may be investigated. The Commission has extensive powers to order the production of documents and to require witnesses to give evidence, and a person who wilfully alters, suppresses or destroys a document may be fined. On completion of an investigation, the EHRC will produce a report in which there may be recommendations for changes applicable to an individual or organisation, or it may recommend changes in the law to the Secretary of State. After the investigation is complete, the Commission may decide to issue a non-discrimination notice. To do so it must have found a breach of section 60 or section 111, or a breach of a sex equality clause. The body on which the notice is served will then have the opportunity to make representations to the EHRC and may appeal against any requirement in an employment tribunal. The notice may be enforced by a county court injunction if within five years of its issue the respondent commits an unlawful act. Before the whole process begins, however, the Commission must be sure it has grounds to begin an investigation and allow the body investigated to make representations. In *CRE v Prestige Group* [1989] IRLR 166, the House of Lords declared an investigation by the Commission for Racial Equality unlawful and the subsequent non-discrimination notice ultra vires and void. The investigation had started without a belief that a discriminatory act had occurred and without giving the company the opportunity to make representations.

In addition to its role in relation to investigations, the EHRC has the power to provide legal assistance to an individual. Given that the Commission does not have an unlimited purse, such assistance is given in only a few cases deemed to be of importance, where the Commission may want to test the Act for future complainants.

5.15 Part-time workers

While many part-time workers are women and therefore had protection under the Sex Discrimination Act (now the Equality Act 2010) as seen in the cases noted above, in addition to such protection the government implemented the Part Time Work Directive (97/81/EC) by the Part-time Workers (Prevention of Less Favourable Treatment) Regulations 2000 (see Section 5.1). These Regulations give part-time workers the right not to be treated less favourably, as to the terms and conditions of their employment, than a full-time comparator, unless the employer can justify the less favourable treatment on objective grounds. Objective grounds are that the less favourable treatment is necessary and appropriate to achieve a legitimate business objective (Reg 5(2)). As with a lot of modern legislation, the Regulations apply to workers and not just employees, and therefore apply to anyone who has agreed to perform any work or services personally. The definition of 'full-time' and 'part-time' is by reference to the practice of the employer.

A part-time worker must compare his or her treatment to that of a full-time comparator. That comparator must be:

1. employed by the same employer and under the same type of contract;
2. engaged in the same or broadly similar work, having regard where relevant to qualifications, skills and experience; and
3. based at the same establishment or another establishment operated by the employer and employed at the same time as the part-time worker (Reg 2(4)).

There is no requirement that the comparator must be of the opposite sex to the part-time worker, because the basis of the less favourable treatment is that the worker works part-time and is not based on the worker's sex. However, unlike other anti-discriminatory legislation, the comparator must be an actual full-time worker and not a hypothetical one (*Carl v University of Sheffield* [2009] IRLR 616). In *Matthews v Kent and Medway Towns Fire*

Authority [2006] IRLR 367, part-time firefighters took an action to gain access to the same benefits as full-time firefighters. There were two issues for the House of Lords to address. First, whether the part-time workers were on the same contract as the full-time workers, which the House of Lords stated in the affirmative. Second, whether the two groups were employed on work which was broadly similar. The employer argued this was not the case, as the full-time firefighters had extra duties over and above fighting fires, which was the only duty required of the part-time workers. The House of Lords stated that if both groups spent a large proportion of their time pursuing the core activities of the organisation, the work was broadly similar.

If a full-time worker becomes part-time or returns to work part-time after an absence of less than 12 months, the worker can choose her former full-time post as comparator (Regs 3 and 4). However, the Regulations do not give a full-time worker the right to return to work part-time, neither do they give a woman returning from maternity leave the right to return to work part-time, although a refusal in respect of the latter may be the basis of a claim under the Equality Act 2010.

A part-time worker has the right not to be treated less favourably than a comparable full-time worker as regards the terms of contract, or by being subjected to a detriment by any act, or deliberate failure to act by her employer (Reg 5(1)). In *McMenemy v Capita Business Services Ltd* [2007] IRLR 400, McMenemy worked Wednesdays, Thursdays and Fridays. The employer allowed people to have bank holidays off, but only if they actually worked on the bank holiday. McMenemy claimed this amounted to less favourable treatment on the grounds of his part-time status as most bank holidays fell on a Monday. The Court of Session held that the treatment must be solely on the grounds of part-time status. As the employer would have treated a full-time worker who did not work on Mondays in the same way, there was no discrimination.

Regulation 5(1) is subject to a defence of justification on objective grounds. In *Gibson v Scottish Ambulance Service* (2004) EAT S0052/04, the EAT had to determine whether rostering a part-time worker for a greater number of stand-by hours, pro rata, than a full-time worker was less favourable treatment. While the EAT found that it was, it found that the reason for the stand-by hours was need and varied between region. As such, there was objective justification. In *O'Brien v Ministry of Justice* [2013] UKSC 6, the issue for the Supreme Court was whether a part-time judge was protected by the Regulations and entitled to a judicial pension on retirement. The Supreme Court ruled that a part-time judge was a worker for the purposes of the Regulations, and that there was no objective justification for different treatment between part-time and full-time judges. The fact that such payments would reduce the pension pot for full-time judges was no justification.

In determining whether there is less favourable treatment, the pro rata principle applies. This is defined in Regulation 1(2):

> 'pro rata principle' means that where a comparable full-time worker receives or is entitled to receive pay or any other benefit, a part-time worker is to receive or be entitled to receive not less than the proportion of that pay or other benefit that the number of his weekly hours bears to the number of weekly hours of the comparable full-time worker ...

Regulation 5(4) specifically states that it is not less favourable treatment to pay a part-time worker a lower hourly rate for overtime than a comparable full-time worker for hours which, added on to the part-time worker's normal hours, constitute less than the full-time worker's normal hours excluding overtime. This merely adopts the ECJ decision in *Stadt*

Lengerich v Helmig [1995] IRLR 216, and was applied in *Jones v Great Northern Railways* (2005) IDS 780.

Where the less favourable treatment is not dismissal, the worker can request in writing that the employer provides her with written reasons for the less favourable treatment within 21 days. The statement is admissible in any tribunal hearing. Failing to do so, or providing an evasive statement, allows a tribunal to draw an adverse inference against the employer, including an inference that the employer has discriminated against the part-time worker (Reg 6).

The part-time worker has a right not to suffer a detriment by any act, or deliberate failure to act, by her employer, on the grounds that:

- she has brought proceedings under the Regulations;
- she has requested a written statement from her employer;
- she has given evidence or information in connection with such proceedings brought by another worker;
- she has otherwise done anything under the Regulations;
- she has alleged that the employer has infringed the Regulations, unless the allegation is false and not made in good faith;
- she has refused or proposed to refuse to forgo a right under the Regulations; or
- the employer believes or suspects that the worker has done one of the above (Regs 7(2) and (3)).

Dismissal on any of the above grounds is automatically unfair (Reg 7(1)). No continuity is needed (ERA 1996, s 108(3)(i)).

An employee may complain to a tribunal within three months of the act or last act. Where the complaint is of less favourable terms, the less favourable treatment takes place on each day during which the terms are less favourable. Where the employee goes from full-time to part-time, the three-month period starts to run with the first day of the varied contract; and where the employee returns from an absence to part-time work, the three months starts on the day of the employee's return (Reg 8(4)).

The tribunal, if it finds the complaint well-founded, may make a declaration as to the employee's rights, compensation which the tribunal considers just and equitable, or order the employer to take steps to obviate or reduce the adverse effect on the worker (Reg 8(7)). Compensation may be reduced for contributory conduct, and the worker is under a duty to mitigate her loss (Reg 8(12) and (13)). Failure to comply with a tribunal order can lead to an increase in compensation (Reg 8(14)).

While in the vast majority of situations part-time workers who are women would already have protection under the Equality Act 2010, the Regulations provide a quick and speedy remedy for all part-time workers, including men, suffering less favourable treatment which cannot be objectively justified. In some cases, however, the worker may wish to use the Equality Act 2010 rather than the Regulations as it is likely that any financial compensation awarded under that legislation will be higher.

5.16 Fixed-term employees

Regulations to implement the Fixed Term Work Directive (99/70/EC) were put to consultation in March 2001. The Directive prohibits discrimination against fixed-term employees as compared to permanent employees, unless there is objective justification. The deadline for implementation was 10 July 2001, but the DTI stated that it needed more time to analyse responses to the draft and was taking advantage of the 'special difficulties' provision in the Directive which allows Member States to delay implementation for up to a year. As such, from October 2002, the Fixed-term Employees (Prevention of Less Favourable Treatment) Regulations 2002 came into force (see Section 5.1 above).

Regulation 1(2) defines a 'fixed-term contract' as one which expires after a specific time, expires after a specific task, or expires on the occurrence or non-occurrence of an event other than retirement. The comparator is the same as under the Part-time Worker Regulations, that is a permanent employee employed by the same employer, at the same establishment or a different establishment operated by the employer, and employed on the same or broadly similar work (Reg 2). The comparator must be an actual employee and cannot be someone who used to be employed.

A fixed-term employee has a right not to be treated less favourably as regards:

- terms of the contract;
- being subjected to any other detriment by any act or deliberate failure to act;
- period of service qualification relating to any condition of service;
- the opportunity to receive training;
- the opportunity to secure permanent employment.

All the above is subject to justification on objective grounds (Reg 3). The pro rata principle applies (see Section 5.15 above) and the employee has the right to be informed of vacancies (Reg 3(5) and (6)). Objective justification exists if the fixed-term employee's terms, taken as a whole, are at least as favourable as the comparator's terms (Reg 4). In *Cure and Another v Coutts and Co plc and Another* (2004) *The Times*, 25 October, fixed-term employees at the bank were not awarded a discretionary bonus which had been awarded to permanent employees. The EAT held that a detriment under the Regulations 'will occur when a reasonable worker might take the view that he had been disadvantaged in the circumstances in which he had, thereafter to work'. However, in *Webley v Department for Work and Pensions* [2005] IRLR 288, the Court of Appeal held that the non-renewal of a fixed-term contract did not amount to less favourable treatment, pointing out that it 'was of the essence of a fixed-term contract that it came to an end at the expiry of the fixed term'.

Where a fixed-term employee has been employed on a fixed-term contract for four years, or a succession of shorter fixed-term contracts which together amount to four years, then the employee will become permanent, unless the continuation of fixed-term employment can be objectively justified (Reg 8). Where the employee satisfies the test for permanent status, there is a right to a written statement of variation within 21 days of a request being made (Reg 9). However, the Court of Appeal, in *Hudson v Department of Work and Pensions* [2012] EWCA Civ 1416, has ruled that periods of time worked under a government-funded training scheme does not count as part of the four years in order for the employee to gain permanent status.

As with the Part-time Worker Regulations, a fixed-term employee has the right to receive written reasons for the less favourable treatment (Reg 5) and has the same protection from unfair dismissal and detriment (Reg 6). The same remedies are available on application to an Employment Tribunal within three months of the act complained of (Reg 7). In *Cure*, the EAT decided that the three months ran not from the time when the employer decided not to pay the bonus to fixed-term employees, but when it had decided on the detail and application of the bonus to relevant employees.

While the Regulations seem extensive, two points should be noted. First, they only apply to employment under a fixed-term contract from 10 July 2002. Second, unlike the Part-time Workers (Prevention of Less Favourable Treatment) Regulations 2000, these only apply to employees and not the wider class of workers.

Summary

5.1 While international law protects against discrimination in a large number of areas, national law at present only protects against discrimination on the grounds of age, disability, gender reassignment, marriage and civil partnership, pregnancy and maternity, race, religion or belief, sex and sexual orientation.

5.2 The Equality Act 2010 recognises four types of discrimination: direct discrimination, indirect discrimination, victimisation and harassment.

5.3 Direct discrimination is treating someone less favourably on one of the prohibited grounds.

5.4 Indirect discrimination is imposing a provision, criterion or practice which applies to all but places a particular group at a disadvantage. The defence to an indirect discrimination claim is that the provision, etc is a proportionate means of achieving a legitimate aim.

5.5 Victimisation is treating someone less favourably because that person has taken part in proceedings under the legislation or alleged breaches of the legislation.

5.6 Harassment is violating a person's dignity or engendering an intimidating, hostile, degrading, humiliating or offensive environment. The perception of the victim is important and no intention is necessary.

5.7 European Union law has had a major impact in this area, particularly in the implementation and interpretation of the Equal Treatment Directive and the Framework Employment Directive.

5.8 There are specific acts of discrimination that an employer may commit against a person.

5.9 The 2010 Act sets out the concept of an occupational requirement when discrimination is permitted.

5.10 The remedy for discrimination is financial compensation or a declaration of the complainant's rights. In addition, the Equality and Human Rights Commission may undertake an investigation, and may issue a non-discrimination notice against an employer.

Exercises

5.1 What do you consider to be the main deficiencies in the present laws on discrimination?

5.2 Ms Brown applied for a temporary social work post in an old people's home on the island of Anglesey in Wales. Her application was turned down because she could not speak Welsh. On Anglesey itself, 62 per cent of the population are Welsh-speaking. In all other respects, Ms Brown was qualified for the job. In fact all social work posts on Anglesey were advertised on a 'Welsh essential' basis. In the event no one was actually appointed to the post because no suitable applicant applied. Ms Brown has now entered a complaint of discrimination against the Council on Anglesey. Advise Ms Brown.

5.3 Hilda and Annie work for Mike's Fashions Ltd, a firm producing ladies wear. The firm also has a factory shop. Hilda has worked in the factory for six years on a part-time basis. The majority of the women in the factory work part-time. Women make up 30 per cent of the workforce.

- ▶ Today the firm has announced that it will be making 25 per cent of the workforce redundant, laying off part-time workers first. Advise Hilda.
- ▶ Annie has been working in the factory shop for six months. The shop is run by a manageress who has a firm policy that, as it is a ladies wear shop, men should not be served. She tells Annie not to serve men, arguing that they always buy the wrong things and create extra work when the goods are returned. Annie thinks this is a ridiculous order and today serves Terry, who bought a set of lingerie for his wife. His wife returned the goods this afternoon and the manageress was tied up for one hour sorting out all the paperwork involved in returned goods. She has now sacked Annie for refusing to obey orders. Advise Annie.

Further reading and references

Baker, 'Proportionality and Employment Discrimination in the UK' (2008) 37 ILJ 305

Barrett, 'When Does Harassment Warrant Redress?' (2010) 39 ILJ 194

Bell, 'Achieving the Objectives of the Part Time Work Directive? Revisiting the Part Time Workers Regulations' (2011) 40 ILJ 254

Bowers, Moran and Honeyball, 'Justification in Direct Sex Discrimination: A Reply' (2003) 32 ILJ 185

Collins, 'Discrimination, Equality and Social Inclusion' (2003) 66 MLR 16

Connolly, 'Rethinking Victimisation' (2009) 38 ILJ 149

Cunningham, 'Discrimination Through the Looking Glass: Judicial Guidelines on the Burden of Proof' (2006) 35 ILJ 279

Cunningham, 'Indirect Discrimination: Between the Wheat and the Chaff' (2009) 38 ILJ 209

Davies, 'A Cuckoo in the Nest? A "range of reasonable responses", Justification and the Disability Discrimination Act 1995' (2003) 32 ILJ 164

Docksey, 'The Principle of Equality Between Men and Women as a Fundamental Right Under Community Law' (1991) 20 ILJ 258

Forshaw and Pilgerstorfer, 'Direct and Indirect Discrimination: Is There Something Inbetween?' (2008) 37 ILJ 347

Gill and Monaghan, 'Justification in Direct Sex Discrimination Law: Taboo Upheld' (2003) 32 ILJ 115

Hand, 'Employers' Liability for Third Party Harassment: An "Unworkable" and Superfluous Provision?' (2013) 42 ILJ 75

James, 'The Meaning of Disability: Physical and Mental Impairment' (2002) 31 ILJ 156

Lawson, 'Disability and Employment in the Equality Act 2010: Opportunities Seized, Lost and Generated' (2011) 40 ILJ 359

Manknell, 'Discrimination on the Grounds of Sexual Orientation, Harassment and Liability for Third Parties' (2003) 32 ILJ 297

McColgan, 'The Fixed Term Employees (Prevention of Less Favourable Treatment) Regulations 2002: Fiddling while Rome Burns?' (2003) 32 ILJ 194

McColgan, 'Class Wars? Religion and (in)equality in the Workplace' (2009) 38 ILJ 1

McCrudden, 'Rethinking Positive Action' (1986) 15 ILJ 219

Further reading and references cont'd

Monaghan, *Equality Law* (Oxford University Press 2007)

Petts, 'Prognosis for Disability Discrimination Following *McDougall*' (2008) 37 ILJ 268

Pilgerstorfer and Forshaw, 'Transferred Discrimination in European Law' (2008) 37 ILJ 384

Pitt, 'Keeping the Faith: Trends and Tensions in Religion or Belief Discrimination' (2011) 40 ILJ 384

Reynold and Palmer, 'Case Comment: What Place for Hindsight in Deciding Whether a Claimant was Disabled?' (2007) 36 ILJ 486

Sargeant, 'Age as an Equality Issue: Legal and Policy Perspectives' (2004) 33 ILJ 208

Sargeant, 'The Employment Equality (Age) Regulations 2006: A Legitimisation of Age Discrimination in Employment' (2006) 35 ILJ 209

Skidmore, 'Sex, Gender and Comparators in Employment Discrimination' (1997) 26 ILJ 51

Skidmore, 'Anti-discrimination Law and the European Union' (2003) 32 ILJ 132

Swift, 'Justifying Age Discrimination' (2006) 35 ILJ 228

Vickers, 'The Employment Equality (Religion or Belief) Regulations 2003' (2003) 32 ILJ 188

Vickers, 'Is all Harassment Equal? The Case of Religious Harassment' (2006) CLJ 579

Vickers and Manfredi, 'Age, Equality and Retirement: Squaring the Circle' (2013) 42 ILJ 61

Watt, 'Goodbye "but-for" Hello "but-why"' (1998) 27 ILJ 121

6.1 Introduction

The Equality Act 2010 repealed the Equal Pay Act (EPA) 1970. In respect of the equal pay provisions, very little has changed, and thus it is likely that existing case law is applicable under the 2010 provisions. There is a difference in the title of the provisions, though. The Equality Act 2010 refers to equality of terms rather than equal pay. In reality, however, the Equal Pay Act 1970 covered contractual terms, and thus the heading 'equality of terms' is more apt.

Equality of terms, particularly pay, for women did not become a relevant issue in the law of the United Kingdom until 1975. The EPA was introduced in 1970, but employers were given five years in which to implement equality, and so the Act came into force in 1975. The present law is now the Equality Act 2010. While the normal applicant for equal pay will be a woman, obviously the rules of statutory interpretation apply and a man can sue for pay equal to that earned by a woman. This is shown by the case of *Hartlepool Borough Council v Llewellyn and Others* [2009] IRLR 796. There, female workers argued that their work was of equal value to that of a group of male council employees. Men who worked alongside the women, doing the same job, put in a contingent claim using the female workers as comparators doing like work. The Employment Appeal Tribunal (EAT) held that as the men could not claim against fellow male workers, they could piggyback on the female workers' claims, albeit that their claim was contingent on the women's success. In addition, the men would be entitled to any arrears granted to the women.

The Act was brought in to adopt the European principle of equal pay which is now found in Article 157 TFEU. This not only states the principle but, in addition, gives a wide definition of pay:

> For the purpose of this Article, 'pay' means the ordinary basic or minimum wage or salary and any other consideration, whether in cash or in kind, which the worker receives directly or indirectly, in respect of his employment, from his employer.

The Article is directly applicable in UK law and creates, along with the Equality Act 2010, an independent right to equal pay, as was established in the cases of *Defrenne v SABENA* [1976] CMLR 98 and *McCarthy v Smith* [1981] QB 15. Furthermore, the Equal Pay Directive (75/117/EEC), which expands the principle of equal pay in the Article, outlines the law that Member States of the European Union should adopt; and as will be seen in Section 6.8.2, the Directive creates a right for certain employees to sue under EU law, expanding their rights under the Article. These employees are those employed by an emanation of the state. This means that in relation to equal pay, the nature of the employer determines how many routes there are to claim equality:

National law	EU law
Equality Act 2010 (all employees)	Article 157 TFEU (all employees)
	Equal Pay Directive (public employees)

6.2   Equality Act 2010

National law provides three methods of claiming equal pay: like work, work rated as equivalent and work of equal value. In this chapter, unless stated otherwise, for the sake of brevity it will be assumed that the employee claiming equality of terms is female. The way in which a woman's pay will change, should she be successful in her claim, is novel. By section 66 of the 2010 Act, all contracts of employment are deemed to include a 'sex equality clause'. If a complainant proves her right to equal pay, the clause will be activated. This means that on a term-by-term comparison between her contract and a man's, any term in her contract which is less favourable than the terms in his becomes as favourable, and any term in his contract which is not included in hers will become incorporated (s 66(2)). The tribunal does not look at the employee's pay package as a whole but at each individual term – this is the principle derived from *Hayward v Cammell Laird Shipbuilders* [1988] AC 894. It is important to note that if her contract contains a term which is more favourable than his, she will retain it and it will not go into the man's contract unless he pursues an equal pay claim using her contract as a comparison.

Obviously, as can be seen from the discussion above, the female employee needs a contract with which to compare terms. Her claim will start, therefore, by her finding a male comparator.

6.3   The comparator

A comparator is defined in section 79 of the Act. The comparator must be:

- employed by the employee's employer or an associated employer (that is, an employer over whom her employer has control, or where her employer and his employer are under the control of a third); *and*
- employed at the same establishment; *or*
- employed at a different establishment in Great Britain, and where common terms and conditions are observed for that class of employee.

In addition, the comparator must be of the opposite sex to the claimant. It will be seen that there must be a common employer plus a common workplace; or, if that is not the case, common terms and conditions must be observed for that class of employee. It was observed by the EAT in *Scullard v Knowles* [1996] IRLR 344 that the need for a common employer meant that the definition of a comparator under section 1(6) of the EPA 1970 (now section 79 of the 2010 Act) was much more restrictive than the definition of a comparator under Article 141 TEC (now Article 157 TFEU), which does not state that there must be common employment. In *Scullard*, the EAT, overturning the employment tribunal, held that the broader definition applied by virtue of the doctrine of direct effect. Thus a manager of a training unit, which was one of a number of units run by a regional education council, could compare herself to male managers of other units run by another regional education council, even though neither the organisation nor the units were limited companies, as all of the councils were funded by the Department of Employment and there was a common collective agreement applying to the employees (see also *South Ayrshire Council v Morton* [2002] IRLR 256). However, in *Lawrence v Regent Office Care Ltd* [2002] IRLR 822, Mrs Lawrence was transferred to Regent Office

Care after North Yorkshire County Council put its catering services out to tender. Her pay was reduced and she claimed equal pay with her former male council employees. While Morison J in the EAT held that it was necessary for an applicant to establish only that she and her comparators were employed at the same establishment in a loose and non-technical sense, he went on to say that he did not consider the principle wide enough to cover Mrs Lawrence's case. She appealed to the Court of Appeal, and that Court referred the case to the European Court of Justice (ECJ) to determine whether Article 141 TEC (now Article 157 TFEU) allowed Mrs Lawrence to compare herself to employees of her former employer with whom her work had previously been rated equivalent in *Ratcliffe v North Yorkshire County Council* [1995] IRLR 439 (see Section 6.7 below). The ECJ stated that comparisons under the Article were not confined to men and women who work for the same employer, but there had to be a single source, such as a common collective agreement, which caused the discrepancies, so that one body was responsible for the discrimination and had the power to prevent it. In Mrs Lawrence's case there were different arrangements for negotiating terms and a comparison could not be made.

The Court of Appeal also referred the case of *Allonby v Accrington and Rossendale College* [2004] IRLR 224 to the ECJ. In *Allonby*, the issue referred was whether a man employed by a college was in the same employment as a woman employed by a company which supplied services to the college. Again the ECJ stressed that although Article 141 TEC (now Article 157 TFEU) was wider than the EPA 1970 (now the Equality Act 2010), where differences could not be attributed to a single source, there was no body responsible for the inequality that could restore equal treatment and thus it did not come within the scope of the Article. Applying these principles, in *Robertson and Others v Department of Environment, Food and Rural Affairs* [2005] IRLR 363, the Court of Appeal held that male civil servants could not use female civil servants working for another government department as comparators. Mr Robertson's claim that there was a common source of payment – the Crown – was dismissed. The Court held that following the Civil Service (Management Functions) Act 1992, each government department was authorised to agree the terms and conditions of employment of its civil servants, therefore the source of the anomalies was the individual departments and not the Crown; there was no common source. Likewise in *Armstrong v Newcastle upon Tyne NHS Hospital Trust* [2006] IRLR 124, the Court of Appeal held that although there were some common terms across the different hospitals, others were determined at a local level, and thus a comparison could not be made across hospitals. However, in *South Tyneside Council v Anderson and Others* [2007] EWCA Civ 654, female school support staff were paid at a rate determined by their contractual grades set out in a collective agreement known as the White Book. Their male comparators were employed by the local authority doing identical work, although none worked in schools. The employment tribunal and the EAT upheld the equal pay claims, but the council appealed in respect of employees who were employed on the recommendation of the governing body of a community school (as opposed to being directly employed by the local authority). The local authority argued that the women and their comparators were not in the same employment because it was open to each governing body to establish terms and conditions of employment. The Court rejected the argument and held that the women were employed by the same employer as their comparators, and were paid by reference to the White Book to which governing bodies referred, and thus they were entitled to equal pay.

Conversely, in *Dumfries and Galloway Council v North and Others* [2009] IRLR 915, classroom assistants, learning support assistants and nursery nurses claimed equal pay with manual workers based elsewhere, such as refuse collectors and refuse drivers. There were also men employed at the same schools as the claimants, but they did not choose these as their comparators. The Honourable Lady Smith held that the claimants were not in the same employment as their comparators, in particular because the head teachers at the schools had no control over those comparators. She stated that for men at a different establishment to be valid comparators, the claimant had to show one of two things. First, that common terms and conditions were observed, for example by showing there was a common collective agreement as in *Leverton* (below). Second, a woman might show that the women doing the same class of job at her establishment were employed on common terms and conditions, and that the men doing her comparators' job at the other establishment and any men employed, or who would be employed, to do that class of job at her establishment would be on common terms and conditions. In the case the claimants could not show that their male comparators could be employed at their schools, given the jobs that they did, and so did not comply with what is now section 79. However on appeal to the Supreme Court ([2013] UKSC 45), their Lordships held that the requirement that the comparators be employed 'at establishments in Great Britain which include the claimant's and at which common terms and conditions of employment are observed either generally or for employees of the relevant classes' means merely that the claimants must show that if employed at the claimant's establishment, however unlikely, the comparators would be employed under broadly similar terms to their existing ones. To be fair to Lady Smith, in *City of Edinburgh v Wilkinson and ors* [2010] IRLR 756 she did say that she felt her analysis in *Dumfries* was wrong and that it did not have to be shown that there was a real possibility that the comparators would be employed at the claimant's establishment.

The Court of Appeal has held that a claimant cannot limit her choice of comparator artificially. In *Cheshire and Wirral Partnership NHS Trust v Abbott* [2006] IRLR 546, a group of domestic staff which was predominantly female sought an equal value claim using as their comparators hospital porters who were all male, in respect of a bonus scheme which applied to porters but not domestic staff. The Court of Appeal upheld the employer's argument that the comparative group should also contain catering staff, who were on work of equal value to that of the porters, a group that was predominantly female and which also had access to the bonus scheme. As such, the domestic staff could not show the scheme had an adverse effect on women.

While some of the above cases seem to limit the definition of comparator, in *Alabaster v Woolwich plc* [2004] IRLR 486 the ECJ stated that the principle of non-discrimination required that a woman who still has an employment relationship during maternity leave must benefit from any pay rise awarded during that leave, and that should be taken into account in the calculation of the earnings-related element of her statutory maternity pay. On hearing the case after the reference, the Court of Appeal in *Alabaster v Barclays Bank and the Department of Work and Pensions* [2005] EWCA Civ 508 held that the then Equal Pay Act 1970, in so far as it required a woman to cite a male comparator, should be disapplied if the reason for not paying a pay increase was based on the woman's pregnancy. This is now reflected in section 74 of the Equality Act 2010, which provides that every woman's contract shall contain a maternity equality clause, which means that any maternity-related pay shall include any increase in pay or bonus she would have received had she not been pregnant or on maternity leave.

The issue of common terms and conditions has also been subjected to wide judicial interpretation. In *Leverton v Clwyd County Council* [1989] IRLR 28, a nursery nurse sought to compare herself with higher-paid clerical workers employed by the county council at a different establishment. The Court of Appeal originally held that the clerical workers were not valid comparators. The complainant worked 32 hours a week and had 70 days' holiday. The comparators worked a 37-hour week with 20 days' holiday. The Court held that although 'common terms and conditions' did not mean identical terms, there had to be a sufficient amount of commonality to enable a proper comparison to be made. In the *Leverton* case two fundamental terms – hours and holidays – were different, and consequently the clerical workers were not valid comparators within what is now section 79. The House of Lords, however, held that the clerical workers were valid comparators, Lord Bridge holding that where there was a common collective agreement, as in *Leverton*, that would 'seem to represent the paradigm, though not necessarily the only example, of the common terms and conditions contemplated by the Act'. In *O'Sullivan v Sainsbury plc* (1990) IRLIB 393, although some terms were different, hours, holidays, maternity and sick provisions were the same. It was held that there was sufficient commonality for what is now section 79 to apply. In *British Coal Corporation v Smith* [1996] IRLR 404, the House of Lords decided that common terms and conditions meant terms and conditions 'that were on a broad basis substantially comparable rather than identical'.

It is for the woman to choose her male comparator and not the tribunal (*Ainsworth v Glass Tubes and Components* [1977] IRLR 74), and there is no requirement that the choice must be fairly representative of a group of workers (*Thomas v National Coal Board* [1987] IRLR 451). In addition, from the case of *McCarthy v Smith* (see Section 6.1 above), the complainant may choose a man who used to do her job before being promoted, but not a hypothetical man. *Diocese of Hallam Trustee v Connaughton* [1996] IRLR 505 held that she could also use a successor. However, in *Walton Neurological Centre v Bewley* [2008] IRLR 588, the EAT held that using a successor is too hypothetical and that *Connaughton* was wrongly decided. Apart from these restrictions, it means that the woman can choose whomever she wishes and is not constrained because a man does the same job as she does. Her choice of comparator determines her avenue for an equal pay claim, from *Pickstone and Others v Freemans plc* [1988] IRLR 357, not vice versa. This prevents an employer from putting a token man into work that is usually exclusively performed by women.

While *Pickstone* has alleviated some of the problems women have in choosing a comparator, it should be noted that there is still a problem when a woman has gone on maternity leave. Given that the ECJ in *Webb v EMO Cargo* (see [1993] IRLR 27) decided that you cannot compare a pregnant woman with a man on long-term sick leave, a claim that maternity pay is less than an employee's sick pay is unsustainable according to the Northern Ireland Court of Appeal in *Todd v Eastern Health and Social Services Board* [1997] IRLR 410. In *Gillespie v Northern Health and Social Services Board* [1996] IRLR 214, the ECJ held that although statutory maternity pay fell within the definition of 'pay' in Article 141 TEC (now Article 157 TFEU), it was not a breach of the Article to set a level of maternity pay which was less than that earned normally by the woman, as this was not unequal treatment based on the sex of the individual (see also *Edwards v Derby City Council* (1998) IDS Brief 624). Furthermore, the Northern Ireland Court of Appeal in *Gillespie v Northern Health and Social Services Board (No 2)* [1997] IRLR 410 held that statutory maternity pay which was higher than statutory sick pay could not be classed as inadequate for the purposes of Article 11(3) of the Pregnant Workers Directive (92/85/EC), which requires that maternity pay should not be less than statutory sick pay.

Once a woman has chosen her comparator, that will then determine her route to equal pay. The route will either be like work, or work rated equivalent or work of equal value.

6.4 Like work

'Like work' is defined by section 65(2) of the Equality Act 2010. Work is like work if:

(a) A's work and B's work are the same or broadly similar nature, and
(b) such differences as there are between their work are not of practical importance in relation to the terms of their work.

Regard shall be had to the frequency or otherwise with which such differences occur in practice, as well as to the nature and extent of the differences (s 65(3)).

Two things should be noted. First, the work does not have to be identical, merely broadly similar. Second, an employer cannot insert differences in the comparator's contract if in practice these differences never arise. In *Capper Pass v Lawton* [1977] ICR 83, the EAT explained how the section should be applied. In that case, Mrs Lawton was employed in the director's dining room, on her own, cooking 10–20 meals a day. She sought equal pay with the assistant chefs in the staff canteen who cooked 350 meals a day. The assistant chefs were supervised. Phillips J said that in applying what is now section 65(2) the job should not be dissected minutely. First, the tribunal should consider if the work is the same or broadly similar by looking at the duties and responsibilities; and, second, the tribunal should look to see what in practice is done, whether there are differences and whether these are of practical importance. What is done and when are therefore important, and a job may be split into three basic areas – duties, hours and responsibilities.

6.4.1 Different duties

In *Electrolux v Hutchinson* [1977] ICR 252 there was a contractual obligation in the male employees' contracts to work overtime, at weekends or at night if so required. In other respects the work was broadly similar. In practice the men rarely performed those extra duties, and it was held that female employees were entitled to equal pay. Likewise in *Coomes (Holdings) Ltd v Shields* [1978] IRLR 263, Mrs Shields was paid 62p an hour, her male counterpart £1.06 an hour. The employers argued that the male employees had the extra duties of removing unruly customers and carrying cash between different shops. The Court of Appeal, however, discovered that in practice there were few unruly customers, and the Court decided that transporting cash between the shops was not a difference of practical importance. Mrs Shields was entitled to equal pay. By contrast, in *Thomas v National Coal Board* [1981] IRLR 451, the fact that the male comparator worked permanent nights unsupervised was a difference of practical importance, and Ms Thomas was therefore not on like work.

6.4.2   Different hours

In *Dugdale v Kraft Foods* [1977] ICR 48, men and women were doing the same work but the men had to work compulsory overtime. It was held that the fact that the men worked overtime did not justify a higher hourly rate for all the working hours, merely for those which were unsociable, as long as overtime was available to women should they wish to do it (see also *Kerr v Lister* [1977] IRLR 259).

6.4.3   Different responsibilities

If a man has more responsibility than a woman doing broadly similar work, this is a difference of practical importance and again will justify a difference in pay. In *Eaton Ltd v Nuttall* [1977] IRLR 71, a man and woman were doing the same work but the woman handled items valued at less than £2.50 whereas the man handled items valued between £5 and £1,000. It was held that the man had more responsibility, in that if he made a mistake the loss to the company would be much greater. Ms Nuttall was not entitled to equal pay. A similar conclusion was reached in *Capper Pass v Allan* [1980] IRLR 236.

On the wording of section 65(3), however, the different responsibility must exist for the whole of the working year and not just at particular times. In *Redland Roof Tiles v Harper* [1977] ICR 349, a man and a woman were doing similar jobs, but the man was paid more because he deputised for the transport manager for five weeks a year. It was held that this did not justify a difference in pay for the whole year – he could be given additional pay when he had the extra responsibility.

6.5   Work rated as equivalent

A second route to equal pay is found in section 65(4) of the 2010 Act where the woman's job and the man's job have been rated as equivalent under a job evaluation study (JES).

The Act does not lay down detailed requirements for a JES but, once it has been carried out, it will be upheld unless the tribunal feels that it was made on a sex-specific system (in other words it is discriminatory – *Green v Broxtowe DC* [1977] IRLR 34; *Neil v Ford Motor Co* [1984] IRLR 339). A sex-specific system is defined in section 65(5) as one which 'for the purposes of one or more of the demands made on a worker, … sets values for men different from those it sets for women'.

Guidance on the nature of a JES was given by the EAT in *Eaton v Nuttall* (see Section 6.4.3 above). It was said that it had to be:

> thorough in analysis and capable of impartial application. It should be possible … to arrive at the position of a particular employee at a particular point in a particular salary grade without taking other matters into account except those unconnected with the nature of the work.

In other words, subjective views on the value of work are not permissible but objective factors such as seniority are relevant. Relative weightings on 'whole job' comparisons are thus inadequate for this purpose, according to the Court of Appeal in *Bromley v H & J Quick* [1988] IRLR 249. In *Redcar and Cleveland Borough Council v Bainbridge (No 2)* [2008] IRLR 776, the Court of Appeal held that the woman is entitled to equal pay with her comparator when the JES gives her job a higher rating than his.

Once both sides have accepted the validity of the JES, it comes into effect and operates the equality clause (*Arnold v Beecham Group Ltd* [1982] IRLR 307). In *O'Brien v Sim-Chem Ltd* [1980] IRLR 373, a JES was carried out by the company, but before they paid Mrs O'Brien her increased salary the government announced a voluntary incomes policy and so the implementation of the scheme was postponed. The House of Lords ruled that once the scheme had been completed, the comparison of the respective terms in the man's and woman's contracts could be made, thus the equality clause was operated. Note, however, that claims for back pay go back only to the date of the JES and not six years, as is the case in a like work or equal value claim (*Redcar and Cleveland Borough Council v Bainbridge (No 2)* [2008] IRLR 776).

6.6 Work of equal value

The original legislation in this area had only 'like work' and 'work rated equivalent' as the routes to equal pay. As such, it did not comply with the Equal Pay Directive which included the concept of equal pay for equal work. This was because an employee could not compel her employer to carry out a JES. In *Commission of the European Communities v United Kingdom* [1982] IRLR 333, the ECJ held that the original Equal Pay Act 1970 did not satisfy the principle of equal pay for equal work. As a result, the existing legislation was amended and introduced the third route to equal pay under national law – that of 'work of equal value'.

A specific procedure was introduced for equal value claims. This procedure was amended by the Employment Tribunals (Constitution and Rules of Procedure) (Amendment) Regulations 2004. The changes were designed to reduce the lengthy delays that were a main criticism of the original procedure. The Rules of Procedure are contained in Schedule 6 to the 2004 Rules.

Rule 8(5) authorises the Presidents of Employment Tribunals to establish specialist panels of chairmen and members. The Rules also contain an indicative timetable for dealing with claims which envisage that where no independent expert is appointed the claim should take 25 weeks, and if one is appointed a claim should take 37 weeks. The Rules also provide for standard orders at each stage of an equal value hearing, and give extensive powers to tribunals to make case management orders. These include the power to order that no new facts shall be admitted unless disclosed to all parties in writing by a specified date; that parties send copies of documents to all parties and the expert; that the employer should grant access to its premises to the expert; and, where there is more than one expert, that they must provide a statement to the tribunal stating areas where they agree and disagree.

6.6.1 Stage 1 hearing

The stage 1 hearing will take place in all equal value claims and will decide if there is a claim. This means that the tribunal must decide whether the claim should proceed and, if so, whether to hear the claim itself or appoint an independent expert. It also means that a tribunal can no longer strike out a claim purely because it considers there are no reasonable grounds to determine that the complainant's work is of equal value to that of her comparator. If a JES has given the complainant's work a different value, this will be upheld unless the tribunal has reasonable grounds to believe that it discriminates because of sex or that it is otherwise unreliable (Equality Act 2010, s 131(6)). By the Employment

Tribunals (Constitution and Rules of Procedure) (Amendment) Regulations 2008 an employment judge may sit alone to hear a stage 1 equal value hearing.

The standard orders require that within 28 days of the stage 1 hearing, the parties shall provide each other with written job descriptions for the complainant and comparator, and identify any relevant facts. Within 56 days the parties must provide the tribunal with a joint statement covering job descriptions and relevant facts. At least 28 days before the hearing the parties must produce a joint statement for the tribunal stating the facts on which they agree and those on which they disagree, giving reasons for the disagreement. The tribunal may order an employer to grant access to its premises to the independent expert if appointed (Rule 3(1)(d)) or, if no expert is appointed, to the complainant and her representative to enable them to interview any comparator (Rule 5(1)(c)). If no expert is appointed, the next stage is a full hearing. If one is appointed, there is a stage 2 hearing.

6.6.2   Stage 2 hearing

The aim of a stage 2 hearing is to resolve disputed facts so that the expert can evaluate the jobs. The tribunal must make a determination on facts upon which the parties disagree, and require the expert to prepare a report based on the agreed facts and those determined by the tribunal. The Rules provide that the tribunal sets a date by which the report is to be produced (normally within eight weeks of the stage 2 hearing). Section 131 of the Equality Act 2010 provides that the tribunal can withdraw the requirement for an expert report and decide the case itself.

6.6.3   Full hearing

This will occur within 18 weeks after the stage 1 hearing if no expert is appointed, and 20 weeks after the stage 2 hearing if there is an independent expert. The tribunal hears the case along with the expert's report, if there is one, and the employer's defence.

Since the introduction of the equal value route, there have been some important rulings on interpretation. The first of these was the House of Lords decision in *Hayward v Cammell Laird Shipbuilders* (Section 6.2 above). Ms Hayward was a canteen assistant in a shipyard and claimed her work was of equal value to that of the shipyard workers who were paid as skilled tradesmen. The independent expert ruled that her job was of equal value, but the tribunal, the EAT and the Court of Appeal held that she was not entitled to extra cash as she had free luncheons and two days' additional holiday compared to her male comparator and, taking the pay package as a whole, her non-cash benefits equalised her pay. This decision was reversed by the House of Lords. Their Lordships said that what is now section 66(2) states that if the equality clause operates, any term in A's contract which is less favourable shall become as favourable and any favourable term in B's contract shall become a term of her contract. Thus, for example:

Woman	Man
£99	£150
20 days' holiday	18 days' holiday

The term in the woman's contract above which is less favourable is the pay, therefore her pay becomes the same as the man's pay (£150). All her other terms remain because they are more favourable than his. This is an important case on the interpretation of the legislative provisions; it does, however, leave the way open for the men to claim equal pay with Ms Hayward!

A further important House of Lords decision in this area is *Pickstone and Others v Freemans plc* [1988] IRLR 357. Mrs Pickstone was employed as a warehouse operative and claimed her work was of equal value to that of a male warehouse checker. Unfortunately, there was one man doing the work of a warehouse operative, and the employers argued that Mrs Pickstone could not claim equal value under what is now section 65(1)(c) as that route applied only where what is now section 65(1)(a) (like work) or section 65(1)(b) (work rated as equivalent) does not apply. Freemans were therefore arguing that as Mrs Pickstone had a like work comparison with a man doing her job, she could not take an equal value comparison with another man doing a different job. This interpretation of the legislation was rejected by the House of Lords. Their Lordships agreed that what is now section 65(1) gave mutually exclusive routes to equal pay, but this was only after the applicant had chosen her male comparator. Had Mrs Pickstone chosen a man doing similar work as her comparator, she would have had to opt for a 'like work' claim. As her male comparator did a totally different job, she could use the 'equal value' route. This is an important decision, as it prevents employers from placing a 'token' man in work which is usually performed by women to prevent equal value claims.

Some critics of the new route were concerned that 'equal value' would be interpreted strictly. In other words, if the woman's job was assessed at a higher value than that of her male comparator, she would lose her equal value claim. The case of *Murphy v Bord Telecom Eireann* [1988] IRLR 267 decided that a woman is entitled to equal pay if her work is of at least equal value to that of her comparator. However, although a woman may choose a comparator who is less than her equal, she is only entitled to equal pay with that comparator and not more. In *Evesham v North Hertfordshire Health Authority* [2000] IRLR 257, a speech therapist successfully compared herself to a clinical psychologist. The Court of Appeal held that she should have been on the same pay scale as her comparator and should receive the same rate of pay, but stated that she was not entitled to be assessed further up the scale because of her longer service. There was no requirement in the legislation that the employer modify an individual term so that it became more favourable than that of her comparator. While this is a correct interpretation of the Act, which talks about the term of the woman's contract becoming as favourable as that of her comparator, it fails to remedy the injustice that Mrs Evesham would have been higher up the scale if the employer had not discriminated against her in the first place.

6.7 Defence

The defence for an employer to an equal pay claim in section 69 of the Equality Act 2010 is that of 'material factor'. Section 69 states that the sex equality clause has no effect with regard to a difference in terms if the employer shows that the difference is because of a material factor, reliance on which:

1. does not involve treating the woman less favourably than her comparator because of her sex; and
2. if the factor is within section 69(2), is a proportionate means of achieving a legitimate aim.

Section 69(2) provides that a factor is within that subsection if the employer shows that, as a result of this factor, the complainant and persons of the same sex doing work equal to the complainant's are put at a particular disadvantage when compared to persons of the opposite sex doing equal work ('equal work' means like work, work rated as equivalent or work of equal value). However, section 69(3) states that a long-term objective of reducing inequality between men's and women's terms of work is always to be regarded as a legitimate aim.

The material factor must be a material difference between the woman's case and the man's (s 69(6)). The EAT in *Financial Times Ltd v Byrne (No 2)* [1992] IRLR 163 held that the burden is on the employer to show both that the difference in terms is genuinely due to a material factor and that the factor is not due to a difference in sex.

There are no cases under the Equality Act 2010 as yet, therefore cases under the old law will be discussed in order to try and ascertain how section 69 will be interpreted. The defence was initially given a narrow interpretation by the Court of Appeal in the case of *Clay Cross (Quarry Services) v Fletcher* [1979] ICR 1. Mrs Fletcher was earning £35 per week and her employer appointed a man, doing the same job, at £43 per week. The employer argued that he had to offer the man this salary because that was the salary in his old job, therefore market forces dictated that he should pay the man more than Mrs Fletcher. The Court of Appeal rejected the employer's claim that there was a material difference between the man's case and Mrs Fletcher's. The Court stated that, on interpretation, the difference had to be in the 'personal equation', in other words, something different in the people doing the job, other than sex. As such, more experience or better qualifications would be a defence, but not the fact that men traditionally are paid more in an industry. As Lord Denning MR remarked, if an employer could pay men more because they asked for more, the legislation would be rendered impotent. Since the decision in *Fletcher*, however, the defence has been widened considerably, and it can now be argued that this widening has allowed what are essentially market forces arguments to be used as a defence.

If the man's salary has been 'red circled', that is, his higher salary has been protected because, for health or other reasons, he has had to take a lower-paid job, this is a material factor (*Methven v Cow Industrial Polymers Ltd* [1980] IRLR 289). Likewise, a difference in pay based on the difference in the cost of living between certain geographical areas is also permitted (*NAAFI v Varley* [1976] IRLR 408). Perhaps two more controversial areas where the defence has been permitted are in the case of part-time workers and situations where there is an approved pay body which has decided the pay scales, such as the Whitley Council. In *Jenkins v Kingsgate Clothing Productions Ltd* [1981] IRLR 388, the employer offered a lower hourly rate to part-time workers. This was for economic reasons, as machinery lay idle for part of the week when operated by part-time workers and there was a higher rate of absenteeism among the employer's part-time workers. The employer therefore hoped to encourage full-time working by paying the higher rate for more hours. The EAT, after a reference to the ECJ, held that economic necessity was a material factor defence as long as there was evidence that this was a valid reason for the difference in pay, that reason existed and the employer did not intend to discriminate. In *Rainey v Greater Glasgow Health Board Eastern District* [1987] AC 224, Mrs Rainey was a prosthetist working in the National Health Service. The Health Board needed to attract extra prosthetists into the Service and offered jobs to practitioners in the private sector, but on their existing salaries, not on NHS rates. This created a pay difference between Mrs Rainey and her male comparator of £2,790 per year. The House of Lords 'regretted' the narrow interpretation given to the defence in *Fletcher* (which Rainey's case resembled on the facts). Their Lordships held that the defence allowed an employer to take into account circumstances outside the personal equation and argue that the difference was necessary to achieve a result such as economic necessity or administrative efficiency.

The case of *Ratcliffe v North Yorkshire County Council* [1995] IRLR 439 suggests, however, that there may be a limit to how far the defence will be extended. In the case, the female employees employed by the council's direct service organisation had successfully claimed equal pay with male comparators. The organisation, however, cut the pay rate in order to make its bid competitive when a contract was put out for tender. The Court of Appeal upheld the employer's defence under what is now section 69 but this was rejected by the House of Lords. Lord Slynn, echoing the words of Lord Denning MR in *Fletcher*, stated that reducing women's wages below that of their male comparators 'was the very kind of discrimination in relation to pay which the Act sought to remove'. In other words, the courts will not allow the market forces defence to become too wide.

A limit imposed by the House of Lords in *Rainey* was that the factor raised by the employer had to be objectively justified; however, a later House of Lords decision in *Strathclyde Regional Council v Wallace* [1998] 1 WLR 259 suggests that where the woman cannot show that the difference in pay is due to a practice which has an impact on a particular group, the employer merely has to show why the difference exists but does not have to justify it objectively. In the case, women who were acting up as principal teachers but not getting the pay rate of permanent principal teachers claimed equal pay on a 'like work' comparison. Of the group acting up, 81 were men and 53 were women. The applicant could not therefore establish that there was discrimination, and therefore the employer's explanation, that is, financial constraint, did not have to be objectively justified (see the EAT in *Tyldesley v TML Plastics* [1996] IRLR 395 and *Parliamentary Commissioner for Administration v Fernandez* [2004] IRLR 22). The approach was endorsed again in *Armstrong v Newcastle upon Tyne NHS Hospital Trust* (Section 6.3 above).

In *Reed Packaging Ltd v Boozer* [1988] IRLR 333, it was held that different pay structures were a material factor defence as long as these were non-discriminatory and the employer was required by law to comply with the pay differentials (*R v Secretary of State for Social Services and Others, ex parte Clarke and Others* [1988] IRLR 22). In *Barber v NCR (Manufacturing)* [1993] IRLR 95, however, a reduction in hours bargained for by the union representing women workers brought about an inequality in the hourly rates of the women and another group of workers. There was no intention to produce this result and the employment tribunal upheld a material factor defence because the difference in pay had been caused by a different history of collective bargaining. The EAT held that the tribunal had posed the wrong question. It was insufficient to isolate the cause of the pay differential and see if it was tainted by discrimination. It was necessary to go further and decide if the cause constituted a material factor justifying a difference in pay on objective grounds.

This interpretation is supported by the ECJ decision in *Enderby v Frenchay Health Authority and Secretary of State for Health* [1994] 1 All ER 495. The case was brought by a speech therapist alleging that her work was of equal value to that of principal grade pharmacists and clinical psychologists. Under the NHS Whitley Council negotiating procedures, the pay rates of speech therapists, who are predominantly women, were negotiated by a different committee from that representing clinical psychologists, who are predominately men. The same is true for pharmacists, who are predominately male. Enderby was therefore on £10,106 per year, whereas a clinical psychologist with the same experience was on £12,527 per year and a pharmacist on £14,106 per year. The Authority argued on three points. First, Enderby's pay was negotiated by a separate bargaining unit from that of her comparators on a non-discriminatory basis. This was a material factor defence. Second, the agreements arising out of the negotiations were non-discriminatory, so Enderby could not complain of direct discrimination. Third, she could not complain of indirect discrimination as there was no barrier to her becoming a pharmacist or clinical psychologist. The ECJ rejected all three arguments. It decided that when bringing an equal pay claim, a woman employed in a female-dominated profession could compare herself to a male-dominated profession, even where there was no barrier between the two, where on statistical evidence there was a significant difference in pay. The burden then fell to the employer to show that the differential was objectively justified irrespective of sex. The ECJ further held that different non-discriminatory bargaining procedures or collective agreements did not necessarily amount to an objective justification, otherwise employers could avoid equal pay claims by using separate bargaining procedures. This point has been furthered enforced in the recent decision of *Kenny v Minister of Justice* (2013) [2013] WLR (D) 87. In the case, civilian clerical workers, who were predominantly women, were paid less than police officers, who were predominantly men, doing clerical duties. The respondent amongst other things argued that the number of posts held by police officers was determined by collective agreement. The ECJ held that collective agreements on their own cannot justify a difference in pay, but they are a factor in determining whether the difference is due to objective factors unrelated to sex.

The last point in *Enderby* was that the fact that part of the pay differential is justified for genuine economic reasons, such as recruitment difficulties, will not justify the whole of the differential, and the claimant is entitled to receive the balance. This will involve tribunals in identifying the part of pay to which the differential relates.

The case has established important points and should affect the section 69 defence as a whole and not just in equal value claims. In *Redcar & Cleveland Borough Council v Bainbridge* (Section 6.5 above), some 1,400 women claimed equal pay with higher-paid male workers employed as roadsweepers and gardeners. The Council argued that under job evaluations carried out with the unions, the men's jobs were given a lower status than the women's jobs and their pay had been protected. As such there was no claim. The Court of Appeal disagreed. The fact that the men and not the women would have suffered a drop in salary after the evaluations was because the women had been discriminated against in terms of their pay. If they had been paid their entitlement, they too would have suffered a pay drop and would have been entitled to the same pay protection as the men.

Enderby also made serious inroads into one major criticism of the legislation – that it does not protect women employed in female-dominated work. The application of *Enderby* may be seen in *British Road Services v Loughran* [1997] IRLR 92. There, the applicant was a clerical officer in an office of nine female clerical officers and seven men. In respect of all the employees employed by her employer, 75 per cent of clerical staff were female. The applicant sought equal pay with warehouse operatives whose pay was covered by a different collective agreement. The employer argued that the different bargaining structures created a defence, unless the principle in *Enderby* applied. The employer, however, argued that *Enderby* would apply only if the group including the applicant was exclusively or almost exclusively composed of women. The Northern Ireland Court of Appeal held that the phrase used in *Enderby* that the applicant's group was 'almost exclusively' composed of women referred to the facts of the particular case. In the present case, 75 per cent of clerical workers were women and the employment tribunal was entitled to conclude that the proportion, compared to 100 per cent of the warehouse operatives being male, provided a reliable indication of unequal treatment and that the different bargaining structures on their own did not justify the pay difference.

While the difference in *Loughran* was considerable, the Court of Appeal decision in *Home Office v Bailey* [2005] IRLR 369 shows that a much smaller difference can still establish a claim. In that case the EAT held that prison administrators could not put in an equal pay claim comparing themselves with prison officers and support staff, because the group consisted of 49 per cent men and 51 per cent women, and as such the women could not show that they were paid less because of their sex. The Court of Appeal, however, overturned the EAT, saying that as long as the number of women exceeded the number of men, that established a prima facie case and so the claim could proceed. Further, in *Gibson v Sheffield City Council* [2010] EWCA Civ 63, the Council argued, on the basis of *Armstrong* (see Section 6.3), that as it had shown that the differences between the pay of female care workers and the pay and bonuses paid predominantly to male workers were not tainted by sex discrimination, it did not have to justify the decision. The claimants argued, however, on the basis of *Enderby*, that given there was a significant disparate impact on women, the burden shifted to the Council to show objective justification. The Court of Appeal agreed with the claimants and remitted the case to the tribunal to consider whether objective justification existed.

Prior to *Enderby*, if the defence was raised, the employer did not have to justify every penny of the pay differential. In *Calder v Rowntree Mackintosh Confectionery* [1993] IRLR 212, male employees worked a rotating shift system. Male and female employees received the same basic pay but the men received a shift premium. The female applicants, while not working rotating shifts, did work unsocial hours. The employers accepted that part of the shift premium paid for the rotating shifts was for unsocial hours, but not all. The women therefore argued that as the whole of the shift premium was not for working unsocial hours, the defence was not made out. The Court of Appeal held that the tribunal was entitled to find that there was a material difference because of the different shift patterns, and the fact that some of the premium covered unsocial hours did not negate the defence. This must now be subject to the *Enderby* decision.

6.8 European law and equal pay

In addition to the three routes to equal pay under national law (Section 6.2 above), EU law gives two further ways in which a complainant may achieve equal pay.

6.8.1 Article 157 TFEU

Article 157 TFEU (ex Article 141 TEC) provides:

> Each Member State shall … ensure that the principle of equal pay for male and female workers for equal work or work of equal value is applied.

In *Defrenne v SABENA* [1976] CMLR 98, the ECJ held that then Article 141 EC (now Article 157 TFEU) was directly effective in the national courts, but only where there was direct and overt discrimination. As such, all employees in Member States have the right to sue under the Article for equal pay for equal work.

The definition of 'pay' within Article 157 TFEU is also wide. It is defined as:

the ordinary basic or minimum wage or salary and any other consideration, whether in cash or in kind, which the worker receives directly or indirectly, in respect of his employment, from his employer.

As such, it covers not only a weekly or monthly wage, but also any benefit which the worker receives as a result of the employment relationship, whether the contract is still subsisting or not. The ECJ has therefore ruled that payment of wages during sickness is covered (*Rinner-Kuhn v FWW Spezial Gebaudereinigung GmbH* [1989] IRLR 493), as are concessionary travel benefits for retired employees (*Garland v British Rail Engineering Ltd* [1982] IRLR 257, although note the important decision in *Grant v South-West Trains Ltd* [1998] IRLR 206) and occupational pension schemes (*Vroege v NCIV Instituut voor Volkshuisvesting BV* [1995] ICR 635 and *Fisscher v Voorhuis Henglo BV* [1994] IRLR 662).

There have been a number of cases in respect of part-time employees. It is not a breach of the Article, however, to offer overtime only to those working 39 hours a week so long as the same overtime rates are paid to part-time and full-time workers (*Stadt Lengerich v Helmig* [1995] IRLR 216). In *Barry v Midland Bank* [1999] IRLR 581, an employee who had worked full-time for 11 years returned to work part-time after maternity leave. She took voluntary redundancy after two years. The redundancy package was based on her final salary and thus took no account of her 11 years of full-time working. She claimed this had an adverse impact on women. The House of Lords held, however, that as full-time and part-time workers were treated the same (that is, redundancy package was based on final salary), there was no discrimination. This seems hard to justify, however, after the case of *Elsner-Lakeburg v Land Nordrhein Westfalen* [2005] IRLR 209. In this case both full-time and part-time teachers were treated as working overtime after they had worked their contractual hours (unlike *Stadt Lengerich*, above). Under German law, however, workers were paid for overtime only if they worked at least three additional hours a month. A part-time worker complained that this meant that she had to work 5 per cent more than her usual hours, whereas a full-time worker had to work only 3 per cent over the normal hours, and as such the rule had a disparate impact on women. The ECJ upheld the complaint, showing that the same treatment of full-time and part-time workers can create discrimination.

Given the above, the case of *Cadman v Health and Safety Executive* [2006] IRLR 969 seems a surprising decision of the ECJ. In 1989 the ECJ stated in *Handels- og Kontorfunktionaerernes Forbund i Danmark v Dansk Arbejdsgiverforening, ex parte Danfoss A/S* [1989] IRLR 532 that length of service is an acceptable criterion for determining pay, even if it has an adverse effect on women. Given *Elsner-Lakeburg* (above), it was to be hoped that this position would have moved forward, but it was confirmed in *Cadman*, the ECJ arguing that the legitimate objective achieved was that the worker performed better.

Perhaps the most important decision in this area is *Barber v Guardian Royal Exchange Assurance Group* [1990] IRLR 240. Mr Barber was made redundant at age 52. Under the provisions of his non-contributory pension scheme, a man, if made redundant before the age of 62, could claim an immediate pension at age 55; women, however, if made redundant, could claim a pension at age 50. Mr Barber alleged sex discrimination, but under the then Sex Discrimination Act, retirement and pension provisions were excluded from its operation. The Court of Appeal, however, asked the ECJ to give a preliminary ruling on certain issues – in particular whether a pension payable under a redundancy scheme could be 'pay' within the meaning of then Article 141 EC (now Article 157 TFEU). The ECJ ruled:

1. Benefits paid by an employer under a compulsory redundancy constituted pay and fell within the Article, whether paid under a contract of employment, by virtue of a statutory provision or on a voluntary basis.
2. Private pensions constituted 'pay' within the Article.
3. It was contrary to the Article for a man who had been made redundant to be entitled to a deferred pension, whereas a woman would be entitled to an immediate pension – 'the application of the principle of equal pay must be ensured in respect of each element of remuneration'.
4. The Article could be relied upon in the national courts.
5. The direct effect of the Article on entitlement to pensions might not be relied upon for entitlements arising prior to 17 May 1990 (the date of the decision) unless legal proceedings had already been initiated.

The effect of the decision was dramatic. A problem arose, however, in relation to point 5. above. The implications were not clear, and as a result the government supported the firm Coloroll in a reference to the ECJ for an interpretation of the point – in particular whether back pension was payable only to 17 May 1990 or to the date of the original act of discrimination. At Maastricht in 1991, all Member States signed a protocol limiting the effect of *Barber* to cases initiated before the judgment or those arising after the judgment, and limiting back pension to the date of the decision. A protocol, however, is not legally binding. In *Ten Oever v Stichting Bedriffspensionfunds voor het Glazenwassers* [1993] IRLR 601, however, the ECJ gave a narrow interpretation to the *Barber* decision. It ruled that benefits have to be equal only if they are earned by periods of employment falling after 17 May 1990; thus the ECJ has confirmed the result required by the protocol. The limitation was further tested in the case of *Quirk v Burton Hospitals NHS Trust and Secretary of State for Health* [2002] Emp LR 469. In this case, until *Barber* the rules of the health service pension scheme allowed women to retire at age 55 but men could not retire until age 60. After *Barber*, the ages were aligned, but women who retired before age 60 were entitled to receive benefits calculated by reference to all of their pensionable service, whereas men retiring before age 60 were only entitled to benefits calculated by reference to service after 17 May 1990, the date of the *Barber* decision. The Court of Appeal held that this was a correct interpretation of *Barber*.

While *Barber* decided that statutory redundancy pay was 'pay' for the purposes of (now) Article 157 TFEU, the position in relation to unfair dismissal compensation was unclear until the decision in *R v Secretary of State for Employment, ex parte Seymour-Smith and Perez* [1999] IRLR 253, where the ECJ decided that unfair dismissal compensation constituted 'pay' within the meaning of the Article.

6.8.2   Equal Pay Directive

The Equal Pay Directive (75/117/EEC) states that the principle of equal pay (now in Article 157 TFEU) means:

> for the same work or for work to which equal value is attributed, the elimination of all discrimination on grounds of sex with regard to all aspects and conditions of remuneration.

A directive establishes a result it wishes Member States to achieve through national legislation. As such, should national legislation fail to provide that result, an individual who is employed by a government authority acting in the capacity of an employer may sue under the directive in the national courts, as long as the directive is sufficiently precise. In other words the government, acting as an employer, should not benefit from its wrongdoing in failing to implement the directive in full. Private employers, however, should not be punished for merely complying with inadequate national law.

The concept of the government as an employer is wide. It covers area health authorities (*Marshall v Southampton & South West Hampshire Area Health Authority* [1986] QB 401) and nationalised industries (*Foster v British Gas plc* [1991] ICR 84). It does not, however, include public limited companies (*Doughty v Rolls-Royce plc* [1992] IRLR 126). This means, in effect, that public employees have an additional route to claim equal pay – the Directive – which is not available to private employees. The Directive, however, may assist private employees in so far as the courts will look to the Directive when interpreting provisions of national law, and should seek to interpret the Equality Act 2010 in line with the Directive and Article 157 TFEU.

6.8.3   Time limits and retrospective claims

The cases necessitate a discussion of time limits and retrospective claims. It has been seen from the discussion above that the ECJ has decided that more and more benefits fall within the definition of 'pay'. *Vroege* and *Fisscher* (see Section 6.8.1) held that the exclusion of part-time workers from occupational pension schemes was potentially contrary to (now) Article 157 TFEU. Those cases also decided that the time limits placed by *Barber* (Section 6.8.1) did not apply to the right to join an occupational pension scheme. This means potentially that part-time workers have claims going back to 1976 when *Defrenne* held that the principle of equal pay had direct effect.

However, there is a distinction between those employees who have left their employment and those employees still employed. In respect of those employees whose contracts have terminated, there is the issue of the relevant time limit for bringing claims. In relation to employees in the private sector, this was extensively discussed in *Biggs v Somerset County Council* [1996] IRLR 203, a case involving a retrospective unfair dismissal claim after the decision of *R v Secretary of State for Employment, ex parte EOC* [1994] IRLR 176 (see Chapter 9). In the case the applicant was dismissed in 1976, two years before the implementation of the Equal Treatment Directive. She was not protected at the time of her dismissal by unfair dismissal provisions because she was a part-time worker. The issue was whether she could pursue a retrospective claim, given that the House of Lords had decided that the limitations relating to part-time workers were contrary to the Equal Treatment Directive and (now) Article 157 TFEU. Given the date of her dismissal, her claim was relying on the Article in force at the time. The Court of

Appeal held that a claim under the Article should be seen as a claim under the relevant domestic law, the Court having the ability to disapply the offending provisions. As such, the relevant time limit under national law applied in relation to the presentation of a claim. In Biggs's case this was three months from the effective date of termination of her contract, and it was not impossible for the applicant to present her claim in time, given that the right to claim unfair dismissal arose from the Article which had direct effect since the decision in *Defrenne* in 1976. This decision has an impact on part-time workers claiming access to occupational pensions retrospectively after their contract has terminated. This is because, on the basis of *Biggs*, their claim will lie under the Equality Act 2010. Section 129(3) of that Act states that claims must be brought within six months of the last act complained of, that is within six months of the effective date of termination of the contract, with no discretion on the part of the tribunal to extend the time limit. This interpretation was upheld by the Court of Appeal in *Preston v Wolverhampton Healthcare NHS Trust* [1997] IRLR 233, effectively wiping out the claims of 60,000 part-time workers who were excluded from pension schemes because of their part-time status. An alternative argument is that it would be impossible for the applicant to enforce her EU law rights until the date of *Vroege* and *Fisscher* (1994), and that the time limits run from that date. *Preston* was appealed to the House of Lords. Their Lordships decided to refer a number of questions to the ECJ ([1998] IRLR 197). First, were the time limits in the then EPA 1970 compatible with EU law? Second, what were the criteria for determining whether the time limits are compatible? Lastly, did the six-month time limit run from the end of the individual contract? In making the reference, the House of Lords was mindful of the ECJ's decision in *Margorrian v Eastern Health and Social Services Board* [1998] IRLR 86 (see further below).

The argument in relation to employees in the public sector is different. There is an argument that until the Occupational Pension Schemes (Equal Access to Membership) Regulations 1995 (now the Equality Act 2010, section 61) came into force, the Equal Pay Directive had not been properly implemented, and therefore on the basis of *Emmott v Minister for Social Welfare and Attorney-General* [1991] IRLR 387 the time limit did not start to run until the Regulations came into force. The principle in *Emmott* is that time limits do not start to run until the Directive is fully implemented.

A second issue was whether the (then) section 2(5) of the EPA 1970 applied and thus restricted back pensions to two years. The section referred to 'arrears of remuneration or damages', and there was an argument that any applicant would not be claiming remuneration or damages and thus section 2(5) did not apply. An alternative argument, which had wider implications, was that, since *Marshall* (Section 6.8.2 above), limits on compensation for discriminatory acts were inconsistent with the Equal Treatment Directive and thus the two-year rule should be disregarded. The ECJ in other areas has held that it is not a breach of EU law to place a restriction on how far back the award can be made (see, for example, *Johnstone v Chief Adjudication Officer (No 2)* [1995] IRLR 157), although those cases were based on the implementation of the Social Security Directives. In a reference from the Northern Ireland Court of Appeal in *Margorrian* (above), the ECJ decided that similar time limits in Northern Ireland's legislation were contrary to EU law, both in the restriction on an application to six months after the termination of the contract and on the two-year limit in respect of back pay; however, the decision related specifically to pension claims, which is why the House of Lords in *Preston* referred wider questions to the ECJ. The EAT referred the more general question to the ECJ in *Levez v T H Jennings*

(Harlow Pools Ltd) [1996] IRLR 499. The ECJ decided ([1999] IRLR 36) that a limit which operates in the field of equal pay, where limits do not apply in respect of other claims, for example recovery of arrears of pay in breach of contract claims, and where the national legislation gives the court no discretion to increase the two-year limit, is contrary to (now) Article 157 TFEU.

The long-awaited ECJ ruling in *Preston* came in the millennium year. The ECJ ruled ([2000] All ER 714) that the statutory limitation period which restricted compensation for the unlawful exclusion of women from the membership of occupational pension schemes to two years was incompatible with EU law. The House of Lords ([2001] 2 WLR 448) confirmed, therefore, that the two-year recovery rule in the then Occupational Pension Schemes (Equal Access to Membership) Regulations 1995 was incompatible with the Directive and what is now Article 157 TFEU, and future pension benefits had to be calculated using both full-time and part-time periods of service arising after 8 April 1976 (the date of *Defrenne*). Their Lordships went on to say, however, that the six-month time period in which to present a claim was not unreasonable and it could not be said to be less favourable than the rules existing in contract. Where there were intermittent contracts, with no stable employment relationship existing, the six-month period ran from the date each contract ended, but where there was employment in the same employment, interrupted at regular intervals, the six-month period ran from the end of the last contract.

Now the Equality Act 2010 takes into account the ECJ decisions and provides that where an employee is employed on a series of contracts, the six-month time limit for bringing a claim runs from the end of the employment relationship (s 129(3)), unless the employer has deliberately concealed facts or the employee is incapacitated in which case the time limit starts to run from the date the employee is aware of the facts or the day the incapacity ceases, and extends the period for recovery of arrears from two years to six. In *Slack and Others v Cumbria County Council* [2009] EWCA Civ 293, the Court of Appeal held that the six-month time limit starts to run at the end of a period of a stable relationship, and this relationship is not broken by issuing a new contract. In the case, Mrs Slack had been employed by the Council from 1971, but in 2000 reduced her hours and a new contract was issued reflecting this change. She brought an equal pay claim, but the Council disputed the claim in relation to the period prior to 2000, arguing that as a new contract had been issued, any claim between 1971 and 2000 was out of time as Mrs Slack had not claimed within six months of her old contract's expiring. The Court of Appeal, while accepting that new contracts had been issued in 2000 (rather than a variation of an existing contract), found for the claimant on the basis of a stable relationship, the concept introduced by the ECJ in *Preston*; consequently, Mrs Slack could take into account periods prior to 2000. However, the EAT ruled in *Foley v NHS Greater Glasgow and Clyde* (2012) UKEAT 0007/12/BI that when there was a reorganisation of NHS Trusts, the six-month time limit started to run from the dissolution of the trust and so the claimants were out of time in their equal pay claim.

There may be some hope on the horizon for those claimants who are unsure of their position. In *Birmingham City Council v Abdulla and ors* [2012] UKSC 47, claimants achieved equal salaries on the basis of work rated as equivalent, but the Council would not pay them the bonuses and additional payments stipulated in their comparators' contracts. The claimants left employment on various dates between August 2004 and November 2008, and their initial claims – that failing to grant them the bonuses and additional payments was discriminatory – were struck out as being out of time. The claimants then took action in the High Court for breach of contract to take advantage of the civil court time limit of six years. Birmingham City Council tried to have the claims struck out under the then applicable Equal Pay Act 1970, section 2(3) of which stated that cases should be struck out where the court considers that claims could be more conveniently disposed of by an employment tribunal. The claimants won on a 3:2 majority vote. Lord Wilson (with Lady Hale and Lord Reed) decided that since the effect of striking out the claims would effectively mean that the claims died, it could not be said that the claims could more conveniently be disposed of in a tribunal. Parliament allowed the claims to be brought in the civil courts as well as before tribunals, and therefore must have accepted that the six-year limitation period would apply. However, while the majority felt that Parliament should consider relaxing the six-month time limit, it warned that claimants who were found to have deliberately delayed bringing their claims to gain an illegitimate advantage by bringing court proceedings risked having their claims struck out; and if a court decided that an individual should reasonably have presented a claim in the tribunal, this was something to take into account when awarding costs.

The Equality Act 2010, however, only entitles the complainant to claim arrears. In *Degan v Redcar and Cleveland Borough Council* [2005] IRLR 504 and *Council of Newcastle upon Tyne v Allan* (2005) IDS 781, the Court of Appeal (*Degan*) and the EAT (*Allan*) held that the law does not provide for a tribunal to award compensation for injury to feelings. Claims under the Act are based on contract law where damages are restricted to financial loss.

Summary

6.1 By section 66 of the 2010 Act, all contracts of employment are deemed to include a 'sex equality clause' which, if activated, makes any term in A's contract relating to pay as favourable as the equivalent term in B's contract.

6.2 In order to claim equal pay, A must find a comparator within the definition in section 79 of the Act, although Article 157 TFEU gives wider protection.

6.3 A is on 'like work' if her/his work is the same or broadly similar and the differences between A's case and B's are not of practical importance. The tribunal will look at duties, hours and responsibilities.

6.4 A is entitled to equal pay if a JES has given the job a rating equal to that of B.

6.5 Equal value is the third route to equal pay. An independent expert may be appointed by the tribunal, who will evaluate the complainant's job and that of the comparator. If an expert is not appointed, the tribunal will assess whether the jobs are of equal value.

6.6 The defences to an equal pay claim are a material factor which is not the difference of sex and where the employer is using a proportionate means to achieve a legitimate aim.

6.7 It is a legitimate aim to reduce the inequality of terms between the sexes.

6.8 In addition to national law, all employees have a route to equal pay under Article 157 TFEU. In addition, public employees can claim under the Equal Pay Directive.

Exercises

Hilda works in the Sales Office at Coronation Products Ltd as a Grade 2 clerical worker. She earns £310 per week. Two months ago the company took on Mike as a clerical worker. In order to attract him to the job, they offered it to him at Grade 3 with a salary of £350 per week. Mike was one of a group of men who came from a local firm which had closed down, and Coronation was anxious to attract them into employment. All were offered jobs at higher grades. There is no difference between the job Hilda does and Mike's job, but the company argues that to re-grade Hilda's job, and that of the other 60 Grade 2 clerical workers (all of whom are women), would involve a great deal of administrative work in restructuring the grading system and would prove to be very expensive. Advise Hilda whether she can claim equal pay with Mike.

Further reading and references

Fredman, 'Equal Pay and Justification' (1994) 23 ILJ 37
Fredman, 'Marginalising Equal Pay Laws' (2004) 33 ILJ 281
Fredman, 'Reforming Equal Pay Laws' (2008) 37 ILJ 193
Gregory, 'Dynamite or Damp Squib? An Assessment of Equal Value Law' (1997) 2 IJDL 167
Kilpatrick, 'Deciding When Jobs of Equal Value Can Be Paid Unequally' (1994) 23 ILJ 163
McColgan, *Just Wages for Women* (Clarendon 1997)
Rowbottom, 'Justifying Service-Related Pay in the Context of Sex Discrimination Law' (2010) 39 ILJ 382
Steele, 'Tracing the Single Source: Choice of Comparators in Equal Pay Claims' (2006) 35 ILJ 338
Steele, 'Beyond Equal Pay' (2008) 37 ILJ 119
Steele, 'Sex Discrimination and the Material Factor Defence Under the EPA 1970 and EQA 2010' (2010) 39 ILJ 264
Thomas, 'Equal Pay and Redundancy Schemes' (2000) 29 ILJ 68

Chapter 7

Employment protection

7.1 Introduction

Since 1963, there has been a transformation in employment law. Until then, the rights of employees were contained almost exclusively within an individual contract of employment, with very little statutory intervention other than in the areas of health and safety and the payment of wages. However, 1963 saw the introduction of the Contracts of Employment Act, which introduced minimum notice periods and the right to written particulars, and since then various pieces of legislation have given employment protection rights which are enforced through the tribunals rather than the ordinary courts. Many of these rights, such as the right not to be unfairly dismissed and the right to redundancy payments, are discussed more fully in Chapters 9 and 10. In addition to these major rights, however, there is a variety of disparate individual rights which were created by the Employment Protection Act 1975 and the Employment Relations Act 1999, and which can now be found in the Employment Rights Act (ERA) 1996. It is these rights that the following will discuss.

7.2 Guarantee payments

The provisions relating to a guarantee payment are contained in sections 28–35 of the ERA 1996. The original provisions were intended to ensure that when an employer temporarily laid off workers, those employees would be entitled to a minimum payment from the employer for a limited period of time. Section 28 lays out the general entitlement and states that where an employee is not provided with work by his employer because of a diminution in the requirements of the employer's business for work of the kind the employee is employed to do, or any other occurrence affecting such work, the employee shall be entitled to a guarantee payment. To claim, the employee must have at least one month's continuous employment. The employee is entitled to a payment where there is a workless day, that is, a day when he would normally have worked, and therefore holidays are not included.

Section 29 goes on to deal with the exclusions from payment. Where the employee is on a fixed-term contract of three months or less, or on a contract for a specific task which was not expected to last for more than three months, the entitlement arises only if the employee has more than three months' continuity. In addition, an employee loses entitlement if the workless day is due to a strike, lock-out or any other industrial action affecting his employer or an associated employer (s 29(3)), or where the employer has offered suitable alternative work which the employee has unreasonably refused, whether the employee is contractually obliged to perform the work or not (s 29(4)(a)). Furthermore, the employee will not be entitled if he fails to comply with reasonable requirements imposed by his employer with a view to ensuring that his services are available (s 29(5)).

There are rather complicated provisions in section 31 as to the amount of and limits on a guarantee payment. In essence, these mean that an employee is entitled to a maximum of five one-day payments in any three-month period at the statutory daily rate. In other words, the employee is entitled to one normal working week's pay at the statutory rate. If normally he works only four days, that is the extent of his entitlement in any three-month period (s 31(3)). If normally he works for six days, the statutory maximum applies and he will receive payment for only five of those days. The employee is not entitled to jobseeker's allowance for the days he receives a guarantee payment, and such days do not count as waiting days for the purpose of such benefit. However, a collective agreement which gives better rights than the statute will take precedence over the statutory entitlement. The right to a guarantee payment is enforced through the employment tribunals within three months of the day in question.

7.3 Medical suspension pay

Under section 64 of the ERA 1996, an employee who is suspended from work on certain specified medical grounds is entitled to receive medical suspension pay for up to 26 weeks of suspension. This applies where the employee is suspended because of a requirement imposed by statute or due to any provision in a code of practice issued under section 16 of the HASAWA 1974 (s 64(2)). In other words, the provisions are not another form of sick pay but are providing an employee who is suspended because, for example, he has been dealing too long with a particular chemical, with a salary during his suspension. In such cases the employee is entitled to be paid his normal week's pay by his employer. The same exclusions apply to a medical suspension payment as apply in the case of a guarantee payment (Section 7.2 above), with the added exclusion that the employee will not be entitled to medical suspension pay in respect of any period during which he is incapable of work by reason of disease or bodily or mental disablement (s 65(3)).

By sections 66–68, if a woman who is pregnant, has recently given birth or who is breast-feeding would otherwise be suspended from work under these provisions and there is no suitable alternative work, she is entitled to her full remuneration. Similar provisions apply if the woman is suspended from work on health and safety maternity grounds. In other words, if, because she is pregnant, she is suspended because of health and safety considerations, this is treated in the same way as any other medical suspension on those grounds.

7.4 Maternity rights

Apart from the important protection from unfair dismissal because of pregnancy discussed in Chapter 9, the ERA 1996, as amended by the Employment Relations Act 1999, the Maternity and Parental Leave Regulations (MPLR) 1999 and the Work and Families Act 2006, provides three further protections in relation to pregnancy:

1. the right to maternity leave;
2. the right to time off for ante-natal care; and
3. the right to maternity pay.

7.4.1 Right to maternity leave

Since April 2007, all pregnant employees are entitled to 52 weeks' maternity leave, regardless of length of service. Such leave is continuous and consists of ordinary maternity leave (OML – see further Section 7.4.3) and additional maternity leave (AML – see further Section 7.4.4).

7.4.2 Compulsory maternity leave

All employees are entitled to a period of two weeks' compulsory maternity leave which is part of OML and which commences on the day childbirth occurs (ERA 1996, s 72; MPLR 1999, Reg 8). An employer must not allow an employee to work during this period and commits a criminal offence if he or she does so.

Note that in September 2013 Advocate-General Kokott gave an opinion in *CA v ST* (2013) Case C-167/12. In the case, the claimant and her partner had a child via a surrogate. The claimant was breast-feeding the child within an hour of its birth, and she lodged a complaint with an employment tribunal that her employer refused to grant her paid maternity or adoption leave on the basis that she had not given birth to or adopted a child. In the opinion of the Advocate-General, the ECJ should find that the claimant has the right to receive maternity leave under the Pregnant Workers Directive (92/85/EC). In his opionion compulsory leave of at least two weeks must be granted to both mothers. However, surrogacy cannot result in doubling the leave under the Directive, therefore four weeks' leave must be deducted from the minimum and the rest of the leave entitlement divided between the two mothers. The ECJ normally follows the opinion of the Advocates-General.

7.4.3 Ordinary maternity leave

The amended section 71 of the ERA 1996 and the MPLR 1999 implement the Pregnant Workers Directive. Section 71 refers to the first 26 weeks of maternity leave as 'ordinary maternity leave'. Leave may not begin until the fifteenth week before the expected week of childbirth, or the first day of the beginning of the fourth week before the expected week of childbirth if the employee is absent wholly or partially because of pregnancy (MPLR 1999, Reg 6(1)(b)). The latest day that leave can commence is the day of childbirth (MPLR 1999, Reg 6(2)).

During OML the employee is entitled to all the terms and conditions of her contract excluding pay, and all her benefits will continue (s 71). In *Hoyland v Asda Stores Ltd* [2006] CSIH 21, the Scottish Employment Appeal Tribunal held that a pro rata reduction of a bonus for absence on maternity leave was not sex discrimination nor pregnancy-related detriment, as such a bonus was remuneration and therefore not a benefit to which the claimant was entitled during her maternity leave. She was, however, entitled to receive a bonus for the two-week compulsory maternity leave period. This is obviously a complex area. If there is no contractual right to pay, a woman will be entitled to statutory maternity pay if she meets the qualifying conditions (see Section 7.4.8 below). Ordinary maternity leave will count as continuous service when assessing pension rights or other benefits based on length of service.

To be entitled to OML the employee must comply with certain notification provisions. She must inform her employer no later than the end of the fifteenth week before the expected week of childbirth (EWC) of the fact that she is pregnant and the date she intends to start taking leave (MPLR 1999, Reg 4(1)(a)). She must also provide a certificate from a midwife or general practitioner stating the expected week of childbirth (MPLR 1999, Reg 4(1)(b)). Failure to comply with the notification provisions may mean she loses her right to statutory maternity pay and to start her leave on her intended date (MPLR 1999, Reg 4(2)). If her maternity leave starts at the beginning of the fourth week before the expected week of childbirth because of a pregnancy-related absence, she does not have to notify the employer of the expected week of childbirth or the date on which her leave starts (it will have started by MPLR 1999, Reg 6(1)(b)). She will, however, lose her rights if she does not inform her employer as soon as reasonably practicable that she is absent wholly or partly because of pregnancy (MPLR 1999, Reg 4(2)). If the illness is not related in whole or in part to her pregnancy, she can remain off work on sick leave up to the date of birth or the date she has notified.

Once she has informed her employer of the date she intends to start OML, the woman can change the date if she notifies the employer (in writing if so requested) by whichever is the earlier of 28 days before the date she originally intended to start her leave or 28 days before the new date she wishes to start her leave, unless it is not reasonably practicable to do so, in which case she should notify the employer as soon as it is reasonably practicable.

7.4.4 Additional maternity leave

All employees, regardless of length of service, are entitled to AML (ERA 1996, s 73; MPLR 1999, Reg 5). Additional maternity leave is 26 weeks starting from the end of OML (MPLR 1999, Reg 7(4)). This means that the total maternity leave which may be taken is 52 weeks, although it could be longer if there is a late birth. Until October 2008 a woman had considerably fewer rights during AML. The employee was entitled to the benefit of the implied obligation of trust and confidence, and terms in the contract relating to notice, redundancy compensation, and disciplinary and grievance procedures. She was bound by terms relating to notice and good faith, and unlike OML, AML did not count as continuous service for pensions or other benefits based on length of service, but did count as continuous service for the purpose of qualifying for statutory employment rights. However, in *EOC v Secretary of State for Trade and Industry* [2007] IRLR 327 the High Court ruled that preventing an employee on AML from receiving the same benefits that applied to her while on OML was sex discrimination, and the Maternity and Parental Leave, etc and Paternity and Adoption Leave (Amendment) Regulations 2008 provide that a woman with an EWC on or after 5 October 2008 is entitled to benefit from the same terms and conditions as those available while on OML, including the fact that AML counts as continuous service for the purpose of qualifying for statutory employment protection rights. The only difference is that whereas after OML she is entitled to return to the same job, after AML she is entitled to return to her previous job or, if that is not reasonably practicable, another job which is suitable for her to do and appropriate for her to do in the circumstances (MPLR 1999, Reg 18(2)).

7.4.5 Return from leave

Unlike under the previous provisions, the employee does not need to inform her employer about her date of return. The employer, after he has received notification of the start date of her leave, should inform the employee within 28 days of the date. If she has not been properly informed of when her leave is due to end, and does not return on time, she is protected against victimisation and dismissal. If she wishes to return before the end of the 52-week period, she must give at least eight weeks' notice of her intention to do so. If she intends to return immediately after the 52 weeks there are no notification requirements. At the end, she is entitled to return to her previous job with her seniority and all other benefits in place as if she had not been absent (ERA 1996, s 71(7)). If when her leave ends it is no longer practicable to continue to employ her because of redundancy, she is entitled to be offered suitable alternative employment (ERA 1996, s 74 and MPLR 1999, Reg 10). If her contract gives her more favourable rights than the statutory provisions, she is entitled to choose the more favourable rights (MPLR 1999, Reg 21(2)). If she wishes to return to different working conditions, she has no statutory right to do this, although she does have the right to request flexible working (see Section 7.8 below).

7.4.6 Contact during maternity leave and keeping-in-touch days

During maternity leave, employers and employees may make reasonable contact with each other. What is reasonable will depend on the nature of the job and the nature of information which may need to be communicated. It is useful if, before leave commences, the parties discuss what contact should be made, how frequently, how contact should be made and the type of information to be communicated. The Maternity and Paternity Leave, etc and the Paternity and Adoption Leave (Amendment) Regulations 2006 allow women or adopters to work for up to 10 mutually agreed keeping-in-touch days, during their leave, without losing entitlement to statutory maternity or adoption pay for those days. The type of work undertaken is a matter of agreement between the parties. An employer may not require an employee to work during maternity leave, nor does an employee have the right to keeping-in-touch days if the employer does not agree to them. Any amount of work on one day counts as a day and the employer cannot, for example, ask an employee to work 20 half days. There is no legal requirement that the employee is paid for the keeping-in-touch days, although government guidance suggests that she should be paid.

7.4.7 Time off for ante-natal care

To qualify for this right the employee must have made an appointment for ante-natal care on the advice of a doctor, midwife or health visitor (ERA 1996, s 55(1)). The employer may not refuse time off for the first appointment, but for succeeding appointments the employer may ask for a certificate certifying that the employee is pregnant and for an appointment card or some other document showing that the appointment has been made (ERA 1996, s 55(2)). The employee is entitled not to be unreasonably refused time off with pay to keep such appointments. Any complaint in relation to refusal of time off or refusal to pay for the time taken must be made to a tribunal within three months of the date of the appointment.

7.4.8 Statutory maternity pay and maternity allowance

The Social Security Act 1986 and the Statutory Maternity Pay Regulations 1986 (as amended) entitle certain employees to statutory maternity pay (SMP). If the employee does not have the qualifying conditions to claim SMP, she is entitled to maternity allowance. If the employee has been working for the employer for 26 weeks by the fifteenth week before the expected week of confinement, she is entitled to SMP for 39 weeks. Maternity allowance is also payable for 39 weeks. The rate of SMP is fixed by the 1986 Regulations. The employee is entitled to nine-tenths of her pay for the first six weeks of the 39, and to the flat rate of SMP for a further 33 weeks.

To claim, the employee's earnings in the last eight weeks ending with the qualifying week must not be less than the lower earnings limit for the payment of NICs. She must produce a certificate (not earlier than the fourteenth week before her expected week of confinement) stating her expected week of confinement, and inform her employer 28 days before her absence begins that she is stopping work because of pregnancy. The maternity pay period starts when she wishes it to. The employer recoups the payments he has made on the 12-week element by making deductions from his NICs. Restrictions on recoupment which exist in relation to statutory sick pay also apply to SMP (see Section 4.2.6).

A woman who does not qualify for SMP is entitled to a maternity allowance from the state. This is payable to women who have been employed or self-employed for at least 26 weeks in the 66 weeks ending with the EWC, who have paid 26 weeks' NICs and have earned on average £30 per week. It is a weekly benefit paid by the government rather than the employer and is paid at a flat rate, or at 90 per cent of weekly earnings if this is less than the flat rate. It continues for 39 weeks and stops if the woman returns to work before the end of the maternity allowance period.

To pay a woman less than she would otherwise have been paid because of her pregnancy or maternity leave is discriminatory. Therefore, any pay increase or bonus achieved while on maternity leave must be reflected in her maternity pay.

7.5 Parental leave

The Parental Leave Directive (96/34/EC) was implemented by the UK in December 1999. The rights are contained in sections 76–80 of the ERA 1996, the detail of the rights being set out in the MPLR 1999. The rights contained in the Regulations represent a fall-back position, the legislation encouraging employers to develop workplace arrangements. As such, the statutory provisions apply only if no workplace agreement exists.

Originally the right to parental leave applied to parents of children born on or after 15 December 1999, the date that the provisions came into force. This excluded parents with young children born before that date. The Trades Union Congress (TUC) mounted a legal challenge, arguing that under the Directive the right should apply to all parents of children who were under the age of 5 when the Regulations came into force (*R v Secretary of State for Trade and Industry, ex parte TUC* [2000] IRLR 565). The Divisional Court referred the question to the ECJ, as a result of which in April 2001 the government extended the right to parents of children who were under 5 on 15 December 1999, and thus the legal challenge was withdrawn.

The Regulations provide that an employee with one year's continuous employment can take up to 18 weeks' unpaid parental leave in respect of each child for which the employee has responsibility (MPLR 1999, Regs 13 and 14). The leave may be taken up to the child's fifth birthday. In respect of disabled children, 18 weeks' leave can be taken up to the child's eighteenth birthday. Where a child has been adopted, leave may be taken up to the five-year anniversary of the placement, or the child's eighteenth birthday, whichever is the earlier (MPLR 1999, Reg 15). During parental leave an employee is entitled to the benefit of the same contractual terms as an employee on AML (Section 7.4.4 above), and is bound by the same contractual terms (MPLR 1999, Reg 17). If an employee returns to work after her AML followed by parental leave, she is entitled to return to the same job, unless it would not have been reasonably practicable to return to the same job after AML; if this is not possible then she has a right to a similar job.

As mentioned above, the Regulations encourage workplace agreements and set out default provisions which are applicable if such agreements do not exist (MPLR 1999, Reg 16). Schedule 2 to the Regulations lists the default provisions and provides for leave to be taken in blocks of multiples of one week, with a maximum of four weeks' leave a year. Any leave amounting to less than a week is classed as a whole week for the purposes of entitlement. The employee must give 21 days' notice before taking leave, and the employer can postpone leave for up to six months if the leave required by the employee would unduly disrupt his business. However, the employer must agree alternative dates on which the leave may be taken.

To prevent the default provisions operating, the employer must have a collective or workforce agreement governing parental leave which is incorporated into the contracts of employment of his employees. A collective agreement is one made with an independent trade union. A workforce agreement may be made only if there is no collective agreement governing terms and conditions of employment. It must be made in consultation with workforce representatives, be in writing and be effective for a period not exceeding five years. The employer must send written copies of the agreement, together with guidance, to relevant employees.

7.6 Paternity leave and pay

New fathers are entitled to one or two weeks' paternity leave paid at the same rate as SMP (Section 7.4.8 above) and may claim any remaining maternity pay which has not been claimed by the mother (see below). This is in addition to parental leave. Eligibility for paid paternity leave is the same as for SMP. The right is lost unless the father has informed his employer of his intention to take leave by the fifteenth week before the expected week of childbirth, and he will have to give 28 days' notice if he wishes to change the start date. To qualify for the right, the employee must have 26 weeks' service before the expected week of childbirth and he must have, or expect to have, responsibility for the child's upbringing or be the mother's husband, partner or civil partner. This applies in relation to natural or adopted children. The qualifying week for adopters is the week the adopter is matched to a child (see Section 7.7).

The leave period will start on or after the onset of labour (or in the case of adopters the week they are matched to a child) and leave will have to be taken in a single block within the first 56 days of the child's life (unless otherwise agreed with the employer). There is protection from detriment and dismissal for taking paid paternity leave, and a father will be able to take unpaid parental leave immediately afterwards.

The Additional Parental Leave Regulations 2010 amend the MPLR 1999 and give fathers a maximum of 26 weeks' leave if the mother has not taken all of her maternity leave. In addition if the mother has not taken all of her 39 weeks' maternity pay, the father can claim the remainder. Additional paternity leave starts 20 weeks after the birth or date of adoption.

7.7 Adoption leave and pay

Couples who have a child placed with them for adoption are able to choose which of them is entitled to take 52 weeks of adoption leave. The first 39 weeks is paid at the same rate as the flat rate of SMP (Section 7.4.8 above). The other adoptive parent is able to take two weeks' paid paternity leave at the time of the adoption. Parental leave may also be taken in addition to adoption leave. The right is available to adoptive parents who have 26 weeks' continuous service.

Adoptive parents have to inform their employer when they have been approved for adoption and the indicative matching time given by the adoption agency. Adoption leave starts as soon as the child is placed with the parents. There is a right of return which is the same as the right to return after AML (Section 7.4.4 above). As with maternity leave, should an employee wish to return before the end of the 52 weeks, the employee must give the employee at least eight weeks' notice of the date on which he or she intends to return. In addition there is protection from detriment or dismissal. The right is not available to step-adoption or adoption by foster-parents.

7.8 Right to request flexible working

Originally the Employment Act 2002 introduced a right to request flexible working, in order to care for a child under the age of 6, by the insertion of a new section 80F into the ERA 1996. This right was extended by the Work and Families Act 2006 to include an employee who cares for a spouse or partner, adult relatives or an adult living at the same address as the employee, and was extended to all parents with children up to the age of 16 in April 2009.

The right allows a qualifying employee to apply to his employer for a change in his terms and conditions of employment in relation to:

- the hours he is required to work;
- the times he is required to work;
- as between his home and place of work, the place he is required to work; or
- any other such aspect of his terms and conditions.

A qualifying employee is an employee who has been employed for 26 weeks. If an employee has already made an application to his employer, he may not make a further application for 12 months.

An employer can refuse an application only on specified grounds, which are:

- costs;
- detrimental effect on ability to meet customer demand;
- inability to reorganise existing staff;
- inability to recruit additional staff;
- detrimental impact on quality;
- insufficiency of work during the periods the employee proposes to work; and
- planned structural changes.

Such refusals should be in writing.

An employee has two weeks in which to appeal against a decision not to allow flexible working, setting out the reasons for the appeal. The appeal should be part of the ordinary company procedures, and the employer must respond in writing within two weeks of the appeal.

The procedural steps are:

1. An employee should make a request in writing setting out the work pattern he or she wants and how it could work.
2. The employer should consider the business case for accepting or rejecting the request.
3. There should be a meeting within 28 days to consider the request.
4. The employer should respond in writing within 14 days of the meeting, either accepting the request, or putting forward the compromise agreed at the meeting, or rejecting the request with the business reasons for doing so and informing the employee of the procedure for an appeal.

There is a right to apply to a tribunal where the employer has failed to comply with the statute or has rejected the application on incorrect facts. Such a complaint must be made within three months either of the date the employee was informed of the employer's decision, or of the date the employer committed a breach of the statute. A tribunal, should it find the complaint well founded, may make either an order that the employer reconsider the application or an award of compensation it considers to be just and equitable in the circumstances.

7.9 Right not to suffer a detriment

Sections 43M–47 of the ERA 1996 create the right not to suffer a detriment in certain cases. 'Detriment' is an act or any deliberate failure to act by the employer. These rights complement the protection against unfair dismissal in these situations discussed in Chapter 9.

7.9.1 Jury service

The Employment Relations Act 2004 inserted a new section 43M into the ERA 1996. This provides that an employee has the right not to suffer a detriment by any act, or deliberate failure to act, on the grounds that he or she has been summoned to attend as a juror or has been absent because of such a summons. Detriment does not include non-payment of salary during such service, unless the contract gives an entitlement to payment.

7.9.2 Health and safety cases

Section 44(1) of the ERA 1996 provides that an employee has the right not to be subjected to any detriment by an act, or a failure to act, on the grounds that:

▷ as a health and safety representative he was carrying out his duties; or
▷ he was carrying out, or proposed to carry out, his duties as a health and safety committee member; or

- where there was no such representative or it was not reasonably practicable to raise the matter with such a representative, he brought to his employer's attention safety risks; or
- in circumstances of danger he could not reasonably avert, which he reasonably believed to be serious and imminent, he left or proposed to leave his place of work, or took steps to protect himself and others from danger. Whether the action is reasonable is up to the tribunal, taking all the circumstances into account, including the employee's knowledge and the advice available. However, the EAT, in *Kerr v Nathan's Wastesavers Ltd* (1995) IDS Brief 548, stressed that tribunals should not place too onerous a duty on the employee to make enquiries to establish if his belief was reasonable.

In *Barton v Wandsworth Council* (1995) IDS Brief 549, an employee was disciplined when he voiced concerns over the safety of patients as a result of what he considered to be the lack of ability of newly introduced escorts. The tribunal held that he had been unlawfully disciplined, showing that the legal protection is triggered when the employee raises concerns.

The employee must complain to an employment tribunal within three months of the act, or failure to act, complained of (ERA 1996, s 48(3)), unless this is not reasonably practicable. The burden is on the employer to show why he acted as he did. If the tribunal finds the complaint well founded, it may make a declaration and an award of compensation. The amount of compensation is what is just and equitable in the circumstances, taking into account any loss sustained by the complainant. The complainant is under a duty to mitigate his loss, and the tribunal may reduce the award for contributory conduct (ERA 1996, s 49).

7.9.3 Sunday working for shop and betting workers

An employee who is a protected shop or betting worker, or an opted-out shop or betting worker, has the right not to suffer a detriment on the ground that he refused or proposed to refuse to work on Sundays (ERA 1996, s 45). 'Protected', under this provision, means that the worker was under a contract, at the date of the commencement of the provision, which did not require him to work on Sundays (ERA 1996, s 36). An 'opted-out' worker is a worker who by his contract is required to work on Sundays and who has given his employer written notice that he objects to Sunday working (ERA 1996, s 40). Such workers are not protected in relation to acts on the part of the employer during the opted-out notice period. The remedies are the same as in relation to health and safety cases (Section 7.9.2 above).

7.9.4 Working time cases

By section 45A of the ERA 1996, a worker has the right not to be subjected to a detriment on the grounds that:

- he refused to comply with a requirement imposed upon him by his employer in contravention of the Working Time Regulations 1998;
- he refused or proposed to refuse to forgo a right conferred on him by the Regulations;

- he failed to sign a workforce agreement, or to vary or extend any other agreement provided for by the Regulations;
- he was a workforce representative for the purposes of the Regulations, or a candidate in a representative election, and performed or proposed to perform activities in relation to that role; or
- he brought proceedings against the employer under the Regulations, or he alleged that the employer had infringed a right under the Regulations.

For the purpose of the last protection, it is irrelevant whether the worker has the right or whether it has actually been infringed, as long as the worker's claim is made in good faith. It will be noted that the section brings together a number of rights listed in the other sections but relates them particularly to breaches of the Working Time Regulations 1998.

7.9.5   Trustees of occupational pension schemes

By section 46 of the ERA 1996, an employee has the right not to suffer a detriment by his employer on the ground that, being a trustee of a relevant occupational pension scheme which relates to his employment, he performed or proposed to perform any of his functions as a trustee. A 'relevant pension scheme' means an occupational pension scheme as defined in section 1 of the Pension Schemes Act 1993.

7.9.6   Employee representatives

By section 47 of the ERA 1996, an employee has a right not to be subjected to any detriment by his employer on the ground that, being an employee representative for the purposes of the TULR(C)A 1992 or the Transfer of Undertakings (Protection of Employment) Regulations 2006, or a candidate in elections for such a representative, he performed or proposed to perform any functions or activities.

7.9.7   Employees exercising the right to time off work for study or training

By section 47A of the ERA 1996, employees who have exercised rights under section 63A to take paid time off for study or training are entitled not to suffer a detriment because they have exercised such rights.

7.9.8   Protected disclosures

By section 47B of the 1996 Act, an employee who has made a protected disclosure (see Section 4.3.5) under the Public Interest Disclosure Act 1998 has a right not to have action short of dismissal taken against him. *Bolton School v Evans* [2007] ICR 641 discusses what is meant by a 'disclosure'.

Changes introduced by the Enterprise and Regulatory Reform Act 2013 make employers vicariously liable for detriments suffered by a worker by another worker, although there is a defence that the employer has taken all reasonable steps to prevent such detrimental action.

7.9.9   Leave for family and domestic reasons

Section 47C of the ERA 1996 creates a right not to suffer a detriment, by any act or deliberate failure to act, for a prescribed reason. A prescribed reason is one prescribed by the Secretary of State that relates to:

- pregnancy, childbirth or maternity leave;
- ordinary, compulsory or additional maternity leave;
- parental leave, paternity leave or adoption leave;
- time off for dependants;
- an application (or proposed application) made for flexible working, a right to flexible working exercised or proceedings brought for breach of such rights;
- disciplinary and grievance hearings.

Section 12 of the Employment Relations Act 1999 provides the right not to suffer a detriment (which is defined as an act or a failure to act) on the grounds that as a worker he exercised his right to be accompanied at a disciplinary or grievance hearing, or he acted as a representative at such a hearing.

7.9.10   Collective agreements

The Employment Relations Act 2004 inserted two sections into the TULR(C)A 1992. Section 145B protects a worker from being offered an inducement to come out of collective bargaining, and section 146(2C) protects a worker from being subjected to a detriment on the grounds that he has refused to enter a contract which includes terms that differ from the terms of a collective agreement which applies to him. Again, 'detriment' means an act or a failure to act (for example, by not granting a pay rise). This amendment was made as a result of *Wilson v UK* (2002) 35 EHRR 20, in which the ECJ held that an essential part of the right given in Article 11 ECHR (freedom of association) was the fact that an employer could not offer financial inducements to persuade an employee to give up his rights.

7.9.11   Recognition

Schedule 1 to the Employment Relations Act 1999 gives details on statutory recognition of trade unions and inserted Schedule A1 into the TULR(C)A 1992. Trade unions are discussed in Chapter 12. Paragraph 156 of Schedule A1 protects a worker from suffering a detriment by an act or failure to act because he has taken action or refused to take action in respect of trade union recognition. The provisions complement similar protection against unfair dismissal contained in paragraph 161, which is discussed more fully in Chapter 9.

7.10   Time off provisions

In addition to the time off provisions for ante-natal appointments (Section 7.4.7 above), the law creates other rights to time off in respect of specified duties or activities. These are discussed below. Any complaint in relation to refusal of time off or refusal to pay for the time taken (if relevant) must be made to a tribunal within three months of the alleged act.

7.10.1 Trade union duties

By sections 168 and 169 of TULR(C)A 1992, an employee who is an official of an independent trade union recognised by the employer is entitled to reasonable time off with pay during working hours to carry out those duties and undergo training. If an employer refuses to allow such time off, the official may complain to an industrial tribunal and obtain a declaration and compensation. 'Official' is defined in section 119 of TULR(C)A 1992 as any officer of the union or branch, or any other person elected under union rules to represent members. The statute creates the right to reasonable time off. The ACAS Code of Practice gives factors to be taken into account when assessing what is reasonable, such as the amount of time already allowed. In *Wignall v British Gas Corporation* [1984] IRLR 493, it was held not to be unreasonable to refuse an employee 10 days off when he had already been granted and taken 12 weeks to pursue union duties.

7.10.2 Time off for union learning representatives

Section 43 of the Employment Act 2002 introduced a new type of trade union representative called a 'union learning representative' (ULR). Under section 168A of TULR(C)A 1992, such a representative is a member of a recognised independent trade union who has been elected or appointed, in relation to members of the union, to analyse learning or training needs, provide information or advice about learning or training matters, arrange learning or training, or promote the value of learning or training. The ULR is entitled to reasonable time off with pay, but only if the union has given the employer written notice that the person is the ULR and that the ULR has undergone sufficient training to fulfil the role, or will have undergone relevant training within six months of the notice. If the employer is required to give the ULR time off to perform his role, he is also required to give him time off to undergo training. Members of the union are entitled to unpaid time off during working hours to access the services of a ULR (TULR(C)A 1992, s 170(2B)).

7.10.3 Trade union activities

By section 152 of TULR(C)A 1992, a member of an independent recognised trade union is entitled to reasonable time off without pay but during working hours to take part in trade union activities.

7.10.4 Health and safety duties

The Safety Representatives and Safety Committees Regulations 1977, made under the HASAWA 1974, provide that an employer shall allow an employee who is a safety representative time off with pay during normal working hours to perform his statutory functions and undergo training.

7.10.5 Public duties

An employee has the right to reasonable time off, without pay, to perform specified public duties. These duties are found in section 50 of the ERA 1996, and include magistracy, membership of a local authority, membership of a statutory tribunal, membership of a health authority, duties as a school governor or membership of a water authority. The right to time off extends to attendance at meetings and doing anything approved by the body for the purpose of discharging its functions.

Criteria for establishing reasonable time off include how much time the employee has already had, the effect of the employee's absence and so on. In *Walters v British Steel Corporation* IDS Brief 150, the employee was transferred to another job and agreed that his public duties would take second place. Safety considerations meant that there had to be certain manning levels and his colleagues refused to cover for him. It was held that, taking into account the circumstances of his employer's business, he was not entitled to time off. In *Emmerson v Inland Revenue Commissioners* [1977] IRLR 458, the employee had already had 18 days' paid leave for public duties and his request for further unpaid leave of absence was refused by his employers. The tribunal held that as the applicant was prepared to use some of his own holidays, a further 12 days' unpaid leave was not unreasonable. Conversely, in *Borders Regional Council v Maule* [1992] IRLR 199, the EAT reiterated that a tribunal has to achieve a balance in the situation of an employee claiming time off in relation to several public commitments. In the case the employee, who was a member of a social security tribunal, sought a day off to attend a training session. The employers refused to allow her the time off. The employment tribunal upheld her complaint under section 50 on the basis that, as the employers had allowed her the time off to sit on the tribunal, they also had to allow her the time off to attend training sessions. The EAT disagreed. The EAT said that the tribunal should look at all factors, including time off taken for other purposes. Lord Coulsfield added that where an employee had a variety of public duties, the employee had a responsibility to scale the level of duties to one which might be regarded as reasonable in all the circumstances. In other words, the fact that the employer has allowed an employee time off to participate in certain public duties does not mean that he is acting unreasonably if he sometimes refuses time off in relation to those duties. All the circumstances must be taken into account. The employee must be allowed time off, however, and it is insufficient for the employer to alter times of the employee's work to fit in with his public commitments (*Ratcliffe v Dorset County Council* [1978] IRLR 191).

7.10.6   Time off to look for work

By section 52 of the ERA 1996, an employee who is under notice of redundancy is entitled to reasonable time off with pay during working hours to look for new employment or make arrangements for training, before the expiry of his notice. However, this right applies only to employees who have been continuously employed for two years on the date the notice is due to expire. The employee does not need to provide his employer with proof of appointments and so on, but if the employer feels that the request is not genuine, it may not be unreasonable to refuse the time off (*Dutton v Hawker Siddeley Aviation Ltd* [1978] IRLR 390).

7.10.7   Time off for occupational pension scheme trustees

A trustee of an occupational pension scheme is entitled to time off during working hours to perform any of his duties as trustee or to undergo training (ERA 1996, s 58). Such time off is what is reasonable in the circumstances having regard to the effect of the time off on the employer's business. It is time off with pay (s 59). Failure to comply with section 58 entitles the trustee to apply to a tribunal within three months of the refusal. The tribunal, if it finds the complaint well founded, can award such compensation as it considers just and equitable (ERA 1996, s 60).

7.10.8   Time off for employee representatives

By section 61 of the ERA 1996, an employee who is an employee representative, or a candidate in an election for such a representative, is entitled to reasonable time off during working hours in order to perform his functions as a representative or candidate. Since 1999 such a representative is also entitled to reasonable time off for training. Time off is also provided to accompany a worker in a disciplinary or grievance hearing. The time off must be with pay (ERA 1996, s 62). By section 63 of the Act, any complaint in relation to a breach of the provisions must be presented within three months of the breach, and the tribunal may award the remuneration the employee would have received if the time off had been allowed.

7.10.9   Time off for study or training

Section 63A of the ERA 1996 gives an employee who is 16 or 17 years old, and who is not receiving full-time secondary or further education, the right to time off with pay, during working hours, in order to undertake study or training leading to a relevant qualification. If an employee is 18 years old and was undergoing such study or training prior to commencing employment with the employer, he is entitled to paid time off during working hours to complete that study or training.

7.10.10   Time off for dependants

The Employment Relations Act 1999 inserted a new section 57A into the ERA 1996 and created a right to reasonable time off for dependants. There is no requirement that such time off be paid. Reasonable time off should be given:

- to allow an employee to provide assistance to a dependant because of illness, injury or giving birth;
- to allow an employee to make arrangements for the provision of care for a dependant who is ill or injured;
- in consequence of the death of a dependant;
- because of the unexpected disruption or termination of arrangements for the care of a dependant; or
- to allow an employee to deal with an incident involving the child of the employee which occurs unexpectedly at an educational establishment which the child is attending (s 57A(1)).

'Dependant' means, in relation to the employee, a spouse, child, parent or any person who lives in the same household other than by reason of being an employee, tenant, lodger or boarder of the employee (s 57A(3)). Where the incident requires the employee to provide assistance or make provision for the care of a person because of illness or injury, the definition of 'dependant' also includes any person who reasonably relies on the employee (s 57A(4)). Where the incident is the unexpected disruption or termination of arrangements for care, the definition of 'dependant' also includes any person who reasonably relies on the employee to make such arrangements (s 57A(5)).

In *Qua v John Ford Morrison Solicitors* [2003] ICR 482, the EAT heard the case of a single mother claiming automatically unfair dismissal for taking dependant leave 17 times in a nine-month period. The EAT held that the right did not entitle an employee to take more time off than would be reasonable to deal with an immediate crisis. Similarly, in *Forster v Cartwright Black* [2004] IRLR 781, the EAT held that an employee was entitled to time off under these provisions to deal with the funeral arrangements following the death of a relative, but not time off to grieve. From this it can be seen that employees have the right to reasonable time off to make care arrangements, but not to deal with the dependant themselves.

An employee is not entitled to exercise the right to time off unless he tells his employer the reason for his absence as soon as reasonably practicable and tells his employer his expected length of absence (unless it was not possible to tell the employer before the incident occurred) (s 57A(2)). In *MacCulloch and Wallis Ltd v Moore* [2003] All ER (D) 37, the EAT stated that where an employee had given the reason and the length of the absence to the employer, there would be a breach of the provisions if circumstances changed and the employee did not inform the employer of the changes. In *Truelove v Safeway Stores plc* (2005) IDS 774, an employee who frequently worked on Saturdays asked for a day's leave one particular Saturday when his babysitting arrangements fell through. Leave was refused, but he took it anyway. He was disciplined and lost a £250 bonus. The tribunal held that the employer did not have enough information to decide if the request was reasonable. The EAT disagreed. It was sufficient that the employer knew that the request was because of childcare. This was an unforeseen eventuality and reasonableness was not applicable, although it would be applicable when considering the number of times the employee had taken time off for childcare. In *RBS v Harrison* [2009] IRLR 28, the employer argued that when an employee had two weeks' notice that her child minder was unavailable, the termination in her childcare arrangements could not be said to be unexpected. The EAT disagreed and stated that the word 'unexpected' does not involve a time element, although in deciding whether it is necessary to take such time off, the length of time between the employee's knowledge of the forthcoming disruption and the disruption happening was to be taken into consideration.

Summary

7.1 There are various employment protection rights which apply to employees.

7.2 These rights apply independently from any contractual provision, unless the contract gives more favourable rights.

7.3 The rights divide into: right to a guarantee payment, right of pay for medical suspension, maternity rights, paternity rights, adoption rights, parental rights, rights not to suffer a detriment in certain cases, and rights to leave and time off.

Exercises

Martin, Ronnie and Phil work as teachers for Middlewich School. The recognised union in the school is the National Union of Teachers (NUT).

Martin has been a member of the governing body of the local university for the past four years. During that time he has had, on average, 14 days off a year to attend meetings during term time. Because of a recent scandal involving the University's Vice-Chancellor, the governing body has met frequently in the past three months, and Martin has had 21 days off to date. The chair of the governing body has just informed him that he will be required to attend meetings on at least another 15 days during the rest of the academic year. Martin's headmaster has refused to allow him any more time off, saying that it is unfair to other colleagues who cover his classes. Martin has never been paid for his time off.

Ronnie is the union health and safety representative at the school. Given that the school has just opened a chemistry department, Ronnie has had three weeks off in the past six months to attend training courses in the handling of chemicals. He now requires a further seven days off to train the chemistry teachers. The headmaster has refused to allow Ronnie the time to train the teachers, and has said that he must train them during the vacation. In addition, Ronnie's class size has doubled recently, and he has been given extra classes to teach to make up for the time he has been away from the school on courses.

Phil is a member of the NUT. The union has held regional meetings in the past to discuss action against national curriculum changes. These meetings are normally held at lunchtime, or in the evenings, and Phil has always attended them. He has just been informed that the next two regional meetings will be held on two mornings during term time when Phil has classes. The union also wishes him to be a member of a party which is being sent to London for a week, again in term time, to lobby Parliament. The headmaster has refused to allow Phil to attend the meetings or join the lobby.

Advise Martin, Ronnie and Phil.

Further reading and references

Anderson, 'Sound Bite Legislation: The Employment Act 2002 and New Flexible Working "rights" for Parents' (2003) 32 ILJ 37

Di Torella, 'New Labour, New Dads: The Impact of Family Friendly Legislation on Fathers' (2007) 36 ILJ 318

Dickens, 'Equality and Working Life Balance. What's Happening in the Workplace?' (2006) 35 ILJ 445

Ewing, 'The Implications of *Wilson and Palmer*' (2003) 32 ILJ 1

James, 'The Work and Families Act 2006: Legislation to Improve Choice and Flexibility?' (2006) 35 ILJ 272

James, 'Enjoy Your Leave but Keep in Touch: Help to Maintain Parent/Workplace Relationships' (2007) 36 ILJ 315

Mortimer, 'Strenghthening Workers' Rights: A New Agenda' (2003) 32 ILJ 129

Vallely and Quinn, 'The Family Friendly Workplace: A Right for all or a Prize for Few?' (2001) 12(5) PLC 43

Part IV

Termination of employment

Chapter 8

Termination at common law

8.1 Termination by operation of law

Although the most common way the contract of employment will come to an end is by an act of the parties, in some circumstances the law will operate to end the relationship automatically on the happening of an event. Should the contract terminate in this way, there will be no liability on either side. The ways in which the contract will terminate by operation of law are discussed below.

8.1.1 Frustration

Frustration occurs when, without the fault of either party, the contract becomes either impossible to perform or fundamentally different from what the parties originally intended. The recognition that an employment contract could be frustrated happened over 100 years ago in the case of *Poussard v Spiers & Pond* (1876) 1 QBD 410, where an opera singer caught a cold and as a result was unable to take part in a week of rehearsals and the first few performances. The replacement hired by the management was prepared to perform only if she was given a month's contract. The opera singer sued the management for breach. It was held that the contract had been frustrated and there was no breach by the management. The circumstances were unusual, in that a few days' illness would not usually frustrate an employment contract which would normally last for some years. In the Poussard case, however, the opera was not due to run for a long period of time and the only replacement the management could get insisted on a contract exceeding the period of illness of the original singer.

The two major events that will frustrate an employment contract are illness and imprisonment. Normally it is only when these events strike the employee that frustration can occur, because often, in today's employment relationships, the employer is not a person but a company, although there is special protection for an employee if a company is wound up or a partnership is dissolved (see Section 8.1.2 below).

The original test in employment cases to see if illness had led to a frustration was formulated by Donaldson P in *Marshall v Harland & Wolff Ltd* [1972] 1 WLR 899, when he said that the tribunals had to ask whether the nature of the employee's incapacity was such that further performance of his obligations was impossible or radically different from that originally intended when he entered the contract. He then gave a list of factors the tribunals should consider when looking to see if a frustration had occurred. These factors were added to in the later case of *Egg Stores Ltd v Leibovici* [1977] ICR 260, by Phillips J and were then summarised and approved by the EAT in the case of *Williams v Watsons Luxury Coaches Ltd* [1990] IRLR 164, as follows:

1. The court must be careful not to use the doctrine too easily, as it may mask a dismissal for disability.
2. It is useful to decide the date on which frustration occurred to determine whether it is a true frustration.

3. There are a number of factors that should be considered, which include the length of the employment prior to the event and the length of future foreseeable employment, the nature of the job and the terms of the employment, the nature, length and effect of the illness and the prospect of recovery, the employer's need for a replacement, the risk of the employer's acquiring statutory obligations to a replacement, the conduct of the employer, whether wages or sick pay have been paid and whether in all the circumstances a reasonable employer would have waited longer.

4. The frustrating event has not been caused by the party seeking to rely upon it.

The operation of the doctrine may perhaps be demonstrated by the comparison of two cases. In *Hart v AR Marshall & Sons (Bulwell) Ltd* [1977] IRLR 51, a night-service fitter, who was described as a key worker by his employer, was ill for 20 months. He sent in regular sick notes but on his return was informed that he had been replaced. The EAT held that, given he was such an important employee, the contract had been frustrated by the illness. By contrast there is the case of *Hebden v Forsey & Sons* [1973] IRLR 344. Here, the employee was one of two sawyers employed by the employer. In total he was away from work for almost two years after an operation. During that time he was in contact with his employer, his employer had agreed to his taking the time off and there was insufficient work for him to do until he had fully recovered. It was held that the contract had not been frustrated.

Imprisonment is another event which may frustrate the contract, but the courts' attitude towards this has changed over the years. The problem that has arisen is that it will normally be the employee's fault that he is serving a prison sentence, and a self-induced frustration is not a frustrating event because it is caused by the fault of one of the parties. In *Hare v Murphy Brothers* [1974] IRLR 342, imprisonment was held to frustrate the contract, Lord Denning MR pointing out that, similarly, an opera singer sitting in a draught may lose her voice, and it could be said that she had induced this, but her contract would still be frustrated. In *Norris v Southampton City Council* [1982] IRLR 141, however, the EAT decided that as the imprisonment had been caused by the employee's own misconduct, there could be no frustration, and the employee was guilty of a repudiatory breach which, if accepted by the employer, would lead to a dismissal. This failed to recognise, however, that the employee did not commit the offence with the intention of breaking the contract and could have received a fine rather than a prison sentence. The position was clarified by the Court of Appeal in *Shepherd (FC) & Co Ltd v Jerrom* [1986] 3 WLR 801. The Court decided that a six-month prison sentence could frustrate a four-year contract of apprenticeship. However, in *Four Seasons Healthcare Ltd v Maughan* [2005] IRLR 324, a care worker who was suspended without pay for 11 months while police investigated complaints of patient abuse, claimed wages for the period. The employer argued the contract was frustrated because the care worker was banned from entering the care home as part of his bail conditions. The EAT held that the contract was frustrated only when the worker was convicted and imprisoned, and as the contract allowed for only seven days' unpaid suspension, he was entitled to wages for the rest of the period. This pushes an employer to make an early decision to dismiss.

Although illness and imprisonment are the commonest forms of frustrating events in an employment relationship, there have been other events that have led to frustration of a contract. In *Morgan v Manser* [1948] 1 KB 184, a 10-year management contract entered into in 1940 was frustrated by the call up into the army of the employee. In *Tarnesby v Kensington, Chelsea & Westminster AHA* [1981] IRLR 369, suspension from medical practice for 12 months was deemed a frustrating event. In contrast, in *Gryf-Lowczowski v Hinchingbrooke Healthcare NHS Trust* [2006] IRLR 100 it was held that the contract of a consultant was not frustrated when he was suspended for two years following allegations of incompetence. The High Court held that there was a likelihood that the consultant would return to work after retraining; given his length of service, there was no frustration. This was despite the fact that the suspended employee was one of only two consultants in the field.

Note that as the contract terminates on the frustrating event and without fault on either side, any rights under the contract cease. Therefore, in *GF Sharp & Co Ltd v McMillan* [1998] IRLR 632, it was held that where the contract of an employee had been frustrated by the employee's injury, he was not entitled to a payment in lieu of notice, despite the fact that the employer had 'kept him on the books' in order to ensure that he received enhanced pension benefits. This did not keep the contract alive after the frustrating event.

8.1.2 Liquidation of the employer or dissolution of a partnership

At common law the liquidation of a company or dissolution of a partnership is clearly a frustrating event because the contract becomes impossible to perform. The common law rules are, however, superseded by statute. By section 139(4) of the ERA 1996, the death or liquidation of an employer or the dissolution of a partnership shall be treated as a dismissal for redundancy, unless the business is taken into new ownership and the employee's contract is renewed. If there is a transfer of an undertaking and the employee objects to being transferred, his contract terminates and there is no dismissal (Transfer of Undertakings (Protection of Employment) Regulations 2006, Reg 4(8)).

8.2 Termination by agreement

If the parties mutually agree that the contract should come to an end then neither party has ended the agreement and there will be no dismissal (employer termination) or resignation (employee termination). Courts will look at the wording of any correspondence between the parties to elicit their true intentions. In *Francis v Pertemps Partnership Recruitment Ltd* (2013) UKEAT 0030/13/BI, Francis was employed by an agency (Pertemps) which placed him with a client who was specified in his contract. When the client no longer needed him, Pertemps offered him the choice of either two weeks' notice and redundancy pay, or two weeks' notice with the agency with the view to his working for another client. At first he chose the latter option, but then he changed his mind. The agency wrote and told him his position was redundant and he should treat the letter as 'formal notice of redundancy'. It also stated that he had a right of appeal 'against the decision to terminate your employment'. Francis claimed unfair dismissal, but Pertemps argued that there had been a mutual agreement to terminate. The EAT held that a dismissal was where the contract had been terminated by the employer and all the language used was consistent with that. Francis had been dismissed.

If there is a genuine agreement there is no problem, but it is important to discover whether the 'agreement' to end the relationship has been brought about by employer pressure, in which case it will be a dismissal. In *McAlwane v Boughton Estates Ltd* [1973] ICR 470, Donaldson J said that tribunals should be careful when finding a mutual agreement to terminate, and should ensure that the employee was aware of the financial implications in so agreeing. Thus if there is some financial consideration, the tribunals will be more prepared to accept a genuine agreement. In *Scott v Coalite Fuels and Chemicals Ltd* [1988] IRLR 131, the employees took early voluntary retirement while under notice, in order to claim a lump sum under a pension scheme. It was held that there was a mutual agreement to terminate. In *Birch and Humber v University of Liverpool* [1985] IRLR 165, the employees were invited to volunteer for early retirement. Two employees volunteered and received a reply from the University that the institution confirmed 'that it is in the managerial interests for you to retire and requests that you do so'. The vacancies created by the retirement were not filled and the two employees argued that they had been dismissed for reasons of redundancy and were entitled to a redundancy payment in addition to any payment for early retirement. The Court of Appeal disagreed and held that there was no dismissal but a mutual agreement to terminate. *Scott*, however, was distinguished in the case of *Gateshead Metropolitan Borough Council v Mills* (1995) IDS Brief 551. The case on its facts was similar to *Scott*, in that the employee was under notice of redundancy, although the employer had stated that there might be alternative employment and therefore the notice might not be acted upon. Mills applied for a variety of other jobs within the Council but was unsuccessful, and so he successfully applied for early retirement. He then applied to a tribunal for a redundancy payment. The employer argued, on the basis of *Scott*, that the subsequent agreement to take early retirement had impliedly withdrawn the notice of dismissal, and that Mills's contract had terminated by agreement. The EAT disagreed. Any withdrawal of the dismissal notice had to have the consent of the recipient. There was no evidence that Mills had so consented, and the fact that he agreed to take early retirement did not indicate that he had impliedly consented. As such, Mills was dismissed and entitled to a redundancy payment.

While the cases seem difficult to reconcile, it could be argued that a distinction might be made between those situations where redundancy would be inevitable should the employee not volunteer and those where it would not. In *Morton Sundour Fabrics v Shaw* (1966) 2 KIR 1, the employee had been warned of the possibility of redundancy and therefore found himself another job. It was held that he had resigned and not been dismissed as his redundancy was not inevitable. By contrast, in *Morley v CT Morley Ltd* [1985] ICR 499, the employees were a father and two sons who had incorporated their family business. The father volunteered for redundancy, and afterwards the sons decided to wind up the business. It was held that there had been a dismissal. Furthermore, the courts will be unsympathetic to an employer who tries to force his employees to leave because of the threat of redundancy, as a cheap way of reducing his workforce. In *Caledonian Mining Co Ltd v Bassett and Steel* [1987] IRLR 165, the employer had told his employees that there would be a reduction in manpower on the site and asked them if they were interested in alternative employment. The men expressed interest in alternative employment but the employer failed to respond, and eventually the men were offered work by the National Coal Board which they accepted. They informed their employer, who then argued that they had resigned and as such were not entitled to redundancy payments. The EAT held that there had been a dismissal. The men had been encouraged to take other jobs by their employer with the intention of avoiding redundancy payments. The employer had caused the men to resign and therefore had terminated the contract. Consequently, the men had been dismissed.

Some years ago, it was possible for the employee to agree that his employment would terminate automatically on the happening of an event, and as such there would be no dismissal or resignation. The authority for such a proposition was the case of *British Leyland (UK) v Ashraf* [1978] IRLR 330, where the employee was given five weeks' unpaid leave to visit his family in Pakistan. He signed a document that if he failed to return on a due date, for whatever reason, his contract would terminate immediately. When he did not return at the appointed time the employers treated the contract as terminated in accordance with the agreement. The EAT held that there had been a consensual termination and no dismissal. This decision, however, is very hard, and takes no account of the reasons for failure to return. Later decisions tried to mitigate the harshness. In *Midland Electric Manufacturing Co Ltd v Kanji* [1980] IRLR 185, the employee's leave of absence was granted with the warning that if she failed to return, the company would consider that she had terminated her employment. Talbot J distinguished *Ashraf* on the basis that the wording in *Kanji* was ambiguous and was merely a statement of intention by the employer that the employee would be dismissed. In *Tracey v Zest Equipment Co* [1982] IRLR 268, the EAT stressed that very clear words were needed to constitute a mutual agreement to terminate.

These cases must now be read subject to the Court of Appeal decision in *Igbo v Johnson Matthey Chemicals Ltd* [1986] IRLR 215. In this case there was an agreement similar to that in *Ashraf*. Both the tribunal and the EAT held that there was no dismissal despite the fact that the employee had failed to return because of illness and had a medical certificate. The Court of Appeal held that *Ashraf* was wrong. It did this by applying section 140(1) of the Employment Protection (Consolidation) Act 1978 (now s 203 of the ERA 1996) to automatic termination clauses. This section renders any agreement to restrict the operation of any provision of the Act void. As such, any agreement purporting to exclude the provisions on unfair dismissal or redundancy has no effect, and this is precisely what automatic termination clauses purport to do. This decision means that in situations such as *Ashraf*, the employer makes the decision that the contract has terminated and therefore there is a dismissal. This does not mean that the dismissal is unfair, merely that the tribunal then has the jurisdiction to look at the fairness or otherwise of the employer's decision.

The decision in *Igbo*, however, applies only to agreements where the termination occurs on the happening or non-happening of an event. It does not restrict the freedom of the parties to negotiate a separate agreement to terminate if that is supported by consideration. In *Logan Salton v Durham County Council* [1989] IRLR 99, the employee had been redeployed as a result of disciplinary proceedings. Further disciplinary proceedings were to be initiated, and there was a recommendation that at the conclusion of the proceedings the employee should be summarily dismissed. Prior to those proceedings, his union representative negotiated with the employer that the employment be terminated and an outstanding car loan of £2,750 be wiped out. Both parties signed an agreement to that effect. The employee subsequently claimed unfair dismissal on the basis that the agreement was void because of what is now section 203 of the 1996 Act. The EAT held that the case could be distinguished from *Igbo* in that here there was a separate agreement to terminate which did not depend on the happening of some future event and which was supported by consideration. The parties had thus mutually terminated their contract.

8.3 Repudiation

A repudiatory breach may terminate the contract if the innocent party so decides. If the innocent party is the employee and the employee decides to end the contract, then unless the employee has two years' continuous service, the contract will have come to an end by resignation, leaving the employee with a claim for damages. If, however, the employee has two years' continuity and is protected by unfair dismissal provisions, the law steps in to protect him, and the resignation will be treated as a dismissal because it was caused by the employer's conduct. This is known as a 'constructive dismissal' and will be discussed in detail in Section 9.4.3. If the employee commits the repudiatory breach and the employer decides to end the contract, the contract has terminated by dismissal. Such a situation is always a dismissal, irrespective of the length of employment of the employee, as the law has no concept of a constructive resignation.

One of the problems that has exercised the judges in this area is the precise time at which the contract comes to an end. A breach which is repudiatory rejects the original contract and may produce a variety of results. It may reject the original contract and bring into play new terms. The innocent party has two options in this case: he can reject the new terms, or he can accept them and continue the relationship. In the latter case, he has decided not to treat the action by the other party as terminating the contract but has agreed to waive the breach and treat the contract as varied (see, however, *Hogg v Dover College* [1990] ICR 39 and *Alcan Extrusions v Yates* [1996] IRLR 327 in Chapter 9). On the other hand, the breach may be a rejection by one party of the contract with no alternative terms offered. Again, the innocent party has the two options, but in reality his choice may be an illusory one if, for example, performance of the contract has been made impossible by the party in breach. If the employer locks out his employees, for example, in practical terms the employees have no real choice as to whether they continue to work or not.

The question of deciding at what precise time the contract comes to an end when there is a repudiatory breach is not a purely academic one. The answer will have implications for both parties in terms of whether the employee has the continuity to claim an unfair dismissal should the employer be in repudiatory breach, what compensation he may claim if he has been unfairly dismissed and what damages either party may claim at common law for the breach.

The normal contractual doctrine is that a repudiatory breach will not operate to terminate a contract until the innocent party accepts it as so terminating (*Howard v Pickford Tool Co Ltd* [1951] 1 KB 417). While many cases have decided that the normal doctrine applies in employment law, this can cause difficulties, in that often the choice given to the innocent party is no real choice at all, for example in a strike or a lock-out; and further, as has already been seen (Section 4.1 above), the courts cannot award the normal contractual remedy of specific performance in an employment contract, to compel the parties to continue the contract.

As a result of the unique nature of an employment contract and the remedies available to the parties, judges originally argued that the normal doctrine did not apply and that a repudiation terminated the relationship automatically. Megarry VC rejected this argument in the case of *Marshall (Thomas) (Exports) Ltd v Guinle* [1979] Ch 227, because this gave the guilty party the right to decide when the contract would come to an end and would allow the wrongdoer to profit from his wrongdoing. (An employer could, for example, commit a repudiatory breach just before the employee had the continuity to claim unfair dismissal and so exclude the employee's rights.) To argue that the innocent party should always accept the breach as terminating before the contract ends is somewhat false where the party has no choice, and therefore the Court of Appeal in the later case of *Gunton v Richmond-upon-Thames London Borough Council* [1980] IRLR 321 tried to find a middle ground between the automatic termination theory and the acceptance theory. Shaw LJ said that in some situations the nature of the repudiatory act was such that it automatically destroyed the contract and acceptance is therefore unnecessary, for example a dismissal by the employer. In other situations, however, the repudiation is not so straightforward, for example a change of contractual terms, and in these situations an acceptance of the termination would be needed by the innocent party before the contract came to an end. The House of Lords, while accepting this argument in *Rigby v Ferodo Ltd* [1988] ICR 29, declined to comment on situations such as a wrongful dismissal by the employer or a walk-out by the employee who then fails to return. In *Smith v Phil's TV Service* (1991) IDS Brief 447, the employee walked out after a dispute with the employer. When he did not return for work the next day, the employer assumed he had resigned and wrote a letter to that effect. The EAT held that the repudiatory breach by the employee would terminate the contract only when the employer accepted it as doing so. Here the employer had accepted it by his letter, and therefore the employer had terminated the contract. It was up to the tribunal to decide if the dismissal was fair (see also *Boyo v Lambeth London Borough Council* [1994] ICR 727).

The position has now been conclusively decided by the Supreme Court in *Geys v Société Générale* [2012] UKSC 63. In the case, Geys was a banker. His contract allowed the employer to terminate by making a payment in lieu of notice (PILON). On 29 November 2007, Geys was called into a meeting and told his contract was being terminated; he was then escorted from the building. On 18 December, after his solicitors asked what his severance package would be, he received a lump sum payment into his bank account which stated it was a PILON, but with no breakdown as to how it had been calculated. Geys asked for a breakdown, which he received on 6 January 2008. The issue for the court was when his contract had terminated: in November, when he was told that it was being terminated, or in January, when his employer complied with Geys' request and thus it could be said he had accepted the repudiatory breach? The issue was important, because the later date was past the trigger date for a bonus payment. The Supreme Court, by a majority, held that the date of termination was the date when it could be said that the employee had accepted the repudiatory breach as ending the contract.

Consequently, a strike by an employee is a repudiatory breach, but it will not end the contract until the employer treats it as so doing by dismissing the strikers. This position is confirmed by statute, in that by section 238 of TULR(C)A 1992, unfair dismissal protection is afforded to strikers where there are selective dismissals for striking. Such protection would not be available if the fact of the strike terminated the contract automatically, as there would be no action by the employer needed to end the relationship.

While the law is now clear since *Geys*, it does lead to a somewhat odd result in relation to different claims. It was clear from the judgments, particularly that of Lady Hale, that the employer must not only make a payment, but also explain to the employee that such a payment has been made, that it is paid in exercise of a contractual right to terminate and how that payment has been calculated. However, settled case law (see Chapter 9) has established that where there is a PILON, the date of termination for unfair dismissal purposes is the date the notice is given and not when it expires. The judgment appears to create two different dates of termination. For unfair dismissal purposes, the date will be when the notice is given, but for a contractual claim for damages, it will take effect only when the innocent party accepts the breach.

It follows that if the breach will not end the contract until it is accepted as so doing by the innocent party, if the breach is rectified before the acceptance then the contract continues as normal. In *Norwest Holst Group Administration Ltd v Harrison* [1985] IRLR 240, the employee worked for the employer in a post which included a directorship. The contract was renewed every year. On 14 June he was told that he was to be transferred to another post which did not include a directorship. He replied by a letter headed 'without prejudice' that he assumed his contract had been terminated, and asked if the employer wanted a meeting to sort out the matter amicably. The meeting was held on 24 June, where the employee was offered his original post plus a directorship. He purported to accept the original repudiatory breach by the employer and claimed unfair dismissal. It was held that there had been no dismissal. A repudiatory breach terminates the contract when it is unequivocally accepted as such by the innocent party. Here the employee had not unequivocally accepted the breach because his letter had been headed 'without prejudice'. It therefore followed that the employer could rectify his breach up to the time of the employee's acceptance, and this is what had happened in this case. The employee had therefore resigned and there had been no breach by the employer entitling him to do so.

8.4 Resignation

An employer termination of the contract is called a 'dismissal'. An employee termination of the contract is a 'resignation', and unless he has the statutory protection of constructive dismissal (see Section 9.4.3) the tribunal will have no jurisdiction in relation to unfair dismissal or redundancy. It follows, therefore, that if an employee accepts a repudiatory breach by the employer and terminates the contract, if he has less than two years' continuity he may only claim damages for the breach.

If the words used by the employee are clear and unambiguous then there is no problem legally. In *Secretary of State for Justice v Hibbert* (2013) UKEAT 0289/13/3007, the EAT held that a letter from a claimant which stated, 'I am of the view that there has been a fundamental breach of my employment contract by my employer and have no alternative but to resign my position' was an unambiguous resignation which had the effect of terminating the contract immediately. If, however, the words are ambiguous then the test is that of a reasonable employer and his interpretation of the employee's intention. If the employee is given the option of resigning or being dismissed and chooses the former option, he is treated as dismissed in law (*Robertson v Securicor Transport Ltd* [1972] IRLR 70); but if the employee chooses to resign for other reasons, for example to avoid disciplinary procedures or because a financial inducement has been given, then that is a resignation and not a dismissal. In *Sheffield v Oxford Controls* [1979] IRLR 133, the director of a small company fell out with the owner who asked him how much money he wanted to leave. They agreed on £10,000 and the director resigned. He then claimed unfair dismissal. It was held that there had been no dismissal. The offer of £10,000 had induced his resignation, and not the fear of dismissal.

To be effective, the resignation must have an ascertainable date. If an employee states that he is resigning without the date of the resignation being clear, either expressly or impliedly, it is merely a statement of an intention to perform an act sometime in the future. Where there is such ambiguity, however, the employer would be better advised to insist on confirmation in writing before assuming the contract is at an end. This is also the safest course of action when the employee resigns in the heat of the moment because of an argument with the employer or because he is upset, even if the words are clear and unambiguous. In *Kwik-Fit (GB) Ltd v Lineham* [1992] IRLR 156, Lineham was a manager. One night, on his way home from the pub, he used the depot toilet. This was not contrary to any rules and he reactivated the alarm. The security staff reported the visit. A director of the company felt that Lineham had committed a disciplinary offence and gave him a written warning in the presence of a junior employee. Lineham threw his keys on the counter and walked out. When he did not return the next day, the employer sent a letter confirming the termination of employment. In the claim for unfair dismissal, the employer argued that the employee's actions constituted a resignation. The tribunal found that where there was an ambiguous resignation, the onus was on the employer to establish the true intention of the employee. The EAT held that the employer was not under such a heavy burden unless there were special circumstances. Where these existed, the employer should allow a reasonable period of time before accepting the resignation at face value. Here, special circumstances existed and the employer should have not assumed that there was a resignation. Lineham was unfairly dismissed. However, in *Ali v Birmingham City Council* [2008] All ER (D) 260, Ali handed a resignation letter to his manager. As he seemed upset he was given 20 minutes to reconsider his position, and at the end of that time, as he was still upset, he was given a further 10 minutes to reconsider. After this he affirmed that he still wanted to resign and was escorted off the premises. He later tried to rescind his resignation, claiming it was made in the heat of the moment and 30 minutes was not a reasonable time in which to reflect on his decision. The EAT held that in the circumstances he had been given a reasonable amount of time to so reflect.

8.5 Common law dismissal

The common law recognises only one act that can constitute dismissal, and that is a termination by the employer with or without notice. It will be seen in the next chapter that where the employee has the protection of the provisions governing unfair dismissal or redundancy, the legislation recognises two other situations where dismissal is deemed to have occurred. These will normally come into effect, however, only if the employee has two years' continuous service; until then, the employee has the protection of the common law alone. Once an employee gains the required continuity, however, the statutory protection is in addition to the protection at common law, and thus an employee may be able to claim for unfair dismissal in the tribunal and sue for a wrongful or unlawful dismissal. Given that termination by the employer is recognised by the statutory provisions on dismissal, it follows that the discussion below on what constitutes a dismissal is also relevant in the context of an unfair dismissal.

If the contract is terminated by the employer, this is a dismissal at common law, but it leaves the question: When is the action by the employer deemed to be an intention to terminate the contract? Just as the employee may use ambiguous words which may appear to be a resignation (see Section 8.4 above), so too the employer may use ambiguous words which the employee construes as a dismissal but where that was not the intention of the employer. In *Futty v Brekkes Ltd* [1974] IRLR 130, the tribunal was asked to interpret language used in a disagreement which took place on Hull docks. During the disagreement a fish filleter was told: 'If you don't like the job you can fuck off!' The employee left and presented a claim for unfair dismissal. The employer argued that the words meant that if the employee did not like the job he was doing, he could clock off and come back the following day. The employer also pointed out that colourful language was a normal occurrence within the context of the employment. The tribunal agreed with the employer and held that the words did not constitute a dismissal. The same conclusion with the same choice of words was also reached in the case of *Davy v Collins Builders Ltd* [1974] IRLR 324. It should be noted that the industry is relevant, as is the type of employee. In some cases such language would be construed as a dismissal (for example, if used to a secretary), and the use of swear words themselves may also be the basis of a claim for a constructive dismissal (see Section 9.4.3), if the employee has the correct continuity, on the basis of a breach of the implied duty of mutual respect.

If the words used do not display such dialectal originality as those above, then normally a dismissal will have occurred. Therefore, more common phrases such as 'You're fired', or 'Collect your cards' or 'You are dismissed' will all constitute a dismissal. The tribunals, however, will again look at the circumstances in which the words are spoken and deduce the intention of the employer from them. In *Tanner v Kean* [1978] IRLR 110, the employer lost his temper with an employee who had taken the company van without consent. He ended a barrage of abuse with the words: 'That's it, you're finished with me.' The EAT decided these words were spoken in anger and were not intended to be a dismissal. Likewise in *Martin v Yeoman Aggregates Ltd* [1983] IRLR 49, the employer told the employee to leave after the employee had refused to perform a task. Within five minutes, however, the employer had recanted his words and suspended the employee instead so that a more rational decision could be made. The employee insisted on treating himself as dismissed. Kilner Brown J said that it was a matter of common sense vital to industrial relations that either party should be able to retract words spoken in the heat of the moment.

8.5.1 Summary dismissal

At common law the employer is required to give notice of termination to his employee; however, the law has always been of the opinion that in some cases the employee's conduct justifies dismissal without notice, and should that situation arise the employer will not be in breach of contract. Such dismissals are known as 'summary' or 'instant' dismissals. While earlier cases gave the employer considerable latitude in this area, Edmund Davies J in *Wilson v Racher* [1974] IRLR 114 said that the older cases treated the employee–employer relationship as akin to that of czar and serf, and they would be decided differently today. This demonstrates that the attitude of the judges in relation to the type of conduct that allows the employer to dismiss without notice is constantly changing, as is the attitude towards the relationship itself.

Certain things do remain constant, however, and the law has always regarded dishonesty within employment as gross misconduct justifying summary dismissal. In *Sinclair v Neighbour* [1967] 2 QB 279, a manager took £15 from a till and left an IOU. He intended to replace the money, but his employer regarded his actions as dishonest and instantly dismissed him. The dismissal was held to be lawful. Serious breaches of duty will justify dismissal without notice (*Ross v Aquascutum Ltd* [1973] IRLR 107), as will a refusal to obey a lawful and reasonable order and gross neglect. In relation to the last category, however, the consequences of the neglect and the position of the employee will be considered when the courts look to see if the dismissal is lawful. One single act of neglect is unlikely to justify instant dismissal unless the consequences are very serious.

The employer will often in his own procedures lay down instances of conduct he considers will justify instant dismissal. While the court will allow an employer to lay down his own rules, it will not allow him to act in an autocratic manner. It is the court which eventually decides whether the conduct was serious enough to warrant instant dismissal, not the employer. Should the employer instantly dismiss in circumstances where he is not entitled to do so, the dismissal is wrongful or unlawful, and the employee is entitled to damages for the employer's breach of contract. These damages will normally be the wages he would have received if he had been given notice.

8.5.2   Dismissal with notice

The protection given to employees at common law is that terminations by the employer should normally occur with notice. The notice the employer is required to give will be found in the contract of employment, but this may be ousted if the employer is giving less than the statutory minimum periods of notice laid down by section 86 of the ERA 1996, in which case the statutory minimum notice periods will apply. Those notice periods are as follows:

- ▶ employees with between four weeks' and two years' continuity: one week;
- ▶ employees with more than two years' continuity: one week for every year of service subject to a statutory maximum of 12 weeks;
- ▶ employees should give a minimum of one week's notice.

Should the contract give greater rights than the statute, the contract prevails; on the other hand, if the contract gives lesser rights than the statute, the contractual term is void and the statutory term is the one to be applied. If the contract is silent as to the notice period, the common law imposes a reasonable period, which could be in excess of the statutory minimum. The fact that the statutory minimum will override lesser contractual periods may be important for the employee who is dismissed shortly before acquiring continuity for unfair dismissal or redundancy (see Section 9.2.6 on effective date of termination). The EAT has held that where the employee is dismissed by letter, the date of dismissal is the date that the employee reads the letter and not the date of delivery. There is no such concept as 'constructive knowledge' of the contents of the letter (*McMaster v Manchester Airport plc* [1998] IRLR 112).

There are two situations where the contract will terminate before the expiry of the notice given. The first is when the employee accepts payment in lieu of notice. This will terminate the contract immediately on the receipt of the wages. In *Locke v Candy & Candy* [2010] EWCA Civ 1350, the claimant was entitled to a bonus of £160,000 after he had been employed for 12 months. The employer terminated his contract by making a payment in lieu of notice 10 days before he had completed the 12 months. The Court of Appeal held that the payment in lieu terminated the contract immediately and consequently the employee was no longer employed when the bonus became payable. The employee will lose any rights to payment in lieu if the right to notice has been waived or lost (*Trotter v Forth Ports Authority* [1991] IRLR 419 and *Baldwin v British Coal Corporation* [1995] IRLR 139) given that the payment is in place of the notice the employee has the right to receive. The employee cannot insist on working his notice and refuse to accept payment in lieu (*Marshall (Cambridge) Ltd v Hamblin* [1994] IRLR 260) since there is no duty to provide work. The case of *Abrahams v Performing Rights Society* [1995] IRLR 486 has stated, however, that if the contract gives the employer a right to pay in lieu, such a payment is not damages for a breach of contract (because there has been no breach) but the employer exercising a contractual right to make a lump sum payment. As such, although the employee will not gain the tax advantages associated with receiving contractual damages, as he is receiving a payment he is entitled to under the contract, it is not subject to the rules of mitigation and therefore the employer cannot reduce the amount because the employee has failed to mitigate his loss.

The second situation comes from the EAT decision in *Palfrey v Transco plc* [2004] IRLR 916. In this case, Palfrey was given notice of redundancy, his contract terminating on 19 May. He asked to leave on 31 March, and Transco agreed and confirmed this would be his final day of employment. The EAT held that, on the facts, this was a withdrawal of the original notice date and agreement of a new date. It would appear, however, that each case will depend on its own particular facts, as in this case the effect of the decision was that Palfrey was out of time to claim unfair dismissal as his date of termination was 31 March and not 19 May. Clear evidence has to be available that any change is mutually agreed.

The wages the employee is entitled to receive during his notice period is laid down by section 87 of the ERA 1996. The employer must pay the normal week's pay, even if the employee does not work because no work is provided, or because he is sick or because he is on holiday. The employee is not entitled to payment, however, if he takes time off, breaks his contract during the notice period or goes on strike.

8.6 Reasons for dismissal

The common law does not require that the employer has a fair reason to dismiss the employee, only that if the employee has been instantly dismissed, gross misconduct or gross neglect should have occurred. In relation to dismissals with notice, the reason for the dismissal is irrelevant. This has repercussions in relation to a dismissal which is originally wrongful, in that if before the employee leaves the employment the employer discovers a reason which would justify instant dismissal, that reason can retrospectively legalise an original unlawful act. This is the complete reversal of the law on unfair dismissal, when the reason for the dismissal is investigated by the tribunal at the time the dismissal occurred. While it may affect the issue of compensation if the employer had no reason to dismiss at the time he made that decision, it is irrelevant to the issue of fairness if he discovers a reason during the employee's period of notice or after the employee has left.

This means that the employee who is protected only by the common law may lose his right to damages, depending on his reaction to hearing of his dismissal. In the old case of *Ridgeway v Hungerford Market* (1835) 3 Ad & El 516, the employee was dismissed in the morning and told that his employment would terminate at the end of the day. This dismissal at the time was wrongful, as the employee had not been given the correct amount of notice. The employee was asked to take notes at a meeting just before his employment ended and the meeting discussed the appointment of his successor. He wrote what the report describes as a protest on the minute book. It was held that although the original dismissal had been unlawful, his subsequent conduct was gross misconduct which justified instant dismissal, and thus the original unlawful act had been rendered lawful retrospectively. This is also the case at common law where the employer discovers the gross misconduct only after he has unlawfully dismissed the employee. Again, the discovery will render the dismissal lawful retrospectively (*Boston Deep Sea Fishing and Ice Co v Ansell* (1888) 39 Ch 339). It should be emphasised again, however, that this is the position at common law. Once the employee is protected by unfair dismissal provisions, the employer must have a statutory fair reason to dismiss, and that reason must exist and be known to the employer at the time he dismisses, otherwise the dismissal will be unfair.

8.7 Procedure for dismissal

At common law, unlike statute, normally no procedure for dismissal is laid down – as long as the employer gives the correct amount of notice, the employee will have no claim. This position is vastly different once the employee is protected by unfair dismissal provisions, in that a fair employer will have certain procedures laid down to deal with discipline, including dismissal, and if he has no procedures, the law will expect him to comply with the ACAS Code of Practice on Disciplinary and Grievance Procedures. In two situations, however, even though the employee has common law protection only, his employer may be required to comply with a procedure before dismissal. These situations are, first, where a disciplinary procedure has become part of the employee's contract and, second, where the employee is an office-holder or the occupant of a statutory position.

8.7.1 Contractual procedures

If the employee has had the employer's disciplinary procedures incorporated as part of his contract then a failure to observe those procedures is a breach of contract. This may affect the remedy available to the employee, as we have already seen in Section 4.1 above that while the courts are reluctant to force the parties to continue the contract, they have, on occasion, awarded an injunction against an employer to protect an employee and ensure that the contractual procedures are adhered to before the termination takes effect. It is unusual for the court to grant an injunction however. In *Marsh v National Autistic Society* [1993] ICR 453, the employee was the principal of a special school. By his contract he was entitled to three months' notice of termination. After an internal disagreement, the employee was dismissed with three months' wages in lieu of notice. He sought an injunction restraining the employers from treating him as dismissed, and requiring them to continue paying his wages on the basis that he had not accepted their repudiatory breach of contract and so the contract continued. Ferris J refused the injunction on the basis that although there was authority for the acceptance theory at common law, those cases which supported the theory had the caveat that if the employment had ceased de facto, the employee could no longer perform his part of the bargain and therefore no action lay in debt for wages – there lay only an action for damages for breach of contract. The measure of damages was the wages due under the notice period, which in this case had been paid. In some cases the damages awarded for any breach may also include a sum to cover the period when the employee would have remained in employment had the contractual procedures been complied with (see Chapter 4).

8.7.2 Public law

In addition to any contractual procedures, if the employee is an office-holder or occupies a statutory position, the law provides further protection in that the employer must comply with the rules of natural justice. Breach of the rules of natural justice will render any decision void and so leave the innocent party in the position he was in before the decision to dismiss was taken, that is, still employed, and he can seek a declaration to that effect. In the famous case of *Ridge v Baldwin* [1964] AC 40, the dismissal of a chief constable was declared void because he had not been given the opportunity to make representations before the dismissal took place.

While it will be seen in Chapter 9 that in employment cases the elements of natural justice which must be adhered to are similar, if not identical, to the rules of a fair hearing under unfair dismissal provisions, it is important to note that the consequences of breach are vastly different. If the rules of a fair hearing are broken in an unfair dismissal situation, normally the dismissal will be found to be unfair and compensation awarded as a remedy. The decision to dismiss is still a valid one, even though it has been found to be unfair in law. If the rules of natural justice are broken, the decision to dismiss is void and therefore, legally, never happened, and the employee is still employed. The rules of natural justice, however, do not apply in a normal employment situation. As Lord Wilberforce said in the case of *Malloch v Aberdeen Corporation* [1971] 1 WLR 1578:

> One may accept that if there are relationships in which all requirements of the observance of rules of natural justice are excluded – these must be confined to what have been called pure master and servant cases, which I take to mean cases in which there is no element of public employment or service, no support by statute, nothing in the nature of an office or status which is capable of protection.

The elements of the rules which apply in employment cases are:

- the right of a person to know the case against him;
- the right to an unbiased hearing;
- the right of a person to put his side of the case; and
- the right to an unbiased appeal.

While this may seem to give the office-holder greater remedies than an employee, recent cases have limited the application of the rules. Certainly it appears that mere employment by a public authority does not mean that the employee holds a statutory position, and thus he will be protected only by the normal unfair dismissal rules and not the rules of natural justice (*R v East Berkshire Health Authority, ex parte Walsh* [1984] IRLR 278); it also appears that only if the relationship is excluded from the normal statutory provisions, leaving the employee with no other protection, will natural justice apply (*R v Secretary of State for the Home Office, ex parte Benwell* [1985] IRLR 6). Many Crown employees are now on contracts of employment, and on the basis of *Walsh* will thereby be protected by unfair dismissal provisions only in relation to their employment.

Having said that, should an office-holder fall within the ambit of public as opposed to private law, his remedies are considerable. In addition to a declaration that his employment continues because of a breach of natural justice, other public law remedies of judicial review are open to him. Judicial review will lie on the basis of illegality, unreasonableness or procedural impropriety (*Council for the Civil Service Unions v Minister for the Civil Service* [1985] AC 374), giving the availability of certiorari to quash the decision.

Remedies for wrongful dismissal

While the employment relationship is contractual, it has already been noted in Chapter 4 that because it is a personal contract, the courts are unwilling to grant an injunction which would force the parties to continue the contract and are prevented by statute from issuing an order of specific performance. This means that, apart from in the circumstances in which contractual procedures are broken and the court may issue an injunction, by far the most common remedy is damages.

The measure of damages is limited to the amount of notice the employee would have received had the contract been adhered to, and no account is taken of any prospective periods of unemployment he might have to endure as a result of the loss of his job. In *Janciuk v Winterite Ltd* [1998] IRLR 63, the EAT held that although damages may be awarded for failing to comply with a contractual disciplinary procedure, these damages will reflect only the period of time the employee's contract would have continued had the procedure been followed and cannot take into account the fact that had the procedure been adhered to, the employee might have not been dismissed. Furthermore, no account is taken of the manner of the dismissal, for example, a dismissal because of a false allegation of theft, or injury to feelings, even if the dismissal has affected the employee's future job prospects (*Addis v Gramophone Co Ltd* [1909] AC 488 and *Meatyard v St Edmunds College* (1998) IDS Brief 624). In *Malik v BCCI* [1997] IRLR 462, however, the House of Lords held that where the employer conducts his business in a dishonest manner, and the employment relationship comes to an end, damages for breach of contract may include financial losses where the former employee's future job prospects are prejudiced by the damage to his reputation caused by the stigma of having worked for a dishonest employer.

While it was thought that *Malik* might lead to a challenge to *Addis*, the House of Lords affirmed the principle in *Johnson v Unisys Ltd* [2001] IRLR 279, confirming that no damages are available in wrongful dismissal for any distress caused by the unfair manner of the dismissal or the damage caused to the employee's reputation. Furthermore, their Lordships decided in *Johnson* that an employee claiming wrongful dismissal could not also bring a claim for a breach of mutual trust and confidence based on the same facts (called the '*Johnson* exclusion zone'). This is explained by the Court of Appeal in *McCabe v Cornwall CC* [2003] IRLR 87 as meaning that if there is identifiable damage caused by the breach which is separate from the damage caused by the dismissal, it will be compensated (endorsed by *Dunnachie v Kingston upon Hull City Council* [2004] EWCA Civ 84). *Eastwood v Magnox Electric* [2004] IRLR 733 has extended this principle to unfair dismissal claims, thus an employee cannot use facts for the basis of an unfair dismissal claim and use the same facts to support a claim of a breach of mutual trust and confidence.

In *Monk v Essex County Council* [2013] EWCA Civ 826, Monk was a primary school administrative assistant who on 10 July 2008 was asked to leave the premises immediately. She pursued a High Court personal injury claim in which she stated that the humiliation of her public removal had caused her psychiatric injury. She argued that she was dismissed on 31 August 2008 as she was paid to this date. The High Court considered that dismissal had occurred on 10 July and struck out the claim as falling within the *Johnson* exclusion zone. On appeal, Moore-Bick LJ stated that if her dismissal had occurred on 10 July her claim would be prevented by the *Johnson* exclusion zone, but if it had occurred on 31 August it would be difficult to argue it was dismissal-related and thus excluded. The decision to strike out the claim was overturned and Monk was allowed to amend her claim to argue she was dismissed on 31 August 2008.

The rules above reflect the contractual position that damages for breach of contract should reflect the actual loss sustained. Note, however, the unusual case of *Gregory v Wallace* [1998] IRLR 387, where the contract provided for two years' notice and allowed the employee not to attend during the notice period and take other full-time employment. The Court of Appeal held that, given the clause in the contract allowing the employee to take on other work during the notice period, he was entitled to full contractual damages for a breach of the notice provision and no account would be taken of his earnings from his new employment.

Apart from lost wages, extra damages may be claimed where the contract envisages more than merely the pay, for example publicity or reputation, or where there are other contractual benefits such as a car (*Shove v Downs Surgical plc* [1984] ICR 532), and it was stated obiter in *Robert Cort v Charman* [1981] IRLR 437 that damages may include a sum to cover the loss of unfair dismissal compensation if the nature of the dismissal was such that the employee had been excluded from such protection, for example by the employer's insisting on payment in lieu to avoid the employee gaining continuity for unfair dismissal (*Raspin v United News Shops Ltd* [1999] IRLR 9). In addition, given that the damages reflect actual loss, should the employee be on a fixed-term contract with no notice provision, the damages will reflect the loss of earnings for the rest of the unexpired term.

As with all contractual claims for damages, the employee is under a duty to mitigate his loss, and therefore will be expected to look for other work, although he is entitled to look for work of a similar kind and at a similar level (but note *Gregory v Wallace*, above). In *Yetton v Eastwoods Froy* [1967] 1 WLR 104, a dismissed managing director had turned down the offer of a job as a junior manager. It was held that he had not failed to mitigate his loss by his refusal. However, if there is a contractual right to pay in lieu, there is no duty to mitigate on the part of the employee (*Abrahams*, Section 8.5.2 above).

Again, because contractual damages are paid for actual loss, the court will deduct from the award the amount the employee would have paid in income tax and NICs. In addition, any benefits the employee might have received during his period of unemployment, such as jobseeker's allowance or income support, will be deducted. Note the decision in *Fraser v HLMAD* [2007] 1 All ER 383, where the Court of Appeal held that where the loss exceeds the £25,000 limit on breach of contract jurisdiction in the employment tribunal, but the claimant chooses to take a claim to a tribunal, a claim for the remainder cannot be brought in the High Court.

Summary

8.1 Although the most common way for an employment relationship to end is an act of the parties, the law will operate in some circumstances to end the relationship automatically without liability on either side.

8.2 The most common way the relationship ends automatically is by frustration, and the usual frustrating event is long-term sickness.

Summary cont'd

8.3 The parties may seek to end the relationship by agreement. The courts will protect an employee by ensuring that there is genuine agreement, and an employee cannot contract out of his rights to sue in the tribunals or courts unless the employer has given consideration for such an agreement.

8.4 Breach by either party which goes to the root of the contract is repudiatory. The contract ends when the innocent party accepts the breach as a termination.

8.5 If the employee has less than two years' continuity and accepts a repudiatory breach by the employer as terminating the contract, he can only sue for damages for a breach of contract. After two years the law calls such a breach a 'constructive' dismissal.

8.6 A repudiatory breach may be withdrawn before acceptance by the innocent party.

8.7 If the employee ends the relationship it is called a 'resignation'. If he is forced to resign or be dismissed, the law will treat his resignation as a dismissal.

8.8 Words of resignation or dismissal spoken in the heat of the moment may not be construed as such by the courts. The law looks to the intention of the party.

8.9 If the employer ends the relationship, it is a dismissal, and in some situations the common law allows the employer to dismiss instantly.

8.10 Apart from the situations of instant dismissal at common law, the only right of the employee is the right to notice. Contractual notice which is less than the statutory minimum is void and the statutory notice period will apply.

8.11 Acceptance of wages in lieu of notice terminates the contract on the date of acceptance and not when the notice expires.

8.12 At common law, information discovered by the employer during the notice period or after the employee has left is relevant to the issue of whether the dismissal was lawful or not.

8.13 If the employee is deemed to be an office-holder or the occupant of a statutory position, he will have increased protection in the form of the rules of natural justice and the availability of judicial review.

Exercises

8.1 Mary and Kath work for Keith's DIY shop. Both have been employed for six months.

Mary was given three days' notice of termination of contract last week. After she left, the employer discovered that for the last six weeks the till in the shop had been down by £50 per week. Mary is one of seven shop assistants.

Kath was told last Friday morning that her employment would finish that afternoon. She screamed abuse at the manager and stormed off the premises, shouting 'I'll get in first, I'm going and you know what you can do with your job.'

Both Mary and Kath now wish to sue for a breach of contract. Advise them.

8.2 Bill has worked for Fred's Fashions for 103 weeks operating a machine that cuts out patterns. Last week he was told that because the manager's son needed a job, he was being given two days' notice as per his contract. He has never had any complaints about his work. He worked his notice and now wishes to know if he can claim unfair dismissal.

Would your answer differ if, after he had left, Fred's Fashions discovered that because of Bill's negligent use of his machine, they had to spend £1,500 on repair costs?

Further reading and references

Burrows, 'What is the Effect of a Repudiatory Breach of a Contract of Employment?' (2013) 42 ILJ 281

Brodie, 'Specific Performance and Employment Contracts' (1998) 27 ILJ 79

Brodie, 'Wrongful Dismissal and Mutual Trust' (1999) 28 ILJ 260

Fredman and Lee, 'Natural Justice for Employees: The Unacceptable Face of Proceduralism' (1986) 15 ILJ 15

Fredman and Morris, 'Public or Private? State Employees and Judicial Review' (1991) 107 LQR 298

Halson, 'Claims for Non-Pecuniary Loss in Employment Tribunals Following *Johnson v. Unisys*' (2003) 32 ILJ 214

McMullen, 'Extending Remedies for Breach of the Employment Contract' (1997) 26 ILJ 245

Sargeant, 'Protecting Employees with Insolvent Employers' (2003) 32 ILJ 53

9.1 Introduction

The concept of unfair dismissal was introduced into British law by the Industrial Relations Act 1971 as a result of the International Labour Organization's Recommendation 119, which Britain accepted in 1964. The provisions within the Industrial Relations Act were the only ones to survive when the Labour government came into power in 1974, and were re-enacted in the Trade Union and Labour Relations Act of the same year. The present law relating to unfair dismissal is to be found in the Employment Rights Act (ERA) 1996.

The reason for its introduction was that by 1970 there were a great number of unofficial strikes, many of which were a protest against dismissals. The common law has always provided inadequate remedies against dismissal, in that provided the employer complies with the relevant notice provisions within the contract, the employee has no protection against arbitrary dismissal. The introduction of the concept of an unfair dismissal was intended to give protection against the harshness of the common law, and thus give rights in addition to the common law. These rights, however, do not apply to all employees but only to those who satisfy the qualifying criteria to make a claim. In essence, this means that all employees have the minimal protection of the common law and some employees have the additional protection of statutory unfair dismissal provisions.

Created by statute, unfair dismissal bears no relation to a common law breach of contract claim, and thus a dismissal may be lawful, in that the contract has been complied with, and still be unfair. Conversely, a dismissal may be unlawful, in that a breach of contract has occurred, but be fair according to the statute. In *Treganowan v Robert Knee & Co Ltd* [1975] IRLR 247, Ms Treganowan had been fairly dismissed but had been given insufficient notice. Her dismissal was therefore fair but unlawful (wrongful). Unfair dismissal does not look for a breach of contract on the part of the employer but a breach of the statute, and the remedies which lie against an employer are not remedies which rely on a contractual claim but rather recognise that the dismissed employee has a property right in his job. This means that the first remedy the tribunal should consider is reinstatement, that is, giving the employee his job back, and the second is re-engagement, that is, giving the employee an alternative job; and if those remedies are not practicable, financial compensation should be awarded based on age, years of service and, to some extent, actual loss.

It has already been noted, however, that not all people have the statutory protection. First, only employees are protected and not the self-employed. The distinction between an employee and an independent contractor has already been discussed (see Section 2.1). For these purposes the definition of 'employment' is found in section 230(1) of ERA 1996, which defines an employee as an individual who works under a contract of employment and which defines a contract of employment as a contract of service or apprenticeship, whether express or implied, oral or in writing. Employees must have been continuously employed for two years generally before they get the statutory protection, although there are certain exceptions where no continuity is needed. It used to be the case that part-time employees had to work for longer periods before they gained protection, and part-time workers who worked less than eight hours a week had no protection at all. These restrictions were challenged in *R v Secretary of State for Employment, ex parte EOC* [1994] IRLR 176, where the House of Lords issued declarations that such restrictions on part-time workers were contrary to the Equal Treatment Directive, the Equal Pay Directive and Article 141 of the Treaty of Rome (now Article 157 TFEU). As a result, the Employment Protection (Part-Time Employees) Regulations 1995 were enacted, removing all such restrictions from the right to claim unfair dismissal and redundancy, and now all employees need two years' continuity whatever their number of working hours.

Until 1999 the continuity period which applied in unfair dismissal cases was two years. It was reduced to one year when the Labour government came to power, and restored to two years by the Coalition Government in April 2012. The two-year rule was originally challenged in *R v Secretary of State for Employment, ex parte Seymour-Smith and Perez* [1997] IRLR 315 (HL). The Court of Appeal issued a declaration that at the time of the applicants' dismissals, the two-year requirement was indirectly discriminatory against women and contrary to the Equal Treatment Directive. On appeal to the House of Lords, their Lordships discharged the declaration but referred various questions to the European Court of Justice (ECJ):

▶ Was unfair dismissal compensation 'pay' for the purposes of Article 141 EC (now Article 157 TFEU)?

▶ If so, did the continuity requirements fall within the scope of Article 141 EC (now Article 157 TFEU) or the Equal Treatment Directive?

▶ What was the legal test for establishing whether a measure adopted by a Member State has such a degree of disparate impact between men and women as to amount to indirect discrimination unless objectively justified?

▶ When must this legal test be applied to the measure – when the measure is adopted, when it is brought into force, when the employee is dismissed or at some other time?

▶ Lastly, what were the legal conditions for establishing objective justification for the purposes of indirect discrimination under Article 141 EC (now Article 157 TFEU), and in particular what material must the Member State adduce in support of its argument of justification?

As has been noted (Section 6.8.1), the decision of the ECJ impacted not only on this area but also on discrimination generally.

The ECJ gave its decision in *Seymour-Smith* on 9 February 1999 ([1999] IRLR 253). In respect of the questions referred, the Court decided as follows:

▶ Unfair dismissal compensation is 'pay' for the purposes of the Treaty.

▶ The conditions determining whether an employee was entitled, where he had been unfairly dismissed, to obtain compensation fell within the scope of Article 141 EC (now Article 157 TFEU), but the conditions determining whether he could claim reinstatement or re-engagement fell within the scope of the Equal Treatment Directive.

▶ It was for the national court to determine the point at which the legality of the two-year rule was to be assessed.

- In order to establish whether the rule was indirectly discriminatory to women, the national court must determine whether the statistics indicated that a considerably smaller percentage of women than men were able to comply with the rule.
- Lastly, if the rule was discriminatory, it was for the Member State to show that the rule reflected a legitimate aim of its social policy, that that aim was unrelated to any discrimination based on sex and that it considered that the means chosen were suitable for attaining that aim.

The ECJ further stated that it was insufficient to consider the number of persons affected since that depended on the number of working people in the Member State; the national court had to look at the proportions of the relevant groups to determine whether the rule had a disparate effect. It further stated that on the relevant percentages in 1985 when the rule was introduced, there did not appear to be a disparate impact (77.4 per cent of men and 68.9 per cent of women could comply with the rule at that date). However, the ECJ added that a lesser difference might indicate indirect discrimination if it showed 'a persistent and relatively constant disparity over a long period'. It would, nevertheless, be up to the national court to determine the conclusions to be drawn from such statistics.

The House of Lords decided the case in the light of the ECJ ruling ([2000] IRLR 263). Their Lordships seemingly disagreed with the ECJ which appeared to be saying that the difference in the proportion of men and women who could comply with the two-year rule was not sufficiently great to constitute indirect discrimination. Lord Nicholls, with whom Lords Goff and Jauncey agreed, appeared to adopt the second test of indirect discrimination advocated by the ECJ by saying:

> I find myself driven to the conclusion that a persistent and constant disparity … in respect of the entire male and female labour forces of the country over a period of seven years cannot be brushed aside as insignificant or inconsiderable … I think these figures are adequate to demonstrate that the [two-year] qualifying period had a considerably greater adverse impact on women than on men.

Their Lordships went on to say, however, that the government had introduced the two-year rule to increase employment (the argument being that employers were more likely to take on staff if they had a reasonable length of time during which they could dismiss without penalty), and it was not unreasonable for the government to wait a period of time to assess whether the introduction of the two-year service requirement had achieved the goal of increased employment. As such, although the two-year rule was indirectly discriminatory to women, the government had objectively justified its introduction.

In addition to the restrictions above, certain classes of employee are excluded from the legislation (see Section 9.3 below).

The relevant statutory provision is now section 108(1) of the ERA 1996. If the employee shows that he has the required continuity and he is not an excluded employee, he must prove that he has been dismissed, and Chapter 8 has already shown the variations that can occur in that regard. He must also present his claim to the tribunal within three months of the effective date of the termination of his employment, unless the tribunal feels that it was not reasonably practicable for the employee to present a claim within that time period (ERA 1996, s 111(2)). In *London International College v Sen* [1993] IRLR 333, the employee had been dismissed on 9 July 1990 and, having gone through the internal appeal procedures, he asked a solicitor the time limit for bringing an unfair dismissal complaint. He was told that he should submit his complaint on or before 9 October 1990. He also contacted the Central Office of Industrial (Employment) Tribunals, where a member of staff confirmed that the relevant date was 9 October. In fact 9 October was a day late and his complaint should have been submitted by 8 October. The employment tribunal found that it was not reasonably practicable for Sen to present his claim within three months of the effective date of termination of his contract. The employer appealed, arguing on the basis of *Jean Sorrel v Rybak* [1991] IRLR 153 that as Sen had consulted a solicitor, the exception to the three-month rule did not operate. (The *Rybak* case is authority for the proposition that professional advice from a solicitor which is wrong, does not make it impracticable to present a claim in time and that therefore the claim should not be heard and the employee must sue his solicitor for negligence. Incorrect advice from the tribunal office, on the other hand, will allow the exception to operate.) The EAT held that the employment tribunal was entitled to find that the substantial cause of Sen's failing to present his case in time was advice from the tribunal and not the solicitor. The employer appealed to the Court of Appeal which upheld the decision of the EAT, adding that there was no cut-and-dried rule that consulting a skilled adviser will always prevent an employee from presenting a claim outside the three-month limit.

These cases are now subject to *Chohan v Derby Law Centre* [2004] IRLR 685 and *Marks and Spencer plc v Williams-Ryan* [2005] EWCA Civ 70. In *Chohan*, the EAT ruled that extending the time limit can be just and equitable where a claimant can show that the failure to lodge in time was the result of a legal adviser's giving the wrong advice. In *Williams-Ryan*, the claimant contacted the Citizens' Advice Bureau (CAB) after being dismissed for gross misconduct. The CAB told her to complete the company's internal appeal procedure, but did not tell her of her right to complain to a tribunal. Her letter of dismissal outlined her right of appeal and told her of her right to lodge a complaint of unfair dismissal, but did not mention the three-month time limit. The claimant thought she had to go through the procedures before lodging a claim. The internal appeal took three and a half months, and she lodged her claim four months after her dismissal. The Court of Appeal reviewed the authorities and ruled that although a claimant cannot have a time limit extended where a solicitor has given negligent advice (*Rybak*), the situation is less clear where the negligent advice is given by the CAB. However, the Court of Appeal did not deal with the issue that it was the negligent failure of the CAB to tell her of her right to claim, nor the fact that the employer had told her of such a right but did not mention the time limits. The Court of Appeal found that as there was no authority on advice from the CAB, the original tribunal had not given a perverse decision when holding it was not reasonably practicable to present her case in time. It is debatable whether this is a softening of the law, as if the employer had not delayed in the appeal, Williams-Ryan would have presented her claim in time, and this influenced the Court of Appeal.

Account now has to be taken of technology. In *Tyne and Wear Autistic Society v Smith* [2005] IRLR 336, Smith submitted his claim via the Employment Tribunal Service's (ETS's) website on the last day of the time limit. He received a receipt from the website, but the claim did not reach ETS until the next day because the website was hosted by a commercial provider. The EAT held that because the claim had reached the website and been accepted there, the claim had been presented in time.

In *Aniagwu v London Borough of Hackney* [1999] IRLR 303, it was held that it was just and equitable to extend the three-month time limit when the complainant had delayed presenting his claim until he knew the outcome of an internal grievance procedure or appeal; and in *Schultz v Esso Petroleum Company Ltd* [1999] IRLR 488, the Court of Appeal held that an employment tribunal had erred in finding that it was reasonably practicable for an applicant to bring his claim in time when, although well for the first seven weeks after his dismissal, he had been too ill to contact his solicitor in the last six weeks. The Court held that the tribunal should take account of events at the end of the three-month period and not at the beginning, and take all the circumstances into account (in that case, the fact that the applicant was hoping the employers would settle without recourse to a tribunal). A similar conclusion was reached in *Harris v Towergate London Market Ltd* (2007) IDS 832 where, on selection for redundancy, Harris made a grievance complaint during which there were further discussions about her selection. The EAT held that the discussions meant it was reasonable for Harris to assume that the dismissal procedure was still continuing, and thus the time limit ran from the date the procedures ended and not the date of dismissal. However, the Court of Appeal took a much stricter approach in *London Underground Ltd v Noel* [1999] IRLR 621. In this case the applicant was dismissed but then offered a lower grade job on a reduced salary within the three-month period. She accepted the offer which was withdrawn shortly after the limitation period had expired. The Court of Appeal held that it was reasonably practicable for her to present her complaint in time and the offer of re-employment did not make it reasonably impracticable. This seems to be a harsh decision which could be abused by unscrupulous employers.

Once the employee has surmounted these hurdles the burden shifts to the employer, who must prove that his reason for dismissal was one of the statutory fair reasons, and during the whole of the hearing the tribunal must consider whether the employer acted reasonably in how he handled the dismissal and whether dismissal was an appropriate sanction in the light of the employee's 'offence'. While all of this may seem complex, it means that any unfair dismissal case nicely divides itself into certain questions:

- Has the employee the required continuity?
- Is the employee excluded from the statute?
- Has the employee been dismissed?
- Has the employer got a statutory fair reason for dismissal?
- Has the employer acted reasonably?

9.2 Continuity of employment

Most employment protection rights require a period of continuous employment before the right can be claimed. In most cases of unfair dismissal, the necessary period of continuous employment is two years. Continuity is defined in sections 212–218 of the ERA 1996, and the aim is to exclude the common law rule that a change of terms means a new contract comes into force. Such a rule operating would mean that, for example, every time an employee received a pay rise, a new contract would come into being and the old contract would cease to exist. Given that many employees receive annual pay rises, to acquire rights based on the length of the contract would mean that employees who received annual pay rises would never acquire the protection from unfair dismissal. The provisions therefore base eligibility on the length of employment and not the contract. In *Wood v York City Council* [1978] IRLR 228, the employee had a variety of jobs with the City Council for three years and then he resigned to take up a position with the Council's York

Festival Office. He was made redundant one year later. It was held that he had sufficient continuity to claim redundancy pay. His employment was with the same employer even though there had been a change of job, a change of location and a change in the terms of employment. *Wood* has been followed in *Cranston v Harwich Dock Co Ltd* [1998] IRLR 567. In this case the employee resigned on Friday and was re-engaged on the following Monday to take advantage of a pension scheme. He agreed with his employer that his resignation would break his continuity. When he was dismissed some months later and claimed unfair dismissal, the employers argued that he did not have the continuity to claim. The EAT, overturning the employment tribunal, stated that section 203 of the ERA 1996 states that it is not generally possible for employers and employees to enter a contract which deprives the employee of his statutory rights. *Morris v Walsh Western UK Ltd* [1997] IRLR 562 confirms that this means that the parties cannot agree to disapply the continuity rules. As such, Cranston had the requisite continuity to claim unfair dismissal.

Continuity starts when the contractual employment starts and not the actual employment (*General of the Salvation Army v Dewberry* [1984] IRLR 222.) In *Welton v Deluxe Retail Ltd* [2013] IRLR 166, Welton worked in a shop in Sheffield and was dismissed when the shop closed. The following week he was offered a job in another shop owned by the same employer and started work one week later. It was held that his continuity started when the contract came into operation and not at the later date of when he started work. The converse is also true, however. In *Koenig v The Mind Gym* [2013] All ER(D) 261, the claimant was dismissed. Her contract provided that she had started work on 1 October and so she did not have the continuity to claim unfair dismissal. She argued, however, that two days previously she had attended a meeting with a client of the respondent, and that this should be taken as the date her continuity began. The EAT, upholding the employment tribunal, dismissed the appeal. There was no contract operating when she met the client as she was not obliged to attend the meeting, she was not there as an employee of the respondent, she was not paid and it was her choice to attend.

Normally continuity continues until the employment comes to an end. As will be seen in Section 9.2.1 below, certain breaks in the period will not stop the running of the continuity and will be counted in the final computation. Other breaks will not stop the running of the period but will be discounted in the final computation. In one case, continuity will stop altogether. This is when the contract involves an illegal act. In *Hyland v JH Barker (North West) Ltd* [1985] IRLR 403, a lorry driver who had been employed for 16 years received a tax-free lodging allowance for one month in the 12 months prior to his dismissal. It was held that he did not have the continuity to claim unfair dismissal because the illegality wiped out the period when the contract was legal, and continuity started from scratch once the illegality ceased. (Note, however, *Hewcastle Catering Ltd v Ahmed* [1992] ICR 626 where it was held that where the illegality was at the instigation of the employer, eg a VAT fraud, and the employees were threatened with dismissal if they did not comply, it was not against public policy to allow the employee to claim unfair dismissal as to hold otherwise would be to benefit the employer.) The cases of *Enfield Technical Services v Payne/Grace v BF Components Ltd* [2007] All ER 394 may throw doubt on this. In the cases, the EAT held that to defeat an unfair dismissal claim on the grounds of an illegal (and therefore void) contract, there must be some misrepresentation or some attempt to hide the true nature of the relationship, and the fact that the parties have wrongly labelled the relationship or have an arrangement which has the effect of depriving HMRC of monies is not enough to render the contract illegal and void. This decision was upheld by the Court of Appeal ([2008] EWCA Civ 393) and is important, in that a mislabelling of the relationship, rather than a deliberate attempt to misrepresent it, will not render the contract void and deprive the worker of the protection granted to an employee, even if the worker has received benefits from being self-employed in the past. Further, in *Lairikyengbam v Shrewsbury NHS Trust* [2010] ICR 66, the EAT held that a contract renewed in contravention of NHS regulations was *ultra vires*; however, an employee who continues to work under such a contract is nevertheless entitled to be treated as an employee.

9.2.1 Weeks which do not break continuity and count towards the final computation

The provisions envisage situations where the employee will not be at work but his continuity will continue. Section 212(3) of the ERA 1996 states that where there is:

- incapability due to sickness or injury;
- a temporary cessation of work; or
- an absence due to an arrangement or a custom,

these absences shall not break the continuity and shall count in the final computation.

In relation to sickness or injury, the employee will retain continuity for 26 weeks of illness. In *Donnelly v Kelvin International Services* [1992] IRLR 496, the EAT discussed whether the incapability is in relation to the employee's particular work or any work. It opted for the former interpretation and thus Donnelly, who while ill had taken a less demanding job for a month and then returned to his employer when his health improved, had not lost his continuity. It must be the illness which is the cause of the absence for the provisions to apply, however; if after the illness the employee remains off work for some other reason, if that reason does not fall within section 212(3), there will be a break in the continuity period (*Pearson v Kent County Council* [1993] IRLR 165).

A temporary cessation of work envisages situations where, because of no fault of the employee, no work is available for him. It is work for the particular employee which must have temporarily ceased and not work (say) in the factory itself. In *Fitzgerald v Hall, Russell & Co Ltd* [1970] AC 984, the employee, a welder, was laid off temporarily, even though others of his colleagues were still employed to weld. The House of Lords decided that the section required the court to look at the situation of the individual employee, and not the situation of the employer as a whole. In *Holt v EB Security Ltd* (2012) UKEAT /0558/11, Holt was made redundant when the pub he worked in closed. He started work in another pub run by a different company in the same group two weeks later. The EAT held that there was a temporary cessation of work for the purposes of continuity. It is questionable whether this is a correct interpretation of section 212(3), as the cessation of work was permanent since the pub had closed; it was Holt's absence from work which was temporary. Note, however, that if the employee's work is given to someone else, there is no cessation for the purposes of the section (*Bryan v Birmingham City District Council* [1987] IRLR 191).

The section will operate only if the cessation of work is temporary, and this leaves the question of how long 'temporary' is. The aim of section 212 was to protect workers in particular industries where lay-offs are common, but the effect has been much wider. In *Bentley Engineering Co Ltd v Crown* [1976] IRLR 146, a period of absence of two years was held to be temporary as it was a relatively short period in the context of the whole employment history. This means that the decision as to whether the cessation is temporary takes place at the end of the break, when all factors are taken into account. What the parties intend is, to a large extent, superfluous, as circumstances may change during the absence. If the employee resigns or is dismissed during the absence, it ceases to be a temporary cessation, even if the employee resumes employment with the same employer (*Wessex National Ltd v Long* (1978) 13 ITR 413). In the important decision of *Ford v Warwickshire County Council* [1983] 2 AC 71, the employee was a teacher who was employed on a session basis. Her contracts ended in July and were renewed in September. This arrangement continued for eight years. The House of Lords stated that the holidays were a temporary cessation of work and that the employee had eight years' continuity, given the length of the employment and the length of the holidays. 'Temporary', according to the House of Lords in the case, means 'transient'. Although the EAT has stated that a strict mathematical approach is wrong (*Flack v Kodak Ltd* [1986] IRLR 255), in *Berwick Salmon Fisheries Co Ltd v Rutherford* [1991] IRLR 203 the same tribunal held that it would not be possible to call a cessation temporary when the periods of lay-off were longer than the periods of working.

Where the absence is by arrangement or custom, again section 212(3) will preserve continuity, although for the section to apply the agreement or custom must be that continuity is so preserved. In *Lloyds Bank Ltd v Secretary of State for Employment* [1979] IRLR 41, an employee worked one week on, one week off, for five years. When she became pregnant, the employers paid her SMP and sought to recover from the Maternity Fund. It was held that she had been continuously employed for five years and her employers were entitled to recover. From *Morris v Walsh Western UK Ltd* (Section 9.2 above) it appeared that the arrangement with the employer must be in place when the employee is absent; it cannot be entered into retrospectively when the employee returns to work. However, in *London Probation Board v Kirkpatrick* [2005] IRLR 443, the EAT said that an arrangement in place before the gap in service was unnecessary, which suggests that retrospective arrangements fall within section 212(3). The EAT did go on to say that if this interpretation was wrong, the existence of the disciplinary procedures could be described as an arrangement in place before the gap in the employment. The most common example under this provision is that of secondment to another employer, or where the employee is allowed time off for personal reasons. Continuing to pay the employee is strong evidence that there is an arrangement that continuity should continue. If an employee is engaged under a series of short-term contracts then section 212 will not protect them, as the parties do not consider the contract to be continuing during the break. In *Booth v United States of America* [1999] IRLR 16, the EAT held that employees who worked on a series of short-term contracts, with a two-week gap in between each one, were not protected by section 212(3).

In addition to the situations listed in section 212, if a person is reinstated or re-engaged after an unfair dismissal or redundancy, he can count the period between his dismissal and reinstatement or re-engagement for continuity purposes (s 219).

9.2.2　Weeks which do not break continuity, but which do not count in the final computation

Any period during which the employee is on strike or locked out by his employer does not break his continuity, but such weeks will be deducted from the final computation of his continuity period (ERA 1996, s 216). The question of when an employee is deemed to be on strike is discussed in Section 9.8 below. Likewise, periods spent in the armed forces do not break the continuity but are not part of the final calculation (ERA 1996, s 217).

Should the employee not fall within the paragraphs above, any break in employment will break the continuity period and a new period will begin when the employment next starts. Any illegality in the contract may stop continuity running, and a new period will start when the illegality ceases (*Hyland v JH Barker (North West) Ltd*, although note *Enfield Technical Services v Payne/Grace v BF Components Ltd* – see Section 9.2 above).

9.2.3　Change of employer

Under the common law, only service with the same employer is calculated for continuity purposes. This means that should the employee change his job, the continuity he acquired with his old employer is ignored and a new period commences with the start of his new employment. This is also the situation when his employer sells his business to another employer. Again, the employer has changed and therefore continuity is broken. This can be hard on the employee, who, through no decision of his own, may lose years of continuous service and with it a great deal of statutory protection. The law therefore protects certain employees when a business is sold as a going concern. The protection will not apply, however when only the assets of a business are sold, even if the new employer takes on the old employees. In that case, the employees must claim a redundancy payment from their old employer and start continuity afresh with their new employer.

Protection for employees comes from two sources: section 218 of the ERA 1996, and the Transfer of Undertakings (Protection of Employment) Regulations 2006 ('TUPE Regulations 2006'). While two sources exist, it should be noted that in fact the Act and the Regulations overlap and often a transfer will be covered by both. The provisions of the 1996 Act and the TUPE Regulations 2006 are examined in further detail in Sections 9.2.4 and 9.2.5 below.

9.2.4　Employment Rights Act 1996

Continuity of employment will be preserved under the ERA 1996 in the following circumstances:

1.　A trade, business or undertaking is transferred (s 218(2)).
2.　A body corporate is substituted for another body corporate by statute (s 218(3)).
3.　An employer dies and the employee is retained by the employer's personal representatives or trustees (s 218(4)).
4.　There is a change of partners, personal representatives or trustees (s 218(5)).
5.　The employee is taken on by an associated employer of his employer (s 218(6)).

For section 218(2) to apply the business must be transferred as a going concern. If only the assets are transferred, this does not fall within the section and continuity will not be preserved. In *Woodhouse v Peter Brotherhood Ltd* [1972] 2 QB 520, the employers manufactured diesel engines. On moving part of their operation to Manchester, they sold the factory and machinery to Peter Brotherhood, which manufactured spinning machines, compressors and steam turbines, although that firm completed four engines begun by the original employer before engaging in their own work. Woodhouse was employed on the engines before being made redundant. The Court of Appeal held that there was not a transfer of a business but only of physical assets, as the business of the new employer, while using the same machinery, was totally different from that of the old. A similar conclusion was reached in *Melon v Hector Powe Ltd* [1981] ICR 43 where, despite the fact that the new employers finished the work of the old employers before starting their own business, there was not a relevant transfer for the purposes of section 218(2). How different the new business must be to prevent the operation of the provision is for the court to decide. In *Crompton v Truly Fair (International) Ltd* [1975] IRLR 250, the old employers manufactured children's clothes while the new employers manufactured men's trousers. It was held that there had been no transfer of the business. Likewise, it has been held that the transfer of a franchise is not within the section.

For section 218(2) to operate, the business and physical assets must be transferred to the new employer, along with the goodwill. In *Blumestead v John Cars Ltd* (1967) 2 ITR 137, the employee worked for successive owners of a concession at a petrol station. It was held that he did not have continuity because only the right to sell petrol had been transferred and no physical assets.

The section provides that 'the period of employment of an employee … at the time of the transfer counts as a period of employment with the transferee', but this leads to the question: When does the transfer actually take place? This is a vexed question , as shown by the Court of Appeal decision in *Teesside Times Ltd v Drury* [1980] IRLR 72, where the employee was dismissed during negotiations for a transfer when an oral agreement had been reached but before the contract was signed. The Court held that continuity continued with the new employer. While Stephenson LJ thought that the transfer is not necessarily the actual transfer but also the processes which are part of it, Goff LJ thought that transfer meant the moment when the transaction of transfer was effected. The later EAT decision of *Macer v Abafast Ltd* [1990] IRLR 137 said that tribunals should lean in favour of that interpretation which best gives effect to the preservation of continuity of service. In *Clark Tokesley Ltd t/a Spell Brook Ltd v Oakes* [1998] IRLR 577, the Court of Appeal interpreted the phrase to mean during the course of the transfer, given that two out of three judges in *Drury* interpreted 'transfer' as the date of the actual transfer and so created ambiguity. The purpose of the provision was to provide a period of continuous employment for the purposes of the Act, even though the person at the particular time might not be in employment.

While the rest of section 218 is, to a large extent, self-explanatory, some clarification of section 218(6) is needed. This states that continuity will be preserved if the employee is employed by an associated employer of the original employer. The definition of 'associated employer' is found in section 231 of the ERA 1996. In essence, employers are associated if one has control over the other, or if both are under the control of third party. 'Control' means legal control rather than ownership of shares (and therefore the voting power of the shares is important – *South West Launderettes Ltd v Laidler* [1986] IRLR 305) and does not include negative control, so that a person who holds 50 per cent of the voting shares does not have control because he can thwart the other shareholders. Singular denotes the plural, therefore control may be exercised by a group of individuals; however, to be associated employers, the same group must be present in both companies (*Poparm Ltd v Weeks* [1984] IRLR 388). Thus if a husband and wife own 60 per cent of the shares in X Ltd, and the husband and his brother own 80 per cent of the shares in Y Ltd, they are not associated employers for the purposes of section 218(6). The subsection is, however, wide enough to include overseas companies. In *Hancill v Marcon Engineering Ltd* [1990] IRLR 15, the employee had worked abroad for an American firm and then in England for a British company which dismissed him. Both were wholly-owned subsidiaries of a Dutch company. The employee sought to include his time worked for the American company in his continuity period. At first instance his claim was dismissed, because the tribunal argued that an American company could not be a limited company under section 231. The EAT overruled the decision. In perceiving the intention of Parliament, the EAT said:

> It seems to us here that a coach and four could easily be driven round a few corners and then straight through the provision of this legislation if the word company [in section 231] were only to include a UK Ltd company when the overseas vehicle is to all intent and purposes identical.

9.2.5 Transfer of Undertakings (Protection of Employment) Regulations 2006

Further rights are contained in the TUPE Regulations 2006. The original Regulations, which were enacted in 1981, were brought in to give effect to EC Council Directive 77/187 (the Acquired Rights Directive). This Directive has now been codified by the Acquired Rights Directive 2001 (2001/123/EC) and transposed into UK law by the TUPE Regulations 2006. The aim of the Directive is to ensure that on the transfer of an undertaking, the contractual rights of the employees are maintained.

9.2.5(a) The history of the Regulations

Some detail about the original Regulations, and the case law thereunder, is necessary to understand the 2006 Regulations. Until amendments introduced by section 33 of the Trade Union Reform and Employment Rights Act 1993, the original Regulations defined an 'undertaking' as any trade or business, and did not include an undertaking which was not in the nature of a commercial venture. This meant that undertakings which had a charitable status did not fall within the Regulations (*Woodcock v Committee of the Friends School* [1987] IRLR 98), neither did the transfer of services in local government to private contractors. It could be argued, however, that there is no requirement that the business must be a commercial venture under ERA 1996 when looking at the interpretation provisions in section 235. Therefore, even if the employee was not protected by the Regulations, his continuity could still be preserved by section 218 of the Act. The EAT in *Stirling v Dietsman Management Systems Ltd* [1991] IRLR 368 held, however, that the definition of 'business' within the (now) ERA 1996 could not be used to widen the definition of a commercial venture under the Regulations. Further, what was or was not a commercial venture was a question of fact for the tribunal.

The restriction of the Regulations to commercial ventures did not fully implement the EC Acquired Rights Directive. The amendments made by the 1993 Act were by no means in the original bill and were introduced during the parliamentary process after the decision of the ECJ in *Dr Sophie Redmond Stichting v Bartol* [1992] IRLR 366. In this case the Sophie Redmond Foundation carried out certain local council functions in relation to drug addicts. The local authority decided to switch the functions to another foundation, and some of the employees from Sophie Redmond were transferred to the second foundation. The issue for the ECJ was whether the Dutch provisions implementing the Directive applied to the transfer of the functions between the two foundations. The ECJ held that a legal transfer was wide enough to include the situation when a public body terminated a subsidy to one body and transferred it to another with similar aims. Second, the Court held that there would be a transfer of an undertaking as long as whatever unit was being transferred retained its factual identity, thus qualifying as a business or part of a business.

Bartol (above) and other cases show that the ECJ, in the early years of the Directive, took a broad view of what constituted a business. In *Watson Rask and Christiansen v ISS Kantineservice A/S* [1993] IRLR 133, the issue came before the ECJ again. When deciding whether a business had been transferred, previous UK decisions had looked for some transfer of ownership (for example *Stirling*, above) and therefore had decided that the contracting out of a service which was peripheral to the main activity of the organisation, such as catering or security, was not the transfer of an undertaking. In *Watson Rask*, Philips A/S contracted out its canteen service to ISS. The terms of the contract were that ISS would receive a fee from which labour, management and administrative costs would be met. Philips would provide the premises, equipment, refuse collection and cleaning products. ISS would offer employment to Philips's employees. ISS made minor changes to the terms of employment and two employees complained. ISS argued that there was no contract involving a change in ownership, merely a transfer of an internal service to an outside contractor. That contractor had so many restrictions placed upon him that there was no change in the ownership of the service. ISS also argued that no assets were transferred, no customers were transferred and there was no profitable objective because ISS was merely providing a service to Philips's staff. The ECJ rejected all the arguments and held that the Directive applied where, following a legal transfer or merger, there is a change in the legal or natural person who is responsible for carrying on the business and who by virtue of that fact incurs the obligation of an employer vis-à-vis the employees of the undertaking, regardless of whether or not ownership of the undertaking is transferred. The Court continued that it was necessary to consider all the factual circumstances, including:

- the type of business or undertaking concerned;
- whether the business's tangible assets are transferred;
- whether or not the majority of the employees are transferred;
- the value of the intangible assets at the time of the transfer;
- whether or not customers are transferred;
- the degree of similarity of activities before and after the transfer;
- the period, if any, for which those activities are suspended.

These were all questions which an earlier ECJ (in *Spijkers v Gebroeders Benedik Abattoir CV* [1986] CMLR 296) stated must be asked when looking to see if there was a relevant transfer under the Directive. Furthermore, the Court in *Spijkers* stated that 'the decisive criterion for establishing the existence of a transfer within the meaning of the EU Acquired Rights Directive is whether the entity in question retains its identity'.

Watson Rask was followed in the UK by the cases of *Dines v Initial Health Care Services* [1994] IRLR 336 and *Kelman v Care Contract Services* [1995] ICR 260, and was applied to first- or second-generation contracting out. In addition, the Directive was held to apply where there was a transfer of one employee (*Schmidt v Spar- und Leihkasse der Früheren Amter Bordesholm, Keil und Cronshapen* [1995] ICR 237 (ECJ)), but does not apply where there is a transfer to complete a one-off contract (*Ole Rygaard v Dansk Arbejdsgiver-forening* [1996] ICR 333, although see below).

The cases above established that the Directive, and hence the original TUPE Regulations, applied to the contracting out of local authority services under the Compulsory Competitive Tendering policies of the then UK government. However, an unexpected decision from the ECJ led to a restriction in the application of the Directive and created uncertainty once again. In *Suzen v Zehnacker Gebaudereinigung GmbH Krankenhausservice and Lefarth GmbH* [1997] ICR 662, Suzen was a cleaner working for a company that had a contract to clean a school. When the contract came to an end, Suzen, along with seven of her colleagues, was dismissed. The school entered into a contract with another company to provide cleaning services, but that company did not take on Suzen and she commenced legal proceedings in the national court which referred a number of questions to the ECJ, the most pertinent being whether the circumstances gave rise to the transfer of an undertaking. The Court stated that the question was to be determined by reference to the criteria laid down in *Spijkers*.

The ECJ further stated that the Directive applied only where the transfer involved the transfer of significant tangible or intangible assets, or a major part of the workforce who provided the service prior to the transfer.

Suzen was followed in the UK courts in *Betts v Brintel Helicopters* [1997] ICR 792 and *Superclean Support Services plc v Lansanna and Wetton Cleaning Services* (1997) IDS Brief 596. However, there were cases where the contracting out of services was held to be covered by the Directive, and thus the Regulations, despite *Suzen*. In *Highland Council v Walker* (1998) IDS Brief 606, the EAT refused to overturn the decision of the employment tribunal that the transfer of dog warden services from a contractor back to the local council, which involved the transfer of one employee, was a transfer under the Regulations. Although the employment tribunal had decided on the basis of *Schmidt* (above) and prior to *Suzen*, the EAT said that the employment tribunal, after careful consideration of the facts, had decided that the lack of transfer of assets did not preclude the transfer of an undertaking, and such an approach was not precluded by *Suzen* (see also *Holmes v Sita (GB) Ltd & FM Conway* (1998) IDS Brief 606). Indeed, the Court of Appeal in *Betts* acknowledged that where there is a labour-intensive undertaking, there can be a relevant transfer where a major part of the workforce is transferred even though no physical assets are transferred. In *ECM (Vehicle Delivery Services) Ltd v Cox* (1998) IRLB 596, the tribunal decided that a transferee could not avoid the operation of the Regulations by refusing to take on the transferor's workforce. In the case, the transferor had lost a business and not merely a customer, therefore the decision is consistent with *Suzen*.

It can be seen that what constituted the transfer of an undertaking was therefore highly complex. On 4 June 1998, the EU Social Affairs Committee reached an agreement on a Directive amending the original Acquired Rights Directive. The new Directive (98/50/EC) amended Articles 1–7 of the 1977 Directive and was implemented by the UK in 1999. Article 1 of the new Directive stated that:

there is a transfer within the meaning of this Directive where there is a transfer of an economic entity which retains its identity, meaning an organised grouping of resources which has the objective of pursuing an economic activity, whether or not that activity is central or ancillary.

The amendments made to the original Directive gave a clearer definition of what was meant by a transfer.

In *Cheesman v R Brewer Contracts Ltd* [2001] IRLR 144, which concerned the loss of a maintenance contract, Lindsay J gave a list of factors a tribunal should consider to establish whether there had been a transfer of an undertaking:

1. There needs to be a stable economic entity whose activity is not limited to performing one specific works contract, and an organised grouping of persons and of assets enabling (or facilitating) the exercise of an economic activity which pursues a specific objective.
2. In order to be such an undertaking it must be sufficiently structured and autonomous, but will not necessarily have significant assets, tangible or otherwise.
3. In certain sectors such as cleaning and surveillance, assets are often reduced to their most basic and the activity is essentially based on manpower.
4. An organised grouping of wage-earners who are specifically and permanently assigned to a common task may, in the absence of other factors of production, amount to an economic entity.
5. An activity of itself is not an entity; the identity of an entity emerges from other factors such as its workforce, management staff, the way in which its work is organised, its operating methods and, where appropriate, the operational resources available to it.

See also *ADI (UK) Ltd v Willer* [2001] IRLR 542. In other words, to establish the transfer of an economic entity, a multi-factor approach should be taken.

In *Argyll Training Ltd v Sinclair* and *Argyll & The Islands Enterprise Ltd* [2000] IRLR 630, the Scottish EAT also held that *Suzen* could not be relied upon to establish that there was no transfer if significant assets or a major part of the workforce were not transferred. Furthermore, in *Argyll* the EAT held that the decision in *Ole Rygaard* (above), that there can be no transfer within the meaning of the Directive where the transfer is to complete a one-off contract, would, if given a broad interpretation, 'give rise to many doubts and difficulties', and thus refused to accept that a transfer of an entity whose activities were limited to one specific contract could not be a protected transfer under the TUPE Regulations.

As seen above, there was still confusion where there were service provision changes. The TUPE Regulations 2006 specifically cover such transfers.

9.2.5(b) What is a 'relevant transfer'?

Regulation 3 of the TUPE Regulations 2006 lists two situations which constitute a relevant transfer. Regulation 3(1)(a) is very similar to the wording in the 1981 Regulations and states that a 'relevant transfer' is:

a transfer of an undertaking, business or part of an undertaking or business situated immediately before the transfer in the United Kingdom to another person where there is a transfer of an economic entity which retains its identity.

Regulation 3(2) defines an 'economic entity' as an 'organized grouping of resources which has the objective of pursuing an economic activity whether or not that activity is central or ancillary'. Regulation 3(4)(a) states that the Regulations apply to both private and public bodies, whether or not they are operating for gain. As such, it is clear that the Regulations are picking up on the old case law discussed above, such as *Argyll Training Ltd* and *Cheesman*.

Regulation 3(1)(b) defines the second type of relevant transfer, which is called a 'service provision change'. This applies to a situation in which:

1. activities cease to be carried out by a person (a client) on his own behalf and are carried out instead by another person on the client's behalf (a contractor);
2. activities cease to be carried out by a contractor on a client's behalf (whether or not those activities had previously been carried out by the client on his own behalf) and are carried out instead by another person (a subsequent contractor) on the client's behalf; or
3. activities cease to be carried out by a contractor or subsequent contractor on a client's behalf (whether or not those activities had previously been carried out by the client on his own behalf) and are carried out instead by the client on his own behalf,

and in which the conditions set out in Regulation 3(3) (below) are satisfied.

Amendments introduced in 2014 by the Collective Redundancies and Transfer of Undertakings (Protection of Employment) (Amendment) Regulations 2014 now provide that for a service provision change, the service provision must be fundamentally or essentially the same as pre-transfer.

A service provision change will fall within the Regulations only if Regulation 3(3) is satisfied. This states:

> The conditions referred to in paragraph (1)(b) are that—
> (a) immediately before the service provision change—
>   (i) there is an organised grouping of employees situated in Great Britain which has as its principal purpose the carrying out of activities concerned on behalf of the client;
>   (ii) the client intends that the activities will, following the service provision change, be carried out by the transferee other than in connection with a single specific event or of a short-term duration; and
> (b) the activities concerned do not consist wholly or mainly of the supply of goods for the client's use.

Again, it can be seen that the Regulations are picking up on the case law discussed above, such as *ECM*. The Regulations would also seem to endorse *Ole Rygaard* (Section 9.2.5(a) above).

In *Metropolitan Resources v Martin Cambridge* [2009] ICR 1380, there was the transfer of the provision of services to asylum seekers. The transferee provided the services in a different way at a new site. The EAT stated that whether there was a service provision change called for a common sense and pragmatic approach. A fundamental question is whether the activities by the transferee are fundamentally or essentially the same as those carried out by the transferor. The EAT stated that there was no call for a formal list of factors which a tribunal must consider, and where one contractor ceases and another commences service provision with differences in time, manner and/or place, there can still be a service provision change under the Regulations. Similarly, in *Wood v London Colney Parish Council* (2010) UKEAT 0528/09/1203, the employer employed the claimant as a bar steward. The employer dismissed the claimant after it surrendered the lease to the second employer and surrendered its licence. The second employer obtained its own licence and began trading using its own employees. The EAT held that the economic entity, the bar, was temporarily suspended by the loss of the licence but did not cease. As such there was a valid transfer and the claimant had protection under the TUPE Regulations 2006. In the case of *Rynda (UK) Ltd v Rhijnsburger* [2013] All ER (D) 73, the EAT held that a single employee can be a 'grouping' under Reg 3(3)(a)(i), in that the employer had made a conscious decision to assign her to the particular activity. Conversely, in *Ceva Freight Ltd v Seawell Ltd* [2013] CSIH 59, the Court of Session ruled that the organised grouping of employees had to be a conscious decision on the part of the employer to put the employees into a group which has as its principal purpose the carrying out of the activity in question. However, in *OCS Group Ltd v Jones and another* (2009) EAT/0038/09, OCS lost a contract to provide a catering service at the BMW plant. The service was a restaurant serving hot food, four satellites and a shop. BMW awarded the contract to MIS, which agreed to provide five kiosks selling sandwiches. The EAT held that the tribunal was entitled to find that the activity carried out by OCS was a 'full canteen service' and as such did not transfer to MIS. If however, the tribunal had classed the activity as the provision of food, the activity might have been caught by the TUPE Regulations 2006. This shows that the classification of the activity is just as important as the activity itself. Likewise, Regulation 3(3)(a)(ii) excludes a service provision change when the client for whom the services are provided intends that the activities are in connection with a single event or a task of a short duration. Therefore in *Liddell's Coaches v Cook* [2012] EmpLR 167, Liddell's Coaches had a contract to provide after-school transport for a year, although normally contracts of this kind were awarded for two to three years. The EAT agreed with the employment tribunal that the contract was for a short-term duration and the TUPE Regulations 2006 did not apply.

9.2.5(c) The effect of a transfer

If there is a transfer which falls under the TUPE Regulations 2006, employees have certain rights. 'Employee' is defined by Regulation 2(1) as an individual who works for another person under a contract of service or apprenticeship or otherwise. In *Cowell v Quilter Goodison Co Ltd* and *QG Management Services Ltd* [1989] IRLR 392, the Court of Appeal held that an equity partner in a firm which had transferred its business was not an employee for the purposes of the Regulations as he worked under a contract for services and not a contract of service.

The effect of the transfer on the relevant employees' contracts is found in Regulation 4. This states that the transferee takes over 'all rights, powers, duties and liabilities under or in connection with any such contract'. There was an exception relating to occupational pension schemes and invalidity and survivors' benefits (Reg 10). While the effect of the original exception was called into question in the case of *Perry v Intec Colleges Ltd* [1993] IRLR 56, it was overruled by the EAT decision in *Walden Engineering v Warner* [1993] IRLR 420 where the EAT held that the Regulation meant what it said and should not be given a gloss. As the Regulation was worded, it did not require the new employer to provide equivalent provision. The Court of Appeal confirmed this interpretation in *Adams v Lancashire County Council and BE Catering Services* [1997] IRLR 436. However, in *Beckman v Dynamco Whicheloe MacFarlane* [2003] ICR 50, the ECJ held that although benefits paid at the end of a working life under a pension scheme were excluded, early retirement benefits paid in the event of redundancy were not, even if they were calculated using normal pension benefit rules. As such, the relevant provision under the superannuation scheme operated by the employee's old employer transferred, and Beckman was entitled to an early retirement pension and lump sum on being made redundant.

While old age, invalidity and survivors' benefits do not automatically transfer because of Regulation 10, the Transfer of Undertakings (Pension Protection) Regulations 2005, which came into effect in April of that year, impose an obligation on transferees to make provision for transferred employees in respect of old age, invalidity and survivors' benefits, in that the transferee must match the contributions of employees of up to 6 per cent of salary.

Under Regulation 4, therefore, the contract transfers lock, stock and barrel to the new employer, including any continuity which has been acquired. In *MITIE Managed Services Ltd v French* [2002] IRLR 512, a question arose on the application of the earlier TUPE Regulations and the liability of a transferee where the transferor provided a profit-sharing or share option scheme. The employment tribunal stated that under Regulation 4, the clause in the contract transferred and the transferee had to honour it. The EAT, however, allowed the employer's appeal, stating that in a case like this, the entitlement of the transferred employees is to 'participation in a scheme of substantial equivalence but one that is free from unjust, absurd or impossible features'. It is suggested that this does little to clarify the law.

Regulation 11 imposes a duty on the transferor to notify the transferee of the transferring employees and of all the associated rights and liabilities which will transfer. This information must be accurate not more than 28 days before the date the information is notified to the transferee, even if the transferor is unaware that the TUPE Regulations apply, and transferees can sue defaulting transferors. Tribunals may award compensation, if the claim is well founded, which it considers just and equitable, although it cannot be less than £500 per employee unless the tribunal feels a lesser sum is just (Reg 12).

While Regulation 4 states that all rights and liabilities transfer, Regulation 4(3) states that the Regulations protect only those persons employed immediately before the transfer, or who would have been so employed if they had not been dismissed in the circumstances described in Regulation 7. This wording is again picking up on existing case law. In *Secretary of State for Employment v Spence* [1987] QB 179, the Court of Appeal held that employees who were dismissed at 11 am one morning when the business was transferred at 2 pm the same day were not employed immediately before the transfer according to the wording of the Regulations. The question of interpretation came before the House of Lords in *Litster v Forth Dry Dock and Engineering Co Ltd* [1989] IRLR 161. In this case, Forth Dry Dock was in receivership and another company had agreed to buy the business. The transferee did not want to take on the employees of Forth Dry Dock because some redundant employees from another company had agreed to accept lower wages. The transferee therefore arranged with the receivers that the employees were to be dismissed an hour before the transfer took place. The transferee then argued that Regulation 4 did not apply, and liability for the dismissals lay with the transferor, which was, of course, in receivership. The House of Lords held that, in order for the purpose of the Directive to be realised in full, it was necessary to imply into the Regulations the words 'or would have been so employed but for being unfairly dismissed under Regulation 7'.

Regulation 7 provides that a dismissal will be fair if it is for an economic, technical or organisational (ETO) reason requiring a change in the nature of the workforce. Thus if the employees have been dismissed for a reason other than those in Regulation 7, they will be deemed to have been employed immediately before the transfer. However, in *Bangura v Southern Cross Healthcare* (2013) UKEAT 0432/12/1203, the EAT ruled that an employee who had been instantly dismissed and who had an appeal pending, was not employed immediately before the transfer. A summary dismissal terminates the contract immediately, and such a dismissal is negated only if an appeal against dismissal is successful, as was the case in *G4S Justice Services (UK) Ltd v Anstey* [2006] IRLR 588.

While *Litster* and Regulation 7 are to be welcomed, in *Ibex Trading v Walton* [1994] IRLR 564 the EAT held that the dismissal of employees of an insolvent company by the receiver, when there was no purchaser on the scene, was not a dismissal connected with a transfer and thus the Regulations did not apply. Furthermore, it should be noted that *Litster* deals only with the question of liability for compensation (that is, the transferee is liable) and does not render the dismissal void. This would seem to go against the ECJ decision in *Bork (P) International A/S v Foreningen af Arbejdsledere i Danmark* [1989] IRLR 41, which made it clear that the Acquired Rights Directive was meant to prevent dismissals before the transfer. The case of *Celtec Ltd v Astley* (2005) ECJ Case C-478/03, however, has implications for employees. The case concerned civil servants seconded to Training and Enterprise Councils during the 1990s and subsequently employed by them. Astley was seconded in 1990 and employed from 1993. The issue was whether his continuity of service was protected by either section 218 of the ERA 1996 or the TUPE Regulations. The ERA 1996, as seen, protects those employed at the time of the transfer, and the Regulations protect those employed immediately before the transfer, so the question was whether the transfer took place at one point in time, 1990, or over a period of time ending when the last secondee was employed (in the case, 1996). The EAT held that it was at one point in time, 1990, while the Court of Appeal held that a transfer could happen over a period of time. The House of Lords referred the issue to the ECJ. The ECJ held that the use of the word 'date' in the Directive meant that a transfer could not happen over a period of time. As such, the House of Lords ([2006] UKHL 29), when it heard the case, concluded that the transfer took place in 1990. However, Regulation 4(3) states that 'an employee employed immediately before the transfer' includes where the transfer is effected by a series of two or more transactions. Whether this has an impact in situations such as *Astley* remains to be seen.

The ECJ also stressed the automatic effect the Directive had on the date the transfer takes place irrespective of the parties' wishes, in line with its decision in *Rotsart de Hertaing v Benoidt* [1996] IRLR 127. This may well have implications for the duty on transferors to inform transferees of all employees and rights and liabilities which are transferring, discussed above. Regulation 11 provides that this information should be given not less than 28 days before the transfer. The ruling in *Astley* is that the transfer takes place when the new employer assumes responsibility for the transferred employees, which will obviously be some time after the contracts, and thus a transferee could find that he receives important information only after he is legally committed to the transfer, and the transferor will not be in breach of his duty.

While the TUPE Regulations are discussed further below and in Chapter 10, two further points should be made here. If liability has transferred and the new employer changes the terms of the contract, the employee may argue that he has been constructively dismissed, but only if there are changes in terms 'which involve a substantial change in working conditions to the material detriment of a person' (Reg 4(9)). In *Berriman v Delabole Slate Ltd* [1985] IRLR 305, the Court of Appeal held that a reduction in salary to bring the transferred employees' pay into line with that of the transferee's employees was a substantial change and not an economic reason within Regulation 7; but in the *Watson Rask* case (Section 9.2.5(a) above) the changes to terms were minor and the ECJ still upheld the employees' complaint, suggesting that Regulation 4(9) does not comply with the Directive, which refers to a 'significant', not 'substantial', change. However, in the later case of *Rossiter v Pendragon plc* [2001] IRLR 256, the EAT held that section 95(1)(c) of the ERA 1996 (see Section 9.4.3 below) had to be construed purposively to give effect to the Acquired Rights Directive, and while the section might be construed differently in the context of domestic law, this did not preclude a broader construction to give effect to the Directive. Therefore a tribunal was not required to find a fundamental breach of contract in order to give rise to a claim of constructive dismissal under the TUPE Regulations. It was sufficient for the applicant to show that there had been a substantial and detrimental change to his working conditions. The Court of Appeal, however, in the joined appeals of *Rossiter and Air Foyle Ltd v Crosby-Clarke* [2002] IRLR 483, overruling the EAT, held that a change to employees' terms and conditions following a transfer does not automatically amount to a constructive dismissal, and the employee still has to establish a fundamental breach of pre-transfer rights. In *Rossiter*, the contract allowed changes in commission which the transferee instigated, resulting in a loss of £3,000 per year. In *Crosby-Clarke*, the transferee moved the business to Belgium, which allowed pilots to work for 11 days without a break whereas in the UK the maximum was four days. Both the employees' contracts allowed the changes and so there was no fundamental breach. Thus, the transferee may vary terms in the same way as the original employer, as long as the variation is allowed by the contract, although the EAT in *Tapere v South London & Maudsley NHS Trust* [2009] IRLR 912 held that the test for whether a substantial change to working conditions is to the material detriment of the transferred employee was to look at the impact of the change from the employee's reasonable viewpoint and not to balance the views of the employee and the employer. In addition, transferee employers cannot use a substantial equivalence argument to defend breaches of pre-transfer terms, except where the terms present practical difficulties like share options. As such, changing a transferred employee's place of work, to his detriment, constituted a dismissal.

In *Power v Regent Security Services* [2007] ICR 970, the EAT held that the principle that any changes to contracts made as a result of transfers under the TUPE Regulations are void, does not apply where the change is to the benefit of the employee but only when the change is to the employee's detriment. This ruling was confirmed by the Court of Appeal ([2007] EWCA Civ 1188). However, *Jackson v Computershare Investor Services* [2007] All ER 448 shows that there are limits to this. In the case Mrs Jackson was transferred to Computershare in 2004 and was dismissed for redundancy in 2005. Computershare had an enhanced severance scheme which it paid to employees who had joined the firm before 2002. The Court of Appeal held that Mrs Jackson was not entitled to the enhanced severance pay, stating that Regulation 4 does not give a transferred employee access to benefits other than those to which the employee was entitled before the transfer.

The Advocate-General in *D'urso v Ecole Marelli Elettro-meccanica Generale SpA* [1992] IRLR 136 expressed an opinion that a constructive dismissal caused by a change in terms would be fair only if such a change would have occurred despite the transfer. This appears to raise doubts as to the validity of Regulation 7. However, the Court of Appeal in *Wilson v St Helens Borough Council* and *Meade and Baxendale v British Fuels Ltd* [1997] IRLR 505 decided that where an employee is dismissed by the transferor for a reason connected with the transfer and is taken on by the transferee on less favourable terms, the dismissal is ineffective and the original terms still apply. This does not apply, however, to dismissals for an 'economic, technical or organisational reason entailing changes in the workforce' (Reg 7(2)). The argument of the Court of Appeal was that Regulation 7 states that a dismissal before or after a relevant transfer is unfair unless it is for an ETO reason. The Court then concluded that if it is unfair within the Regulation, it must therefore be void. The Court went on to hold that in *Meade* the dismissal was void and thus the change of terms by the transferee was ineffective, despite the fact that the employees had agreed to the change and had worked under them. Conversely, in *Wilson* the dismissal was for an ETO reason and therefore effective, leaving the employees free to agree a change in terms. After the decisions, the EAT in *Cornwall County Care Ltd v Brightman* [1998] IRLR 228, while acknowledging it was bound by *Wilson* and *Meade*, held that, in certain cases, the employee may be taken to have accepted his dismissal. Thus, if the employee worked under the new terms for some time, he could be said to have accepted that he has been constructively dismissed, albeit the dismissal is unfair by Regulation 7(1), and the employee should be paid compensation to buy out his old terms.

It must be said that the above cases left the law in a confused state. *Wilson* and *Meade* were appealed to the House of Lords. Their Lordships ([1998] 3 WLR 1070) reviewed the views of both the EAT and the Court of Appeal in the cases. In the EAT, *Foreninggen af Arbejdsledere i Danmark v Daddy's Dance Hall a/s* [1988] ECR 739 was cited, in which the ECJ said that the employment relationship may be changed by a transferee, provided it was done lawfully, but that the relationship could not be altered if the transfer itself was the reason for the change. Similarly in *Watson Rask* (Section 9.2.5(a) above), the employees successfully argued that the transferee could not change their pay day from the last Thursday of the month to the last day of the month. The ECJ held that if a term is altered to the employee's detriment because of a transfer, the alteration is invalid. In *Meade*, the EAT held that as the employees had been made redundant by the transferor and offered new terms by the transferee which they accepted, there had been an effective dismissal and the employees could not argue that they were employed under their original terms. *Daddy's Dance Hall* was irrelevant as a variation case, but was relevant on the facts as presented to the Appeal Tribunal in *Wilson*. In the Court of Appeal, it was discovered that the facts relied on by the EAT in *Wilson* were incorrect, as the employees had been made redundant and offered new contracts by the transferee.

The House of Lords upheld the Court of Appeal decision in *Wilson*, stating that although the dismissal was transfer-related it was for an ETO reason. In respect of *Meade*, however, the House of Lords felt that there was nothing in the Regulations which rendered a dismissal ineffective, even if it was connected with the transfer. The dismissal was therefore effective but unfair. The employees' claim, however, fell outside the three-month time limit required. This leaves the law in the curious position that if the employer dismisses the employees and then offers new terms, the dismissal will be effective but unfair unless it is for an ETO reason affecting changes in the workforce. The new terms, however, will be valid. If, on the other hand, the employer takes on the transferred employees and negotiates a change in terms, such a change will be invalid (*Daddy's Dance Hall* and *Watson Rask*, above) and the old terms will continue. Note, however, *Power v Regent Security Services* (above).

Since 2002, however, the ECJ appears to be relaxing its position. In *Boor v Ministre de la Fonction Publique et de la Réforme Administrative* ECJ Case C-425/02, Boor was transferred when a non-profit organisation in the private sector moved to Luxembourg. Public sector pay rates were set by legislation and were lower than those in the private sector. The ECJ said there was nothing to prevent the new employer reducing Boor's salary to comply with national laws relating to public sector employees. However, if the change was substantial, the employee could resign and claim constructive dismissal. This seems to allow for some harmonisation of terms and supports the Court of Appeal findings in *Rossiter*.

Changes made to the Regulations by the Collective Redundancies (Transfer of Undertakings (Protection of Employment) (Amendment) Regulations 2014 provide that any terms agreed by collective agreement can be renegotiated one year after the transfer, provided any changes are not less favourable to employees. In addition, the 2014 Regulations now clarify that an ETO reason includes a change of location of the workforce.

9.2.6   Effective date of termination

For the purposes of unfair dismissal (and redundancy), it is necessary to know the exact date when the employment relationship ended. There are two reasons for this:

1. to calculate the period of continuous employment; and
2. because the complainant has a short time period after the termination of the employment in which to present his claim (three months for unfair dismissal, six months for redundancy).

For unfair dismissal purposes, the date the relationship is deemed to end is known as the 'effective date of termination'. The date which applies is given in section 97(1) and (4) of the ERA 1996. The effective date of termination is:

1. if the contract is terminated by notice on either side, the date that notice expires, whether it is of the proper length or not;
2. if the contract is terminated without notice, the date on which the termination takes effect;
3. if a fixed-term contract expires without being renewed, the date on which it expires;
4. if the employee gives counter-notice which is shorter than the employer's notice, the date the counter-notice expires.

The only problem area is 2. above. Two problems can arise in this area. First, the employer may instantly dismiss the employee to prevent him acquiring the continuity for unfair dismissal. The Court of Appeal in *Stapp v Shaftesbury Society* [1982] IRLR 326 confirmed that the actual date of termination is the effective date of termination, and this has since been supported in *Batchelor v BRB* [1987] IRLR 136. Second, if the employee accepts wages in lieu of notice then again the date of termination is when the employee leaves and not when the notice expires, unless there is some ambiguity, for example the employee being given written notice but orally agreeing to accept wages in lieu (*Robert Cort v Charman* [1981] IRLR 437).

If the employee is given contractual notice which is shorter than the statutory minimum to which he is entitled then the date of termination is the date when the statutory notice expires for certain purposes by section 97(2) of the Act. These are:

- calculation of the qualifying period for unfair dismissal;
- calculation of the basic award in unfair dismissal;
- calculation of the period of continuous employment on which the award is based.

9.3 Excluded employees

The legislation excludes certain employees from protection from unfair dismissal. We have already seen in Section 9.1 above that the employee must normally have the requisite amount of continuity of employment to claim, and unless the reason for the dismissal is one where no continuity is required, employees without the minimum amount of service will not be protected. In addition, certain other classes of employee are excluded. The main areas of exclusion are discussed below.

9.3.1 An employee who has agreed to waive his rights to unfair dismissal

Normally an employee cannot sign away his rights to unfair dismissal or redundancy compensation, and any such agreement which purports to exclude such rights is void by section 203 of the ERA 1996 (*Igbo v Johnson Matthey Chemicals Ltd* [1986] IRLR 215). There are two exceptions to section 203. The first is where an officer of ACAS has promoted an agreement between the parties and the employee accepts that agreement in full settlement of his claim. The normal procedure is for the parties to sign an ACAS agreement, but the fact that the form has not been signed by the employee although his agreement has been registered is sufficient (*Gilbert v Kembridge Fibres Ltd* [1984] IRLR 52). If the employee's representative signs on the employee's behalf this may be insufficient if the tribunal does not recognise the authority of the representative to so sign. While solicitors, barristers and members of the CAB will have that authority (*Freeman v Sovereign Chicken Ltd* [1991] IRLR 408), trade union representatives may not, and this could render the agreement void.

The second exception is in section 203(2)(f). This allows an employee to enter a settlement agreement which is legally binding provided that:

1. the agreement is in writing;
2. the agreement relates to the particular complaint;
3. the employee has received independent advice from a relevant independent adviser;
4. the adviser has in force a contract of insurance or an indemnity provided for members of a profession or professional body, covering the risk of loss by the employee;
5. the agreement identifies the adviser; and
6. the agreement states that the conditions regulating compromise agreements under the Act are satisfied (s 203(3)).

It appears that a problem with settlement agreements is that they have to be particularly well worded to be effective. In *Bank of Credit and Commerce International SA v Ali* [2001] IRLR 292, a settlement agreement expressed to be 'in full and final settlement of all or any claims whether under statute, common law or in equity of whatsoever nature that exists or may exist' did not bar an action for stigma damages which the parties could not have contemplated when drawing up the agreement. The House of Lords said that clear language would be needed, leaving no room for doubt that the employee intended to surrender rights and claims of which he could not have been aware when signing the agreement. In *Hinton v University of East London* [2005] EWCA Civ 532 a more detailed 'catch-all' phrase was used. The compromise agreement (the previous name of a settlement agreement) contained the statement that the agreement:

> was in full and final satisfaction of all claims in all jurisdictions (whether arising under statute, common law or otherwise) … arising out of or in connection with his employment with the university, the termination of his employment or otherwise, including in particular the following claims which have been raised by or on behalf of the employee as being claims he may have …

The list that followed contained 11 different kinds of claims, but did not include a claim of continuing detriment arising from whistle-blowing, despite Hinton's having raised this in correspondence. The Court of Appeal held that the statutory claims to which the agreement related must be identified. Generic words such as 'unfair dismissal' will suffice, as will referring to a particular section of a relevant statute, but a general phrase such as 'all statutory rights', or naming the statute without identifying the relevant sections, is not sufficient and an employee is free to pursue a claim. As such, Hinton had not compromised his detriment claim and was free to pursue it. The case shows that employers should specify all claims mentioned by the employee in some detail, and a general settlement agreement, used for all employees, is likely to leave an employer exposed. This is definitely not a case of one size fits all!

The fact that section 203(2)(f) refers to an agreement relating to a particular complaint does not mean that it is limited to complaints that have been presented to the tribunal, according to the EAT in *Lunt v Merseyside TEC Ltd* [1999] IRLR 458, although Parliament did not intend to permit a blanket settlement agreement compromising claims which had never been indicated in the past. Therefore, in the case, it included claims the applicant had indicated (by letter) she would not pursue if a settlement was reached. This is endorsed by *Hinton*.

If a settlement agreement does not comply with section 203(2)(f) it is void and the claim has not been settled. This, for example, would at present be the case if a settlement agreement purported to be in final settlement of any claim, as it must relate to a particular complaint. However, according to the EAT in *Sutherland v Network Appliance Ltd* [2001] IRLR 12, this will not invalidate the whole of the agreement but renders it void only in respect of statutory claims as it falls foul of the restrictions in section 203(1). Thus it is still enforceable in settlement of any breach of contract claims.

It can be seen that settlement agreements have to be worded very specifically to achieve their aim.

There are two further exceptions where an employee may agree to exclude his rights to go to an employment tribunal. The ERA 1996 introduced the concept of dismissal procedures agreements in section 110. Such an agreement, if recognised by the Secretary of State, is in substitution of the right to claim unfair dismissal in a tribunal. To date only one industry, the electrical contracting industry, has a designated dismissal procedures agreement which has now lapsed. This was thought to be because of the many hurdles that had to be surmounted under the original Act. As such, the Employment Rights (Dispute Resolution) Act 1998 amended section 110. The section provides for a greater number of reasons for dismissal to be covered by a dismissal procedures agreement, provides that such agreements include provision for arbitration and provides for legal enforcement of any award made under the procedures. These changes may encourage more industries to set up agreements and prevent unfair dismissals being heard in the employment tribunals.

A further method whereby an unfair dismissal will not be heard by a tribunal is if the parties use the arbitration scheme established by ACAS and discussed in Chapter 1.

9.3.2 An employee who falls within the category of excluded persons

Certain classes of employee are excluded by sections 198–200 of the ERA 1996. These include share fisher persons, employees employed for less than a month, members of the police and mariners. Police includes the British Transport Police Force (*Spence v British Railways Board* [2001] ICR 232).

9.3.3 An employee whose dismissal is to safeguard national security and the minister has issued a certificate to that effect

9.3.4 An employee outside the territorial scope of UK labour legislation

Section 196 of the ERA contained a further restriction where the employee ordinarily worked outside Great Britain, but this section was repealed by the Employment Relations Act 1999. However, the Rome Convention on the Law Applicable to Contractual Obligations 1980 (80/934/ECC) was incorporated into UK law by the Contracts (Applicable Law) Act 1990.

Territorial limits are seen in other legislation, but the repeal of section 196 of the 1996 Act apparently removed such restrictions from unfair dismissal provisions. However, the Court of Appeal held in *Crofts v Cathay Pacific Airways Ltd* [2005] EWCA Civ 599 that in order to gain protection, an employee must be employed in Great Britain. Nevertheless, in the case a liberal interpretation was given to the phrase. The Court had to decide whether there was jurisdiction to hear unfair dismissal claims from international airline pilots who were employed by a UK subsidiary of a Hong Kong registered company, to fly aircraft operated by Cathay Pacific. The pilots had Hong Kong licences and contracts subject to Hong Kong law, and were paid in Hong Kong dollars into a Hong Kong bank, but their contracts required them to be based in England. The Court said that where the contract bases the employee is likely to shed light on where the employment is when the job is international and mobile. As the pilots by their contracts were based in England, there was jurisdiction to hear the claim.

The House of Lords discussed the issue in *Lawson v Serco Ltd* [2006] UKHL 3. In the case their Lordships heard three joined appeals involving a security officer working for a British company at an RAF base on Ascension Island, a youth worker employed by the Ministry of Defence at British Army bases in Germany and an air crew member, based in the UK but employed by a company resident in Hong Kong. In all three cases the House of Lords held that the employee had the right to claim unfair dismissal. The House of Lords said that in three situations an employee working abroad may be protected from unfair dismissal:

- peripatetic employees who are based in Britain;
- employees working in a British enclave abroad;
- an employee posted abroad by a British employer 'for the purposes of a business carried on in Great Britain'.

While the last example was *obiter*, as it covered none of the employees in question, the EAT applied it in the case of *Williams v University of Nottingham* UKEAT 0124/07/RN. The case concerned a Nottingham University lecturer who was employed to work for the University of Nottingham in Malaysia, which was a totally separate company. He resigned and claimed unfair dismissal. The EAT held that he was unable to claim, but confirmed that employees posted abroad would have such a right if they fitted the House of Lords' description above.

9.3.5 An employee shareholder

As seen in Section 2.1.7, such persons have no rights to unfair dismissal.

9.4 Has there been a dismissal?

In order to claim unfair dismissal the employee must obviously show that he has been dismissed. The different types of termination of the contract at common law have already been discussed in Chapter 8. For the purposes of unfair dismissal there is a statutory definition of 'dismissal' in section 95 of the ERA 1996. This states that dismissal will occur in the three situations discussed below.

9.4.1 Employer terminating with or without notice

This is, of course, the classic termination at common law. It involves the employer ending the relationship, and the question of whether the dismissal is wrongful or not is irrelevant to the issue of fairness. Thus a lawful dismissal may be unfair, and likewise a wrongful dismissal may be fair. All the situations discussed in Chapter 8 which constitute a dismissal at common law will be a 'dismissal' under section 95.

9.4.2 Fixed-term contract which expires and is not renewed

Section 95(1)(b) identifies this specifically as a dismissal.

9.4.3 Constructive dismissal

While the previous two situations are more or less self-evident, this third category is not. It picks up on the common law situation of a repudiatory breach by the employer which forces the employee to resign (Section 8.3); therefore, on the face of it, there appears to be a resignation. The law is aware, however, that this construction can leave employees with little protection against an unscrupulous employer who makes life so bad as to force them out, therefore statute calls this situation a dismissal. The breach by the employer must have caused the employee's resignation (*Jones v F Sirl & Son (Furnishers) Ltd* [1997] IRLR 493). However, it is sufficient that the employer's repudiatory breach played a part in the dismissal; it did not have to be the principal reason for the employee's resignation, according to the EAT in *Wright v North Ayrshire Council* (2013) UKEAT 1117/13/BI, following the Court of Appeal in *Nottinghamshire County Council v Meikle* [2004] IRLR 703 (Section 5.6 above).

It should be noted, however, that statute has created this concept and therefore two very important points should be borne in mind. First, the concept of constructive dismissal arises only if the statutory protection applies, therefore the concept protects only those with the requisite continuity; until the employee has been employed for two years by his employer, if the employee ends the relationship for whatever reason, it will be construed as a resignation. While resignation by the employee is the normal position in constructive dismissal, two cases suggest that this might not always be so. In *Hogg v Dover College* [1990] ICR 39, a full-time member of staff received a letter following an illness, offering him part-time work on a reduced salary. He lodged a complaint of unfair dismissal while still working under the new terms under protest. The EAT held that the letter from the employer terminated the contract even though the employment continued. Alternatively, there was a new contract, the old one terminating by Hogg's acceptance of the employer's repudiatory breach. *Hogg* was followed in *Alcan Extrusions v Yates* [1996] IRLR 327, where the imposition of a new shift system, which also involved changes in pay and holidays, was a repudiation which the employee accepted as terminating the old contract even though he worked to the new terms under protest. The EAT held that whether the change in terms is radical enough to amount to a termination of the original contract and the substitution of a new contract is a question of fact for the tribunal. While the cases protect employees without the need to resign, they create uncertainty, as each case must be decided on its own facts. *Edwards v Surrey Police* [1999] IRLR 426 makes it clear, however, that there must be some communication, by words or conduct, to inform the employer that the existing contract has ended. In the absence of such communication the relationship continues.

Second, statute has created the concept of a constructive dismissal but has chosen not to create the corollary – a constructive resignation. This means that if the employee commits a repudiatory breach and the employer chooses to end the relationship, as the employer has terminated the contract it is a dismissal, although the reasons for the dismissal will obviously be relevant when looking at the issue of fairness.

Section 95(1)(c) of the ERA 1996 states that it is a dismissal if the employee terminates the contract, with or without notice, in circumstances in which he is entitled to do so because of the employer's conduct. This leads to the question of what conduct entitles the employee to leave and claim constructive dismissal.

In the early days of the concept, judges argued that any unreasonable behaviour on the part of the employer could form the basis of a constructive dismissal claim, but Lord Denning MR decided that the test was a contractual test in *Western Excavating (ECC) Ltd v Sharp* [1978] IRLR 27. Here the employee was suspended without pay as a disciplinary sanction. As he had no money, he asked his employer for his holiday pay, which was refused, and then asked for a loan, which was also refused. He then resigned, claiming constructive dismissal because of unreasonable conduct on the part of his employer. The Court of Appeal held that because the employer had committed no breach of contract, there was no dismissal and the employee had resigned. Lord Denning MR said:

> If the employer is guilty of conduct which is a significant breach going to the root of the contract of employment or which shows that the employer no longer intends to be bound by one or more of the essential terms then the employee is entitled to treat himself as discharged from any further performance. If he does so, then he terminates the contract by reason of the employer's conduct. He is constructively dismissed.

While other cases tried subtly to reintroduce the reasonableness test, the Court of Appeal reiterated the contractual importance in *Courtaulds Northern Spinning Ltd v Sibson* [1988]

IRLR 305, where the employee had resigned when his employer told him to move sites. The employee argued that as there was no contractual mobility clause, the order was unreasonable and that therefore he had been constructively dismissed. The Court rejected this argument, first on the basis that unreasonable conduct on the part of the employer was not the test for constructive dismissal and, second, because, as the employee had moved sites in the past, there was an implied mobility clause in his contract.

The breach must be fundamental, and minor changes in terms would not set up a constructive dismissal claim. In *Irving v Thwaite Holme Kitchens* (1995) IRLB 518, a persistent breach of a contractual right to a pay rise entitled the employee to resign and claim constructive dismissal. Likewise, reducing pay, fundamentally altering hours and a major alteration of job duties have all been successful constructive dismissal claims. A breach of the duty of trust and confidence will also found a constructive dismissal claim, as we have already seen in Chapter 4. In certain circumstances the employer may rectify the breach of mutual trust and confidence. In *Buckland v Bournemouth University Higher Education Corporation* [2010] EWCA Civ 12, Buckland was a professor who resigned when his marks were changed and his grievance was not upheld by the university. The EAT held that the employment tribunal had been wrong to find that the grievance process had not cured the breach of the implied term of mutual trust and confidence. However, the Court of Appeal disagreed. The Court stated that an employer who has committed a fundamental breach cannot cure it while the employee is considering whether to treat it as dismissal. Note, however, the case of *Aberdeen City Council v McNeill* [2010] IRLR 374, where the EAT held that if an employee is in breach of the duty of trust and confidence at the time of his resignation, he cannot claim constructive dismissal on the basis of the employer's breach of that duty.

Although sometimes a one-off act is the breach, very often it is a series of acts where the final act is the last straw. In *London Borough of Waltham Forest v Omilaju* [2004] EWCA Civ 1493, the Court of Appeal stated that the last straw did not have to be an unreasonable or blameworthy act but it could not be a blameless act. The act has to contribute, however slightly, to the breach of trust and confidence. In the case, the claimant resigned and claimed constructive dismissal, claiming that the last straw was the fact that the council did not pay him for his attendance at tribunal proceedings that he brought against his employer. The Court of Appeal held that it could not be the last straw as the council, under its rules, was not entitled to pay him in such circumstances. In *Wishaw & District Housing Association Ltd v Moncrieff* (2009) UKEAT 0066-08-2204, the EAT held that a tribunal must clearly identify what is the final straw when determining whether it entitles the employee to resign. It held that a letter from the employer threatening to consider dismissing the claimant because of long-term absence, and a letter from the employer's representative offering to deal with the claimant's grievance internally when previously he had been offered external mediation, could not be considered a last straw entitling the employee to resign.

A strange situation arose in *Warnes v Trustees of Cheriton Oddfellows Social Club* [1993] IRLR 58. Warnes was employed as a steward and secretary of a social club. There was a resolution to remove his secretarial duties at the club's Annual General Meeting (AGM). On learning of this, Warnes wrote a letter claiming he had been constructively dismissed. The employment tribunal found that, while taking away the secretarial duties could be a constructive dismissal, the resolution by which it was done was invalid under the club rules because it had not been submitted 14 days prior to the AGM. The tribunal concluded that the resolution therefore did not take away Warnes' secretarial duties and his claim for constructive dismissal failed. The EAT allowed Warnes' appeal. It held that if an officer of the employer dismissed an employee where, as a matter of contract, he did not have the power to do so, in general it would not be open for the employer to rely on the abuse of power. Therefore, the fact that the resolution was invalid did not prevent a finding of constructive dismissal.

A constructive dismissal may arise out of an anticipatory breach as long as the breach has not been withdrawn (*Norwest Holst Group Administration Ltd v Harrison* [1985] IRLR 240; but also see *Kerry Foods Ltd v Lynch* [2005] IRLR 680). There can be no claim, however, if the terms of the contract are in dispute and the employee argues that the employer has broken a disputed term. In *Frank Wright & Co (Holdings) Ltd v Punch* [1980] IRLR 217, the employee resigned when he did not receive cost of living increases. His original contract said he was entitled to such increases, but his statutory statement said he was not. The EAT said there could be no constructive dismissal when the employer genuinely believed that he was complying with the contract, however erroneous that belief was. This shows that intention is important in this area, but leaves the employee in somewhat unsatisfactory position that it is up to him to prove that the employer was not mistaken and knew what the terms really were.

If the employee wishes to treat the employer's breach as terminating the contract, he must do so quickly or he may find that he has, by his conduct, accepted the variation in his terms. In *Jeffrey v Laurence Scott & Electromotors Ltd* [1977] IRLR 466, the employee waited some three and a half months after the breach before he resigned, and it was held that there was no constructive dismissal. Note, however, *Hogg* and *Yates* (above) and *El-Hoshi v Pizza Express Restaurants Ltd* (2004) IDS 768, where a restaurant worker, who made a public interest disclosure to management about employing illegal workers, was transferred to kitchen work which he found humiliating and went off sick as a result. He asked for the manager to be disciplined but nothing was done, so after two months he resigned and claimed unfair dismissal. The EAT held that the delay was understandable in the light of his illness and allowed his constructive dismissal claim.

It does not follow that, because the employer is in breach of contract, the constructive dismissal is unfair. In *Hall v Lodge* (1977) IRLIB 76 an employee was promoted, but it soon became apparent that she was unable to do the job. The employers demoted her to her original grade at another shop, and she resigned and claimed unfair dismissal. While there had clearly been a breach by the employer and therefore a constructive dismissal, it was fair in the circumstances. On the other hand, if the breach by the employer is an excessively harsh sanction imposed after a disciplinary offence, the employer is not acting within the band of reasonable responses as a reasonable employer would do and this will be unfair. This is because, for a dismissal to be fair, the employer must have a fair reason and act reasonably in the circumstances, as will be shown in Section 9.5 below. If he has acted as no reasonable employer would do and this is the repudiatory breach, logic dictates that the dismissal must be unfair (*Cawley v South Wales Electricity Board* [1985] IRLR 89).

9.5 Reasons for dismissal

In any unfair dismissal claim the employee must show that he is eligible to claim and that he has been dismissed. This means that the burden of proof starts with the employee to show that a dismissal has taken place. Of course, in practice, in the majority of cases this is obvious, and normally the employee will have the burden of proof only when he alleges constructive dismissal, or when the situation is ambiguous and the employee is alleging that the words of the employer constituted a dismissal and the employer alleges that he did not intend to dismiss.

The burden is always on the employer, however, to prove he had one of the statutory fair reasons to dismiss, and this means that in any tribunal hearing the employer must bring forward evidence that the reason existed. From the famous case of *British Home Stores v Burchell* [1978] IRLR 1379, the employer must show that he had a genuine belief, based on reasonable grounds following a reasonable investigation, that the employee should be dismissed. This was approved by the Court of Appeal in *Weddel v Tepper* [1980] IRLR 96. This means that although, in theory, the employer does not have to prove he acted as a reasonable employer (see Section 9.6 below), in practice reasonableness and the reason for the dismissal are closely linked, and an employer who has not investigated will find it hard to prove a reason existed. Furthermore, it is only the reason known to the employer at the time of the dismissal which is relevant (*Devis and Sons Ltd v Atkins* [1977] IRLR 314). This means that should the employer have no reason at the time of the dismissal, but before the case comes before the tribunal a reason emerges, the dismissal must be unfair, although compensation may be reduced. This is interpreted strictly. In *Alboni v Ind Coope Retail Ltd* [1998] IRLR 131, the employer gave notice to a pub manageress after the pub manager resigned. The reason for the notice given to the manageress was that the employer did not think that she could do the job single-handedly, but the employer was prepared to keep an open mind until the end of the notice period. During the notice period, the employer received no application from her to do the job alone nor did she submit a business plan, and so the dismissal went ahead. The EAT held that the dismissal was unfair because the employer had taken into account events after the notice had been given. The Court of Appeal held that this was a misinterpretation of *Devis v Atkins*, which holds that if a reason becomes known to the employer after the employment has actually terminated, that cannot be used retrospectively to justify the dismissal. It should be noted that the position is totally the opposite when looking at common law dismissal, as seen in *Ridgeway v Hungerford Market* (1835) 3 Ad & El 516 (see Section 8.6 above).

In addition, the tribunal will ignore any pressure put upon the employer to dismiss the employee (for example, the threat of industrial action), although should the union put pressure to bear on the employer, either the employer or the employee may join the union as a party to the unfair dismissal proceedings and the tribunal may apportion compensation between the employer and the union, so that the union may end up paying the whole of the award to the employee (TULR(C)A 1992, s 160).

The list of statutory fair reasons is to be found in sections 98(1) and (2) of the 1996 Act. These will be discussed in detail below.

9.5.1   Capability and qualifications

9.5.1(a) Capability

Inherent incapability Capability is defined as 'capability assessed by reference to skill, aptitude, health, or any other physical or mental quality'. This indicates that the statute envisages that the capability reason may be based on inability to do the job, that is, failing to reach acceptable standards for whatever reason, or that illness or accident may render a person who was once capable now unable to do the job. A tribunal will expect an employer to handle the two categories in different ways, for while it is reasonable to warn an employee that he should improve his standards, it may not be so reasonable to warn a genuinely sick employee that he must get well or else. In addition, there is a difference between the employee who is inherently incapable and the one who is incapable because of negligence, laziness or just sheer bloody-mindedness! The latter categories fit more neatly into the second reason, that is, conduct (see Section 9.5.2 below).

The 'skill' part of the provision includes both managerial and manual skills, but obviously the expectations of the employer need to be communicated to the employee. Failing to reach a standard he does not know about is hardly a fair reason to dismiss an employee. In *Davison v Kent Meters Ltd* [1975] IRLR 145, an employee was dismissed for assembling the majority of 500 components wrongly. She said that she was merely following the instructions laid down by the charge hand. The charge hand gave evidence that he had never shown her how to assemble the components. Not surprisingly it was held that her dismissal was unfair. She could hardly be expected to do something if no one had shown her how to do it. This does not mean, however, that the standard must remain static, although a reasonable employer will train and allow a reasonable length of time for the employee to adjust. The incapability, however, must relate to the job he is employed to do, that is the job and duties laid down by his contract.

'Aptitude' may mean that the employee is unsuited to the particular job because of a facet in his character. He may, for example, lack interpersonal skills – hardly a good point for a salesman. Aptitude may also cover aptitude tests, although it will be unfair if the employer dismisses before the employee has completed all the attempts allowed. In *Blackman v Post Office* [1974] IRLR 46, a telegraph officer was dismissed when he failed an aptitude test after the maximum number of attempts. It was held that his dismissal was fair.

The employer will have to prove that the employee was actually incapable of doing the job he was employed to do. The *Burchell* test (Section 9.5 above) means that the employer must show he genuinely believed, on reasonable grounds, that the employee was incapable. This means that he must produce evidence for the tribunal that the employee was failing to meet standards. Such evidence will come from a comparison with employees doing the same work, or with results such as sales figures.

The tribunal will look to see whether the employee knew that he was failing to achieve the correct standards, or whether he was left in blissful ignorance. Just as it will be unfair not to lay down the standards, it will be unfair not to warn the employee that his standards are dropping or not reaching an acceptable level. As Donaldson J pointed out in *Winterhalter Gastronom v Webb* [1973] IRLR 120, many do not know they are capable of jumping the five-barred gate until the bull is close behind them. This means that in the majority of cases, dismissals for incapability will be fair only if there is a period of inability, with evidence of warnings and evidence of the employee's lack of improvement. In some cases, however, a one-off act will justify dismissal if the consequences are serious. In *Alidair v Taylor* [1978] IRLR 82, a pilot was dismissed after a bad landing in fair weather conditions. The landing caused damage to the plane but the passengers were uninjured. It was held that his dismissal was fair.

Ill-health   Incapability because of ill-health requires different considerations on the part of the employer, because no amount of training or warnings will make the employee get well again. In situations of sickness, the starting point is the reason for the illness. If the sickness is caused by the working conditions then the employer must try to take steps to alleviate the conditions or provide alternative employment, and only if neither of these is possible will a resultant dismissal be fair. A risk of illness may result in a fair dismissal if the employee is in an important position and a sudden illness could be potentially dangerous. In *Converform (Darwen) Ltd v Bell* [1981] IRLR 195, however, it was held unfair to dismiss the works director who had had a heart attack when the employer discovered he had been warned that he was in great danger of having another.

The law distinguishes between persistent short-term illness and a single long-term illness. In relation to the former, the EAT has said that in such cases the procedure to be adopted is akin to that adopted in misconduct cases (*International Sports Co Ltd v Thomson* [1980] IRLR 340). In such cases a warning as to the consequences of persistent absence will normally be reasonable, as well as a review of the employee's attendance record. There is usually no point in requiring a medical investigation, although should the review reveal an underlying cause for the absences, the tribunal will expect a medical investigation to have been carried out.

In relation to long-term sickness the situation and procedure are different. First, the nature and length of the illness may frustrate the contract, in which case issues of dismissal and fairness are irrelevant as there has been no termination; the contract has come to an end by operation of law rather than by the actions of either party (see Chapter 8). Where the illness does not frustrate the contract, the tribunal will look for sympathetic treatment by the employer, including consultation with the employee.

The starting point is again evidence. Reliance on medical certificates is unlikely to suffice, and consultation with the employee's doctor and a company doctor or an independent specialist is normally essential. As the reason for the dismissal is that the employee's illness makes him incapable of doing the job, it is necessary that the doctors know the nature of the job that the employee is employed to do. The employee's doctor cannot give information to an employer without the employee's consent, and by the Access to Medical Reports Act 1988, the employee has a right to see any report prepared by his doctor and can veto its transmission to his employer. Furthermore, an employer does not have an implied right to require his employees to undergo a medical examination by a company doctor or a specialist (*Bliss v South East Thames Regional Health Authority* [1987] ICR 700). If the employee refuses, however, a tribunal might well find any subsequent dismissal fair. Should the medical evidence conflict, the employer should normally seek the opinion of a third doctor, although this may be unnecessary where there is a conflict between the employee's general practitioner and the company doctor who will be more aware of the nature of the employee's job.

Once the medical evidence has been obtained, the employer should consult with his employee. In *Luke v Navy, Army & Airforce Institutes* (1990) EAT 223/90, the employee worked for NAAFI, installing and maintaining billiard tables. On 31 October 1988, he had a road accident in which he sustained a severe whiplash injury. In February 1989, NAAFI's medical officer examined him and concluded that he could not resume the work for which he was employed but that he could do alternative lighter work. The employee's own doctor agreed with this assessment. In June 1989, the employee was warned that if he did not return to work within three months his contract would be terminated.

Meanwhile the employer had looked for alternative work but could find none, and in September the employee was dismissed. The EAT held that while there was sufficient evidence of incapacity to do the job, the employer had failed to consult adequately with the employee and the dismissal was unfair. On the other hand, if the employer can show that there was good reason not to consult, he may escape a finding of unfair dismissal, but only if the circumstances are exceptional. By contrast with *Luke* there is the case of *Eclipse Blinds Ltd v Wright* [1992] IRLR 133. In this case the employee's health had gradually deteriorated. In 1987 her employment had been made part-time, and in 1989 she was off work for a long period. Her doctor considered that her health was not good and that she would not return to work in the near future. The company decided that a permanent replacement was needed. The manager did not consult with the employee but wrote to her instead. He thought it would be difficult to talk to her as, unlike her doctor, she thought she was improving. The tribunal found that in the circumstances the failure to consult was not unfair, and the decision was supported by the EAT.

The different treatment of long-term illness and persistent short-term sickness is well illustrated by comparing two EAT decisions. In *Mitchell v Arkwood Plastics (Engineering) Ltd* [1993] ICR 471, Mitchell was absent from work after fracturing his shin as a result of an accident at work in May 1990. For four months, apart from sick certificates, there was no communication between Mitchell and his employers. On 27 September, the employers wrote to him and asked when he would be fit to return to work. Mitchell went to see his doctor and replied on 5 October, stating that he did not know his date of return as he was due to see a consultant. One week later Mitchell was dismissed. The employment tribunal held that the dismissal was fair as the employee had a duty to keep his employer informed as to his progress. The EAT, allowing Mitchell's appeal, held that the employee was under no such duty. The employers should have discovered the true medical position before dismissing on health grounds, and should have considered the possibility of Mitchell's undertaking light duties until he was fully recovered. By contrast, in *London Borough of Tower Hamlets v Bull* (1993) *Personnel Today*, 10 August, Bull was absent from work with a variety of unconnected illnesses for a total of 110 days between October 1987 and February 1990. In February 1990 he was called in to see the council's doctor, who reported that Bull was not suffering from any underlying medical condition. In May 1990, after another period of absence, Bull was warned that unless his attendance improved, he would be dismissed. In June he was absent for a further four days and was sacked. After his dismissal, Bull's trade union representative told the council that Bull had a drinking problem and that that was the reason for his absences. The council, however, refused to reconsider its decision and did not activate its special procedure for dealing with alcohol-related problems. The employment tribunal found that Bull had been unfairly dismissed because the council had not consulted Bull's doctor. The EAT disagreed. There was no duty to consult the employee's doctor in these circumstances in the light of the absence record. Furthermore, the council was entitled to ignore Bull's alcohol problem as it had not been raised until after the dismissal.

Employers should also be aware of the impact of the Equality Act 2010. If the illness falls into the definition of 'disability', as discussed in Chapter 5, then a dismissal may be discrimination.

9.5.1(b) Qualifications

Qualifications are defined as any degree, diploma or other technical or professional qualification relevant to the employee's job. This was interpreted in *Blue Star Ship*

Management Ltd v Williams [1979] IRLR 16 as meaning qualifications which have a bearing on ability or aptitude, such as an HGV licence, and not merely permits or authorisations and so on. There should, however, be a contractual requirement to hold such a qualification. In *Lister v Thom & Sons Ltd* [1975] IRLR 47, the employee was employed as a fitter/driver. He was required to hold an HGV licence if he drove heavy goods vehicles, but he failed the necessary test. He continued in employment, however, as a fitter. His contract did not require him to hold a licence. After a disagreement with his employer, he was told that if he did not obtain his licence he would be sacked. He tried again and failed, and was dismissed. It was held that his dismissal was unfair.

However, the requirement to hold the qualification may be implied into the contract. In *Tayside Regional Council v McIntosh* [1982] IRLR 272, the employers advertised for a vehicle mechanic, saying that a driving licence was essential. The applicant was appointed to the post but no mention was made of a driving licence. He subsequently lost his licence and was dismissed. It was held that his dismissal was fair, as the nature of the job clearly required a driving licence.

9.5.2   Conduct

Conduct, or more correctly misconduct, is one of the most common reasons for dismissal. Yet again, it is for the employer to provide evidence that the reason exists, and so an investigation is essential. In relation to this reason in particular, the procedure used by the employer will be closely scrutinised by the tribunal, particularly how far the employer's procedure complies with or adopts the principles of the ACAS Code of Practice on Disciplinary and Grievance Procedures. The Code and the employer's procedures will be discussed in Section 9.6 below when looking at aspects of reasonableness.

While the statute lays down no guidelines as to the type or seriousness of misconduct that may justify dismissal, some principles seem to have emerged from the cases. First, the conduct does not have to be gross, only substantial in relation to the circumstances of the case, so that relatively minor acts may, in certain circumstances, justify dismissal. Second, the conduct does not have to be blameworthy. In *Jury v EEC Quarries Ltd* [1980] EAT 241/80, the employee refused to retrain as a Class 2 HGV driver when all Class 3 vehicles went out of service, and he was dismissed. It was held that although he was in no way to blame, his dismissal was fair. Third, if the employer has a number of suspects for misconduct and after an investigation cannot discover which one is guilty, but knows at least one must be, it appears that it is fair to dismiss all. This was stated by the Court of Appeal in *Monie v Coral Racing Ltd* [1981] ICR 109 and was applied to the dismissal of four employees in *Parr v Whitbread plc t/a Threshers Wine Merchants* [1990] IRLR 39. Care must be taken, however, to ensure that the employer has narrowed the group down to only those who could have committed the act, and his investigation must show how he has discounted other potential suspects.

For the purposes of looking simply at the reason for dismissal for the moment, by an analysis of the cases we can see the type of conduct which may justify dismissal. The tribunal will usually be looking at misconduct committed within employment, but in some circumstances conduct committed outside the employment situation may justify dismissal.

9.5.2(a) Conduct inside employment

Absenteeism and lateness As a general rule, absenteeism and lateness are not gross misconduct, and therefore the employer cannot fairly dismiss for a first offence. If, however, the consequences are serious, such as the loss of a big order, dismissal may be fair (*Galloway v K Miller (Contractors)* (1980) COIT 243/80). In the majority of situations the employer must warn his employee and investigate the reasons for the lateness or absenteeism before dismissing.

Disloyalty We have already seen (see Sections 4.3.4–4.3.6) that the employee owes a duty of loyalty to his employer, and should he act disloyally, he will be in breach of contract. Disloyalty may take a number of forms. The employee may disclose confidential information to an unauthorised person, he may be working for his employer's competitor in his spare time or actually conducting a rival business. In all of these situations, provided the employer has the evidence that the employee is guilty, dismissal, in some cases instant dismissal, will be fair. In *Carson v John Lewis & Co* (1977) EAT 266/77, a manager failed to tell her employers that she was working in competition to them in her spare time (she was required to inform them of outside work by the work's rules) and then lied about her activities when she was found out. It was held that she was fairly dismissed. Likewise in *Pintorex Ltd v Keyvanfar* [2013] EWPCC 36, the Patents Court held there had been a breach of confidence when an employee copied his employer's database onto a laptop owned by his new employer, who then used the information to approach two clients of the claimant and undercut his prices. The outside work must be potentially damaging to the employer, however. In *Nova Plastics Ltd v Froggatt* [1982] IRLR 146, an odd-job man did work for a competitor of his employer in his spare time and was dismissed when this was discovered. It was held that, given his position in the firm, he was unlikely to know or pass on information which could damage his main employer and so his dismissal was unfair. Dismissal for working for a non-rival in his spare time will almost certainly be unfair unless it affects the employee's performance.

One major problem in this area occurs when the employee intends to leave his employment and does work preparatory to setting up on his own. In *Marshall v Industrial Systems and Control Ltd* [1992] IRLR 294, the employee was the managing director of a company which distributed software. The company's major customer was a large American plane-maker. The employee had been warned of poor performance in autumn 1990, although not actually threatened with dismissal. In December 1990, the company discovered that the employee and another manager intended to set up in competition and had approached the American customer, and had sought to induce another employee to join them. The managing director was dismissed. The employee argued that his dismissal was unfair because it was obvious that the respondents were waiting to dismiss him on poor performance and it was reasonable for him to take steps to secure his own future. He relied on the previous decision of *Laughton and Hawley v Bapp Industries Supplies Ltd* [1986] IRLR 245, where it was held that writing to suppliers and asking for price lists was not a breach of duty, even though it indicated the employee was going to set up in competition when he left. The EAT so decided because there was no evidence of an intention to abuse confidential information, and no evidence that the employee had not devoted the whole of his time to the employer's business before leaving. The EAT rejected the analogy in *Marshall*, the important distinction between the two cases being that it is not a breach of duty to hold an intention to set up in competition or to find out prices from suppliers, but it becomes a breach of duty when key employees are approached to leave, and when direct and definite approaches are made to the employer's customers. From *Marshall* it appears that such conduct will justify dismissal, even if there is no evidence of a danger of future misuse of information or connections; in other words, it is irrelevant if the customers approached would not leave the existing employer. It is the approach which is the breach of duty, not the consequences. This is supported by *Tithebarn Ltd v Hubbard* (1992) (unreported), where the employee was dismissed for trying to entice other employees to join him when he set up in competition. The EAT held that this conduct did not amount to a breach of duty and his dismissal was unfair.

Disobedience   It has been seen that another duty in the employment contract is that the employee shall obey the lawful, reasonable orders of his employer (see Section 4.3.2) and thus refusal to do so is a breach of contract and misconduct. Chapter 4 has already demonstrated that not all orders are reasonable even if they are within the employee's contract and, likewise, some orders will be deemed reasonable even though they go outside the employee's contractual duties. What constitutes a reasonable order is often a question of fact for the tribunal, looking at the circumstances of the case. In any case of dismissal for disobedience, therefore, the tribunal will look to see if the order is lawful and reasonable, and at whether the employee had valid grounds for refusing to comply with it.

The starting point will be the contractual duties. As a rule of thumb, refusal to obey a contractually binding order will normally be fair unless the employee has very good reasons for his refusal. In *Osborn Transport Services v Chrissanthors* (1977) EAT 412/77, a driver refused to pick up a load from a customer with whom he had had a bad experience. He was dismissed for disobedience and the tribunal ruled that his dismissal, in the circumstances, was unfair. Conversely, refusal to do something which is outside the contract may still constitute disobedience. We have already seen in *Horrigan v Lewisham London Borough Council* [1978] ICR 15 (Section 4.3.2 above) that refusal to do non-contractual overtime may justify a dismissal if there are no valid reasons for the refusal.

Many refusals will come from employees whose duties or hours have changed because of a business reorganisation. In *Ellis v Brighton Co-operative Society Ltd* [1976] IRLR 419, the employee, after returning to work following an illness, discovered that the employer had agreed a reorganisation with the union which involved the employee's working additional hours. He refused to work over his contractual hours and was dismissed. The EAT held that while the employee was not bound to work those hours, the employer, having consulted with the union, could not be expected to make an exception for one employee and therefore the dismissal was fair under 'some other substantial reason' (see Section 9.5.5 below).

Refusal to relocate may amount to misconduct if there is a mobility clause in the contract, although the tribunal may imply a provision of reasonable notice, depending on the extent of the move and the circumstances of the employee (*United Bank v Ahktar* [1989] IRLR 80; see Section 3.1.1). Even without an express mobility clause, if the move will not affect the employee's travelling time or expenses, the order will be reasonable. In some circumstances, the court may imply a mobility clause if that is the way the parties have operated the contract in the past (*Courtaulds Northern Spinning Ltd v Sibson*, Section 9.4.3 above).

Breach of company rules may also amount to disobedience even though they are not contractual, although just because the rules state that certain conduct will result in dismissal it does not necessarily follow that the dismissal will be fair. In *Laws Stores Ltd v Oliphant* [1978] IRLR 251, it was held to be unfair to dismiss an employee with eight years' service for till irregularities, even though the work's rules stated that such irregularities constituted gross misconduct. This was supported by the Court of Session in *Ladbroke Racing Ltd v Arnott and Others* [1983] IRLR 154, when three employees broke the company rule against placing bets at their own place of work. While such conduct was stated in the rules to be a dismissible offence, the court held that the dismissals of the employees were unfair. To apply the rule rigidly, without taking all the circumstances into account, was unreasonable.

Where the rule broken is one of the company's health and safety rules, the tribunal is more likely to find that the dismissal is fair, given the employer's safety duties towards his employees. In *Lindsay v Dunlop Ltd* [1980] IRLR 93, a group of employees refused to work in an area which contained hot rubber fumes which were believed to cause cancer. The employer was waiting for a report from the Health and Safety Executive to see what changes were necessary, and asked the employees as a temporary measure to wear masks. All the employees agreed apart from Lindsay. It was held that his subsequent dismissal was fair. It was reasonable for the employer to wait for a specialist report before making major changes.

Dishonesty Although dishonesty is a criminal matter, the employer does not have to produce evidence that establishes beyond a reasonable doubt that the employee is guilty. As with all of the reasons, he merely has to show that he has a genuine belief in the employee's guilt. The fact that the employee is charged, however, is not sufficient to establish a genuine belief without investigation by the employer (*Scottish Special Housing Association v Cooke and Others* [1979] IRLR 264). The major problem in this area is that the employer needs to investigate to discover the evidence he needs to establish his reason, but often the police are also investigating and the employee will have been instructed by his solicitor to say nothing during the employer's investigation. It appears that if the employer has enough evidence without the employee's statement to come to a reasonable belief, the dismissal will be fair even if the employee is subsequently acquitted of criminal charges. In *Harris and Shepherd v Courage* [1981] IRLR 153, two drivers loading stolen beer were identified by witnesses. The police later charged them with theft, and on the advice of their solicitor, the employees refused to take part in the employer's investigation. The employer dismissed them and they were later acquitted. It was held that the dismissals were fair because the employer had enough evidence to form a reasonable belief in their guilt. It is the employer's belief at the time of the dismissal which is important, not what happens afterwards.

Violence and fighting In relation to fighting, the employer must gather all the evidence available before he can establish his reason for dismissal. Interviewing only one or two witnesses will be insufficient. Again, many employers will class fighting as gross misconduct within the work's rules, but as in other areas, rigid enforcement of the rules without taking all the circumstances into account will render a dismissal unfair. Issues such as the status of the employee, where the fight took place, provocation and past work record should all be considered.

Other misconduct While it is impossible to go through every act of misconduct which could justify dismissal, a general point should be noted. Dismissal will be fair if it is within the range of reasonable responses that a reasonable employer would adopt (*Rolls-Royce Ltd v Walpole* [1980] IRLR 342), therefore it is not within the remit of the tribunal to find that a dismissal is unfair because it would not have dismissed in those circumstances. If a reasonable employer would have dismissed, the dismissal is fair. In *East Berkshire Health Authority v Matadeen* (1992) *The Times*, 1 July, the employee, a charge nurse in a hospital for the mentally and physically handicapped, admitted to making a number of nuisance telephone calls to members of the nursing staff. The health authority found this to be gross misconduct and dismissed him. The employment tribunal felt that his conduct was not serious misconduct and found that his dismissal was unfair. The Court of Appeal found the tribunal's decision to be perverse. The question is whether a reasonable employer would have dismissed him, not whether the tribunal would have acted in that way. Likewise *in Brito-Babapulle v Ealing Hospital NHS Trust* [2013] All ER (D) 211, the EAT held that the fact that an employer has found the employee guilty of gross misconduct does not automatically mean that dismissal is within the band of reasonable responses. In the case, a hospital consultant was dismissed for gross misconduct when it was discovered that she had been treating private patients while off sick. The EAT held that while the tribunal was entitled to find that it was reasonable for the employer to find the employee guilty of gross misconduct, it had erred in assuming this meant that dismissal was within the band of reasonable responses. It had to decide whether, in all the circumstances, it was reasonable for the employer to dismiss for *this* misconduct.

9.5.2(b) Conduct outside employment

As a general rule, conduct outside the employment hours has nothing to do with the employer and he cannot therefore discipline his employee. In some circumstances, however, the conduct may so reflect on the relationship that the employer loses all trust and confidence in the employee. In these situations, dismissal may be fair if the employer can show that the conduct outside working hours has a direct effect on the employment relationship. For example, if a lorry driver is convicted of a drink-driving offence and loses his licence, it will be fair to dismiss him if there is no alternative work he can do. But whereas that example is fairly self-explanatory, others are not.

It appears that if the conduct is such that it makes the employee unsuitable for his job, or unacceptable to other employees, or could cause potential harm to the employer's business, dismissal will be fair. In *Moore v C&A Modes* [1981] IRLR 71, a section leader was dismissed after 20 years' service after being convicted of a shoplifting offence in another store. It was held that her dismissal was fair. In *Gardiner v Newport Borough Council* [1974] IRLR 262, a lecturer of boys aged 16–18 was convicted of committing an indecent act with another man in a public toilet. His subsequent dismissal was fair. And in *Whitlow v Alkanet Construction Ltd* [1975] IRLR 321, the dismissal of an employee who was sent to do work in one of his director's houses and who used the opportunity to begin an affair with the director's wife, was also held to be fair. The director felt that if he could not trust him with his own wife, he certainly could not trust him with customers' wives! On the other hand, in *Bradshaw v Rugby Portland Cement Ltd* [1972] IRLR 46, the dismissal of an employee after his conviction for incest was held to be unfair. The conduct had no bearing on his work and there was no evidence that his colleagues found him unacceptable to work with (see also *Securicor Guarding Ltd v R* [1994] IRLR 633). However, the Court of Appeal has more recently held that a risk of damage to an employer's reputation by allegations of child abuse against one of its employees, even if the allegations were unproved and even though the employee did not work with children, may be a fair reason for dismissal. In *Leach v OFCOM* [2012] EWCA Civ 959, Leach was an internal policy adviser for OFCOM. OFCOM has a statutory duty to have regard to the vulnerability of children. Leach was arrested in Cambodia on suspicion of sexual abuse of children; however, after an internal disciplinary hearing, OFCOM concluded that Leach was innocent of the offence. Some time later the Manchester Child Abuse Investigation Command contacted OFCOM with allegations which went far and beyond what had been alleged before. As a result, OFCOM held another disciplinary hearing and dismissed Leach, because of the risk of damage to its reputation and its feeling that Leach had not been honest with OFCOM at the previous disciplinary hearing. The Court of Appeal upheld the finding that the dismissal was fair because of the risk of reputational damage, and on the ground that there had been a breakdown of trust and confidence.

9.5.3   Redundancy

Redundancy is the third fair reason for dismissal that may be pleaded by an employer. If the employee claims a redundancy payment, there is a presumption that the dismissal was due to redundancy by section 163(2) of the ERA 1996, but the presumption will not apply if the employee claims unfair dismissal (*Midland Foot Comfort Centre v Moppett* [1983] All ER 294). In this case the employer must show that redundancy was the reason for the dismissal. Even if redundancy is the reason, if the employee shows that he was chosen for a reason which is automatically unfair, or there was lack of consultation or warning, he will win his claim for unfair dismissal. In addition, the law requires that the employer has a fair procedure when dealing with redundancies, and even though the employer may show that the reason exists and that there was fair selection, he may still find himself at the end of a ruling of unfair dismissal if he has not handled the redundancies reasonably. Aspects of reasonableness in respect of redundancies are discussed below.

To establish the reason, the employer must show that a redundancy situation exists within the statutory definition in section 139(1) of the ERA 1996. While the definition will be discussed fully in Chapter 10, at present it is sufficient to state that this means that the employer must show that he is ceasing business, moving his place of business, or that work of the particular kind which the employee was employed to do has ceased or diminished, or is expected to cease or diminish. Even though the reason may exist, however, there will be an unfair dismissal if the employee can show that he falls within the provisions relating to an automatically unfair redundancy. The provisions are contained in the ERA 1996 and the TULR(C)A 1992. The ERA 1996, section 105 provides that an employee will have been unfairly dismissed if the reason (or, if more than one, the principal reason) for the dismissal is that the employee was redundant and:

- where the circumstances constituting the redundancy applied equally to one or more other employees in the same undertaking who held positions similar to that held by him and who have not been dismissed by the employer and he was selected for dismissal because he was carrying out health and safety duties;
- he was a shopworker or betting shopworker who refused to work Sundays;

- he asserted a statutory right;
- he was an employee representative;
- he was a trustee of an occupational pension scheme;
- he made a protected disclosure;
- he asserted working time rights;
- he asserted rights under the National Minimum Wage Act 1998;
- he asserted tax credit rights;
- he asserted part-time worker rights;
- he asserted fixed-term employee rights;
- he took leave for family reasons (including parental leave, dependant leave and, if female, maternity leave);
- he was absent on jury service;
- he requested flexible working or, in the case of a female employee, she was selected because of her pregnancy or because she had recently given birth.

The 1992 Act, section 153 adds further reasons. That is, that selection was for:

- membership or non-membership of a trade union;
- participation in the activities of an independent trade union at the appropriate time;
- use of trade union facilities or services at an appropriate time; or
- refusing an inducement to come out of collective bargaining, including certain dismissals in connection with statutory recognition and certain dismissals during industrial action.

All the above provisions show that there are three stages involved: the employees must be in the same undertaking, similar employees must have been retained and selection for redundancy must have been on the basis of one of the reasons above.

9.5.3(a) The same undertaking

The meaning of 'undertaking' is not clear, but it is probably wider than an establishment at a particular location and could mean the whole of the employer's business if run in a unified way. A common management will be a relevant factor, but flexibility of labour and different skills could also affect the decision. Thus departments could be considered in isolation in some circumstances.

9.5.3(b) Similarly placed employees

At least one other employee must remain employed in a position similar to that of the dismissed employee. The tribunal will look at the type of work, as well as at the status of the employee, his skills, and the terms and conditions of employment (*Simpson v Roneo Ltd* [1972] IRLR 5). If others are capable of doing the work of the redundant employee, they will be in similar positions only if they have covered the work in the past or there is a great deal of interchange of labour at the workplace (*Dorrell v Engineering Developments Ltd* [1975] IRLR 234).

9.5.3(c) Automatically unfair reasons

Once the employee has established that similarly placed employees in the same undertaking were not selected, he must then show that the reason for his selection was one of the automatically unfair reasons listed above. These reasons are discussed later in Section 9.7. In all of the cases of automatically unfair reasons for selection, the normal continuity requirement does not apply (ERA 1996, s 108).

9.5.4　Statutory restriction

The penultimate potentially fair reason for dismissal is that the employee could no longer continue to work in the position which he held without contravention by himself or his employer of a duty or restriction imposed by or under any enactment. The provision is objective and there must be potential contravention of a legislative provision – an employer's misguided belief in such a contravention will not suffice. In *Bouchaala v Trusthouse Forte Hotels Ltd* [1980] IRLR 382, the employer was mistaken as to the legality of a work permit obtained by the employee and dismissed him. It was held that it was not a dismissal for statutory contravention.

The statutory provision must specifically relate to the work the employee was actually employed to do. Thus, if an employee is employed solely or substantially to drive a vehicle, he might be fairly dismissed should he be disqualified from driving. In *Appleyard v Smith (Hull) Ltd* [1972] IRLR 19, a mechanic in a small garage was banned from driving. A substantial part of his job was road-testing vehicles, and after his ban the employer could not find him sufficient work to do which did not involve driving. It was held that his dismissal was fair. An employer must show, however, that the prohibited part of the employee's duties constituted a significant part of his job and that the employer considered whether he could continue to employ him until the disqualification ceased. By contrast, in *Mathieson v WJ Noble & Son Ltd* [1972] IRLR 76 a travelling salesman was disqualified from driving and had arranged for a driver to drive him for the period of his ban. The employer dismissed him without seeing if the arrangement would work, and it was held that the dismissal was unfair.

9.5.5　Some other substantial reason

The final potential fair reason in section 98(1)(b) of the ERA 1996 seems almost to be a catch-all, in that if the reason does not fall within the first four listed, it will be caught by this one, bearing in mind that almost anything will fall under this heading. While cases do show that a variety of different situations will fall within section 98(1)(b), the two most common situations which arise in the tribunals and courts are business needs and pressure from third parties.

9.5.5(a)　Business needs

This is the situation where the employer is changing the terms of the employee's contract and thus is in breach, and the employee refuses to accept the change. It should be stressed that the fact that the employee has a right to refuse to accept the change has no bearing on the fairness or otherwise of the dismissal, and in many cases the needs of the business will be overriding. In *RS Components v Irwin* [1973] IRLR 239, the employer was losing business because his sales staff were leaving and working for competitors. The employer unilaterally imposed restrictive covenants on the existing sales staff and the employee was dismissed when he refused to accept the change in his contractual terms. It was held that his dismissal was fair.

Originally, to justify a change in terms and conditions, the employer had to show that the business was in serious danger of being brought to a standstill (*Ellis v Brighton Co-operative Society Ltd* [1976] IRLR 419), but the standard is not so high today and the employer must show only that there is a sound business reason for the reorganisation. It is not sufficient, however, for the employer to show merely that the change was a good idea. He must show what advantages or benefits the policy will bring. The tribunal does not need to be convinced that it would have taken similar measures, only that a sound business reason existed, necessitating changes, and that the changes could reasonably have either alleviated the problem, or improved the business or maximised its potential. In *Hollister v National Farmers' Union* [1979] ICR 542, the union reorganised its insurance business so that the terms of the employees who sold the insurance changed. In deciding that the dismissal of one who refused to accept the changes was fair, the Court of Appeal said that a tribunal only had to ask 'whether the reorganisation was such that the only sensible thing to do was to terminate the employee's contract unless he would agree to a new arrangement'. The decision as to what reorganisation takes place is therefore a management decision alone. In *McGibbon and McCoy v OIL Ltd* (1995) IDS Brief 541, the EAT said that it was for the tribunal to carry out a balancing exercise, whereby the disadvantages to the employee and the advantages to the employer in the offer of new contracts have to be weighed up.

A dismissal arising from a change in terms is more likely to be fair if:

▷ many or all the other employees have agreed to the change (*Robinson v Flitwick Frames Ltd* [1975] IRLR 261);
▷ the union has agreed to the change (*Bowater Containers Ltd v McCormack* [1980] IRLR 50);
▷ the change is trivial (*Baverstock v Horsley Smith & Co* COIT 910/112).

While reorganisation is the most common business need, the tribunals do accept others. In *Farr v Hoveringham Gravels Ltd* [1972] IRLR 104, the employee, who was on 24-hour call-out, moved to a house some 40 miles from his place of work. It was held that his subsequent dismissal was fair. In *Foot v Eastern Counties Timber Co Ltd* [1972] IRLR 83, the employee was dismissed when it was discovered that she was married to an employee of a rival firm. Again the dismissal was fair.

9.5.5(b) Pressure from third parties

Where other employees refuse to work with a colleague, or customers put pressure on the employer, it may be fair to dismiss even though the employee has done nothing wrong. In *Scott Packaging Ltd v Paterson* [1978] IRLR 465, the EAT held that it would be justifiable to dismiss an employee in response to an ultimatum from the company's major customer. In *Dobie v Burns International Security Services (UK) Ltd* [1984] ICR 812, the employee was employed by the company which provided the security service at Liverpool airport and was based at the airport as a security officer. Following two incidents for which he was not to blame, the airport refused to have him working there. The employers offered him alternative work at a lower rate of pay which he refused, and he was dismissed. The Court of Appeal held that his dismissal was fair. This decision, while within the statutory provisions, seems particularly harsh as the customers' reasons for their reaction are never brought into question, and it means that the employee, who may be blameless, can be fairly dismissed because of a whim of a person outside the employment relationship. If work colleagues refuse to work with the employee, this too can constitute some other substantial reason. In *Treganowan v Robert Knee & Co Ltd* [1975] IRLR 247, a woman upset other staff she worked with by describing in detail her affair with a younger man. Eventually they refused to work with her and it was held that her consequent dismissal was fair. However, in *Bancroft v Facilities Management Ltd* [2013] All ER (D) 183, the EAT held that before dismissing at the request of a third party, the employer should consider whether the request is justified. In the case the employer had a contract with the Home Office to provide catering for a bail hostel. Under the terms of the contract, the Home Office could require removal of contractor staff 'whose admission would be undesirable', without giving reasons for the request. When the claimant fell out with the hostel manager, the Home Office asked for him to be removed, and the employer dismissed him. The EAT held that the extent of injustice to the employee was an important consideration in deciding whether the dismissal was fair. The employment tribunal had failed to address the issue of why the employer had failed to look at the issues between the manager and the claimant, and to mitigate the injustice caused to the claimant.

In one situation, however, pressure put upon the employer will be ignored for the purposes of determining whether the dismissal is fair or not. This is where the pressure is brought by a union in the form of the threat of a strike or other industrial action (ERA 1996, s 107). Furthermore by section 160 of TULR(C)A 1992, either the employer or the employee may join the union as a party to the unfair dismissal proceedings, and the tribunal may apportion any compensation to be paid between the employer and the union, so it may be that the union pays all of the award to the complainant.

9.6 The concept of reasonableness

Although the employer has to prove only that he has a fair reason for dismissal, in some ways this is deceiving. Section 98(4) of the ERA 1996 states:

> Where the employer has fulfilled the requirements of subsection (1) … the determination of the question of whether the dismissal was fair or unfair (having regard to the reason shown by the employer)—
> (a) depends on whether in the circumstances (including the size and administrative resources of the employer's undertaking) the employer acted reasonably or unreasonably in treating it as a sufficient reason for dismissing the employee, and
> (b) shall be determined in accordance with equity and the substantial merits of the case.

In other words, having a fair reason to dismiss is only one step. The employer must show the tribunal that he acted reasonably in dismissing the employee, and he can do that only by ensuring that the members of the tribunal have considerable information before them as to how he dealt with the employee and how he has dealt with similar cases in the past. Thus, while the employer does not have to prove that he acted reasonably in the circumstances, he will certainly have to bring forward much evidence of his conduct in the particular case before the tribunal and of his conduct in previous cases, to allow the tribunal to come to a decision. It must be stressed, however, that just because the tribunal would not have dismissed in those circumstances, this does not make the dismissal unfair. This was pointed out by Browne-Wilkinson J in *Iceland Frozen Foods v Jones* [1983] ICR 17. In that case he set out the correct five-stage approach for an employment tribunal to adopt when considering the question of reasonableness:

(1) the starting point should always be the words of section 98(4) themselves; (2) in applying the section an industrial tribunal must consider the reasonableness of the employer's conduct, not simply whether they (the members of the industrial [employment] tribunal) consider the dismissal to be fair; (3) in judging the reasonableness of the employer's conduct an industrial [employment] tribunal must not substitute its decision as to what was the right course to adopt for that employer; (4) in many, though not all, cases there is a band of reasonable responses to the employee's conduct within which one employer might reasonably take one view, another quite reasonably take another; (5) the function of the industrial [employment] tribunal, as an industrial jury, is to determine whether in the particular circumstances of each case the decision to dismiss the employee fell within the band of reasonable responses which a reasonable employer might have adopted.

The oft-quoted phrase 'band of reasonable responses' is the essence of any unfair dismissal case, and you might be forgiven for thinking that this allows employers considerable latitude and that only the most unreasonable dismissals will be judged to be unfair. While this would perhaps be overstating the situation, it is only later cases laying down principles in relation to consistency and fair procedure that have perhaps limited total autocratic action on the part of the employer. On the other hand, it does allow the employer some latitude. In *Weston Recovery Services v Fisher* (2010) UKEAT 0062/10/0710, the claimant had been dismissed for returning a car in an unsafe condition. The tribunal found the dismissal to be unfair as it did not consider the claimant's conduct to be gross misconduct. However the EAT disagreed; it held that as a matter of law, in line with section 98(4), the dismissal was fair. The employer had complied with the *Burchell* test (see Section 9.5 above) and the sanction, dismissal, fell within the range of reasonable responses. However, the EAT agreed with the tribunal's finding of fact that the conduct was not gross misconduct, and thus the employer was guilty of wrongful dismissal as it should have terminated the contract with notice. The case illustrates that dismissal may still be fair even if the claimant is not guilty of gross misconduct. It also shows that employment tribunals are kept in check by the higher courts, and should they substitute their own decision for that of the employer, their decision will be perverse and an appeal will lie.

In the case of *East Berkshire Health Authority v Matadeen* (Section 9.5.2(a) 'Other misconduct', above), the Court of Appeal discussed the issue of perverse decisions. The applicant was a charge nurse, and in 1988 he admitted to making nuisance calls to other members of nursing staff. The Health Authority found this to be gross misconduct and dismissed him. The tribunal upheld his complaint of unfair dismissal because it did not feel that his conduct constituted serious misconduct, and therefore dismissal was not in the band of reasonable responses which the employer was entitled to make. The Health Authority appealed against the decision and eventually the case came before the Court of Appeal. The Court found that the EAT could not find the employment tribunal's decision to be perverse simply because it would have reached a different decision. However, the employment tribunal had found the employer's decision to be irrational and to defy logic. It was therefore wrong in law and thus perverse. In *Neale v Hereford & Worcester County Council* [1986] ICR 471, the Court of Appeal said that an employment tribunal's decision might be said to be perverse if the appeal tribunal could say of the decision, 'My goodness, that was certainly wrong'. However, in *Piggott v Jackson* [1992] ICR 85, a later Court of Appeal urged caution when applying this definition because it allowed the appeal tribunal to take the impermissible step of substituting its own decision for that of the tribunal. A finding of perversity had to be supported by other evidence, that is, that the tribunal had misdirected itself in law or had reached a conclusion which was unsupported by the facts.

Section 98(4) of the ERA 1996 refers to the tribunal deciding whether the employer acted reasonably in treating the reason as sufficient cause to justify dismissal, 'in accordance with equity and the substantial merits of the case'. In practice, this means that a tribunal will look at two aspects when looking at reasonableness: the actual fairness of the decision, that is, whether dismissal was outside the range of reasonable responses for this type of conduct; and procedural fairness, that is, whether the employer used a fair procedure before the employee's eventual dismissal. In looking at the employer's procedures, the tribunal must take into account the size and administrative resources of the employer's undertaking, so that a larger employer might be expected to employ different standards from those of a smaller one. In practice, of course, the two aspects are invariably interlinked.

9.6.1   Fairness of the decision

It has been noted already that the decision of the employer must be within the band of reasonable responses that a reasonable employer would choose, but this leaves the questions of what a reasonable employer is, and what he takes into account when making his decision. The tribunal will look at a variety of factors, such as how the employer has treated such cases in the past, whether he has taken the employee's past work record into account, whether he has taken the length of the employee's service into account and whether he has looked to see if there is an alternative to dismissal in appropriate circumstances.

9.6.2   Consistency

An employee must know where the goal posts are and what penalty he can expect for certain conduct. If the employer is inconsistent in the way he applies his sanctions, employees will not know where they stand, and this in itself may render a dismissal unfair. If the employer treats employees differently, or has treated certain conduct leniently in the past and then decides to raise standards, this will leave employees in an uncertain position and feeling a sense of injustice when they are treated differently for the same act. In *Post Office v Fennell* [1981] IRLR 221, an employee was dismissed instantly after assaulting a colleague in the staff canteen. He argued that other workers who had committed the same offence in the past had not been dismissed. The Court of Appeal held that his dismissal was unfair. In *Hadjioannou v Coral Casinos Ltd* [1981] IRLR 352, the EAT limited the operation of *Fennell* by saying that consistency was relevant only where employees had been misled into thinking that certain conduct would be overlooked or that dismissal would not be the sanction. This was followed in *Levenes Solicitors v Dalley* [2007] All ER 52.

The EAT reviewed consistency in the case of *Proctor v British Gypsum* [1991] *Personnel Today*, 3 December. In the case, Proctor was a foreman of a team of vehicle loaders who were paid a bonus which depended on the rate of loading. When one of the team refused to resume work after a break, Proctor began arguing with him and eventually hit him. During the disciplinary hearing, the company looked at sanctions it had imposed in the past for similar conduct. While it had imposed lesser sanctions than dismissal previously, the company took the decision to dismiss Proctor. The employment tribunal dismissed his claim of unfair dismissal and he appealed to the EAT, which upheld the earlier decision on the basis that the decision could not be faulted, but at the same time took the opportunity to review the law surrounding inconsistency and comparability. From *Wilcox v Humphrey & Glasgow Ltd* [1975] IRLR 211 it was established that before making a decision to dismiss, the employer should consider truly comparable cases which he knew about or ought reasonably to have known about. However, small companies may not keep records, and there was no requirement to do so. The EAT then stressed that situations within an undertaking may change. Dishonesty or fighting, for example, may have increased, in which case the employer would have to go back only a few years and not since records began, because the policy might have changed. In each situation, however, the comparison must be a true one where the circumstances of the relevant employees were the same. An untrue comparison is as dangerous as no comparison at all. In simple terms, the employer is under a duty to review past sanctions, but only by comparing like with like. One thing that is clear, however, is that it is the employer's policies which are relevant and not the policies of individual managers who work for the employer. Consistency within a department but not within an undertaking will not satisfy the requirement of reasonableness (*Cain v Leeds Western Health Authority* [1990] IRLR 168). If the employer considers the case not to be comparable, however, the tribunal cannot substitute its own opinion and say that it is (*Paul v East Surrey Health Authority* [1995] IRLR 305).

9.6.3 Past work record and length of service

In misconduct cases in particular, failure to take account of the employee's past record and length of service may render a dismissal unfair. In *Johnson Matthey Metals Ltd v Harding* [1978] IRLR 248, the employee, who had been employed for 15 years with an unblemished record, was dismissed when a colleague's watch, which had gone missing some time before, was found in his possession. The EAT held that his dismissal was unfair given the length of his previous good service. A good work record may also justify different treatment of employees who have committed the same act of misconduct. In *Sherrier v Ford Motor Co* [1976] IRLR 146, two employees were caught fighting, and despite an investigation by the employer, the instigator could not be established. One of the employees had a 15-year unblemished record and the employer suspended him for five days without pay. Sherrier, on the other hand, had been employed for two years and had six disciplinary offences on his record, and the employer dismissed him. His claim for unfair dismissal was dismissed. A similar situation arose in *Airbus (UK) Ltd v Webb* [2008] IRLR 309, where five employees were found watching television when they should have been working. Four had good records and were given final warnings. The fifth had a final warning which had expired three weeks beforehand and he was dismissed. The Court of Appeal held the dismissal to be fair. The four other employees had good records but Webb had not, and it was reasonable for the employer to take the expired final warning into account.

9.6.4 Alternative employment

In some cases a reasonable employer will look to see if there is alternative work for the employee to do. This is particularly so in the case of illness or redundancy, but the principle may be applied to almost any situation bar serious misconduct. An employee, for example, may have been over-promoted and demotion back to his original grade is a possibility (*Hall v Lodge* [1977] IRLIB 76); however, a tribunal will not expect an employer to demote a person who is clearly incompetent at any level. On the other hand, a tribunal will expect an employer to have considered alternative employment actively where the dismissal is for illness, and failure to do so may well render the dismissal unfair, particularly if there is light work that the employee can do (*Todd v North Eastern Electricity Board* [1975] IRLR 60). In *McAdie v Royal Bank of Scotland* [2007] EWCA Civ 806, McAdie was dismissed after being on long-term sick leave as a result of stress caused by bullying and mismanagement at work. The Court of Appeal held that the fact that the employer had caused the incapacity in question did not preclude the dismissal being fair. However, the question for the tribunal was whether the employer had acted reasonably in the circumstances, and the tribunal had to include in its considerations that the employer was to blame for the absence. Where the employer was responsible for an employee's incapacity, it should normally be expected to 'go the extra mile' in finding alternative employment, or put up with a longer period of absence than would be otherwise reasonable. On the facts of the case, given she was adamant that she did not want to return to work, McAdie's dismissal was fair, although the judgment is clear as to the responsibilities of an employer when incapability is caused by the working environment.

In relation to redundancy, ERA 1996 envisages alternative employment being offered, and by section 138 allows the employee a trial period in the new employment without the loss of redundancy compensation should it prove to be unsuitable (see Chapter 10). Certainly, refusing to allow an employee a trial period if alternative employment is offered in a redundancy situation is an unfair dismissal (*Elliot v Richard Stump Ltd* [1987] IRLR 215).

The Court of Appeal looked at the question of alternative employment in conduct dismissals in the case of *P v Nottinghamshire County Council* [1992] IRLR 362. There, P was employed as an assistant groundsman at a school. After a complaint by his 14-year-old daughter, he was arrested and charged with indecent assault, and released on bail. The Council suspended him on full pay until the outcome of the criminal case. At his trial he pleaded guilty and asked for other offences to be taken into account. At the subsequent disciplinary hearing, P argued that he had pleaded guilty only to prevent his daughter from having to attend court. The Council was concerned about the risk to school children and told P he would be dismissed with 12 weeks' notice, but that an attempt would be made to find him alternative employment in the highways department. He was not required to attend for work during his notice period, and during his notice he received a letter saying that the highways department would not consider him because of his sickness record. P claimed unfair dismissal. The employment tribunal found that P had been unfairly dismissed. The EAT held that the tribunal had erred in law in its answers to certain questions, and remitted the case back to the tribunal for a rehearing. The Court of Appeal held that the tribunal had erred in relation to certain questions, but concentrated on the issue of alternative employment. The employment tribunal had found that the Council had not reasonably investigated the possibility of alternative employment, but the EAT had found that because the tribunal's answers to questions it had asked itself were wrong, this could have coloured its view on this issue. The Court of Appeal held that where an employee's conduct rendered him unsuitable to continue in employment in a particular capacity, in an appropriate case and where the size and resources of the company permitted, it might be unfair to dismiss without first considering if the employee could be offered an alternative job. This does not have to occur before notice of dismissal is given, however; it is dismissal which is the operative act.

9.6.5   Fair procedure

While the tribunals will have regard to the factors listed above, without doubt one of the most important aspects of fairness is the procedure the employer uses before dismissing the employee. Failing to use a procedure or using a procedure unfairly will almost certainly mean that a dismissal is unfair. A reasonable employer has a fair procedure and adheres to it. While there are certain basic principles which apply to any of the reasons for dismissal, the tribunal will look for different procedures applying in different cases. A reasonable employer does not invoke disciplinary procedures against an employee who is long-term sick, for example. The following discussion will therefore look at procedural fairness in relation to each reason for dismissal, in order to highlight both the differences and the similarities.

Until April 2009, statutory disciplinary procedures existed which an employer had to follow; otherwise, in the majority of cases, the dismissal would be automatically unfair and compensation would be increased. The procedures were introduced in 2004, and it would be fair to say they were not a success. As a result, a review of the procedures by Gibbons, on behalf of the government, led to their abolition in 2009 and to an increased emphasis on statutory codes of practice.

One effect of the abolition of the procedures is the resurrection of the House of Lords decision in *Polkey v AE Dayton Services Ltd* [1987] IRLR 503. In *Polkey*, the House of Lords overturned the infamous decision in *British Labour Pump Co Ltd v Byrne* [1979] IRLR 94 and the notorious 'no difference' rule, which allowed an employer to show that even if he had followed his procedures, he would still have dismissed the employee, thus his failure had made no difference to the final outcome. The House of Lords in *Polkey* stated that this was a misinterpretation of the statute, which looked at the reasonableness of the employer's behaviour and not the unfairness to the employee; thus, except in very few cases, a failure to follow a laid-down procedure would render a dismissal unfair. However, if an employee would have been dismissed had the procedure been followed, this will lead to a reduction in the compensation awarded (a *Polkey* reduction).

In the case of both the disciplinary and grievance procedures, there is a requirement that meetings should be held within a reasonable time. In addition, employees are entitled in both sets of procedures to be accompanied by a companion. This right was introduced by section 10 of the Employment Relations Act 1999 and applies to workers. In *Toal v GB Oils Ltd* [2013] IRLR 696, the EAT held that the request for a particular person to accompany the worker does not have to be reasonable, and an employer cannot refuse to allow a worker to be accompanied by a particular companion. The right in relation to disciplinary hearings is to be accompanied to any meeting which may result in the administration of a warning, confirmation of a warning or other disciplinary action. In relation to grievance hearings, the right arises in relation to hearings which are about a 'duty by an employer in relation to a worker' (Employment Relations Act 1999, s 13(5)). The companion is entitled to paid time off to prepare for and attend the hearing. Originally under the 1999

Act, the companion had a right to address the hearing on the worker's behalf but could not answer questions. The Employment Relations Act 2004 extended the companion's right. Section 10(2B) of the 1999 Act now allows a companion to put the worker's case, sum up that case and respond on the worker's behalf to any view expressed in the hearing; however, by section 10(2C) an employer is not required to permit the companion to answer questions on behalf of the worker. It is submitted that the distinction between responding to a view expressed by the hearing and answering questions, may, in reality, be difficult to make.

In some cases the employee is entitled to legal representation at internal disciplinary hearings. In *R (on the application of G) v Governors of X School* [2011] UKSC 30, the employee, who was a music assistant at a school, was alleged to have kissed a 15-year-old boy. If the employee was found guilty, the school had a duty to report him to the Secretary of State for Children, Schools and Families in order for the department to decide whether he should be entered on the register of those who are unsuitable to work with children. The claimant sought to have a legal representative to accompany him in the disciplinary hearing. The school refused, and after the hearing the claimant was dismissed. The claimant sought judicial review, claiming that the school's refusal constituted a breach of Article 6 of the ECHR (the right to a fair trial). The High Court held that the school was required to have regard to Article 6 and that the internal procedures were to be regarded as part of the Secretary of State's procedures relating to whether someone was suitable to work with children. As such, the claimant was entitled to legal representation, and the potential of an unfair dismissal claim in a tribunal was not an adequate alternative remedy. This was rejected by the Supreme Court, however, which held in a majority decision that Article 6 was not engaged. In *Kulkarni v Milton Keynes Hospital NHS Trust* [2009] EWCA Civ 789, the Court of Appeal has held that an NHS doctor facing charges of misconduct or capability is entitled to legal representation, and it also stated *obiter* that where charges are such that if proved an employee might be unable to work, then the employee has a free-standing right to legal representation under Article 6. In other words, if the internal process could lead to a loss of livelihood, then Article 6 applies and legal representation must be permitted.

9.6.6 The procedures

The procedures, many coming from the original ACAS Code of Practice, have built up over the years. A number of points should be noted before discussing the procedures in any detail, though. First, case law has established that different procedures apply for different reasons. Second, in almost all cases, case law has established that an employer should conduct a thorough investigation before conducting a disciplinary hearing. Third, there are established rules in relation to fair hearings and fair appeals. All of these points are contained in the revised ACAS Code on Disciplinary and Grievance Procedures 2009. As noted, case law envisages different procedures applying to the fair reasons, therefore it is proposed to discuss each reason separately (see Sections 9.6.7–9.6.12 below). Failure to observe any Code of Practice on the part of the employer can lead to an increase in compensation of up to 25 per cent. Likewise, if an employee fails to observe the Code in relation to grievances, this can lead to a decrease in compensation of up to 25 per cent.

9.6.7   Capability and qualifications

9.6.7(a) Inadequate work

The starting point for the employer is to decide whether this is deliberate incapability, that is, laziness or deliberate negligence, or inherent incapability. The former case is really misconduct and should be treated as such. Where the reason appears to be inherent incapability, the tribunal will normally look for three stages in the employer's procedure: an investigation, reasonable opportunity to improve and warnings.

9.6.7(b) Investigation

Instant dismissal without an investigation will almost always be unfair. When the employee is the subject of an investigation, he should be told the scope of the investigation and the facts and the matters alleged against him (*British Midland Airways Ltd v Gilmore* [1981] EAT 173/81). The employer should normally give the employee the opportunity to explain, particularly if the incapability is sudden after years of acceptable work. It may be, for example, that the nature of the job has changed and the employee needs training, or something may have happened in his personal life which is affecting his work. In *Davison v Kent Meters Ltd* (see Section 9.5.1(a)) the employee had never been shown how to assemble the components. Not surprisingly, her dismissal was found to be unfair. A proper investigation by the employer would have revealed her lack of training.

9.6.7(c) Reasonable opportunity to improve

If after the investigation the employer can detect no reason for the incapability, for example lack of training, a failure to allow the employee opportunity to improve will often render a dismissal unfair (*Mansfield Hosiery Mills Ltd v Bromley* [1977] IRLR 301). The employee must know, however, where his standards fall down and what he must do to improve. In other words, the employer must tell him specifically what standards to reach – a general comment that he must improve is not likely to get either of them anywhere. The length of time given to the employee will depend on a variety of factors, such as the employee's seniority, length of service and past performance. The employee should be told the date by which he has to improve and be warned that his job is in jeopardy.

9.6.7(d) Warnings

Normally, the employer should warn the employee before dismissal, but failure to do so may not always render the dismissal unfair. The EAT pointed out in *Littlewoods Organisation Ltd v Egenti* [1976] IRLR 334 that there is a distinction between disciplinary procedures and capability procedures. Whereas disciplinary procedures should always be followed strictly, this is not necessarily the case in relation to capability. The aim of a warning in capability cases is to improve the employee's performance, and if the warning would not have this effect, one does not have to be given. Thus in *Lowndes v Specialist Heavy Engineering Ltd* [1977] ICR 1, the employee was dismissed after five serious and expensive mistakes. He was not warned and was given no opportunity to make representations. It was held that his dismissal was fair. Having said that, the employer must ensure that his evidence shows that a warning would not have improved the employee. If the tribunal feels that a warning would have made a difference, failing to warn will render the dismissal unfair.

9.6.8 Sickness and injury

The aim of a fair procedure in these cases is the gathering of sufficient information to form an accurate picture of the employee's present and future health, and his ability to do the job. This will involve the employer in the gathering of medical evidence and consultation with the employee, giving the employee the opportunity to bring forward his own evidence. Failure to obtain evidence or consult will normally render the dismissal unfair.

9.6.8(a) Medical evidence

Reliance on medical certificates is unlikely to suffice as evidence. The employer should gain as much evidence as possible from the employee, the employee's doctor and, if appropriate, the company doctor (*East Lindsey District Council v Daubney* [1977] IRLR 191). To ensure that the evidence is pertinent, the employer should inform the doctor of the nature of the employee's job, although the decision to dismiss will ultimately be a managerial and not a medical one. Any fresh evidence which comes to light after the employer has taken the decision to dismiss but before the notice period has expired should be taken into account, and the employer should review his initial decision (*Williamson v Alcan (UK) Ltd* [1977] IRLR 303). The employer must get the employee's permission to obtain evidence from the employee's own doctor under the Access to Medical Reports Act 1988, and the employee may refuse or veto part of the report before it reaches the employer. In such circumstances it will probably be fair to dismiss the employee if the veto is unreasonable and the employer reasonably believed the employee was and would be incapable of performing his job. If there is a conflict between the employee's own evidence and that of the company doctor, the employer will normally be expected to obtain a third opinion, although this may not be necessary where, for example, the company doctor's report is likely to be more accurate because of his knowledge of the nature of the job.

9.6.8(b) Consultation with the employee

The employer should consult with the employee before making his decision, and the *Daubney* case (Section 9.6.8(a) above) says that only in exceptional cases will dismissal be fair where there has been no consultation. Consultation does not mean warnings, however, because you cannot warn a person to get well. Consultation means treating the employee with sympathetic consideration, although this does not mean keeping the job open for an unreasonable length of time, or creating a job for him if one does not exist. An employer should also not dismiss the employee because of the risk of a recurrence or future illness without strong evidence that a recurrence is likely. In *Converform (Darwen) Ltd v Bell* [1981] IRLR 195, the employee had suffered a heart attack and his employers refused to allow him to return on his recovery because they feared he would have another attack. It was held that in the circumstances his dismissal was unfair. If, however, it was the work environment which had caused the illness, subject to the possibility of alternative employment, it may be fair to dismiss (*Taylorplan Catering (Scotland) Ltd v McInally* [1980] IRLR 53).

Some firms place employees in a holding department, and the employees will return when they are fit and a suitable vacancy occurs. The exact position of such an employee will depend on the arrangements made. If the effect is to terminate the contract, with the employer under a moral obligation to provide work when the employee is fit again, there is a dismissal and the employee may sue (*Marshall v Harland & Wolff Ltd* [1972] 1 WLR 899); however, it has been held that if the employee agrees to such action there is no dismissal. In *Parker v Westland Helicopters Ltd* IDS Supp 15, an employee was put into a holding department with her consent until a suitable vacancy occurred. It was held that no dismissal had taken place.

9.6.9 Conduct

Every employer must give his employees a copy of the disciplinary procedures which apply to them, or refer them to a document stating the procedures. In practice, where an employer has his own disciplinary procedures they will break down into three constituent parts: the rules, the procedures and the sanctions.

9.6.9(a) Rules

Disciplinary rules will either be part of the employer's disciplinary procedures, or be contained in a separate document such as the work's rules or a company handbook. Wherever they are, they must be communicated to the employee so that he knows exactly what conduct is or is not acceptable to the employer. Given that this is the purpose of the rules, it follows that a lack of communication of the rules to the employee or insufficient communication may render a dismissal unfair. In *Brooks & Son v Skinner* [1984] IRLR 379, the employer had agreed with the union that any employee who, as a result of overindulgence at the Christmas party, failed to turn up for work the next day would be dismissed. This agreement was not communicated to the employees and Skinner was dismissed when he failed to show up the next day. It was held that his dismissal was unfair as he would not have realised, without being told, that such conduct could lead to dismissal. This leads to the question, however, of how far the employer must communicate obvious rules, for example that theft is gross misconduct. In *Parsons (CA) & Co Ltd v McLoughlin* [1978] IRLR 65, a dismissal for fighting was fair even though it was not included in the employer's rules as gross misconduct, because everyone would know that such conduct would be looked upon gravely by management. It should be stressed, however, that in the particular case the fighting took place by dangerous machinery on the shop floor, and where the potential consequences are not so serious, failure to communicate the rule may lead to the dismissal being unfair (see, for example, *Meyer Dunmore International Ltd v Rogers* [1978] IRLR 167).

In addition, the employee must understand that what is being communicated to him is a standard to which he must conform. Vague and badly drafted rules which might be misunderstood by an employee could again lead to a finding of unfair dismissal. Even if the rule has been adequately made known to the employee and has been broken, the employer may still be acting unreasonably if the rule breached has no relevance to the employment. The law will not allow an employer to act in an autocratic manner and will always question whether the punishment fits the crime. In *Talbot v Hugh M. Fulton Ltd* [1975] IRLR 52, the employee was dismissed for having long hair contrary to the rules. It was held that his dismissal was unfair. There was no safety risk involved and no definition of what was meant by 'long'. On the other hand, in *Higham v International Stores* [1977] IRLIB 97 there was a company rule requiring employees to wear a tie and proper shoes and socks. The employee was dismissed for continually wearing clogs and sandals, and failing to wear a tie. It was held that his dismissal was fair. The shop had a middle-class clientele in a conventional town, and it was reasonable for the employer to lay down standards of dress.

9.6.9(b) Procedures

Even if the rule is clear and well communicated but has still been broken, the employer will lose the case if he has not gone through the correct procedure before dismissing the employee. Normally, if the employer has followed his own procedures the dismissal will be fair, although if the tribunal feels that the procedures themselves are unfair it will lead to a finding of unfair dismissal. In *Vauxhall Motors Ltd v Ghafoor* [1993] ICR 370, the employee was dismissed for fighting. Under the disciplinary procedure agreed with the union, he could appeal against his dismissal only with the consent of the union convenor, who in this case refused his consent. The EAT held that this constituted procedural unfairness, because the right to appeal is the right of every individual and such a right should not be taken away without the individual's express consent. The fact that the employee was a union member did not mean he had given this consent.

In the majority of cases the tribunal will look for a thorough investigation, a fair disciplinary hearing and an appeal. At one time it was thought that failing to follow a fair procedure would not render the dismissal unfair if the employer could show that the breach of procedure had made no difference to the employee, that is, if the procedure had been followed, the employee would have been dismissed anyway so that the breach of procedure had made no difference to the final outcome (*British Labour Pump Co Ltd v Byrne* [1979] IRLR 94). This so-called 'no difference' rule was deemed to be a misinterpretation of section 98(4) of the ERA 1996 by the House of Lords in *Polkey v AE Dayton Services Ltd* [1987] IRLR 503, their Lordships arguing that the rule concentrated on the unfairness of the decision to the employee rather than the reasonableness of the employer's action. In the case, the employers decided to make three out of four van drivers redundant. Polkey was asked to drive two of the drivers home after they had been given the news of their redundancies, and when he returned to his place of work he was called into the office and told that he was the third redundant driver! The employee claimed unfair dismissal on the basis that he had never been warned or consulted about his redundancy (see Section 9.6.11 below). The employers pleaded the 'no difference' rule, arguing that even if they had warned and consulted, Polkey would have been made redundant anyway. The House of Lords said that that was irrelevant. A reasonable employer would have warned and consulted whether the redundancy was inevitable or not, and by failing to do so the employer had not acted reasonably. The dismissal was unfair. Since this decision, even greater emphasis has been placed on fair procedures and adherence to them by the tribunals, although in *Cabaj v Westminster City Council* (1996) IDS Brief 567, where the procedure allowed for an appeal to be heard by a three-member panel but only two members turned up and the appeal was heard anyway, the EAT held that this was a fundamental defect and as such rendered the dismissal unfair. The Court of Appeal overturned the decision on the basis that the panel reached a majority decision.

9.6.9(c) Investigation

We have already seen that the employer must have a genuine belief based on reasonable grounds after a reasonable investigation that the employee is guilty of misconduct (see Section 9.5 above). In other words, the employer must gather all the evidence he can so that he can make a reasoned and fair decision (*Scottish Daily Record & Sunday Mail (1986)*

Ltd v Laird [1996] IRLR 665). This means, for example, that if the employee has been caught fighting, the employer should investigate who started the fight, whether there was any provocation, whether it was a subordinate who started the fight against someone more senior or vice versa, whether the fight was in potentially dangerous circumstances and whether it was in work time on work premises. All of these factors will be relevant and the employer cannot discover the answers without an investigation, that is, making sure he has questioned anyone who saw the fight.

The importance of a thorough investigation is seen in the EAT decision in *Stuart v London City Airport* [2013] All ER (D) 33. Stuart was employed in a position of trust as a Ground Services Agent. He entered a duty-free store within the airport to buy some presents. He was holding them in his hands when he was called outside of the shop by a member of staff for a chat, at which point he was apprehended for stealing the goods. In dismissing him the employer relied on the fact that he had left the shop with the goods and the evidence of a shop assistant who claimed she had seen Stuart conceal the goods – evidence strongly disputed by Stuart. During the internal procedure the employer did not interview the shop assistant or the member of staff who had called Stuart outside, nor had the employer looked at CCTV footage of Stuart's movements inside the shop. The EAT stated that allegations of serious misconduct required careful investigation, and the employer had acted unreasonably in failing to carry out further investigation which would have supported Stuart's assertion that he was innocent of the alleged offence.

Normally an employer will suspend the suspected employee pending the outcome of the investigation. The Court of Appeal, however, has stated that suspension should not be an automatic reaction to allegations against employees. In *Crawford v Suffolk Mental Health Partnership NHS Trust* [2012] EWCA Civ 138, the Court said that suspending claimants and then forbidding them from contacting anyone involved should not be a knee-jerk reaction, and any employer who suspends without good reason is likely to be in breach of the duty of mutual trust and confidence. In the case, two nurses were accused of assaulting a patient in their care who had dementia. They were suspended when the allegations were made. They were accused of tying a patient to a chair. They stated that they had tied the chair to a table but had not tied the patient to the chair, saying that a sheet had become wrapped round the patient through struggling. After an investigation and hearing, they were dismissed for gross misconduct. The investigation was poor in that the conclusion that the sheet could not have become wrapped round the patient in the way the claimants described was reached by the chair of the disciplinary hearing conducting an experiment which was not discussed with the claimants, and they were not asked to demonstrate what had happened. As such the dismissal was unfair. In addition, the Court of Appeal that the employer should not have suspended the employees, as it was difficult to believe that a reasonable employer could have considered that there was any risk of the treatment of which they were accused being repeated.

Any suspension should be with pay, unless there is a contractual right to suspend without pay, otherwise the employer will be in breach of his common law duty to pay wages. Having said that, even if such a contractual right exists, a person is innocent until proved guilty, and to suspend without pay almost seems like a punishment and prejudging the issue, and this could be seen as unreasonable in the circumstances by a tribunal. As soon as an employer suspects an employee, he should suspend him and begin an investigation. Memories fade quickly, and witnesses may not remember everything if there is too long a delay between the event and the investigation. In *Marley Home Care Ltd v Dutton* [1981] IRLR 380, a delay of one week before the start of the investigation made the dismissal unfair because the employee could not remember the incident clearly. A delay may also lead the employee to think that the incident is being ignored, or that it has blown over.

Although normally an employer should conduct as thorough an investigation as possible, in one set of circumstances this may not be possible, that is where the conduct is a criminal offence and the police are also investigating. In this case the employee will often remain silent on the advice of his solicitor, and therefore the employer does not hear the employee's version of events. In these circumstances, as long as the employer has enough evidence to form a reasonable belief in the guilt of the employee, the dismissal will be fair. In *Harris and Shepherd v Courage* (Section 9.5.2(a) above), it was held that the dismissals were fair, because the employer had enough evidence to form a reasonable belief that the employees were guilty as alleged. If the employee does confess, he may retract his confession when he knows that criminal proceedings are being brought. In this situation the employer is entitled to rely on the original confession if it is reasonable to do so (*University College of Buckingham v Phillips* (1981) EAT 608/81).

While there has been authority stating that a dismissal may be fair even when the employee is dismissed without an investigation in cases of admitted dishonesty (*Royal Society for the Protection of Birds v Croucher* [1984] ICR 604), this should be treated with caution. In *John Lewis plc v Coyne* (2001) *The Times*, 5 January, it was discovered that the employee had made two to three personal telephone calls a week. She had a 13-year unblemished work record. Following the discovery, she was interviewed without warning and, on admitting the allegation, was dismissed. The EAT upheld the employment tribunal decision that the dismissal was unfair. The appeal tribunal distinguished *Croucher* on the basis that the dishonesty in that case was on a far greater scale and the dismissed employee was a director. Furthermore, although the employer in *Coyne* considered that making personal telephone calls fell within the dishonesty policy, the appeal tribunal did not agree that the employee's actions satisfied the test for dishonesty.

9.6.9(d) Hearing

Once the employer has gathered the evidence, he must conduct a disciplinary hearing to make a decision as to the sanction he will impose. The procedures will normally lay down who will conduct the hearing. Many books state that the hearing must comply with the rules of natural justice. While the principles of a fair hearing are similar if not identical to the rules of natural justice, it should be noted, as stated in Chapter 8, that the consequences of a breach are not the same. If natural justice applies and its principles are breached, the decision is void. If the rules of a fair hearing are broken, the decision to dismiss still stands but the dismissal without doubt will be found to be unfair. The rules of a fair hearing are as follows:

1. The employee must know the case against him to enable him to answer the complaint (*Hutchins v British Railways Board* [1974] IRLR 303). In *Celebi v Compass* (2010) UKEAT 0032/10, the claimant was believed to have stolen money but the allegation made against her was the 'loss of £3,000'. She knew she was being accused of theft and after a disciplinary hearing she was dismissed. The EAT held that the dismissal was unfair as the allegation lacked precision, and the employee had not been told specifically that

she was accused of stealing the money. Given that the aim of this rule is that the employee should have a chance to prepare his case, he should be told the basis for the hearing in sufficient time for him to prepare adequately. It has also been held (in *A v Company B Ltd* [1997] IRLR 405) that as well as knowing the allegations against him, an employee must know the identity of his accuser. However, in *Hussain v Elonex plc* [1999] IRLR 420 the Court of Appeal held that there was no obligation on the employer to show witness statements to the employee during the disciplinary hearing. It would be unfair not to tell the employee of the existence of the statements, but not unfair not to show those statements to him.

2. The employee should have the opportunity to put his side of the case, that is, the employer should listen to the employee's side of the story and allow him to explain his conduct or put forward mitigating circumstances. In *Budgen & Co v Thomas* [1976] IRLR 174, the employee was dismissed after she signed a confession that she had stolen a sum of money. She was dismissed after the security officer had sent his report to the head office, which took the dismissal decision without allowing the girl an opportunity to put her side of the case. She was a diabetic and claimed that she was confused at the time she made the confession and that the confession was untrue. It was held that her dismissal was unfair. She had not been given a hearing and, in view of her circumstances, had she been given the hearing, the decision to dismiss might not have been taken. The employee's right to put his side of the case arose again in the case of *Clarke v Trimoco Motor Group Ltd* [1993] IRLR 148. Here, Clarke and another employee were accused by a customer of billing for petrol which had not been put into the customer's lorries. In the course of the investigation Clarke denied fraud, but admitted that he had post-dated some fuel vouchers at the request of drivers. He was given a written warning but told that the employers might take further action if the police came up with new evidence. Two lorry drivers confessed to fraud to the police and implicated Clarke. The employers therefore suspended Clarke pending the outcome of the court case against him and the lorry drivers. After the case was adjourned twice, Clarke was dismissed for the original offence of altering fuel vouchers. The tribunal found that the real reason for the dismissal was the suspicion that Clarke was involved in the fraud, although this was not the reason given, and the dismissal was fair because Clarke knew that this was the reason. Furthermore, the employer had not acted unfairly in not giving Clarke an opportunity to answer the allegation of fraud, as Clarke could have raised it in the grievance procedure between his suspension and dismissal. The EAT, while agreeing with the employment tribunal that Clarke knew the real reason for his dismissal, held that the dismissal was unfair. The fact that Clarke could have used the grievance procedure was no excuse for the employer's failure to allow Clarke to answer the allegations of fraud.

3. The employee must be allowed representation at the hearing if he wishes. Denying the employee this right may well render the dismissal unfair (*Rank Xerox Ltd v Goodchild and Others* [1979] IRLR 185), although the employer can specify the type of representation he will allow and in most cases there is no right to legal representation (although see *R (on the application of G) v Governors of X School* and *Kulkarni v Milton Keynes Hospital NHS Trust*, in Section 9.6.5 above). The right to be accompanied at both disciplinary and grievance hearings has been enhanced by the Employment Relations Act 1999. Sections 10–13 create rights for workers to be accompanied at a disciplinary or grievance hearing by a single representative who may address the hearing and

confer with the worker, but who cannot ask questions on behalf of the worker. Such a representative may be a trade union official or a worker employed by the employer. There is a complaint to an employment tribunal for denial of this right within three months of the denial, and if the tribunal finds the complaint well founded, it can award compensation of up to two weeks' pay. A worker who exercises the right to be accompanied or who accompanies a fellow worker is protected from suffering a detriment or dismissal. Note that the provisions protect workers as defined in section 13 of the 1999 Act. This definition is wider than 'employee' and includes, for example, agency workers and home workers.

4. The hearing should be unbiased, that is, the employer should approach the hearing with an open mind and not pre-judge the issue. It would clearly be unfair if the employee was accused of hitting a manager and that manager chaired the hearing to decide whether to dismiss him or not. Without doubt the manager would have already made his decision before the hearing started. In *Moyes v Hylton WMC* [1986] IRLR 482, two witnesses to an act of sexual harassment also conducted the investigation, and one chaired the disciplinary hearing which decided to dismiss the employee. It was held that the dismissal was unfair. In *BOC Ltd v McConnon* (1992) EAT 613/89, an employee had been to the pub and was found drunk and asleep in his truck by the foreman. The foreman reported him to the acting branch manager, who sent the employee home and told him to return the following Monday. The Friday before McConnon's return, the foreman, the branch manager and the personnel officer discussed the case, and held a further meeting on Sunday to go over the evidence. On Monday the branch manager conducted the disciplinary hearing which dismissed McConnon. The EAT held that the branch manager should not have conducted the investigation and the hearing. There was another branch manager on the site who could have chaired the hearing. To ensure there is no bias, if possible the person who conducts the investigation should not be the person taking the decision to dismiss. Mr McConnon was unfairly dismissed (see also *Whitbread plc t/a Whitbread Medway Inns v John Hall* [2001] ICR 699).

5. The employee should be informed of his right to appeal to a higher level of management who have not been involved in the previous decision to dismiss. Should an employee fail to exercise his right to an appeal, he will not have failed to mitigate his loss and it will not contribute to the finding of the tribunal in any way (*William Muir (Bond 9) Ltd v Lamb* [1985] IRLR 95); however, by section 127A of the ERA 1996, where an employee fails to make use of an internal appeals procedure, the employment tribunal has the power to reduce the compensation awarded by up to two weeks' pay where the effective date of termination of the contract is after 1 January 1999. On the other hand, refusing to allow the employee to exercise a contractual right of appeal will almost always render the dismissal unfair (*West Midlands Co-operative Society Ltd v Tipton* [1986] IRLR 112). By section 127A, the tribunal may increase the employee's compensation, in this case where the effective date of termination is after 1 January 1999, and in addition the court may place an injunction upon the employer to prevent the contract being treated as terminated until the appeal has taken place (*Jones v Lee and Guilding* [1980] IRLR 67).

9.6.9(e) Appeals

The tribunal is required to consider if the employer has acted reasonably, taking into account the resources of the employer and the size of his undertaking. This means that the tribunal will expect the employer to have provided an appeal against the original dismissal decision. All the principles which apply to a fair hearing (above) also apply to an appeal. Three further points should be noted, however. First, given the rule against bias, a person cannot chair the disciplinary hearing and also chair the appeal. Second, given that the employee should know the case against him, it follows that the appeal cannot endorse the decision to dismiss for another reason. If, therefore, the employee has originally been dismissed for theft and the appeal panel feels that there is insufficient evidence, it cannot confirm the dismissal on the ground that the employee failed to report theft by fellow employees (*Monie v Coral Racing Ltd* [1981] ICR 109). Lastly, given that the aim of the law is to ensure that the employee has a fair hearing before dismissal, an appeal which is a total rehearing of the case, rather than a review of the evidence, can rectify previous breaches of procedure at the disciplinary hearing stage (*Whitbread & Co plc v Mills* [1988] IRLR 501 and *Adivihalli v Export Credits Guarantee Department* (1998) IDS Brief 620).

It has already been noted that the Human Rights Act 1998 has impacted on this area (see Section 1.5). In *Tehrani v UK Central Council for Nursing, Midwifery and Health Visiting* [2001] IRLR 208, the Court of Session looked at the impact of Schedule 1, Part I, Article 6. It held that disciplinary proceedings before the Council's professional conduct committee fell within the scope of Article 6, because they involved the determination of the complainant's civil rights since they could result in the removal of Tehrani's name from the register of nurses. As such, she was entitled to 'a hearing before an independent and impartial tribunal' (Article 6). The Court went on to state, however, that it is not necessary for a professional disciplinary tribunal to meet all of the requirements of an independent and impartial tribunal, if the disciplinary procedure provides a statutory right of appeal to a court of law. Case law from the European Court of Human Rights establishes that there is no breach of the European Convention on Human Rights if the disciplinary tribunal is subject to control by a court which itself complies with Article 6.

9.6.9(f) Sanctions

The employer will normally have a variety of sanctions he may impose for misconduct, the ultimate sanction being dismissal. The variety of the employer's sanctions will be an important consideration for the tribunal in considering whether the decision is a fair one and the punishment fits the crime. Imposing too harsh a sanction short of dismissal may in itself be a repudiatory breach of contract, justifying the employee's resigning and claiming constructive dismissal. The procedures themselves must be clear as to the sanctions which may be applied.

9.6.9(g) Warnings

Generally, apart from serious or gross misconduct, an employee should receive a warning before being dismissed. The ACAS Code recommends three warnings before dismissal, the first oral, the second and the third written, although these are only guidelines, and clearly it depends on the circumstances of the case and the type of misconduct. Whereas it may be unreasonable to depart from that sequence in relation to, for example, an employee's being five minutes late on one occasion, it would not be unreasonable to circumvent the earlier stages of the procedure and issue a final warning for serious acts of misconduct. A warning is both an indication to the employee that his behaviour is disapproved of and an opportunity to improve that behaviour, although a warning for different misconduct may be considered when looking at later misconduct (*Auguste Noel Ltd v Curtis* [1990] IRLR 326).

The ACAS Code urges that, apart from gross misconduct, no one should be dismissed for a first breach of discipline. While the Code no longer stipulates that warnings should remain on the employee's record only for a set time, it does say that employees should be told how long a warning will last, and the Guide to the Code says that warnings should be disregarded after a specified time (often 6–12 months). *Airbus (UK) Ltd v Webb* (Section 9.6.3 above), however, shows that even if a warning has expired, it may be reasonable in some circumstances for the employer to take it into account when looking at sanctions. Therefore after warnings have expired, they will not be taken into account when looking to see if the procedure has been followed in later cases of misconduct, but they may be considered when the employer is looking at the employee's work record when considering what sanction to impose.

There have been a number of recent cases involving warnings. The first is the surprising decision in *Christou (1) and Ward (2) v London Borough of Haringey* [2013] EWCA Civ 178. The case related to the dismissals of a social worker and team leader involved in the Baby P case. Originally both employees received final written warnings for their conduct, but the case became notorious after the conviction of Baby P's mother and her partner, and an inquiry was established by the Secretary of State for Education into Haringey's child protection arrangements, which found that they were inadequate. The inquiry concluded that the original disciplinary procedure was 'blatantly unsafe, unsound and inadequate'. After a new hearing, both employees were dismissed. The Court of Appeal rejected the arguments of the appellants that it was unfair to re-open the disciplinary decisions and that the doctrine of *res judicata* applied. *Res judicata* applies only to court and tribunal proceedings and not to internal disciplinary proceedings. It should be noted, however, that the facts of the case are unusual.

In *Simmonds v Milford Club* [2013] All ER (D) 182, the EAT held that a tribunal in an unfair dismissal case may question the appropriateness of a final warning prior to dismissal where there are grounds for thinking that such a final warning is inappropriate. Simmonds was disciplined when he gave staff a £15 Christmas bonus in cash instead of a bottle of wine to the value of £15 as instructed. As he was already on a final warning, he was dismissed. The final warning was given because he had asked his wife to deposit the club's takings in the bank while he waited outside in the car, as he could not park close enough to the bank. The EAT reversed the employment tribunal decision that the dismissal was fair because it had failed to consider whether the final warning was consistent with the club's procedures, and remitted the case to the tribunal to consider whether the final warning was inappropriate. However, the next month the Court of Appeal, in *Davies v Sandwell Metropolitan Borough Council* [2013] EWCA Civ 135, held that an employer's reliance on a final warning in an unfair dismissal claim may be challenged only in the exceptional case of bad faith or where the warning was manifestly inappropriate. Likewise, the EAT has further ruled, in *Wincanton Group v Stone* [2013] IRLR 178, that a tribunal cannot look behind warnings where a dismissal is based on an accumulation of warnings, unless there is evidence of bad faith or the warnings are manifestly inappropriate.

9.6.9(h) Fines or deductions

The ERA 1996 provides that the employer must have contractual authority to make such deductions, or get the written consent of the employee before such deductions are made (see Section 4.2.5). Failure to obtain the permission of the employee, either through the contract or before the deduction is made, will lead to a possible claim under the 1996 Act and a potential claim for constructive dismissal. In *Lethaby v Horsman, Andrew & Knill Ltd* [1975] IRLR 119, a deduction was made from the employee's salary to cover the loss of company property. There was no contractual authority to deduct and the employee resigned. It was held that the employee had been constructively dismissed.

9.6.9(i)　Suspension without pay

It follows that if deduction from wages without contractual authority or written agreement is a breach of ERA 1996 and a potential constructive dismissal, so too will be a suspension without pay (see also Section 9.6.9(c) above).

9.6.9(j)　Demotion

Given that the employee is employed in a certain capacity to perform certain duties, any alteration in either without the consent of the employee is a fundamental breach by the employer, and again may constitute a potential constructive dismissal. The same is true if the employer imposes a disciplinary transfer on the employee without his consent or the contractual authority to do so.

One point should be noted about all the above sanctions which, if there is no contractual authority to impose such sanctions, may lead to a constructive dismissal claim. It does not necessarily follow that because the employee has been constructively dismissed, the dismissal is unfair. In *Hall v Lodge* (1977) IRLIB 76, an employee was promoted from the role of supervisor to manager. Within a short time, however, it was apparent that she had been promoted too soon and she was unable to do the manager's job. The employer therefore offered her another supervisor's job at a different branch at her old salary. She refused, resigned and claimed constructive dismissal. It was held that although the employer had constructively dismissed the employee, in the circumstances the dismissal was fair. Where demotion is out of proportion to any misconduct committed, even if there is a contractual right to demote, the excessiveness of the employer's actions could lead to a constructive dismissal claim and the dismissal is likely to be unfair. In *Cawley v South Wales Electricity Board* [1985] IRLR 89, an employee was demoted when he was seen urinating from a moving van. Although the employer had a contractual right to demote, it was held that demotion for a first act of misconduct was too harsh a sanction. It therefore followed that the employer had committed a repudiatory breach, which meant that the resignation of the employee was a constructive dismissal. Given that the repudiatory breach was the employer's unreasonable action, it followed that the constructive dismissal was unfair. In other words, if the sanction is too harsh, the consequent dismissal must be unfair.

9.6.10　Statutory restriction

There are no real procedural issues involved when dismissing for this reason. The fairness of the dismissal will turn on the fairness of the decision, for example whether the employer has considered alternative employment, rather than the procedure he adopted.

9.6.11　Redundancy

We have already seen in Section 9.5.3 above that in certain circumstances a redundancy will be unfair if the employee is selected for particular reasons (ERA 1996, s 105;

TULR(C)A 1992, s 153). Even if these sections have not been infringed, a redundancy may still be unfair if the employer has not acted reasonably. In particular the tribunal will look at the unit of selection used, the criteria chosen for selection, the reasonableness of the procedure and the efforts made to find alternative employment.

9.6.11(a) Unfair unit of selection

The employer should define his pool of employees in a reasonable manner before using his selection criteria. If work is interchangeable between groups of workers, for example, the broader unit of selection should be adopted (*Gilford v GEC Machines* [1982] ICR 725). If the union has agreed the selection unit, it is more likely to be held that the unit of selection was reasonable.

9.6.11(b) Unfair selection criteria

The selection criteria should be objective and not subjective. A criterion such as retaining employees who in the opinion of management will keep the company viable was frowned upon by the EAT in *Williams v Compair Maxam Ltd* [1982] IRLR 83 as being too heavily reliant on individual opinion. A good starting point is 'last in, first out' (LIFO), and a selection based on LIFO is unlikely to be unfair. The employer may depart from LIFO as long as he uses other objective criteria such as experience, skill, attendance and so on. He must ensure that any criterion he adopts is not discriminatory, and we have already seen that a criterion selecting part-time workers first may constitute sex discrimination (see Section 5.5).

9.6.11(c) Reasonable procedure

The employer must have a reasonable procedure when dealing with potential redundancies. In *Somerset County Council v Chaloner* [2013] All ER (D) 192, the employer suffered a downturn and proposed that four senior management posts be reduced to two Business Development Managers. Chaloner, based on the job description, applied for one of the new posts. Before the interviews the employer decided to make more redundancies, including the post of finance officer. The job description 'Business Development Manager' was rewritten so as to include additional finance responsibilities, and this information was sent to the finance officer but not to Chaloner. The finance officer was appointed to one of the new posts, but Chaloner, who was unsuccessful, was dismissed. The EAT held that the introduction of a competing candidate and a new job description, of both of which Chaloner was unaware, was unfair and Chaloner had been unfairly dismissed.

The case of *Williams v Compair Maxam* (Section 9.6.11(b) above) laid down guidelines for a fair procedure where there is a recognised trade union. Although the guidelines apply only in a unionised situation, and may be inappropriate for a small business (*Simpson & Son (Motors) v Reid and Findlater* [1983] IRLR 401), some of the principles are appropriate to any business. The guidelines are as follows:

1. The employer should give as much warning as possible of the impending redundancies to the union and employees concerned.
2. The employer should seek the agreement of the union regarding selection criteria and the best means of achieving the necessary result, causing as little hardship and unfairness as possible.

3. The employer should consider any representations made by the union as to the selection.
4. The employer should consider whether, instead of dismissing the employee, he could offer alternative employment.

9.6.11(d) Warning and consultation

Consultation should be the normal rule, whether the employee is a member of a recognised union or not. In *Hough v Leyland Daf* [1991] IRLR 194, failing to consult with the employee, despite consulting with the employee's union, was held to render a redundancy unfair (see also *Rolls-Royce Motor Cars Ltd v Price* [1993] IRLR 203). Consultation, however, requires positive action on the part of the employer, and merely informing the employees of impending redundancies and then telling them what the selection procedure is to be, is not consultation (*Rowell v Hubbard Group Services Ltd* [1995] IRLR 195). Furthermore, the duty to consult applies to all employees, even those on fixed-term contracts which have expired (*University of Glasgow v Donaldson and McNally* (1995) IDS Brief 543). In some circumstances, however, lack of consultation may not affect the fairness of the dismissal if the tribunal accepts that the ensuing publicity could damage the business or result in a loss of faith in the company's products. Failure to consult the union, of itself, is unlikely to make the dismissal unfair, but it will do if accompanied by other procedural shortcomings. There is a statutory duty to consult with a recognised trade union or an elected employee representative in redundancy situations by section 188 of the TULR(C)A1992.

9.6.11(e) Alternative employment

We have already noted at Section 9.6.4 above that the employer should consider whether there is alternative employment he can offer the employee, although he is not required to create vacancies.

9.6.12 Some other substantial reason

Until recently, as with statutory restriction, there were few, if any, procedural issues in relation to 'some other substantial reason' (SOSR). However, in the recent case of *Lund v St Edmunds School* (2013) UKEAT 0514/12/0805, the EAT held that the ACAS Code applies to SOSR reasons. In the case, Lund was dismissed when his frustration with the school's computer equipment alienated colleagues and affected staff morale. The employment tribunal found the dismissal to be procedurally unfair because Lund had no warning of the dismissal meeting and no right of appeal. However, it reduced his compensation for contributory conduct, and refused to allow an uplift of compensation for failure to observe the Code on the basis that the Code did not apply to SOSR. The EAT held that the tribunal was wrong and that the Code did apply, and granted the uplift.

A further relevant issue is in relation to pressure from third parties, when the employer must show he has investigated adequately and has sufficient evidence on which to base his decision.

9.7 Automatically unfair reasons for dismissal

In certain cases of dismissal the issue of reasonableness is irrelevant and, should the employee show the reason for dismissal, the dismissal will be automatically unfair. In all the cases below (with the exception of a transfer under the Transfer of Undertakings (Protection of Employment) Regulations 2006 ('TUPE Regulations 2006')) the normal continuity rules are disapplied.

9.7.1 Leave for family reasons

A dismissal for pregnancy, a reason connected with pregnancy or for taking family leave is automatically unfair. By section 99 of the ERA 1996, an employee dismissed for these reasons needs no continuity of employment to claim unfair dismissal. There must, however, be a causal link between the dismissal and the exercise of the rights. Therefore, if the employee can no longer do her job because of pregnancy, or it would be a breach of a statutory provision to keep on employing her, the dismissal will not be automatically unfair but the question of reasonableness may still mean that the tribunal finds the dismissal unfair in the circumstances, because, for example, there is alternative work she could do. Where a woman is selected for redundancy because of her pregnancy, this is a dismissal for pregnancy and not redundancy (*Brown v Stockton-on-Tees Borough Council* [1988] IRLR 263 and ERA 1996, s 105). Leave covered by section 99 of the ERA 1996 is maternity leave, parental leave, paternity leave, and adoption leave, and section 57A of the 1996 Act covers time off to look after dependants.

9.7.2 Spent convictions

The Rehabilitation of Offenders Act 1974 was enacted to ensure that those convicted of a criminal offence who had genuinely tried to rehabilitate themselves should not be handicapped by having to disclose their past. Consequently, under the Act, certain rehabilitation periods are laid down, at the end of which the conviction is deemed to be spent. The rehabilitation period depends on the seriousness of the offence, but generally when a conviction is spent the employee does not have to reveal it. For employment purposes, section 4(3)(b) of the Act states that a spent conviction or failure to disclose it shall not be grounds for dismissing or excluding a person from any office, profession, occupation or employment, or for prejudicing him in any way in any occupation or employment.

The main rehabilitation periods are:

Sentence	Rehabilitation period
Imprisonment of more than 6 months and up to $2^1/_2$ years	10 years
Imprisonment of 6 months or less	7 years
Youth custody	7 years
Fine or community service order	5 years
Detention centre	3 years
Probation order, conditional discharge, binding over, care order or supervision order	1 year, or when order expires, whichever is the longer
Absolute discharge	6 months

The rehabilitation period runs from the date of conviction, not the expiry of the sentence. The periods of imprisonment are the sentence imposed and not the time served. Certain professions, such as nurses, solicitors and accountants, are exempt from the Act by the Rehabilitation of Offenders (Exception) Order 1975.

The 1974 Act provides no remedy if a person is refused a job because of a spent conviction, or if a person is discriminated against because of such a conviction. However, a dismissal for a spent conviction is unfair within the meaning of section 98 of the ERA 1996. In *Hendry v Scottish Liberal Club* [1977] IRLR 5, the employee was dismissed when it was discovered he had a spent conviction for possession of cannabis. It was held that the reason for his dismissal did not fall within the fair reasons for dismissal and was therefore unfair.

9.7.3 Transfer of undertakings

The Transfer of Undertakings (Protection of Employment) Regulations 1981, Regulation 8 rendered a dismissal automatically unfair if the transfer or a reason connected with it was the reason or the principal reason for the dismissal. In *Milligan v Securicor Cleaning Ltd* [1995] IRLR 288, the EAT held that as Regulation 8 rendered such a dismissal unfair, normal continuity rules did not apply. The last government swiftly reacted and amended Regulation 8 by the Collective Redundancies and Transfer of Undertakings (Protection of Employment) (Amendment) Regulations 1995. The TUPE Regulations 2006, Regulation 7(6) now makes it clear that an employee must have two years' continuity to claim. *Milligan* has also now been overruled by the Court of Appeal in *MRS Environmental Services Ltd v Marsh* [1997] ICR 995.

There is an exception in Regulation 7(2) of the 2006 Regulations when the dismissal will not be automatically unfair. This is where the reason was economic, technical or organisational (ETO), entailing changes in the workforce of either the transferor or the transferee before or after the relevant transfer, in which case it is a fair dismissal. The ETO defence appears to be wide and could defeat the purpose of the Regulations. As such, the courts have tried to keep the defence as narrow as possible. In *Whitehouse v Blatchford & Sons Ltd* [1999] IRLR 492, Whitehouse was a prosthetic technician employed by a company providing services for a hospital. At the end of the contract the new contract was awarded to another company, which agreed to take on the existing employees, although a condition of the contract inserted by the hospital was that the number of employees was reduced by one to reduce the contract price. Consequently, Whitehouse was made redundant by the transferee after the transfer. The employment tribunal held that the dismissal was fair on the ETO defence and Whitehouse appealed. The EAT reviewed the authorities in this area, namely *Berriman v Delabole Slate Ltd* [1985] IRLR 305 and *Wheeler v Patel* [1987] ICR 631. In *Berriman*, there was not an ETO defence when the transferee dismissed an employee for failing to accept a reduction in pay, so standardising the pay of all the transferee's employees. The action did not involve changes in the workforce and therefore the ETO defence did not apply. In *Wheeler*, the dismissal of all the staff prior to the transfer to achieve an enhanced price similarly was not an ETO defence as it did not relate to the conduct of the business. In *Whitehouse*, the majority of the EAT found that the employment tribunal was entitled to find an ETO defence existed, because the reduction in the number of employees had been at the insistence of the hospital and the transferee would not have obtained the contract without that reduction, a decision upheld by the Court of Appeal. It does seem on the facts, however, that *Whitehouse* is difficult to distinguish from *Wheeler*, in that in *Wheeler* the business would not have been sold without the dismissal of the employees.

9.7.4 Trade union membership or activities

By section 152(1) of TULR(C)A 1992, a dismissal is automatically unfair if the reason for the dismissal was that the employee:

1. was, or proposed to become, a member of an independent trade union; or
2. had taken, or proposed to take, part in the activities of an independent trade union at an appropriate time; or
3. was not a member of any trade union, or of a particular trade union, or of one of a number of particular trade unions, or had refused, or proposed to refuse, to become or remain a member.

For the purposes of 3. above, this includes the refusal of a non-union member to make payments in lieu of union dues, or his objection or proposed objection to such payments (TULR(C)A 1992, s 152(3)). Dismissal on this ground does not require any continuity as a prerequisite to any claim.

The tribunals have given a wide interpretation to the provisions. In *Discount Tobacco and Confectionery Ltd v Armitage* [1990] IRLR 14, the employee enlisted the help of her trade union representative to secure a written contract from her employer. She wished to raise certain discrepancies between the written terms and the terms originally offered, but the employer dismissed her. She argued her dismissal was for her trade union membership, and this was confirmed by the EAT who ruled that dismissal for using the services provided by a trade union fell within section 152 (see also *O'Dea v ISC Chemicals* [1995] IRLR 599).

There is also protection for taking part in trade union activities at an appropriate time. This leads to two questions: What are trade union 'activities'? And what constitutes an 'appropriate time'? 'Activities' is given its normal meaning, so that union meetings, recruitment and so on are all union activities. In *Controlled Demolition Group Ltd v Lane and Knowles* (1991) EAT 418/91, the employees were employed as asbestos strippers. Lane was a member of the union and took an active part in it. Knowles was not a member of the union. The union held a meeting to recruit new members, but neither employee attended. Shortly afterwards both were given notice of redundancy and both claimed unfair dismissal, despite the fact that neither had the requisite continuity. The tribunal found that there was a genuine redundancy situation and that the employer needed to reduce the workforce by 13 employees. However, 20 employees were made redundant and seven new employees were taken on. The tribunal found that the employer was antagonistic towards the union and had taken the opportunity of redundancy to rid itself of those involved in trade union activities. In Lane's case it was because of his membership and participation, in Knowles's case it was because the employer thought he had intended to join the union. The EAT confirmed the finding. The tribunal was justified in concluding that the principal reason for the dismissal was the membership or proposed membership of the union and not redundancy. If the principal reason had been redundancy, and the reason for selection had not been union activities, then the employees would have needed two years' service, but that was not the case here. The evidence showed that the employer knew of Lane's activities and mistakenly thought that Knowles had attended the meeting, and these were the reasons for their selection. On the other hand, the employee must be indulging in those activities by or on behalf of the union. In *Chant v Aquaboats* [1978] ICR 643, the employee was dismissed for organising a petition about an unsafe machine. Although he was a union member, he was not an official nor was he organising the petition on behalf of the union. It was held that his dismissal was not for union activities. However, in *Fitzpatrick v British Railways Board* [1990] ICR 674 the dismissal of a union activist when her employer discovered that she had been dismissed by her previous employer because the previous employer had found her activities disruptive, was a dismissal within the section.

To gain protection, the activities must have taken place at the 'appropriate time'. By section 152(2) of TULR(C)A 1992 this means outside working hours, or within working hours in accordance with arrangements with or with the consent of the employer. In *Zucker v Astrid Jewels Ltd* [1978] IRLR 385, the employee tried to persuade her colleagues to join the union at every available opportunity while she was working. It was held that she was taking part in union activities at the appropriate time as the employer could hardly restrict topics of conversation. Conversely, in *Marley Tile Co Ltd v Shaw* [1980] ICR 72, a union meeting was not held with the consent of the employer who merely remained silent when informed it was to take place. It should be noted that striking or other industrial action is not taking part in trade union activities for the purposes of the section.

9.7.5 Dismissal for the use of trade union services or refusal of an inducement

The Employment Relations Act 2004 amended section 152(1) of TULR(C)A 1992 to increase the protection of employees who are dismissed if the reason or principal reason is that they had made use of, or proposed to make use of, trade union services at an appropriate time, or that they have failed to accept an inducement to come out of collective bargaining. 'Trade union services' are defined in section 152(2A) as being services made available to an employee by an independent trade union by virtue of his membership of the union, and include 'consenting to the raising of a matter on his behalf by an independent trade union of which he is a member'.

9.7.6 Dismissal in connection with recognition

The Employment Relations Act 2004 introduced a new right to be protected against unfair dismissal in respect of recognition disputes. The Act added Schedule A1 to TULR(C)A 1992. Paragraph 161 renders a dismissal of an employee automatically unfair if the reason for the dismissal was that:

- the employee acted with a view to obtaining or preventing recognition of a union;
- the employee indicated that he supported or did not support recognition of a union;
- the employee acted with a view to securing or preventing the ending of bargaining arrangements;

- the employee indicated that he supported or did not support the ending of bargaining arrangements;
- the employee influenced or sought to influence the way in which votes were to be cast by workers in a ballot in connection with recognition;
- the employee sought to influence other workers to vote or not to vote in such a ballot;
- the employee voted in such a ballot;
- the employee proposed to do, failed to do, or proposed to decline to do, any of the above.

9.7.7 Dismissal in health and safety cases

By section 100 of the ERA 1996, a dismissal will be unfair if the reason for the dismissal was that:

- the employee was a health and safety representative and performed or proposed to perform any of the functions of such; or
- there is no such representative and the employee brought to his employer's attention circumstances which the employee reasonably believed were harmful or potentially harmful to his health and safety; or
- in circumstances of danger he reasonably believed to be imminent and which he could not avert he left or proposed to leave his workplace, or refused to return to his workplace while the danger continued; or
- in circumstances of danger he reasonably believed to be imminent he took or proposed to take steps to protect himself and others from danger.

Such a dismissal will not be unfair if the employer can show that it was or would be so negligent for the employee to take those steps that a reasonable employer would have dismissed him.

Selection for redundancy for any of the above reasons is an automatically unfair redundancy.

9.7.8 Dismissal of shop workers or betting workers who refuse Sunday work

By section 101 of the 1996 Act, when a shop worker or betting worker is protected or has opted out, it is an automatically unfair dismissal to dismiss him for refusing to work on Sundays. A protected worker is one who was not contracted to work on Sundays unless he has given his employer written notice that he does not object to Sunday working (s 36). An opted-out worker is one who has given written notice to his employer that he objects to Sunday working (s 40). The dismissal is not, however, automatically unfair if the reason for the dismissal was the employee's refusal to work on a Sunday during the opted-out notice period (s 101(2)).

9.7.9 Dismissal in working time cases

Section 101A of the 1996 Act provides that it is an automatically unfair dismissal if the reason or principal reason for the dismissal was that:

- the employee refused or proposed to refuse to comply with a requirement which the employer imposed or proposed to impose in contravention of the Working Time Regulations 1998;
- the employee refused or proposed to refuse to forgo a right under those Regulations;
- the employee failed to sign or enter into, vary or extend an agreement under the Regulations; or
- as a candidate or representative under the Regulations, the employee performed or proposed to perform any functions or activities.

9.7.10 Dismissal of trustees of occupational pension schemes

By section 102 of the ERA 1996, it is an automatically unfair to dismiss an employee who is a trustee of an occupational pension scheme where the reason or principal reason for the dismissal was that the employee performed or proposed to perform any of his functions as trustee.

9.7.11 Dismissal of an employee representative

By section 103 of the 1996 Act, it is an automatically unfair dismissal if the reason or principal reason for the dismissal is that the employee is an employee representative or a candidate in an election for such a representative, and he performed or proposed to perform any functions or activities pertinent to his role.

9.7.12 Dismissal for acting as a companion

Section 12 of the Employment Relations Act 1999 renders a dismissal automatically unfair if a worker is dismissed because he has acted as a worker's companion in a disciplinary or grievance hearing.

9.7.13 Dismissal for making a protected disclosure

By section 103A of the ERA 1996, it is an automatically unfair to dismiss an employee who makes a protected disclosure under the Public Interest Disclosure Act 1998.

9.7.14 Dismissal on the grounds of assertion of a statutory right

Section 104 of the 1996 Act states that a dismissal is automatically unfair if the reason for it is that the employee brought proceedings to enforce a relevant statutory right, or alleged that the employer had infringed his relevant statutory rights. Relevant statutory rights for the purposes of the section are any rights conferred by the ERA 1996 where the remedy for infringement is a complaint to an employment tribunal, minimum notice rights (see Chapter 7), and rights in relation to union activities and rights to time off conferred by TULR(C)A 1992, including the rights to time off for union learning representatives (see Section 9.7.4), rights conferred by the Working Time Regulations 1998 (see Section 4.2.12) and rights conferred by the TUPE Regulations 2006 (see Section 9.2.5(c)). In addition, under the Part-time Workers (Prevention of Less Favourable Treatment) Regulations 2000 (Reg 7) (see Section 5.15) and the Fixed-term Employees (Prevention of Less Favourable

Treatment) Regulations 2002 (Reg 6) (see Section 5.16), it is automatically unfair to dismiss a person exercising his rights. It is irrelevant for the purposes of the section and the Regulations whether the employee has the right or not, and whether it has been infringed, as long as the allegation or proceedings were made in good faith. As before, selection for redundancy for this reason is also an automatically unfair dismissal.

9.7.15 Dismissal in national minimum wage cases

Section 104A of the ERA 1996 provides that it is an automatically unfair dismissal if the reason for the dismissal was that action was proposed or taken to enforce or secure a right under the National Minimum Wage Act 1998, the employer was prosecuted for an offence under section 31 of the Act as a result of action taken by or on behalf of the employee, or that the employee qualifies or will qualify for the national minimum wage.

9.7.16 Dismissal in tax credit cases

Similar provisions exist in section 104B of the 1996 Act in respect of an employee enforcing a right, etc under the Tax Credits Act 1999.

9.7.17 Dismissal for requesting flexible working

Section 104C of the ERA 1996 makes it an automatically unfair to dismiss an employee who has requested, or proposes to request, flexible working, or who has brought proceedings against the employer in respect of such.

9.7.18 Dismissal for jury service

Section 98B of the 1996 Act renders it an automatically unfair dismissal if the reason or the principal reason for the dismissal was that the employee had been summoned for, or had been absent attending, jury service. It will not be automatically unfair if the employer can show that the undertaking would suffer substantial injury if the employee was absent, that he made this known to the employee, and that the employee unreasonably refused or failed to apply to be excused jury service or have service deferred.

9.7.19 Dismissal for a reason relating to a prohibited list

Section 104F of the ERA 1996, introduced by the Employment Relations Act 1999 (Blacklists) Regulations 2010, makes dismissal for a reason relating to a prohibited list an automatically unfair dismissal (see Section 13.6).

9.8 Dismissal during a strike, lock-out or other industrial action

When the concept of unfair dismissal was introduced by the Industrial Relations Act 1971, the legislature decided that tribunals should have a neutral position when the reason for the dismissal was that the employee was taking industrial action; thus tribunals had no jurisdiction to hear an unfair dismissal claim unless there were selective dismissals or selective re-engagement. This used to be the position in any situation, but the Employment Act 1990 took away the tribunal's jurisdiction in any circumstance where the action was unofficial, and the provision was re-enacted in section 237 of TULR(C)A 1992. That section states that an employee has no right to complain of unfair dismissal if at the time of the dismissal he was taking part in an unofficial strike or unofficial action. Section 237(2) states that action is unofficial if it is not authorised or endorsed by the trade union. The meanings of 'authorised' and 'endorsed' are discussed in Chapter 13. Thus, in relation to unofficial action, the employee now has no protection whatsoever.

In relation to official industrial action, the starting point is section 238A of TULR(C)A 1992 (as amended by the Employment Relations Act 2004). This provides that an employee who is dismissed for taking part in protected industrial action shall be regarded as unfairly dismissed if one of the sets of circumstances below applies. Protected industrial action is action which, under section 219 of the 1992 Act, the union has lawfully organised and which is therefore protected from liability in tort for inducement to break or interfere with contracts (s 238A(1)). The circumstances are:

- the dismissal takes place within a period of 12 weeks (the basic protected period) beginning on the day the employee first took part in the industrial action; or
- the dismissal takes place after the end of that period and the employee had ceased to take industrial action before the end of that period; or
- the dismissal takes place after the end of that period, the employee had not ceased to take part in industrial action before the end of that period and the employer has not taken reasonable procedural steps for the resolution of the dispute to which the industrial action relates.

Where the employee is locked out during the action, any days of lock-out do not count towards the protected period (TULR(C)A 1992, s 238A(7C)), so if the employee is locked out for one week he is protected for a total of 13 weeks (the basic 12-week protected period plus the one week of lock-out, known as the 'extension period'). 'Dismissal' means the date on which the employer's notice was given (not the date it ended) and in other cases the effective date of termination.

In deciding whether the employer had taken reasonable procedural steps for the resolution of the dispute, regard shall be had to:

- whether procedures established by collective agreement, or any other agreement, had been complied with by the employer or union;
- whether either party offered or agreed to negotiate or resume negotiations after the start of the protected action;
- whether the employer or union unreasonably refused, after the start of the protected action, a request for conciliation services to be used;
- whether the employer or union unreasonably refused, after the start of the protected action, a request that mediation services be used in relation to the procedures to be adopted for resolving the dispute (TULR(C)A 1992, s 238A(6)).

Where the parties have agreed to use the services of a conciliator or mediator, section 238B of the 1992 Act sets out further matters to which the tribunal must have particular regard:

▶ whether the conciliation or mediation meetings have been attended on behalf of the employer and union by an appropriate person;
▶ whether the employer and union have co-operated with the conciliator or mediator in making arrangements to set up meetings;
▶ whether the employer and union have carried out any actions agreed with the conciliator or mediator and whether such actions were done in a timely manner;
▶ whether the employer and union answered all reasonable questions asked of them in meetings with all the parties.

The normal continuity rules do not apply. A claim must be presented to an employment tribunal within six months of the dismissal. A tribunal cannot order reinstatement or re-engagement until after the conclusion of the protected industrial action (TULR(C)A 1992, s 239).

If section 238A of the 1992 Act does not apply, or there is a dismissal in relation to a lock-out by the employer, then section 238 comes into play. This states that a tribunal has no jurisdiction to hear an unfair dismissal complaint unless:

▶ one or more of the relevant employees have not been dismissed; or
▶ a relevant employee has before the expiry of three months beginning with the date of his dismissal been offered re-engagement and the complainant has not been offered re-engagement.

This leads to two questions: What action is covered? And what is the definition of 'relevant employee'?

9.8.1 Action covered

Section 238 of the 1992 Act refers to a lock-out, strike or other industrial action. None of these words is defined by the 1992 Act, but definitions of 'lock-out' and 'strike' are provided in section 235(4) and (5) of the ERA 1996. Under section 235(4) of the 1996 Act:

'lock-out' means —
(a) the closing of a place of employment,
(b) the suspension of work, or
(c) the refusal by an employer to continue to employ any number of persons employed by him in consequence of a dispute,
done with a view to compelling persons employed by the employer, or to aid another employer in compelling persons employed by him, to accept terms or conditions of or affecting employment.

A 'strike' is defined in section 235(5) as:

(a) the cessation of work by a body of employed persons acting in combination, or
(b) a concerted refusal, or a refusal under a common understanding, of any number of employed persons to continue to work for an employer in consequence of a dispute,
done as a means of compelling their employer or any employed person or body of employed persons, or to aid other employees in compelling their employer or any employed person or body of employed persons, to accept or not to accept terms or conditions of or affecting employment.

While these definitions are relevant only to the 1996 Act (*Express and Star v Bunday* [1988] ICR 379), they may be used for guidance in the interpretation of other legislation. They indicate that it is important to look at not only the action, but also at the purpose behind it.

Nothing in the ERA 1996 suggests that the action must be a breach of contract. While invariably a strike or a lock-out will involve a breach, other industrial action may not. This does not mean that the employee is not taking industrial action for the purposes of section 238 of the 1992 Act. This is shown by *Power Packing Casemakers Ltd v Faust* [1983] IRLR 117, where the employees were engaged in a voluntary overtime ban. The employees were threatened with dismissal and all but three employees lifted the ban. The three employees were dismissed and the Court of Appeal, confirming the EAT, held that the employment tribunal had no jurisdiction to hear an unfair dismissal complaint as the employees were taking part in industrial action at the time of their dismissals. It was irrelevant that the employees were not in breach of contract if the object of the action was to apply pressure to the employer or disrupt the employer's business.

Section 235(5) refers to 'a cessation of work by a body of employed persons', but a wide definition was given to the phrase in *Lewis v Mason & Sons* [1994] IRLR 4. In this case an individual driver was dismissed when he refused to do an overnight trip in an unheated van in December. Other workers threatened to go on strike and they were dismissed. It was held that they were all taking part in industrial action at the time of their dismissals, even though the original driver was acting on his own when he was dismissed.

For section 238 of TULR(C)A 1992 to apply, the employee must have been taking part in a strike or industrial action. The meaning of the phrase 'taking part' has led to the courts deciding that it is the employee who must disprove that he is taking industrial action. In *Coates v Modern Methods and Materials* [1982] IRLR 318, the employee was frightened to cross picket lines, and after refusing to do so on the first day of the strike, she was then ill for the remainder of the action, although she did attend strike meetings. Despite the fact that her illness was certified, the Court of Appeal held that she was taking part in the action because she had not openly disagreed with it. By not attending work there was a presumption she was taking part which she had failed to rebut. So too in *McKenzie v Crosville Motor Services Ltd* [1989] IRLR 516, an employee and trade union member who had worked during a previous dispute but failed to show up for work during the dispute in question, was deemed to be taking part and therefore excluded from unfair dismissal protection, the EAT holding that it was an implied contractual obligation on the employee to maintain contact with his employer and disassociate himself from the action. In *Rogers v Chloride Systems* [1992] ICR 198, the employee was sick throughout the period of the dispute. The employer, in seeking to establish the intentions of his employees, sent a letter to those not at work requiring them to sign undertakings that they would return on a specific date. Rogers was telephoned at home and asked her views on the strike. She stated that if she was not sick she would support her colleagues, and when she refused to sign the undertaking she was dismissed with the rest of the strikers. She sued for an unfair dismissal. While the tribunal in the case could not make a finding because the employee had not given evidence in person, the tribunal established how an employer should deal with the situation of sick employees during a strike. If only a few employees were sick, they should be visited and their views elicited. Where there were more than a few and their views were determined by letter, then specific questions should be asked to which the employee would be required to give 'yes' or 'no' answers. These questions should ask specifically if the employee would have returned to work by the due date if he or she had not been sick, and whether the employee is prepared to return to work as soon as he or she is fit to do so.

9.8.2 Relevant employees

The tribunal will have jurisdiction if one or more of the relevant employees have not been dismissed or are re-engaged (TULR(C)A 1992, s 238(2)). The definition of 'relevant employees', however, differs depending on whether there is a lock-out, a strike or other industrial action.

9.8.2(a) Lock-out

In relation to a lock-out, 'relevant employees' mean those employees directly interested in the dispute (TULR(C)A 1992, section 238(3)(a)). This has been interpreted to mean all those employees who have been locked out at any time during the dispute. In *Campey & Sons v Bellwood* [1987] ICR 311, the company wished to bring in new working conditions and, because of the threat of industrial action, closed the factory on 18 October. On 22 October, the employers sent notices to its employees telling them to return on 24 October. Those who did not return on that date were told to return or be dismissed, and eventually a group of employees was sacked. It was held that the date of the lock-out was 18 October, and the relevant employees for the purposes of the statute were the employees locked out at that date. As some of those employees were not dismissed, there had been selective dismissals, and the tribunal had the jurisdiction to see if those dismissals were unfair.

9.8.2(b) Strike or other industrial action

In this case the definition of 'relevant employees' means those employees who at the date of the complainant's dismissal were taking part in the action (TULR(C)A 1992, s 238(3)(b)). This means that if the situation in *Campey* (Section 9.8.2(a) above) had involved a strike, the tribunal would not have had jurisdiction. The date the tribunal must look to is that of the complainant's dismissal, and it must then see if all the other employees taking part in the strike or other industrial action at that time have been dismissed. It appears, however, that as long as those other employees have been dismissed by the conclusion of the tribunal hearing, the employer will have immunity. The reason for the dismissal of the other employees appears to be irrelevant. This must be the conclusion from *McCormick v Horsepower* [1981] IRLR 217, where an employee who was taking part in the industrial action was dismissed for redundancy after the other strikers had been dismissed but before the hearing. It was held that because all the employees, including McCormick, had been dismissed, the tribunal had no jurisdiction to hear the other strikers' claims. This interpretation obviously gives the employer a great deal of leeway, as there may be a substantial time period between the date of the dismissals and the date of the hearing. In addition, the group of relevant employees is taken from the establishment at which the dismissed employee works. This means that if the employer owns two factories and employees at both go on strike, he can dismiss all the strikers at one factory while retaining those at the other, without losing the immunity from unfair dismissal proceedings.

While the majority of cases revolve around the interpretation of 'relevant employees', one case has concentrated on the interpretation of the phrase 'offered re-engagement' in section 238(2)(b) of the 1992 Act. In *Tracey v Crosville (Wales) Ltd (No 2)* [1997] IRLR 691, all 119 employees were dismissed when they went on strike. The employers then recruited replacement staff by placing advertisements in the local press and on local radio, and in jobcentres. All applications were considered, including those from the dismissed strikers, of whom 22 were re-engaged. Tracey was not re-engaged and claimed unfair dismissal.

The employers argued that the tribunal did not have jurisdiction as the advertising campaign constituted an offer of re-engagement to all the dismissed employees. It was held that a general advertising campaign did not constitute an offer of employment to any individual. The advertisements were invitations to treat. As such there had been selective re-engagement of relevant employees for the purposes of section 238 and the tribunal had the jurisdiction to hear the claim.

Should the tribunal have the jurisdiction to hear a claim, the normal standards of reasonableness apply (see Section 9.6 above). Just because the employee has been dismissed during industrial action does not mean that the employer does not have to act as a reasonable employer. In *McClaren v National Coal Board* [1988] IRLR 215, the employee allegedly committed an assault while taking part in industrial action. The employer reported the matter to the police, and after the employee was convicted the employer dismissed him. At no time had the employee been given a hearing or an opportunity to put his side of the case. The Court of Appeal held that the dismissal was unfair. The fact of industrial action did not justify failing to give the employee the opportunity of offering an explanation. The tribunal may, however, reduce the award for contributory conduct. While *TNT Express v Downes* [1993] IRLR 432, suggests that in some cases the industrial action may be contributory conduct, the Court of Appeal in *Crosville* stated that there has to be individual conduct over and above the collective industrial action, a decision confirmed by the House of Lords.

Again, if the tribunal does have the jurisdiction, the time limit is different for the presentation of a claim. The limit in a normal unfair dismissal is three months after the effective date of termination of the contract, but the tribunal does have the discretion to allow a claim outside that limit in exceptional circumstances (see Section 9.9 below). In relation to a claim under section 238 of TULR(C)A 1992, the time limit is six months (s 239), the tribunal having the same discretion to extend.

9.9 Remedies for unfair dismissal

Apart from claims under sections 238 or 238A of TULR(C)A 1992 (see Section 9.8 above), a claim for unfair dismissal must normally be presented within three months of the effective date of termination of the contract. However, by section 111(2)(b) of the ERA 1996, the tribunal may hear complaints out of time if it is satisfied that it was not reasonably practicable to present the complaint in time.

There may be a variety of reasons why the tribunal will allow a complaint to be presented outside the three-month period. In *Cavaciuti v London Borough of Hammersmith & Fulham* (1991) EAT 246/91, the EAT ruled that where the effective date of termination is ambiguous, the tribunal should take the date most favourable to the employee to see if the complaint is presented within the time period. Cavaciuti was dismissed on 4 July 1990. A letter of 6 July stated that he would be paid during his notice period but he did not have to work. After a series of letters, a final letter was sent on 19 July stating that his paid notice ended on 5 August 1990, and with his holiday entitlement he would be paid up to and including 22 August. His final payslip showed the normal deductions as if he remained a local authority employee. The issue was whether his date of termination was 5 August or 22 August. The tribunal ruled that this was not a summary dismissal with payment in lieu, as the employee had been employed during his notice period. The important letter was that of 19 July, and the natural interpretation of that letter was that the employee remained employed up to and including 22 August. Likewise, if the employee has been given incorrect advice by a competent person such as a tribunal officer, the tribunal will allow a claim out of time. We have already seen in *London International College v Sen* (Section 9.1 above) that the tribunal decides the cause of the applicant's failure to present the claim in time and that the Court of Appeal has stated that there is no cut-and-dried rule that advice given by a solicitor which is wrong does not necessarily prevent the tribunal from exercising its discretion.

In addition to erroneous advice or ambiguous termination letters, there are other situations when a tribunal will allow a late complaint. In *Rogers v Northumbria Leisure Ltd t/a Border Travel* (1990) EAT 321/90, Rogers was informed that she would be made redundant in June, but at the request of the employer she began work on a temporary contract on 3 July. On 14 August she was informed that the office would close on 31 August, and she stopped work immediately, receiving a month's pay in lieu. In January 1990 she discovered that the business was still operating, and presented a complaint to the tribunal in February 1990. She argued that it was only in January that she was aware, and could reasonably be aware, that the business was still trading. The tribunal, however, found that Rogers had visited the premises on 31 August and 12 September, therefore she knew the business was still trading on those dates and she should have enquired whether the business was actually closing down. As such, it was reasonably practicable for her to present her complaint in time. She appealed. The EAT dismissed her appeal but considered the law in this area. In *Walls Meat Co Ltd v Khan* [1979] ICR 52, it was held that it would be reasonably practicable to present a complaint in time if the fault lay in the complainant's not making the enquiries that he reasonably should. In *Palmer v Southend-on-Sea Borough Council* [1984] ICR 373, it was held that misrepresentations on the part of the employer were relevant, and in *Machine Tool Industry Research Association v Simpson* [1988] ICR 559 the tribunal held that the question to ask was whether the continuation of the business was something which was reasonably unknown to the complainant. In *Rogers*, the employee was a manageress and had been told by her employer on 31 August that he considered it worthwhile to continue trading. As such, it was reasonably practicable for Rogers to present her complaint in time.

Should the applicant be successful in his claim for unfair dismissal, there is a variety of remedies that may be awarded by the tribunal.

9.9.1   Reinstatement

Reinstatement is an order that the employer shall treat the employee in all respects as if he has not been dismissed, and it must include all the benefits payable in the period since his dismissal including seniority and pensions (ERA 1996, s 114(2)). In exercising its discretion to make an order for reinstatement, the tribunal must have regard to:

- the wishes of the complainant;
- whether it is practicable for the employer to comply with the order;
- if there is contributory conduct, whether it is just to make the order (s 116(1)).

In *Central & NW London NHS Trust v Abimbola* (2009) UKEAT 0542/08/0304, the EAT said that a tribunal should not take too narrow a view of section 116, and that the existence of trust and confidence between the employer and the ex-employee was a factor to consider when making a reinstatement order. As such, it set aside an order when there was a finding that the claimant was evasive and dishonest when giving evidence in the remedies hearing, and there were unproven allegations of misconduct prior to his dismissal.

In *Coleman v Magnet Joinery Ltd* [1974] IRLR 343, the Court of Appeal held that 'reasonably practicable' meant reasonably practicable in the industrial relations sense. A redundancy or reorganisation which has arisen after the dismissal will normally render it impracticable to order reinstatement, as will tension between the parties or the situation of a small employer who would have to work closely with the reinstated employee (*Enessy Co SA v Minoprio* [1978] IRLR 489). In the more recent case of *Arriva London Ltd v Eleftheriou* [2013] All ER (D) 60, Eleftheriou was a bus driver who was dismissed from his job in May 2010 while awaiting surgery following an injury which prevented him from driving. His claim was heard in February 2012, by which time he was fully recovered and was working for another company as a driver at a lower salary. The tribunal found that he had been unfairly dismissed as the employer had not sought medical advice before dismissing him. He asked for reinstatement which the tribunal granted . The tribunal, however, deducted 60 per cent from his compensation on the basis that if Arriva had sought medical advice, there was a 60 per cent chance that Eleftheriou's dismissal would have been fair. Arriva appealed, arguing that the orders were inconsistent, in that it was unfair to order reinstatement when there was a 60 per cent chance the dismissal would have been fair. The EAT rejected this argument. While certain factors such as employee misconduct are relevant to reinstatement, the employer's procedural failings were irrelevant to the issue. Furthermore, the fact that the claimant had another job did not prevent the tribunal from making the order.

The fact that the employer has appointed a replacement to do the employee's job does not make it impracticable to order reinstatement, unless the employer shows that it was not practicable for him to arrange for the dismissed employee's work to be done without engaging a replacement, he waited a reasonable time before engaging the replacement without having heard from the dismissed employee that he wished to be reinstated, and when he engaged the replacement it was no longer reasonable for him to arrange for the work to be done except by a replacement (ERA 1996, s 116(5) and (6)). While reinstatement is rarely ordered, if the tribunal exercises its discretion, failure to comply will lead to an additional award (see Section 9.9.3(c) below).

9.9.2   Re-engagement

If the tribunal declines to award reinstatement it must then consider re-engagement. Such an order means that the employee is returned to a comparable job rather than to his old job, but the job must be as favourable as the old (ERA 1996, s 115(2)). The job must not be more favourable, however (*Rank Xerox (UK) Ltd v Stryczek* [1995] IRLR 568).

In deciding whether to exercise its jurisdiction, the tribunal takes into account factors similar to those necessary when considering reinstatement. In *Nairne v Highland & Islands Fire Brigade* [1989] IRLR 366, the employee was found to be unfairly dismissed because of a procedural irregularity. The employee was a fireman where it was a contractual requirement that he was able to drive, and his dismissal occurred when he had been banned from driving for three years. His contributory conduct was assessed at 75 per cent, and given that it was so high and that there was no suitable alternative work, an order for re-engagement was unsuitable. However, in *Wolff v Oasis Community Learning* [2013] All

ER (D) 20, Wolff was a teacher with Oasis, which was an institution responsible for a number of schools across the country. Wolff had made allegations of misconduct against Oasis and its human resources department, and was dismissed. The dismissal which was found to be unfair and the tribunal ordered re-engagement at a different school in another part of the country. The EAT held that such an order was not impractical since it covered a different workplace and different colleagues.

9.9.3 Financial compensation

Given that orders of reinstatement or re-engagement are made in less than 1 per cent of cases, this means that the main remedy for unfair dismissal is financial compensation. Until 1999 the various heads of award were increased annually (ERA 1996, s 208, now repealed). While this is still the case, section 33 of the Employment Relations Act 1999 provides that the limits on such awards are index-linked, and thus they may rise considerably in any one year. As such, in the discussion below, the specific limits on the heads of awards will not be given.

9.9.3(a) Basic award

The basic award is to compensate the employee for the loss of his job. It is calculated in the same way as redundancy pay (see Section 10.8), and is based on the employee's age and years of service in the following way:

- service below the age of 22: half a week's pay for each year of service
- service between 22 and 41: one week's pay for each year of service
- service over the age of 41: one and a half week's pay for each year of service (ERA 1996, s 119(2)).

The above is subject to a statutory maximum weekly rate and 20 years' service. In addition, the award may be reduced for:

- conduct (whether it contributed to the dismissal or not)
- unreasonable refusal of an offer of reinstatement
- any redundancy pay received
- any ex gratia payments (ERA 1996, s 122(1), (2) and (4)).

The award cannot be reduced, however, as a result of conduct committed by the employee after his dismissal (*Soros v Davison* [1994] IRLR 264).

9.9.3(b) Compensatory award

The award is to compensate the employee for the loss he has suffered as a result of the dismissal (ERA 1996, s 123(1)). As from 29 July 2013 the figure is 52 weeks' pay or £74,200, whichever is the lower. While the award should reflect the employee's loss, it must be just and equitable in the circumstances; therefore, if the employee would have been dismissed even if the procedures had been followed, for example, the compensation will be reduced (a *Polkey* reduction – see Section 9.6.5 above). In *Hill v Governing Body of Great Tey Primary School* [2013] IRLR 274, the employment tribunal found that Hill's dismissal was unfair, but had the proper procedure been followed she would have been dismissed two months later and therefore the tribunal reduced her compensation by 80 per cent. The EAT held that the tribunal had erred in its assessment. The correct approach is to ask whether this particular employer would fairly dismiss, not whether a hypothetical fair employer would. In addition, if the employee has contributed to his own dismissal, the tribunal can rule that it is not just or equitable to grant any compensation, even if there are procedural failings on the part of the employer, according to the EAT in *Ladrick Lemonious v Church Commissioners* (2013) UKEAT 0253/12/2703.

The tribunal will look at a variety of factors when assessing compensation under this head, such as immediate loss of earnings, future loss of earnings, loss of fringe benefits, expenses in looking for work, loss of pension rights, loss of employment protection and the manner of the dismissal (*Norton Tool Co Ltd v Tewson* [1972] IRLR 86). *Norton Tool* also established that where an employee is dismissed without notice and without pay in lieu of notice, he is entitled to compensation equal to net pay for that period without deduction in respect of other earnings derived from alternative employment. However, the Court of Appeal in *Stuart Peters Ltd v Bell* [2009] EWCA Civ 938 held that the *Norton Tool* principle does not apply to employees who are constructively dismissed. Elias LJ noted that this leads to differences in compensation between those constructively dismissed and those whose contracts are terminated by the employer. He continued (at paragraph 14):

> The *Norton* principle is not designed to give full compensation during what would have been the notice period had the contract been terminated on notice. Rather it is to uphold expectations that will result from the application of good industrial relations practice where the employer has chosen to terminate the contract with no (or inadequate) notice, even where he genuinely believes that he is entitled to do so.

In the case Mrs Bell was found to have been constructively dismissed. Under her contract she was entitled to six months' notice, but under the *Norton* principle any earnings she acquired in the first six months since she resigned were not deducted from her compensatory award by the employment tribunal, a decision upheld by the EAT and reversed by the Court of Appeal. This is something which needs consideration by the Supreme Court.

Immediate loss of earnings will involve the tribunal in a calculation as to the loss between the date of the dismissal and the date of the hearing, less any unemployment or other benefits received. Future loss of earnings involves the tribunal in an estimate of how long the employee is likely to remain unemployed, given the area and the prospects of future employment. In *Cumbria County Council v Bates* [2013] All ER (D) 165, Bates was found to have been unfairly dismissed but the tribunal was made aware at the remedies hearing that he was facing prosecution for assaulting a pupil. Cumbria CC asked for a postponement of the hearing until the outcome of those proceedings. The tribunal refused, citing *Soros v Davidson* (Section 9.9.3(a) above). The EAT held that in respect of a compensatory award, Bates's subsequent conviction and imprisonment for six weeks may have affected his future job prospects, and thus the compensatory award would be substantially reduced. The case was remitted to a new tribunal.

In *James W Cook & Co (Wivenhoe) Ltd v Tipper* [1990] ICR 716, it was held that if the employee's dismissal arises from the closure of the employer's business, the future loss element should not extend beyond the date of the closure of the business. In *Dunnachie v Kingston upon Hull City Council* [2004] EWCA Civ 84, the Court of Appeal held that damages could be awarded under this head for non-economic loss such as damage to reputation or psychiatric injury. However, this was overruled by the House of Lords ([2004] UKHL 36) which held that the word 'loss' in section 123 of the ERA 1996 covered only pecuniary loss. The employee is under a duty to mitigate his loss under this head.

9.9.3(c) Additional award

Where the employer has ignored an order for reinstatement or re-engagement, the dismissal was discriminatory or the dismissal was for certain specified statutory reasons, the tribunal may make an additional award. In the case of refusing to comply with or fully comply with an order for reinstatement or re-engagement, or if a discriminatory dismissal, the award will be between 26 and 52 weeks' pay (ERA 1996, s 117(5) and (6)), subject to the statutory maximum weekly pay rate. This limit does not apply where the award would not reflect the true loss of benefits (ERA 1996, s 124(3) and (4)), so reflecting the view of Lord Donaldson MR in *O'Laoire v Jackel International Ltd* [1990] IRLR 70 that the limit can discourage employers from complying with a reinstatement order and creates injustice to higher-paid employees. An additional award may also be made when the employer takes back the employee but on terms different from the tribunal order (ERA 1996, s 117(1)(b)). In *Artisan Press v Strawley and Parker* [1986] IRLR 126, the tribunal found that two security staff had been unfairly dismissed and ordered their reinstatement. The employer re-employed them in fundamentally different jobs involving very minor security duties. The EAT held that there was no difference, when assessing the additional award, between an employer refusing to allow an employee back and an employer who did not give the employee his old job back. When assessing the award, however, the issue of practicability may be looked at again (*Port of London Authority v Payne* [1994] IRLR 9). The monetary provisions of a reinstatement order cannot be enforced through court action (*O'Laoire v Jackel International Ltd*, above).

Where the dismissal is due to membership or non-membership of a trade union or union activities, the complainant is entitled to a minimum basic award by section 156 of TULR(C)A 1992. The applicant is also entitled to a minimum basic award where the dismissal is for health and safety reasons, because the employee is a trustee of an occupational pension scheme or because the employee is an employee representative. This gives a minimum basic award plus, where reinstatement or re-engagement is not ordered, an award of 104 weeks' pay with a statutory minimum and maximum figure. Should the tribunal order reinstatement or re-engagement and the employer fails to comply, the award is 156 weeks' pay with a statutory minimum but no statutory maximum. The award may be reduced for conduct on the part of the complainant, the amount of the reduction being at the discretion of the tribunal, and the reduction being what is just and equitable according to the circumstances of the case.

9.9.3(d) Interim relief

If the dismissal is in connection with trade union activities, membership or non-membership of a trade union, or because the employee did certain actions in relation to recognition, an application may be made for interim relief under section 161 of TULR(C)A 1992 and Schedule A1, paragraph 161(2) to the same Act. Such an application may also be made if the dismissal is on health and safety grounds, or because the employee is a trustee of an occupational pension scheme, the employee made a protected disclosure or is an employee representative by section 128(1) of the ERA 1996. In all instances an application must be made within seven days of the dismissal. In the case of a dismissal on trade union grounds, the application must be supported by a signed certificate from a trade union official that there are reasonable grounds to believe that this is the true reason for the dismissal. A tribunal, if satisfied that on the hearing of the unfair dismissal complaint it will find the complaint well founded, can ask the employer if he will reinstate or re-engage the employee. If the employer so agrees, the tribunal will make an order to that effect. If the employer refuses, the tribunal may make an order for continuation of employment. Such an order preserves the employee's benefits under the contract until the case is determined or settled. Failure to comply with any order under these provisions allows the tribunal to award compensation to the employee such as is just and equitable in the circumstances, reflecting the infringement of the employee's rights and the loss he has suffered.

Summary

9.1 Unless there is an automatically unfair dismissal, at present only employees with two years' continuity who are not excluded by the legislation can claim unfair dismissal.

9.2 'Continuity' means that a contractual relationship exists for the requisite time.

9.3 The law allows certain breaks in the continuity to count in the final computation.

9.4 Depending on what is being transferred, a change of employer may or may not break continuity.

9.5 The requisite period of continuity must exist at the effective date of termination of the contract.

9.6 In addition to employer termination recognised at common law, statute recognises two other situations where a dismissal will have occurred for unfair dismissal purposes: non-renewal of a fixed-term contract and constructive dismissal.

9.7 The employer must prove he had one of the statutory five fair reasons to dismiss.

9.8 It is sufficient for the employer to prove that he had a genuine belief, based on reasonable grounds after a reasonable investigation.

9.9 'Capability' can mean inherent incapability or incapability due to illness.

9.10 Qualifications can include aptitude tests.

9.11 'Conduct' normally means conduct within the employment, but in some circumstances, conduct outside the employment may justify dismissal.

9.12 Redundancy can be automatically unfair or unfair because the employer has not acted reasonably when dismissing.

9.13 'Statutory restriction' means it is a breach of law to continue to employ the employee.

9.14 'Some other substantial reason' tends to fall into two categories: business needs and pressure from third parties.

9.15 Pressure from a union will be ignored when deciding the issue of fairness.

9.16 The tribunal must also be satisfied that the employer has acted reasonably. This involves looking at the fairness of the decision and compliance with disciplinary procedures.

Summary cont'd

9.17 'Fairness of the decision' means looking at all factors and seeing if dismissal was within the band of reasonable responses that a reasonable employer would choose.

9.18 Procedural fairness will rely heavily on the ACAS Code of Practice and the employer's own procedures.

9.19 Statute recognises some reasons are automatically unfair.

9.20 The remedies for unfair dismissal are reinstatement, re-engagement or financial compensation.

9.21 Financial compensation is divided into the basic award, the compensatory award and the additional award.

9.22 Certain employees may claim interim relief until the case is heard.

Exercises

9.1 Alf, Mike and Jack work for Coronation Products Ltd, and have done so for four years. Five weeks ago, the company decided to streamline production. It therefore looked at the shop floor workers and decided to ignore the redundancy selection policy of 'last in first out' that had been agreed with the unions. The company dismissed for reasons of redundancy all workers over the age of 50, despite the fact that many younger workers had less continuity. If the policy had been observed, Alf would have been retained, but because he is 52 years old, he has been selected for redundancy. There is an internal appeals procedure which all employees can use to appeal against selection for redundancy. Coronation Products has refused to allow any of the selected men to use the procedure on the basis that nothing they could say would alter the decision. Alf has been told he may not use the procedure.

Mike and Jack were caught fighting by Mr Ogden, the personnel manager. Red, the trade union representative, dislikes both men because they disagree with how he negotiates for his members. Mr Ogden investigates the fight, and having got Red's version of events (he was one of 10 witnesses), Mr Ogden dismisses Mike and Jack. There is an internal appeals procedure. Mike chooses not to use the procedure, but Jack appeals. The appeal panel consists of senior managers. On the evidence, they decide that as it is difficult to apportion blame for the fight, Jack's appeal against dismissal on that ground should be upheld. However, there has been a problem of stock shortages in Jack's department and Jack has been suspected of being responsible. The appeal therefore endorses Jack's dismissal on the grounds of the stock shortages.

Advise Alf, Mike and Jack in respect of unfair dismissal.

9.2 Unfair dismissal is perhaps a misnomer. It would be truer to call it unreasonable dismissal, since it is the concept of reasonableness which causes most employers to lose their cases. However, the new statutory procedures may render the common law concepts a thing of the past. Discuss.

Further reading and references

Anderman, 'The Interpretation of Protective Employment Statutes and Contracts of Employment' (2000) 29 ILJ 223

Bowers and Clarke, 'Unfair Dismissal and Managerial Prerogative: A Study of "other substantial reason"' (1981) 10 ILJ 34

Bowers and Lewis, 'Non-Economic Damage in Unfair Dismissal Cases: What's Left After *Dunnachie*?' (2005) 34 ILJ 83

Brodie, 'Fair Dealing and the Disciplinary Process' (2002) 31 ILJ 294

Ewing and Hendy, 'Unfair Dismissal Law Changes Unfair?' (2012) 41 ILJ 115

McMullen, 'An Analysis of the TUPE Regulations 2006' (2006) 35 ILJ 113

Morris, 'Fundamental Rights: Exclusion by Agreement?' (2001) 30 ILJ 49

Pollard, 'Pensions and TUPE' (2005) 34 ILJ 127

Reynold and Palmer, 'Proving Constructive Dismissal: Should One Be Concerned with What Was in the Employer's Mind?' (2005) 34 ILJ 96

Sargeant, 'TUPE – The Final Round (2006)' JBL 549

Vickers, 'Unfair Dismissal and Human Rights' (2004) 33 ILJ 52

Chapter 10

Redundancy

10.1 Introduction

Compensation for redundancy was one of the first employment protection rights introduced into British law. The first piece of legislation was the Redundancy Payments Act 1965. The law is now contained in the main in the Employment Rights Act (ERA) 1996. The aim of a redundancy payment has never been to cushion a person over a period of unemployment but rather to recognise an employee's stake in his job. This means that it is irrelevant if the employee has another job to go to once he has been made redundant; he is still entitled to a redundancy payment. In addition, the employee's stake increases the longer he has worked for the employer, and as such his payment increases with age and years of service. A redundancy payment is calculated in the same way as the basic award in unfair dismissal (see Section 9.9.3(a)).

10.2 Qualification to claim

In order to claim a redundancy payment an employee must have two years' continuous service and be dismissed for reasons of redundancy. The requirements and complications in continuity have been previously discussed (see Section 9.2). In addition, the same classes of employee are excluded from claiming a redundancy payment as are excluded from claiming unfair dismissal (see Section 9.3).

The definition of 'dismissal' for redundancy purposes is contained in section 136 of the ERA 1996. The situations in which an employee is 'dismissed' are the same as for unfair dismissal, that is:

employer termination with or without notice;
a fixed-term contract expiring; and
constructive dismissal.

In addition, by section 139(4), if the employment is terminated by the death, dissolution or liquidation of the employer, or the appointment of a receiver, there is a dismissal for reasons of redundancy. Entitlement to claim, however, is dependent on the dismissal being because of redundancy and not for any other reason. In *Saunders v Earnest A. Neale Ltd* [1974] IRLR 236, the employees conducted a work-to-rule. The employer sacked them and eventually the factory closed down. It was held that there was not a dismissal for redundancy; the work-to-rule had caused the dismissals, which had in turn led to the factory closing down, and not the other way round. There is a statutory presumption in section 163(2) that if an employee is dismissed and claims a redundancy payment, the dismissal is for reasons of redundancy, and it falls to the employer to rebut the presumption. In *Willcox v Hastings* [1987] IRLR 298, two employees worked for an employer who sold the business to a married couple. The new owners wanted only one employee so that one of the existing employees would be redundant. However, the new owners intended that their son should work for them, and so dismissed both of the original employees. They stated that one of the employees was redundant but did not specify which one. The Court of Appeal held that both were entitled to a redundancy payment. The presumption arose in respect of both employees, and the new employers had not rebutted the presumption in relation to either of them.

The definition of 'redundancy' is found in section 139(1) of the 1996 Act. This states that a redundancy has occurred if the employee's dismissal is wholly or mainly attributable to:

1. the fact that his employer has ceased, or intends to cease, to carry on the business for the purposes for which the employee was employed by him, or has ceased, or intends to cease, to carry on that business in the place where the employee was so employed; or
2. the fact that the requirements of that business for employees to carry out work of a particular kind, or for employees to carry out work of a particular kind in the place where the employee was so employed, have ceased or diminished or are expected to cease or diminish.

This means that redundancy occurs in three situations:

the employer's ceasing business;
the employer's moving his place of business; or
the employer's reducing his labour force.

10.3 Definition of redundancy

10.3.1 Cessation of business

Where there is a closedown of the business there are few legal problems. The tribunal is merely required to see if in fact the business has been shut down and is not required to look at the reasons behind the closure (*Moon v Homeworthy Furniture (Northern)* [1976] IRLR 298).

10.3.2 Moving place of business

Where the employer moves his place of business or closes down in one particular place but continues elsewhere, there is a redundancy for the purposes of the 1996 Act. Two points should be noted, however. First, the move must be substantial and affect the employee's travelling costs and so on. In *Managers (Holborn) Ltd v Hohne* [1977] IRLR 230, the employee was employed at Holborn and the employers moved premises to Regent Street which was a short distance away. It was held that there was no redundancy situation. Both premises were in central London and neither the applicant's work nor travelling expenses were affected by the move. Second, before deciding whether the move constitutes a redundancy, it is necessary to see if the employee has a mobility clause in his contract. The phrase 'in the place where the employee was so employed' in section 139(1) means the place where the employee can be required to work under his contract, according to the court in *United Kingdom Atomic Energy Authority v Claydon* [1974] IRLR 6. This means that if there is a clause requiring the employee to work at any of the employer's establishments, on the face of it the employee will be in breach of contract if he refuses to move, and his dismissal will be for disobedience to lawful, reasonable orders rather than for redundancy. The contract must require the employee to move, however, in the particular situation. In *Provincial Insurance plc v Loxley* (1990) EAT 161/90, the employee had been employed by the company in a variety of locations, but in 1977 was moved to East Grinstead where he had settled. His son was to sit GCSE examinations in June 1989 and the employee was told that, because of a restructuring of the company, he would be required to move to Reading in July 1989. The employee's contract contained a mobility clause, but with a provision that this would not be enforced against employees who produced evidence of hardship. Examples of hardship included children who were about to sit public examinations. The employee refused to move because his son wished to proceed to A-levels, and so he resigned and took up employment elsewhere. The employee claimed a redundancy payment. The tribunal, relying on the case of *Marley v Forward Trust Group Ltd* [1986] IRLR 369, held that where there was a mobility clause and a redundancy clause, the two could not coexist and the redundancy clause predominated. The Employment Appeal Tribunal (EAT) held that the tribunal had misdirected itself, and while on the interpretation of the contract in *Marley* the redundancy clause had overridden the mobility provision, the Court of Appeal in that case did not say that as a matter of law this would always be so. The tribunal had to decide whether the employee fell within the hardship provisions of the mobility clause to see if he was required to move or not. The case was therefore remitted back. The decision demonstrates that even an express mobility clause may not be enforced against an employee in some circumstances (see also *United Bank v Ahktar*, Chapter 3).

If there is no mobility clause in the contract, the courts will rarely imply one unless that is the way the contract has been worked by the parties in the past. In *O'Brien v Associated Fire Alarms* [1968] 1 WLR 1916, the employee had always worked within commuting distance of Liverpool. His work was administered from the Liverpool office which was part of the north-western area of the employer's business. Because of a reduction in work in Liverpool, the employer tried to move the employees from Liverpool to Barrow-in-Furness (some 120 miles away), arguing that Barrow was still within the region and that there was an implied term that the employees would work anywhere within the region. The Court of Appeal would only imply a term that the employee should work within daily travelling distance of his home. By contrast, in *McAndrew v Prestwick Circuits Ltd* [1988] IRLR 514, the employee was taken on in 1975 and the employers acquired another factory some 15 miles away in 1983. All the contracts of new employees after that date contained mobility clauses, but in practice employees worked between the two factories, regardless of whether there was a mobility clause or not. The Court of Session held that there was an implied mobility clause in McAndrew's contract.

Even if there is no mobility clause, express or implied, if the job at another site is deemed to be an offer of suitable, alternative employment and the employee unreasonably refuses it, he will disentitle himself to a redundancy payment (see Section 10.5 below).

10.3.3 Excess labour

This is probably the most difficult provision within the statute. Section 139(1)(b) of the 1996 Act refers to the requirements of the employer for employees to carry out 'work of a particular kind', and it is this phrase which has caused the most problems. The first point to note is that the statute talks about the employer's requirements for employees. It therefore follows that if the employer no longer requires employees to do the tasks because, for example, he is putting out the work to self-employed people, the requirements of the employer for employees has ceased (*Bromby v Hoare & Evans* [1972] ICR 113). Apart from that obvious fact, the questions for the tribunal are: What is the particular work for which the employee is employed, and have the employer's requirements for that work ceased or diminished? In *Vaux Breweries Ltd v Ward* [1968] ITR 385, the employer decided to replace barmaids with bunny girls. The question was whether the work of the bunny girls was of a different kind from that of Ward, an older barmaid who was dismissed. The answer had to be 'No'. The work had not changed, merely the type of person that the employer required to do that work. So too in *North Riding Garages v Butterwick* [1967] 2 QB 56, the employee had been a manager of a garage for 30 years. He had always been heavily involved in the repair work of the garage, but the new owners wanted him to do much more paperwork and less of the practical work. The manager was not very good at the paperwork and after eight months he was dismissed. He argued that the employer now needed a different type of manager and that he was redundant. The court held that the tasks of a manager had been reallocated but essentially the work remained the same. The new employer had merely introduced different methods of doing the same job, and the employee was dismissed for reasons of incompetence (see also *Hindle v Percival Boats* [1969] 1 WLR 174). In *Safeway Stores plc v Burrell* [1997] IRLR 200, the EAT stated that tribunals have to ask themselves three questions: Was the employee dismissed? If so, had the requirements of the employer's business for employees to carry out work of a particular kind ceased or diminished? If so, was this diminution in the requirement for employees the reason for the dismissal? This was applied when an employee was dismissed because the employer decided that he required someone with more experience, the EAT holding that the dismissal was for redundancy (*BBC v Farnworth* (1998) IDS Brief 624).

While normally a change in emphasis in the tasks comprising the job will not be a redundancy, in rare situations the court may find that the change in emphasis means that the employer does require different work. In *Murphy v Epsom College* [1985] ICR 80, the employee was employed as a general plumber. The employer updated the heating system by introducing an electronic control system, and Murphy was made redundant on the basis that the employer now needed a heating technician who could deal with both electrics and plumbing rather than a general plumber. The Court of Appeal upheld the tribunal's decision that Murphy was redundant. It has also been held that night-shift work as opposed to day-shift work is work of a particular kind, and therefore moving night work into daytime hours is a redundancy (*Macfisheries Ltd v Findlay* [1985] ICR 160).

The starting point to discover what kind of work the employee is employed to do will be his job duties under his contract. This could mean that if there is a wide flexibility clause, the employee can never be redundant because there will always be work he is contracted to do. However, the courts have limited the application of flexibility clauses by stating that they must be interpreted by reference back to the main job duties (*Haden Ltd v Cowan* [1982] IRLR 314).

At one time it was thought that a change in the terms of the contract meant that the employer now required a different type of work. In *Chapman v Goonvean & Rostowrack China Clay Ltd* [1973] 1 WLR 678, seven employees resigned and claimed constructive dismissal by reason of redundancy when works transport which was provided by the employer ceased when it became uneconomic to run. Although the terms of the contract had changed, this did not mean that the type of work required by the employer had changed, according to the Court of Appeal. The employer still required seven employees, and had taken on seven new employees to replace the ones who had resigned. This appears to be the test. Does the employer still need the same number of employees to do that particular type of work? If the work is increasing, but the employer requires fewer employees to do the work (for example, because of new technology), there is a redundancy situation. Conversely, if there is a reorganisation, but overall the employer still needs the same number of employees to do that particular work, there is no redundancy. In *Johnson v Nottinghamshire Combined Police Authority* [1974] IRLR 20, two women had worked as clerks from 9.30 am to 5.30 pm. The authority wanted them to work shifts, from 8 am to 3 pm and from 1 am to 8 am. Both women refused and were dismissed. The Court of Appeal held that there was no redundancy. The employer still required two employees doing the same amount of work, albeit at different times. It follows, therefore, that if a dismissed employee is replaced, the dismissal cannot be for redundancy because the requirements of the employer have not diminished. This is also the case if the employer takes on extra staff in the hope of increased production which never materialises (*O'Hare v Rotaprint Ltd* [1980] IRLR 47). In *Shawkat v Nottingham City Hospital NHS Trust (No 2)* [2001] IRLR 555, the Court of Appeal held that the mere fact of a reorganisation, as a result of which the employer requires employees to do a different job, is not conclusive of redundancy. The tribunal must then decide whether there is a change in the requirements of the employer for employees to carry out work of a particular kind.

Lastly, under these provisions, redundancy must be the whole or the main reason for the dismissal. Therefore, if the employer decided to redeploy the redundant employee and give him another employee's job, the employee who was eventually dismissed could claim a redundancy payment as redundancy was the reason for his dismissal, even though it was not his job which was made redundant (*North Yorkshire County Council v Fay* [1985] IRLR 247). This is the situation known as 'bumping'. A later case, however, has now placed doubt on this interpretation. In 1997 in the case of *Safeway Stores plc v Burrell* (above), the EAT said that a bumped dismissal was a redundancy because the dismissal is caused by a diminution in the requirements of the employer for employees to carry out work of a particular kind and it was irrelevant that there was not a diminution in the kind of work the dismissed employee was employed to do. However, in *Church v West Lancashire NHS Trust* [1998] IRLR 492, the EAT reconsidered bumped redundancies and the meaning of the words 'work of a particular kind'.

In the case, Church was employed in a particular department where the Trust decided that there had to be some redundancies. As no one volunteered for redundancy, the Trust decided to interview staff for the retained jobs, and those who failed the interview would be made redundant. Church was told that he would have to attend interviews for two posts available to him, one of which was his own. The union was not happy at the way the redundancies were being handled and advised their members not to take part in the interviews. As a result, Church did not attend and was deemed to have failed the interview; he was made redundant. He claimed that he had been unfairly dismissed. The employment tribunal found that although Church's post existed after the reorganisation, it was filled by an employee who would otherwise have been made redundant, therefore Church had been bumped out of his job and was therefore dismissed by reason of redundancy. The tribunal also found, however, that he had been fairly selected in that there had been proper consultation before his dismissal. Church appealed, arguing that he had not been dismissed by reason of redundancy.

The EAT regarded the previous decisions on bumped redundancies and concluded that it was not bound by any Court of Appeal decisions in the area. In the tribunal's opinion, 'work of a particular kind' in section 139 of the 1996 Act meant work of the kind done by the employee being made redundant. The appeal tribunal said that it was a matter of causation. The reason for the bumped employee's dismissal was not redundancy but the application of a procedure which required the dismissal of that employee in order for the employer to complete a reorganisation. Church's dismissal was not wholly attributable to a diminution in the employer's requirements; rather it was attributable to the method selected by the employer to handle the redundancy situation. The EAT also stated that the test for deciding whether the employee was employed to do work of a particular kind was a mixture of a functional and a contractual approach, as stated by the Court of Appeal in *High Table Ltd v Horst* [1997] IRLR 513. As such, Church's appeal was allowed.

The contractual test looks at the work specified in the employee's contract; the functional test looks at the work the employee was actually doing. While in *Safeway Stores plc v Burrell* the EAT laid emphasis on the contractual test to establish the particular kind of work that the employee undertook, *Horst* and *Church* both talk of a mixture of the two tests, which is a more flexible approach. This was endorsed by the House of Lords decision in *Murray v Foyle Meats Ltd* [1999] IRLR 562. In this case the employees worked as meat plant operatives. They normally worked in the slaughter hall, but under their contracts they could be required to work elsewhere and had occasionally done so. Because of a decline in business, the employers had decided that fewer employees were needed in the slaughter hall and the applicants were made redundant. The applicants argued that the selection pool was too narrow. As they were required to work elsewhere under their contracts, selection should have been across the whole of the business and not just the slaughter hall. The House of Lords upheld the original tribunal decision that the requirements of the employer for employees to work in the slaughter hall had diminished and that this was the reason that the applicants were redundant. The pool for selection was therefore correct. Lord Irvine LC, however, commented that:

> both the contract test and the function test miss the point. The key word in [section 139(1) of the ERA 1996] is 'attributable' and there is no reason in law why the dismissal of an employee should not be attributable to a diminution in the employer's need for employees irrespective of the terms of his contract or the function he performed.

This, it is suggested, goes further than the previous decisions and looks to the cause of the employee's dismissal.

The main criticism of the decision in *Church* is that it leaves employees in Church's position with no redress. Church wanted to dispute the employer's redundancy claim to strengthen his complaint of unfair dismissal, but given the 'some other substantial reason' category of fair dismissal (see Section 9.6.12), it is likely any dismissal of bumped employees would be found to be fair. Furthermore, the procedure used in Church's case to select for redundancy, that is, getting employees to apply for their own jobs, is becoming a more common way of selecting those to be dismissed. If they are not dismissed for redundancy and the dismissal is fair for 'some other substantial reason', this decision leaves those employees with no compensation for the loss of their jobs. The wider definition given by Lord Irvine LC in *Murray* may allow a bumping situation to constitute a redundancy. Thus in *Contract Bottling Ltd v Cave* (2013) UKEAT 0525/12/DM, the claimants worked in the accounts department and were dismissed when they were put into a redundancy pool, the four lowest-scoring employees being dismissed for redundancy regardless of job function. Remaining staff were retrained to fill the gaps. Cave's job still existed, but as he was one of the lowest-scoring employees he was dismissed and another employee trained to take his place. The EAT applying, *Murray v Foyle Meats*, held that this was a dismissal for redundancy as a form of bumping had taken place. Furthermore, in the EAT decision in *Leventhal Ltd v North* (2004) EAT 0265/04, the EAT said that in a redundancy situation employers should consider bumping a more junior colleague and offering the job to a more senior member of staff at risk of redundancy. The case concerned a publishing firm in severe financial difficulties, and the quickest way of reducing overheads was to make the senior editor's job redundant. At no time did the company consider making the subordinate editor redundant and offering the job, with less pay, to the senior editor. The EAT held that the company had acted unfairly. While an unfair dismissal case, this clearly shows that bumping not only falls within the definition of redundancy, but also that an employer may face an unfair dismissal claim if it fails to consider it.

10.4 Misconduct and redundancy

Section 140(1) of the ERA 1996 provides that in certain situations the employee will be disentitled to a redundancy payment. This occurs when the employer terminates the contract where:

1. the employee commits an act of misconduct and the employer dismisses without notice; or
2. the employee commits an act of misconduct and the employer dismisses with shorter notice than the redundancy notice; or
3. the employer, when the redundancy notice expires, gives the employee a statement in writing that the employer is entitled, by virtue of the employee's conduct, to dismiss without notice.

In such cases the dismissal is for reason of the employee's conduct and not redundancy.

There are two exceptions to section 140(1). By section 140(2), where an employee, while under notice of redundancy, takes part in a strike or other industrial action, section 140(1) does not apply. This allows employees to take industrial action to protest against the redundancies. If, however, an employee who is on strike is selected for redundancy, the tribunal will have no jurisdiction to hear the case unless it falls within the special provisions on unfair dismissal (*Simmons v Hoover Ltd* [1977] QB 284). By section 143 of the 1996 Act, the employer can extend the redundancy notice period and require the employees to work in order to make up the days lost by the industrial action; and if the employees refuse, they disentitle themselves to a redundancy payment. By section 140(3), if an employee while under notice of redundancy commits an act of misconduct and is dismissed for this misconduct, the tribunal may award him such part of his redundancy payment as the tribunal considers just and equitable. The employee must have actually committed the misconduct however; a reasonable belief by the employer is insufficient. In *Bonner v Gilbert (H) Ltd* [1989] IRLR 475, an employee, while under notice of redundancy, was dismissed for suspected dishonesty. The tribunal held that as the employer genuinely believed in the employee's guilt, what is now section 140(3) applied. The EAT held that the test for the section was whether the employee was actually guilty and not the employer's belief in his guilt. What is now section 140(3) did not apply and the employee was entitled to a redundancy payment. Thus an employee who commits an act of misconduct during notice of redundancy may get some, if not all, of his redundancy payment, whereas the employee who has committed misconduct before being given notice of redundancy and is then made redundant will get nothing if he is dismissed with short notice or the employer gives the necessary statement.

10.5   Suitable alternative employment

If the employer offers the employee his old job back or a different job which is suitable alternative employment, the new contract starts on the termination of the old contract or within four weeks of the old contract's expiring, and the employee unreasonably refuses the offer, he is disentitled to a redundancy payment by section 141(2) and (3) of the ERA 1996. The provisions therefore mean that two questions must be asked: Is the offer of suitable alternative employment? And is the employee's refusal of that offer unreasonable?

The first question is an objective one based on all the circumstances. Obviously, if the employer offers the employee his old job back, it must be an offer of suitable alternative employment. If the employer offers a different job, however, a variety of factors must be looked at together to see if the employment is suitable. For example, the alternative work may be at a lower salary but include a bonus which will offset the difference. It may involve extra travelling expenses but give a higher salary, or the employer may be prepared to pay travelling expenses. A drop in status or responsibility will often mean that the offer is unsuitable even if salary is unaffected. In *Taylor v Kent County Council* [1969] 2 QB 560, the headmaster of a boys' secondary school was, on its closure, offered a post in a pool of mobile staff at the same salary. It was held that the drop in status meant that the offer was unsuitable (see also *Cambridge & District Co-operative Society Limited v Ruse* [1993] IRLR 156). The court said in *Carron Co v Robertson* (1967) ITR 484 that all factors should be considered, such as the nature of the work, hours and pay, the employee's strength and training, experience and ability, and status in the employer's premises. Thus in *Standard Telephones & Cables v Yates* [1981] IRLR 21, an offer of unskilled assembly work was unsuitable alternative employment for a skilled card-wirer. One thing which is clear, however, is that the employer must actually offer alternative work and that work must be specific. In *Curling v Securicor Ltd* [1992] IRLR 549, the employers lost a contract to provide security at a detention centre. The employees' contracts contained wide mobility clauses, and after the loss of the contract at the detention centre, the employer circulated a list of alternative jobs and interviewed employees as to whether they were prepared to accept any of them. No attempt was made to invoke the mobility clause. Curling left to take up employment with the company that gained the contract at the detention centre, and claimed a redundancy payment. The company argued that Curling had resigned because he had refused to comply with the mobility clause. The EAT held that there was a dismissal. The employer had not attempted to invoke the mobility clause at the time and could not do so as an afterthought. As such, there was a dismissal and the employer had sought to offer alternative work. The offers, however, were not of suitable alternative employment. No specific offers had been made, merely a list distributed which contained a multiplicity of insufficiently specified jobs.

If the offer is unsuitable, that is the end of the matter and the employee is entitled to a redundancy payment. If the offer is deemed to be suitable then the employee will still be so entitled if his refusal is reasonable in the circumstances. While the court will look at features of the job to see if it is suitable, when looking at the employee's refusal it will examine broader issues, for example the employee's domestic circumstances. In *Paton, Calvert & Co v Westerside* [1979] IRLR 108, the employee, who was under notice of redundancy, was offered his old job back when his employers got a Temporary Employment Subsidy from the government. The employee was 61 years old and had already found a new permanent job. His refusal was held to be reasonable. The offer was of temporary work and, given his age and the difficulty a person of his age had in getting work, the permanent nature of the job he had accepted was very important. Note, however, *Devon Primary Care Trust v Readman* [2013] EWCA Civ 1110. Readman was a senior manager in community nursing. In November, due to a restructuring, she was told that her job was at risk. She completed her statutory trial period (see Section 10.6 below) at a lower grade as a community nursing manager, but felt that the post was unsuitable and resigned. She was then offered a job at her original grade as a matron, but she refused the post because she did not want to work in a hospital. The EAT held that the position was suitable, but Readman's refusal was within the band of reasonable responses as her career was in community nursing and she did not want to go back into a hospital. As such the original tribunal decision was plainly wrong. The Court of Appeal, however, held that the band of reasonable responses test was inappropriate for section 141 cases and remitted the case to another tribunal.

A personal fad will not render the refusal reasonable. In *Fuller v Stephanie Bowman Ltd* [1977] IRLR 7, the employer moved offices from Mayfair to Soho. The employee refused to move because the new office was above a sex shop. The tribunal found that the refusal to move was based on undue sensitivity and was unreasonable in the circumstances.

10.6 Trial period in new employment

If the terms of the new contract differ (wholly or in part) from those of the old contract then, by section 138 of the 1996 Act, the employee is entitled to a trial period. By section 138(3), the statutory trial period is four weeks, but this may be extended by the employee's contract as long as the period is in writing and specified precisely. If the employee is dismissed during the trial period, he is treated as being dismissed for the reason his original contract ended, that is redundancy, and on the date his original contract ended, so entitling him to claim a redundancy payment. If the employee resigns, he is treated as dismissed for redundancy unless his resignation was unreasonable. The four weeks is interpreted strictly and means four calendar weeks, whether the employee worked or not. In *Benton v Sanderson Kayser Ltd* [1989] IRLR 19, four calendar weeks ended on 18 January. The employee resigned on 19 January when he had worked less than four weeks because of the Christmas break. It was held that he had lost his entitlement to a redundancy payment. If, however, the employer does not terminate the employee's old contract but merely moves him to different work, then there is a variation which the employee can accept or reject. At common law, he will be entitled to a reasonable period of time to make up his mind, and this may well exceed four weeks. In *Shields Furniture Ltd v Goff* [1973] ICR 187, the employees were transferred because of lack of work in their own department and left after more than four weeks. Their employer had never terminated their old contracts. The EAT held that at common law they were entitled to a reasonable period of time to see if they accepted the variation. After that acceptance they were entitled to the statutory four-week trial period, and if they resigned before that period had expired, they were entitled to a redundancy payment. In *McKindley v William Hill (Scotland) Ltd* [1985] IRLR 492, it was held that this meant that a resignation 12 months after the employee was moved to another job entitled him to a redundancy payment.

10.7 Lay-off and short-time working

In order to prevent redundancies, the employer may temporarily lay off his workers or put them on short time. By section 147 of the ERA 1996, a lay-off is where no work or pay is provided by the employer. Short-time working is where less than half a week's pay is earned. By section 148, where the lay-off or short time has lasted for more than four consecutive weeks, or six weeks in any 13 weeks, the employee may give notice to his employer that he intends to claim a redundancy payment. He must give the notice in writing and he must give the correct notice needed to terminate his contract. The employer has a defence if he can show that he reasonably expects to provide full-time work for the next 13 weeks, and if he raises this defence in a written counter-notice served within seven days of the receipt of the employee's intention to claim.

10.8 Redundancy compensation

A redundancy payment is calculated in the same way as the basic award for unfair dismissal (see Section 9.9.3(a)) and is therefore based on age and years of service. Unlike the basic award, there is no deduction for contributory conduct.

To make a claim, the employee must have two years' continuous employment at the relevant date. The problems involved with the calculation of the period of continuity have already been discussed in Chapter 9. Should the employee claim unfair redundancy and be successful, any redundancy payment is deducted from the basic award to prevent double compensation (ERA 1996, s 122(4)). If the payment exceeds the basic award it is also set off against the compensatory award (*Roadchef Ltd v Hastings* [1987] IRLR 142).

The employer must give his redundant employee a written statement setting out how his redundancy compensation has been calculated (ERA 1996, s 158). Failure to do so renders the employer liable to a fine.

If the redundancy is caused by the employer's insolvency, the employee may make a claim for a redundancy payment to the Department for Work and Pensions under section 166 of the 1996 Act. While the employee ranks as a preferential creditor in his employer's insolvency, this will not be much use if the employer has no assets, and therefore additionally the Department may pay certain sums directly to the employee from the National Insurance Fund. The following payments may be made from the Fund (ERA 1996, s 184):

up to eight weeks' wages, including guarantee pay, medical suspension pay, maternity suspension pay, pay for statutory time off and a protective award, up to the existing statutory maximum weekly pay in a redundancy calculation;

minimum pay during notice under section 86 of the ERA 1996 (subject to statutory weekly maximum);

up to six weeks' holiday pay accumulated in the previous 12 months (subject to statutory weekly maximum);

basic award issued by a tribunal;

reimbursement of fees paid for apprenticeship or articles (subject to statutory weekly maximum).

10.9 Consultation

We have already seen in Chapter 9 that a failure to consult and warn the employee about his redundancy may render the dismissal unfair. In addition to the procedural requirements for unfair dismissal, statute creates an obligation on employers to consult with unions or elected employee representatives in certain cases of redundancy. The original legislative provisions were contained in the Employment Protection Act 1975, which was implemented to give effect to the EC Directive on the Approximation of Laws Relating to Redundancies (EEC/75/129). The relevant provision is now section 188 of TULR(C)A 1992 (as amended). The amendments were enacted after *Commission for European Communities v United Kingdom of Great Britain and Northern Ireland* [1994] ICR 664, which held that the provisions on consultation did not fully implement EC Directives EEC/75/129 (above) or 77/187 (Acquired Rights Directive), in that they did not provide for consultation where there was not an independent recognised trade union. The original provisions created an obligation on the employer to consult with independent recognised trade unions before the redundancies occurred. Amendments in 1995, 1999 and 2014 now provide that the employer is under a duty to consult with representatives of an independent recognised trade union, or employee representatives where there is no independent recognised trade union, where he proposes to dismiss as redundant 20 or more employees at one establishment in 45 days or less. However, the EAT, in *AEI Cables v GMB* (2013) UKEAT 0375/12/0504, has stated that a tribunal must also look to practicalities, and if the employer is insolvent and cannot lawfully trade for the full period then a shorter period is more appropriate. In so finding, it overturned a protective award granted to each employee by the tribunal for 90 days (the old consultation period) and substituted a 60-day protective award.

It should be noted that the government at the time of the amendments took the opportunity to remove from consultation provisions the situation where fewer than 20 employees are being dismissed for redundancy, a removal unsuccessfully challenged by the trade union movement (*R v Secretary of State for Trade and Industry, ex parte UNISON* [1996] IRLR 438). However, problems where there is an establishment with fewer than 20 employees may be seen in *USDAW v Ethel Austin Ltd (in administration)* [2013] IRLR 686 (the 'Woolworth case'). When Woolworths and Ethel Austin became insolvent there was collective consultation. Each store was treated as a separate establishment, and thus there was consultation only at stores which employed more than 20 employees. McMullen J stated that section 188 of the 1992 Act does not accurately reflect the Acquired Rights Directive (which does not refer to single establishments) and that there should be a purposive interpretation of section 188. The employers should have consulted with all of the employees, as employers cannot get out of their duty to consult by employing small numbers of employees at different establishments throughout the country. As such all employees were entitled to a protective award. Leave has been given for the Secretary of State to appeal the decision.

At the time of the amendments, protection from detrimental treatment and dismissal was introduced for employee representatives (see Chapters 7 and 9).

The statutory definition of an 'independent trade union' is given in section 5 of TULR(C)A 1992. The concept of a recognised trade union is wider than that of a union recognised under the statutory procedure (see Chapter 12). Section 178(3) of the 1992 Act states that 'recognition' means the recognition of the union by the employer, to any extent, for the purposes of collective bargaining, and collective bargaining is defined in section 178(1) as negotiations relating to or connected with one or more of a list of specified matters.

Where there is no written agreement, the question of recognition is a question of fact for the tribunal. In *NUTGW v Charles Ingram & Co Ltd* [1977] IRLR 147, it was held that the tribunals should consider five points when deciding if a union is recognised for the purposes of the statute:

1. Recognition is a mixed question of law and fact.
2. Recognition requires mutuality.
3. There must be an express or implied agreement for recognition to exist.
4. If an agreement is implied, there must be clear conduct to establish the agreement, usually over a period of time.
5. There can be partial recognition for some purposes but not all.

Thus, in the case, the employer was a member of a trade association which bargained with the union, the manager had discussed terms and conditions with the union official over a substantial period of time, and the firm had stated on a government form that the union was recognised. All of these factors indicated that the employer recognised the union for collective bargaining purposes. On the other hand, it would appear that, in the absence of a written agreement, membership of a trade association which has negotiated with the union is not sufficient for recognition (*National Union of Gold, Silver and Allied Trades v Albury Brothers Ltd* [1979] ICR 84); likewise one-off negotiations on particular topics do not constitute recognition.

As noted above, if there is no recognised independent trade union, the employer is required to consult with elected employee representatives. Original amendments in 1995 did not specify the criteria for how the election of such representatives was to be conducted – it was up to the employer to choose. Further amendments in 1999 now require the employer to make suitable arrangements for the election and take reasonable steps to ensure that it is carried out sufficiently early enough for information to be given and consultation to take place in good time (TULR(C)A 1992, s 188(7A)). While it is up to the employer to decide the number of representatives to be elected and the amount of time they serve, the number must be sufficient to represent all of the employees properly, and the period of office must be long enough to complete the consultation (s 188(A)(1)(b) and (d)). The representatives must be members of the affected workforce (s 188(A)(1)(e)) and no one who is a member of the affected workforce may be unreasonably excluded from standing for election (s 188(A)(1)(f)). Everyone who is a member of the affected workforce must have a right to vote and the voting must be in secret (s 188(A)(1)(g) and (h)). In the event of a dispute as to the validity of the election, any of the affected employees may complain to a tribunal, and the burden is on the employer to show that the election conditions were complied with (s 189(1) and (1B)). The definition of 'affected employees' was also changed in 1999 and now includes any employee who may be affected by the redundancies and not only those who will be dismissed (s 188(1)).

Further amendments made by the Collective Redundancies and Transfer of Undertakings (Protection of Employment) (Amendment) Regulations 2014 allow employers who employ less than 10 employees (called micro-businesses) to consult with the employees directly rather than elect representatives, although it does not prevent an employer from holding an election should it wish to do so.

The duty in section 188(1A) of the 1992 Act requires the employer who proposes to declare redundancies to begin consultation in good time. This leads to two questions: When does the employer propose to make redundancies? And what constitutes 'in good time'? In *Re Hartlebury Printers Ltd* [1992] ICR 559, the employer was experiencing financial difficulties in May 1990. Consideration had been given to declaring redundancies but the idea was rejected. On 25 June, a prospective buyer indicated that it would require some employees to be made redundant. The union was informed on 27 June and agreed the figures on 29 June, although the redundancies were not implemented. On 3 July the company went into liquidation. The union sued. One of the arguments turned on when the duty to consult arose. The legislation refers to the employer 'proposing' redundancies, but the Directive refers to an employer 'contemplating' redundancies, which arguably is sooner. The court in *Re Hartlebury Printers Ltd* declined to pursue that argument and concluded that the legislation complied with the Directive until the ECJ decided otherwise. The point then turned on when it could be said that this employer proposed to make redundancies. The court held that as no definite decision had been made until 25 June, the consultation had been at the time the employer proposed to make redundancies and the consultation requirements had been met. However, in *MSF v Refuge Insurance* [2002] IRLR 324, the union claimed that the consultation period on planned redundancies implemented by Refuge Insurance following a merger was too short. Refuge Insurance argued that, under section 188 of the 1992 Act, consultation did not have to begin until a proposal on redundancy had been made. The EAT agreed, but stated that the UK does not comply with the Directive.

Unless the minimum consultation periods apply (see below), previously the law set out what was not 'in good time' instead of stating what the time limit was. Consultation at the time of the issue of redundancy notices did not comply with the original provisions (*NUT v Avon County Council* [1978] IRLR 55), nor did a meeting half an hour before such notices were issued. Likewise, two or three days before the issue of redundancy notices was held to be useless (*TGWU v Nationwide Haulage Ltd* [1978] IRLR 143). In *Junk v Kuhnel* [2005] IRLR 310, the ECJ held that an employer should begin the statutory consultation procedures when he intends to terminate contracts, and this was interpreted by the EAT in *Leicestershire County Council v UNISON* [2005] IRLR 920 as meaning that consultation must begin when the employer proposes to give notice of dismissal.

The time when the duty to consult begins has now been the subject of judicial discussion in the case of *UK Coal Mining Ltd v National Union of Mineworkers and The British Association of Colliery Management* [2008] IRLR 4. The facts of the case are quite complicated. After debates about the viability of a colliery, the government in April 2004 gave the company £19 million to develop it, and the managing director announced, in May 2004, that the colliery would remain open as long as it met production targets and operating costs were kept to a minimum. On 12 January 2005, water began to rise at the face of the seam being worked, and although pumps were installed, the water was rising more quickly than it could be pumped out and production had to stop. By 25 January the water level was falling; however, on 21 January the managing director had contacted the Department of Trade and Industry (DTI) and informed it that the company was close to announcing the closure of the colliery, stating that the economic and risk cases for developing a new coal face were not satisfactory. He also stated that for safety reasons the company would not restart the damaged face. A number of meetings were held with the National Union of Mineworkers (NUM) and British Association of Colliery Management (BACM) representatives from 26 January until 26 February, when the first compulsory redundancies were made. The company did not respond to any suggestions made by the representatives, and although the company reiterated that the colliery would close on health and safety grounds, it produced no evidence of any surveys or reports it had commissioned to support this.

The employment tribunal found that the company had misled the unions as to the true reasons for the dismissals, which were economic rather than on health and safety grounds. This finding was not overturned by the EAT. The EAT also upheld the finding that since *Leicestershire Council v UNISON* (above), the words 'proposing to dismiss' in section 188(1) of the 1992 Act must be interpreted as 'proposing to give notice of dismissal', and therefore consultation must be completed before notices of dismissal are given to the workforce. Since the number of redundancies was over 100, this meant that the required 90-day consultation period (at the time) had not been complied with. However, the EAT overturned the employment tribunal on one point. The tribunal had been bound by the earlier case of *R v British Coal and Secretary of State for Trade and Industry, ex parte Vardy* [1993] ICR 720, which stated that the then section 188 did not require an employer to consult over the reasons for the closure of the colliery. However, an amendment to section 188 introduced in 1995 was a definition of 'consultation'. This is found in section 188(2), and requires an employer to consult on ways of avoiding the dismissals, reducing the number of employees to be dismissed or mitigating the consequences of the dismissals. The EAT therefore held that, given this amendment, there must now normally be a duty on an employer to consult on the reasons for closure, otherwise it would make a mockery of section 188(2).

Where there are a substantial number of redundancies, section 188(1A) of the 1992 Act lays down minimum consultation periods. If 100 or more employees are to be made redundant within 90 days, at least 45 days' consultation must take place. If between 20 and 99 employees are to be made redundant within 90 days, at least 30 days' consultation must take place. The employer must disclose to the employee representatives in writing the reasons for his proposals, the numbers and descriptions of those employees affected, the total number of employees of that description employed, the method of selection and the proposed method of carrying out the dismissals (TULR(C)A 1992, s 188(4)). Consultation should be undertaken with a view to obtaining agreement with the representatives, and the definition of redundancy for consultation purposes is widened to include dismissal for reasons not related to the individual (s 195(1) of the 1992 Act), that is, it covers bumping. Representatives must also be told the method of calculation of redundancy payments other than those required by law (TULR(C)A 1992, s 188(2)(f)).

The employer may plead special circumstances as a defence to a failure to consult. By section 189(6) of the 1992 Act, if the employer can show that it was not reasonably practicable to comply with any of the consultation requirements and he took all steps towards compliance with the requirements as were reasonably practicable in the circumstances, he will reduce and may even extinguish his liability. The most common situation pleaded is that the business has suddenly gone into liquidation which was unforeseeable. If the employer continues to trade in the hope that he will avoid liquidation, and this is a reasonable expectation, then special circumstances will exist. A foreseeable liquidation, however, will not constitute special circumstances and the employer will be liable. The employer who shuts his eyes to the obvious will have no defence (*Association of Patternmakers and Allied Craftsmen v Kirwin Ltd* [1978] IRLR 318). Since 1993 there has been no defence available to the employer that he failed to consult because information was not provided by a controlling employer (s 188(7)).

Where the employer has broken his statutory duty to consult, the union or the employee representatives may apply to a tribunal for a protective award which is payable to those employees in respect of whom the representatives should have been consulted (TULR(C)A 1992, s 189(2)). The award is for the protected period, that is, beginning at the date the first dismissals took place and continuing for as long as the tribunal considers just and equitable, but in all cases subject to a statutory maximum of 45 days if 100 or more were made redundant and 30 days if 20 to 99 were made redundant (s 189(4)). In *Spillers-French v USDAW* [1980] ICR 31, the EAT held that as the section requires the tribunal to consider the seriousness of the employer's default, the purpose of the section is compensatory rather than punitive, and if the employees had suffered no loss as a result of the failure to consult, no award should be made. However, in the case of *Smith and Another v Cherry Lewis Ltd* [2005] IRLR 86, a later EAT has stated that the purpose of the award is punitive and intended to have a deterrent effect. In the case the employer went into receivership and told the staff to contact the DTI for payment arrears. There was no consultation. The employment tribunal held that it could not make a protective award as the employer could not pay, but the EAT made an award of 90 days' pay (the consultation period at the time) because of the employer's blatant breach of the requirements. It stated that the ability of the employer to pay was irrelevant when the objective was to punish and deter. How far this would help employees in the situation of a bankruptcy, however, may be more theoretical than real. Since 1993 the requirement on a tribunal to offset any award made against wages or payment in lieu of notice has been removed.

Similar provisions relate to consultation where there is a transfer of an undertaking under the TUPE Regulations 2006. The issues of dismissal and liability for redundancy have already been discussed in Chapter 9. Where such a transfer takes place, the employer must arrange for an election of employee representatives to take place where there is no recognised trade union. Regulation 13 creates a duty on both the transferor and the transferee to inform the representatives. The representatives must receive information about the transfer and the legal, economic and social implications of it, the measures that the employer envisages it will take in relation to the employees and, if the employer is the transferor, the measures the transferor envisages the transferee will be taking. Furthermore, consultation is more strictly defined, in that the employer must consult with the representatives, consider any representations they make and give reasons if they reject the ideas (Reg 13(7)). In *Baxter and Others v Marks and Spencer and*

Others [2005] All ER 26, the EAT made some observations on the issue of consultation before a transfer under the TUPE Regulations 2006. It stated that, unlike consultation on collective redundancies (above), there is no minimum consultation period for TUPE consultation. It also stated that where the issue was an inevitable administrative change, there is no need to consult. The duty to consult applies to matters of principle only.

By Regulation 6 of the TUPE Regulations 2006, where the transferor recognises a union then when, after the transfer, the undertaking remains a distinct identity separate from the remainder of the transferee's undertaking, recognition is transferred so that the transferee is deemed to recognise the union which may, therefore, transfer a duty to consult. By Regulation 6(2)(b), however, the transferee may vary or rescind any agreement for recognition so transferred.

The remedy for failure to comply with the consultation provisions under the Regulations, including holding an election of employee representatives, is found in Regulation 15. Again, the employer may raise the defence of special circumstances. The maximum award which may be made under the Regulations is 13 weeks' pay. In *Shields Automotive v Langdon and Brolly* [2013] EmpLR 034, the employer called an election at 2 pm with voting closing at 5 pm. Brolly was unable to vote as it was his day off. The employer gave no explanation as to why the election had to be done so quickly, and Langdon did not vote in protest. The election resulted in a tie, and the employer selected one of the tied candidates. The EAT held that the employer's duty is to ensure that an election is fair, and to do so the employer must ensure that employees have an opportunity to vote. However, where an employer has taken some steps to comply with its duty, the starting point for any award should be less than the 13 weeks. As such Langdon's award was two weeks' pay and Brolly was awarded three weeks' pay.

Regulation 15(9) of the TUPE Regulations 2006 states that the transferor and transferee are jointly and severally liable for a failure to consult. However, in *Country Weddings Ltd v Crossman* [2013] All ER (D) 46, the EAT held that a tribunal cannot apportion liability. This is the job of the county court or High Court under the Civil Liability (Contribution) Act 1978.

Summary

10.1 Redundancy payments are a recognition of a worker's property right in his job.

10.2 To claim a redundancy payment, an employee must have two years' continuity and be dismissed for reasons of redundancy.

10.3 'Redundancy' is defined as the employer's ceasing business, moving his place of business, or reducing the number of employees employed to do particular work.

10.4 If the employee has committed misconduct and is selected for redundancy, or commits misconduct during the redundancy notice, the dismissal is for misconduct if the employer so elects.

10.5 If the employee who has been selected for redundancy goes on strike or participates in other industrial action, the dismissal is still for redundancy.

10.6 If the employer offers suitable alternative employment which the employee unreasonably refuses, the employee becomes disentitled to a redundancy payment.

Summary cont'd

10.7 If the employee accepts alternative employment, he is entitled to a statutory trial period; and if during this trial period he reasonably resigns, he may still claim a redundancy payment.

10.8 In certain situations of lay-off and short-time working the employee may claim a redundancy payment.

10.9 Redundancy compensation is calculated in a way similar to that for the basic award in unfair dismissal.

10.10 There is a statutory duty on an employer to consult with employee representatives when making a certain number of employees redundant and a statutory duty to inform the government when making mass redundancies.

10.11 Failure to consult with the union or employee representatives, when there is no justification for the failure, entitles the affected employees to a protective award.

10.12 There are similar consultation duties on both the transferor and transferee when there is a transfer of an undertaking.

Exercises

10.1 Good Nosh Ltd is a contract catering company. One of the units they operate is Westshire Hospital, where three weeks ago they changed all their food preparation to cook-chill. Cook-chill involves prepared food being delivered from a production kitchen 50 miles away. The food is then regenerated at the unit.

Den has been employed for eight years. He was the chef at Westshire. As a chef, his duties included the preparation of 1,000 meals a day. As a result of cook-chill, he now prepares only 20 meals a day from their raw state for senior management at the hospital. His post has been renamed 'Kitchen Supervisor', and his duties are the preparation of food for senior management and the supervision of the kitchen staff. His hours have been reduced by five a week, with a consequent reduction in pay. Today Den handed in his notice.

Ethel has worked there for four years. She is a general assistant. Before cook-chill her duties involved the preparation of vegetables and salads, but since cook-chill was introduced, her duties have been altered so that she now puts out the prepared food and serves it. Her hours and pay are the same, but she feels she is no longer using her creative skills.

Pete is a delivery man for Good Nosh Ltd and has worked for the company for three years. Since the introduction of cook-chill his hours have radically altered. Before, he started at 8 am and finished at 3.30 pm for five days a week. Now he works from 5 am to midday for six days a week (the sixth day being Sunday). This is because the prepared chilled food has to be delivered for use within 24 hours. His pay has remained the same. He feels aggrieved because he feels that he is working unsociable hours which are disrupting his domestic life.

Advise Den, Ethel and Pete.

10.2 What is the relationship between section 218 of the ERA 1996 and the TUPE Regulations 2006?

Further reading and references

Armour and Deakin, 'The *Rover Case (2)*: Bargaining in the Shadow of TUPE' (2000) 29 ILJ 395

Collins, 'Transfer of Undertakings and Insolvency' (1989) 18 ILJ 144

Eady, 'Collective Dismissals, Consultation and Remedies' (1994) 23 ILJ 350

Hall and Edwards, 'Reforming the Statutory Consultation Procedure' (1999) 28 ILJ 299

McMullen, 'Takeovers, Transfers and Business Reorganisations' (1992) 21 ILJ 15

Njoya, 'The Interface Between Redundancy and TUPE Transfers' (2003) 32 ILJ 123

Wedderburn, 'Consultation and Collective Bargaining in Europe: Success or Ideology?' (1997) 26 ILJ 1

Chapter 11

Duties of ex-employees

Introduction

In Chapter 4 we saw that the employee owes a duty of faithful service to his employer and part of that duty is not to divulge, or otherwise misuse, confidential information. This duty is either implied into the contract by the common law, or it may be an express term of the contract. This raises the question, however, of the protection afforded to the employer once the relationship has come to an end. The damage that may be caused to an employer's business by a third party's learning trade secrets or secret processes is just as serious whether passed on by a present or a past employee. We have already seen that the courts grapple with the problem of distinguishing between what is confidential to the employer and what may be said to be part of the skills acquired by the employee during his period of employment. This problem becomes more acute once the employment relationship has ended, for the new employer will be 'buying' the employee for his skill and knowledge. Consequently, the courts are wary of any attempt to restrict the employee after the termination of his contract. Having said that, some restrictions are allowed, and there are two methods which may be invoked. These are discussed below.

11.2 Express/implied duty of fidelity

While there is a term in the contract restricting the employee from divulging confidential information while he is employed, in some circumstances this duty will continue after the relationship has ended. It appears from *Faccenda Chicken Ltd v Fowler* [1987] Ch 117 (Chapter 4 at Section 4.3.5), however, that the duty is limited when applied to ex-employees and will extend only to the divulgence of trade secrets and, possibly, customer connections. Furthermore, the contractual duty will prevent only the divulgence of information and will not prevent the employee from working for a competitor or setting up in competition.

Whereas a blatant transfer of information, for example, giving the new employer a formula, will be protected, other use of information will not be. What of the ex-salesman who visits his old customers rather than give the list to his new employers, as in the *Faccenda Chicken* case? He is not divulging any information, merely using his existing contacts. *Faccenda Chicken* demonstrates that such action is not a breach of the contractual duty. It is because of these limitations of the contractual duty in relation to ex-employees that employers rely on the second method of protection, restraint of trade covenants.

11.3 Restraint of trade covenants

A covenant is merely a promise. A restraint of trade covenant is a promise contained within a contract of employment, whereby the employee undertakes that he will accept a restraint upon where he works and for whom, for a period of time after he has left the employment relationship. This may at first sight appear to be the panacea to all employers' problems in relation to the misuse of confidential information. Would that it were that simple! The courts are notoriously wary of such covenants because they are required to balance conflicting interests – the interests of the employer on the one hand, who wishes to protect his business, and the interests of the employee on the other hand, who has a legitimate right to be free to pursue his career where and with whom he wishes.

The starting point will be whether the covenant is enforceable on contractual principles before the court will look at the validity of the covenant itself. If the covenant has been agreed at the end of the relationship, it is likely to be unenforceable as the employer is giving no consideration for the employee's promise to restrict his future employment. Likewise, a repudiatory breach on the part of the employer repudiates the whole contract, including the covenant, and therefore the covenant becomes unenforceable. In *Briggs v Oates* [1990] IRLR 472, a solicitor had been employed by two partners. The partnership changed, which meant that his contract terminated. This was done without notice and was thus a repudiatory breach of contract. It was held by the High Court that the solicitor was therefore no longer bound by the restraint clauses in his contract. The employer must commit a repudiatory breach of contract, however. By contrast, in *Rex Stewart Jefferies Parker Ginsberg Ltd v Parker* [1988] IRLR 483, the employee had been joint managing director of an advertising agency. There was a covenant in his contract which prevented him from soliciting clients of the agency for 18 months after his employment had ended. The employee left and set up his own agency. He argued that the employer could not rely on the covenant because he had been dismissed and paid wages in lieu of notice. The Court of Appeal held that paying wages in lieu of notice was not a breach of contract, therefore the covenant was valid and enforceable. The employer cannot, however, write into the covenant that it will be enforceable whether the termination of the contract is lawful or not (*Living Design v Davidson* [1994] IRLR 69). The covenant does not have to be reiterated, however, every time the contract is varied. In *Marley Tile Co Ltd v Johnson* [1982] IRLR 75, the employee's original letter of appointment contained a number of restraints which prevented him from seeking employment with rival organisations, or competing with his employer, for a period of 12 months after leaving his employment. On promotion to area manager, his letter of appointment contained the same restraints, but when he was promoted a second time the letter made no reference to the restraints. The Court of Appeal held that the restraints in his original letter of appointment applied to any subsequent promotions. The Court said that as the employee had remained with the same company, each time his contract varied the parties must have assumed that the same terms applied unless anything was said to the contrary. No reference was made, for example, to his company car or expense account because both parties assumed that they were still part of the contract. Thus the covenants were part of each successive contract. They were, however, too wide and therefore void.

Even if the clause is technically enforceable, the courts may still render it void if they feel it is not reasonable. Whereas the courts are prepared to protect an employer against the misuse of confidential information by existing employees, they are less happy in giving protection against ex-employees by upholding a provision that limits the employee's choice of future employment. The current law on restraint of trade covenants is to be found in *Nordenfelt v Maxim Nordenfelt Guns and Ammunition Co* [1894] AC 535. The case was not an employment case but involved the sale of a business. The contract contained a provision preventing the vendor from setting up in competition. The House of Lords established that a restraint of trade covenant is to be considered void unless the party alleging its validity can prove it is:

1. reasonable as between the parties; and
2. reasonable in the public interest.

Since the later case of *Esso Petroleum Ltd v Harper's Garage (Stourport) Ltd* [1968] AC 269, the courts have emphasised that both aspects are equally important, and therefore both must be proved for the covenant to stand.

'Reasonable between the parties' has been interpreted to mean that the employer must have a recognisable interest to protect and is not merely attempting to prevent normal competition (see further Section 11.4 below). 'Reasonable in the public interest' means that even if the employer has a legitimate interest to protect, he may give himself only the protection he needs (see further Section 11.5 below). Therefore if the covenant is so wide in area or time that it gives more protection than is needed, it will be unreasonable in the public interest and will fail. If the covenant is not drafted as separate provisions, if one part offends the test of reasonableness, the whole covenant will be void even if the rest is giving only the necessary protection.

11.4 Reasonable between the parties

To establish that the covenant is reasonable between the parties, the employer must show he has some proprietary right to protect. In other words, he must show that he has a trade secret, secret process or customer connections, the disclosure of which could damage his business. In addition, he must show that the ex-employee has knowledge of the trade secret or secret process, or be in a position where customers are likely to follow him to his new employment. The employer cannot restrain all his employees merely because he has a trade secret, secret process or customer connections to protect. He can restrain only those employees who have the necessary knowledge or connections to do harm to the employer's business. Further, the employer can restrain the employee only in relation to those aspects of the business in which the employee was employed and of which he thus has knowledge, and cannot impose a restraint covering all aspects of the employer's business (*Turner v Commonwealth and British Minerals Ltd* [2000] IRLR 114). If, therefore, it is shown that the employee does not have the knowledge or connections, the covenant will be seen as a blatant attempt to prevent competition and will be void. In *Herbert Morris Ltd v Saxelby* [1916] 1 AC 688 there was a provision in the employee's contract preventing him from working for a competitor for seven years after leaving his employment. The employee had no knowledge of the employer's trade secrets and had no personal contact with the employer's customers. All the employee had was his own technical skill and knowledge. It was held that the covenant was an attempt to prevent competition and therefore void. Similar conclusions were reached in *Strange v Mann* [1965] 1 All ER 1069 and *Faccenda Chicken Ltd v Fowler* (above).

A trade secret or secret process does not have to be patented to be able to be protected, but it must be confidential, that is, outside the sphere of public knowledge, and it must be more than the employee's knowledge of the trade which he has acquired through his employment. Valid restraints have covered secret processes and formulas (*Forster & Sons v Sugget* (1918) 35 TLR 87), the design of a machine (*Ansell Rubber Co v Allied Rubber Industries* [1967] VR 37) and detailed knowledge of the workings of a specialised business (*Littlewoods Organisation Ltd v Harris* [1978] 1 All ER 1026).

The law is even more restrictive in relation to the employer's customers. The employer may protect himself only in relation to employees who have established a relationship with the customers so that there is a real danger that the customers will follow the employee when he leaves (*International Consulting Services (UK) Ltd v Hart* [2000] IRLR 227). In *Strange v Mann* (above), the contract of a manager of a firm of bookmakers included the provision that he was not to engage in a business similar to that of his employers within a 12-mile radius once his employment had terminated. It was held that, given that the manager had little influence over the customers, most of whom placed bets by telephone rather than face to face, the employer had no legitimate interest to protect. A similar conclusion was reached in *Bowler v Lovegrove* [1921] 1 Ch 642, where a restraint against an estate agent who mainly dealt with customers by telephone was also held to be void. In addition, in the *Bowler* case the nature of the employer's business was relevant. Customers rarely build up long-term relationships with estate agents.

Salespeople, in particular, will have built up relationships with customers, and therefore the customers may follow the employee when he leaves. In *Coppage v Safety Net Services* [2013] EWCA Civ 1176, the Court of Appeal held that a six-month restraint, preventing the former employee from approaching his former employer's customers to solicit business from them, was reasonable. He had been the 'face' of the business, and the length of the restraint was not excessive. In unusual cases, the employee may have influence over customers with whom he has no direct contact, and it will be legitimate to protect the employer against the possibility of the loss of such customers (*John Michael Design plc v Cooke* [1987] ICR 445). Generally, however, the employer should protect himself only in relation to customers who have had direct contact with the employee. In the old case of *Mason v Provident Clothing and Supply Co* [1913] AC 724, a restraint covenant purported to prevent the employee from competing with her ex-employers within a 25-mile radius of the centre of London. The employee had had contact with customers only in a specified area of London. Consequently, the House of Lords stated that the covenant covered customers she had not met, and was therefore too wide and void. More recently, in the complex case of *Office Angels Ltd v Rainer-Thomas and O'Connor* [1991] IRLR 214, there were two restraint clauses which the employer sought to enforce. Relevant to this discussion was clause 4.5(a), which stated that the employees would not, for six months after the termination of employment, solicit custom from any person who had been a company client during the employees' employment. The Court of Appeal held that the clause was too wide in itself. It covered all clients (6,000–7,000), of which the employees had dealt with about 100. As such, the clause was void (see also *Scully UK Ltd v Lee* [1998] IRLR 259).

11.5 Reasonable in the public interest

Even if the employer proves he has a legitimate interest to protect, the covenant will still be declared void if the court feels that it is not reasonable in the public interest. There are three ways in which a covenant may infringe public interest considerations.

First, the covenant may be drafted too broadly and give the employer more protection than he actually needs because, on construction, it prevents the employee from entering non-competitive employment. In *Fellowes & Son v Fisher* [1976] 2 QB 122, a conveyancing clerk, employed by a firm of solicitors in Walthamstow, agreed that for five years after the termination of his employment he would not be employed in, or concerned with, the legal profession anywhere within the postal district of Walthamstow and Chingford, or solicit any person who had been a client of the firm while he had worked there. The Court of Appeal held that, on construction, this prevented him from working in any part of the legal profession, including local government. As such, the restraint was wider than that needed by the employer and void. Likewise, in *Commercial Plastics Ltd v Vincent* [1965] 1 QB 623, an employee's contract contained a restraint covenant which prevented his working in the PVC calendering field for one year after leaving his employment. The employee had only ever been employed in the adhesive tape side of the business, and therefore the covenant, which prevented the employee from working in any aspect of the industry, was too wide and void.

Second, the covenant may cover too wide an area and therefore give the employer more protection than he actually needs. This may be because there is no area limit and therefore the restriction is deemed to be worldwide, or because the employer is preventing the employee from working in an area in which the employer has no interest and therefore where he does not need protection. In *Spencer v Marchinton* [1988] IRLR 392, the restraint covered an area of 25 square miles, but the employer had not expanded into that area by the time the employee left. It was held that the clause was too wide and unenforceable. In the *Office Angels* case (Section 11.4 above), clause 4.5(b) provided that the employees would not, within six months after the termination of their employment, 'engage in or undertake the trade or business of an employment agency' in Greater London within a one kilometre radius of the branch at which they had been employed. The employees left and formed another employment agency within the one kilometre limit. On interpretation of the clause, the Court of Appeal recognised that the employers did have a legitimate interest to protect – their clients and the temporary workers which the agency sent out to organisations. The employers, however, specifically protected themselves only in relation to clients in clause 4.5(a) (see Section 11.4 above), therefore clause 4.5(b) obviously also related to clients and was set up with the intention of preventing the employees from diverting business from their ex-employers by taking advantage of the influence they had over clients while they were still employed. Clause 4.5(b), however, did not do this. Although the branches of the employer's agency did have area boundaries, these boundaries were not absolute. Furthermore, whereas temporary workers were influenced by the location of the office, clients were not. They merely telephoned, and the branch could be located anywhere. As such, all the clause did was prevent competition; it did not protect the legitimate interests of the employer. It was therefore void.

Whether the area is too wide will depend on a variety of factors. The fact that the employer has not expanded into the area will mean that he is overprotecting himself. While this may look like an attempt to prevent competition, it should be remembered that normally a covenant will be inserted into the contract at the beginning of the relationship, at a time when the employer may genuinely believe that he will expand. In *Greer v Sketchley Ltd* [1979] IRLR 445, the employer, who operated a business in the Midlands and London, intended to expand nationwide, and inserted a covenant preventing the employee from competing on a nationwide basis. It was held that as the employer had not yet expanded by the time the employee left, the clause was too wide and void. This demonstrates the problems if the employer thinks ahead. The decision in *Greer* left the employer with no protection at all in the areas in which he operated.

The density of population within the area will also affect the decision of the court. In the *Fellowes* case (above) the area was not particularly wide but was densely populated, which was a factor taken into account by the court when holding the clause to be void. On the other hand, in *Fitch v Dewes* [1921] 2 AC 158, a lifelong restraint on a solicitor's clerk which prevented him from working within a seven-mile radius of Tamworth Town Hall was held to be valid. The House of Lords decided that it was a modest area which was not densely populated, and so a lifetime restraint was not unreasonable.

The last way in which the covenant might offend public interest is if its duration is too long. To a large extent, however, the geographical and time factors are looked at together. Generally, the more extensive the area, the shorter the time limit should be. In *Commercial Plastics* (above), a one-year restraint was too long given that the restriction was worldwide, and in *Scully* (Section 11.4 above), a 24-month worldwide restriction was unenforceable. By contrast, in *Fitch v Dewes* (above), the small area involved led the court to find that a lifelong restraint was reasonable. In *Kynixa Ltd v Hines* [2008] EWHC 1495, there was a restraint of trade covenant contained in a shareholders' agreement. Kynixa was a company providing rehabilitation and case management services for injured persons, and its principal customers were solicitors and insurance companies. All three employees were shareholders and two were directors of the company. They were all known by the principal customers of the company as part of its senior management. All three left to work for another company in competition to Kynixa. Part of the covenants contained clauses against solicitation and competition. The non-solicitation clause was for six months, whereas the non-competition clause was for 12 months; and all three defendants argued that the non-competition clause was unenforceable as it was for too long a period of time. Wyn Williams J analysed the law in respect of restrictive covenants. He concluded that, given the senior positions held by the defendants, and given that often contracts to provide services between Kynixa and its customers were only for two years before they came up for renewal, 12 months was not unreasonable, and therefore the covenants were reasonable and enforceable. Note, however, that the Court of Appeal in *Beckett Investment Management Group v Hall* [2007] EWCA Civ 613 stated that the mere fact that the duration chosen (in that case 12 months) is arbitrary, does not prevent the clause from being enforceable.

In practice, all the factors are looked at together and each case turns on its own particular set of facts. As Pearson LJ said in *Commercial Plastics v Vincent* (above): 'It would seem that a good deal of legal know how is required for the successful drafting of a restraint clause.'

11.6 Enforceability

It may appear from the above that it is difficult to draft a valid restraint of trade provision in a contract. To some extent this is right, as the courts do not particularly like enforcing a provision which will restrict an employee's future job prospects for some time after leaving his employment, and we have already seen that even the courts recognise that it takes a great deal of skill to draft a clause which the courts will enforce. Having said that, even if the clause does offend the principles of reasonableness, there are two methods that the court may use to save it.

First, the court may look at the reality and effect of the provision. However, it will not allow an employer to try to get a covenant imposed 'by the back door'. For example, the employer may not disguise the covenant by providing that the employee must pay the employer a commission if he solicits customers after leaving the employment, for this is just another way of restraining him (*Stenhouse Australia Ltd v Phillips* [1974] AC 391). Neither may the employer enter into an agreement with another employer to prevent the employment of his ex-employees. In *Kores Manufacturing Co v Kolok Manufacturing Co* [1959] Ch 108, two employers manufacturing similar goods entered into an agreement that neither would employ a person who had been employed by the other in the preceding five years. The Court of Appeal held that as neither employer had a valid interest to protect, if such a provision had been in an employee's contract it would have been void as unreasonable between the parties. The employers could not do covertly what the courts would not allow them to do overtly, and the agreement between them was void. Furthermore, the employer cannot prevent the ex-employee from poaching the employer's employees (*Hanover Insurance Brokers Ltd v Schapiro* [1994] IRLR 82).

However, given that the courts look to the effect of the provision, they have been prepared, in some cases, to interpret the provision in the way the parties intended and not in the way it strictly reads. This happens only rarely and will occur only where the clause is ambiguous. The courts will not normally go against a strictly worded clause. Should they interpret an ambiguous clause, however, it may save the covenant. In *Home Counties Dairies Ltd v Skilton* [1970] AC 403, there was a restraint clause in the contract of a milkman which stated that he should not 'serve or sell milk or dairy products' after leaving his employment. On a strict interpretation of the clause, this restricted his future employment beyond acting as a milkman. He would be in breach of the provision if he worked, for example, in a supermarket. As such, it was too wide and void because the employer did not need that amount of protection. It was obvious, however, that the employers wanted to restrict his future employment as a milkman only, and the clause was interpreted in this way and upheld. Similarly, in *White (Marion) Ltd v Francis* [1972] 3 All ER 857, a restraint provision in the contract of a hairdresser prevented the employee from taking future employment in the hairdressing business 'in any way'. Again, the parties obviously intended the restriction to apply only to employment as a hairdresser, and the covenant was interpreted as the parties intended and was saved. In *Ward Evans Financial Services v Fox* [2002] IRLR 120 there was a restraint clause in financial advisers' contracts preventing them from inducing customers to leave the company. Two advisers intended to leave the company and set up in competition, and had purchased a dormant company with this aim. A client asked if it could transfer business to the new company, and it was agreed that the business would transfer on the setting up of the new company. This eventually happened. The Court of Appeal held that although the advisers had not solicited the client, by saying that the business could transfer to the new company, they had failed to put the interests of the employer first and thus had to pay damages. In other words, the spirit of the covenant was upheld. In the *Hall* case (above), the Court of Appeal rejected the literal interpretation of the words 'the company' and held that the words also protected the clients of subsidiary companies within a large corporate group. Maurice Kay LJ stated that the law would recognise the reality of big business and not take a 'purist approach to corporate personality'.

Perhaps the most surprising case is *Littlewoods Organisation Ltd v Harris* [1978] 1 All ER 1026. There, the employee had been employed as a director by Littlewoods. His employer's main competitor in the mail order business was Great Universal Stores Ltd, and there was a provision in the contract of employment that, for 12 months after leaving his employment, he would not be employed by Great Universal Stores Ltd or any of its subsidiaries. Littlewoods was, by this restraint, protecting confidential information relating to the preparation of its mail order catalogue, in which capacity the employee had been employed. As Great Universal Stores operated all over the world and in businesses other than mail order, the ex-employee argued that the restraint was too wide and therefore void. He argued that Littlewoods required protection only in relation to mail order in Great Britain, but that the clause gave much greater protection. The Court of Appeal, however, said that, looking at the ex-employee's job and the employer's intention, the clause could be interpreted to relate only to Great Universal Stores' mail order business in Great Britain. As such it was valid and enforceable.

While the court may interpret ambiguous clauses favourably, such cases are rare. We have already seen in the *Office Angels* case that the court felt that the employer had a legitimate interest to protect but that the wording of the covenant did not afford that protection, and the court would not interpret it so that it could be saved (see Section 11.4). The Court of Appeal stated that restraint covenants totally restricting employment should be used only as a last resort, and normally a non-dealing clause would be looked upon more favourably by the courts. Furthermore, it should be noted that in that case the Court of Appeal felt that the employer needed protection against the poaching of other employees. This had not been written into the covenant and the Court was not prepared to imply that the restriction on setting up in competition related to other employees (which probably would have been valid) rather than clients. The clause was ambiguous and was therefore construed in favour of the ex-employees. This case could be seen as a change in attitude to ambiguous covenants on the part of the courts.

There is another way in which the court may save a potentially void covenant which does not involve issues of interpretation. This is known as the 'blue pencil rule' and involves the court severing the offending part of an otherwise valid covenant, so leaving one which is reasonable and enforceable. It must be stressed, however, that the courts will not rewrite a covenant and will use this technique only if the severance will leave a valid covenant. Therefore, a court cannot sever an area provision which is too wide, for to do so will leave a worldwide covenant which will still render the covenant void. The same would apply to the severance of a time limit which is void because it is too long. Severance would leave a lifelong restraint which will also fail the test of reasonableness. This means that there are only certain types of covenants in which the rule may be used, that is, covenants which have individual clauses. In *Lucas (T) & Co Ltd v Mitchell* [1974] Ch 129, a salesman covenanted that for a year after the termination of his employment he would not:

1. solicit orders within his trading area from present customers and those whom his employer supplied during the previous 12 months; and
2. deal in the same goods or goods similar to those that he had sold.

The court held that the second clause was unreasonable and unenforceable. That clause could, however, be severed from the first clause and still leave a valid, enforceable covenant. A similar severance was performed in *Stenhouse Australia Ltd v Phillips* (above). How the clause is drafted, therefore, can be the deciding factor in whether the covenant falls or is saved.

The cases discussed above have been confirmed in *TSF Derivatives Ltd v Morgan* [2005] IRLR 246. There, the High Court deleted part of a covenant it felt was excessive and enforced the remainder. It also stated that if a clause is capable of two interpretations, one too wide and the other reasonable, a court should always adopt the latter. Lastly, a court should not rewrite a clause, but if part can be deleted and an enforceable covenant remains, a court should grant an injunction as long as the employer can show a legitimate business interest requiring protection.

11.7 Enforcement

Should a clause be upheld by the courts, the question to be asked by the employer is: Which is the best method to enforce the covenant against the ex-employee? Two remedies are available – injunction or damages – both, however, are fraught with difficulties.

If the employer chooses injunctive relief, he will wish to apply for an interim injunction before the case is heard by the full court. This is obviously the quickest and most effective form of protection as it will prevent any immediate breaches of the covenant which could severely damage the employer's business by the time of the full hearing. The rules governing the granting of interim injunctions were discussed at length by the Court of Appeal in the case of *Lansing Linde Ltd v Kerr* [1991] IRLR 80. Kerr had been employed by Lansing Bagnall and had transferred when the company was taken over by Linde AG. His new contract contained various restraint clauses. In contravention of those clauses, he left to work for a competitor. The employer sought an interim injunction. The Court of Appeal looked at the guidelines laid down by *American Cynamid Co v Ethicon Ltd* [1975] AC 396, that is, that before such an injunction can be granted there must be an arguable case and damages would not be an appropriate remedy. If both parties would be inconvenienced by the injunction and damages are an inadequate remedy for either party, then the injunction should be given to the party who would suffer the most inconvenience if it is not granted. In deciding this last point, the Court of Appeal in *Lawrence David Ltd v Ashton* [1989] IRLR 22 stated that one of the most relevant criteria is whether or not the employer would have any real prospect of winning his case.

In the *Lansing Linde* case the Court found that Kerr was in charge of marketing, and although he did not regularly visit customers, he did have access to trade secrets in relation to the UK marketing operation. However, the company did not operate on a worldwide basis and the restraints were worldwide. The Court felt this was giving the employer more protection than was needed and that a restriction on employment in Western Europe would have been more reasonable. In relation to the balance of convenience test, the Court identified three situations which might apply. First, there would be the situation where only one party would suffer loss which damages could not compensate, and in that case an injunction would be granted. Second, there would be the situation where there would be a rapid full trial and then the injunction would be granted to the party who would suffer the most loss before the trial. Third, there was the situation when a full trial would be unlikely, either because the interim action would effectively decide the issue, or because, given time delays on a full hearing, the time period within the restraint would be exhausted. In the case in hand, the Court thought it unlikely the parties would go to a full trial given that the time restraint was only 12 months and that it was unlikely that there would be a full hearing before that date. Even if there was such a hearing, the Court thought it unlikely that the employer would succeed, given the geographical restraint. As a result, the injunction was refused.

Given this ruling and the fact that the majority of restraint covenants are not for long periods of time (indeed, they may well fail the test of reasonableness if they are for too long a period), injunctive relief would seem to be difficult to obtain.

If the employer does not seek an injunction to prevent the breach of the covenant, he may seek damages to compensate the loss he has incurred as a result of the breach. While this is an easy proposition to state, in practice it may be difficult for the employer to quantify his loss in financial terms, which is why in practice the majority of employers will seek injunctive relief. Should the employer seek to claim damages, however, the House of Lords in *Attorney-General v Blake* [2001] IRLR 36 extended the damages for which an employer may claim. The case has established that a defendant may be required to pay to the employer the profit that he has received as a result of the breach, even if the employer has suffered no actual financial loss. It was envisaged by their Lordships that the return of profits would apply only in exceptional circumstances where the normal remedies of specific performance or injunction are not compensation for the breach of contract.

One further point should be noted. We have already seen in Chapter 9 that if the employer's undertaking is transferred to another and the employees are taken on by the new employer, the contracts transfer with the employees. In *Morris Angel & Son v Hollande* [1993] ICR 71, the Court of Appeal held that where there was a transfer of an undertaking and by Regulation 4 of the TUPE Regulations all the employee's contractual terms were transferred to the transferee, this included the transfer of a restraint covenant entered into with the transferor. Thus the new employer could rely on the covenant.

Summary

11.1 A restraint covenant will be enforceable only if the employer can prove that he has a legitimate interest to protect, that is, that the clause is reasonable between the parties.

11.2 Even if the clause is reasonable between the parties, the employer must also prove that it is reasonable in the public interest, that is, it is not for too long a time period or for too wide an area.

11.3 A clause will be interpreted strictly, and normally any ambiguity will be interpreted to the advantage of the employee.

11.4 If one part of the clause is unreasonable the whole clause will fall, unless the covenant contains severable parts and the courts, using the 'blue pencil rule', can sever the offending part and still leave an enforceable covenant.

11.5 If the employer commits a repudiatory breach of contract then the covenant is also repudiated.

11.6 Even if the covenant is upheld, effective enforcement by the employer may prove to be problematical.

Exercises

Tweedledum and Tweedledee work for Rooftec Ltd, a manufacturer of a revolutionary new roofing material with outlets throughout the United Kingdom.

Tweedledum works in the laboratory which developed the new material, as a technician. He has the following provision in his contract of employment:

The employee undertakes that for 12 months after leaving his employment, he will not work within the roofing industry anywhere in the United Kingdom.

Tweedledee is a salesman. There is a provision in his contract which states the following:

The employee undertakes that for 12 months after leaving his employment, the employee will not:

(a) work in the roofing industry anywhere in the United Kingdom;
(b) solicit any customers of Rooftec Ltd with whom he has dealt during his period of employment;
(c) set up in business in roofing anywhere in the United Kingdom.

Both employees now want to leave and work for another roofing manufacturer. Advise Tweedledum and Tweedledee as to the likelihood of the court upholding the covenants.

Further reading and references

Brodie, 'Health and Safety, Trust and Confidence and *Barber* v *Somerset County Council*: Some Further Questions' (2004) 33 ILJ 261

Cabrelli, 'Post-Termination Covenants in the Spotlight Again' (2004) 33 ILJ 167

Edwards, 'Restrictive Covenants and Employment' [1991] BLR 3

Hepple, 'Employee Loyalty in English law' (1999) Comp Lab LJ (20) 204

Jefferson, 'Restraint of Trade: Dismissal and Drafting' (1997) 26 ILJ 62

Korn, 'Losing Staff and Trade Secrets' (1991) 135 SJ 484

Korn and Small, 'Confidential Information' (1991) 2 IPB 2

Sales, 'Covenants restricting recruitment of employees and the doctrine of restraint of trade' (1988) 104 LQR 600

Part V

Trade unions and the law of industrial action

Chapter 12

Trade unions

Introduction

The idea of a group of people associating for mutual protection and benefit in relation to employment is a common enough one today, but this was not always the case. The Industrial Revolution saw the birth of trade unions as we know them today, but that birth was met with hostility from both the legislature and the judges. The Combination Acts 1799–1800 made any agreement with the purpose of improving working conditions an offence and imposed criminal sanctions upon those who called or attended a meeting for that purpose, so essentially undermining the very essence of a union. The major legal obstruction to unions during the early part of the nineteenth century was that, as their main purpose was to improve the working conditions of their members, they were seen to be in restraint of trade and therefore illegal if they performed this function. The Combination Laws Repeal Act 1824 meant that unions were not criminal per se, but after a series of strikes the Combination Act 1825 rendered unions criminal except where their sole purpose was the determination of wages or hours. Major advances were made by the introduction of the Trade Union Act 1871 and the Criminal Law Amendment Act of the same year. The former provided that trade union activity was not to be regarded as in restraint of trade, and gave unions the power to enforce certain contracts and hold property. The latter modified the offences of intimidation, obstruction and molestation in relation to trade union activity, but this was thwarted somewhat by the judiciary's increased use of the offence of criminal conspiracy in relation to industrial action. The Conspiracy and Protection of Property Act 1875 defined the ambits of lawful industrial action and created immunity from criminal conspiracy where the act was done in furtherance of a trade dispute, and was not criminal if done by one person alone. So began the system of immunity from the law in certain circumstances, rather than the creation of specific rights.

The judiciary, however, was, and some would argue still is, hostile to the unions. Despite legislative intervention, judges found ways to find that industrial action was against the law by extending the common law and creating what have come to be known as the economic torts. We shall see in Chapter 14 that this was not confined to the early part of the twentieth century but has continued. This development was limited, however, in that, as a trade union was not a body corporate, the union itself could not be sued, only the individual members, thus trade union funds were protected. This position, however, was overturned by the famous House of Lords decision in *Taff Vale Railway Company v Amalgamated Society of Railway Servants* [1901] AC 246. In this case, their Lordships ruled that the Trade Union Act 1871 had enabled unions to be sued in their own name, and as such the Amalgamated Society of Railway Servants was ordered to pay £23,000 in damages and £19,000 in costs. The implications of the judgment were far-reaching and meant that union funds were at risk. As a result, the Trade Disputes Act 1906 was passed. Rather than providing that unions could not be sued, the Act continued the theme of immunity from tortious liability. This immunity remained until the Industrial Relations Act 1971 was resurrected in the Trade Union and Labour Relations Act 1974, and was again removed by the Employment Act 1982. In addition, the 1906 Act gave immunity to individual members from conspiracy and inducing breaches of contract, provided such actions were done in contemplation or furtherance of a trade dispute, the so-called 'golden formula' which is present in modern-day legislation.

This battle between the judiciary and the legislature is one that has continued during various stages of trade union history, and will be referred to in more detail in this and the following chapter. What this brief introduction hopes to show is that a union is a strange hybrid, in that it is a separate entity for certain purposes only. In addition, the introduction lays down the basis on which a union or its members can take industrial action. Unlike in any other European country, no one has the right to take action, he or she is merely immune from certain civil liability in certain situations, that is, when the action is within the golden formula. This means that successive governments can radically alter the protection enjoyed by both unions and their members simply by changing the statutory definition of a trade dispute.

12.2 Status of trade unions

The statutory definition of a trade union is now found in section 1(a) of the Trade Union and Labour Relations (Consolidation) Act (TULR(C)A) 1992, which provides that a trade union means an organisation (whether temporary or permanent):

> which consists wholly or mainly of workers of one or more descriptions and whose principal purposes include the regulation of relations between workers of that description or those descriptions and employers or employers' associations ...

The definition is wide and concentrates on the purpose of the body. Thus a body which had a subsidiary purpose of regulating relations between workers and employers would not be a trade union within the above definition. In *Midland Cold Storage v Turner* [1972] ICR 230, a shop stewards' committee drawn from various trade unions was not a trade union within the definition since its purpose was to discuss whether industrial action should be taken and it did not engage in negotiations with employers. Likewise in *Akinosun v The Certification Officer* (2013) UKEAT 0180/13/0507, the EAT held that the General Healthcare Workers Union, whose principal purpose was representing workers at internal disciplinary proceedings, was not a trade union. Langstaff J set out three points of construction when looking at section 1. First, whether an organisation's principal purposes include the regulation of relations between workers and employers or employers' associations is a question of fact for the Certification Officer. Second, the definition looks at whether the principal purpose of the organisation is collective in nature, even if it may also provide services to individuals. Third, the question of whether an organisation is a trade union is framed in the present tense, not one which looks at what might happen at a future date. On the other hand, the body may have other purposes and still fall within the definition, which says that the principal purposes must *include* the regulation of relations, and so on. In *BAALPE v NUT* [1986] IRLR 497, BAALPE was a small organisation representing the interests of advisers and lecturers in physical education. Its constitution stated that it was concerned with the professional interests of its members. As such, it fell within the statutory definition and was entitled to representation on a teachers' national negotiation committee.

The fact that the body is temporary will not prevent its being a union if its purposes fall within the definition. In the *Midland Cold Storage* case (above), the committee had been set up during a particular dispute with no official status within the unions from which the members came. This was irrelevant when considering whether it was a union within the definition. From section 1(a), a body may be temporary and still be a union.

The definition describes a union as consisting of workers. The definition of 'worker' is to be found in section 296 of the 1992 Act, which states:

> In this Act worker means an individual who works, or normally works or seeks to work—
>
> (a) under a contract of employment, or
> (b) under any other contract whereby he undertakes to do or perform personally any work or services for another party to the contract who is not a professional client of his ...

As such, professional bodies such as The Law Society are not trade unions within the definition (*Carter v Law Society* [1973] ICR 113).

Section 1(b) of the 1992 Act widens the definition of 'trade union' to include 'constituent or affiliated organisations which fulfil the conditions in paragraph (a)'. This means that federations of unions are to be regarded as trade unions themselves.

While section 1 helps to identify which groups are trade unions and which are not, it does nothing to explain the precise legal status of such a body. We have already seen that for many years a union as an unincorporated body could not be sued, and that therefore union funds were protected. This protection ended with the House of Lords decision in the *Taff Vale* case (above), when it was decided that as the Trade Union Act 1871 allowed unions to hold property and enter certain contracts, the union could be sued in its own name. But if a union can be sued in its own name, logically it can also sue in its own name. That this is clearly the case was established in *NUGMW v Gillian* [1946] KB 81, where a union successfully sued the general secretary of another union for defamation.

This means that, as already mentioned, a union is a kind of hybrid organisation. Lord Parker in *Bonsor v Musicians' Union* [1956] AC 104 called the union a 'near corporation'. In other words, it has many of the characteristics of a body corporate without actually having corporate status. The Industrial Relations Act 1971 tried to resolve this anomaly by giving corporate status to all unions that registered under the Act. For reasons well documented elsewhere and which will not be rehearsed here, the unions were totally opposed to the Act and simply did not register, so thwarting the purpose of the provision. Unions opposed corporate status to avoid the scrutiny of accounts, to which all companies are subject. While they have been successful in the former, they have not been so successful in the latter, as will be seen. The present position is therefore that unions are still unincorporated associations but have certain advantages which corporate bodies enjoy. This statutory regulation began in the Trade Union and Labour Relations Act 1974 and is now contained in sections 10 and 12 of TULR(C)A 1992. Section 10 provides that although a trade union is not a body corporate it is capable of:

- making contracts;
- suing and being sued in its own name;
- having criminal proceedings brought against it.

In addition, section 12 allows the union to hold property vested in trustees, and section 12(2) provides that any judgment or award made against the union is enforceable against its property to the same extent and in the same manner as if it were a body corporate. Furthermore, section 23 protects the personal property of members and trustees in the same way that shareholders within a company obtain protection through the concept of limited liability. The clarification of the law, however, does not mean that the union has a legal personality within the legal definition of such in certain circumstances. In *EEPTU v Times Newspapers* [1980] 1 All ER 1097, the union sued for defamation. O'Connor J held that as the statute specifically states that the union is not and is not to be treated as a body corporate, the union does not have a legal personality which must be protected through the law of defamation.

12.3 Listing

The concept of maintaining some kind of voluntary listing of trade unions was introduced in the Trade Union Act 1871. Such a list continued with the compliance of the unions until the Industrial Relations Act 1971 which introduced a very different system of registration. Under that Act, only unions that registered were entitled to statutory immunity against certain industrial action (something the unions had enjoyed since 1906). In addition, any unions that registered under the 1971 Act had to 'pay' for their immunity by subjecting their constitution, rules and accounts to outside scrutiny. Union opposition to the Act demonstrated itself by a policy of non-compliance, and very few unions registered – indeed those that did, were expelled from the Trades Union Congress (TUC). The Trade Union and Labour Relations Act 1974, which repealed the Industrial Relations Act, reintroduced the concept of voluntary listing similar to that which existed under the 1871 Trade Union Act. The provisions are now in sections 2 and 123 of TULR(C)A 1992. These provide that the Certification Officer shall maintain a voluntary list of trade unions and employers' associations. Any union may apply for inclusion on the list. A body may be removed from the list by the Certification Officer if at any time it ceases to fall within the statutory definition. An appeal against refusal to list or removal from the list lies to the Employment Appeal Tribunal (EAT).

While there are few advantages to being listed, it is the first requisite to obtaining a certificate of independence. It is this certificate which brings considerable advantages to both the union and its members.

12.4 Independent trade unions

The Certification Officer can issue any union on the list with a certificate of independence (TULR(C)A 1992, s 6). Such a certificate is conclusive evidence that the union is independent (s 8). An independent trade union is one which is not under the control of an employer or liable to interference from an employer arising out of financial, material or other support (s 5). While financial support is easy to identify, the other aspects of the definition are more subjective, and the Court of Appeal in *Squibb UK Staff Association v Certification Officer* [1979] ICR 235 held that the test was whether the union was exposed to or vulnerable to the risk of interference rather than interference as a fact.

The *Squibb* case (above) demonstrates that the test for determining independence is not a clear-cut one and involves looking at a variety of factors. The EAT in *Blue Circle Staff Association v Certification Officer* [1977] ICR 224 approved the criteria listed by the

Certification Officer in his 1976 annual report. The report states that the following should be considered:

1. History: the union's past links with the employer are relevant. The more recent those links, the less likely that the union is truly independent. In the *Blue Circle* case, the association had been formed six months earlier with total employer control, one of the factors leading the EAT to agree with the refusal of the certificate of independence.
2. Finance: any direct financial assistance from the employer will mean dependency.
3. Employer facilities: if the employer provides facilities for the union such as a free office or telephone, this will be a factor to be considered, and this was a major reason in the *Squibb* case for deciding that the union was not independent. It should be noted, however, that the ACAS Code of Practice on Time Off for Trade Union Duties and Activities suggests in paragraph 24 that management should provide facilities, such as accommodation and telephones, to enable officials to perform their duties effectively.
4. Membership: if membership is limited to one company, this may raise the question of total independence from the employer. It has been pointed out, however, that members of the National Union of Mineworkers (NUM) used to be employed by one employer, and yet it is unthinkable that the independence of that union would ever be challenged.
5. Negotiation record: the Certification Officer will take into account whether there is a 'robust attitude in negotiation'. In other words, regular compliance with the employer's wishes may indicate a lack of independence.
6. Organisation: one of the arguments against Blue Circle was that ordinary members had a restricted role. Only members of three-years' standing could be elected as area committee representatives and the employer nominated the chairperson of the Joint Central Council. In addition, members of management had originally been committee members and had helped draft the rules, which removed them as such in the bid for independence.

On an application for a certificate of independence, the Certification Officer will make such enquiries as necessary, including listening to representations from other unions. An appeal against the refusal of a certificate lies to the EAT. A certificate may also be withdrawn if the nature of the union changes.

The certificate of independence gives certain rights to the members of the union. It will be seen below that members of independent trade unions are protected against dismissal and detriment on the grounds of trade union activities or membership (sections 146 and 152 of the 1992 Act). However, more rights pertain to both the union and its members if it is independent and recognised by the employer for collective bargaining purposes.

12.5 Recognition of trade unions

The major purpose of any union is to protect and promote its members' interests, and the way it will do this is by collective bargaining. Many workers in Britain still have their terms and conditions agreed collectively rather than individually. Obviously, however, for the union to perform this function the employer must accept it as the bargaining agent for the workforce. Prior to 1979, successive governments felt that collective bargaining was the best way to conduct industrial relations, and as such it was supported. The Industrial Relations Act 1971 introduced a statutory procedure whereby if the majority wanted recognition in a workplace the employer had to comply, and the National Industrial Relations Court had the jurisdiction to force the employer to do so. These rights were only given to registered unions, however, and given that the majority of unions refused to register, the procedure was little used. A more complicated procedure was introduced by the Employment Protection Act 1975, whereby an independent trade union could refer a recognition dispute to ACAS who, after investigation, could then order the employer to recognise the union. These powers were not enforceable, however, and ACAS could not coerce the employer to comply, as demonstrated by the famous Grunwick dispute (*Grunwick Processing Laboratories v ACAS* [1978] AC 655). As such, rather than give ACAS more teeth, the recognition procedures were abolished by the Employment Act 1980, and until 1999 nothing was put in their place.

Recognition, however, is still an important issue for the union. Apart from meaning that it can fulfil its primary purpose of regulating relations between its members and employers, a recognised independent trade union and its members have certain rights. We have already seen that only members of independent recognised trade unions are entitled to time off without pay for trade union activities, and only officials of such unions are entitled to paid time off for trade union duties (see Chapter 7). Recognised independent trade unions are entitled to information for collective bargaining purposes. Thus recognition is vitally important for a union to perform its functions. It is also important for individual members, who will acquire extra rights.

The above discussion therefore raises the question of when a union is recognised. Since the Employment Relations Act 1999, there are two ways by which this can occur:

1. where the employer recognises the union voluntarily; or
2. where the union has invoked the statutory recognition procedure and thus the employer has to recognise the union for collective bargaining purposes.

Different consequences apply to the two situations. Where recognition is voluntary, the employer may vary or withdraw recognition unilaterally (unlike where a union is recognised under the statutory procedure). Furthermore, an employer may recognise a union which represents only the minority rather than the majority of his workforce. By contrast, as will be seen below, once a union has gained statutory recognition it may not normally be derecognised for a period of three years, and if recognition was granted because of a ballot of the majority of affected workers, derecognition may occur only after a ballot supporting derecognition has been conducted.

12.5.1 Voluntary recognition

The starting point is section 178(3) of the 1992 Act, which defines recognition as 'recognition of the union by the employer ... to any extent, for the purposes of collective bargaining'. Collective bargaining means negotiations relating to or connected with one or more matters specified in section 178(2). These are:

▶ the terms and conditions of employment, or the physical conditions in which workers are required to work;

- engagement or non-engagement, or termination or suspension of employment or the duties of employment, of one or more workers;
- allocation of work or the duties of employment as between workers or groups of workers;
- matters of discipline;
- a worker's membership or non-membership of a trade union;
- facilities for officials of trade unions;
- machinery for negotiation or consultation and other procedures, relating to any of the above matters, including the recognition by employers or employers' associations of the right of a trade union to represent workers in such negotiation or consultation or in the carrying out of such procedures.

The phrase in section 178(3) that the union is recognised 'to any extent' for the purposes of collective bargaining means that an employer may recognise a union for only one of the matters listed above. Where there is no express agreement, however, the section does not state what conduct constitutes recognition. We have already seen in Chapter 10 that recognition is a mixture of law and fact when looking at issues of consultation with recognised trade unions when declaring redundancies. Where there is an express agreement normally no problems arise; however, the law may imply recognition from the parties' conduct. In *National Union of Gold, Silver and Allied Trades v Albury Brothers Ltd* [1979] ICR 84, discussions between a union and an employer concerning whether a particular individual's wages came within agreed pay scales, where no agreement was reached, did not amount to recognition. Conversely, in *Joshua Wilson & Bros Ltd v USDAW* [1978] IRLR 120, the cumulative effect of a number of contacts over a year with the employer led the EAT to imply recognition. These contacts included allowing the union to put up notices detailing a pay rise negotiated nationally, allowing an official to collect union payments from workers during working hours and consulting the union over a reallocation of duties. The appeal tribunal stressed that separately none of the incidents would have led to a conclusion of recognition, it was the cumulative effect of all of the incidents which led the tribunal to its conclusion.

12.5.2   Statutory recognition

The procedures outlined in brief below were introduced by the Employment Relations Act 1999, which inserted a new Schedule A1 into TURL(C)A 1992 which itself has been amended by the Employment Relations Act 2004. The Central Arbitration Committee (CAC) cannot accept an application for recognition where there is already a collective agreement in force covering pay, hours and holidays, but can accept an application if the agreement covers only one or two of those issues (TULR(C)A 1992, Sch A1, para 35). As such, in *Pharmacists Defence Association v Boots Management Services Ltd* (2013) Case No TURI/823, a recognition agreement between the employer and the Boots Pharmacists Defence Association, which allowed the Association to collectively bargain for facilities for officials and machinery for collective consultation, could not block an application by another trade union for recognition for collective bargaining on pay, hours and holidays. However, in *R (on the application of the NUJ) v CAC and MGN* [2005] IRLR 28, the National Union of Journalists (NUJ) had been discussing recognition for sports journalists with MGN. MGN, however, accepted an approach from the British

Association of Journalists (BAJ), which had recognition for some MGN titles but which only had one member in the sports area. The CAC refused to accept the NUJ application for recognition because there was a voluntary collective agreement with the BAJ covering pay, holidays and hours, even though BAJ did not have many members in the bargaining unit.

The steps described below are cumulative, that is, if the first step is successful then that is the end of it; if not, step two applies and if that is not successful step three applies. Any application for recognition is made to the CAC.

12.5.2(a) Recognition by agreement

The process begins with a request for recognition which must satisfy certain conditions. First, the request must be received by the employer (TULR(C)A 1992, Sch A1, para 5). Second, the request must be made by an independent trade union (Sch A1, para 6). The request can only be made to an employer who employs, on the day the request is received, 21 employees, or an average of 21 employees in the 13 weeks ending on the day the request for recognition is received. The number of employees includes those employed by an associated employer (Sch A1, para 7). In *Graphical Paper and Media Union v Derry* [2002] IRLR 380, the majority of shares in two printing companies were owned by one person. The employees had the same contracts and one management, and workers employed by both companies had been used in calculating the minimum number of employees needed for a recognition claim. The union claimed that the companies were one bargaining unit and sought joint recognition. The CAC held that normally joint recognition could not be granted even where employees at the associate employer had been used to calculate the number of employees. However, in the particular circumstances, the CAC concluded that there was one employer and the union claim was allowed.

Third, the request must comply with the minimum criteria laid down by Schedule A1, paragraph 8, that is, it must be in writing, it must identify the union or unions and the bargaining unit, and it must state that it is made under Schedule A1. If the employer refuses within 10 days but wishes to negotiate, then negotiation begins (which may involve ACAS). If after 20 days (or a longer period if the parties agree) there is still failure to reach agreement, the steps below apply.

12.5.2(b) Recognition by application to the Central Arbitration Committee

If the employer refuses a request for recognition, fails to respond in the time limits set out in Section 12.5.2(a) above or negotiations fail, the union may apply to the CAC. The CAC must decide whether the bargaining unit is appropriate within the terms of Schedule A1, paragraph 19B(2) and (3). The CAC must try to help the parties reach agreement as to the appropriate bargaining unit within 20 days of receipt of the union's application, or a shorter period if both parties so request or the CAC sees no reasonable prospect of the parties reaching agreement on the bargaining unit (Sch A1, para 18). The CAC may extend the period it has previously shortened at the parties' request if it feels this will allow the parties to reach an agreement (Sch A1, para 18(5)). In both cases (shortening or lengthening the period) the CAC must state the reasons for the action. Paragraph 18A of Schedule A1 requires the employer to provide information to the union and the CAC within five working days after the CAC gives notice of acceptance of the union's application. The employer must provide:

- a list of the categories of worker in the proposed bargaining unit;
- a list of the workplaces at which the workers in the proposed unit work;
- the numbers of workers the employer reasonably believes to be in each category at each workplace in the proposed unit.

The union can request the CAC to appoint an independent person to communicate formally with the relevant workers on behalf of the union, after the application for recognition has been accepted. Once appointed, the employer must within 10 working days give the CAC the names and home addresses of the relevant workers, and the CAC must pass this information on to the independent person. Should an employer fail to give the information, the CAC may either issue a declaration that the union is recognised or order a ballot.

If the parties have not reached an agreement, the CAC must decide the appropriate unit within 10 working days, starting with the end of the negotiation period stated above (Sch A1, para 19). By paragraph 19A, if the employer has failed to give the information listed in paragraph 18A, the union can ask the CAC to decide the appropriate unit before the end of the 20-day period in paragraph 18 (above).

In addition, the CAC must decide whether the union is likely to have the support of the majority of the workers constituting the unit, and must not proceed with the application if this is not the case. If the CAC is satisfied as to worker support, it must issue a declaration that the union is recognised and is entitled to conduct collective bargaining on behalf of the workers constituting the bargaining unit.

12.5.2(c) Recognition after a secret ballot

A secret ballot must take place instead of a declaration in three situations:

- where the CAC feels that the ballot will be in the interests of good industrial relations;
- where a 'significant number' of union members in the bargaining unit inform the CAC that they do not want the union to conduct collective bargaining on their behalf;
- where membership evidence is provided which leads the CAC to conclude that there are doubts whether a 'significant number' of union members within the bargaining unit want the union to conduct collective bargaining on their behalf (Sch A1, para 22).

The ballot must be conducted by a qualified independent person appointed by the CAC, and must take place within 20 days of that person's being appointed unless that period is extended by the CAC. An extension may be granted if both parties request, to enable them to reach an agreement voluntarily. The ballot may take place in the workplace or by post. The employer is under a duty to co-operate with the ballot and to give the union reasonable access to the workers constituting the bargaining unit. The Code of Practice on Access to Workers during Recognition (and Derecognition) Ballots gives guidance on this, as does Schedule A1, paragraph 26(4D). The employer must also give the CAC the names and addresses of the workers constituting the bargaining unit and any worker who later joins that unit, and must inform the CAC if a worker leaves the unit. In addition, the employer is under a duty not to induce workers not to take part, nor take action or threaten to take action against workers taking part (Sch A1, para 26(4A)). If the employer fails to comply with these obligations the CAC may order the employer to remedy this or issue a declaration that the union is recognised.

If the ballot shows that the union is supported by a majority of the workers voting and at least 40 per cent of the workers constituting the bargaining unit, the CAC must issue a declaration that the union is recognised (Sch A1, paras 25–29). The Court of Appeal, in *R (on the application of Ultraframe (UK) Ltd) v CAC* [2005] IRLR 641, stated that where there has been a problem with a ballot (in the case the GMB and United Road Transport Union complained that not all staff had received ballot papers), the CAC can order a re-run. The statute refers to a 'ballot', and that means a ballot conducted in accordance with the statutory provisions. In the case, not all relevant workers had received ballot papers, and it was irrelevant that the qualified independent person had announced the result of the ballot. As it had not complied with the statutory procedures, the CAC could annul it and order a new ballot.

The costs of the ballot are met 50:50 between the employer and the union.

12.5.2(d) Consequences of recognition

The parties must within 30 days of the declaration come to an agreement as to the method by which they will conduct collective bargaining. 'Collective bargaining' means bargaining in relation to pay, hours and holidays, although the parties may change this by agreement. If no such agreement is reached, the CAC must specify the method. Such a specified method is legally enforceable, although the parties may agree in writing to vary or replace the method specified by the CAC, and that agreement shall be legally enforceable (Sch A1, para 31). The remedy for breach of either of the above is specific performance, not damages. If the CAC has specified the method of bargaining, the employer must invite (on at least a six-monthly basis from the date of recognition) trade union representatives to discuss:

- the employer's policy on training members of the bargaining unit;
- plans for training them in the next six months; and
- training which has taken place since the last meeting (TULR(C)A 1992, s 70B(2)).

The employer must provide certain information to the union at least two weeks before such meetings take place. Failure to comply allows the union to apply to an employment tribunal, which may make a declaration and award compensation to members of the bargaining unit which does not exceed two weeks' pay (TULR(C)A 1992, section 70C(1), (3) and (4)).

12.5.2(e) Derecognition if fewer than 21 employees

If three years after the agreement or declaration to recognise, the employer has fewer than 21 employees on average, the employer may serve notice of derecognition on the union as required by Schedule A1, paragraph 99(3), and if the union does not apply to the CAC, the collective bargaining arrangement shall cease after 35 days. In addition, a union may be derecognised in the same way as it may be recognised, except that the CAC may not proceed with a secret ballot unless it decides that at least 10 per cent of the workers constituting the bargaining unit are in favour of ending the arrangement and there is prima facie evidence that the majority of workers constituting the bargaining unit would be likely to favour the ending of the bargaining arrangement. Such a ballot may be held on the request either of the employer, or of the workers falling within the bargaining unit (Sch A1, paras 112 and 128).

12.6 The political fund

The labour movement in the early years was reliant on a sympathetic Liberal government to give it legal protection. While this partnership worked well, it soon became apparent that the movement required working-class Members of Parliament (MPs) who would fully understand the problems and provide truly representative views in Parliament. Consequently, the movement decided to fund such MPs through union funds, and introduced the idea that part of each member's contribution to the union would support working-class MPs. This subsidy to promote political aims was declared illegal by the House of Lords in *Amalgamated Society of Railway Servants v Osborne* [1910] AC 87, since under the Trade Union Act 1871 a union could pursue only those objects listed in the Act, that is, the regulation of relations between workers and employers. Pursuance of political aims was not subsumed within those objects. The Liberal government again came to the aid of the unions by the passage of the Trade Union Act 1913, which by section 3 allowed unions to pursue any object listed within its constitution, although insisting that such a fund supporting political objectives should be a separate fund and it should be called the 'political fund'. This fund is supported by trade union members' contributions and is automatic unless the member contracts out of paying into the fund.

Substantial amendments were made to the Act by the Trade Union Act 1984, although at the time the government insisted that unions ballot their members every 10 years to see if the members wished the political fund to be maintained. The Trade Union Reform and Employment Rights Act 1993 introduced the contracting-in system by amending the 1992 Act. Section 68 of TULR(C)A 1992 provided that an employer should not deduct union subscriptions from a worker's wages (the so-called 'check off' system) unless the worker had authorised the deduction in writing within the previous three years, the employer had notified the worker of any increases at least one month before the deduction was made and the employer had notified the employee of his right to withdraw his authorisation at any time. The worker had a right of complaint in an employment tribunal in the case of unauthorised deductions. Since the Deregulation (Deduction from Pay of Union Subscriptions) Order 1998, new members need give written authorisation only once, and it continues indefinitely, subject to the right to withdraw authorisation. Existing members may give notice in writing to the employer that they wish their authorisation to last three years. After that period, any further authorisation will be indefinite, again subject to the right to withdraw authorisation.

The 1993 Act also introduced stringent balloting provisions in relation to the maintenance of a political fund (TULR(C)A 1992, ss 75–78), requiring such ballots to be conducted in the same way as the ballot for the election of trade union officials (see Section 12.11 below).

The present law is contained in the 1992 Act. Section 71(1) of TULR(C)A 1992 lays down that payment for political purposes, whether made directly or indirectly, may be made only from a separate political fund. Political purposes are then defined in section 72(1) as the expenditure of money:

(a) on any contribution to the funds of, or on the payment of expenses incurred directly or indirectly, by a political party;

(b) on the provision of any service or property for use by or on behalf of any political party;

(c) in connection with the registration of electors, the candidature of any person, the selection of any candidate or the holding of any ballot by the union in connection with any election to a political office;

(d) on the maintenance of any holder of a political office;

(e) on the holding of any conference by or on behalf of a political party or of any other meeting the main purpose of which is the transaction of business in connection with a political party;

(f) on the production, publication or distribution of any literature, document, film, sound recording or advertisement the main purpose of which is to persuade people to vote for a political party or candidate or to persuade them not to vote for a political party or candidate.

Section 72(2) states that attendance at a conference as a delegate or participator falls within paragraph (e) above.

A challenge on expenditure goes to the Certification Officer or the High Court, with an appeal to the EAT. Many cases have discussed the meaning of the present section 72(1)(f). In *Coleman v Post Office Engineering Union* [1981] IRLR 427, the Certification Officer ruled that affiliation to the Canterbury District Trades Council Campaign Against the Cuts was not political activity since there was no expenditure on literature and the meetings were not held by a political party, nor directly or indirectly in support of a political party. It was also relevant that there was a great deal of support from unions not affiliated to the Labour Party. This decision may be contrasted with the cases of *Richards v NUM* [1981] IRLR 247 and *Paul v NALGO* [1987] IRLR 43. In *Richards*, the Certification Officer held that money spent on a march and a parliamentary lobby against government cuts should have come from the union's political fund. In *Paul*, NALGO distributed leaflets and posters highlighting cuts in public services and the effects of privatisation, urging people to use their vote in the forthcoming local elections. All the publicity stated that NALGO was not affiliated to any political party. Browne-Wilkinson VC decided that payment for the campaign should have been made out of the political fund. Given the closeness of the local election, he held that the purpose of the leaflets and posters was to dissuade people from voting Conservative. Contributions to funding Labour Party Headquarters is a political object and not a commercial investment (*Association of Scientific, Technical and Managerial Staff v Parkin* [1984] ICR 127). The political fund can operate on an overdraft as long as the interest is charged to the fund (TULR(C)A 1992, s 83).

The 1992 Act lays down conditions for the establishment and maintenance of a political fund. A political resolution must be passed by a majority of members voting on a ballot conducted according to the provisions of the Act, that is, it must comply with the union's political ballot rules as approved by the Certification Officer (s 73). The Certification Officer cannot approve such rules unless they include the appointment of an independent scrutineer, entitlement of all the members to vote, voting complies with section 77 (that is, it is postal and secret) and the rules provide for a scrutineer's report. Additional provisions introduced by the 1993 Act include the requirement that the scrutineer sees a register of members and the requirement of an independent person to count the votes (TULR(C)A 1992, s 77A). By section 73(3), the union must ballot its members every 10 years to maintain the fund. If it fails to do so or the resolution is lost, the fund lapses and any levy collected after that date must be returned to the members. The remaining fund may be transferred to any other union fund.

12.7   Trade union accounts

The 1992 Act, as amended by the Trade Union Reform and Employment Rights Act 1993, lays down stringent rules for the organisation of a trade union's financial affairs. By section 32 of TULR(C)A 1992, the union must make annual returns to the Certification Officer, including a profit and loss account, a balance sheet, an auditor's report and any other documentation he may require. Following the case of *Taylor v NUM (Derbyshire Area) (No 2)* [1985] IRLR 65, the Employment Act 1988 placed a duty on unions to allow their accounts to be inspected for at least a six-year period after their creation, and gave members the right to be accompanied by a qualified accountant (TULR(C)A 1992, ss 29 and 30). Failure to keep accounting records, failure to allow such records to be inspected, failure to allow a member to inspect the accounts, failure to submit an annual return and failure to keep a separate fund for members' superannuation are all criminal offences (TULR(C)A 1992, s 45). Section 45A of the Act lists the penalties and prosecution time limits for such offences, and section 45B allows for disqualification of offenders from union office (that is, a member of the executive, the president or the general secretary) for a period of up to 10 years. Failure on the part of the union to disqualify convicted persons from office allows a member of the union to complain to the Certification Officer or the court for a declaration that the union has failed to comply with section 45B.

Following allegations in the press of irregularities in relation to the NUM's funds, the union established an enquiry under the chairmanship of Gavin Lightman, QC. The subsequent report was critical of some of the dealings of the senior officials of the union. Criminal charges were commenced by the Certification Officer under what is now section 45, but the charges were subsequently dismissed. As a result of the Lightman Report, the Trade Union Reform and Employment Rights Act 1993 introduced more rights for members and gave greater powers to the Certification Officer. By section 32A of the 1992 Act, information about the salary and benefits of each member of the union executive, the president and the general secretary must be included in the annual return. The trade union must take reasonable steps to ensure that all its members, within eight weeks of the submission of the annual return, are provided with a written financial statement of income and expenditure. A copy must also be given to the Certification Officer. Section 37A gives the Certification Officer new powers to order an investigation into the conduct of a union's financial affairs and publish a report after such an investigation. Failure to comply with such an investigation will be a criminal offence. In addition, new offences are created arising out of such an investigation, and persons convicted of such offences may be disqualified from being a member of a union executive, or from being the president or general secretary of a union, for between five and 10 years, depending on the gravity of the offence.

At first sight, it appears that the legislature is merely attaching the same rights to trade union members as are enjoyed by shareholders of a company, and making senior trade union officials responsible in the way that company directors are responsible, including imposing the sanction of disqualification. It should be noted, however, that the information available to trade union members under these provisions is much greater than that available to shareholders.

12.8 The rule book

The rules of a trade union form the terms of a contract between it and its members. They become part of the contract in the same way that collective agreements become part of the individual employment contract between the employer and the employee. The rule book, however, will form the express terms in that contract and, as in every other type of contract, terms may be implied. Custom and practice may add to the rules and so too add to the terms in the contract of membership. In *Heaton's Transport Ltd v TGWU* [1973] AC 15, the House of Lords held that shop stewards had customary power to call industrial action even though the express provisions of the union's constitution did not give this power. In addition, the 'Oh of course' test so common in other areas of contract (see Section 3.6) may be used to imply terms into the contract of membership and amend the rules. In *MacLelland v NUJ* [1975] ICR 116, the courts implied into the rule book of the NUJ the requirement of reasonable notice before important meetings.

Apart from contractual devices, other areas of law impact on the union rule book. Statute has now impacted in a variety of ways. By section 69 of TULR(C)A 1992, for example, there is a rule in all union rule books allowing a member to terminate his membership on the giving of reasonable notice. The Equality Act 2010 renders it unlawful to discriminate on the grounds of a protected characteristic (see Section 5.2) in relation to membership, access to benefits or subjecting members to a detriment on those grounds.

The rules cannot be contrary to the common law, so that in *Drake v Morgan* [1978] ICR 56 the House of Lords stated that a union policy to pay the fines of members convicted of unlawful picketing was illegal because such a policy supported the criminal actions of its members (now TULR(C)A 1992, s 15). By contrast, however, it appears that rules which support members in the commission of breaches of contract or torts are not unlawful. In *Porter v NUJ* [1979] IRLR 404, the House of Lords held that the provision of funds to members on strike or taking other industrial action was not illegal. The distinction between supporting the commission of criminal and civil acts arose again in the case of *Thomas v NUM (South Wales Area)* [1985] IRLR 136. In the case it was alleged that the strike was bound to result in the commission of both crimes and torts. Scott J stated that while it would be unlawful for the union to organise and support criminal activity, he was not clear what the position would be in relation to the organisation of tortious activity. Given that in the normal situation, the activity organised and supported by the union may result in torts or criminal acts being committed rather than such being inevitable, he did not feel that he had to decide the point.

The basis of the decisions above may be looked at in another way, however. Although the union is not a body corporate, in some ways it is treated as if it is, for example in the making of contracts and suing and being sued in its own name. This has led courts to impose certain company principles upon unions, more particularly the *ultra vires* doctrine, that is, that the union has only the power given to it by the rules and therefore has no power to act outside them. Thus, any payment of fines for criminal acts, for example, is *ultra vires*. The rule which allows such payment is unlawful and void, therefore the union has no power to act under its auspices. A strike, for example, must be called only after a proper ballot has been conducted. If the ballot is illegal, the union has no power to call a strike; and if the union has no power to call a strike, it has no power to pay strike pay. Thus in *Taylor v NUM (Derbyshire Area) (No 3)* [1985] IRLR 99, Vinelott J ruled that payment of strike pay to members involved in a non-balloted strike was *ultra vires*. Similarly, in *Clarke v Chadburn* [1984] IRLR 350, a resolution of the NUM conference to change the disciplinary rules was *ultra vires* because this could not be done without a prior meeting of the Nottinghamshire Area Council; and in *Hopkins v National Union of Seamen* [1985] IRLR 157 the imposition of a levy on members by the National Executive Council was declared *ultra vires* and void as that body had no power to raise a levy. While many have argued that as unions are not corporations the *ultra vires* rule should not apply, the courts continue to use it to control the unions' exercise of their power under the rules. This means that, given the analogy with companies, on occasion the courts have also used the so-called rule in *Foss v Harbottle* (1843) 2 Hare 461, which has implications for individual members who wish to sue for breaches of the rules. This will be discussed more fully in Chapter 13.

12.9   Inter-union disputes

Unions may clash over the organisation of workers or rights within a particular factory or industry, for example as to which union has the right to organise a particular group of workers, or as to which union should have recognition rights within a particular industry or workplace. In addition, disputes may arise between unions because of 'poaching' of members from one union to another. Such disputes may arise because in the UK there is no tradition of single-union workplaces; for example, there were some 15 unions operating in Ford workplaces in 1969 and eight unions covering Austin Rover workers in 1985. Foreign companies establishing workplaces within the UK are more prone to try to reach a single-union deal – often offering recognition rights to one union in return for flexible working patterns or no-strike clauses. These trends mean that the risk of inter-union disputes remains high.

To prevent government intervention in this area, the Trades Union Congress (TUC) polices such disputes. To do so it operates a series of principles known as the Bridlington Agreement, which was first adopted in 1939 in Bridlington. The agreement has been amended in subsequent years. Breach of the agreement is dealt with by the TUC Disputes Committee and the ultimate sanction for breach of the agreement is expulsion from the TUC.

To prevent dual membership of unions, Principle 2 laid down that on receipt of an application for membership, a union must check the record of the applicant. If the applicant is the subject of a disciplinary sanction or has outstanding subscriptions, or there are other reasons why he should not be accepted, the union should reject the application. In addition, the existing union must agree to the transfer, and if the agreement is withheld the new union should not take on the member unless it feels that permission is being withheld unreasonably, in which case the matter must be referred to the Disputes Committee. The principle, at one time, did cause problems when there was an abundance of closed shops operating (see Section 12.14 below), and cases often came before the Committee arising from the transfer of an employee who was the member of one union to another site where a different union was operating a closed shop. Changes in the law which have now rendered the operation of a compulsory closed shop illegal have alleviated the number of cases on this issue.

Apart from issues involving individual members transferring between unions, Principle 5 is designed to prevent unions from going into competition with each other in a workplace or industry in relation to membership or recognition. The principle provides that no union may organise at an establishment where another union has the majority of workers as members and engages in negotiations on wages and conditions for those workers, unless that union agrees.

It appears that in relation to the individual member, the principles are not implied as terms in his contract of membership but are merely a code of conduct (*Spring v National Amalgamated Stevedores and Dockers Society* [1956] 2 All ER 221). However, even though the principles comprise voluntary self-regulation, the courts may still get involved in relation to their supervisory jurisdiction to ensure that the Disputes Committee acts within the law. This is demonstrated by *Rothwell v APEX* [1976] ICR 211. The case arose after an attempt by the TUC to avoid the implications of the *Spring* decision (above). In *Spring*, the plaintiff had been enrolled as a member of NASDS contrary to the Bridlington Agreement, and the TUC Disputes Committee ordered the union to expel him, which it did, despite the fact that there was no power to expel under its own rules. It was held that the expulsion was void. As a result, the TUC invited all affiliated unions to adopt a model rule (Model Rule 14) covering expulsion in compliance with a Disputes Committee ruling. In *Rothwell*, members of a staff association called SAGA voted to merge with APEX, but this amalgamation was objected to by the Association of Scientific, Technical and Managerial Staff (ASTMS). The Disputes Committee then ruled that ASTMS was the appropriate union for those workers, and the General Council therefore called upon APEX to expel all those who had already joined under Model Rule 14. It was held that the expulsions were invalid for three reasons. First, ASTMS had less than 50 per cent membership, and therefore under the Bridlington Agreement APEX was right to proceed with the merger. Second, the merger had been conducted in accordance with the relevant statutory provisions and the General Council had no power to undo what had lawfully been done by statute. It therefore followed that APEX had no power to expel because the decisions of both the Disputes Committee and the General Council were *ultra vires* and void. Section 174(4) of TULR(C)A 1992 now provides individuals with the right not to be expelled or excluded on the basis of membership of another union.

12.10 Trade union amalgamations

By section 97 of TULR(C)A 1992 there are two ways in which unions may become one – either by an amalgamation, or by a transfer of engagements. If there is a transfer of engagements (that is, the new union undertakes to fulfil all the engagements of the old), there must be an instrument of transfer submitted to the Certification Officer and approved by him, and a resolution approving the instrument must have been adopted by a simple majority vote, after seven days' notice, of the members of the transferor union (s 97(2)). In relation to an amalgamation, the requisite notice and vote must be conducted by both the transferor union and the transferee union (s 97(1)). The Trade Union Reform and Employment Rights Act 1993, amending section 100 of TULR(C)A 1992, requires that any vote on union mergers or transfers shall be fully postal and subject to independent scrutiny. A member of a union passing a resolution to approve an instrument of amalgamation or transfer may complain to the Certification Officer that the statutory provisions have not been complied with within six weeks of the application to register the instrument (s 103(2)), and the Certification Officer cannot register the instrument until he has investigated and determined the complaint or the complaint is withdrawn. The Certification Officer may make a declaration that he finds the complaint to be justified, or may order that the union take certain steps before the instrument can be registered. An appeal lies against the Certification Officer's decision to the EAT on a point of law only (s 104). When the instrument of transfer takes effect, the property of the old union is immediately vested in the new union without the necessity for any conveyance (s 105). Further, by section 101A of TULR(C)A 1992, if the amalgamated unions are already listed, the Certification Officer must enter the name of the newly amalgamated union onto the list and remove the old names, and section 101A(3) and (4) provide for the issue of a new certificate of independence if the amalgamating unions had such certificates prior to amalgamation.

12.11 Trade union elections

One of the tenets of recent legislation in this area has been democratising the trade union movement, and to this end the legislation has introduced the requirement of balloting in respect of many issues. We have already seen above that a ballot complying with the statutory requirements is required for an amalgamation or transfer and for the maintenance of the political fund. We shall see in Chapter 14 that members must also be balloted before industrial action is undertaken, and failure to hold a legal ballot before such action has severe consequences for the union. So, too, the law requires balloting of all relevant members in the selection of the officials of the union, but further requires that such ballots and elections must take place every five years.

The first piece of legislation to introduce the idea of full membership balloting for union officials was the Trade Union Act 1984. This required that all voting members of the principal executive committee, whatever it was called, be elected every five years. The principal executive committee is the main committee of the union exercising executive functions. The government obviously intended that this should prevent certain union officials, not least Arthur Scargill, then president of the NUM, from holding his job for life. Many union presidents however, including Mr Scargill, merely gave up their vote so that they were not caught by the legislation. As a result, the Employment Act 1988 amended the 1984 Act by the so-called 'Scargill clause', so that the president, the general secretary and every member of the principal executive committee had to be re-elected every five years. 'Member of the executive' includes any person who by the rules or practice of the union may attend and speak at some or all of the meetings of the executive, except in the capacity of giving advice or information upon which the executive may act. These provisions were consolidated in section 46 of TULR(C)A 1992. This was amended by the Employment Relations Act 2004 so that a union is allowed to appoint a president in accordance with its rule book and without the need for an election, if the president already holds the position of general secretary or is a member of the executive and has been properly elected to that position. In other words, the union is not required in those circumstances to hold a second election. Section 47 of the 1992 Act further provides that no member of the trade union shall be unreasonably excluded from standing as a candidate and no candidate shall be required to be a member of a political party. In *Ecclestone v NUJ* [1999] IRLR 166, the national executive committee refused to accept a candidate for election to general secretary because, although he had held the post for 17 years, he had been dismissed following a dispute with the National Executive Committee (NEC) which claimed it no longer had confidence in him. The court held that this was the same as saying the NEC could block anyone it did not want to stand, and was thus a breach of section 47.

By section 50 of TULR(C)A 1992, all members of the union are entitled to vote, with three important exceptions: those who are unemployed, those who are in arrears with their subscriptions, or those who are apprentices, trainees, students or new members. The union rules may restrict entitlement to vote to members of a class determined by occupation or geographical area, but may not do so if the effect is to disentitle a member from voting at elections for officials (s 50(4)).

By section 51 of the 1992 Act, voting must be postal; however, section 54 of the Employment Relations Act 2004 gives a power to the Secretary of State to widen the means of voting as long as it always includes postal voting. The 1992 Act also lays down the requirements which must be complied with on the ballot paper, for example the name of the independent scrutineer appointed and a number marked on the paper. At present, the union must provide the candidates with the opportunity of preparing an election address and if such addresses are prepared the union must distribute them to the voters (TULR(C)A 1992, s 48(1)).

Section 49 of the 1992 Act requires the union to appoint an independent scrutineer. The functions of the scrutineer are listed in the section, and he must prepare a report on the election to the trade union as soon as reasonably practicable after the last date for the return of the voting papers. The report must contain items such as the number of returned voting papers, the number of valid votes, the number of invalid papers and a statement that there are no grounds for believing that there was a contravention of the statute, that the arrangements for the election minimised the risk of unfairness or malpractice and that he was able to carry out his functions free from interference (s 52(2)). The union cannot issue the results of the election until the receipt of the scrutineer's report, and must bring the contents of the report to the attention of its members. The union is obliged to maintain a register of the names and addresses of its members (s 24). By section 49, the union must require the scrutineer to inspect the register of members, and the scrutineer must state in his report that an inspection has been requested and completed. In addition, section 51A of TULR(C)A 1992 requires an independent person to count the votes; and if this person is not the scrutineer, the scrutineer must receive the voting papers once they have been counted, and his report must identify the independent counter and whether the scrutineer was satisfied with his performance.

The 1992 Act provides two remedies for failure to comply with the statutory provisions. The first, contained in section 55, is an application to the Certification Officer. Any member or candidate, up to a year after the default, may apply to the Certification Officer for a declaration. The Certification Officer must make a determination within six months of the application, and if a declaration is granted, it may state the steps that the union must take to remedy the declared failure. The second remedy is an application to the High Court (s 56). The advantage of turning to the court is that it has the additional power to make an enforcement order (s 56(4)), and this may be an order that the election be held again within a specified time period. In addition, the court may grant interim relief.

12.12 The right to information

The Employment Protection Act 1975 recognised that to be able to collectively bargain effectively, unions needed certain information from the employer. As a result, the Act introduced a right to receive certain information. This right has been retained, the provisions now being found in sections 181–185 of TULR(C)A 1992.

By section 181, an employer who recognises an independent trade union is required to disclose certain information to representatives of the union at their request. 'Representative' means a trade union official or any other person authorised by the union to carry on collective bargaining. The information which must be disclosed is any information about the employer's undertaking or that of an associated employer, without which the representatives would be materially impeded in carrying on collective bargaining, and such information which would be in accordance with good industrial relations practice to disclose (s 181(2)). The major limitation on this right is that by the wording in section 181, the employer has to disclose information only in relation to those matters for which the union is recognised for collective bargaining. Thus, if the employer recognises the union only for collective bargaining on pay, this is the only issue on which he is required to disclose information. In *R v CAC, ex parte BTP Tioxide Limited* [1982] IRLR 60, the company negotiated with the union on pay awards. It sought to introduce a job evaluation scheme without consulting the union, although the company gave the union the right to represent workers who wished to appeal against their gradings under the scheme. The union sought information about the scheme. It was held that that information need not be disclosed as the union was not recognised and did not have negotiating rights on job evaluation.

Section 181 of the 1992 Act further limits the rights by restricting the information to topics within the statutory definition of 'collective bargaining' found in section 178. This states that collective bargaining means negotiations relating to one or more of the following matters:

- terms and conditions of employment, or the physical conditions in which any workers are required to work;
- engagement or non-engagement, or termination or suspension of employment or the duties of employment, of one or more workers;
- allocation of work or the duties of employment between workers or groups of workers;
- matters of discipline;
- a worker's membership or non-membership of a trade union;
- facilities for trade union officials; and
- machinery for negotiation or consultation, and other procedures, relating to any of the above matters, including the recognition by employers or employers' associations of the right of a trade union to represent workers in such negotiation or consultation or in the carrying out of such procedures.

ACAS has produced a Code of Practice (ACAS Code of Practice 2: Disclosure of Information to Trade Unions for Collective Bargaining Purposes) which in paragraph 11 lists the type of information it would be good industrial relations practice to disclose. This includes:

- pay and benefits (including job evaluation systems, distribution of pay and total pay bill);
- conditions of service (including policies on recruitment, appraisal systems, and health and safety);
- manpower (including numbers, grades and labour turnover);

▶ performance (including productivity data, sales and return on invested capital); and
▶ financial information (including cost structures, and gross and net profits and loans).

Paragraph 12 states that this is not intended to be a checklist, neither is it intended to be exhaustive.

While the Code provides a wide-ranging list, it is important to remember that it is merely a code and therefore is not binding, although section 181(4) of TULR(C)A 1992 makes particular reference to it. Section 182, however, provides for restrictions on the general duty to disclose, and therefore an employer does not have to disclose information:

▶ the disclosure of which would be against the interests of national security, or
▶ which he could not disclose without contravening a prohibition imposed by or under an enactment, or
▶ which has been communicated to him in confidence, or which he has otherwise obtained in consequence of the confidence reposed in him by another person, or
▶ which relates specifically to an individual (unless that individual has consented to it being disclosed), or
▶ the disclosure of which would cause substantial injury to his undertaking for reasons other than its effect on collective bargaining, or
▶ obtained by him for the purpose of bringing, prosecuting or defending any legal proceedings.

Section 182(2) of the 1992 Act further provides that the employer need not produce or allow an inspection of the originals or copies of any documents for the purpose of conveying or confirming information. Nor is the employer obliged to compile or assemble information, if to do so would involve work or expenditure which is out of proportion to the value of the information in the conduct of collective bargaining. Given these restrictions, it is valid to question the value of the right to the information.

Section 183 of TULR(C)A 1992 provides a remedy for a trade union where the employer has failed to provide information, or failed to confirm information in writing when the union has requested such. The union may complain to the CAC. If the CAC feels the matter can be dealt with by conciliation, it will call upon ACAS to promote a settlement. If conciliation is unsuccessful or inappropriate, the CAC may make a declaration that the complaint is well founded and require the information to be disclosed by a particular date. If the employer ignores the declaration, the union may make a further complaint by section 184. The union may present a claim to the CAC in writing in respect of one or more descriptions of employees, that their contracts should contain the terms and conditions specified in the claim (s 185). If the CAC finds for the union, it may make an award that the employer shall observe those terms and conditions which by the award become part of the individual employee's contract. No award may be made if the employer discloses the information which is the subject of the complaint.

The rights to information have been further enhanced by the Transnational Information and Consultation of Employees Regulations 1999 (as amended by the Transnational and Consultation of Employees (Amendment) Regulations 2010), which were brought in to implement the European Works Council Directive (EC 94/45). The Regulations require a European Works Council (EWC) or an information and consultation procedure (ICP) to be established in every EU-scale undertaking. An 'EU-scale undertaking' is one which has at least 1,000 employees and at least 150 employees in each of two Member States (Reg 2(1)). Central management is responsible for starting negotiations to establish an EWC or ICP, and they must be initiated if at least 100 employees or representatives of at least 100 employees who represent employees in at least two Member States so request (Reg 9). Employee representatives are either representatives of an independent recognised trade union, who represent the relevant employees, or elected employee representatives who are expected to receive, on behalf of employees, information relevant to terms and conditions of employment of those employees or information about the activities of the undertaking which may significantly affect the interests of those employees (Reg 2). The scope, function, composition and term of office of an EWC or the implementation of an ICP are determined by a special negotiating body (SNB) in conjunction with central management (Regs 16 and 17). The SNB must consist of a representative of each Member State where the undertaking is based and up to three additional members (Reg 12). Central management must convene a meeting of the SNB to reach a written agreement on the arrangements for the information and consultation of employees (Reg 16(1)).

There are default provisions. If central management refuses to begin negotiations within six months of a request from employees or their representatives, or if the parties are unable to agree information and consultation procedures within three years of such a request, an EWC may be established with between three and 30 members. The information and consultation that the EWC can receive is, however, limited to matters concerning the group of undertakings as a whole. This EWC has the right to meet with central management once a year and receive a report on the progress and prospects of the undertaking or group. Paragraph 7 of the Schedule to the Regulations specifies issues which should be covered at this annual meeting.

If the parties agree to establish an EWC or ICP, or the default provisions become applicable, and no EWC or ICP has been established because of a failure by central management, the SNB, a former SNB member or employee representative may complain to the EAT. That tribunal may require central management to establish an EWC or ICP, and may also order the payment of a penalty to the Secretary of State of up to £75,000. This will be payable unless the failure resulted from a reason beyond the control of central management or there is other reasonable excuse for the failure (Reg 4).

There are two important limitations on the information to be disclosed. First, members of an SNB, EWC or ICP representatives owe a duty not to disclose information which has been given to them on confidential terms. Disclosure of such information is a breach of statutory duty unless it is a protected disclosure under the ERA 1996 (Reg 23). Second, central management do not have to disclose information which would 'seriously harm the functioning of, or would be prejudicial to, the undertaking or group of undertakings concerned'. A challenge to a decision by management that information falls within this category may be made to the CAC, which may order disclosure if it feels the information is not protected (Reg 24).

In addition to the Transnational Information and Consultation of Employees Regulations 1999, the Information and Consultation Directive (2002/14/EC) was agreed in 2002 and implemented by the Information and Consultation of Employees Regulations 2004. At the date of implementation the Regulations applied to employers with at least 150 employees; in March 2007 they applied to those employing 100 or more; and from March 2008 to those employing 50 or more.

The 2004 Regulations provide a fall-back statutory scheme if there are no voluntary arrangements in place. This will apply on a request in writing from 10 per cent of the workforce. The statutory procedure involves the establishment of an information and consultation committee consisting of one representative per 50 employees, up to a maximum of 50 members. The committee must be given information and be consulted about: the development of the undertaking's activities and its economic position; the state of employment in the undertaking and measures to be taken if there is a threat to employment; and any decisions likely to lead to substantial changes in work organisation where consultation must be with a view to reaching agreement. Where there are voluntary arrangements in place, the employer can ballot the workforce to see if new arrangements should be negotiated. If 40 per cent wish to change the arrangements, the employer has six months to negotiate with elected employee representatives as to the new arrangements. If negotiations fail, the statutory provisions apply. Where there are voluntary arrangements, the parties can decide the areas for consultation and information. Complaint on failing to release the information is to the CAC, which may then refer a case to the EAT if a penalty judgment is required.

There is evidence that the courts are interpreting the 2004 Regulations against employers who drag their feet. In *Amicus v Macmillan Publishers Ltd* [2007] IRLR 378, Macmillan had been before the CAC in 2005 for failing to provide information and was ordered by the CAC on its second appearance to give Amicus more precise information about employee numbers (a right granted by the Regulations so that a union can determine whether it has 10 per cent support for a request). Amicus therefore put in a second request in March 2006. Macmillan declined to ballot all employees to ascertain the level of support or start negotiations with employee representatives. Macmillan argued that the existing arrangements complied with the requirements for a pre-existing arrangement, but the EAT disagreed. As such, the standard information and consultation procedures came into play within six months of a valid request. The standard procedures give timescales for negotiations which require an employer to ballot employees to assess support for the request, and then enter negotiations. Macmillan should have arranged for the election of employee representatives by September 2006, but failed to do so. The EAT assessed the award on the basis that there had been a significant failure, 'because it must have been plain, reading the legislation, that the relevant provisions were being ignored at almost every stage' (*per* Elias P), and decided that Macmillan should pay £55,000. The maximum possible award is £75,000.

12.13 Financial assistance

The Employment Relations Act 2004 introduced a new section 116A into TULR(C)A 1992. This lists five purposes for which the Secretary of State may give money to enable or assist a trade union. That is, to:

1. improve the carrying out of any of its functions;
2. prepare to carry out any new function;
3. increase the range of services it offers to persons who are or who may become members;
4. prepare for an amalgamation or the transfer of any or all of its engagements;
5. ballot its members (whether as a result of a statutory requirement or otherwise).

The union must be independent (unless a federation of unions applies), and the Secretary of State can determine the way the assistance is provided and any terms relating to its disbursement. Section 116A(4) prohibits such assistance being added to the union's political fund, and if there is a breach of this, the Secretary of State must take such steps as are reasonably practicable to recover such sums from the political fund.

12.14 The closed shop

No discussion of unions is complete without mentioning closed shops. Although they cannot be legally enforced anymore, they were a powerful tool in the traditional industries. A closed shop was the situation where in a particular workplace, or workplaces if the employer operated a multi-site operation, membership of a particular union was necessary in order to work. If there was a pre-entry closed shop, this meant that the potential employee had to be a member of the union before he could be offered a job, and so essentially the union controlled the pool of applicants. A post-entry closed shop meant that employees had to join the union after acquiring the job. The closed shop raised many emotional arguments. Those who defended it argued that it prevented free-riders from obtaining the benefit of union representation (for example, on wage rises) without paying any union dues. Employers too argued that a closed shop made collective bargaining easier and prevented the problems of many unions representing disparate groups of workers on one site. By contrast, opponents of the closed shop argued that it took away freedom of the individual to choose the union to which he wished to belong, and also took away the right of an individual not to belong to any union. Certainly, where a closed shop existed, the union had a great deal of strength against the employer. When the Donovan Commission reported in the 1960s, it found that industries where the closed shop was prevalent were more strike-prone than those where union membership was not compulsory, and many people believed that the existence of a closed shop inevitably led to more industrial action.

There was no legal control over the closed shop until the Industrial Relations Act 1971. This Act introduced the concept of unfair dismissal, and it was through this concept that the closed shop was controlled. It was an unfair dismissal to dismiss a worker who would not join a union, although certain approved closed shops (or agency shops) could exist if on a majority vote the workers wanted one.

The fall of the Conservative government and the repeal of the Industrial Relations Act by the Trade Union and Labour Relations Act 1974 brought with it statutory protection for the closed shop. The original Act defined a closed shop as a union membership agreement which required a group of workers to belong to a specified union or unions. Protection came in the form that it was a fair dismissal to dismiss an employee who refused to join a union when a union membership agreement had been signed, but allowed a worker to be protected from dismissal if he objected to joining the union on religious grounds. These provisions meant that the union could coerce employees to join and put pressure on the employer to dismiss those employees who refused.

The Thatcher government which was returned in 1979 made the closed shop one of the targets of its industrial legislation policy and began slowly to dismantle any protection. The Employment Acts 1980 and 1982 increased protection for those employees who did not wish to join the union by making any dismissal unfair, while retaining the idea of a fair dismissal for those employees who refused to join but who did not fall within the categories of protection. This applied, however, only where a legal closed shop was operating, that is, one that had complied with the complicated balloting provisions introduced in 1980 and extended by the 1982 Act. In addition, where there was a claim of unfair dismissal, the union could be joined as a co-respondent in the claim and could be ordered to pay some, if not all, of the compensation awarded. While some would argue that this was a deliberate attempt to destroy the power of the unions, the European Court of Human Rights in *Young, James and Webster v United Kingdom* [1983] IRLR 35 had ruled that the legislation which allowed for compulsory membership of a particular union was an infringement of Article 11 of the European Convention on Human Rights as it restricted the freedom of the individual to join the union of their choice.

Despite the ruling, it remained possible to enforce a legal post-entry closed shop until 1988, when the Employment Act of that year rendered any dismissal for union or non-union membership unfair in any circumstances (now TULR(C)A 1992, s 152). As such, while post-entry closed shops can still exist, no one can legally be compelled to join a union.

The legislation of 1988, however, did nothing to prevent pre-entry closed shops operating, and while it was unlawful to dismiss or otherwise discriminate against an existing employee who refused to join the union, it still remained legal to discriminate against potential employees by insisting that they were union members before offering them employment. It was obvious that the government would not allow this situation to exist for very long, and the Employment Act 1990 finally destroyed any protection which existed for the pre-entry closed shop by rendering any action to discriminate in the appointment of persons on the grounds of union membership or non-membership illegal (now TULR(C)A 1992, ss 137–143). It should be noted that it was not part of government policy at the time to give protection to union members who were refused work because the employer wanted a union-free workplace. The European Social Charter, however, recommended that Member States prohibit discrimination on the grounds of non-union membership or union membership, and the government felt obliged to comply. This policy did not continue, however. Two Court of Appeal decisions (*Associated Newspapers Ltd v Wilson* [1993] IRLR 336 and *Associated British Ports v Palmer*, same reference), discussed below, decided that where an employer gave the employee the choice of a collectively bargained contract and an individual contract, the individual contract giving 4.5 per cent more pay than the collectively bargained one, then this amounted to discrimination on the grounds of trade union membership. While the decisions were reversed by the House of Lords ([1995] IRLR 258), the then government, in response to the Court of Appeal decisions, inserted a new clause in the Trade Union Reform and Employment Rights Bill (now s 148(3) of the 1992 Act) allowing employers to offer better terms to non-union members. Section 17 of the Employment Relations Act 1999 reversed these decisions and amended the legislative provisions by redefining 'detriment' as an act or any deliberate failure to act. This amendment, however, only applied in the context of collective agreements and pay. As a result of *Wilson v UK* (see Chapter 7), the Employment Relations Act 2004 provided protection against being offered an inducement or suffering detriment or dismissal for refusing to come out of collective bargaining (now TULR(C)A 1992, ss 145A and 145B).

Summary

12.1 A union is not a body corporate but it has certain powers which are also given to incorporated associations.

12.2 The legal definition of a union is that it must be a body of workers whose principal purpose is the regulation of relations between those workers and an employer or employers' association.

12.3 A union may be temporary or permanent.

12.4 A union must be listed and obtain a certificate of independence to enable its members to acquire certain rights.

12.5 In addition to independence, it is important for the union to be recognised by the employer for collective bargaining purposes.

12.6 Maintenance of a political fund by the union must be the subject of a membership ballot.

12.7 Unions must comply with stringent statutory rules regarding their accounts.

12.8 While the rule book lays down the express terms of the contract of membership between the union and its members, such terms may be augmented by custom and practice, or by the officious bystander test discussed in Chapter 3.

12.9 Unions must act within their stated objects for their actions to be *intra vires*.

12.10 The unions have adopted voluntary regulation in the form of the Bridlington Agreement.

12.11 Unions must comply with the statutory balloting provisions if they wish to amalgamate. In addition, all voting officials must be elected by membership ballot every five years.

12.12 Recognised independent trade unions are entitled to certain information from an employer for collective bargaining purposes, and independent trade unions are entitled to financial assistance from the Secretary of State.

12.13 A union can no longer enforce a pre-entry or post-entry closed shop by compulsory union membership.

Exercises

12.1 Why did it take unions in the UK so long to establish an ability to pursue their aims?

12.2 How far is the present legislation reminiscent of the Industrial Relations Act 1971?

12.3 Do you feel that the current legislation meets the then government's (2008) stated aim of democratising unions?

12.4 Good industrial relations should involve a balance of power between both sides. Many would argue that the balance has shifted in favour of the employer to the detriment of the unions. Do you feel that this is an accurate reflection of the present legislation?

Further reading and references

Bercusson, 'The European Social Model Comes to Britain' (2002) 31 ILJ 209 *Democracy in Trade Unions*, Cmnd 8778 (1983)

Dukes, 'The Statutory Recognition Procedure 1999: No Bias in Favour of Recognition?' (2008) 37 ILJ 236

Ewing, 'The Strike, The Courts and the Rule Books' (1985) 14 ILJ 160

Ewing, 'Trade Union Recognition and Staff Associations – A Breach of International Labour Standards?' (2000) 29 ILJ 267

Ewing, 'The Implications of *Wilson and Palmer*' (2003) 32 ILJ 1

Ewing, 'The Function of Trade Unions' (2005) 34 ILJ 1

Gall, 'The First Five Years of Britain's Third Statutory Recognition Procedure' (2005) 34 ILJ 345

Hall, 'Assessing the Information and Consultation of Employees Regulations' (2005) 34 ILJ 103

Kidner, 'Trade Union Democracy: Election of Trade Union Officers' (1984) 13 ILJ 193

Laulom, 'Flawed Revision of the EWC Directive' (2010) 39 ILJ 202

Simpson, 'Trade Union Recognition and the Law: A New Approach – Parts I and II of Schedule A1 to the Trade Union and Labour Relations (Consolidation) Act 1992' (2000) 29 ILJ 193

Trade Unions and Their Members, Cmnd 95 (1987)

Wedderburn, 'Collective Bargaining or Legal Enactment? The 1999 Act and Union Recognition' (2000) 29 ILJ 1

Chapter 13

The rights of trade union members

13.1 Introduction

For many years the legislature adopted a non-interventionist approach in the area of trade union activity, and apart from giving trade unions immunity from liability in certain situations to enable them to take industrial action, very little legislation was passed. This meant, however, that while individual members were protected should they take industrial action, very few other rights accrued. The Industrial Relations Act 1971 showed a departure from the previous non-interventionist approach, and although the Act was short-lived, its successor, the Trade Union and Labour Relations Act 1974, introduced strong protection for the union and its members engaging in industrial action, and gave legal protection to the closed shop. The Labour government which introduced that piece of legislation, however, saw it as part of a three-part plan in this field. The second part was the introduction of employment protection rights which were enacted in the Employment Protection Act 1975 and which also, for the first time, gave rights to trade union members vis-à-vis the employer. The final part was to be legislation on industrial democracy, which did not get very far owing to the party losing power.

The government which took office in 1979 was anxious to protect non-union members and democratise the unions; therefore, while retaining many of the rights union members had against an employer, it introduced rights for non-union members to protect them in situations where the union was putting pressure on the employer either to dismiss or to discriminate against them because of their non-union membership. In addition, it introduced new rights for union members vis-à-vis the union, and a special Commissioner to enforce these newly created rights. While the post of Commissioner was abolished in 1999, jurisdiction passed to the Certification Officer.

Thus the trade union member now has two groups of rights – those against his employer to ensure that he is not treated less favourably than a non-unionist and that he is allowed time off to pursue his trade union activities, and those against his union to ensure that the union acts within the bounds of the rule book and that it does not unreasonably discipline or exclude him. Some of these particular rights have been discussed elsewhere in this book. The time-off rights were more logically discussed with employment protection rights in general in Chapter 7. So too dismissal for trade union membership or activities was more logically discussed with unfair dismissal in Chapter 9. The discussion below deals with the rest of the rights that a trade union member is now granted by law.

13.2 Enforcement of the union rule book

While there is special statutory protection for union members in relation to rules concerning discipline and exclusion or expulsion (see Section 13.3 below), a member must rely on the common law to enforce any other rule in the rule book. Although the rule book forms the contract of membership between the individual member and the union, this will not always provide him with a remedy. Rather, the trade union member is treated in a way similar to a shareholder in a company and, as such, his remedies against the union are similar to those imposed against incorporated associations.

The simple proposition is that because a union as an entity exists only as a creation of statute, its legal capacity to act comes from its rules (and to some extent from statute when talking about industrial action, elections, amalgamations and so on). As such, if the rules or statute lay down when a union can act (for example, after a majority vote of members) then should the union act without fulfilling the requirements, it has no capacity to do so and hence its actions are *ultra vires*. *Ultra vires* actions, as we have already seen in Chapter 12, are void, and a member may challenge the union. In certain cases the member may do this by application to the Certification Officer, a right introduced by the Employment Relations Act 1999. So, for example, a member may apply to the Certification Officer where a breach or threatened breach relates to the appointment, election or removal of a person from office, disciplinary proceedings, balloting of members on any issue other than industrial action and the constitution or proceedings of any decision-making body (TULR(C)A 1992, s 108A). Should the complaint be upheld, the Certification Officer may make an enforcement order requiring the union to take steps to remedy the breach, withdraw the threat of the breach and abstain from action which would mean that the breach would occur in the future (s 108B). However, apart from the statutory specified actions, the member's right to enforce the rule book is a negative one, and the member may only obtain a declaration stating that the rule has been broken rather than restraining a breach or compelling the union to observe it. This is well illustrated by the case of *Taylor v NUM (Yorkshire Area)* [1984] IRLR 445. Although this case has now been superseded by the statutory requirements concerning balloting before industrial action (TULR(C)A 1992, s 226) the principle is important. The case arose out of the national miners' strike of 1984–85. Under the national union rules, a national strike could not be called without a ballot which obtained a 55 per cent majority vote in favour of such a strike. This rule was reiterated in the rules of each of the area unions. Taylor challenged the strike because there had been no national ballot. In relation to the Yorkshire branch there had been a ballot, but this had been held in 1981, although there was a vote in favour of a strike with an 85.6 per cent majority. The court held that the union's argument that the strike was a series of local strikes rather than a national strike was arguable. Even if that was the case, however, the ballot in 1981 in Yorkshire was too distant from the strike to authorise it and as such the strike was *ultra vires*. Taylor's remedy, on the other hand, was a declaration that the strike was unofficial; he could not obtain an injunction to prevent the strike continuing, or insist that a proper ballot was conducted. Nicholas J held that a member's right under the rules was confined to being able to insist that a strike could not be held lawfully without the requisite ballot. In other words, the best a member can do is restrain *ultra vires* behaviour, not force the union to act *intra vires*.

Enforcement of the rules is further complicated by the introduction of company law concepts in this area. It has already been mentioned in Chapter 12 (see Section 12.8) that the rule in *Foss v Harbottle* (1843) 2 Hare 461 has, on occasion, been applied to unions. In simple terms, the rule states that if a breach of the rules controlling the organisation is really a wrong done to the organisation, only the organisation can sue. It therefore follows that if the wrongful act is capable of ratification, the individual member may have no action, because the majority can override his wishes by ratifying the act. To prevent useless actions being taken against companies, therefore, the rule has developed that if the action is capable of ratification the individual loses his right of action whether it is ratified or not, unless there is a fraud on the minority members. By applying this rule to trade unions (unincorporated associations, remember), the individual trade union member may therefore be deprived of his right to challenge a breach if the court feels that, for example, the union had the power to do the act but performed it in an irregular way.

A contrast with *Taylor* (above) is *Cotter v NUS* [1929] 2 Ch 58, where an official challenged a resolution made by a Special General Meeting to make an interest-free loan to the Miners' Non-Political Movement. The basis of the challenge was that the delegates at the meeting had not been properly elected and the meeting had not been properly convened in accordance with the union rules. The Court of Appeal held that, given that such a loan could be made by such a meeting, the irregularities were minor and the loan was capable of ratification. As such, the member was prevented from challenging the loan by *Foss v Harbottle*.

On the other hand, if the union had no power to act in the first place, for example by calling a strike without first holding a ballot, the union has no power to call a strike and hence that act can never be ratified. It therefore follows that the rule in *Foss v Harbottle* cannot apply and the member may take action, although his remedy may be limited. While the proposition may be easy to state, it is far from easy to apply in practice, and although the rule in *Foss v Harbottle* has been applied only infrequently to unions, the fact that it has been applied to unincorporated associations at all has been the subject of criticism.

13.3 Exclusion and expulsion

We have already seen in Chapter 12 that essentially a trade union cannot legally enforce a closed shop, and therefore it may appear that any discussion on exclusion and expulsion may be redundant. Closed shops still exist, however, in certain industries, and whereas the employee may have a remedy against the employer for refusing to employ him because he is not a trade union member, that will not help him if the reason he is not such a member is that the union does not want him or has expelled him, particularly as other rights arise from trade union membership. In addition, there may be other reasons why a member is excluded or expelled, such as non-membership of a trade.

While the principle of freedom of association is well established and protects those who are union members, the question arises as to how far the law can intervene when an employee wishes to associate with a union which does not want to associate with him. Article 8(a) of the International Covenant on Economic, Social and Cultural Rights states that the freedom to join an association is subject to the rules of the association, and the European Court of Human Rights held in *Cheall v United Kingdom* [1986] 8 EHRR 74 that an expulsion did not infringe Article 11 of the European Convention on Human Rights (giving the right of freedom of association with others, including the right to form and join a trade union) if the expulsion was conducted to comply with the Bridlington Agreement (see Section 12.9). Thus it appears that the organisation itself may regulate its membership.

You may feel that this should be the case, particularly when a union is a voluntary organisation. This ignores the fact, however, that unions are very powerful, both politically and economically, and this is a fact which has not escaped the notice of the courts. The problem in this area is that the member is complaining that the union will not enter a contract with him rather than the more normal complaint that a contract has been broken. He is not complaining that he is deprived of a right, but rather that he has lost the chance of acquiring a right, and until fairly recently, such a complaint had no legal remedy in the English courts. The Court of Appeal, however, and Lord Denning MR in particular, have suggested that a right to work exists which may be infringed by exclusion or expulsion from a union. (Consideration of whether there is a duty to provide work to enforce this right has already been given in Chapter 4.)

Lord Denning began to establish that a right to work might exist in the case of *Nagle v Fielden* [1966] 2 QB 633. In the case the plaintiff, a woman, complained that she had been refused a trainer's licence by the Jockey Club because she was a woman. The importance of the licence lay in the fact that no horse could be entered for a race unless the trainer had a licence, and Mrs Nagle's head lad had to obtain the licence in his name. Lord Denning opined that, given that the Jockey Club operated a monopoly, in that it was the only body to grant licences, and given that without a licence Mrs Nagle could not carry out her living of training race horses, a rule the operation of which unreasonably prevented Mrs Nagle from obtaining a licence was in restraint of trade and void. While the other judges did not go so far, they were prepared to concede that the point was arguable.

While the association in *Nagle* was not a trade union, it was operating a monopoly, and it was not long before Lord Denning used the analogy in a closed-shop situation. In *Edwards v SOGAT* [1971] Ch 354, a case involving expulsion from a trade union, Lord Denning said that he did not feel that a trade union could give itself an unfettered discretion to expel or exclude a member. He continued: 'The reason lies in a man's right to work ... The courts ... will not allow so great a power to be exercised arbitrarily or capriciously or with unfair discrimination, neither in the making of rules nor in the enforcement of them.' While the idea of a right to work may be questionable, the comments help to explain the reasoning behind Lord Denning's judgment. He decided that the union could not rely on its immunity from restraint-of-trade claims because the union's action destroyed the right of an individual to earn his living and so was *ultra vires*. Whereas a rule of a union cannot be unenforceable by the reason only that it is restraint of trade (TULR(C)A) 1992, s 11), Lord Denning's comments that a union cannot exercise its rules arbitrarily or capriciously have been adopted by statute. Originally, section 65 of the Industrial Relations Act 1971 made it unlawful to exclude 'by arbitrary or unreasonable discrimination' a worker from a trade union. When that provision was repealed in 1976, the TUC set up its own Independent Review Committee to hear complaints from people about exclusion or expulsion from unions that were members of the TUC. The government which came to power in 1979 was not happy with this self-regulation, and in the Employment Act 1980 it introduced the right not to be excluded or expelled from a trade union unless a person does not satisfy the membership requirements, he no longer qualifies on geographical grounds, he is no longer employed by a relevant employer, or the expulsion or exclusion is entirely attributable to his conduct. Protection is now found in section 174 of the 1992 Act, as amended by the Employment Relations Act 2004.

By section 174(2)(d), a union may expel or exclude where the reason for that expulsion or exclusion is entirely attributable to conduct, and the conduct is neither excluded conduct nor protected conduct. There are no rights to expel or exclude where it is to any extent related to excluded conduct, but there are limited rights to expel or exclude where such is attributable to some extent to protected conduct. However, section 174(4) of

TULR(C)A 1992 (as amended by the Employment Relations Act 2004) specifies that excluded conduct is:

- current or former membership of a trade union;
- current or former employment by a particular employer or at a particular place; or
- conduct for which disciplinary action taken by a union would be regarded as unjustifiable (see Section 13.4 below).

Protected conduct is found in section 174(4A) and was defined as being or ceasing to be, or having been or ceased to be, a member of a political party. Political activities of any kind are not protected conduct (s 174(4B)).

The relationship between section 174 of the 1992 Act and the European Convention on Human Rights was tested in the case of *ASLEF v UK* [2007] IRLR 361 (ECtHR) 448. Lee, a train driver, joined the union ASLEF in 2002 and a few months later stood as a British National Party (BNP – formerly the National Front) candidate in local elections. ASLEF had a formal policy to 'campaign vigorously to expose the obnoxious policies of political parties such as the National Front' and expelled Lee from membership. However, because of section 174, ASLEF was forced to take him back or face a huge compensation claim. ASLEF considered this to be a breach of Article 11 of the Convention, which provides that the right to form and join a trade union may be subject to such restrictions 'as are necessary in a democratic society in the interests of national security or public safety, for the prevention of disorder or crime, for the protection of health or morals or for the protection of the rights and freedoms of others'. ASLEF claimed that section 174 was a breach of Article 11 and the European Court of Human Rights agreed. The Court held that forcing a private body to accept Lee as a member was an infringement of Article 11. The UK government was ordered to pay ASLEF's costs. The case led to amendments to section 174. The Employment Act 2008 inserted section 174(4C)–(4H) into TULR(C)A 1992. By section 174(4C), membership or past membership of a political party is not protected conduct if membership of that party is contrary to a rule or objective of the union, although a union cannot rely on conduct being against an objective of the union if, in relation to exclusion, such objective could not be reasonably ascertained by a person working in the same trade, industry or profession; in the case of expulsion, it must not be reasonably ascertainable by a member of the union (s 174(4D)). Likewise, if at the time of the conduct the objective was not reasonably ascertainable by a member of the trade, industry or profession (in the case of exclusion), or by a union member (in the case of expulsion), it cannot be relied upon by the union (s 174(4E)). Furthermore, the union has no protection if the decision to expel or exclude is taken otherwise than in accordance with the union rules, would cause the individual to lose his livelihood or suffer exceptional hardship, or the decision is taken unfairly (s 174(4G)). A decision is taken unfairly if and only if before the decision the individual has not been given notice of the proposal and the reasons for it and a fair opportunity to make representations about the proposal, or if such representations are not considered fairly. It has to be said that the provisions are worded in such a way that there is the potential for litigation and judicial interpretation.

A claimant has the right to go to an employment tribunal. If the complaint is well founded, the tribunal may make a declaration and an award of compensation which, although it is based on unfair dismissal figures, exceeds the statutory maximum imposed in unfair dismissal cases (TULR(C)A 1992, s 176(6)). Where a declaration is made, a tribunal must state the ground (that is, protected or excluded conduct) and must also make a declaration if the breach of section 174 is because of conduct which is contrary to the rules of the union (section 176(1A), (1B), (1C) and (1D)). A tribunal must award the statutory minimum where, at the time of the decision, the claimant had not been admitted or readmitted into the union. But the minimum does not apply where the tribunal has issued a declaration that the exclusion or expulsion was for excluded or protected conduct (section 176(6A) and (6B)). Compensation may be reduced for contributory conduct. An appeal lies to the EAT.

An expulsion where there is no right to expel in the circumstances will be *ultra vires* and the tribunal will grant the complainant a remedy (*Bonsor v Musicians' Union* [1956] AC 104); and likewise the refusal of an appeal where one is granted by the rules will render the expulsion invalid (*Braithwaite v Electrical, Electronics and Telecommunications Union* [1969] 2 All ER 859). In addition, if the rules are vague, the courts will place their own interpretation upon them. In *Kelly v NATSOPA* (1915) 84 LJKB 2236, the court held that an expulsion based on a rule which allowed such action if the member was guilty of conduct prejudicial to the union's interests had been misapplied when the union expelled the plaintiff when he obtained a part-time job. By contrast, in *Evans v National Union of Bookbinding and Printing Workers* [1938] 4 All ER 51, the rules provided for expulsion of a member who acted contrary to the interests of the union. Evans was absent from work on a number of occasions, contrary to an agreement between the union and employers. It was held that his expulsion was a valid exercise of the union's power under the rules.

While the above cases are examples of the common law rather than statute operating, the principles are the same when applying the statutory provisions. Furthermore, when dealing with exclusion cases, the EAT has stated that the provisions should not be read in a restrictive way. In *Clark v NATSOPA (SOGAT '82)* [1986] ICR 12, Clark had taken voluntary redundancy from the printing industry in 1976 as part of an agreement to reduce over-manning in the industry. Part of the agreement was that he should not seek work in the printing industry in the United Kingdom. Some years later, he wished to work again in the printing industry and tried to re-join the union. His application was rejected and he complained that he had been unreasonably excluded. The union argued that as he had not applied for a job which required union membership, he had no cause of action. The EAT disagreed. It was sufficient that a person was seeking employment generally to invoke the protection. The complainant did not have to show that the exclusion had lost him a job before he could sue.

13.4 Discipline of union members

Although expulsion from the union may be imposed as a disciplinary sanction, it is not the only form of sanction imposed by a union on its members. Nevertheless, the courts' powers are wide enough to control a union's use of its power when the sanction is something other than expulsion. The main form of control exercised by the courts is that the union must comply with the rules of natural justice. While these rules are normally applied to judicial or quasi-judicial bodies, it has been clear since *Lee v Showman's Guild of Great Britain* [1952] 2 QB 329 that trade unions must abide by the rules when making decisions in relation to their members. Lord Denning MR stated in *Breen v AEU* [1971] 2 QB 175 that although a union hearing was operating in an administrative way, it must still act fairly, and the courts had the power to issue declarations and injunctions to ensure fair treatment.

The rules of natural justice involve four elements:

1. Notice: A person must be given adequate notice of the charge against him and the potential penalty so that he has an opportunity to answer it. In *Annamunthodo v Oilfield Workers Union* [1961] AC 954, the plaintiff knew that he was charged with making allegations against the union president and knew he could be fined. He did not know that such conduct was treated as prejudicial to the union and that he could be expelled. It was held that his subsequent expulsion was void.

2. Opportunity to put his case: A person must be given the opportunity to put his side of the case and to answer the charges against him.

3. Unbiased hearing: The hearing should be unbiased. This is probably easier to state in theory than operate in practice, as often the members of the hearing who are judging, for example, prejudicial conduct are union officials. Although the rule is stringently adhered to in judicial hearings, it is modified in the case of domestic tribunals, and as long as there is no obvious bias, for example a person involved in the dispute is also involved in the hearing, the rule will not be offended. In *White v Kuzych* [1951] AC 585, the plaintiff was expelled from the union because of his opposition to the closed-shop policy that the union had adopted. The fact that those who were involved in the hearing had spoken in support of the policy did not render the decision void for bias. On the other hand, in *Roebuck v NUM (Yorkshire Area) (No 2)* [1978] ICR 676, two union officials had given evidence to a newspaper in a libel action taken by the union president Arthur Scargill on behalf of the union. Mr Scargill presided over the hearing which recommended that the two officials be suspended from office for conduct prejudicial to the union, and then chaired the area council meeting which, not surprisingly, confirmed that decision. It was held that the suspensions were void. Mr Scargill had in reality been the complainant, and had made up his mind on the matter before the first hearing commenced, let alone the second. So too in *Taylor v NUS* [1967] 1 WLR 532, the union's general secretary dismissed an official and then chaired the appeal against the dismissal. It was held that the decision to dismiss was void.

4. Representation: The rules do not specifically state that a person should be allowed legal representation, and it appears from *Enderby Town Football Club v Football Association* [1971] Ch 591 that such representation may be specifically excluded by the rules as long as some kind of representative is allowed.

While the rules are the basis of the contract of membership between the union and its members, and the courts do not like to interfere in that contract, a rule ousting the jurisdiction of the courts is void. This was the position at common law and is now to be found in section 63(1) of the 1992 Act. A rule which purports to require a member to exhaust internal procedures before seeking a remedy in the courts is not void under this provision, but by section 63(2) such a rule will be ignored by the court if a member has asked for the matter to be dealt with by the union and six months after such application the union has not completed the internal procedures.

In addition to the common law controlling the conduct of disciplinary hearings and the statutory provision preventing the rules from ousting the courts' jurisdiction, statute has further provided a right for all trade union members not to be unjustifiably disciplined.

The original right was introduced by the Employment Act 1988 and is now contained in sections 65–67 of TULR(C)A 1992. Section 64 lists the sanctions which are defined as discipline, which includes expulsion, fines, refusal of access to benefits or any other detriment. Section 65 then defines what is meant by 'unjustifiably', which includes disciplinary action in respect of:

- failing to participate in industrial action;
- failing to contravene a provision in the contract of employment;
- asserting breaches of the legislation by an official or union representative unless that allegation was made in bad faith;
- making representations to the Certification Officer; and
- encouraging a person to perform their contract of employment contrary to union instructions;
- failing to agree or withdrawing agreement to deduction from wages of union fees;
- resigning or proposing to resign membership, or proposing to join or refuse to join another union;
- working with non-union members;
- working for an employer who employs non-union labour; and
- requiring the union to perform an act which by statute it must perform on the requisition of a member.

If the action complained of is an exclusion or expulsion under section 174 and the reason is a breach of section 65, the expulsion or exclusion is automatically unreasonable (TULR(C)A 1992, s 66(4)).

A breach of the provisions allows a member to complain to the employment tribunal, which may make a declaration and award compensation. The amount of compensation is the same as that awarded under section 176 of the 1992 Act (that is, 30 times the maximum weekly pay in the basic award for unfair dismissal, plus the maximum compensatory award, with a statutory minimum). The EAT has held in *NALGO v Courtney-Dunn* [1991] IRLR 114 that if a member is successful in obtaining a declaration and compensation, the union must put him in the position he was in before the unjustifiable discipline was imposed. The compensation awarded should, however, reflect the actual loss sustained by the member and not be punitive. In *Bradley v NALGO* [1991] IRLR 159, the complainant was expelled for failing to take part in industrial action and claimed compensation. The union did not contest the declaration, nor did it revoke the expulsion. The EAT awarded the minimum award only. The expulsion did not affect the complainant's job prospects and would not affect his joining another union.

13.5 The Certification Officer

The office of the Commissioner for the Rights of Trade Union Members was created by the Employment Act 1988 as a body to give assistance to trade union members who wished to take action against their union for infringement of certain statutory rights. The post was abolished by the Employment Relations Act 1999 and jurisdiction over specified contractual matters passed to the Certification Officer. The matters are listed in Ch VIIA (sections 108A–108C) of the 1992 Act.

13.6 Action short of dismissal

So far this chapter has dealt with the rights of individual members against the union, but the law also affords a certain amount of protection against an employer.

The Employment Relations Act 1999 (Blacklists) Regulations 2010 give protection for trade union members against employers who operate blacklists, ie lists of trade union members whom they will not employ. Regulation 3(1) states that no person shall compile, use, sell or supply a prohibited list. A prohibited list is defined in Regulation 3(2) as a list (in any form – written, electronic, etc) which contains details of persons who are or have been trade union members, or who are taking part in or have taken part in trade union activities. Note that there is no definition of 'trade union activities' in the Regulations, although there are similar phrases in other statutes. The government's response to the consultation stated that it would include participation in official but not in unofficial industrial action. In addition, the list must have been compiled with a view to use by employer or employment agencies for the purposes of discriminating in relation to the recruitment or treatment of workers. 'Discrimination' has the same definition as in the Equality Act 2010, ie treating someone less favourably than another due to (in this context) their trade union membership or activity (Reg 3(3)).

Where there is a breach of Regulation 3, Regulation 13 provides for enforcement by a person affected in the county court for breach of statutory duty. The court may award unlimited damages that may include compensation for injury to feelings (Reg 13(3)(b)). In addition, the court may make an order restraining the defendant from breaching the Regulations. The Regulations also provide a remedy in the employment tribunal where an employer refuses employment to a claimant or an employment agency refuses to offer its services. The list of what constitutes 'refusing to employ' is wide and includes refusing to process an application or making an offer no reasonable employer would make (Reg 5(2)). In addition, a claim lies where the employer has dismissed a worker or subjected him to a detriment (Reg 9) for a reason relating to the prohibited list (Reg 12, inserting a new s 104F into the ERA 1996). This constitutes an automatic unfair dismissal. A claim lies within three months of the action complained of. As with discrimination claims, the burden of proof is reversed. The tribunal may award compensation up to the maximum for unfair dismissal with a minimum award of £5,000 (Reg 8). In addition, the tribunal has the power to make a recommendation that the employer or employment agency take action to eliminate or reduce the adverse effect of their unlawful conduct. An unreasonable failure to comply may result in an increase in compensation. The tribunal may also reduce compensation where it considers that the conduct of the claimant makes it just and equitable to do so (Reg 8(5)).

In addition to the rights discussed above, we have already seen in Chapter 9 that the law will protect an employee who is dismissed for trade union membership or non-membership, or for taking part in trade union activities at the appropriate time. Protection against dismissal, however, is complemented by protection against action short of dismissal for one of the above grounds, and is now found in section 146 of TULR(C)A 1992. Should a tribunal find a complaint well founded, it may make a declaration to that effect and award compensation to offset any loss caused by the action (s 149(2)). In addition, either the complainant or the employer may join the union as a co-respondent if it was union pressure which induced the action, and the tribunal may order that some or all of the compensation be paid by the union(s 150(1) and (3)).

The original provisions were contained in the Employment Protection (Consolidation) Act 1978, and under that legislation, refusal to grant a benefit on these grounds was action short of dismissal for the purposes of protection. In *NCB v Ridgway* [1987] ICR 736, it was held that refusal to give a pay rise negotiated with the Union of Democratic Mineworkers (UDM) to NUM members was unlawful action short of dismissal. In other words, it is sufficient if the employer discriminates against members of a particular union, and it is not necessary to show discrimination against union members as a whole. Whether there is protection against threats, however, is more in doubt. The EAT in *Brassington v Cauldron Wholesale Ltd* [1978] ICR 405 stated *obiter* that it felt that the threat to close down a factory, sack the workforce and open under a different name if the workers joined a union was not sufficient to be caught by the statute.

Despite earlier interpretations, the provisions on action short of dismissal came under scrutiny in a number of cases. In *Associated British Ports v Palmer* and *Associated Newspapers Ltd v Wilson* [1995] IRLR 258, an action arose in both cases as a result of 'sweeteners' paid to employees who agreed to give up their rights to have their wages determined collectively and to switch to individual contracts. The converse obviously applied, that is, those who still wished to have their wages negotiated collectively did not receive these payments. As such, the question in both cases was whether such payments were contrary to section 146 of the 1992 Act. The EAT held in both cases that there was no breach of section 146 because it was not shown that the employer had the purpose of 'preventing or deterring [an employee] from being or seeking to become a member of an independent trade union, or penalising him for doing so' (s 146(1)). The Court of Appeal, however, decided that the necessary purpose was shown, that is, the purpose of the payments was to persuade employees to abandon their trade union representation and deter them from trade union membership. These cases went against the then government's stated policy of encouraging the development of individual contracts, and consequently the Trade Union Reform and Employment Rights Act 1993 amended section 148 by providing that such conduct is not action short of dismissal if it is intended to further a change in the employers' relationship with any class of employee, unless it is action that no reasonable employer would take. After this amendment, the House of Lords reversed the decisions in *Palmer* and *Wilson*, and further restricted any protection by holding that action short of dismissal envisaged a positive act on the part of the employer and did not include an omission to act (for example, by not giving a pay rise). As such, the employers' conduct did not amount to action short of dismissal for the purposes of section 146. Wilson and Palmer took their case to the European Court of Human Rights, which ruled ([2002] IRLR 568) that the UK was in breach of Article 11 of the ECHR by permitting employers to use financial incentives to persuade employees to relinquish their rights to trade union representation for collective bargaining purposes. The Court said:

> It is the essence of the right [under Article 11] that employees should be free to instruct or permit the union to make representations to their employer. If workers are prevented from so doing the freedom to belong to a trade union becomes illusory.

While the Employment Relations Act 1999 overturned the House of Lords decisions, the government felt that the amendments did not cover the judgment in *Wilson* and *Palmer*, and the Employment Relations Act 2004 introduced further protection, as discussed below.

Gallacher v Department of Transport [1994] IRLR 231 was another case involving section 146 of the 1992 Act. In this case, the applicant was a civil servant who was elected to a full-time union post in 1986. Until 1990 he had no management functions and was not fully under the staff appraisal system. In 1990 he applied for promotion, but was rejected because there were doubts as to his management capabilities after a four-year gap. He was told that he would need more management experience, which would mean a reduction in his union activities. The employment tribunal upheld the complaint of detriment, but the EAT held that the tribunal had erred in making that decision because it had failed to consider what 'action' had been taken and what the 'purpose' was behind it. The Court of Appeal upheld the decision of the EAT.

In order to pursue a claim under section 146 of TULR(C)A 1992, the employee must be subjected to a detriment as an individual, and therefore action taken against the union is not covered, although action taken against a group who are members of the union could be covered if it affects them as individuals. Cases like *Gallacher*, *Palmer* and *Wilson*, however, show a difficulty in the provision, in that in order for a claim to be successful, the act or failure to act on the part of the employer must be for the purpose of preventing or deterring the employee from union membership or activities. Thus, in *Gallacher*, the purpose of not promoting him was not to deter him from trade union activities even though the effect was precisely that. This may now be subject to the later decision of *London Borough of Southwark v Whiller* [2001] EWCA Civ 808, where the employer offered a promotion to a union official, but on the basis that she would receive the higher rate of pay applicable to the grade only when she was able to undertake the duties of the grade. The Court of Appeal held that the tribunal was entitled to conclude that the purpose of the employer was to deter her from union activities.

Given the problems with section 146, and the *Wilson* and *Palmer* decision, the Employment Relations Act 2004 inserted new sections 145A–145F into the 1992 Act. Section 145A gives a worker the right not to have an offer made to him by his employer where the employer's sole or main purpose is to induce the worker not to be or seek to be a member of an independent trade union; not to take part in the activities of an independent trade union at an appropriate time; not to make use of the services of a trade union at an appropriate time and to be or become a member of a trade union. Section 145B gives a right to a worker who is a member of an independent union seeking recognition or recognised by the employer, not to have an offer made to him, where similar offers are being made to other workers, the sole or main purpose of which is to secure that the terms of the workers will no longer be determined by collective agreement. These sections mean that, along with section 146, workers are now protected against detriment and inducement.

In addition to existing statutory protection, it has been seen above that the Human Rights Act 1998 impacts on this area. As noted in Chapter 12 (in Section 12.14), in *Young, James and Webster v United Kingdom* [1983] IRLR 35 (a case under the now repealed closed-shop provisions), the European Court of Human Rights ruled that legislation which allowed for compulsory membership of a particular union was an infringement of Article 11 ECHR as it restricted the right of an individual to join a union of his choice; and in *Ahmed v UK* [1999] IRLR 188, the same Court held that the threats of disciplinary action would also constitute an interference with the right to join a trade union and freedom of expression. The decision in *Wilson* and *Palmer* adds to this list of actions which constitute an infringement of Article 11.

Summary

13.1 The rule book forms the contract of membership between the trade union member and the union.

13.2 Enforcement of the rule book by a member is governed by the common law and not by statute.

13.3 The remedy for a member where a breach of the rules is alleged is the restraint of *ultra vires* behaviour. A member cannot force a union to act *intra vires*.

13.4 The rule in *Foss v Harbottle*, which comes from company law, has on occasion been applied to trade unions.

13.5 *Foss v Harbottle* can never be applied when the union acts *ultra vires*.

13.6 Statute provides individual members with a right not to be excluded or expelled from a union.

13.7 The common law rules of natural justice apply to trade unions, and if they are breached, the decision is void.

13.8 Statute has also created a right for trade union members not to be unjustifiably disciplined by their union.

13.9 Regulations protect workers who have been refused employment or been dismissed, or who suffered a detriment because their details have been included on a prohibited blacklist.

13.10 In addition to giving protection from dismissal on the grounds of non-membership of a trade union or union membership or activities, statute protects employees who have had action short of dismissal taken against them on these grounds.

Exercises

13.1 Do you consider that the rule in *Foss v Harbottle* can legitimately be invoked against a trade union member? If not, why not?

13.2 The Domestic Bus Company was involved in a dispute with the Travel Union over proposed redundancies. The union had concluded a union membership agreement with the company which covered drivers only. The union decided to take industrial action and held a ballot of its members. A majority of 79 per cent voted in favour of industrial action. The union then called on all its members to strike, despite the fact that the union rule book stipulated in Rule 84 that 'all negotiating procedures should be exhausted before industrial action is taken on any issue'. In a collective agreement concluded the previous year between the company and the union, three distinct stages were spelled out in a 'Grievance Procedure'. In this instance, only the first stage of the procedure had been completed before industrial action was taken.

Fred, a conductor, was expelled from the union for failing to obey the union's instructions to strike under Rule 9, which stated that: 'Any union member acting contrary to the interests of the union is liable to expulsion.' He was informed that the local committee had met and, after considering his refusal, had decided to expel him.

Jim, another union member, wishes to challenge the Travel Union in respect of two payments made from the union's general fund. One was a payment of £10,000 to a strike committee to support pickets, where no rule specifically authorised such payment, and the second was a payment of £5,000 to support the 'Troops Out of Afghanistan' movement's meetings. The union's political fund rules authorised funds to be made generally available for political purposes.

Advise Fred and Jim.

Further reading and references

Barrow, 'The Employment Relations Act 1999 (Blacklists) Regulations 2010' (2010) 39 ILJ 300

Bogg, 'Employment Relations Act 2004: Another False Dawn for Collectivism?' (2005) 34 ILJ 72

Corby, 'Limitations on Freedom of Association in the Civil Service and the ILO's response' (1986) 15 ILJ 161

Ewing, 'The Implications of *Wilson* and *Palmer*' (2003) 32 ILJ 1

Ewing, 'The Employment Act 2008: Implementing the *ASLEF* Decision: A Victory for the BNP?' (2009) 38 ILJ 38

Hendy and Ewing, 'Trade Unions, Human Rights and the BNP' (2005) 34 ILJ 197

Kidner, 'Unjustified Discipline by a Trade Union' (1991) 20 ILJ 284

Mead, 'To BNP or not to BNP: Union Expulsion on the Ground of Political Activity – A Commentary on *ASLEF* v. *Lee*' (2004) 33 ILJ 267

Morris, 'Fundamental Rights: Exclusion by Agreement?' (2001) 30 ILJ 49

Removing the Barriers to Employment, Cmnd 655 (1989)

Trade Unions and Their Members, Cmnd 95 (1987)

Wedderburn, 'Freedom of Association and Philosophies of Labour Law' (1989) 18 ILJ 1

Chapter 14

Industrial action

Introduction

Since the growth of trade unionism after the Industrial Revolution, the strength of the employee has been in his freedom to associate with fellow employees and to negotiate collectively with the employer. This may seem to be a bold statement at first sight, but its basis is the foundation stone of industrial relations. An employer has economic strength when compared to an employee. He has the job, and if the employee does not comply with the employer's wishes then, unless the law prevents it, the employer can easily replace him. Any protest by the individual employee is unlikely to have much effect. If the employee, however, is one of a large group, all of whom protest against the employer, then the impact will be much greater, and the possibility of such a protest could keep the employer from making unreasonable demands. Thus, simplistically, the power of employees to organise balances the economic power of the employer. This power to organise, however, is only half the story. The body of workers must be able to protest in a way which will be effective and which will persuade the employer to see their point of view. Hence, industrial action in one form or another, be it a go-slow, a work-to-rule or ultimately a strike, gives the body of workers bargaining power. It is therefore the power to organise plus the power to take industrial action that is the balance to the employer's economic power. Good industrial relations policy tries to achieve an equal balance of power. Too much power on the part of the unions will shift the balance in their favour; too little power on the part of the unions will shift the balance the other way and increase the strength of the employer.

We have seen already in Chapter 12 that unions in the UK did not have a political base until the early part of the twentieth century, and so were dependent upon political parties which did not consist of workers to support and help them. This fact, coupled with the fear in the UK caused by revolutions in Europe, led to protection for unions being developed in a strange way. In most European countries, workers have rights to take industrial action which are protected by a written constitution. In the UK, the law developed a series of immunities rather than rights. In other words, all industrial action will break the law, either civil or criminal, but the law gives immunity from civil liability in certain situations. This system of immunities has two important consequences. First, a right enshrined in a written constitution cannot easily be taken away once granted. On the other hand, an immunity may be widened or narrowed merely by redefining the situations where it will apply. To give an example, a union and its members have immunity when taking industrial action if they are acting in contemplation or furtherance of a trade dispute – the so-called 'golden formula'. In 1974 the definition of a 'trade dispute' covered disputes between employers and workers, and between workers and workers. In 1982 the definition was altered to refer to a dispute between workers and their employer. By removing four words and inserting the word 'their' into the first part of this definition, immunity was removed from tertiary action, most forms of secondary action and inter-union disputes.

The second important consequence of immunities is that they create no rights. The media often talk about the 'right to strike', but jurisprudentially this is wrong. If a person has a right to do something, there must be a corresponding duty on the part of someone else to allow that person to exercise the right. If someone has a right of way over my property, I have a legal duty to allow him to exercise that right, and I can be sued if I refuse to do so. The law will protect the right. In the area of industrial action no such protection of rights exists. We shall see below, for example, that while union members may peacefully picket their own place of work if it is in contemplation or furtherance of a trade dispute, and have immunity from civil liability if they commit any torts, the police can disperse pickets at any time if they fear that a public order offence may be committed or they fear a breach of the peace. Thus the law gives a freedom to picket which may be exercised only at the discretion of the police.

The present law on industrial action has had a chequered history. For many years the law was, to a large extent, non-interventionist in this area. The main piece of legislation governing industrial action was the Trade Disputes Act 1906, which created the basic immunities, defined the golden formula and gave trade unions total immunity from civil liability in all situations. Apart from the odd statute to overrule judicial decisions which increased liability, the law kept out of industrial relations.

Change in this policy came with the Conservative government of the early 1970s. Despite the recommendations of the Donovan Report, the government decided to alter the policy of non-intervention in this area at one fell swoop, with the introduction of the Industrial Relations Act 1971. We have seen already in Chapter 12 that this Act introduced a system of registration for trade unions, and it was only by such registration that unions kept the immunity they had until then enjoyed. In addition, the Act attacked the closed shop which had been the basis of union strength for so long, and introduced new concepts such as 'unfair industrial practices' and 'cooling off' provisions. In short, overnight the Act tried to alter totally the system of industrial relations which had been in force for most of the century.

The result of this and the consequent demise of the government are best recorded in history books. It is sufficient to say here that the unions at the time were very strong, and the policy of non co-operation they adopted did much to aid the government's downfall. The Labour government which came into power repealed the Act by the Trade Union and Labour Relations Act 1974 (amended in 1976), and tried to restore labour relations to their pre-1971 position. Conflict with the unions, culminating in the 'winter of discontent' in 1979, meant the return of a Conservative government in that year.

That government had learned from its mistakes in the 1970s and so set about reforming the law by a 'softly, softly' approach. In other words, rather than introducing a one-off piece of legislation changing everything overnight, the government reformed step by step. This is evidenced by the amount of legislation it passed during its time in office – 10 Acts of Parliament in 18 years. In addition to the approach, the policy basis of the legislation changed. It has already been stated that a good industrial relations policy should seek to balance the power between both sides. The Conservatives argued that this was their aim in 1971, when, alarmed by the growing number of strikes, they felt that the power had shifted too far into the lap of the unions. The 1979–97 government, however, had a totally different rationale behind its industrial relations policy. It saw employment legislation as part of a broader economic policy. That policy was one of market forces, that is, the market should be free to conduct itself. Legislation was needed, therefore, to remove obstacles to the market. Unions distort the market because, when strong, they can demand high wage rises and cause financial loss to an employer by taking industrial action. The costs caused by this are therefore put on to goods, so making Britain less competitive in the marketplace. Reduce the power of the unions and you remove one of the major obstacles to competitiveness.

This discussion is necessary to understand the law in this chapter and elsewhere. Increasing continuity periods for unfair dismissal, for example, was another way of increasing competitiveness by allowing an employer to dismiss more people without incurring the expense of legal compensation (see Section 9.2). Curbing the situations where a union's funds will be protected when it takes industrial action is another, so too is preventing a union from enforcing a closed shop. This policy, however, means that the balance of power is ignored, because the policy predicates that the employer must have the greatest power. Many would argue that by the time the Trade Union Act 1984 was passed, the law was in the same position as in 1971. After that, the law went much further than the Industrial Relations Act. Many felt that the law had gone too far, and indeed both the Confederation of British Industry and the Institute of Personnel Management felt that the Trade Union Reform and Employment Rights Act 1993 was unnecessary. The Labour government which was elected in 1997 enacted a number of legislative provisions introducing rights at an individual level, discussed elsewhere in this text. While the government introduced some collective provisions in the Employment Relations Acts, most particularly recognition rights, it did not repeal much of the legislation brought in by the previous administration.

14.2 Industrial action and the contract of employment

Virtually all forms of industrial action will constitute a breach of contract on the part of the employee. While often when talking of industrial action it is assumed that this means a strike, striking is only one type of industrial action, and it will be useful at the outset to look at the common forms of industrial action and their effect on the contract of employment.

14.2.1 Go-slow

A go-slow is a breach of an implied term to work at a reasonable pace in the absence of justifying circumstances. In *General Engineering Services Ltd v Kingston & St Andrew's Corporation* [1989] IRLR 35, a case on vicarious liability, the Privy Council held that fire officers operating a go-slow were not acting within the course of their employment. The go-slow was an unlawful act which repudiated their contracts of employment.

14.2.2 Work-to-rule

Prior to 1972 it was thought that a work-to-rule could not constitute a breach of contract because the employee was merely doing what he was legally obliged to do, that is, carrying out instructions to the letter. However, the leading case of *Secretary of State for Employment v ASLEF (No 2)* [1972] 2 QB 455 decided that such action could constitute a breach of contract. The facts of the case have been discussed in Chapter 4. The reasons why the Court of Appeal held that was a breach of contract are important for our discussion here. First, the rule book which the employees were following comprised merely instructions from the employer and not terms of the contract. As such, the rules could be unilaterally altered by the employer. Second, the employees were in breach of an implied duty not to interpret orders in an unreasonable manner. Third, one of the rules stated that they should prevent avoidable delay, so the action was a breach of this rule. And lastly, if the intention of the work-to-rule was to disrupt the employer's business, this made the action a breach of contract. Whichever reason is adopted, it would appear that any work-to-rule will result in breach, and this is further supported by the later case of *Ticehurst v British Telecommunications plc* [1992] IRLR 219 (see Chapter 4 at Section 4.3.1).

14.2.3   Overtime ban

Whether this an overtime ban constitutes a breach of contract depends on whether the overtime is compulsory or voluntary, and involves looking at the terms of the contract itself. Even if there is no express term relating to overtime, there may be an implied term based on past practice. If the term refers to 'reasonable overtime', the courts will interpret the word 'reasonable'. In *NCB v Galley* [1958] 1 WLR 16, the employee was required to do reasonable overtime and refused to work on Saturday mornings. It was held that he was in breach of contract. Even if overtime is purely voluntary, it is arguable that there may still be a breach of contract. The *ASLEF* case (Section 14.2.2 above) shows that if the effect of the action is a disruption of the employer's business, a breach will have occurred. *ASLEF* also introduces the concept of intention, so that a lawful act may become unlawful if the intention behind that act is unlawful (that is, a breach of contract). While the Court of Appeal in *Ticehurst* left open the issue of whether an act which did not disrupt the employer's business could be actionable, *ASLEF* seems to suggest, given the importance of intention, that a ban on voluntary overtime which does not affect the employer's business will be actionable if the intention behind it was to so disrupt. However, in *Burgess v Stevedoring Services Ltd* [2002] IRLR 810, a Privy Council case, Lord Hoffmann said that intention alone would not make lawful conduct unlawful.

14.2.4   Blacking

Blacking may take a variety of forms. An employee may refuse to handle goods from a particular supplier or goods that are destined for a particular customer. If employees are instructed to handle such goods and refuse to do so, they are refusing to obey a reasonable lawful order and are in breach of contract. Another form of blacking is refusing to work with particular employees, for example non-unionists. In *Bowes & Partners v Press* [1894] 2 QB 202, miners refused an order to go down in a cage with a non-unionist. It was held that their refusal was a breach of contract.

14.2.5   Strike without notice

A strike is a situation where the employee is withdrawing his labour and refusing to work. As such, he is failing to perform his part of the work–wage bargain, and therefore is committing a repudiatory breach.

14.2.6   Strike with notice

Traditionally the view is that if a strike takes place after due notice has been given, that is, the notice needed to terminate the contract, then the strike is legal (*Allen v Flood* [1898]

AC 1). This view means that the employee has effectively resigned. This, however, is not what the employee intends, and the traditional view was questioned by Donovan LJ in *Rookes v Barnard* [1964] 1 All ER 367 and by Lord Denning MR in *Stratford v Lindley* [1965] AC 269. Both their Lordships considered that strike notice was, in fact, notice to break the contract of employment as the employees did not intend to terminate their contracts. While the traditional view may hold where the correct notice is given, a problem arises when the employee gives short notice or ambiguous notice. Does this constitute notice to terminate, notice to break the contract or notice to suspend the contract? If the notice is taken as notice to break the contract, it will amount to an anticipatory breach, the view taken by Lord Devlin in *Rookes v Barnard* and by Lord Denning in *Stratford v Lindley*. However, Lord Denning observed later in *Morgan v Fry* [1968] 2 QB 710 that such a view would do away with the 'right to strike'. For this reason, in *Morgan v Fry*, Lord Denning interpreted strike notice as notice to suspend the contract, focusing on the fact that there is no duty to pay wages during a strike. This was by no means the majority view in *Morgan*, however. Russell LJ considered strike notice to be notice of a breach of contract, Davies LJ thought it was notice to terminate and Lord Denning MR thought it was notice to suspend. The Donovan Commission considered Lord Denning's proposition, but rejected it because of the difficulties which could arise from such an interpretation. For example, what happens if the strike never ends, or if the employer dismisses the strikers? Despite this, the view that strike notice suspends the contract was adopted by the Industrial Relations Act 1971. After that Act was repealed, however, the view was rejected in *Simmons v Hoover Ltd* [1977] QB 284, where the EAT decided that a strike with or without proper contractual notice is a repudiatory breach on the part of the employee and the notice given is notice to break the contract, Phillips J stating that he did not think that *Morgan v Fry* was intended to revolutionise the law in the area. Thus, the employer can choose to treat the repudiation as terminating the contract by dismissing the strikers, or can treat the contract as continuing.

One other analysis is possible. This rests on the distinction between notice to terminate the contract, which is intended, and notice to terminate the employment, which is not. This was the view expressed by Davies LJ in *Morgan v Fry*, who saw strike notices as notice to terminate present contractual conditions coupled with an offer to work on new terms. This view may be questioned, however, since the House of Lords decision in *Miles v Wakefield Metropolitan District Council* [1987] IRLR 193, where their Lordships suggested that all industrial action is a repudiatory breach since there is an intention to harm the employer's business which goes fundamentally against the duty of loyalty and co-operation which the employee owes to the employer. If this view is correct and the intention behind the action is the test of legality, it would suggest that any strike notice, whether of correct length or not, is notice of a breach of contract, and it will be construed as notice to terminate only if it is expressed to be so.

Two cases in the European Court of Human Rights challenged this position. In *Demir and Baykara v Turkey* (Application No 34503/97, 12 November 2008), the Court decided that Article 11 ECHR, which protects the right of freedom of association, also protected a right to collective bargaining. Further, in *Enerji Yapi-Yol Sen v Turkey* (Application No 68959/01, 21 April 2009), the Court went further and stated that Article 11 protects a right to strike. In reaching these conclusions the Court in Strasbourg made reference to the conventions of the International Labour Organisation (ILO) and the European Social Charter (ESC). However, the recognition of a right to strike in English law was rejected by the Court of Appeal in *Metrobus Ltd v UNITE* [2009] EWCA Civ 829. While the specifics involved in the arguments in *Metrobus* are discussed in Section 14.7 below, an argument put forward on behalf of the union was that the complicated balloting and notice provisions with which the union must comply to gain immunity from liability (again discussed in detail below) effectively were an unjustified interference with the right to strike established by *Enerji*. The Court of Appeal rejected these arguments, stating that *Demir* was not authority for the proposition that the nature of a right to strike had to be decided with reference to ILO and ESC standards; they had merely provided the context for the decision. Further, in *Enerji*, although the European Court of Human Rights had stated that an interference with the right to strike had to be justified under Article 11(2), it had not explained its reasoning for so deciding.

Despite the courts' reluctance to recognise a right to strike, the Labour Government White Paper, Fairness at Work considered that it is an anomaly that employees taking industrial action risk dismissal for a breach of their employment contracts, particularly as employees can lose the right to claim unfair dismissal in certain circumstances (Chapter 9). The government therefore reinstated protection against unfair dismissal for those involved in official industrial action by Schedule 5 to the Employment Relations Act 1999 (see Chapter 9).

14.3 Industrial action and the economic torts

14.3.1 Inducement of a breach of contract

If a person induces or persuades a party to a contract to break that contract, the injured party may sue the inducer in tort for inducement of a breach of contract. For example, a trade union official persuading members to go on strike is inducing those members to break their contracts of employment, therefore the employer can take action in tort against the official. This form of inducement only involves the breach of one contract, and is called a 'direct inducement' because the pressure is being exerted on the party who is in a contract with the person the inducer wishes to harm, in this case the employer. The tort is also committed if a person induces a party to break a commercial contract or a contract for services.

The tort of inducement first emerged in *Lumley v Gye* (1853) 2 E&B 216. Gye, an impresario, induced an opera singer to break her contract with Lumley and sing for him for higher wages. The court found Gye liable as he had induced the breach of contract. Prior to the case, the only recourse was against the actual contract breaker. The principle was extended further in *Bowen v Hall* (1881) 6 QBD 333, when the Court of Appeal held that it applied to inducement of breaches of all types of contract and not just breaches of contracts for personal services. In addition, *Allen v Flood* [1898] AC 1 makes it clear that malice is not the essence of the tort. In *Thomson v Deakin* [1952] Ch 646, Jenkins LJ stipulated the elements of the tort of inducement: the defendant knew of the existence of the contract and intended its breach; the defendant persuaded or procured employees to break their contracts with this intention; and the employees did break their contracts. These were restated in the joined appeals of *OBG v Allan, Douglas v Hello! Ltd* and *Mainstream Properties v Young* [2008] 1 AC 1. In *OBG*, receivers were appointed to a company under a floating charge which turned out to be invalid, but before they realised this, they sold the company property. The company sued them for, amongst other things, interference with contractual relations. In *Douglas*, *OK* magazine sued *Hello!* magazine for interference with contractual relations as *Hello!*'s publishing of photos of Michael Douglas and Catherine Zeta-Jones's wedding, taken by an undercover photographer, ruined *OK*'s exclusive coverage. In *Young*, two employees of Mainstream Properties Ltd passed a development opportunity, which they should have offered to the company, to another they both had an interest in. Young had financed the venture and Mainstream Properties sued for inducing a breach of the employees' contracts.

The requirements of the tort are set out in the Sections 14.3.1(a)–(f) below.

14.3.1(a) Unlawful act

In order to be liable, the defendant must have induced an unlawful act. If the unlawful act is a breach of contract, the contract must exist and be valid in law at the time of the inducement (*Long v Smithson* (1918) 118 LT 678). Liability has since been extended to cover inducements of other unlawful acts. In *Cunard SS Co Ltd v Stacey* [1955] 2 Lloyds Rep 247, the court granted an injunction preventing union officials from inducing seamen to break their duties under the Merchant Shipping Act 1894 (see also *Meade v Haringey London Borough Council* [1979] 2 All ER 1016). Similarly, in *Prudential Assurance Co Ltd v Lorenz* (1971) 11 KIR 78 a union instructed insurance agents to withhold payment of premiums that they had collected from their employer. It was held that the union was guilty of inducing breaches of contracts of employment and inducing breaches of the agents' fiduciary duties.

Because it is necessary to induce an unlawful act, it therefore follows that if the inducement is to terminate the contract lawfully there can be no liability, neither is there a tort of inducing a party not to enter a contract (*Midland Cold Storage v Steer* [1972] Ch 630). This leaves the question, however: What if a breach would occur but for an exclusion clause? In other words, does the tort extend to interference with a contract rather than breach? Until 1969, it was clearly the case that an actual breach had to have occurred before the tort was committed; however in *Torquay Hotels Ltd v Cousins* [1969] 2 Ch 106, the Court of Appeal extended the tort. In the case, the managing director of the Imperial Hotel at Torquay refused the Transport and General Workers Union (TGWU) recognition, and as a result the union cut off oil supplies to the hotel by picketing and a series of strikes. The managing director told a reporter that the Hotel Association was determined to stamp out the TGWU's intervention in the hotel trade, and the union reacted by placing pickets outside the hotel. Furthermore, a union official telephoned Esso, which supplied the hotel with oil, and informed them that an official dispute existed at the hotel and that the union would be calling on the delivery drivers, who were members of the TGWU, not to deliver the oil. In the hotel's contract with Esso, there was a *force majeure* clause, that is, a clause which exempted Esso from liability for breach if they were prevented from delivering because of an industrial dispute. All three members of the Court of Appeal held that the TGWU was guilty of the tort of inducement. Russell LJ and Winn LJ both stated that a breach had occurred and that the clause only prevented liability arising. Lord Denning MR went further. He stated that despite the fact that there was no breach of contract, the tort was satisfied as there had been an interference with the performance of the contract. However, in *OBG* (Section 14.3.1 above), the House of Lords stated that over the years there had been a blurring of certain torts, so that inducing a breach of contract was a specific application of a wider tort of causing loss by unlawful means. Their Lordships stated that this blurring was wrong and that the specific tort of inducing a breach of contract had to involve an actual breach. As such *Torquay Hotels* should no longer be regarded as good law. There can be no liability if the act induced is not unlawful (*Patrick Stevedores Operation Pty Ltd v ITWF* (1998) IDS Brief 613).

14.3.1(b) Knowledge

It is further necessary to show that the defendant knew that there was a contract between the parties, and that he knew enough of its contents to realise that what he was doing involved the risk of its breach. It is unnecessary to prove that the defendant knew all of the terms of the contract, but if the inducement is to break one specific term then knowledge of that term must be proved, although that knowledge may be implied. In *Bents Brewery v Hogan* [1945] 2 All ER 570, a union official persuaded a brewery manager to obtain financial information about the company to aid the union in collective bargaining. This was a breach of the duty of fidelity implied into the contract of employment of the manager. It was held that as the official knew that the manager was an employee, he must have been aware of the duty of fidelity. This idea that the defendant must have known of the existence of the term has been developed through the cases. In *Stratford v Lindley* [1965] AC 269, Lord Pearce stated that it seemed unlikely that the union would be ignorant of the commonplace terms that existed in a normal contract in the industry. In *Greig v Insole* [1978] 1 WLR 302, Slade J stated that it would be sufficient to prove that the defendant knew of the existence of the contract, provided it was shown that the defendant intended the contract to be breached. However, in *OBG* (Section 14.3.1 above), the House of Lords stated that the defendant must actually realise his inducement will have the effect of breaching the contract. Whether this will limit the application of implied knowledge is yet to be seen, although the House did approve the principle that deliberately turning a blind eye will be interpreted as having the requisite knowledge (see *Emerald Construction Ltd v Lowthian* [1966] 1 All ER 1013 and *Merkur Island Shipping Co v Laughton* [1983] IRLR 26). Further, in *Young* (Section 14.3.1 above), the defendant did not realise the employees were in breach of contract and therefore could not be liable for the tort.

14.3.1(c) Intention

Closely coupled with the requirement of knowledge is the need to intend to cause the breach. This means that the defendant must have foreseen the possibility of breach, as well as wishing to achieve that end. If the defendant did not appreciate that there was a risk of breach, even though he knew a contract existed, there will be no liability. In *British Industrial Plastics Ltd v Ferguson* [1938] 4 All ER 504, an employee left British Industrial Plastics and contacted a rival firm, telling it that he had knowledge of a particular moulding process. The rival thought that disclosure may be a breach of contract and told the ex-employee to get a patent before revealing the information, believing this would avoid the breach. It was held that there was no liability for inducement as the company honestly thought that it would not cause a breach of contract. Thus if the defendant intends that the contract be terminated lawfully, there is no liability. If, however, the defendant knew enough about the contract to realise that a breach was inevitable, yet persists in what he is doing, the court will infer that he intended the breach.

The standard required was relaxed over the years and it appeared that recklessness was enough to establish intention, in that if the defendant was indifferent as to whether the contract was terminated lawfully or not, he was deemed to have intended the breach. In

Emerald Construction (Section 14.3.1(b) above), Higgs and Hill were the main contractors on a site. Emerald Construction was engaged as a labour-only subcontractor. The union did not like labour-only contracts and tried to get Higgs and Hill to get rid of Emerald Construction. In the union's experience such contracts were terminable upon short notice, but Emerald Construction's contract needed longer notice than was usual. The union called a strike to pressure Higgs and Hill to end the contract. It was held that the union intended that the contract be terminated unlawfully if it could not be terminated lawfully. It had deliberately turned a blind eye to the specific terms and just wanted Emerald Construction out. In other words, the union was reckless as to the actual term relating to notice. However, in *Young* and *OBG* (Section 14.3.1 above), the House of Lords held that it was an essential prerequisite of the tort that the wrongdoer specifically intended to interfere with the contract. Therefore, in both cases, as the defendants had no such intention (in *OBG* they had made an honest mistake), the tort had not been committed. As such, it now appears that the wrongdoer must deliberately, and not just carelessly or negligently, induce a breach for the requirements of the tort to be met.

14.3.1(d) Inducement

The word 'inducement' implies pressure being put on an unwilling party, but what amount of pressure does the law require? In *Allen v Flood* (Section 14.3.1 above), it was held that communicating the view of employees to the employer was not an inducement. Similarly, a statement of the facts was not an inducement in *Thomson v Deakin* (Section 14.3.1 above). However, again, the standard has been relaxed over the years, and the line between communicating information and an inducement is now difficult to draw. In *Torquay Hotels Ltd v Cousins* (Section 14.3.1(a) above), it was held that the union had induced Esso to break the contract by telling them that there was a dispute at the hotel. The key factor appears to be the intention of the speaker, and if the speaker intends that the contract be broken, then there is an inducement even if the speaker is merely communicating a set of facts to the recipient of the information. This, however, raises another issue. What if the recipient is willing to get out of the contract anyway? For example, what of the situation when the employee votes in favour of a strike and after the ballot is then called out on strike by the union? Is there an inducement? It is probably sufficient that there is an agreement to act inconsistently with the terms of the contract. This view is supported by *British Motor Trade Association v Salvadori* [1949] 1 All ER 208, where the seller of new cars induced purchasers to re-sell to him in breach of a term of the purchasing contract. In fact the purchasers were willing to do this because they received a good price, but it was still held to be an inducement.

14.3.1(e) Causation

There must be a causal connection between the inducement and the breach. Thus if the contract breaker intended to break the contract anyway and was not influenced by the inducement, there will be no liability. Lord Pearce in *Stratford v Lindley* (Section 14.3.1(b) above) said that the breach had to be a reasonable consequence of the inducement. This suggests that if the inducement is one of a series of factors which persuaded the contract breaker, there will be sufficient causation.

The discussion above has concentrated on direct inducement, that is, pressure being exerted on a party to a contract with the party that the inducer wishes to harm, the typical situation being a union official inducing an employee to break his contract of employment with the intention of harming the employer. Inducement, however, may also be indirect. This involves an inducement of someone who is not in a contract with the party that the inducer wishes to harm, but the consequence of the inducement is a breach of a further contract. For example, a union official may induce the employees at A (a supplier of X, the employer in dispute) to refuse to deliver goods to X. The result is that A cannot perform his contract of supply with X and so X suffers a loss.

14.3.1(f) Defence

There is, in theory, a defence to an action of inducing a breach of contract, that of justification. I say 'in theory' because it has been successful in only one case. In *Brimelow v Casson* [1924] 1 Ch 302, chorus girls in the King Wu Tut Tut Review were paid so poorly that many of them turned to prostitution to increase their earnings. The union ordered a strike. It was held that the union officials were justified in inducing the girls to break their contracts in order to ensure that the employer was obliged to pay the girls a living wage. Russell J said that if justification did not exist in this case, he could hardly conceive the case when it would be present! The fact that no ill-will is intended towards the employer is not sufficient for the defence. In *Greig v Insole* (Section 14.3.1(b) above), the International Cricket Council was found to have induced breaches of cricketers' contracts with the Kerry Packer World Cricket Series. Slade J held that the fact that they acted from impersonal or disinterested motives did not justify the tortious conduct.

14.3.2   Procurement of a breach of contract

This tort is similar in its effect to inducement and, like inducement, may exist in direct or indirect form. In its direct form it involves the same three parties seen in direct inducement, but rather than persuading an employee to break a contract, procurement involves removing the means by which the contract can be performed. For example, if a union official persuaded a lorry driver not to drive, this would be a direct inducement. If, however, the official took away the driver's keys, so that he could not drive, this would be a procurement, because the official has taken away the means by which the driver performs his contract; the driver himself has not made a decision to break his contract. As with direct inducement, there must be an unlawful act, knowledge, intention, procurement and causation. *Thomson v Deakin* (Section 14.3.1 above) recognised that such a tort existed, and examples were given of removing essential tools or kidnapping an essential employee. The only decided case, however, would appear to be *GWK Ltd v Dunlop Rubber Co Ltd* (1926) 42 TLR 376. GWK made cars and contracted with Allied Rubber that whenever their cars were displayed at motor shows, they would be fitted with Allied's tyres. On the eve of a show, someone changed the tyres to Dunlop tyres. Dunlop was held liable to Allied and GWK, having committed the wrongful act of trespass intending to injure Allied. It appears, therefore, that a constituent part of the tort is that the procurement is by unlawful means.

Just as with the case of inducement, there may be an indirect procurement. Again, this involves four parties, as in indirect inducement, and occurs when the procurer takes away the means by which the contract can be performed. Perhaps the most common example is where a trade union official persuades the employees at a supplier of the employer in dispute to black supplies intended for that employer. Hence the supplier is in breach of his commercial contract, not because he has been persuaded to go into breach but because the action of his employees means that he cannot get supplies through. A case which affords a good illustration of the tort is *Stratford v Lindley* (Section 14.3.1(b) above). Stratford was the chairman of Stratford Ltd and Bowker & King Ltd. The latter company owned oil-carrying barges and employed 48 men, 45 of whom were members of the TGWU and three of whom were members of the Watermen, Lightermen, Tugmen and Bargemen's Union (WLTBU). The TGWU obtained recognition from Stratford Ltd, and the WLTBU put pressure on the company to receive recognition too. Stratford Ltd owned barges which it hired to firms which employed their own crews. The crews were members of the WLTBU. The union told the crew members not to return the barges at the end of the hiring contract, and as a result Stratford Ltd was unable to fulfil other contracts of hire. It was held that the WLTBU was liable for procuring breaches of contract between Stratford and the new hirers.

With regard to causation, it appears that the breach must be the necessary consequence of the procurement and not merely the reasonable consequence (as in inducement – see Section 14.3.1(e)).

14.3.3   Causing loss by unlawful means

The basis of this tort is the use of unlawful threats to induce a party to commit a lawful act which causes loss, classically threatening industrial action which causes the employer to lawfully terminate an employee's contract. It differs from inducement because there is no breach of contract. The tort originally was known as 'intimidation' because it was committed only when the threat was a threat of physical injury; however, in 1964 the House of Lords decided the case of *Rookes v Barnard* [1964] 1 All ER 367 and considerably widened the operation of the tort. In *Barnard*, the branch chairman of the union and two other officials told BOAC that if they did not dismiss Rookes, who had resigned from the union, they would strike. Rookes was consequently lawfully dismissed, that is, he was given the correct contractual notice. Rookes sued on the basis that the threat of a strike was the threat of a breach of contract and therefore the threat of an unlawful act. The House of Lords upheld Rookes's argument and decided that the threat of a breach of contract was an unlawful threat for the purposes of intimidation. In *OBG* (Section 14.3.1 above), however, Lord Hoffmann said that the name 'intimidation' had been wrongly ascribed to the facts in *Barnard*. He felt that the tort of causing loss by unlawful means had existed since *Allen v Flood*, and that this was the reason for the decision in *Barnard*.

The requirements of the tort of causing loss by unlawful means are as set out in the following sections.

14.3.3(a) Unlawful threat

There must be a threat. It is uncertain whether there is a distinction between a threat and a warning. There probably is not, as the basis of the tort is the intention to injure by unlawful means. The threatened act must be conditional, however, on action or lack of it. In other words, the threat must be, for example, that there will be a strike unless X is dismissed. There is no case law as to the position if the official merely threatens a strike and the employer works out that he can avoid it by sacking X, if this has not been said to him. Furthermore, the threatened wrong must be unlawful and actionable, so that if the strike would not be actionable because a statutory immunity exists (see Section 14.5 below) then no liability will occur.

14.3.3(b) Intention

The defendant who utters the threat must intend to harm the claimant. This was clearly the case in *Rookes v Barnard*, and will normally be evident as the victim will usually be named in the threat. Recklessness would appear to be insufficient.

14.3.3(c) Causation

While the threat must have persuaded the party to act and so harm the claimant, it is unclear whether the threat must be the sole cause of the action. If in *Rookes*, for example, the employer had already considered sacking the employee for bad workmanship, so that the threat was not the sole cause of his action, it is unclear whether the tort would have been made out.

14.3.3(d) Loss to the claimant

The claimant must have suffered a loss which was caused by the unlawful threat.

14.3.3(e) Unlawful means

In *OBG* (Section 14.3.1 above), the House of Lords held that 'unlawful means' includes an interference with the freedom of the third party in his dealings with the claimant. Thus, in *Douglas, Hello!* magazine was not liable because it obtained the photographs from a freelance photographer, and therefore the magazine's actions had not interfered with the dealings between Douglas and *OK* magazine – it was the actions of the photographer that had so interfered.

It is possible that the defence of justification could apply to the tort. Lord Devlin suggested this in *Rookes v Barnard*, but it is difficult to envisage the situations when it might apply.

14.3.4   Conspiracy

The tort of conspiracy has two forms. The first is a 'simple conspiracy', sometimes called a 'conspiracy to injure', which is a combination to cause injury to a third party without justification. The second form is a 'conspiracy to use unlawful means'. In a simple conspiracy, no unlawful means are required.

The existence of a simple conspiracy was recognised in *Mogul Steamship Company v McGregor Gow & Co* [1892] AC 25, when the House of Lords stated that the tort had three elements: a combination of at least two persons; intentionally causing loss; and the predominant purpose is not to further a legitimate interest. In addition, there must be an agreement to injure, not merely coincidental action. This is a question of fact and should not be inferred from common conduct. To found a claim, the claimant must actually suffer loss. This is different from criminal conspiracy, where the intention to cause loss forms the basis of the offence even if no loss occurs (Criminal Law Act 1977, s 1).

At least two persons, therefore, must agree to injure the claimant and intend to cause him loss. In *Quinn v Leathem* [1901] AC 495, Leathem employed non-unionists. Officials of the union asked him to dismiss one of his non-union workers. Leathem refused and was told that one of his major customers would be warned not to place further orders with Leathem. Leathem offered to pay the fines and joining fees of all his non-union employees, but the union refused and the customer withdrew his custom after the union threatened a strike should he fail to do so. It was held that although there was no unlawful action, the officials were guilty of conspiracy because their intention was to injure Leathem.

The common law, however, has developed the defence of justification. In other words, relating back to the third element of the tort, if the purpose of the combination is to further the legitimate interests of the conspirators then there is no liability. In *Crofter Handwoven Harris Tweed v Veitch* [1924] AC 435, yarn was imported from the mainland because it was cheaper than yarn made on the island of Lewis. The yarn was then woven by crofters. This meant that the cloth so produced was cheaper than cloth produced wholly on the island, and as a result, wages of the mill workers on the island were very low. The mill workers were members of the TGWU. Dockers, who were also members of the TGWU, placed an embargo on yarn from the mainland to ensure that price competition was eliminated, as this was keeping the wages of the mill workers down. It was held that the predominant purpose of the action was to protect the legitimate interests of the combiners and protect the livelihood of the union members. As such the action was justifiable and no liability arose. Thus action to enforce the legitimate interests of the union will never attract liability. Action where the predominant purpose is spite or vengeance will create liability, however, even if it also furthers the aims of the union. In *Huntley v Thornton* [1957] 1 All ER 234, the plaintiff was expelled from the union and hounded out of several jobs after he refused to comply with a union instruction to stop work and after he called the district committee of the union 'a shower'. It was held that the action of certain officials was motivated out of spite and vengeance with the aim of injuring the plaintiff, and hence their action was not justified. Two officials who were not taking action out of spite were not liable for the tort.

The tort of conspiracy to use unlawful means is more complex. As with a simple conspiracy there must be an agreement to injure and intention to cause loss, but in addition there must be the use of unlawful means. Unlike a simple conspiracy, it is enough if damage to the claimant is likely to result, even if that is not the defendant's predominant purpose. This was doubted by the House of Lords in *Lonrho v Shell Petroleum (No 2)* [1982] AC 173 but reaffirmed by a later House of Lords decision in *Lonrho v Fayed* [1991] 3 All ER 303. The most difficult question is: What kinds of unlawful means will be sufficient to constitute the tort? Certainly a conspiracy to commit a crime would suffice, and Lord Wright in *Crofter Handwoven Harris Tweed* (above) thought that a conspiracy to commit an offence under the Conspiracy and Protection of Property Act 1875 would be sufficient. It is not clear whether a conspiracy to commit a breach of contract is enough, although, as already seen (in Section 14.3.3 above), this will found an action for causing loss by unlawful means. One thing is clear, however. The illegal act must be integral to the aims of the conspirators and not peripheral, so, for example, an agreement by two picketers to pilfer will not set up the tort.

14.3.5 Interference with a trade or business by unlawful means

It is sometimes argued that no such tort exists, or that it is merely an umbrella phrase to describe existing torts in this area, although immunity against such a tort was included in the Trade Disputes Act 1906 and later repealed by the Employment Act 1982. It would seem, however, that such a tort does exist, although it is of recent origin. It was declared to exist by the Court of Appeal in *Hadmor Productions Ltd v Hamilton* [1981] 2 All ER 724

(CA), and the House of Lords in the same case appeared tacitly to accept that such a tort existed ([1982] IRLR 162).

The development of the tort of interference with a trade or business by unlawful means can be explained given that since *Rookes v Barnard* there is liability for threatening to use unlawful means to interfere in a person's trade; logically, therefore, the actual interference must also be tortious. In *Hadmor*, it was alleged that ACTT officials threatened to persuade their members to refuse to transmit television programmes produced by Hadmor. Thames Television had acquired a licence to transmit the programmes but was under no contractual obligation to do so. Hadmor therefore had no contract with which the action would interfere, merely a commercial expectation. It was held, however, that a prima facie case that a tort had been committed had been made out.

The essence of the tort is the use of unlawful means, which raises the question of what constitute 'unlawful means'. It has always been the case that inducing someone to break their contract is unlawful means for the purposes of torts which have that requirement. Under the Trade Disputes Act 1906 there was immunity from liability for inducing breaches of contracts of employment if done in contemplation or furtherance of a trade dispute. Section 13(3)(b) of the Trade Union and Labour Relations Act 1974 stated that a breach which was not actionable could not constitute unlawful means. This provision was repealed by the Employment Act 1980, but the House of Lords in *Hadmor* stated that the provision had only stated the law, and that a wrong which was immune from liability could not constitute unlawful means. Therefore, if statutory protection exists, the tort is not made out. Likewise, void acts do not give rise to legal rights or duties and, as such, cannot be unlawful means (*Mogul v McGregor Gow*, Section 14.3.4 above). Certainly, however, any tort which does not attract statutory immunity will provide the basis of the tort, for example trespass, deceit, intimidation, breach of statutory duty, and so on.

From *Hadmor* it appears that in addition to unlawful means there must be an intention to harm the claimant, and the claimant must sustain actual loss. The Court of Appeal expanded upon this in *Lonrho v Fayed* (Section 14.3.4 above) and stated that it was not necessary that the defendant's predominant purpose was to harm the plaintiff, but it must be shown that the defendant's unlawful act was directed against and intended to harm the plaintiff. The kind of interference which will create liability is still unclear. In *Fayed*, Lonrho claimed that the Fayed brothers had fraudulently deceived the Secretary of State for Trade in not referring their bid for the House of Fraser to the Monopolies and Mergers Commission, and therefore Lonrho had been wrongfully deprived of the opportunity to acquire Harrods. The Court of Appeal felt it was arguable that this constituted a tort and that the case should go to a full trial. The tort is therefore a developing one and one which could take over from the more common torts listed above, particularly as no immunity exists apart from the fact that inducement or intimidation cannot be unlawful means if they are not actionable because of statutory immunity.

14.3.6 Economic duress

All industrial action is intended to put economic pressure on the employer. In contract law, economic pressure can amount to duress and, if proved, the contract may be avoided and any money paid under it recovered. Normally, this argument is not used against unions because they have no contract with the employer; however, in *Universe Tankships of Monrovia v International Transport Workers' Federation* [1983] AC 366 such a contract did exist. The Federation, as part of its campaign against flags of convenience, insisted that employers paid a sum into the union's welfare fund as a price for lifting the blacking of a ship. As soon as the blacking was lifted, the employers sought to recover the money they had paid, arguing that payment had been made under duress and therefore was avoidable. The House of Lords said that if the action had been protected by the immunities, that is, was in contemplation or furtherance of a trade dispute, the employer could not circumvent the protection by bringing an action for duress. However, since payment into a welfare fund is not a recognised trade dispute, there was no such protection and the employer's action succeeded. A similar conclusion was reached in *Dimskal Shipping v ITWF* [1992] IRLR 78, where the facts were similar but the money was paid in Sweden where such pressure was lawful. The House of Lords said that as the contract was governed by English law, that prevailed and the employer could recover.

14.4 The impact of EU law

There has been much in the press recently about workers being brought into the UK from abroad because they work for lower pay than UK workers. The Posted Workers Directive (96/71/EC) requires a Member State to observe minimum terms applied in that state in relation to posted workers, but this does not help employees who may be being paid well above minimum rates if foreign workers are prepared to work for less. Recent national events have seen unions taking industrial action against employers who take on such workers, but EU law suggests that such action is illegal, from the cases of *Viking Line ABP v ITF* [2008] 1 CMLR 51 and *Laval un Partneri Ltd v Svenska Byggnadsarbetareforbundet* [2008] 2 CMLR 9. In *Viking Line*, a ferry owned by a Finnish company sailed between Finland and Estonia. When Estonia joined the EU, the company decided to reflag the ship as Estonian and replace its Finnish sailors with sailors from Estonia who would work for lower pay. The Finnish Seamen's Union and the International Trade Federation (ITF) threatened industrial action, and Viking Line sought an injunction on the basis that its rights to free establishment anywhere in the EU under Article 43 TEC (now Article 49 TFEU) would be infringed by the threatened industrial action. On referral, the ECJ held that such action would be an infringement of Article 43 TEC (now Article 49 TFEU) rights.

In *Laval*, a Latvian building company, with a subsidiary in Sweden, won a contract to build a Swedish school and proposed to use Latvian workers who would work for considerably less pay than Swedes. It refused to enter an agreement with Swedish unions to pay the Latvians the Swedish rate of pay, and the union started industrial action which was lawful under Swedish law. Laval argued that the industrial action was an infringement of its rights to provide services anywhere in the EU under Article 49 TEC (now Article 56 TFEU), a claim upheld by the ECJ.

These two cases seem to show that EU law allows cheaper labour to be brought in from one Member State to undermine existing terms and conditions in another Member State. It appears to be contrary to the basic tenets of EU law which seek to protect workers throughout the EU.

14.5 Statutory immunities

It can be seen from the above that unions may commit a great number of economic torts when they take industrial action, but we have already seen that in some circumstances there will be statutory immunity from liability for the commission of certain torts. The immunity is now contained in section 219(1) of TULR(C)A 1992, which states:

> An act done by a person in contemplation or furtherance of a trade dispute is not actionable in tort on the ground only:
> (a) that it induces another person to break a contract or interferes or induces another person to interfere with its performance, or
> (b) that it consists in his threatening that a contract (whether one to which he is a party or not) will be broken or its performance interfered with, or that he will induce another person to break a contract or interfere with its performance.

It will be seen, therefore, that protection is not afforded against the commission of all torts, and that torts such as libel, slander, trespass, breach of statutory duty and so on have no immunity. It can also be seen that immunity does not apply every time one of the protected torts is committed, but only where it is committed 'in contemplation or furtherance of a trade dispute' – the so-called 'golden formula'. It should further be noted that only torts can attract statutory immunity; a union or its members can never be immune from criminal liability.

This means that to discover whether the union and its members have statutory protection from liability, the starting point is to discover whether there is a trade dispute and whether they are acting in contemplation or furtherance of it.

14.5.1 Trade dispute

The definition of a 'trade dispute' is to be found in section 244(1) of the 1992 Act. This provides that a trade dispute is:

> a dispute between workers and their employer which relates wholly or mainly to one or more of the following:
> (a) terms and conditions of employment, or the physical conditions in which any workers are required to work;
> (b) engagement or non-engagement, or termination or suspension of employment or the duties of employment, of one or more workers;
> (c) allocation of work or the duties of employment between workers or groups of workers;
> (d) matters of discipline;
> (e) a worker's membership or non-membership of a trade union;
> (f) facilities for officials of trade unions; and
> (g) machinery for negotiation or consultation, and other procedures, relating to any of the above matters, including the recognition by employers or employers' associations of the right of a trade union to represent workers in such negotiation or consultation or in the carrying out of such procedures.

14.5.2 Workers and their employer

First, it should be noted that a trade dispute can now exist only between workers and their employer. Prior to the change in definition introduced by the Employment Act 1982, the dispute could be between workers and any employer, and workers and workers. Such a broad definition meant that secondary and tertiary action fell within the definition, as did inter-union disputes. This type of industrial action has no protection today. Therefore industrial action cannot be directed at an employer whose employees are not involved in the dispute. The employer, however, cannot change his identity to try to prevent the statutory immunity applying. In *Examite Ltd v Whittaker* [1977] IRLR 312, the AUEW union was in dispute with Baldwins Industrial Services. The company formed a second company called Examite Ltd which took over the entire business of Baldwins. Examite then argued that it was not the employer with whom the AUEW was in dispute. It was held that the court should look at the reality behind the facade. Lord Denning MR was prepared to raise the veil of incorporation, Roskill LJ and Shaw LJ found for the union on other grounds. The corporate veil will not be lifted, however, where long-established companies are involved. In *Dimbleby & Sons Ltd v NUJ* [1984] 1 WLR 427, journalists employed by Dimbleby refused to send printing work to TBF Ltd rather than to their own associated printing house, T Bailey Foreman Ltd, where the printers were on strike. TBF Ltd was also an associated company of T Bailey Foreman Ltd. The journalists were taking sympathy action to support the printers. The NUJ argued, first, that they were employed by the same employer and, second, that the dispute was about the allocation of work under section 244(1)(c) of TULR(C)A 1992 (see Section 14.5.1 above). While the House of Lords accepted that there was a dispute about the allocation of work, the journalists were not in dispute with their employer. All the companies were legitimate separate legal entities and the journalists were not employed by T Bailey Foreman, who was the employer in dispute.

By section 244(2) of the 1992 Act, a dispute between a Minister of the Crown and workers shall be treated as a dispute between those workers and their employer if the dispute relates to matters referred to him by a joint body on which he is represented or, broadly speaking, his approval is required before a settlement can be made. This provision was discussed in the dispute involving teachers and the boycott of national tests arising out of the National Curriculum. In *Wandsworth London Borough Council v NASUWT* [1994] IRLR 241, the question for the Court of Appeal was whether there was a trade dispute. On the issue of the parties, the Court unanimously held that there was a dispute between workers and an employer, by the operation of section 244(2).

'Worker' is defined in section 244(5) of the 1992 Act. It must be noted that the protection is for workers and not merely employees. Section 244(5) gives a definition of 'worker' in relation to a trade dispute, but the general definition in section 296 is wider. In *TGWU v Associated British Ports* (2002) IDS Brief 705, Associated British Port (ABP) was the port authority for the Humber Ports. Under the Pilotage Act 1987 it had the power to authorise suitably qualified persons to act as pilots, and a duty to arrange for the provision of the services of self-employed authorised pilots to be exercised on its behalf. In 1991 it entered an agreement with Humber Pilots Ltd (HPL) for the provision of the services of self-employed pilots. HPL was the collective voice of pilots in the area and not their employer. In 2001, ABP decided that from January 2002 it would employ pilots directly. HPL declared a trade dispute involving the TGWU and threatened strike action. ABP sought an injunction, arguing that self-employed pilots were not workers and thus there was no trade dispute. Section 296(1)(b) of the 1992 Act defines a worker as an individual who works, normally works or seeks to work 'under any other contract whereby he undertakes to do or perform personally any work or services for another party to the contract who is not a professional client of his'. At first instance an interim injunction was granted, Hunt J deciding that the pilots were not workers within the definition. On appeal, the Court of Appeal reversed the judgment. That Court stated that the existence of a statutory duty imposed on ABP to provide pilotage services did not preclude the existence of a contractual relationship between the pilots and ABP. The pilots' authorisation was on terms and conditions on which the offer of authorisation was made, and when a pilot accepted those terms and conditions he had entered a contract with ABP. As such, the pilots fell within the definition in section 296(1)(b). It should be further noted that the definition in section 244(5) covers not only those employed by the employer, but also a person who has ceased to be employed where his employment was terminated in connection with the dispute or the termination of his employment was one of the circumstances giving rise to the dispute.

14.5.3   Dispute

The second question which must be determined is whether there is a dispute between the parties. In *Beetham v Trinidad Cement Ltd* [1960] AC 132, Lord Denning MR said that a dispute exists wherever a difference exists between the parties. But the questions arise: What is the situation if one party concedes to the demand made by the other? Is there a dispute? In the case of *Cory Lighterage Ltd v TGWU* [1972] 1 WLR 792, a case under the Industrial Relations Act 1971, an employee had allowed his union membership to lapse and after pressure from the union, the employer suspended him on full pay. The employee was quite happy to accede to this, and it was held that at the time no dispute existed between the employee and his employer, but there was a dispute between the employee and the union (such a dispute did not have protection under the 1971 Act). Buckley LJ said: '[I]f someone threatens me with physical injury unless I hand over my wallet and I hand it over without a demur, no one could, in my opinion, sensibly say that there had been any dispute about my handing over my wallet.' Such a decision obviously creates problems in relation to the statutory immunities, and so the effect of the decision in *Cory* was reversed in 1974 and is now section 244(4) of the 1992 Act. This provides that:

> An act, threat or demand done or made by one person or organisation against another which, if resisted, would have led to a trade dispute with that other, shall be treated as being done or made in contemplation of a trade dispute with that other, notwithstanding that because that other submits to the act or accedes to the demand no dispute arises.

Thus a threat of industrial action which causes the employer to, for example, dismiss someone, is action in contemplation of a trade dispute.

14.5.4   Related wholly or mainly to

The next step is that the dispute must relate 'wholly or mainly to' one or more of the statutory items in section 244(1) of TULR(C)A 1992 (see Section 14.5.1 above), and it is important to note that it is the dispute which must relate wholly or mainly to those matters, not the action, which should merely further the dispute. This means that the dispute must be identified to discover what the quarrel is really about. If it is not about one of the statutory items in reality, it will not be sufficient to show some theoretical connection. For example, in *Stratford v Lindley* (Section 14.3.1(b) above), the reason for the blacking by the union was not to obtain recognition but to retaliate because the employer had recognised another union, hence was not a trade dispute. Under the 1974 definition, the dispute merely had to be connected with one of the statutory items. This meant that as long as one of the items was part of the reason for the dispute, it did not matter that other non-statutory items were involved, although the courts would not afford statutory immunity to a dispute where the statutory items were peripheral to the main reason for the dispute. In *BBC v Hearn* [1977] 1 WLR 1004, the Association of Broadcasting Staff, to which the majority of BBC staff belonged, objected to racial and political discrimination. The union felt that it would be wrong to broadcast the FA Cup Final to South Africa because of that country's apartheid policy, and when the BBC refused to give an undertaking not to transmit the broadcast, the union instructed members televising the match not to work on the programme. It was held that there was no trade dispute as the real motive for the action was political, and it was over-subtle to say that it was a dispute connected with terms and conditions of employment because there was an issue as to whether a condition should be inserted into the employees' contracts that they would not be compelled to transmit to South Africa.

Under the old definition, therefore, as long as a statutory item was one part of the dispute, a trade dispute existed. A contrast to *Hearn* may be seen in *NWL Ltd v Nelson and Laughton* [1979] 3 All ER 614. In this case a ship was originally registered in Norway but the owners, to save money, decided to employ a Hong Kong crew, and therefore re-registered the ship in Hong Kong, although the ship never went near Hong Kong, ie the ship was flying a flag of convenience. The Hong Kong crew were content with their wages, but the ITWF union blacked the ship when it docked at a British port. It was well known that the ITWF had a campaign against flags of convenience, and the ship owners sought an injunction arguing that the dispute was political. The House of Lords, however, held that the dispute was clearly connected with terms and conditions of employment of seamen, even if other purposes existed behind the dispute.

The change in definition from 'connected with' to 'relating wholly and mainly to' was clearly an attempt to reverse the *NWL* decision, and the effect of the change can be seen in the case of *Mercury Communications Ltd v Scott-Garner* [1984] Ch 37. The dispute arose out of the government's licensing of operators other than British Telecom to operate telecommunications. Mercury planned to establish a communications network partly using the British Telecom network, and the Post Office Engineers' Union instructed their members not to connect Mercury. At first instance it was held that there was a trade dispute because the union was concerned with future job losses. However, when the case reached the Court of Appeal a different conclusion was reached because of the existence of a job security agreement between British Telecom and the union. Lord Donaldson MR said that 'in this context the phrase "wholly or mainly relates to" directs attention to what the dispute is about and, if it is about more than one matter, what is it mainly about'. On this definition, the Court held that the action related to 'a political and ideological campaign seeking to maintain the concept of public monopoly against private competition' (*per* May LJ).

14.5.5 Subject matter

The dispute must be wholly or mainly related to one or more of the items in section 244(1) of the 1992 Act listed in Section 14.5.1 above. This is demonstrated by the *Hearn* case (Section 14.5.4 above). In section 244(1)(a) of the Act, the phrase 'terms and conditions of employment' is given a wide meaning. In section 244(5), 'employment' is defined as 'any relationship whereby one person personally does work or performs services for another', that is, it is not confined to a contractual relationship. 'Terms of employment' obviously refers to all matters covered by the contract whether express or implied, for example hours, pay, holidays and so on. However, the expression has an even wider ambit. In

Hearn, Lord Denning MR said that 'terms and conditions of employment' includes not only the contractual terms and conditions, but also 'those terms which are understood and applied by the parties in practice, or habitually, or by common consent, without ever being incorporated into the contract'. This phrase was approved by Lord Diplock in *Hadmor* (Section 14.3.5 above) and by the House of Lords in *Universe Tankships* (Section 14.3.6 above). Thus in *P v NAS/UWT* [2003] IRLR 307, a union's action in instructing its members not to comply with an instruction to teach a disruptive pupil was held to be a trade dispute. The Court of Appeal held that a dispute regarding the reasonableness of an instruction from an employer could be regarded as a dispute about terms and conditions of employment.

Conversely, however, in *Universe Tankships* their Lordships considered that some things within the contract might not necessarily be part of the terms and conditions. Lord Diplock said:

> But wide as the expression 'terms and conditions of employment' is, it is limited to terms which regulate the relationship between an employee and the person for whom he works ie his employer. It does not extend to terms which regulate a relationship between an employer and some third party acting as principal and not as agent for the employee.

Thus a term that the employer would make a contribution to the union would not, in Lord Diplock's view, be a term or condition of employment even if it was a term in each individual employee's contract. Further interpretation may be seen in *University College London Hospitals NHS Trust v UNISON* [1999] IRLR 31. In the case the union wanted the Trust to enter into a contractual agreement with a consortium that was taking over staff from the Trust, that the consortium would, for a period of up to 30 years, maintain the equivalent terms and conditions for all employees working for the consortium to those employees who had not been transferred. The Trust gained an injunction restraining the union from organising a series of strikes to support its demands. The Court of Appeal rejected the union's argument that the proposed industrial action was in furtherance of a trade dispute within the meaning of section 244(1)(a) of the 1992 Act because the sought-for agreement would not only guarantee the pay of existing staff but, given the 30-year period, would inevitably cover staff who had never been employed by the Trust. Section 244(1)(a) does not cover a dispute over terms and conditions of employees who have never been employed by the employer in dispute.

The problem that arises with the expression is shown in a situation, for example, where the employee is employed by the state and the state imposes a pay freeze to which the employees object. Is that a dispute about terms and conditions, that is pay, or is it a political dispute objecting to government policy? Without doubt, action which purely demonstrates against government policy is political and gains no immunity. The first determination of what constitutes a political dispute was the General Strike of 1926 which received no immunity (*National Sailors and Firemen's Union of Great Britain and Northern Ireland v Reed* [1926] 1 Ch 536). Action taken to protest against the Industrial Relations Act 1971 similarly lost immunity. One factor in these cases is that the employer cannot concede the union's demands. Where the government is also the employer, however, section 244(2) of TULR(C)A 1992 can render the dispute a trade dispute even if the dispute does challenge government policy, provided the main objection to the policy is that it affects terms and conditions. We have already seen in the *Wandsworth* case (Section 14.5.2 above) that the Court of Appeal held that the dispute between the local authority and the NASUWT fell within section 244(2); furthermore, it was held to be a trade dispute relating to terms and conditions of employment because the policy of testing increased teachers' workload, and this had been emphasised as the purpose of the dispute in the strike ballot which had been conducted. So too in *Westminster City Council v UNISON* [2001] IRLR 524, a ballot was held in relation to proposed industrial action in response to a council plan to privatise the housing assessment and advice unit. The Court of Appeal held that a proposal to transfer a unit and its employees to a private employer was a trade dispute within section 244(1) as it was a dispute about the identity of the employer. In other situations, however, the distinction between a trade dispute and a political dispute is not so easy to draw.

Section 244(3) of the 1992 Act states that a trade dispute exists even though it relates to matters outside Great Britain, as long as the persons taking the action are likely to be affected in respect of one or more of the statutory items.

14.5.6 'In contemplation of'

The phrase attempts to place a chronological limit on legitimate industrial action. Two questions have to be answered: Does a trade dispute exist or is one imminent? And when the persons acted, were they contemplating the trade dispute? Thus this part of the 'golden formula' applies when a trade dispute exists or is imminent. Lord Loreburn LC said in *Conway v Wade* [1909] AC 506: 'I come now to the meaning of the words "an act done in contemplation or furtherance of a trade dispute" ... I think they mean that either a dispute is imminent and the act is done in expectation of and with a view to it, or that the dispute is already existing and the act is done in support of one side to it.' In the case, Conway had been expelled from the union for failing to pay a fine. He later rejoined the union at another branch. Wade discovered the earlier expulsion and told the employer (falsely) that there would be a strike if Conway were not dismissed. It was held that Wade was not acting in contemplation of a trade dispute. He may have decided subjectively that he would try to call a strike, but the dispute was all in his mind and it could not reasonably be inferred from the facts that a dispute was likely to occur.

It appears, therefore, that whether the dispute is imminent is an objective test, and there must be evidence that there is or there is about to be a dispute. Furthermore, the dispute must be 'impending or likely to occur', according to Lord Shaw in the case. He went on to say, 'it does not cover the case of coercive interference in which the intervener may have in his own mind that if he does not get his own way he will thereupon take ways and means to bring a trade dispute into existence'. Likewise, action taken which may result in a trade dispute breaking out is not in contemplation of it (*Bents Brewery v Hogan*, Section 14.3.1(b) above). By contrast, *Heath Computing Ltd v Meek* [1981] ICR 24 shows that a dispute may exist even though there has been no confrontation or direct discussions. In the case, NALGO had sent out a circular to its members in the NHS, instructing them not to co-operate with Heath Computing because it foresaw that if the NHS gave computing work to Heath, the members' jobs would be in jeopardy. It was held that such action was in contemplation of a trade dispute which was imminent.

14.5.7 'In furtherance of'

Once again, a dispute must exist or be imminent, and then the test is whether the action is in furtherance of it. Action which does not further the dispute will lose immunity. In

Beaverbrook Newspapers v Keys [1978] ICR 582, a trade dispute existed between the *Daily Mirror* newspaper and the union which resulted in a total stoppage in production. The *Daily Express* decided to print more copies to cater for the increase in demand, but the union told its members not to handle the extra copies. It was held that the action was not in furtherance of the trade dispute at the *Daily Mirror* because it would do nothing to aid the dispute. It may appear that this introduces an objective test and that it is up to the court to decide if the action furthers the dispute. This, however, goes against the judgment of Lord Loreburn LC in *Conway* (Section 14.5.6 above). He said:

> If however some meddler sought to use the trade dispute as a cloak beneath which to interfere with impunity in other people's work or business, a jury would be entirely justified in saying that what he did was done in contemplation or furtherance, not of the trade dispute, but of his own designs, sectarian, political, or purely mischievous, as the case may be. These words do, in my opinion, in some sense import motive, and in the case I have put, quite a different motive would be present.

In other words, the intention behind the action is important. The Court of Appeal, in a series of cases from 1978 to 1980, chose to adopt an objective approach. The House of Lords, however, in reversing the Court of Appeal decisions, reaffirmed the situation in *Conway* that the test is subjective, that is, whether the person honestly believed that his actions would further the dispute. In *Express Newspapers Ltd v McShane* [1980] AC 672, the NUJ was in dispute with provincial newspapers. The NUJ called its members in the provincial newspapers out on strike, but the papers still received news from the Press Association teleprinter. The NUJ called out its members at the Press Association, but not all members complied. The NUJ then instructed its members working on national newspapers to black any copy from the Press Association. The House of Lords, reversing the Court of Appeal, held that whether an act is done in furtherance of a trade dispute depends only upon whether the defendants honestly and genuinely believed that they were furthering the dispute, which was the situation in the case. Reasonableness is only a factor in determining whether the belief is genuinely held, and if no reasonable person could possibly have thought that the action would further the dispute then it calls into question whether the defendant really did so believe. Here, as the defendants genuinely believed that they were furthering the dispute, the action had immunity. The same conclusion was reached in *Duport Steels Ltd v Sirs* [1980] 1 All ER 529, where, after the British Steel Corporation refused a pay claim, the steel unions in the public sector went on strike. As this seemed to have no effect, the unions instructed their members in the private sector to strike. This was designed to compel the government to intercede and make more money available to the Corporation to enable it to meet the pay claim. The House of Lords, reaffirming the decision in *McShane* (above), held that the subjective test applied and that, because the steel unions genuinely believed that they were furthering the dispute by their actions, the action had immunity. Their Lordships particularly regretted this result, but decided that this was the correct interpretation of the law and that it was up to Parliament to change the law if it so wished. Indeed, soon afterwards the Employment Act 1980 made the secondary action in *Duport Steels* illegal, and further legislative intervention has now rendered most secondary action illegal.

While the subjective test prevails, it still remains the case that action taken in consequence of a trade dispute rather than to further it will have no immunity. Arguably, this was the situation in the *Beaverbrook* case (above), and the action there was in consequence of the dispute at the *Daily Mirror* rather than an attempt to further it. This means that action taken after the dispute has ended will have no protection. In *Stewart v AUEW* [1973] ICR 128, the plaintiff, a haulage contractor, had defied pickets on strike at a shipyard. After the strike was settled, the plaintiff was blacked. It was held that the union had no immunity. The action was in consequence of a trade dispute, not in furtherance of it.

14.5.8 Secondary action

It will be noted from the discussion above that if employees at a supplier or customer of the employer in dispute take sympathy action by, for example, refusing to handle goods meant for that employer, as those employees are not in dispute with their employer they do not fall within the definition of a trade dispute and therefore have no immunity. Originally, section 17 of the Employment Act 1980 provided certain immunity for such action, known as 'secondary action', by providing what were known as the 'gateways' to protection. The section was complicated and was repealed by the Employment Act 1990, leaving only protection for picketing which has a secondary effect. In other words, if employees who are in dispute with their employer lawfully picket their own place of work, they are likely to turn back drivers from suppliers or customers. This means that they are inducing those drivers to break their contracts of employment with their employers, who are not parties to the dispute. This secondary effect of picketing, however, will still have immunity under section 219 of TULR(C)A 1992. All other forms of secondary action will have no protection.

14.6 Trade union liability

The Trade Disputes Act 1906 introduced immunity from tortious liability for trade unions. This was brought in to reverse the *Taff Vale* decision (see Chapter 12) and was re-enacted in the Trade Union and Labour Relations Act 1974. This blanket immunity was removed by the Employment Act 1982 and now a union has the same immunity as its individual members, that is the union will be immune if the action is within the 'golden formula' and the acts committed are the torts listed in section 219 of the 1992 Act. There is, however, a statutory limit on the damages that may be awarded against a union, first introduced in 1982 and now contained in section 22 of the 1992 Act. The amount of damages depends on the number of members the union has. If there are fewer than 5,000, the maximum is £10,000. Between 5,000 and 25,000, the maximum is £50,000. Between 25,000 and 100,000, the maximum is £125,000; and over 100,000 members, the limit is £250,000. Each separate action may result in the maximum being imposed, therefore if more than one employer takes action against the union, each employer may be awarded the statutory limit. Furthermore, the limit applies only to damages and not to fines for contempt. Thus in the NGA dispute against the *Stockport Messenger* in 1984, the union was fined £675,000 for contempt.

This means that if the individual member is protected then the union, provided it complies with the balloting and other provisions discussed below, will also have immunity. Furthermore, if the individual member has lost immunity, or it was an act which did not have immunity in the first place, then the union may be liable too. This rider is added because the union will only be liable for action which when taken had been authorised or endorsed by the union. Section 20(2) of TULR(C)A 1992 states that action shall be taken as authorised or endorsed by the union if it was authorised or endorsed by any person empowered by the rules to do so, or by the principal executive committee, the president or the general secretary, or by any other committee or any other official of the union. Further, by section 20(3), a 'committee' is any group of persons constituted in accordance with the rules of the union, and an act is taken to be 'authorised or endorsed by an official' if it was authorised or endorsed by, or by any member of, any group of persons of which he was, at the material time, a member and where the purpose of the group included the organisation or coordination of industrial action. The number of persons who carry the authority of the union was greatly extended by the Employment Act 1990. The reason was that although previously the union had been liable only if it had given authority to a person or committee to authorise or endorse industrial action, a great many strikes were in fact called by shop stewards, who under the old provisions did not have such authority, and as a result, the action was unofficial and the union not liable for torts committed. The government, however, felt that a great deal of unofficial action was tacitly supported by unions, and hence extended the definition of official action to prevent unions from escaping liability. In effect these provisions resurrect the old case of *Heatons Transport Ltd v TGWU* [1973] AC 15, where the House of Lords held that the custom and practice of the union gave shop stewards a general implied authority to institute blacking by their members.

The union may escape liability if it repudiates the act, but the provisions relating to repudiation are very stringent. Section 21 provides that an act shall not be taken to be authorised or endorsed by the union if it is repudiated by the executive, president or general secretary as soon as reasonably practicable after knowledge of the act has come to any of those bodies (s 21(1)). Section 21(2) states that to constitute a valid repudiation it must be written and given to the person or committee which instituted the action without delay, and the fact and date of the repudiation must be given to every member taking part or who might take part in the action and to the employer of such members. Section 21(3) then sets out what the repudiation must say:

> Your union has repudiated the call (or calls) for industrial action to which this notice relates and will give no support to unofficial action taken in response to it (or them). If you are dismissed while taking unofficial industrial action, you will have no right to complain of unfair dismissal.

Repudiation which does not comply with section 21(2) and (3) is ineffective, and the action will be deemed official and the union will be liable. An act is also not treated as repudiated if at any time afterwards the executive, president or general secretary behaves in a manner which is inconsistent with the purported repudiation (s 21(5)). In *Express and Star v NGA* [1986] ICR 589, the general secretary of the union had sent out circulars saying the action should cease, but one official stated at a meeting that he had had a nod and a wink that they should not be distributed and another stated that he had been told that strike pay would be given. While this was not a case concerning repudiation, it gives an example of the type of conduct that section 21 is intended to catch. In addition, section 21(6) states that the executive, president or general secretary shall be treated as acting inconsistently with a repudiation if on a request made to them within six months of the repudiation, by a party to a commercial contract which is affected by the action and who has not received written notice of the repudiation from the union, the union does not give such notice.

14.7 Loss of trade union immunity

It has already been noted that a union has the same immunity or lack of immunity as individual members, thus if the member commits a tort for which there is no immunity, for example slander, then the union will be liable. The union will also be liable if the member, for example, induces a breach of contract but this is after the trade dispute has finished and is therefore outside the 'golden formula'. Even if the member is immune, the union will lose its statutory immunity if it fails to comply with the statutory balloting provisions (below). As such, it is inaccurate to say that the union's immunity reflects that of the individual member. Trade union immunity depends on the 'golden formula', the protected torts being committed, and the balloting and notice requirements being complied with. Breach of any of these conditions will render the union liable for any tortious wrongs committed.

A ballot is required in respect of any act done by a trade union, that is, in respect of any action authorised or endorsed by the union. Entitlement to vote must be accorded to all members of the union that the union reasonably believes will be induced by it to take part in the action, and the ballot will be ineffective if this provision is not complied with (TULR(C)A 1992, s 227). This section was amended by the Employment Relations Act 2004 after the case of *National Union of Rail, Maritime and Transport Workers v Midland Mainline Ltd* [2001] IRLR 813, which showed a lack of clarity about to which union members the union was required to give an entitlement to vote. The section now makes it clear that the union does not have to give an entitlement to those who may take industrial action, even though they have not been induced by the union.

By section 226A, the union must give, no later than the seventh day before the opening of the ballot, written notice to the employer of those members entitled to vote in the ballot, stating the opening day of the ballot and a description of the employees who will be entitled to vote. In *Metrobus Ltd v UNITE* (Section 14.2.6 above), the Court held that where affected members are only partly covered by check-off arrangements, a union is obliged to give sufficient information to the employer to enable the employer to deduce the numbers, types and workplaces of the non-check-off members. The Court of Appeal in *Blackpool and Fylde College v NATFHE* [1994] IRLR 227 held that the union had not complied with section 226A when it had stated that it would ballot all staff who were union members. There were 288 union members in the college, but the employer could identify only 109 who had their union subscriptions deducted from their salary. This suggests that the names of those employees balloted should be given to the employer, in order for him to ascertain which employees are involved. This could obviously lead to employees being singled out by the employer. As a result, the Employment Relations Acts 1999 and 2004 amended section 226A so that a union need only give information to the employer so that he can make plans and bring information to the attention of those of his employees involved. That information must contain a list of the categories of employees who the union reasonably believes will be entitled to vote and a list of the workplaces at which they work (TULR(C)A 1992, s 226A(2A)–(2I)).

However, in *Metroline Travel Ltd and ors v UNITE* [2012] EWHC 1778, the union was seeking a bonus for transport workers in London as a result of increased work caused by the Olympics. The ballot notices went to several employers who provided bus transport to Transport for London (TFL) and stated that those balloted would be 'all members who are drivers, engineering grades and supervisory grades working on the TFL contract either on a full time or part time basis'. The employers asked for clarification, as some of the grades mentioned spent no time on the TFL contract, some worked on it occasionally, and some worked on vehicles which might or might not be used for TFL. UNITE clarified by stating that all drivers would be balloted, including four drivers who worked on call and could be asked to work on TFL, as would drivers who worked non-TFL routes but did some TFL driving for overtime, and that duty manager and engineering grades could be expected to carry out at least some TFL work. The ballot was in favour of strike action and the strike notice under section 234A (see below) contained the same wording. Three employers sought an injunction on the basis that it was not possible for them to establish who had been balloted and who had been called out on strike. The injunction was granted on the basis that 'working on TFL contracts either on a full time or part time basis' was too imprecise even with the subsequent clarification.

Failing to name those employees entitled to vote will not be grounds for declaring that a union has not complied with the legal requirements. In addition, no later than the third day before the opening day of the ballot, the union must send to the same employers a sample of the form of the voting paper which is to be sent to those employees entitled to vote. 'Opening day of the ballot' means the first day that a voting paper is sent to a member. Failure to comply with these provisions means the loss of immunity for the trade union.

Section 228 of the 1992 Act provides for separate workshop ballots for each place of work. Section 228A, inserted by the Employment Relations Act 1999, relieves the union of the duty to hold separate workplace ballots if one of the following applies:

▶ the workplace of each member entitled to vote is the workplace of at least one member who is affected by the dispute;
▶ entitlement to vote is accorded to and limited to all members who according to the union's reasonable belief have a common occupation and are employed by a common employer or number of employers with whom the union is in dispute;
▶ entitlement to vote is accorded to and limited to all the union members employed by a particular employer or number of employers with whom the union is in dispute.

By section 229, the method of voting must be by voting paper, which must be framed in such a way that the member can answer 'yes' or 'no' to the question of whether he is prepared to take part in a strike and whether he is prepared to take part in action short of a strike. Amendments made by the Employment Relations Act 1999 make it clear that an overtime ban and a call-out ban constitute action short of a strike (TULR(C)A 1992, s 229(2A)). The voting paper must specify who is authorised to call for industrial action and must also contain the following statement:

> If you take part in a strike or other industrial action, you may be in breach of your contract of employment.
> However, if you are dismissed for taking part in a strike or other industrial action which is called officially and is otherwise lawful, the dismissal will be unfair if it takes place fewer than 12 weeks after you started taking part in the action, and depending on the circumstances may be unfair if it takes place later. (TULR(C)A 1992, s 229(4))

Section 230(2) of TULR(C)A 1992, which was amended by the 1993 Act, requires that such a ballot must be a postal ballot, the voting paper being sent to the member's address, and that all members should be given a convenient opportunity to vote by post. All those voting should be informed, as soon as reasonably practicable after the vote, of the number of 'yes' votes, the number of 'no' votes and the number of spoiled ballot papers (s 231). By an amendment in 1993, this information must also be given to all relevant employers (s 231A). The Trade Union Reform and Employment Rights Act 1993 amended the legislation so that all industrial action ballots must now have an independent scrutineer (s 226B), and the name and details of the scrutineer must be given on every voting paper (s 229(1A)). A copy of the scrutineer's report shall be available, on request, to any member entitled to vote or any relevant employer. Section 226C of TULR(C)A 1992, introduced by the 1993 Act, excludes the appointment of a scrutineer where the total number of members entitled to vote is fewer than 50.

If the vote supports industrial action, the union will again lose immunity if it is not called by the person specified on the ballot paper as being so authorised (s 233(1)). In *Tanks and Drums Ltd v TGWU* [1991] ICR 1, the union had nominated its general secretary as having authority to call a strike. Negotiations with the employer had been conducted by a district official, and two weeks after a ballot in favour of industrial action, the official obtained permission from the general secretary to call a strike the next day if the employer did not come up with a better offer. The employer did not come up with a better offer and the official called a strike. The Court of Appeal held that the delegation of authority from the general secretary was so specific, and related to such specific events, that it could be said that the general secretary had, in fact, called the action for the purposes of the legislation. This would suggest that a more general delegation of authority would mean that there had been an infringement of section 233 and the union's immunity would be lost.

While the law requires notice to be given to the employer if the ballot approves industrial action, in *Metrobus* (Section 14.2 6 above) it was also stated that the union is obliged to inform the employer of the result of the ballot as soon as reasonably practicable, even if the ballot rejects industrial action or if the union decides not to take industrial action. If the ballot supports industrial action, it will cease to be effective after four weeks or after such longer duration not exceeding eight weeks as agreed between the union and the members' employer (TULR(C)A 1992, s 234, as amended by the Employment Relations Act 1999). If during that time industrial action is prohibited or suspended by a court order or undertaking, the union can apply to the court for an order that the period of suspension or prohibition should not be counted as part of the four-week period, although the court shall not make such an order if it feels that the ballot no longer represents the views of the union members concerned. No application to the court may be made by the union after eight weeks has elapsed from the date of the ballot. The period between making an application and its determination is not counted in the calculation of the period but, in any event, the ballot lapses after 12 weeks. The notice periods can cause problems when the employer wishes to negotiate and so action is suspended and then negotiations break down. In *Post Office v UCW* [1990] 1 WLR 981, a ballot which was held in September 1988 led to industrial action which continued until December 1988. There was no action between January and April 1989, but in May action started again, culminating in a strike in September 1989. The disputes were all over the same issue, but the Court of Appeal held that the dispute which began in May was a new campaign and that a fresh ballot should have been taken before action commenced.

The Trade Union Reform and Employment Rights Act 1993 added section 234A into the 1992 Act which has since been amended by the Employment Relations Act 2004. This introduced the concept of notice of industrial action to employers. Failure to give such notice will result in the trade union losing its immunity for any torts committed during the subsequent action. The notice must be given to an employer whose employees the union reasonably believes will be taking part in the industrial action. By section 234A(3), the notice must be in writing and give a list of the categories to which the 'affected employees' belong, that is, those employees whom the union reasonably believes will be induced to take part in industrial action, and a list of the workplaces at which they work. The notice must also state whether the action will be continuous or discontinuous, and the date when the action will commence or, if discontinuous action is intended, the dates when any affected employees will take part. It must also state that the notice is being given for the purposes of section 234A. The notice period begins on the date that the union informs the employer of the ballot result and ends on the seventh day before the first of the days specified in the notice. The notice must cover all those employees falling within the notified categories and employed at a notified workplace (s 234A(5)). If the action ceases to comply with a court order or undertaking and the union then authorises or endorses the action again at a later date, the original notice lapses and the union must again give notice to the employer stating the date or dates on which the action will take place. This will not apply, however, where the union has suspended action to negotiate with the employer. In this case, the union and employer can agree that the action will cease to be authorised or endorsed from a date specified in the agreement (the suspension date) and that it will resume authorisation or agreement at a date specified in the agreement (the resumption date). This is stated in section 234A(7A) and (7B) of the 1992 Act, introduced by the Employment Relations Act 1999. This means that should negotiations fail, the union will not need to issue a fresh notice to the employer.

The Employment Relations Act 1999 inserted section 232B into the 1992 Act (as amended by the Employment Relations Act 2004), which now provides that minor procedural failures will be disregarded and will not render the union liable. The failures which will be disregarded are: section 227(1) (entitlement to vote accorded to all members who the union reasonably believes will be induced to take part in industrial action); section 230(2) (every person entitled to vote should have the voting paper sent to his home address and be given a convenient opportunity to vote by post); and section 230(2A) (voting provisions for merchant seamen). Such failures can be disregarded only if they are accidental and on a scale which is unlikely to affect the result of the ballot or, if more than one failure has occurred, taken together they are on a scale which is unlikely to affect the result of the ballot (s 232B(1)(b)).

It has already been noted that the Court of Appeal in *Metrobus* rejected the argument that Article 11 of the ECHR provides a right to strike and that the complex balloting and notice provisions are an unjustified interference with that right (see Section 14.2.6 above). However, the then government introduced the Lawful Action (Minor Errors) Bill 2010. This provided that small accidental failures in ballots or notices would be disregarded, as would minor errors in the information about the result of the ballot, and compliance by the union with the procedures would be based on substantial compliance and the burden of proof in injunctions would shift so that evidence would be required to show that substantial compliance had not taken place. If passed, the Bill would have relieved some of the burdens on trade unions and also provided a challenge to claims of a breach of

Article 11 ECHR. Unfortunately, due to the general election in 2010 the Bill was never passed.

In addition to procedural requirements, the legislation removes immunity where industrial action is taken over particular issues. In some ways this is strange, as all of the issues fall within the statutory items which can be the subject of a trade dispute, so the legislation removes them from the general definition. The first issue which may be the subject of industrial action and where immunity is lost is pressure to impose union membership and union recognition requirements. The provisions were first introduced in 1982 and are now contained in sections 144, 145, 186 and 187 of TULR(C)A 1992. These sections render void any terms in a contract which require the other party to recognise a union or to maintain a closed shop among its workers. By sections 222(3) and 225, any industrial action for the purpose of persuading a party to insert such a clause in a contract will lose immunity. Section 222(1) removes immunity if one of the reasons for the action is to pressure the employer to discriminate against non-union members, that is, action to maintain a closed shop will lose immunity. Lastly, protection against unfair dismissal was removed from strikers engaged in unofficial action in 1990 and is now section 237 of the 1992 Act. In addition, by section 223, any industrial action where one of the reasons for it is the dismissal of unofficial strikers loses immunity.

14.8 Picketing

Picketing is a method by which a trade union can strengthen a strike. It can prevent workers from entering the workplace and so increase the disruption to the employer. It can prevent supplies getting in, so that production is affected, and it can prevent goods leaving, so causing problems with any commercial contracts that the employer may have with his customers. In short, it is a very effective industrial weapon. The effectiveness of picketing was demonstrated during the miners' strikes in the 1970s, when coal was prevented from reaching power stations, bringing industry to a halt. Mass picketing was seen at Grunwick in 1977 when workers from all over the UK joined the employees at Grunwick in their fight for union recognition.

The problem with picketing from a legal point of view is that inevitably it involves a consideration of both the criminal and civil law. The criminal law becomes involved not, by any means, because all pickets are violent, although a great many violent acts were committed on the picket lines during the miners' dispute in 1984–85 and the Wapping dispute in 1986, but because the fact that picketing involves a group of people standing around can create criminal liability. In addition, pickets will normally interfere with contracts, be committing a trespass and often commit private nuisance, so rendering them potentially liable in tort. As such, it is necessary to consider all the potential liability and then look at the immunity. This is also an area where the Human Rights Act 1998 is likely to have an impact. Article 11 of the ECHR, which guarantees the right to freedom of peaceful assembly, and Article 10, which guarantees the right to freedom of expression, may be applicable to individual employees who picket, particularly if the pickets are restricted to six, as suggested under the Code of Practice discussed in Section 14.8.5 below.

14.8.1 Criminal liability

14.8.1(a) Obstruction of the highway

It is an offence wilfully to obstruct free passage along the highway without lawful authority or excuse (Highways Act 1980, s 137). Given that inevitably this is the intention of pickets, it should not be surprising that this and the following offence are the ones most frequently levied against such activity. Lawful authority will exist if the picket has statutory immunity (subject to police discretion) and if the use of the highway by the picket is a reasonable exercise of a member of the public's right to pass and repass on the highway. In *Tynan v Balmer* [1967] 1 QB 91, 40, pickets were walking around at the top of a service road to prevent lorries reaching the factory gates. The pickets argued that they were only exercising their right to pass and repass on the highway. It was held that their actions were an unreasonable exercise of that right. Thus the reason for the picket, where it occurs, how long it lasts, why it is done and whether it causes an obstruction are all relevant questions.

The offence, if committed, is one of strict liability, and it is irrelevant that the plaintiff genuinely believes he is exercising his rights. In *Broome v DPP* [1974] AC 587, a picket failed verbally to persuade a lorry driver not to enter a site, and so stood in front of the lorry and refused to move when asked to do so by the police. He was arrested and charged with obstructing the highway. The magistrates felt that as he had delayed the lorry driver only for about nine minutes, this was a reasonable exercise of his right to picket. The House of Lords held that there is no such right, merely a freedom, and the fact that Broome thought he was exercising a right was irrelevant. The delay of the lorry driver was an unreasonable use of the highway, hence an obstruction, and as the offence was one of strict liability, Broome should have been convicted.

14.8.1(b) Obstructing a police officer in the execution of his duty

Under section 51(3) of the Police Act 1964, it is an offence to obstruct a police officer in the execution of his duty. Thus refusal of a police order to stop obstructing the highway is an offence (*Tynan v Balmer*, Section 14.8.1(a) above). The police also have a duty to do what is necessary to prevent a breach of the peace where such a breach is a real possibility. This means that the police have a wide discretion to control pickets by limiting their number when they feel that a breach of the peace is likely. In *Piddington v Bates* [1961] 1 WLR 162, a policeman told the defendant that two pickets were sufficient at a factory gate. The defendant pushed past the policeman, stated that he knew his rights and proceeded to picket. Unfortunately, his knowledge of his rights was limited as he was arrested and charged with obstruction! Lord Parker stated that the police are entitled to take any proper steps to prevent a breach of the peace, including limiting the number of pickets. In *Moss v McLachlan* [1985] IRLR 77, it was decided that the police have a power to disperse pickets some way from their destination if they reasonably believe a breach of the peace will occur should they get to their destination. This gives the police control over so-called 'flying pickets' (that is, pickets travelling all over the country to support other workers in their disputes) and is supplemented by section 4 of the Police and Criminal Evidence Act 1984, which gives police the authority to operate road checks for certain purposes which include ascertaining whether a vehicle is carrying a person intending to commit an offence which a senior police officer has reasonable grounds to believe is likely to lead to a serious public disorder. However, *R v Chief Constable of Gloucestershire* [2006] UKHL 55 suggests that such a power exists only if an offence is imminent. In the case, the Chief Constable knew of demonstrators moving by coaches into Gloucestershire. He had reasons to believe that the demonstration would not be peaceful, and so ordered his officers to intercept the coaches before they reached their destination and to search but not arrest the passengers. After the search the officers concluded that some but not all of the passengers intended to cause a breach of the peace at the demonstration. The officers therefore ordered all the passengers back onto the coaches, and they escorted the coaches back to London. One of the passengers argued that the police officers' actions were an unlawful interference with her rights of freedom of expression and assembly under Articles 10 and 11 of the ECHR. The House of Lords agreed. It held that at the time the coaches were stopped and turned back there was no indication of an imminent breach of the peace and, since the Chief Constable did not think that when the coaches were stopped a breach was likely to occur, the action by the officers was an unlawful interference with the Article 10 and Article 11 freedoms. Consequently, it seems that the power of the police is not as widespread as may at first seem.

14.8.1(c) Breach of the peace

In addition to obstruction of a police officer there is the common law offence of behaving in a manner likely to cause a breach of the peace. Thus stopping vehicles or shouting at employees trying to work may constitute the offence (*Kavanagh v Hiscock* [1974] QB 600). Likewise, refusing to obey a police instruction to disperse may constitute the offence in the same way as the offence of obstructing a police officer.

14.8.1(d) Public nuisance

It is an offence to obstruct the public in the exercise or enjoyment of their common law rights, including the right to free passage along the highway. Originally, in *Lyons (J) & Sons v Wilkins* [1899] 1 Ch 255, it was thought that the picket per se constituted the nuisance; this was doubted by Lord Denning MR in a dissenting judgment in *Hubbard v Pitt* [1976] QB 142, but the rest of the Court of Appeal did not discuss the issue. In *News Group Newspapers Ltd v SOGAT '82* [1986] ICR 716, the High Court held that the conduct of the pickets at the plant in Wapping amounted to an unreasonable obstruction of the highway and so constituted a public nuisance. A public nuisance is also actionable in tort if the claimant can show particular damage other and beyond that suffered by the general public.

14.8.2 The Trade Union and Labour Relations (Consolidation) Act 1992

Originally, certain offences were created by the Conspiracy and Protection of Property Act 1875. These offences have now been consolidated into section 241 of the 1992 Act. The offences are committed by those who try to compel another to do (or not to do) something, without legal authority, by means of:

- using violence towards or intimidating that person, or his family or injuring his property;
- persistently following that person from place to place;
- hiding tools, clothes or any other property, or depriving or hindering the use of such;

- watching or besetting the person's home, workplace or the approach to either;
- following a person with two or more others in a disorderly fashion, in any road or street.

The most common charge is that of watching and besetting. In *Galt v Philp* [1984] IRLR 156, workers were engaged in a sit-in during which they barricaded laboratories and prevented other employees from entering. It was held that they were besetting. In *Thomas v NUM (South Wales Area)* [1985] IRLR 136, it appears that 'wrongfully and without legal authority' means that the act must be independently tortious or criminal for the offence under section 241. Thus if the picket has immunity, it would have to be shown that some wrong outside the immunity had been committed for the offence to be raised.

14.8.3 The Public Order Act 1986

This Act abolished the common law offences of riot, rout, unlawful assembly and affray, and repealed provisions in the Public Order Act 1936 relating to threatening behaviour likely to cause a breach of the peace. The 1986 Act creates a series of statutory offences which may be invoked in an industrial dispute. These are:

1. Riot (s 1): this is where 12 or more persons use or threaten to use violence for a common purpose which could cause a person of reasonable firmness to fear for his personal safety.
2. Violent disorder (s 2): this is the same as riot but occurs where three or more persons threaten, etc.
3. Affray (s 3): this has the same element as riot but only one person is involved. Threats themselves are insufficient and there must be violence.
4. Fear or provocation of violence (s 4): it is an offence to use threatening, abusive or insulting words or behaviour, or to distribute or display any visual representation which is threatening, abusive or insulting, where the intention is to make a person fear immediate violence or provoke immediate violence, or the action is likely to do the above.
5. Harassment, alarm or distress (s 5): this has the same elements as fear or provocation of violence but is committed within the sight or hearing of a person likely to be caused harassment, alarm or distress. It is a defence if the defendant can show he had reasonable cause to believe that a person was not in his sight or hearing.

14.8.4 Civil liability

There are four main torts which may be committed by pickets.

14.8.4(a) Private nuisance

This is an unlawful interference with an individual's enjoyment of his land. The tort was extensively discussed by Scott J in *Thomas v NUM* (Section 14.8.2 above) when he held that mass picketing constituted a nuisance because the sheer volume of numbers had an intimidatory effect which prevented the users of the land from exercising their rights over it. Furthermore, it has been seen that an unreasonable obstruction of the highway is also actionable as a private nuisance by the owner of the land whose right of access to the highway is being restricted by the picket (*News Group Newspapers Ltd v SOGAT '82*, Section 14.8.1(d) above).

14.8.4(b) Trespass to the highway

Using the highway for a purpose other than the exercise of the right to pass and repass is a trespass to the highway. The injured parties are the owners of the soil below the highway, either adjoining landowners or the local authority.

14.8.4(c) Economic torts

It has already been noted that invariably a picket will induce breaches of contracts of employment, procure breaches of commercial contracts and in fact cover the whole gamut of economic torts during the course of the picket.

14.8.4(d) Protection from Harassment Act 1997

The Act has introduced a statutory tort which is relevant to pickets. By section 1, it is an offence for a person to pursue a course of conduct which amounts to harassment of another and which he or she knows or ought to know amounts to harassment. 'Course of conduct' is defined as conduct on at least two occasions (s 7(3)) and 'conduct' includes speech (s 7(4)). 'Harassment' includes alarming a person or causing a person distress (s 7(2)). There is a defence if the person shows that in the circumstances the pursuit of the conduct was reasonable (s 1(3)(c)). In this context the Human Rights Act 1998 may be relevant. A person who is the victim of such conduct may seek an injunction to restrain it, and it is an offence, punishable by up to five years' imprisonment, to breach the injunction without reasonable excuse (s 3). Damages may also be awarded.

14.8.5 Immunity for picketing

The immunity for pickets is contained in section 220 of TULR(C)A 1992. This renders it lawful for a person, in contemplation or furtherance of a trade dispute, to attend at or near his own place of work for the purpose of peacefully obtaining or communicating information, or peacefully persuading a person to work or not to work. In addition, a trade union official may peacefully picket at or near the place of work of a member of the union whom he is accompanying and whom he represents. Unemployed employees are allowed to picket their former place of work if their employment was terminated in connection with the trade dispute or the dismissal gave rise to the trade dispute.

The limit of attending at or near the employee's place of work was introduced after public disquiet about flying pickets (see Section 14.8.1(b) above). Such attendance is now lawful only if done by a trade union official. In the *SOGAT '82* case (Section 14.8.1(d) above), the newspaper proprietor Rupert Murdoch had moved his print works from Fleet Street to Wapping, and when the unions refused the move and took strike action, all those who went on strike were dismissed. They picketed the plant at Wapping. It was held that the pickets' place of work was Fleet Street and therefore the picket was outside section 220. By contrast, in *Rayware Ltd v TGWU* [1989] IRLR 134, the workplace was on an industrial estate which was private property. The roadway was about two-thirds of a mile from the premises, and as the pickets would have committed a trespass if they had gone to the factory entrance, they picketed the entrance to the site instead. It was held that they were picketing near their place of work for the purposes of section 220.

According to the Code of Practice on picketing, 'place of work' means the entrance or exit of the factory, site or office. Even if the picket is lawful as to place, it should be noted that all that can be done is the peaceful obtaining or communication of information or peaceful persuasion of a person. *Broome v DPP* (Section 14.8.1(a) above) makes it clear that a picket has no right to stop a person. Furthermore, while there is no mention in the legislation as to the numbers which may lawfully picket, Scott J in *Thomas v NUM* (Section 14.8.2 above) thought that 50 or 70 miners picketing colliery gates fell outside the immunity on the basis that sheer weight of numbers contradicted the aim of peaceful picketing. He relied on the Code of Practice, which states that mass picketing is not lawful picketing in the sense of an attempt at peaceful persuasion, and states that no more than six pickets should be allowed at each entrance to the workplace. Scott J thought that this provided a guide as to sensible numbers on a picket line so that the weight of numbers should not intimidate those who wish to work. The result of this decision seems to be that more than six pickets will be construed as intimidation and therefore not peaceful. As such, the picket will lose the protection of section 220.

14.9 Remedies

Obviously, although the individual member commits the tort, it is more beneficial for an employer to sue the union, hence the removal of blanket union immunity in 1982. The majority of employers, however, do not want damages, but rather want to prevent the action from commencing or to stop it as soon as possible. Thus the most common remedy sought is that of injunctive relief. Often the relief sought will be for an interim injunction, requiring those who organise the action to call it off until the matter comes to a full trial. This is an important remedy for the employer as often, if an interim injunction is granted and the action is suspended, the case never gets to full trial as support for the action has waned.

The House of Lords in *American Cynamid Co v Ethicon Ltd* [1975] AC 396 laid down the principles which must be applied by the court when considering whether to grant injunctive relief. The court must ask itself three questions: Is there a serious issue to be tried? Has the claimant shown that the defendant's conduct is causing him irreparable harm which cannot be remedied by a subsequent award of damages? On the balance of convenience, is the harm being suffered by the claimant greater than will be incurred by the defendant if he is ordered to cease his activities pending a full trial? This decision represents a relaxation of the previous law in *Stratford v Lindley* (Section 14.3.1(b) above) where the plaintiff had to show at least a prima facie case which was likely to be successful at full trial. The decision, however, works against unions (although see the Court of Appeal in *Viking Line ABP v ITWF* [2006] IRLR 58), as the balance of convenience test is usually in favour of maintaining the status quo, that is, full production, as it is obvious that the employer will lose from the industrial action much more than the union. In *Mercury Communications v Scott-Garner* (Section 14.5.4 above), the plaintiffs succeeded in showing that there was a serious issue to be tried and that they had a real prospect of securing a permanent injunction at full trial. In considering the balance of convenience, the court held that the loss which would have been sustained by the plaintiff would have vastly exceeded the limit of £250,000 which could have been imposed as damages. On the other hand, even if the union did prove that the action was lawful, it would have suffered no loss as the temporary cessation in the industrial action would not hasten or cause any redundancies. The plaintiffs got their injunction. In an attempt to rectify this imbalance, section 221(1) of the 1992 Act provides that if there might be a trade dispute defence to an injunction, the court should not grant the injunction ex parte until all reasonable steps have been taken to inform the defendant and give him an opportunity to put his side of the case, and by section 221(2) the court must have regard to the fact that the defendant would succeed in a trade dispute defence at full trial. The House of Lords in *NWL v Woods* [1979] ICR 867 stated that if it is likely that the defence will succeed then an injunction should not be granted. Such a defence, however, will apply only to the torts for which there is statutory immunity.

If the union fails to comply with an injunction, the two methods of enforcement are committal for contempt or sequestration of the union assets. The court may imprison for contempt, fine or order security for good behaviour. The union may be held in contempt if it does not prevent its officials from acting in contempt by section 20(6) of the 1992 Act.

Sequestration is a discretionary remedy of the court and may be granted if the court is satisfied that the disobedience to the court order, be it an injunction, or an award of damages or a fine, is intentional. The order sequestrates all the property of the union, and commissioners move in to take possession of the property so sequestrated. It was ordered in cases during the miners' dispute of 1984–85, where one area branch was attempting to move money into officials' personal accounts to prevent paying a fine; and when later the trustees of the union's assets were attempting to send money abroad to frustrate the sequestrators, the court removed them as trustees. The remedies against trade union funds mean that officials are less likely to risk unlawful industrial action because they run the risk of bankrupting the union.

Until 1993, remedies against the union were given to employers and members only. The 1993 Act gave, for the first time, protection to an individual who suffered as a result of unlawful industrial action. Section 235A of TULR(C)A 1992 creates a right for an individual, where the industrial action either prevents or delays the supply of goods or services to him, or reduces the quality of goods or services supplied to him, to apply to the High Court. This right arises where the act to induce a person to take part or continue to take part in industrial action is unlawful, that is it is actionable in tort or a union member would have a right to sue the union because the balloting requirements had not been complied with. It is immaterial whether the individual is entitled to be supplied with the goods or services. If the court finds an application well founded, it may make an order requiring the inducer to stop the inducement and requiring him to take steps to prevent further industrial action (s 235A(4)). Any act of inducement shall be taken to be committed by the trade union if it has authorised or endorsed the action (s 235A(6)).

This section creates rights for members of the public to take proceedings when they are affected by unlawful industrial action. *P v NAS/UWT* (Section 14.5.5 above) is an example of the section's being invoked, where a disruptive pupil took action because teachers were refusing to teach him. This section particularly affects the unions in those industries which deal with members of the public, in particular the service industries.

Summary

14.1 The basis of the legal regulation of industrial action under some previous governments was the pursuance of a market forces economic policy rather than the balance of power between the two sides of industry.

14.2 Virtually all forms of industrial action will constitute a breach of the employee's contract of employment.

14.3 All forms of industrial action will involve the economic torts.

14.4 The range of economic torts has been extended since the reduction in the scope of the statutory immunity.

14.5 Unions and their members are immune from liability for certain economic torts only if they are acting in contemplation or furtherance of a trade dispute.

14.6 Because of the definition of 'trade dispute', all tertiary action and the majority of secondary action create liability.

14.7 Trade unions have only the same immunity as their members, and will lose immunity if they fail to comply with the statutory requirements on balloting and notice.

14.8 A trade union is liable, however, only when it has authorised or endorsed the action, and may escape liability if it repudiates the action.

14.9 There is a statutory maximum on the award of damages against a union in any one action. There is no such limit in relation to fines imposed for contempt.

14.10 Picketing may involve both criminal and civil liability; there is no immunity for criminal actions.

14.11 A person can now lawfully pickct only at or near his own place of work, and must be acting within the 'golden formula' to be protected from civil liability.

14.12 The police have a total discretion to disperse pickets if they reasonably fear a breach of the peace. This means that there is only a freedom to picket and not a right.

14.13 Employers normally seek an injunction to prevent or suspend industrial action. In addition, an individual may claim relief against the union if the action disrupts the supply of goods or services to that individual.

14.14 Breach of any court order by a union may lead to a fine or imprisonment for contempt, or ultimately to sequestration of union assets.

Exercises

14.1 At Groanwick Ltd a dispute over pay exists with the employees represented by Bovver Union. The workers refuse to handle goods from the company's suppliers, having also organised a sit-in at the company's premises, where they effected entry by force.

The company has existing contracts for the supply of goods from Conthem Ltd. Bovver Union contacts Aggro, the union representing the majority of workers at Conthem, and informs it of the dispute. Officials of Aggro inform Conthem that its members will refuse to handle goods bound for Groanwick and the company agrees to stop the supplies to Groanwick.

Certain supplies are, nevertheless, still leaving Conthem, being handled by non-union labour. As a result, workers from Groanwick and Conthem mount a picket at the gates of Conthem to prevent supplies leaving the company.

Advise the employers.

14.2 'The past 50 years have witnessed an enormous extension of the scope of the economic torts as they affect industrial action, while simultaneously seeing a significant contraction in the breadth of the golden formula, a combination of events which has considerably extended the scope of potential liability for individual participants in industrial action.' Consider the accuracy of this statement.

Further reading and references

Auerbach, 'Legal Restraint of Picketing: New Trends; New Tensions' (1987) 16 ILJ 227

Beardsmore, 'Labour Disputes in 2005' (2005) 114 LMT 174

Carty, 'The Public Order Act 1986: Police Powers and the Picket Line' (1987) 16 ILJ 146

Carty, 'International Violations of Economic Interests: The Limits of Common Law Liability' (1988) 104 LQR 250

Dukes, 'The Right to Strike Under UK Law: Not Much More than a Slogan?' (2010) 39 ILJ 82

Dukes, 'The Right to Strike Under UK Law: Something More Than a Slogan?' (2011) 40 ILJ 302

Elias and Ewing, 'Economic Torts and Labour Law: Old Principles and New Liabilities' (1982) 41 CLJ 321

Ewing, 'The Dramatic Implications of Demir and Baykara' (2010) 39 ILJ 2

Hendy, 'Caught in a Fork' (2000) 29 ILJ 53

Howarth, 'Against Lumley v Gye' (2005) 68 MLR 195

Miller and Woolfson, 'Timex, Industrial Relations and the Use of Law in the 1990s' (1994) 23 ILJ 209.

Morris, 'Industrial Action in Essential Services: The New Law' (1991) 20 ILJ 89

Prassl, 'To Strike, to Serve? Industrial Action at BA, BAplc v UNITE (the union)' (2011) 40 ILJ 82

Ronnman, 'Laval Returns to Sweden: The Final Judgement of the Swedish Labour Court and Swedish Legislative Reforms' (2010) 39 ILJ 280

Sales and Stilitz, 'Intentional Infliction of Harm Caused by Unlawful Means' (1999) 115 LQR 411

Simpson, 'A Not so Golden Formula: "in contemplation or furtherance of a trade dispute" After 1982' (1983) 46 MLR 463

Simpson, 'The Code of Practice on Industrial Action Ballots and Notice to Employers' (2001) 30 ILJ 194

Wallington, 'Injunctions and the Right to Demonstrate' (1986) CLJ 86

Wedderburn, 'Underground Labour Injunctions' (2001) 30 ILJ 206

Index